A DIGEST
OF THE
HINDULAW

A DIGEST
OF THE
HINDU LAW

OF

INHERITANCE, PARTITION, AND ADOPTION

EMBODYING THE REPLIES OF THE SASTRIS.

WITH

INTRODUCTIONS AND NOTES

THE LATE SIR RAYMOND WEST, K.C.I.E.,

SYED H. R. ABDUL MAJID, M.A., LL.D.,

FOURTH EDITION

OF

WEST & BUHLER.

IN THREE PARTS

PART-3 (ADOPTION)

GYAN

Published by

GYAN

Gyan Publishing House
5, Ansari Road
Daryaganj, New Delhi-110002
Phone: 011-47034999, 9811692060
E-mail: books@gyanbooks.com

Distribution Network
gyanbooks.com
India, USA, Canada, UK, Australia, France

ISBN : 978-81-212-9555-0 (Set)
978-81-212-9552-9 (PB)
First Published, 1919

2nd Impression 2023

Printed at: Gyan Press, Delhi.

A DIGEST OF THE HINDU LAW (PART-3: ADOPTION

Author: RAYMOND WEST, SYED H. R. ABDUL MAJID

A DIGEST

OF THE

HINDU LAW

OF

INHERITANCE, PARTITION, AND ADOPTION

EMBODYING THE REPLIES OF THE ŚÂSTRIS.

WITH

INTRODUCTIONS AND NOTES.

BY

THE LATE SIR RAYMOND WEST, K.C.I.E.,

a Judge of the High Court at Bombay, etc.

AND

SYED H. R. ABDUL MAJID, M.A., LL.D.,

of Gray's Inn, Barrister-at-Law,

Trinity College, Dublin: LL.D.; Cambridge University: Law Tripos, Pts. I. & II., and Oriental Languages (Arabic and Persian) Tripos, and Moral Sciences, Syed Mahmud Prizeman of Christ's College; Calcutta University: Double Honours (Philosophy and Persian), Graduate Scholar of the Presidency College; late Examiner and Lecturer on Mohammedan Law, Colonial Office, London; Fellow and Lecturer on Hindu, Mohammedan, and Colonial Law, the Société Internationale de Philologie, Sciences et Beaux-Arts, London; Author of "England and the Moslem World," "The Historical Study of Mohammedan Law," "The Moslem International Law"; and Translator of "Al-Mowatta of Malik," from the Arabic and of "The Rubáiyát of Hafiz," etc.

FOURTH EDITION

OF

WEST & BÜHLER.

1919.

BOOK III.

ADOPTION.

SECTION I.—SOURCES OF THE LAW.

In their opinions on the cases laid before them the Sastris have in many instances referred to Adoption "made with the ceremonies of the Vedas and the Smritis." No precepts as to such ceremonies are to be found in the Vedic literature, and even in the Smritis the recognition of the "son by gift" is but a part of a scheme in which he holds only a comparatively low place amongst the dozen varieties of substitutionary sons approved by those writings. They present few or no traces of the developed and elaborate system which has come down to our generation enriched and complicated by the inventive suggestions and the subtle controversies of a long series of lawyers, who were at the same time scholastics having unbounded confidence in the methods of a highly technical philosophy (*a*). The fundamental notion indeed on which the institution was afterwards reared is found already in full possession of the Brahmanical mind in the Vedic period. The manes were to be worshipped; the family was to be continued; the householder was to esteem his own being complete only when his home was furnished with a wife and son (*b*). But other means than adoption supply the defects of nature; some further stages on the way to refinement have still to be passed before those means become discredited. In the meantime Adoption is but slightly glanced at. Its fitness for the

---

(*a*) For the methods of interpretation and development brought to bear on the Vedas, see Whitney's Essays, 1st Series, pp. 108 ss.

(*b*) See Whitney's Essays, 1st Ser., pp. 50, 59; comp. Manu IX. 45.

needs of a people of the peculiar mental and spiritual character of the Hindus was not at first perceived. Here, therefore, even more than in other departments of the law, the Veda has, for the practical lawyer of the present day, but little importance as a direct source of the law (*c*). For a complete history of the "origins" of the subject the requisite researches have still to be made, the needful competence has still perhaps to be perfected. The modern edifice, though bearing everywhere the impress of the primitive religion and its early modifications, is planned in the main on ideas of a later time, the growth and variances of which can be gathered from the existing literature with at least an approach to confidence (*d*).

In the long interval between the Veda and the Smritis more had been done towards systematizing than towards refining the theory of paternal and filial relations. The importance of maintaining the family is at the close of this period as strongly recognized as ever; the relations of the living to the dead had, through long meditation, become more vividly conceived than before. But the grossness of a barbarous time is not as yet cast off, nor have the ideas of the people settled down to any final appreciation of the several recognized modes of replenishing the family. Gautama, Baudhayana and Vasishtha, Manu and Yajnavalkya, Harita, Vishnu and Narada present their several lists. The order in which they rank the different substitutionary sons (*e*) will be discussed hereafter. That a substituted son is indispensable, failing one begotten, the rishis agree, with the exception of Apastamba (*f*). In him we have an echo perhaps of the then already ancient objection to the gift or acceptance of a child, an objection which later commentators found no great difficulty by means of distinctions and particular applications in explaining away (*g*).

Another long break in the record follows the period of the Smritis. That a considerable development of the Hindu mind and character took place in the interval is manifest from the works in other departments which have come down to us. Poetry and philosophy awakened higher moral sensibilities, and the myths of the earlier times became enveloped in a mist of sacred

---

(*c*) See above, p. 50.

(*d*) Comp. Whitney, *op. cit.* pp. 62, 70.

(*e*) See Col. Dig., Book V., Chap. IV.

(*f*) Transl., p. 131.

(*g*) Comp. Datt. Mim. Sec. I., 36—47.

association which softened their repulsive features and prevented their exercising an injurious influence (*h*). The uncertain strivings of the nobler minds towards refinement and delicacy in the relations of the sexes and the constitution of the family were gradually in some measure realized by the Brahmanical class, and those in close communication with them, while neither at any time quite lost such a hold of the primitive beliefs and conceptions of duty as served to bind the slow changes of their institutions together in historical continuity. When we come into clear light again we find a marked advance in purity of sentiment. Adoption has in a great measure supplanted the grosser institutions that once competed with it on more than equal terms. The archaic formulas are still preserved, but they have been subtly emptied of their former contents, or have become themes for mere academic disquisitions, which show the learning of the commentators and their tenderness for the sacred writings, but stand apart in a great measure from actual practice and the living law. The far-fetched explanations of the hard sayings which could not be set aside (*i*) show at once the reverential spirit of the commentators, and their resolution to mould even intractable materials to the uses and cravings of a society always in movement, and for centuries in a general movement forward, though not always on lines which led to the best conceivable results, or which entirely commend themselves to European sympathies formed under wholly different influences.

From the time that Adoption comes upon the scene as an established section of the Hindu jural system, many authors have dealt with it either as the subject of separate treatises or along with the other leading topics of the law (*k*). Besides the Vyav. May., which is the most frequently quoted, the Bombay Sastris have referred to the Viramitrodaya, the Samskara Ganapati, to the Samskar, and "Datta" Kaustubha, to the Narnayasindhu and Dharmasindhu, the Dattaka Darpana and the Dvaita

---

(*h*) Comp. for the earlier period Gough's Phil. of the Upanishads, p. 17.

(*i*) On the reconciliation of discrepancies in the sacred writings and the application of reason to establish harmony, reference may be made to *Bhau Nanaji* v. *Sundrabai*, 11 Bom. H. C. R., at pp. 265 ss. See, too, the Datt. Mim., sec. II. 102, where reasoning, it is said, is to be applied to draw out an obvious inferential sense rather than separate revelations assumed for rules resting on one and the same principle.

(*k*) Many of these works are preserved amongst the learned in MS.

Nirnaya (*l*). The doctrines drawn from these authorities are supported by citations from Manu and other Smritis, as well as from the Mitakshara, and the Daya Bhaga of Jimuta Vahana. These last are but infrequent. The Dattaka Mimansa and Dattaka Chandrika are hardly referred to at all. The opinions enunciated agree for the most part with the rules laid down in these treatises, but the remark of Rao Saheb V. N. Mandlik (*m*) seems to be substantially correct, that till quite recent years they were but little known and relied on in Western India (*n*). It does not follow, however, that they are not valuable guides to the law. Though the law of Adoption has, in historical fact, grown up by a process of gradual adaptation, yet the Hindu commentators do not, any more than the English Judges, ever set themselves up as makers of the law They claim to be expositors, and if one of them develops principles in a way more consonant to the general ethical and jural system than another he naturally obtains the preference (*o*). The congruousness of his doctrines with the whole mass of received notions is recognized, and they are received into the legal consciousness of the people as rules which, from their fitness, must be followed (*p*). This fitness implies a due agreement with the traditions that have descended in slowly modified interpretations from the Vedic era, and forms a proper ground on Hindu principles for the acceptance into the common law of the particular phases of doctrine which come thus recommended (*q*). This is more especially so if they are set forth with a clearness and point which makes them readily intelligible. It may seem that the Dattaka Mimansa and Dattaka Chandrika have not any very strong claims on these grounds, but excellence is essentially comparative, and very high authorities have agreed in assigning to the Dattaka Mimansa the first place amongst the treatises on Adoption (*r*). Colebrooke says (*s*) that "the Dattaka Mimansa is

---

(*l*) The one intended is that of Shankara Bhatta, father of Nilkantha, author of the Mayukha.

(*m*) Vyav. May., Introd. lxxii.

(*n*) That the Rao Saheb is a little too sweeping in his assertion may be seen by a reference to the opinions of the Poona Sastris in *Haebutrao's Case*, 2 Borr. R., at pp. 104, 105.

(*o*) See Col. Dig., Book II., Chap. IV., T. 15 Com.; T. 17; Book V., T. 57, 424 Comm.

(*p*) Comp. Mayer, Inst. Jud. Tom. V., p. 7.

(*q*) See *Bhau Nanaji Utpat* v. *Sundrabai*, 11 Bom. H. C. R. 267.

(*r*) *Bhagwan Singh* v. *Bhagwan Singh*, L. R. 26 I. A. 153; S. C., I. L. R. 21 All. 412.

(*s*) 2 Str. H. L. 183.

no doubt the best treatise on Hindu Adoption." By this Sutherland was led to translate it: "The Dattaka Mimansa," he says (*t*), "is the most celebrated work extant on the Hindu law of Adoption." Of the Dattaka Chandrika he says, "it is a work of authority" (*v*). In assigning it to Devanda Bhatta as its author he may probably have been mistaken (*w*), but this does not affect his judgment as to its popular reception as a guide to the law. Sir M. Westropp, C.J., says of the Dattaka Mimansa that "though not quite invariably followed [it] is generally of high authority in this Presidency" (Bombay) (*x*). In Bengal the authority of both works stands still higher. It was said by Mitter, J., that "The Dattaka Chandrika and the Dattaka Mimansa are undoubtedly entitled to be considered, and have always been considered, the highest authorities on the subject of Adoption" (*y*) But that their influence is not thus confined is plain from the description given by Sir W. Macnaghten, cited by the Privy Council in *The Collector of Madura's Case* (*z*): "Again of the Dattaka Mimansa of Nanda Pandita, and the Dattaka Chandrika of Devanda Bhatta, two treatises on the particular subject of Adoption, Sir William Macnaghten says, that they are respected all over India; but that when they differ the doctrine of the latter is adhered to in Bengal and by the Southern jurists, while the former is held to be the infallible guide in the Provinces of Mithila and Benares."

As supplementary to the Mitakshara and the Mayukha, then, these may fairly be regarded as the principal authorities. The others referred to, though in some instances of importance, are not only less accessible, but on the whole less valuable when got at, and less suited to bringing about a general harmony of doctrines and decisions on a subject on which it is specially desirable that the law should be uniform and widely known. Still usage, the ultimate test, has in some instances decisively rejected the doctrines of these two works, as for instance in allowing adoption by a widow without express authority from her husband (*a*),

(*t*) Preface.
(*v*) *Ibid.*
(*w*) See Rao Saheb V. N. Mandlik, *loc. cit.*
(*x*) *In Gopal N. Safray* v. *Hanmant G. Safray*, I. L. R. 3 Bom., at p. 277.
(*y*) In *Rajendro Narain Lahoree* v. *Saroda Soondaree Dabee*, 15 C. W. R. 548.
(*z*) 12 M. I. A., at p. 437.
(*a*) See *Haebutrao Mankur's Case*, 2 Borr., at pp. 104, 105.

while Nanda Pandita insists that Vasishtha's text requiring the husband's assent prevents any adoption at all after his death. The Samskara Kaustubha (*b*) says that the assent of kinsmen cannot properly be withheld, and therefore the widow, who is competent and bound to perform this service for her husband, may act without their concurrence. The Sastris in *Thukoo Baee Bhide* v. *Rama Baee Bhide* (*c*) deduced a like competence from the injunction of the Mitakshara, " a woman must be restrained only from unnecessary or useless acts," and declared that the widow could adopt even against the wishes of her husband's kinsmen. In a previous case (*d*) the Sastris had quoted the Mayukha to prove that the widow might indeed adopt without an express authority from her husband, but after " obtaining the sanction of the kinsmen and informing the ruling authorities." This they said " corresponds with the custom of the country." Yet should the widow have actually adopted a son with due ceremonies, such an adoption conformable to the Vedas could not " be set aside should the person opposing it be ever so near of kin." The Courts, as will be seen, have steered a middle course amongst the conflicting authorities. That they should have had to do so implies that none can be received as absolutely supreme.

In the present day it does not seem likely that the fountain-heads of the law will be much drawn on for new principles in the Law of Adoption. They are, indeed, too meagre to afford such principles save through an elaborate process of constructive inference. To this they have been subjected by the Hindu writers for many centuries, and the rules deduced by these writers have in their turn been tried and sifted by express or tacit reference to the usages and the peculiarities of Hindu society, until those best suited to its needs have been ascertained and appropriated. The Smritis come nearer than the Veda to modern practice, but the most important authorities are the writers, such as have been referred to, whose expositions have partly embodied and partly fashioned the customary law. In the great case of *The Collector of Madura* (*e*) the chief authorities on the law touching a widow's power to adopt had been collected under the four heads of (1) Original Sanskrit texts, (2) Responses of Sastris, (3) Opinions of

(*b*) As to the authority of this work, see 2 Borr. R. *loc. cit.*

(*c*) 2 Borr. R. 488, 499.

(*d*) *Sree Brijbhookunjee Maharaj* v. *Sree Gokoolootsaojee Maharaj*, 1 Borr. R. 202, 214.

(*e*) 12 M. I. A. 397, 411.

European writers, and (4) Decisions of the Courts. The judgments, both in the first instance and in appeal, proceeded almost entirely on the third and the fourth classes of authorities, and of the first the Judicial Committee speak as "a catena of texts, of which many have been taken from works little known and of doubtful authority. Their Lordships concur with the Judges of the High Court in declining to allow any weight to these," while accepting those recognized by the chief European writers on Hindu Law as of unquestionable authority in the South of India, where the case under appeal had arisen.

To the opinions of the Sastris, which the High Court had denounced as having "polluted the administration of Hindu law" (*ee*), their Lordships, as already observed (*f*), attach considerable importance. Those opinions, they say, "which are consistent with [translated works of authority] should be accepted as evidence that the doctrine which they embody has not become obsolete, but is still received as part of the customary law of the country" (*g*).

In dealing with authorities the analogy of the rules accepted by kindred schools may greatly strengthen one of two or more inconsistent doctrines propounded by rival authors (*h*). All rely on the same ancient texts, and the waves of philosophical or moral influence which have moulded the derived notions in one part of India have almost of necessity extended their effect to the neighbouring regions, aided in the case of the learned by their possession of a common language. Through the medium of Sanskrit, ideas having in themselves a fitness for wide reception have been capable at all times of diffusion with something like the same

---

(*ee*) *In Collector of Madura* v. *Anandayi*, 2 Mad. H. C. R., at p. 223.

(*f*) Above, p. 2.

(*g*) *The Collector of Madura* v. *Moottoo Ramalinga Sathupathy*, 12 M. I. A., at p. 438, 439. The Sastris vacillated occasionally in the opinions they delivered. On points of difficulty they naturally differed. When one considers the cobweb structure of the Hindu Law laboriously spun out of a primitive theology by means of a philosophy having but little respect for mere practice, it was impossible that there should not be variances of opinion. One view was in itself as reasonable in many cases as the other. In some instances the Sastris seem to have gone wholly wrong. The same may be said of jurists and Judges everywhere. A reading of the Sastris' responses, as wide as that on which the present work is founded, would convince any unprejudiced student that as Law Officers of the Courts these learned men performed their duties, save in very rare instances, with integrity as well as intelligence.

(*h*) *Ibid.*

striking celerity which obtained through the use of Latin in the Europe of four and five centuries ago.

The tendency of usage to conform to the received scripture standards has been noticed in the first part of this work (*i*). Hindu theory justifies variances from the normal rule of conduct only by a supposition of some lost revelation (*k*) to which they may be referred, except in cases purposely left to individual discretion (*l*), and the Sastris assert the superiority of the Vedas to mere custom (*m*), but when the precept is not decisive they allow custom to replace it (*n*). The Charters of the High Courts and the Regulations of the Legislature give the next place in authority after the Statute law to usage, and however in learned speculation the sacred texts may be exalted above mere human practice there can be no doubt that the Hindu lawyers had arrived substantially at the same conclusion that the British Government has defined. The general force of custom as law is repeatedly asserted by Manu (*o*), as by Katyayana, Yajnavalkya, and the other great Rishis (*p*). The Mitakshara allows that custom has abolished Manu's rules for specific deductions and unequal shares in partition (*q*). The Vyavahara Mayukha declares that the very practice given by Gautama as an example of one that usage could not establish, the marriage of a maternal uncle's daughter, is sanctioned by custom in the Dekhan (*r*). Macnaghten instances the Kshetraja as a legal subsidiary son still recognized by the local law of Orissa (*s*). Mitramisra, following the Mitakshara, says the conflicting texts respecting subsidiary sons are to be reconciled by

---

(*i*) See above, pp. 9, 402, 403. As to the determination of caste rules, see sec. II. below.

(*k*) See 2 Muir's Sanskrit Texts, 165, and references below.

(*l*) Manu II. 12, 18; Gaut. XI. 20.

(*m*) 2 Borr. 488; see M. Müller, H. A. S. Lit., p. 53; Muir's Sanskrit Texts, vol. III., pp. 179, 181; Col. Dig., Book I., T. 50 Comm.; Datt. Mim., sec. I., paras. 10, 11.

(*n*) Apastamba, Transl., pp. 15, 55. At p. 47 is a caution against inferring the former existence of a Vedic passage from a usage which can be accounted for on merely utilitarian grounds, and a caution against following a usage with no higher justification.

(*o*) I. 108, 110; II. 12; IV. 178; VII. 203; VIII. 41, 42.

(*p*) See the quotations in *Rawut Urjun* v. *Sing Rawut Ghunsiam Sing*, 5 M. I. A. 180.

(*q*) Mit., Chap. I., sec. 3, para. 4.

(*r*) Vyav. May., Chap. I., sec. 1, para. 13.

(*s*) Macn. H. L. 102.

referring them to different local customs (*t*). On this principle the Sastri, in a case amongst the Bhatele caste, declared that by the caste custom an adoption could not be allowed while male kinsmen survived to continue the family (*v*). This agrees with the answers preserved in Borradaile's collection, and shows that custom well established is practically supreme. In the particular instance, which is not a solitary one, it may well be that the custom embodies a rule against adoption, which once existed in some sacred writings as Apastamba indicates, but has faded away in the transcriptions of later centuries.

The importance of custom as a source and standard of the law is specially great in the case of adoption, because, this being of comparatively modern development, the Vedic texts, written without respect to it, admit of manipulation very much according to the desires of the interpreters. The Smritis even are far from regarding adoption in the light in which it is now viewed. Thus, though the Sruti and Smriti are to the pious Hindu above all reasoning (*w*), and a rationalist ranks as an atheist (*x*), yet Vijnanesvara, who raises the sacred code above all rules of ethics, has still to admit an adjustment by reference to the general and particular and other modes of interpretation (*y*), and custom and approved usage (*z*) govern the received construction of the texts in proportion as these are in themselves indecisive and incapable of direct application (*a*). This does not exclude a comparison of the relative weight of those who pronounce on the customary law.

(*t*) Viram. Transl., p. 127; Macn. H. L. 188.

(*v*) MS. 405, Surat, 14th June, 1847.

(*w*) Manu II. 10; comp. *ibid*. XII. 105.

(*x*) Manu II. 11; see Smriti Chandr., Chap. III., para. 21; Manu. XII. 106.

(*y*) See Yajn. II. 21; Vyav. May., Chap. I., pl. 112; Col. Dig., Book II., Chap. IV., T. 15 Com.; Book V., T. 332 Com.; Comp. Goldstücker, *op. cit*. p. 2; 2 Muir's Sanskrit Texts, 169, 177, 200.

(*z*) Judicial Committee in *Bhya Ram Singh* v. *Bhaya Ugur Singh*, 13 M. I. A. 390.

(*a*) Vijn. in Roer and Montriou's Yajn. p. 8; Manu I. 110; IV. 155. He goes so far as to say that precepts are not to be followed in a practice that has become repulsive to the community, as, for instance, by raising up seed to a man deceased, and by sacrificing a cow, though these are commended by the Hindu scriptures; Mit., Chap. I., sec. III., para. 4. But Devandha Bhatta censures this looseness of doctrine, and quotes Vasishtha (I. 17) to prove that usage is of authority only where it is not opposed to the Vedas and Sastras, Smri. Chand., Chap. III., p. 21 ss. See Gaut. XI. 20; Baudh. Pr. Adh. 1, Kand. 2, paras. 1-7; Manu VIII. 41; VII. 203.

Superior knowledge is to be recognized in some men, of local usages and of tradition (*b*); they, in fact, are the depositaries of custom, as it is gradually organized (*c*), and reproduce it in its living forms (*d*). It was a consciousness of this which moved the Bombay Government of the early part of the present century to set on foot the enquiries conducted by Steele and Borradaile. The information gathered by the former on adoption is embodied in his Law of Caste. The answers collected by the latter have not been all preserved, but in English and Gujarati a considerable body remain (*e*). These were obtained from the representative members of the several castes. They were given, it is evident, with care and consciousness as well as knowledge. They have for other purposes been frequently referred to in the foregoing pages of this work, and they must be used as additional and valuable authorities on the Law of Adoption (*f*).

It may be necessary to add that a particular custom which is relied on in any case as derogating from the common law, based itself on a more general custom, must be clearly proved (*g*) in this as in other departments of the law (*h*). Of a general custom the Courts take notice without its being proved and without their attention being called to it. Works like the present may make the performance of this duty somewhat easier.

For the application of the law as ascertained from its various sources the Judicial Committee have laid down principles which must always constitute a great part of the science of the Courts. Thus in dealing with the Hindu Law " Nothing from any foreign source should be introduced into it; nor should the Courts interpret the texts by the application to their language of strained

---

(*b*) 2 Muir's S. Texts, 173.

(*c*) See Savigny, System, vol. I., § 12; Goudsm. Pand., Book I., § 15, and notes.

(*d*) Comp. Savigny, System, vol. I., §§ 7, 8, 29, 30; Puchta Gewohnheitsrecht, vol. I., p. 162 ss.

(*e*) The Gujarati collection by Sir Mangaldas Nathubhai.

(*f*) As to the force of custom see further *Rama Lakshmi* v. *Shivanantha*, 14 M. I. A. 576; *Surendra Nath Roy* v. *Hiramani Barmani*, 1 Beng. L. R. 26 Pr. Co.; *Lala Joti Lal* v. *Mussamat Durani Kuar*, Beng. L. R. F. B. R. 67; *Court of Wards* v. *Pirthee Singh*, 21 C. W. R. 89 C. R.; *Bai Amrit* v. *Bai Manek*, 12 Bom. H. C. R. 79; *Damodhur Abaji* v. *Martand Apaji*, Bom. H. C. P. J. 1875, p. 293.

(*g*) See Col. in 2 Str. H. L. 181.

(*h*) See *Neelkisto Deb Burmono* v. *Beerchunder Thakoor*, 12 M. I. A. 523; 14 M. I. A. 576; *supra*, note (*f*).

analogies" (*i*). As to the weight to be given to decisions, "It is entirely opposed to the spirit of the Hindu customs to allow the words of the law to control its long received interpretation as practically exhibited by rules of descent and rules of property founded on the decisions of the Courts of the country" (*k*), and "a new construction ought not to be placed on a text of Hindu Law contrary to the current of modern authority" (*l*).

SECTION II.—NATURE OF ADOPTION AND ITS PLACE IN THE HINDU SYSTEM.

Though Adoption now holds among the Hindu jural institutions a place second in importance only to Marriage, it has won this place only by slow degrees. A craving for a real, and failing that, for a fictitious, perpetuation of the family seems to have prevailed amongst the Hindus from the earliest ages (*m*). This craving has sprung less from a desire to satisfy the capacity for affection and protection—though this has not been absent—than from a sense of the need of a son to save the Brahman from endless discomfort in the other world (*n*). The connexion of putra (= son) with "put" (= hell) even if not well founded etymologically is ancient (*o*), and corresponds to thoughts that have possessed the Hindu's mind in all ages (*p*). "Heaven," says the Veda, "awaits not one destitute of a son" (*q*), and "a Brahman is born under three obligations: to the saints for religious duties, to the gods for

---

(*i*) *Bhya Ram Singh* v. *Bhaya Ugur Singh*, 13 M. I. A. 390.

(*k*) *Kooer Goolab Singh* v. *Rai Kurum Singh*, 14 M. I. A., at p. 196.

(*l*) *Thakoorain Sahibu* v. *Mohan Lal*, 11 M. I. A., at p. 403; *Bhagwan Singh* v. *Bhagwan Singh*, L. R. 26 I. A. 153; *Bai Kesserbai* v. *Morariji*, I. L. R. 30 Bom. 431 P.C.

(*m*) See Ait. Brahm. VII. 3, 9; Vasishtha, Chap. XVII., para. 2; Manu IX. 8, 9, 45, 106; III. 37, 262, 277, IV. 184.

(*n*) See Apast. Pr. II., Khand. 24, paras. 1, 3, 4; Vasish. XVII. 1—4; Baudh. Pr. II., Kand. 11, para. 34; Col. Dig., Book V., T. 270.

(*o*) Col. Dig., Book V., T. 302, 303.

(*p*) See Vishnu XV. 43 ss.

(*q*) Col. Dig., Book V., T. 311; Viram. Transl., p. 115; *Huradhun Mookurjia* v. *Musst. Mookurjia*, 4 M. I. A. 414. Yet in the absence of a son the widow may perform the kriya and sraddha of her deceased husband. Steele, L. C. 34; above, p. 87.

sacrifices, to his forefathers for offspring (*r*). He is absolved who has a son, performs religious duties, and has offered sacrifices" (*s*). When the Brahman dies a son is indispensable "for the funeral cake, the libation, and the solemn rites" (*t*). These obligations of the son are persistently dwelt on in the sacred books, and when we see how the sacerdotal class were interested in the multiplication of ceremonies (*v*) it is easy to understand why the duty of paternity (*w*) was one which they never failed to magnify. The more sacrifices, the more vicarious feasting, and the more distributions to learned Brahmans (*x*), the more prominent the position assigned to them (*y*).

(*r*) See Phil. of the Upanishads, p. 264. Comp. Manu III., 70, 81. Thus it is that "on viewing the fact of his begotten son a father is released from his debt to his ancestors," 2 Str. H. L. 198.

(*s*) Datt. Mim., sec. I. 5; so Baudh. Pr. II., Kand. 11, para. 33; Kand. 16, paras. 2—7.

(*t*) Datt. Mim., sec. I. 3; Vishnu XV. 43; Col. Dig., Book IV., Chap. I., T. 8. If unworthy, however, the son could be replaced. Col. Dig., Book V., T. 263, 264, 278, Comm. "Perpetuated offspring and a heavenly abode are obtained through a son, a grandson, and a great-grandson," Yajn. quoted Col. Dig., Book IV., Chap I., T. 36.

(*v*) See Manu III. 117, 146.

(*w*) Paternity, not Maternity. "Males only need sons to relieve them from the debt due to ancestors," Col. Dig., Book V., T. 273 Comm. Nor is adoption of a daughter warranted by any Smriti; *ibid.*, T. 334 Comm., though it is supported by Puranic legends. In *Gangabai* v. *Anant*, I. L. R. 13 Bom. 690, a case under the Vyav. May., it has been held that a Brahman cannot adopt a daughter conferring on her the right of a real daughter. Manu V. 160, 161, in recommending continence to a childless widow, does not suggest adoption, but promises salvation as the reward of austerity. Comp. Steele, L. C. 34.

Nilkantha gathers from Manu IX. 168 that, according to his precept, only a son, not a daughter, can be given in adoption. Vyav. May., Chap. IV., sec. V., para. 6.

(*x*) See Gaut., Chap. XV. 5—15; Apast. Pr. II., Khand. 16, paras. 3 ss.; Manu I. 95; III. 97, 138, 145, 146, 187, 189, 207, 208, 236, 237. Individual moderation, however, is prescribed; Manu, IV. 186, 190, 195.

(*y*) Marriage is a samskara that is strongly enjoined, see Col. Dig., Book V., T. 252, Comm.; see Manu II. 67; III. 2, 4; Col. Dig., Book IV., Chap. I., T. 17.

The Brahman should marry and light the domestic hearth as soon as possible after leaving his guru or teacher. A girl, it is prescribed, is to be married at from six to eight years of age, Steele, L. C. 26, though the validity of the marriage is not affected if she be under the age of maturity. Col. Dig., Book V., T. 338 Comm. The injunctions laid on the parents and on the husband by Manu show the main purpose of the union (see also Col. Dig., Book V., T. 198, 199; Datt. Mim., sec. I. 5), but in consequence of the legal severance of a girl from her family of birth in some instances for years before her husband's

It is strange to modern feelings how much amongst the ancients sacrifices and religious celebrations were conceived as a bargain (*z*) in which, for a consideration of oblations duly offered (*a*), with formulas duly uttered (*b*), protection and prosperity might be justly claimed (*c*). There was but little bowing down before the sublime conception of Almighty benevolence, less dwelling on a single supreme Creator and controller of events than on partial deifications of persons and of qualities within the reach of a limited intelligence (*d*). In the adoption of a son the Hindu aimed and still aims at satisfying an exacting group of manes greedy in the other world for recognition and offerings in this (*e*). He looks too for appreciable benefits which he is himself to derive

---

unfitness can be discovered, and of her having in the meantime become disqualified by attaining maturity for another marriage, she remains a member of her *quasi*-husband's family, to which the marriage rites have transferred her. See above, p. 418; Manu III. 11, 37, 45; IX. 4, 26, 77, 81; Col. Dig., Book IV., Chap. I., T. 15, 16, 18, 19, 62, 64, 65, 66, 84. The sacred writings readily lent themselves to this, as they generally contemplated the replacement of a husband where necessary by a substitute. See *ex. gr.* Col. Dig., Book V., T. 231. In the case of a marriage ceremony performed between relatives or between persons of different castes whose marriage is forbidden no conjugal connection is recognized, the woman is put away and her children are illegitimate; but she is entitled to maintenance. Steele, L. C. 29, 30. On the other hand, a mere defect in reciting the formulas (mantras) at the wedding is rectified by reciting them again correctly, *ibid.*

(*z*) See Ihne, Hist. of Rome, Book VI., Chap. XIII.; Soury, Etudes Historiques, p. 280; Phil. of the Upanishads, p. 262; Manu III. 63, 67; IV. 155 ss.

(*a*) Manu III. 279.

(*b*) See Baudh. Pr. II., Kand. 11, para. 32; Kand. 14, paras. 4, 5, 11, 12; Manu III. 217, 277 ss.; IV. 99, 100; Apast. Pr. II., Khand. 16, paras. 7 ss.; Phil. of the Upanishads, p. 102.

(*c*) For the purposes sought to be attained by the due utterance of the "mantras" or spells, and their coercive force over the gods, reference may be made to Whitney's Essays, 1st Series, p. 20; see Manu IV. 234.

(*d*) "The innumerable gods of Hinduism are deified ghosts or famous personages, invested with all sorts of attributes in order to account for the caprices of nature. This is the state of the vulgar pagan mind; by the more reflective intelligence the gods are recognized . . . as beings capable of making themselves very troublesome; whom it is, therefore, good to propitiate, like men in office." Sir A. C. Lyall, Asiatic Studies, p. 51.

(*e*) Manu, Chap. III. *passim;* Vasish. XI. 40—44; Gaut. XV. 15 ss. A higher range is attained in such passages as those quoted by M. Müller, Lect. on the Sc. of Religion, pp. 233, 265; comp. *ibid.* 153; Tiele, Anc. Religions, pp. 114, 143. The manes were on particular occasions to be honoured with animal sacrifices. Manu V. 41; comp. v. 35.

from the future ceremonies (*f*), the fruit of which will reach him in the realm of shades (*g*). He shrinks with horror from being left destitute beyond the pyre to suffer the mysterious anguish which awaits the man for whom no son can perform the Sraddhas (*h*). The stronger and more materialistic may resist this tendency (*i*), in some few active faith is lost in metaphysical subtleties (*k*), some are too obtuse to realize the future at which others shudder; but for the most the pressure of a social opinion pervaded everywhere with these ideas, moulds their desires (*l*) and defines their spiritual outlook and their hopes and fears. In somehow acquiring a son the Hindu thinks generally that he is making the best of all possible bargains for himself in this world and the one to come (*m*).

Various means for supplying a natural deficiency of male off-spring were devised, or still adhered to the family in its gradual consolidation on a permanent type from the looser and grosser associations that preceded the dawn of civilization. Amongst these expedients, Adoption, when first admitted, seems to have been received with but doubtful favour (*n*). The levirate and the appointment of a daughter in one or other of the forms of these

---

(*f*) See Manu IX. 180; Col. Dig., Book V., T. 306; Baudh. Pr. II., Kand. 14.

(*g*) See Manu III. 274, 275. As to the sin of the son who omits to satisfy his obligations, see Vishnu XXXVII. 29; LXXVI. 2; Phil. of the Upanishads, p. 264. The enumeration of the right seasons for oblations to the manes in Yajn. I. 217, may remind one of the famous five reasons for drinking amongst the Western nations. So too Vishnu, LXXVI—LXXVIII.

(*h*) Vishnu, XX. 33—37; Col. Dig., Book V., T. 312, 313.

(*i*) Individual Hindus have no hesitation (see the Sarva-Darsana-Sangraha, p. 10) in expressing their contempt for the whole system, but they are rare exceptions. Others think that their duty may be fulfilled and their salvation secured under the Hindu Law by other means than procuring a lineage. They rely on such texts as Yajn. I. 40, 50; III. 190, 204, 205; Manu V. 159.

(*k*) See Phil. of the Upanishads, Chaps. IV., V., p. 263.

(*l*) For the ceremonies and the mantras or spells to be recited see Vishnu, LXXIII—LXXVI.

(*m*) See Manu III. 81, 82, 122, 127; Col. Dig., Book V., T. 270.

(*n*) Apast. Pr. II., Pat. VI., Khand. 13, para. 11, positively forbids the gift equally with the sale of a child. He does not recognize the substitutionary sons. He condemns vicarious procreation, *loc. cit.*, para. 7, at the same time indicating that it was common. Medhatithi, much later, contends that there can be no real substitute for the son, from whose production, not his replacement, the proposed spiritual benefit is to be derived. See Datt. Mim., sec. I. 36, and comp. the alternative rendering of Gaut. IX. 53, quoted under Vasish. XII. 8. This would forbid leaving the family of birth to join another by adoption.

institutions must for generations and even centuries have been the approved modes of obtaining a substitutionary son (*o*). Other methods, still less commendable, according to modern ideas, must have had a certain vogue, seeing that they are recognized in the sacred Smritis (*p*). The final survival of adoption while the rival institutions perished is a mark of its greater suitableness to the moral sensibilities and needs of a society gradually advancing in refinement, yet clinging always to the traditions of the past. The field is here still encumbered with the remains of fallen structures which have engaged a good deal of the attention of the native authors. They have only a partial and occasional influence on the law of to-day, but some observations may be necessary in order to place Adoption in its proper historical relation to the rival, and no doubt older, institutions, which in the end it has supplanted and extinguished.

It is possible to trace in the Vedic literature (*q*) some indications of the appointment of a daughter to produce a son, not for her husband, but for her own father (*r*). This and the levirate (*s*) may be regarded as having in the Vedic period almost completely filled the space now occupied by adoption (*t*). It is impossible to suppose that a subject of such importance as adoption, so stirring to the feelings of the religious, and so calling for ceremonies and sacred ministrations, should not have been frequently mentioned if in fact the institution was generally recognized when the hymns were composed (*v*). Yet that it was creeping into existence

---

(*o*) See Col. Dig., Book V., Chap. IV., sec. III., arts. I. and II.

(*p*) See *ex. gr.* the quotations in Col. Dig. *loc. cit.*, sec. IV.

(*q*) It is necessary to go back so far to find the root of this as of nearly all existing Hindu institutions. See Whitney, Or. and Ling. Studies, 1st Series, pp. 101 ss.

(*r*) Müller, Rigveda, vol. I., p. 232; Transl. Tag. Lect. 1880, p. 249.

(*s*) A passage quoted in Muir's Sansk. Texts, vol. V., p. 459, makes it plain that the young widow of the Vedic period sought the society of her brother-in-law just as amongst the Jews. (See above, p. 397.) The frequent references to the same custom in the Smritis have already been noticed. (See above, p. 394 ss.)

(*t*) Above, p. 394; Rig. Veda, X. 40, referred to above, p. 276. The Vedic passage apparently insisting on a really paternal relation as the condition of celebrating certain sacrifices has to be explained away in the Datt. Mim., sec. I. 44.

(*v*) The myth of Sunahsepa's giving himself to Visvamitra, who already had a hundred sons, is referred to in the Rig Veda, but it is evidently not recognized as a part of the social system. Nor is it connected by any chain of natural development or deduction with adoption. A mere casual and partial similarity does not under such circumstances indicate derivation. Sunahsepa, it appears,

may be inferred even from the exhortation against it as incapable of supplying a deficiency of begotten offspring (*w*).

The levirate, as a means of raising up issue, became in the course of time disreputable amongst the Brahmans (*x*) or at any rate somewhat discredited. It is by Manu made one of the reproaches of king Vena, who appears to have strongly resisted the pretensions of the Brahmans, that he made this practice "fit only for cattle" a law for men (*y*). Yet a few verses later the institution in a modified form is fully recognized (*z*), and a souless woman it is admitted might be legally authorized to take a substitute for her husband (*a*). Thus the ruder arrangements of a half-

---

must have already uttered mantras and must therefore have been initiated. Hence it is said arises an authority for the adoption of a son whose samkaras have been completed in another family. When history admits the legend, logic may accept the inference.

In the comparatively late Yajur Veda there is an instance in the story of Atri of a man's giving away all his children and in place of them adopting a religious ceremony. Such myths sprang merely from the unchecked play of invention. Taken seriously as examples for imitation they would warrant what the law strongly condemns, needless adoption and parting with all sons. The story of Manu's appointment of a daughter though he had sons, Col. Dig., Book V., T. 216, is not by any one held to validate a similar appointment now, nor is Pandu's liberal acceptance of his wife's children a pattern for a less meritorious generation. See Col. Dig., Book V., T. 301 Comm., T. 273 Comm. A further pitch of imaginative licence is reached in the story of Daksha's appointing his fifty daughters and giving twenty-seven to one husband. See Col. Dig., Book V., T. 222.

(*w*) See the passages cited by Zimmer, Altindisches Leben, p. 318; and comp. Rig. Ved. I. 124, 125.

(*x*) Above, pp. 395—6; Manu V. 161, 162.

(*y*) See Muir, Sansk. Texts, vol. I., p. 297; Manu IX. 66.

(*z*) Manu IX. 69, 70; comp. Gaut. Ad. 28, para. 19; Vasish., Chap. XVII., para. 11; Vishnu, Chap. XV., para. 3.

(*a*) Manu IX. 147, 159, 161; Baudh. Pr. II., Kand. 2, para. 12. Not only could a wife be borrowed, but a Brahman might be hired, as well as a relative called in, to supply a suspected defect on the part of the husband desirous of offspring. See the passage quoted Datt. Min., § V. 16. Various bargains could be made between the father and the *quasi*-father; see the texts, Col. Dig., Book V., T. 213, 214, 217, 235, 238, 240, 241, 244, 252.

In the passage quoted Datt. Chand., sec. III. 9, it is provided that a son begotten on the widow by a brother of the deceased husband is to be regarded as a son of the latter only. He is to take precedence as heir over sons begotten by the deceased on other men's wives. As to these see Gautama, quoted Col. Dig., Book V., T. 265. The Brahma Purana, quoted *ibid.* T. 217, would, taken without the gloss, reverse the order of succession.

savage time (*b*) stand recorded side by side with higher conceptions still struggling for admittance. The higher cause prevailed, but its supremacy is even now not completely established amongst the primitive tribes (*c*). Amongst the higher castes the older notions are virtually obsolete, yet in the law books we find rules still based on them with more or less of artificiality (*d*). These instances of adjustment must be taken rather perhaps as proofs of the strong conservative tendency of learned men building on sacred foundations, than as the real grounds of customs which had an obvious recommendation in their fitness; but they give a peculiar turn to the reasonings on some points of the chief authorities which has had a palpable influence on the development of the practical law.

As an example of this, reference may be made to the rule that the place as heir of a member of a family disqualified by some personal defect may be taken by a son begotten either by the man himself or by a kinsman on his behalf (*e*). The specific mention of these substitutes is held by the Mitakshara (*f*) to exclude a son adopted by a man himself disqualified for inheritance, and the Smriti has probably come down from a time when the family might refuse to accept any one not actually born in it under arrangements which provided that a child thus born shared the common ancestral blood (*g*).

(*b*) Polygamy, though the indications of it in the Vedic hymns are not frequent, is yet referred to, see Muir's Sansk. Texts, vol. V., p. 458; Zimmer, Altin, Leb. 324. The seclusion of women seems from other Vedic passages not to have been practised. It is probable that under such circumstances a considerable licence of manners prevailed, and of this there are several indications. Wilson, Rig Veda, 2, xvii.; Zimm. *op cit.* 332, 334.

(*c*) See above, p. 357.

(*d*) Doctor Burnell, Introd. to the Madhaviya, says: "Indian jurists never attempted to record such merely human details" as those of local custom, but the perusal of such a work as the Vyav. Mayukha can leave no doubt that the commentators were no more independent than other human beings of the moral medium in which they lived. An ingenious and laboured interpretation not infrequently leads merely to a corroboration of what custom had already made law.

(*e*) Mit., Chap. II., sec. 10, para. 9.

(*f*) *Ibid.*, para. 11.

(*g*) There was no such thing as a repeal of a Smriti law. See above, pp. 46—50. As the sacred writings were inspired all had authority, and when they clashed had in some way to be reconciled by interpretation (see Manu II. 12—15). Here the precise rule prescribed for the particular case is declared by Vijnanesvara to override the more general law of replenishment of the family,

Another instance is the reference by some authors of the right of a widow to adopt a son without express authorization to the duty in former ages of raising up seed to her deceased husband by an appointed relative (*h*). And as this function was assigned to the brother or other near kinsman, so he, it was said, was the person to concur in an adoption by the widow, without which such an adoption could not be valid (*i*). The Privy Council refused to admit the analogy as affording more than " an explanatory argument for an actual practice " (*k*), and placed the necessity for kinsmen's assent upon the ground of " the presumed incapacity of women for independence," but the logical method pursued by the Indian writers referred to and adopted by the High Court of Madras in this case is extensively applied in the Hindu Law (*l*).

---

and the rule has been preserved, though its effect now is to prevent disqualified persons from supplying their own places at all, comp. pp. 48—50, above; *The Collector of Madura* v. *Muttu Ramalinga Sathupathy*, 12 M. I. A., at p. 435, and S. C. 2 M. H. C. R., at p. 231. It is a canon of construction that when there is a general rule a special one of possible narrower scope is to be interpreted so as not to deprive the wider rule of its general operation. See Datt. Chand., sec. V., 27. This is equally a rule of the English Law; see Co. Litt. 299*a*, and *Ebbs* v. *Boulnois*, L. R. 10 Ch. A., at p. 484. The apparent contradiction is got rid of by a limitation of the one or the other rule as to persons, time, or place of operation.

(*h*) See *Collector of Madura* v. *Srimatee Muttu Ramalinga Sathupathy*, 2 M. H. C. R., at pp. 213, 221, 222, 224, 226, 230.

(*i*) *Ibid.*

(*k*) S. C. 12 M. I. A., at p. 441. The Samskara Kaustubha argues that a woman's necessary dependence does not disqualify her for adopting, but it does not decisively dispense with the assent of kinsmen, though these may incur damnation by wrongly withholding it. The construction given by the Sastris (above, p. 783) is subject to this qualification.

(*l*) The principle of development on which, as a formulated scheme, the whole law of adoption rests, is strongly insisted on at 2 M. H .C. R. 227. The Judicial Committee at 12 M. I. A. 441, says that " as a ground for judicial decision these speculations are inadmissible " : the force of any doctrine depends on its reception. (*Ibid.*, p. 436.) But the character of the doctrine is sometimes virtually conclusive for or against its admissibleness, and the view expressed by the High Court may derive some support from the dicta of Lord Wensleydale in *Morehouse* v. *Rennell*, 1 Cl. & Fin. 546, adopted by Willes, J., in the *Tagore Case*, L. R. Suppl. I. A., at p. 68. On the other hand, in *Reg.* v. *Bertrand*, L. R. 1 P. C., at p. 520, it is said that the Courts cannot make that law which the Legislature or usage has not made so. This is quoted and approved in *Reg.* v. *Duncan*, L. R. 7 Q. B. D., at p. 200. In *Dalton* v. *Angus*, L. R. 6 A. C., at p. 812, Lord Blackburne recognizes fictions as a beneficent usurpation, departure from which would be as great a usurpation by the Courts. That even principles quite foreign to the Hindu Law may thus obtain reception and react on the

It is only necessary to read the Smritis with a little care to perceive that something like a Spartan indifference to mere sexual purity (*m*) prevailed amongst the Hindus whose habits and ideas are recorded in these ancient compositions (*n*). In discussing the punarbhu (twice-married woman) and the svairina (faithless wife) Narada shows that irregular relations were common. The chief care manifested is as to the ownership of the children, which is said to belong to him who has begotten them, if the husband

---

whole system appears from the discussion above, p. 578 ss. See *Suraj Bunsee Koer's Case*, L. R. 6 I. A., at p. 102.

(*m*) Vishnu, Transl. XV. 27, and note. See McLennan, Studies in Anc. Hist., p. 178. For the legend of Vasishtha, called in to his aid by King Saudasa, see Col. Dig., Book V., T. 229, Comm. The controversy pointed at in Vasishtha, Chap. XVII., paras. 6 ss., shows very clearly that in his time it was still an open question whether additions to a family might not allowably be obtained by the aid of an outsider. Vasishtha expresses no decided view. The puritan Apastamba (Pr. II., Pat. 6, Khand. 13, paras. 6, 7) ascribes the son thus obtained to the real father, but the Vedic Gatha quoted by him necessarily implies that procreation by deputy was very common. Manu, IX. 51, ascribes the offspring to the woman's husband, comp. V. 162. He recognizes, IX. 162, that a man may have two heirs, one only of whom was begotten by himself, and takes it as of course that a child of an unknown father belongs to the master of the house in which he is born, V. 170; see above, p. 794, note (*o*). An indication of the same ancient usage is to be found in the Buddhist Law, published by Mr. Jardine, Judicial Commissioner of British Burmah. In Chap. II., sec. 89, it is said that where a daughter, disapproving of the husband chosen for her by her parents, gets a son procreated by another man, such a one is recognized as a Khettadza (*i.e.* Kshetraja) son. This part of the Burmese Law has obviously been introduced from India, and probably reproduces more archaic rules in many instances than those that have been preserved in India itself.

(*n*) The capture of brides by force or pretended force was common. It is noted of a blind daughter that any wooer may carry her off, and no one hurl a javelin at him. Muir's Sansk. Texts, vol. V., p. 458; comp. Manu, III. 33, 34. In Baudhayana, Pr. IV., Adh. I., para. 15, it is said that an abduction gives no marital right. The "mundium" jealously guarded by early European law was a corrective of the rough wooing of capture. It is found insisted on in the "Vagaru Dhammathat," translated from Pali by Dr. Forchhammer; but the law is evaded by three successive elopements.

The passage quoted from the Atharva Veda in Muir's Sansk. Texts, vol. I., p. 280, seems to indicate that Brahman women were sometimes taken from their husbands by powerful men. It shows also that Brahmans married the wives or widows of Rajanyas and of Vaisyas. In such a case the Brahman is to be regarded as the only real husband. See Zimmer, Altin. Leb., p. 326. Such practices are far removed from the Brahmanical usages and ideas of the present day.

has sold his wife's embraces (*o*), but otherwise (*p*) to the husband. Vasishtha (*q*) calmly deals with the case of a woman who, having left the husband of her youth to live with another, afterwards returns to his family. She stands on the same social footing as a widow remarried in the family she joins (*r*).

(*o*) The purchase or hiring of another man's wife to procure offspring for oneself is authorized by the texts of Narada, quoted in Col. Dig., Book V., T. 342, 343. See also T. 257, 264, 265 and Comm. The prevalence of such a custom affords the readiest explanation of the illegality of the adoption of a sister's or a daughter's son. The adopted is "a reflexion of a begotten son." The conditions of legality in the case of the begotten son adhere, therefore, as far as possible to his representative. Now when a sonless man leased another's wife to provide him with offspring, it was impossible that he should take his own sister or daughter : incest was abominable, while other immoralities had not yet assumed that character. When adoption took the place of procreation an imitation of nature was still kept up, and she who could not be to a man the actual mother of a begotten substitutionary son was not allowed to be mother of *his* substitute the son given in adoption.

The Dattaka Mimamsa, sec. V., 16 ss. places the prohibition on the ground that a man could not be called in to procure a son for the husband of his own daughter or sister. The statement is of course quite true. The one form of licence even with its limitation is as revolting to modern ideas as the other. Of the two it seems more reasonable to trace the rule to an extension of the fiction of a natural relation in the adoptive father's own family rather than to limitations on the replenishment of another family. The Roman Law said, "Adoptio demum in his personis locum habet in quibus etiam natura potest habere," Poth. Pand. Li. I. Tit. VII. § XVI.; and the Hindu law of adoption presents many instances of the influence of the same principle, as in preventing a man's adoption of one older than himself, and whom, therefore, he could not possibly have begotten, and adoption by an immature girl who could not be mother of the representative son. See Steele, 388, 44, 48.

(*p*) Hence the story of Pandu in the Mahabharata, quoted Col. Dig., Book V., T. 273, Comm. There was much controversy on the point, as may be seen from Col. Dig., Book V., T. 253 Comm., and many other passages.

One of the laws of the Alamanni provided that where a man had carried off the wife of another he was to pay a fine to the husband. If the captor took her to wife while the fine remained unpaid, any child resulting from the marriage before the fine was paid was to belong to the former husband. So as to the children of a daughter taken without the mundium or guardianship being acquired from her father, see Canciani, Leg. Barb., vol. II., p. 335.

(*q*) Chap. XVII. 19.

(*r*) Along with general censures of adultery (Manu IX. 30) there are in Manu (VIII. 352, ss.) and the other Smritis (Yajn. I. 72, 74; comp. Vishnu XXXVII. 33) such indulgences allowed as show that caste was thought much more of than mere chastity. Girls are indeed encouraged to fornication with men of high class. (Manu VIII. 365; comp. 2 Str. H. L. 162, and p. 376, *supra*.) The penalties provided are for the insolence of those who connect

It is not amongst people of such habits and ideas that we can look for the delicacy which now characterizes the relations of the sexes in advanced communities. The gradual abolition of the grosser means of supplementing a family in favour of the system

---

themselves with members of a class different from their own (Vyav. May., Chap. XIX., para. 6)—in the case of men with their superiors (Manu VIII. 374 ss.), in the case of women (Manu VIII. 371) with their inferiors. To the same effect is Narada. (Pt. II., Chap. XII., Sutra 78; Vyav. May., Chap. XIX., para. 11; comp. 2 Str. H. L. 167.) The object of the restrictions and the indulgences was to maintain the lordly superiority of the twice born (Manu III. 155, 156, 178; IV. 80; V. 104; X. 317, 319; XI. 84, 101; XII. 43) and to prevent their corruption (Manu V. 89; VIII. 353; IX. 7; Col. Dig., Book IV., Chap. I., T. 8, 77, 78, 79, 83) through the infusion of low-caste blood; the sons being supposed to partake more largely of the nature of their fathers (Manu, III. 49; IX. 9, 32, 35, 36; X. 5, 12, 30, 64, 67, 72; Yajn. I. 93).

The notion that male offspring partake more largely of the father's nature, and female offspring of the mother's, has been widely entertained: see *ex. gr.* Lucr. De Nat. Rer. IV. 1229—1232, Ed. Munro; and the denunciations of adultery that occur rest on its tendency to confuse caste, and to deprive the manes of the true ancestors of their due offerings—a privation regarded as a great though undefined calamity. See Thomson's Bhagavadgita, p. 7. Vasishtha says (Chap. XXVIII. 1—9; Chap. V. 1—4) that a woman is not by unchastity made more than temporarily impure. (So Yajn. I. 72.) She imparts no taint of sin during dalliance, and is not to be cast off by her husband for any impurity. A tradition preserved in the Mahabharata commends king Mitrasaha for accommodating the sage Vasishtha with his wife Damavanti.

In the case of unmarried women the state of feeling may be gathered from the functions assigned to the Apsarases in the Vedic heaven (see Muir, Sansk. Texts, vol. V., pp. 307, 308, 345, 430; vol. IV., p. 461). Manu's approval or permission of a sacrifice of modesty to a man of higher class (Manu VIII. 364) is reproduced in the Pali law books of the Burmese. See Notes on Buddhist Law, III., sec. 140, p. 14. And that some men had no troublesome sensitiveness about their wives' chastity is plainly indicated (see Vas. XIV. 6—11). The Taittiriya Brahmana gravely explains the character of the reward given for sexual association, and the sage Yajnavalkya (II. 290, 292) provides against cheating on either side. With "Dasis" or slaves not secluded, Narada thinks connexion innocent (Nar., Pt. II., Chap. XII., paras. 78, 79), and he treats the ornaments of courtesans as exempt from seizure like the instruments of musicians, as the means by which they gain their livelihood. This way of regarding the subject has come down to modern times, and, not to go farther, Nilakantha in the Mayukha ranks courtesans with the members of other business associations. (Vyav. May., Chap. XVII. 2; Chap. XIX. 10, 11; Chap. XXII.) The sisterhoods of dancing women must hence be deemed not wholly foreign to the Hindu system as it was, though that system contains within itself the means of a gradual purification corresponding to the advance in moral and social refinement manifested in the adoption of higher standards in the customary law.

of adoption is itself a striking evidence of progress in civilization. The appointment of a daughter held an intermediate place between this and the coarse materialism of the earliest modes of substitution (*s*). It is no longer recognized (*t*), but traces of the institution still remain in the existing law. From it on the one hand has been derived the right of succession of the daughter and the daughter's son (*v*), while on the other it is connected with the fitness of a daughter's son for adoption. As an imitation of a real son the adopted son ought to be born of some woman whom the adopted father could have married (*w*). This excludes the son of a daughter, and such is the law generally received amongst the higher castes (*x*), but amongst the lower castes sub-divisions of the great Sudra class almost everywhere, and amongst some of the higher castes by thoir customary law, the daughter's son is deemed fit for adoption, and even the most fit on account of the place he might formerly have taken as a son by appointment, as well as of the blood connexion on which the system of appointment itself was founded (*y*).

The passage of Vasishtha (*z*) which directs that a man desiring to adopt shall make his selection from amongst near relatives, and for choice take the nearest (*a*), is so obscurely expressed as to admit of various interpretations (*b*). How the ingenuity of commentators has been exercised upon it may be seen in Colebrooke's note to the Mit. Chap. I., sec. 11, para. 13. The Samskara Kaustubha (*c*), and the Nirnaya Sindhu (*d*), construing the direc-

---

(*s*) Col. Dig., Book V., T. 295, 296, 304.

(*t*) Vyav. May., Chap. IV., sec. IV., para. 46.

(*v*) See above, pp. 79, 405—6; *Bhau Nanaji* v. *Sundrabai*, 11 Bom. H. C. R., at p. 274.

(*w*) See above, pp. 798, note (*o*); *Ramchandra* v. *Gopal*, I. L. R. 32 Bom. 623; *Walbai* v. *Heerbai*, I. L. R. 34 Bom. 491; *Yamnava* v. *Lakshman*, I. L. R. 36 Bom. 533.

(*x*) See Datt. Mim., sec. II. 74; Vyav. May., Chap. IV., sec. V., para. 11; *Bai Nani* v. *Chuni Lal*, I. L. R. 22 Bom. 973.

(*y*) Datt. Mim., sec. II. 74, 93, 105, 107, 108; comp. Vishnu XV. 47; *Ramlinga Pillai* v. *Sadasiva Pillai*, 9 M. I. A. 506.

(*z*) Chap. XV., para. 6; Datt. Mim. II. 15, 75.

(*a*) This is not compulsory now, see *Sreemati Uma Dayi* v. *Gokool Ananddas Mahapatra*, L. R. 5 I. A. 40, 51, unless for Bombay a special local law is constituted by the Vyav. May., Chap. IV., sec. V., paras. 16, 19. This does not seem to be admitted by the Sastris. See below, sec. 4.

(*b*) The Datt. Mim. rests on a passage of Saunaka. See D. M., sec. II. 2.

(*c*) Sec. III., pp. 45*b*, 47*a*.

(*d*) Sec. III., p. 63*a*.

tion most liberally, approve the adoption, failing a sagotra sapinda, of a daughter's or a sister's son (*e*). The Sastris, following the Vyav. Mayukha (*f*), are almost uniformly opposed to this, except in the case of Sudras (*g*). They rely on the impossibility of a real paternal and filial relation between the fictitious father and a son so born; and the decisions in Bombay must be considered perhaps to have confirmed the Sastris' view (*h*), but the customary law seems in a measure at least to have been represented by the doctrine of the two works referred to (*i*). These were no doubt written under the influence of ideas which shaped the customary law, and they afford an example in their divergence from the more generally received authorities of parallel growths of doctrine springing from the same original source, yet taking quite different lines of development according to the medium in which they were placed. The real nearness of the daughter's son once procured ready acceptance for the doctrine of appointment, and this in its turn has facilitated the admission of the daughter's son as fit for adoption. The Sastra had, however, to be interpreted accordingly, and this interpretation, setting aside the ordinary doctrine of a necessary difference in the families of birth of the real mother and the adoptive father, paved a way for the admission of the sister's son (*k*). In the South of India the Brahmanical law was for the most part apparently accepted only with this qualification, adapting it to previously existing customs, as in the case of marriage between the children of a brother and a sister rejected by the stricter law of the North, but allowed in the South, because it could not be prevented (*l*).

The appointment of a daughter appears to have been conceived in two ways. According to the one the appointed daughter herself

---

(*e*) This is opposed to the Datt. Mim., sec. II. 32, 33, 74, 95, 98, 102.

(*f*) Chap. IV., sec. V., para. 36.

(*g*) See *ex. gr.* above, p. 410.

(*h*) *Gopal Narhar Safray* v. *Hanmant G.*, I. L. R. 3 Bom. 273, 298; *Sriramalu* v. *Ramayya*, I. L. R. 3 Mad. 15.

(*i*) Steele, L. C. 44, 46, 183; 2 Str. H. L. 101. See *Gopal Narhar* v. *Hanmant G. Saffray*, Bom. H. C. P. J. 1881, p. 715; S. C. I. L. R. 6 Bom. 107.

(*k*) The sister's son was amongst many of the aboriginal tribes heir to his uncle, see above, pp. 271, 274; and as adoption became regarded as necessary to heirship he would thus appear to the lower castes the most fit for adoption. Amongst the higher castes such adoptions are probably imitations suggested by natural affection.

(*l*) Baudh. Pr. I. Adh. 1, Kand. 2, para. 3; comp. *supra*, pp. 7, 155.

took the place of a son (*m*), and then her son naturally succeeded her by representation. She was given for inheritance the place of a male, a place as a source of further succession, such as the Vyavahara Mayukha assigns her in the devolution of property not included amongst the special varieties of stridhana. According to the other conception she was merely the instrument by which an heir to her father could be produced in the person of her son (*n*). Vasishtha places the appointed daughter third amongst the subsidiary sons, and he says (*o*), " it is declared in the Veda, a maiden who has no brothers comes back to the male ancestors, returning as their son." In Manu IX. 127 ss., the transition may be observed to the second conception. The daughter, it is said, meaning the appointed daughter, is a man's heir failing a son, and as a woman's daughter usually takes the property given to the mother at her marriage, so in the particular case of the appointed daughter her son takes the property of his maternal grandfather through her. That her right is deemed the prior one appears from verse 134, in which it is said she takes equally with the after-begotten son of her father, and from verse 135, which on her death without a son gives the property that has devolved on her to her surviving husband. Yet in verse 136 it is said that by the son whom she produces " the maternal grandfather becomes in law the father of a son (*p*): let that son give the funeral cake and possess the inheritance." This seems to make a subsidiary son of the grandson by the appointed daughter; but again in verse 139 this grandson is placed on the same footing as a son's son, which implies an intervening right through which his own is derived and a consequent precedence of his mother. Apastamba makes no provision for appointment, or for the succession of a widow. He hesitatingly admits the daughter on failure of other heirs (*q*). Gautama recognizes the son of the appointed daughter but not the

(*m*) Col. Dig., Book V., T. 203, 204, 215, 216; Vasish., Chap. XVII., para. 15. See Dr. Bühler's note *ad loc.*

(*n*) Vishnu, Chap. XV., paras. 4—6. The two senses of putrikaputra are dwelt on in the Vyav. May., Chap. IV., sec. VI., para. 43. The institution, though continued in some places down to modern times, is distinctly excluded by Nilkantha from the law of the present day. Vyav. May., *loc. cit.*, para. 46.

(*o*) Sec. 16.

(*p*) Col. Dig., Book V., T. 207 says " sire of a son's son," probably from a different reading. See also T. 209, compared with Manu IX, 131.

(*q*) Pr. II., Pat. 6, Khand. 314, Sutra 4.

daughter herself (*r*). Vishnu has a similar rule (*s*), to which he adds one providing for the daughter's succession as such after the widow (*t*). Baudhayana (*v*) also recognizes the appointed daughter's son, but not the daughter, as a subsidiary son, to whom he assigns the next place after the son lawfully begotten. In his list the adopted son comes fourth.

By the time when the Mitakshara was written the daughter's right as heir had gained general recognition apart from her appointment (*w*). As putrika-putra her place is speculatively recognized (*x*), but as secondary to that of her son born under the prescribed condition. She no longer enjoys an equal right with her own after-born brother as in Manu, and her son ranks but as a subsidiary son, equal, as Visvesvara says, to a lawfully begotten son in the absence of such a son, but inferior in being one degree more distant from the propositus (*y*).

The son by simple adoption had in the meantime been gaining a greater and greater preference to the other substitutionary sons. When, traversing a wide interval, we pass from the Vedic period to that of the Smritis (*z*), we find adoption recognized, but still in a comparatively subordinate rank, as a means of continuing the family. It is mentioned, along with the appointment of a daughter, the levirate, and other means of procuring offspring, in all the principal compilations whose precepts on this subject have been

---

(*r*) Chap. XXVIII., Sutra 33. He gives him only the tenth place, which is explained or explained away by Haradatta *ad loc*, and Vijnanesvara in the Mit., Chap. I., sec. XI., para. 35.

(*s*) Chap. XV., Sutra 4.

(*t*) Chap. XVII., Sutra 5.

(*v*) Pr. LL., Adh. 2, Kand. 3, Sutras 15, 31. See Col. Dig., Book V., T. 213, and Comm.

(*w*) Mit., Chap. II., sec. II., para. 5. See the *Utpat Case*, 11 Bom. H. C. R., at p. 274.

(*x*) Mit., Chap. I., sec. XI., para. 3.

(*y*) The appointed daughter's son, superior to his own mother as heir to her father, had almost a counterpart amongst the Greeks. The heiress given in marriage by her father transmitted to her son a right of succession to her father which excluded herself and her husband, though, failing sons, she was capable of inheriting. See the seventh and ninth speeches of Isaeus, translated by Sir W. Jones in his works, vol. IX., pp. 188, 200, and 226, 231, with the summary of the Attic laws prefixed to the collection. The son born under such an arrangement appears to have been capable of taking both estates unless he had brothers. See Dem. *adv.* Makart; secs. 12, 13, 14.

(*z*) Above, pp. 25 ss.

preserved. The different relative places assigned in these works to the different kinds of sons are due probably to the several modes of affiliation having come into vogue in different families or tribes long before any methodical classification of them was attempted. A reference to some vague principle or a mere convenience in enumeration determined the order of the sons in the earliest lists. In the later ones contained in such systematic compilations as Manu and Vasishtha the different kinds of sons are divided into those who are kinsmen and heirs, and kinsmen without being heirs (*a*). Several lists are given in Colebrooke's Digest, Book V., Chap. IV., sec. 1, and in the Viramitrodaya, Chap. II., Pt. II.

The kinsmen not heirs are described by the Mitakshara (*b*) as not heirs to collaterals. To their fictitious fathers they are in their turn equally heirs as the other substitutionary sons (*c*). The place of the several kinds of sons in the one or the other class differs in different Smritis (*d*). It is probably impossible to find any better ground of reason for the variances than that assigned by Vijnanesvara, who says that precedence must be determined by the character of the subsidiary son (*e*). Visvesvara in the Subodhini says that Manu's list is a mere loose enumeration not aiming at a precise regulation of priority, and that the same observation applies to the other Smritis in which a similar apparent classification occurs.

(*a*) See *ex. gr.* Gautama, Adh. 28, paras. 29—32. This Smriti assigns the third place to the adopted son, making him a kinsman and heir, while the son of an appointed daughter stands tenth, and amongst the kinsmen without heirship.

(*b*) Chap. I., sec. XI., p. 30.

(*c*) It seems probable from the rule evidently derived from the Hindu Law, still preserved amongst the Burmese, that the "sons not heirs" were originally not heirs to their ceremonial father. They may have been taken merely to perform the indispensable exequial rites, as they seem to have had in competition with the other class no higher right than the illegitimate son, a right to what the father gave them. See Notes on Buddhist Law by J. Jardine, Esq., Judicial Commissioner in Burmah, Part V., Chap. II., sec. 85. The dharmaputra or ceremonial son, appointed merely to perform exequial rites, not taking any share in the estate, is a still existing institution, Steele, L. C. 185, 226. The Madhaviya (Trans. p. 21) quotes Vishnu as wholly excluding the four classes of sons of unknown paternity in competition with the legitimate son, refusing them even the quarter of a share allowed to other secondary sons. This passage is wrongly attributed, it seems, to Vishnu, but it may still embody an ancient rule.

(*d*) Comp. Baudh., Pr. II., Kand. 2, para. 23, with Gaut., Adh. 28, paras. 29, 30.

(*e*) See also Col. Dig., Book V., T. 277, Comm.; T. 278, Comm.

This grouping of the several kinds of subsidiary sons in two classes with important differences of rights does not occur in the Smriti of Yajnavalkya on which the Mitakshara is founded. The task of the Hindu expositor was thus made easier; since, taking Yajnavalkya as his guide, he construed the other Smritis with reference to this as the chief, but it forced him to go to other sources for the determination of the right of an adopted son to succeed collaterally (*f*). This is established on the authority of Manu (*g*), in whose list, as well as in Baudhayana's (*h*), the adopted son is placed in the higher class of sons and heirs (*i*).

Yajnavalkya II. 129—133 enumerates twelve kinds of sons as capable of continuing the succession in a Hindu family. These are: (1) the aurasa or ordinary son; (2) the putrika-putra, or son of an appointed daughter; (3) the kshetraja or son begotten by an appointed kinsman; (4) the gudhaja, or one furtively produced in the husband's house; (5) the kanina, the love-child of a damsel taken with her when she is married; (6) the paunarbhava, or son of a twice-married woman; (7) the dattaka, or son given by his father, by both father and mother, or by the mother alone with the father's assent, in his absence or after his death; (8) the krita, or the son bought (*k*); (9) the kritrima, or orphan taken with his own assent only; (10) the svayamdatta, or son self-given either on losing his parents or being abandoned by them; (11) the sahodhaja, or son of a bride pregnant at the time of her marriage; (12) the apaviddha, or son cast out by his father and mother and taken as a son by a protector.

(*f*) Comp. Col. Dig., Book V., T. 277, Comm.

(*g*) Mit., Chap. I., sec. 11, paras. 30, 31.

(*h*) Baudh., Pr. II., Adh. 2, Kandika 3, paras. 20, 31, 32.

(*i*) See Col. Dig., Book V., T. 277, Comm.

(*k*) The sale of children by their parents was a recognized institution amongst the Romans. The gradual spread of Christian ideas made such sales disreputable, but the attempts to prevent them as illegal caused so much infanticide under the form of abandonment, that Constantine allowed sales in cases of distress. Justinian, after much hesitation, at last prohibited all alienations of children. They were still seized and sold by the Roman "revenue department" for some time after private sales had been forbidden. The person who preserved an exposed child (on the exposure of infants at Athens and Rome, see Petit, Leg. Att., p. 144), with its parents' knowledge might keep it either as a son or as a slave (Maynz, Dr., Rom. § 328), and infants might be given in adoption, but arrogation was till a late period limited to those who had attained the age of puberty and discretion (Tomkins and Lemon, Gaius, p. 96).

It will be seen that in the case of the first six there was either an actual connection by blood with the legal father or at least a strong probability of it. In the case of the last six this connection subsisted if at all only accidentally. The son by gift and acceptance stands at the head of this second class, and as the gradual purification of manners brought the other substitutionary sons into discredit, the son lawfully begotten and the son by adoption have now become the only ones recognized by the general Hindu Law. Thus the Hindu Law of the present day (*l*) does not recognize the putrika-putra (*m*) or any kind of subsidiary son (*n*) except the dattaka (*o*), and in some districts the kritrima (*p*). The latter mode of affiliation is still allowed in the Mithila region (*q*), but it does not appear to be much in use (*r*).

(*l*) See Vyav. May., Chap. IV., sec. IV., para. 46; Smr. Chand., Chap. X., para. 5; 2 Str. H. L. 82; Col. Dig., Book V., T. 279, 280, 420, Comm.; Smriti Chandrika, Chap. X., para. 6.

(*m*) It is to be observed that the putrika-putra is not found in Manu's list of subsidiary sons, IX. 159, 160. But vv. 132 ss. leave no doubt that either the appointed daughter herself or else her son took the place of a son to the appointing father. Comp. 2 Str. H. L. 199.

(*n*) Many of the smritis allot to the substitutionary sons various specific aliquot parts of the father's estate. All such rules are inoperative, the Madhaviya says, in this Kali Yuga. See Madhaviya by Burnell, pp. 21, 22, 24.

(*o*) Steele, L. C. 43; Datt. Mim., sec. I. 64; MS. 1633; Col. Dig., Book V., T. 280; Vyav. May., Chap. IV., sec. IV., para. 46.

(*p*) *Nursing Narain* v. *Bhutton Lall*, Sutherland's Rep. for 1864, p. 194. As to the Kritrima adoption, see Col. Dig., Book V., Chap. IV., sec. X. note; *Wooma Daee* v. *Gokoolanand*, I. L. R. 3 Cal. 587 (P. C.) S. C., L. R. 5 I. A. 49, referring at p. 51 to *Ooman Dutt* v. *Kunhia Sing*, 3 C. S. D. A. R. 144; and see the cases under note (*q*) *infra*.

As to the classes (9) and (10), see *Balvantrav Bhaskar* v. *Bayabai*, 6 Bom. H. C. R. 83 O. C. J., deciding that an orphan cannot be adopted, though self-given or given by his brother; *Bashettiappa* v. *Shivalingappa*, 10 Bom. H. C. R. 268; *Subbaluvammal* v. *Ammakutti Ammal*, 2 Mad. H. C. R. 129.

(*q*) *The Collector of Tirhoot* v. *Huropershad Mohunt*, 7 C. W. R. 500; *Mussamut Shibo Koeree* v. *Joogun Singh*, 8 *ibid.* 155; *Baboo Juswant Singh* v. *Dooleechund*, 25 *ibid.* 255; *Wooma Daee* v. *Gookhoolanund Dass*, I. L. R. 3 Cal. 587 (Pr. Co.); Tagore Lect. 1880, p. 527.

(*r*) In 2 Str. H. L. 155 ss. there is an interesting discussion between Colebrooke and Ellis on the legality in the present age of the Krita form of adoption by purchase. Ellis contends that in the South of India usage has sanctioned this form, and that the standard authorities, at any rate in the shape in which they have there been received, do not prohibit it. Sir T. Strange referred the question to the Court of Tanjore, and there thirteen Sastris were unanimous in pronouncing against the validity of such an adoption. In the same discussion

Amongst some of the lower castes the levirate still prevails (*s*) as a source of offspring received as legitimate. In Orissa the usage, once general (*t*), is becoming restricted to the lower orders (*v*). With these exceptions and those arising from the peculiar marriage customs of some of the non-Aryan tribes (*w*), adoption may now be regarded as the only legal means of satisfying the need of a son when natural offspring fails or has perished.

A Svayamdatta, the Sastri said, was not to be recognized in the Kali Yuga, so that though a man of fifty and having children might be deemed apt for adoption, yet he could not be adopted if his parents did not survive to give him away (*x*).

Colebrooke admits that an appointed daughter may take the place of a son, as provided in the Mit., Chap. I., sec. II., para. 23; but the Sastris do not assent to this. They insist that in this Kali Yuga "the competency of any son other than that of the body and one given in adoption is repealed," and that the prohibition extends to all the castes. *Op. cit.*, pp. 188, 189. See to the same effect the Sastri, *ibid.*, p. 82.

(*s*) Above, pp. 395 ss.

(*t*) Col. Dig., Book V., Chap. IV., sec. X. note. The practice in Orissa of raising seed to one deceased is recognized by Jagannatha, Col. Dig., Book V., T. 300, Comm. *ad. fin.*

(*v*) Comp. 2 Str. H. L. 164.

(*w*) These have gained a partial recognition in various parts of India from the Brahmans, who in return have imposed their own doctrines, and especially that of their own superiority, on the classes below them. Proofs of these statements in the province of law we are now considering may readily be found in such works as Buchanan's Mysore, and Wilks's South of India. Mr. Ellis thought that the Krita or son bought was forbidden to Brahmans only, but he was contradicted by Colebrooke and the Sastris. See 2 Str. H. L. 149 ss.

(*x*) MS. 1755; Vyav. May., Chap. IV., sec. V., para. 6. See Col. Dig., Book V., T. 275; the *Maharaj Case*, 1 Borr. 202 (No. 43); *The Collector of Surat* v. *Dhirsingji Vaghbaji*, 10 Bom. H. C. R. 235; *Balvantrao Bhaskar* v. *Bayabai*, 6 Bom. H. C. R. 83; *Subbaluvammal* v. *Ammakutti Ammal*, 2 Mad. H. C. R. 129; *Jogesh* v. *Nritya*, I. L. R. 30 Cal. 965.

The word "putra" employed in the Smriti passages to express "son" see *ex. gr.* Col. Dig., Book V., T. 273, does not properly include an adopted son. Hence these passages cannot be literally cited to justify the gift in adoption of an adopted son, or generally such a gift by a grandfather or other head of the family. Custom conforms to these restrictions, as may be gathered from the absence of cases of attempted gift of the kind in question in the records of the High Courts. Disinheritance is a different thing, and so is separation. See Steele, L. C. 185; Col. Dig., Book V., T. 264; above, pp. 547 ss. It is the parents or the father who must needs give in adoption, and to a father in person or represented by his wife or widow. See Col. Dig., Book V., T. 275 Comm.

The influence of a growing refinement of feeling is seen in the ascription to

A section of the Mitakshara (*y*) is devoted to the subject of the dvyamushyayana, or son of two fathers. As a means of reconciling the texts of Manu which allow and condemn the procreation of a son by a substitute (*z*), Vijnanesvara expounds them as permitting this in the case of a widow who has only been betrothed, not in the case of one whose marriage has been completed. The brother of the deceased husband may beget one son on the widow, who is to be formally married to him for this purpose, and the son thus produced belongs to the husband deceased, unless the procreator is himself destitute of male issue, in which case or by special agreement the son becomes a dvyamushyayana, capable of offering oblations to both fathers and of inheriting from both. Vijnanesvara thus mitigates the coarseness of the ancient rule (*a*).

The raising up of seed in the mannor here contemplated being disallowed in the present age (*b*), it is impossible that there should be a dvyamushyayana of the original type. But the sense of the term has been extended by the commentators on the Mitakshara (*c*) so as to include the only son of one man given in adoption to another on an agreement that he shall retain his filial relation to the giver at the same time that he assumes it to the donee. The Vyavahara Mayukha fully accepts this doctrine, and deals at length with the double relationships that arise from such an adoption (*d*).

Vishnu of the text by which the sons of uncertain origin were to be excluded from the funeral oblation and succession to the estate. See Mit., Chap. I., sec. XI., p. 27, note; Vishnu, Chap. XV., Datt. Mim., sec. II. 61.

The influence of the older on the development of the newer institutions is well seen in the story of Sunahsepa on which the Samskara Kaustubha, by a characteristic argument, founds a justification for the adoption of a man already initiated in his family of birth. The "given son," it is said, must include the son "self-given." Sunahsepa was self-given. It is not to be supposed that he had not been initiated. The transaction in his case cannot be questioned, as it rests on Vedic authority. Hence initiation does not impede "self-gift" nor consequently gift by parents in adoption. The story of Sunahsepa is relied on as an instance of a svayamdatta. See Col. Dig., Book V., T. 300, Comm., which immediately afterwards pronounces against any such substitutionary son in the present age. *Ibid.*

(*y*) Chap. I., sec. X.

(*z*) Comp. Baudh., Pr. II., Kand. 2, para. 12.

(*a*) See Baudh., *loc. cit.*; Narada, Pt. II., Chap. XIII., paras. 14, 23; and Yajn. I. 68, 69.

(*b*) Datt. Mim., sec. I., para. 66.

(*c*) See Mit., Chap. I., sec. X., para. 32, notes.

(*d*) See Vyav. May., Chap. IV., sec. V., para. 21 ss. The translation of Rao Saheb V. N. Mandlik is here greatly superior to that of Borradaile. *Krishna* v. *Paramshri*, I. L. R. 25 Bom. 537.

The giving of a son as dvyamushyayana is recognized by the Judicial Committee as allowed by the existing Hindu Law (*e*). In the case of an only or eldest son it is said the presumption is that his father would not break the law by giving him in adoption otherwise than as a son to both fathers. "This latter kind of adoption would not sever the connection of the child with his own family" (*f*).

The Madras Sadr Court ruled (*g*) that the dvyamushyayana son is not to be recognized in the present age, but from personal en quiries it appears that he is not at all unusual in the Southern districts of Bombay. For this Presidency the Sastris have held that an agreement may be made between the father of a boy and the man receiving him in adoption that he shall represent both as a son (*h*). In a case in which a Brahman had adopted a boy of a gotra different from his own it was said that the boy was to be regarded as a dvyamushyayana. As he would be subject to certain disabilities in his family of adoption, supposing his tonsure had taken place in his family of birth, the Sastri seems to have given him the benefit of a presumption like that relied on by the Judicial Committee in the case referred to (*i*).

It follows that for the Bombay Presidency the answer given to Sir T. Strange (*k*), rigidly limiting succession to the aurasa or the dattaka son, cannot be regarded as an accurate statement of the law. Steele (*l*) includes amongst the rules of the customary law one to the effect that a boy adopted by his father's brother is to perform the Sraddhas of both and to inherit the property of both. subject as to his real father's estate to a prior right of heirship down to a brother's son. This means simply that he is reduced to the rank of a son of his adoptive father; but the Vyav. May (*m*)

(*e*) See *Wooma Daee's Case*, above, p. 806 (*p*).

(*f*) *Nilmadhub Doss* v. *Bishumber Doss*, 13 M. I. A., at p. 100; *Gurulinga Swami* v. *Ramalakshmamma*, L. R. 26 I. A. 116; S. C., I. L. R. 22 Mad. 398.

(*g*) *Oonnamala Awchy* v. *Mungalum*, Mad. S. D. A. R. for 1859, p. 81.

(*h*) MS. 1692; see Steele, L. C. 47. In the case of an adoption by an uncle the boy inherits from him, from his real father also, failing heirs down to brother's sons, *i.e.* to his own fictitious relation to his real father. *Ibid.* This agrees with what Colebrooke says at 2 Str. H. L. 121, that the son of such an adopted son belongs to the family of his father's upanayana (investiture) and consequent grotraship. This form of adoption, and that of an only son, are held valid among the Lingayats, *Chenava* v. *Basangavda*, I. L. R. 21 Bom. 105; *Basava* v. *Lingangauda*, I. L. R. 19 Bom. 331.

(*i*) MS. 1675. In the Datt. Mim. it seems to be assumed as of course that a brother's only son taken in adoption becomes a son of two fathers. See below.

(*k*) 2 Str. H. L. 82.

(*l*) L. C. 47.

(*m*) Chap. IV., sec. V., para. 25.

makes him heir to his real father immediately on failure of other sons, at the same time that he ranks as heir to his adoptive father, though subject to be reduced to a quarter share by the birth of a begotten son.

The son of such an adopted son belongs, Colebrooke says, to the family in which the dvyamushyayana received his investiture of the sacred thread (*n*). In the Bombay Presidency the dvyamushyayana celebrates the sraddhas of both fathers, but his son, it seems, those of the grandfather by adoption only, not of his natural grandfather (*o*). Whether any right of inheritance to the latter passes to him on his father's predecease has not been decided (*p*).

It will be evident from the foregoing discussion how throughout the gradual narrowing of the field of choice a sense of the absolute necessity of a son, actual or representative, has never lost its hold on the Hindu mind (*q*). This central impulse has persisted through every variation of detail and must be recognized as due to the deepest-lying principles of the national character. That character is reverential, affectionate, and speculative, but always or nearly always within narrow limits and with a certain meagreness of thought (*r*). In the family with its roots and its branches extending beyond the present world the Hindu mind has found its appro-

---

(*n*) 2 Str. H. L. 122. He receives his own investiture in that family. Any adoption after investiture is an irregularity which causes the son of the person thus adopted to return to his father's gotra, if different from that of his adoptive family. Such an irregularly adopted son is called anityadatta. *Ibid.* The adoption would probably not be recognized in Bombay. See Steele, L. C. 43.

(*o*) This statement rests on oral information as to the general practice. As to this, however, and the right of succession, see Col. Dig., Book V., T. 262, 263 Comm.

(*p*) As an only son he should not be given, and his succession in his family of birth would be excluded by brothers.

(*q*) The man of perfect life ought, at the close of his "householder" stage, to become a hermit, and hand over his temporal interests to his son. See Tiele, Outlines, &c., p. 128. The craving for a son to celebrate sacrifices is very widely spread. In China it is said that one half the families have adopted children. Only a sonless man can adopt. Nephews are to be taken by preference. The form is that of a sale which may be real or fictitious. See Journal of North China Branch R. A. Soc., Pt. XIII., p. 118.

(*r*) As *ex. gr.* Baudh., Pr. II., Kand. 14, paras. 9, 10; Kand. 15, paras. 1—6. See Tiele, Anc. Rel. 123. On the mixed intellectual character even of the Brahmanas, see Whitney, *op. cit.*, p. 68.

priate centre of interest, in the material perpetuation of the sacra, an intelligible and fit connection to their mutual advantage amongst all the members of the family line (*s*). To it in its vulgar type an interchange of influence between the seen and the unseen is inconceivable except through the palpable connection of sacrifices (*t*). They are indispensable, as the material chain was to Newton for the transmission of physical activity (*v*). The purpose of the interchange that is sought is not of an elevated character, it is not spiritual expansion and enlargement of being (*w*), but rather such limited and prosaic ends (*x*) as may conceivably be furthered by an humble type of divinities (*y*). From the Vedic hymns downwards, boasts of sacrifices offered have been made the ground for never-ending claims to aid in the sordid exigencies of ordinary life (*z*). Those of the family the son can best understand; he by his initiation becomes born again into the unseen family (*a*); he has the traditional formulas and sacred names. Without these little or no material good can be hoped for; failing a son by birth, a substitute must be found to gain it (*b*): fertile fields, long life (*c*), success in lawsuits, continuous male offspring (*d*), and ruin of enemies. The nobler craving for an object of special affection, the desire to perpetuate one's name (*e*) and worldly influence (*f*), the wish to educate a youth who may rule a chief's subjects kindly—all these motives no doubt operate on occasion with more or less strength in inducing adoption, but the persistent cause and basis of the institution is the

---

(*s*) See Gaut., Chap. IV., 30 ss.; Chap. V. 3, 5, 9.

(*t*) See Thomson's Bhagavad Gita, p. 7, and note 36.

(*v*) See Baudh., Pr. II., Kand. 5, paras. 2, 8, 18; Kand. 9; Kand. 11, paras. 2, 3; Kand. 12, paras. 11—15; Kand. 14, para. 12; Kand. 15, para. 12.

(*w*) See Phil. of the Upanishads, p. 266.

(*x*) See Rig. Veda, I. Hymn 9. Apast., Pr. II., Pat. 7, Khand. 16, paras. 24, 26 ss., show the former prevalence of animal sacrifices.

(*y*) See Philosophy of the Upanishads, pp. 10 ss.

(*z*) See Rig. Veda, I. Hymns 12, 14; II. Hymns 4, 12.

(*a*) Manu II. 172.

(*b*) Capable therefore of gaining it or of receiving the requisite qualification by (tonsure and) the sacred thread. 2 Str. H. L. 100; Col. Dig., Book V., T. 273 Com.; *Lakshmappa* v. *Ramava*, 12 Bom. H. C. R. 364.

(*c*) Baudh., Pr. II., Kand. 14, para. 1; Pr. IV., Adh. II., para. 11; Apast., Pr. II., Pat. 7, Khand. 16, paras. 7 ss.

(*d*) Manu III. 262, 263, 277; Vishnu LXXVIII. 9, 19.

(*e*) See Apast., Pr. II., Khand. 24, para. 1; Datt. Chand., sec. I. 3.

(*f*) Col. Dig., Book V., T. 312.

conception of spiritual gain (*g*), an other-worldliness of a special variety (*h*).

It is in this sphere of thought that the procreation of a son is regarded as imperative on a Hindu of the higher castes, or at least an endeavour to that end (*i*). In the event of incapacity or failure it becomes a religious obligation (*k*) to adopt a son in order that the sacrifices may not fail (*l*). The stringency of this religious obliga-

---

(*g*) Col. Dig., Book V., T. 304, 313.

(*h*) "Fathers desire offspring for their own sake, reflecting 'this son will redeem me from every debt whatsoever due to superior and inferior beings.'" Narada, Pt. I., Chap. III., para. 5. Spiritual benefits, however, are not the only reason for adoption. The Jains recognize adoption though they have no sraddha or paksha ceremonies, *Sheo Singh Rai* v. *Musst. Dakho*, L. R. 5 I. A. 87; *Bhagvandas Tejmal* v. *Rajmal*, 10 Bom. H. C. R. 201; *Bhala Nahana* v. *Parbhu Hari*, I. L. R. 2 Bom. 67; *Manik* v. *Jagat*, I. L. R. 17 Cal. 518; *Asharfi* v. *Rup*, I. L. R. 30 All. 197.

Regard being had to the immeasurable benefits to be secured by the adoption of a son, it may be a matter of surprise that any Hindu should, except through accident, die childless. The hope of a begotten son, however, is not readily resigned. The widow can be instructed to adopt. In poor families the expenses caused by an adoption both for the ceremonies and the subsequent maintenance of the adopted son cannot easily be met. In families of wealth and position the natural parents are brought into an intimacy that is not perhaps quite welcome, and there is always a chance of the attachment of the adopted son to his mother and his family of birth making him comparatively indifferent to the one he has entered by adoption. There is room for fear even of his plotting against his adoptive father and endeavouring to get him set aside. Many Hindus, being lukewarm and dilatory, faintly intend to adopt but do nothing. Hence it happens that adoption is less practised than might be expected, and the right of selecting an heir to a chiefdom or a great estate often devolves on the widow. The interest which, in such cases, the representatives of the junior branches have in a good choice has gained general acceptance for the doctrine that their assent is requisite to the validity of the adoption, though this is not by all the Marathas perhaps regarded as absolutely essential. The widow, left to herself, is generally inclined to adopt. She thus in an undivided family gains consideration, and she is anxious to provide not only for her husband's Sraddhas but for her own and her father's, the celebration of which is a duty of the son, though not an absolutely indispensable one. See Vyav. May., Chap. IV., sec. V., paras. 17, 36; Mit., Chap. I., sec. XI., para. 9; Steele, L. C. 47, 48, 187, 394; Viram. Transl., p. 116; *Bhagvandas* v. *Rajmal*, 10 Bom. H. C. R., at p. 265; *Rakhmabai* v. *Radhabai*, 5 Bom. H. C. R. 181 A. C. J.; *Gopal* v. *Naro*, 7 Bom. H. C. R. XXIV. App.; Col. Dig., Book V., T. 273, 275 Comm.

(*i*) See above, p. 789; Baudh., Pr. II., Kand. 16, paras. 10—14; Pr. IV., Adh. I., paras. 17—19; and Manu IX. 137; Col. Dig., Book V., T. 270.

(*k*) 2 Str. H. L. 194, 198

(*l*) Datt. Mim., sec. I., para. 5; Manu IX. 180.

tion is strongly insisted on by Mitter, J. (*m*). It was in the case referred to made a ground for upholding an authority to adopt given by a minor as being an act at once obligatory and beneficial to him. This deduction may be doubtful, and a merely religious obligation is not one that Civil Courts can enforce. Colebrooke says (*n*): " Passages of law recommend, but do not enjoin, adoption for the oblation, the obsequies, and the honour of his name " according to a text said to be of Manu. The sense of the religious obligation felt by a true Hindu raises a presumption of fact which is of weight in cases of conflicting testimony, yet, as has been said by the Judicial Committee: " Their Lordships do not deny the force of that presumption, but they cannot shut their eyes to the fact that childless Hindus die daily without having fulfilled this obligation or made provision for its fulfilment after their death " (*o*).

Were the duty to adopt a son more than a merely moral obligation it would follow apparently that a power to adopt given to a widow (*p*) must be promptly executed. So long as a man lives he may in most cases reasonably hope for offspring, but with his life the possibility ceases, and the duty resting on his widow becomes imperative (*q*) and urgent lest she too should die without adopting. The Judicial Committee, however, approved the judgment of the Sadr Court of Bengal that the " fact of an authority to adopt being possessed by a widow, does not supersede and destroy her personal right as a widow " (*r*), and " the claim of a widow duly authorized to adopt to claim under any circumstances her personal rights until she does adopt is not affected by a consideration of what might be the proper course if she could be proved to have violated any clear and positive legal obligation " (*s*). The widow must fulfil in good faith the direction given to her (*t*), but she is

(*m*) *Rajendro Narain Lahoree* v. *Saroda Soonduree Dabee*, 15 C. W. R. 548.

(*n*) 2 Str. H. L. 83

(*o*) *Nilmadhub Doss* v. *Bishumber Doss*, 13 M. I. A., at p. 100.

(*p*) *Huradhun Mookurjia* v. *Muthoranath Mookurjia*, 4 M. I. A. 414.

(*q*) This is more particularly the case when an express direction has been given by the deceased husband than where he has left the widow merely to fulfil the duty as her own conscientiousness and prudence suggest. *Musst. Subudra Chowdryn* v. *Golooknath Chowdree*, 7 C. S. D. A. R. 143.

(*r*) So *Musst. Tareenee* v. *Bamundoss Mookerjee*, 7 C. S. D. A. R. 533.

(*s*) *Bamundoss Mookerjee* v. *Mussamut Tareenee*, 7 M. I. A., at pp. 178, 190.

(*t*) A testator may bequeath property to a boy designated by him for adoption, and the widows must adopt the boy. They are not allowed to defeat the bequest by not adopting. " Widows " should for Bombay be " the elder allowed a discretion as to time and choice unless restricted by the terms of the power (*v*). In the Bombay Presidency and in Madras a widow may adopt without an express power (*w*), but this is not held to lay her under a positive legal obligation, or to prevent her husband from forbidding an adoption (*x*). Nor are coparceners of the deceased husband, whose assent is generally necessary, compelled to assent to an adoption, as, were this a legal duty, they apparently must do (*y*). The conclusion seems to be that "though it may be the duty of a Court of Justice administering the Hindu Law to consider the religious duty of adopting a son as the essential foundation of the law of adoption and the effect of an adoption upon the devolution of property as a mere legal consequence" (*z*), yet it is only a duty of imperfect obligation to which no right corresponds in any person who can enforce it at law (*a*). Even in the case of a widow authorized, and therefore morally bound to adopt, it was said that "no suit of that kind can be maintained" (*b*).

The adoption of a son being prescribed in order to supply the place of a son begotten (*c*), the duty does not arise until the birth of a son becomes very improbable (*d*). The existence of a son or

---

widow," unless she refuses, and then the younger, Steele, L. C. 187; *Nidhoomoni Debya* v. *Saroda Pershad Mookerjee*, L. R. 3 I. A. 253.

(*v*) *Sreemutty Deeno Moyee Dossee* v. *Doorga Pershad Mitter*, 3 C. W. R. 6 Mis. Rul.

(*w*) Mit., Chap. I., sec. XI., para. 9; *The Collector of Madura* v. *Moottoo Ramalinga Satthupatty*, 12 M. I. A. 397. The Pandit at 2 Str. H. L. 115 does not seem to have thought any sanction essential; Colebrooke did; Ellis thought it might possibly be needless amongst Sudras, *ibid.*

(*x*) *Bayabai* v. *Bala*, 7 Bom. H. C. R. 1 App.

(*y*) The Datta Kaustubha, as construed by the Sastris, see above, pp. 783, 795, says their assent is not essential.

(*z*) Pr. Co. in *Sri Raghunadha* v. *Sri Brozo Kishoro*, L. R. 3 I. A. 191.

(*a*) One does not look for entire consistency in works composed like the Smritis, and thus we find in Manu "many thousands of Brahmans, having avoided sensual pleasures from their youth up, and having left no issue, have nevertheless ascended to heaven." Thus the ground of a compulsory duty is cut away by the highest authority, and salvation pronounced accessible by asceticism as well as by procreation or adoption. See Manu V. 159.

(*b*) *Musst. Pearee Dayee* v. *Musst. Hurbunsee Kooer*, 19 C. W. R. 127. Comp. *Bamundoss Mookerjea* v. *Musst. Tarinee*, 7 M. I. A. 169, 190.

(*c*) Datt. Mim., sec. I.; 3 Col. Dig., Book V., T. 312.

(*d*) Steele, L. C. 43, 182. An adoption by an unmarried man, though improper, is not deemed void. Col. Dig., Book V., T. 273, Comm. But a stricter rule prevails in the Southern Maratha country, Steele, L. C. 182. In *Jamoona* v. *Bamasoondari*, L. R. 3 I. A. 72, it is taken for granted that the age at which a male may adopt is that of discretion according to his law. See

grandson makes an adoption not only needless but illegal (*e*). Loss of caste by the only son or the sole grandson, through an only son deceased, would, according to Hindu authorities, justify an adoption (*f*). The son being bound to perform the funeral ceremonies of his father and the annual Sraddhas to ancestors, besides the daily domestic sacrifices, and the many periodical and occasional celebrations incumbent on a Hindu householder (*g*), the sinful taint attending exclusion from caste makes it impossible that he should fulfil these primary duties. They are all of a religious character and cannot be performed with the intended spiritual effect by one in a state of impurity (*h*). But the outcast son or grandson may be restored to caste (*i*). In some extreme cases it has been held that a father may disinherit his son (*k*); it may be that when this step is taken the father may replace the son thus degraded by adopting another (*l*), but it seems very doubtful whether an adoption would be valid while a son by birth still holds

---

also *Musst. Anundmoyee* v. *Sheeb Chunder Roy*, 9 M. I. A. 287, and *Rajendro Narain Lahoree* v. *Saroda Soonduri Dabee*, 15 C. W. R. 548.

Under the Roman Law males only had the capacity for a true adoption, as they only could exercise the patria potestas under which the child was brought. (Gaius, I. 104.) An imitative institution grew up by which women adopted heirs. The Emperor Galba was thus adopted, and the law was widened so as to recognize the fictitious relation thus created for purposes of succession. (Maynz, Dr., Rom. § 328.) The rights of succession were mutual, but no agnatic relation was created. (Tomk. and Lem., Gaius, p. 98.) Comp. 2 Str. H. L. 128.

(*e*) Steele, L. C. 42; Datt. Mim., sec. I., paras. 3, 5, 45, 47; Dat. Chand., sec. I. 6; Manu IX. 168. A son is to be adopted only to prevent a failure of obsequies, Manu IX. 180; Col. Dig., Book V., T. 301, Comm. But Jagannatha contends that though a son is to be adopted for this particular purpose only, subject to the condition, yet for other purposes he may be adopted though a begotten son exist. This converts the condition imposed by Manu into a mere specification of purpose in a particular case. Kulluka's remark is more cogent, who says that when a temporal consequence (invalidity of the adoption) is deducible from the text, it is an illegitimate process to deduce only a moral one, *i.e.* the impropriety of adoption when a son already exists, while such an adoption may still be regarded as legal.

(*f*) Steele, L. C. 42, 181, 381.

(*g*) Manu IX. 180; Steele, L. C. 225; above, p. 549.

(*h*) See Steele, L. C. 42; Col. Dig., Book V., T. 319, 328, Comm.

(*i*) Steele, L. C. 381, 382.

(*k*) See above, p. 549; Col. Dig., Book V., T. 278 Comm.

(*l*) A grandson takes his father's place on the exclusion of the father, see above, p. 549; Steele, L. C. 224; and his existence prevents adoption; see Datt. Chand., sec. I. 6.

the status of a son, even though expelled from caste (*m*). Should the father die in these circumstances he will have sufficiently intimated that he did not wish to deprive his son, and it would probably be held that the widow could not supplant the son by an adoption. The sacra follow the inheritance (*n*). The non-performance of them, however reprehensible, does not deprive the heir of his estate (*o*). The loss of caste, which formerly operated as a bar to inheritance, no longer has that effect. Competence to perform the sacrifices cannot therefore be deemed a condition precedent to the complete vesting of the estate in the son at the moment of his father's death, and the estate once vested cannot be taken away from him (*p*). An adoption, even if made, would thus not affect the estate; in practice it does not occur. It is said no doubt that total loss of caste is equivalent to death, and may validate a second adoption when the first has in this way become abortive (*q*), but it is clear that the statute law has on this point profoundly modified the Hindu Law (*r*). Full effect must be given to the intentions of the Legislature, and though this may be consistent with a power of disinheritance for good reasons left to the father as a remnant of the patria potestas (*s*), it is obviously inconsistent with a capacity in any one to supersede the heir, become owner, on a ground declared insufficient to prevent his succession.

The disability to inherit arising from loss of caste having been abolished, there is a certain inconsistency in retaining the disqualifications arising from personal defects. These cannot, according to Hindu notions, put the sufferer from them into a worse position than would expulsion from caste (*t*). They have not, however, been touched by legislation, and as we have seen they are still recognized. Sir T. Strange (*v*) thought that in such cases adoption was competent to the father who could not derive spiritual benefit from the incapable son; but by the customary law of Bombay it is said that the insanity of a son by birth is not generally a valid

---

(*m*) The practice of the castes was indulgent except when the inheritance was to a sacred office, Steele, L. C. 225.

(*n*) Manu IX. 142; Vyav. May., Chap. IV., sec. V., para. 21.

(*o*) Steele, L. C. 62, 226.

(*p*) See above, p. 552.

(*q*) Steele, L. C. 45.

(*r*) *See Narayan Ramchunder* v. *Luxmeebaee*, 1 Morr. 61.

(*s*) See above, p. 270.

(*t*) See Col. Dig., Book V., T. 321, 323.

(*v*) 1 H. L. 77.

cause for adoption (*w*). It is consistent with this, that the blindness or dumbness of a son should not justify adoption (*x*). The marriage of Hindu children is a contract made by their parents; the children themselves exercise no volition, so that insanity does not necessarily prevent marriage. Marriage having been once contracted, the son of the disqualified person may take his place down to the partition of the inheritance (*y*); and should he be incapable of adopting, his wife may, according to the Bombay authorities, do so in his stead (*z*). His assent is implied where dissent has not been signified, and the act is one regarded as necessarily beneficial.

The same spirit of foresight which makes the sonless man adopt a son makes him who has but a few sons anxious not to reduce the number (*a*), lest in the end he who stood so well for happiness in the other world should, through improvidence, incur the penalty of endless destitution. If he have but one son, the gift of that one (*b*) is everywhere reprobated as a grave spiritual crime. In every case the parting with a son, like the acceptance of a son, is too serious a step to be taken without the assent of the father (*c*) who so depends on him for all his future. Allowance is made too for maternal love, and thus it is said that both parents ought to concur in giving away a son (*d*). Should no parents survive, a Sastri said an adoption could not be made because they alone could make the ceremonial gift (*e*). A rule almost as strict has been laid down by the

---

(*w*) Steele, L. C. 42, 181; comp. *ibid.* 224.

(*x*) The caste rules vary as to insanity. The only case in which they all concur is that of loss of caste, which as it cannot now affect a son's right of inheritance would probably be held not to make adoption possible during his life. See Steele, L. C., pp. 225, 381.

(*y*) Above, p. 599.

(*z*) Steele, L. C. 182.

(*a*) One of but two sons ought not to be given according to the Datt. Mim. and Datt. Chandrika. See below, p. 818.

(*b*) See 2 Str. H. L. 88, 107. There are some legendary stories of such a gift, but these are of no authority as law.

(*c*) Col. Dig., Book V., T. 273, 274, 275, Comm.; Viram. Transl., p. 115; Vyav. May., Chap. IV., sec. V., paras. 16, 17; Mit., Chap. I., sec. XI., para. 9; Datt. Mim., sec. IV., paras. 10 ss. Balambhatta allows the gift by a mother in distress or after her husband's death, without special authorization. See note to Mit., *loc. cit.* *Rangubai* v. *Bhagirthibai*, I. L. R. 2 Bom. 377, citing *Narayan* v. *Nana*, 7 Bom. H. C. R. 153 A. C. J., *Ibid.* App. *Bashetiappa* v. *Shivlingappa*, 10 Bom. H. C. R. 268, 271.

(*d*) Vyav. May., Chap. IV., sec. V., para. 16; Steele, L. C. 45. The mother's assent is not indispensable, Mit., Chap. I., sec. XI., para. 9.

(*e*) MS. 1755.

High Court of Bombay (*f*), but the customary law has in some few instances been construed as allowing the head of a family to give away a junior in adoption (*g*).

At Madras (*h*), Allahabad (*i*) and Bombay (*k*) it has been held that the gift of an only son is valid, the prohibition being only directory, or on the principle of *factum valet*, and such was Sir T. Strange's opinion (*l*). The Pandits who have maintained the validity of such a transaction have not denied that it was directly opposed to their scriptures, but they have relied on there being "no express provision for setting aside an adoption made with due ceremonies" (*m*). Ellis, too, on whom Sir T. Strange relied, seems to have thought "that if the act be duly completed it cannot be reversed" (*n*). The doctrine of *factum valet* has been discussed by H. H. Wilson in a passage already quoted (*o*). Ellis thinks the exigency which warrants such an adoption must be distress of the giver, but he thinks the ceremony once performed is effectual, as in the case of marriage. In *Radha Mohun* v. *Hardai Bibi* (*p*) the Judicial Committee have held that the adoption of an only son is not null and void under the Hindu Law. Amongst the Lingayats the adoption of an only son is valid (*q*), and so it is according to the Vyav. May. in Gujarat (*r*).

In the case of *Haebutrao* v. *Govindrao Mankur* (*s*), the question was submitted to the Sastris of whether the gift in adoption of both of two sons could be valid. The impossibility of undoing an adoption once completed is insisted on in the answers, but the gift really in question was that of the sole remaining (and the eldest) son to the widow of the donor's brother. In such a case the passages

---

(*f*) *Bashetiappa* v. *Shivlingappa*, 10 Bom. H. C. R. 268; *Lakshmappa* v. *Ramava*, 12 Bom. H. C. R., at p. 376, and the cases therein cited.

(*g*) MS. 1645. Comp. Panj. Cust. Law, vol. II., p. 155.

(*h*) *Chinna Gaundan* v. *Kumara Gaundan*, 1 Mad. H. C. R. 54; *Singamma* v. *Vinjamuri Venkatacharlu*, 4 *ibid*. 165.

(*i*) *Hanuman Tiwari* v. *Chirai*, I. L. R. 2 All. 164; Turner, J., dissenting.

(*k*) *Vyas Chimanlal* v. *Ramchandra*, I. L. R. 24 Bom. 367.

(*l*) 1 Str. H. L. 87.

(*m*) MS. 1695. *Arunachallam Pillai* v. *Ayyasvami Pillai*, 1 Mad. Sel. Dec. 156, quoted 1 Mad. H. C. R. 56.

(*n*) 2 Str. H. L. 108.

(*o*) Above, p. 737.

(*p*) L. R. 26 I. A. 113.

(*q*) *Basava* v. *Lingangauda*, I. L. R. 19 Bom. 428.

(*r*) *Vyas Chimanlal* v. *Ramchandra*, I. L. R. 24 Bom. 367.

(*s*) 2 Borr. R. 83.

which declare that by the existence of a son of one of several brothers all are made fathers, have been variously applied by Hindu lawyers to support the approval and the disapproval of an adoption. Nanda Pandita in the Datt. Mimamsa (*t*) devotes an elaborate argument to proving that where there is a son of a full brother available for adoption, he and no other ought to be taken (*v*). Even the son of a half-brother ought not to be chosen if the nearer relative can be had. And the injunction he contends has such force that even the only son of a brother may be and ought to be adopted (*w*). Without adoption he is not a son in the required sense to his uncle, and is indeed provided for as heir after his uncle's widow, his daughter and her son, while by adoption he does not lose his faculty of ministering spiritually to his real father and the ancestors who are equally ancestors of his adoptive father.

It is obvious that in such a case the manes of progenitors will not be left destitute by the transfer of the boy to another family, while if filial relation to one of a group of brothers involves a similar relation to all, the real father must still benefit, though in a less degree, through the sacrifices of the son adopted by his uncle. The boy becomes in fact a dvyamushyayana (*x*) who will perform his real father's obsequies and take his estate if that father should not have any other son. The Mitakshara and the Vyavahara Mayukha do not discuss this particular case, but as they recognize the dvyamushyayana and the theories connected with his double relations, the adoption of an only son of a brother is permissible (*y*).

The eldest son, if living, should be retained in his family of birth for the celebration of its sacra and the discharge of the father's obligation to his ancestors. This son alone, Manu says (*z*), is begotten from a sense of duty, and on this he grounds a rule of primogeniture which is soon after qualified (*a*), and which, as we

---

(*t*) Sec. II.

(*v*) So Steele, L. C. 182.

(*w*) The possibility of adopting the only son even of a brother is doubted by the Judicial Committee in *Srimati Uma Deyi* v. *Gookoolanand Das Maheeputra*, L. R. 5 I. A. 49, 53. The customary law of Bombay favours this particular kind of adoption, though generally opposed to the adoption of an only son; see Steele, L. C. 183.

(*x*) Datt. Mim., sec. II. 36; above, pp. 808, 809.

(*y*) This was Colebrooke's view, see 2 Str. H. L. 107, where he cites Mit., Chap. I., sec. X., para. 1, and sec. XI. para. 32. So too Sutherland, Synopsis, Head II.

(*z*) IX. 107; see Dayabhaga, Chap. I., para. 36; 2 Str. H. L. 105.

(*a*) IX. 111.

have seen, has not, except in special cases, been retained in the law of inheritance (*b*).

In the case of an eldest son, though the importance of him to his family of birth is so strongly insisted in the earlier authorities, yet more recent writers have in some instances pronounced the gift effectual, though censurable (*c*). After such a gift there is still a son left to perform the father's obsequies, and no one supposes that if an eldest son dies a second son is not perfectly competent to take his place. Why not then when the eldest is removed from the family by gift? This may not be a satisfactory answer to an unqualified prohibition exacting obedience apart from the reasons that may be assigned for it, but it may have influenced the Sastris in forming the opinion now and then expressed (*d*), that the gift of an eldest son out of several is not invalid. The giving, it is said, in such instances is prohibited, but not the taking (*e*). In Bombay it has recently been decided that such a transaction is legally valid (*f*).

As in the absence of a son by birth an adopted son takes his place in relation to the adoptive father (*g*), the same principle which prevents the adoption of a son while a begotten son exists (*h*)

(*b*) See above, pp. 65, 676; Dayabhaga, Chap. I., para. 37. It is pronounced a sin for a younger brother to precede the elder in offering a Srauta sacrifice or in marrying, Baudh., Pr. IV., Adh. 6., para. 7.

(*c*) Vyav. May., Chap. IV., sec. V., paras. 4, 5; 2 Str. H. L. 105. It is not opposed to Hindu notions that a man should benefit spiritually by moving another to an act which in him is sinful. See *ex gr.* Baudh., Pr. IV., Adh. 8, para. 10 and note; Mit., Chap. I., sec. XI., para. 10; Vyav. May., Chap. IV., sec. V., paras. 13, 14.

(*d*) MS. 1612, 1621. So *Janokee Debea* v. *Gopaul Acharjea*, I. L. R. 2 Cal. 365. See 2 Str. H. L. 105.

(*e*) MSS. 1682, 1684.

(*f*) *Kashibai* v. *Tatia*, Bom. H. C. P. J. 1883, p. 40; S. C. I. L.R. 7 Bom. 225. So *Abaji Dinkar* v. *Gangadhar Vasudev*, 3 Morris, 420.

(*g*) Steele, L. C. 47; 2 Str. H. L. 218.

Under the Roman Law the adoptive father could give his adopted son in adoption to another. (Gaius, I. 105.) This was by the earlier law. Justinian deprived an adoption of any one but a descendant of most of its legal effects, especially subjection to the patria potestas, so that an adopted son could not be given away again, nor was it worth while to give him away seeing that the adoptive father was under no particular obligation to him. In the case of sons taken by "arrogation" many safeguards were enacted to prevent their being defrauded by the adoptive fathers. (See Maynz, *op. cit.*, § 328 *ad fin.*) The latter was obliged to leave to his adopted son at least one-fourth of his estate.

(*h*) *Joy Chundra Raee* v. *Bhyrub Chundra Raee*, M. S. D. A. R. for 1849, p. 461.

equally forbids the adoption of a second while a first adopted son is living (*i*). In the important case of *Rangamma* v. *Atchamma* (*k*) the Sastris of the Provincial Courts of Madras pronounced in favour of multiple adoptions. They relied on a passage quoted by Jagannatha to the effect that many sons are to be desired, as the father will get the benefit of the religious acts performed by any one of them, and maintained that several adoptions were as laudable as the procreation of several sons. They are supported no doubt by some of the treatises on adoption which take the passage in this sense (*l*), but Jagannatha appears to limit its meaning to the allowance of taking in adoption sons of the various descriptions—that is, by the several modes of substitution or such as would spring from wives of the different castes (*m*). This cannot be regarded as more than a speculative licence, seeing that a marriage out of a man's own caste, or a substitution otherwise than by adoption, is no longer permitted (*n*), but Sir T. Strange sets forth a double adoption as valid (*o*). The doctrine, however, is entirely opposed to the Dattaka Mimamsa, which allows only the sonless man to adopt (*p*). In Bengal the passage as to several sons had already been limited to sons by birth (*q*), though a second adoption was under peculiar circumstances, and perhaps wrongly, upheld. Sutherland pronounced strongly against the attempted extension of it (*r*), and a similar opinion was expressed by Sir W. Macnaghten (*s*).

(*i*) *Nursing* v. *Khooshal*, 1 Borr. 88; *Lakshmappa* v. *Ramava*, 12 Bom. H. C. R. 364; H. H. Wilson, Works, vol. V., p. 57; *Gopee Lall* v. *Musst. Sree Chundraolee Buhoojee*, L. R. I. A. Supp. 131; *Mohesh Narain* v. *Taruk Nath*, L. R. 20 I. A. 30.

The Athenian laws had such care for the adopted son that they did not allow an unmarried man who had adopted to marry without a special permission from the Judges. (See Petit, Leges Atticæ, p. 141.)

(*k*) 4 M. I. A. 1. See the discussion, 2 Str. H. L. 194.

(*l*) It is taken from the Karma Purana, and being quoted by Hemadri is from him copied by Kamalakara in the Nirnayasindhu.

(*m*) Col. Dig., Book V., T. 408, Comm.

(*n*) See, however, 4 M. I. A., at pp. 95, 96.

(*o*) 1 Str. H. L. 78.

(*p*) Datt. Mim., sec. 1, paras. 3, 6. So also Datt. Chand., sec. 1, para. 3.

(*q*) *Gouree Prosad Raee* v. *Joymala*, 2 C. S. D. A. R. 136, in 4 M. I. A., at p. 67.

(*r*) 2 Str. H. L. 85.

(*s*) P. & P. H. L., vol. I., p. 80. A simultaneous adoption of two sons is not effectual as to either, *Gyanendro Chunder Lahiri* v. *Kalla Pahar Haji*, I. L. R. 9 Cal. 50, referring to *Sidessurry Dossee* v. *Doorga Churn Sett*, 2 In. Jur. N. S. 22; see *Ibid.* 24.

The Judicial Committee on a consideration of the authorities determined, in the case just referred to, that a second adoption during the subsistence of the first was not to be allowed (*t*). This decision, which has recently been reaffirmed (*v*), agrees with the customary law of Bombay (*w*); and the existence of a son's son equally with that of a son makes adoption impossible (*x*), as in the absence of a son his son represents him both in rights and in religious duties towards the family (*y*). In *Surendra Keshav Roy* v. *Doorgasundari Dassee* (*z*) the Judicial Committee has recently held that it is settled law that a Hindu simultaneous adoption is invalid.

The purpose of adoption being such as we have seen, it would seem that consistency with the theory of the institution should have prevented an unmarried man from adopting a son (*a*). Such a man can but seldom be able to say that he cannot have a begotten son (*b*), and at any rate he is bound to marry (*c*). The Dattaka Mimamsa and Chandrika do not contemplate adoption by a bachelor, nor in the rule laid down in the Vyavahara Mayukha (*d*) is there the express provision in favour of a bachelor's capacity that might have been expected, had there been an intention to recognize his right to adopt. Jagannatha, however, (*e*) says there is no law forbidding adoption by an unmarried man, and Sutherland (*f*) thinks such an adoption ought to be admitted. The Sastris have in one or two instances said that a bachelor can adopt (*g*), and the

---

(*t*) *Rangama* v. *Atchama*, 4 M. I. A., at p. 102; *Gopee Lall* v. *Musst. Sree Chundraolee Buhoojee*, L. R. I. A. Supp. 131; *Mohesh Narain* v. *Taruk Nath*, L. R. 20 I. A. 30.

(*v*) *Gopee Lal* v. *Musst. Sree Chundraolee Buhoojee*, L. R. S. I. A. 131.

(*w*) Steele, L. C. 42, 45, 183, 387.

(*x*) Steele, L. C. 42.

(*y*) In *Virbuddra* v. *Baee Ranee*, 2 Morr. 1, the question arose of whether an adopted son could renounce his adoption and return to his family of birth. The Sastri, relying on Manu IX. 142, said he could not, but that he could resign his rights in the family of adoption on which the adoptive mother became free, with the consent of the near relatives, to adopt another son in his place.

(*z*) L. R. 19 I. A. 108.

(*a*) See Steele, L. C. 43.

(*b*) See Steele, L. C. 182.

(*c*) *Ibid.* 25; above, p. 790.

(*d*) Chap. IV., sec. V., para. 36.

(*e*) Col. Dig., Book V., T. 273, Comm.

(*f*) Note iv.

(*g*) MS. 1670.

Sdr Court of Bombay upheld a similar rule as a local usage (*h*). In Madras the question of a widow's capacity to adopt without trying the effect of remarriage has twice been resolved in the affirmative (*i*). In the latter of the two cases an opinion was expressed in favour of the validity of adoption by a bachelor, but this was extra-judicial, and rested entirely on the authorities already discussed. It has been held by the Bombay High Court that a bachelor (*k*) can make a valid adoption. So can a widower (*l*) or a minor (*m*), or a childless Hindu (*n*), although at the time of adoption his wife may be pregnant. In no case the possibility that a son may afterwards be born invalidates the adoption.

It seems probable that adoption in the full sense has been but recently introduced amongst most of the lower castes (*o*)—recently, that is, in comparison with the establishment amongst the twice-born (*p*). It is the Brahmana, not the man of inferior race, who is born with the triple debt to the gods, the manes, and the rishis (*q*). The Vedic study due to the last is forbidden to the Sudra (*r*). The religious ceremonies, the celebration of which is the first duty of a Brahman's son, do not exist for the Sudras, and Vachaspati contended that a Sudra could not affiliate because he could not offer the requisite sacrifice and prayers. The Datt. Mim. refutes this by reference to a text of Saunaka (*s*), which distinctly recognizes the adoption of a Sudra by a Sudra with liberty to take a daughter's or a sister's son—a liberty which the Vyav. May. makes a duty when such a son is available (*t*). The authority (Parasara) relied on by

---

(*h*) *Gunnappa* v. *Sankappa Deshpande*, Sel. Rep. 202 (2nd ed. 229). See Steele, L. C. 182, which states a contrary rule for the Southern Maratha Country.

(*i*) *Nagappa* v. *Subba Sastri*, 2 Mad. H. C. R. 367; *N. Chandrashekarudu* v. *N. Brahmanna*, 4 Mad. H. C. R. 270.

(*k*) *Gopal* v. *Narayan*, I. L. R. 12 Bom. 329.

(*l*) *Nagappa* v. *Subba*, *supra*.

(*m*) *Jamoona Dassya Chowdhrani* v. *Bamasoonderai Dassya*, L. R. 3 I. A. 72; *Rajendro* v. *Saroda*, 15 W. R. 548.

(*n*) *Hanmant Ramchandra* v. *Bhimacharya*, I. L. R. 12 Bom. 105.

(*o*) As to the gradual extension of the Aryan influence, see Whitney's Or. and Ling. Studies, 2nd Series, p. 7.

(*p*) Vasish, II., pp. 1—4.

(*q*) Vasish. XI. 48; Phil. of the Upanishads, Chap. IV.

(*r*) Vasish, XV. 11; XVIII. 12-14; Baudh., Pr. I., Adh. 11, para. 15; Adh. 10, para. 5; Manu II. 115, 116, 173; IV. 81; Apast., Pr. I., Khand. 1, para. 5.

(*s*) Datt. Mim., sec. I. 26; sec. II. 74.

(*t*) Vyav. May., Chap. IV., sec. V., para. 11.

Nilkantha says that the requisite sacrifice may be offered by a Brahmana on behalf of the Sudra, and is effectual for the latter, though a sin in the former. Adoptions by women are made effectual by similar vicarious celebrations of the ceremonies (*v*).

In a passage at 2 Str. H. L., p. 89, Ellis refers to a Dattaka Mimamsa of the Madhaviya in which it is said there is no adoption for a Sudras (*w*). The ceremonial adoption cannot, he shows, be properly performed by Sudras (*x*) who are incapable of celebrating the fire sacrifice (Datta-homam) with the requisite Vedic texts (*y*). But the Sudra having no gotra, the transfer of a boy of that caste from one to another gotra cannot take place, and this transfer it is the purpose of the Datta-homam to effect. He concludes, not that an adoption is impossible, but that the ceremonies necessary in the case of one of the twice-born may be dispensed with and replaced by public acknowledgment.

The Maithila doctrine seems to disallow adoption by a Sudra on the ground of his incapacity to offer the Homa sacrifice and recite the sacred formulas (*z*). The Datt. Mim. (*a*) refutes this by reference to the text of Saunaka; and Ellis, *loc. cit.*, says that a public avowal amongst Sudras takes the place of the ceremonial prescribed for the other castes. Thus amongst Sudras a formal gift and acceptance are sufficient, and may be established by inference. The Datt. Mim., sec. I., 27, says that the express ascription of the power of adoption to Sudras and to women who cannot pronounce the formulas necessarily implies that these may in their case be dispensed with, contrary to the Vivada Chintamani (*b*), and a Sastri said that a Gosavi of the Sudra class could adopt but should omit the Vedic formulas (*c*).

In Bengal it was at one time held (*d*) that even amongst the Sudras the ceremonies of adoption could not be dispensed with. The services of a Brahman it was said were to be obtained to do

---

(*v*) Vyav. May., Chap. IV., sec. V., paras. 12-15; Steele, L. C. 46.

(*w*) Comp. Gaut., Chap. IV. 25—27.

(*x*) See the extracts from the Sudra Kamalakara and from Vyasa at p. 483 of Rao Saheb V. N. Mandlik's Vyav. May.

(*y*) See 2 Str. H. L. 218.

(*z*) 2 Str. H. L. 131. See also the Vyav. May., Chap. IV.. sec. V., paras. 12, 13.

(*a*) Sec. I. 26; sec. II. 74.

(*b*) Transl., p. 88.

(*c*) MS. 1678.

(*d*) *Bhyrubnath Tye* v. *Mohesh Chunder Bhadooree*, 13 C. W. R. 168.

what the Sudras themselves could not do towards the completion of the sacrifices (*e*). But on a further consideration of the matter a Full Bench, upheld on appeal by the Privy Council, determined (*f*) that no ceremonies were essential except the giving and taking of the child. It is certain that Sudras cannot recite the prescribed mantras (*g*); the question really was whether their incapacity in this and other respects did not exclude them altogether from the institution (*h*). This has been resolved in favour of their competence (*i*). The purposes of adoption have been widened so as to embrace objects in which the Sudra is interested equally with the Brahman, and besides the kriya and the sraddhas the Samskara Kaustubha insists on the necessity of preserving the renown of a deceased by alms, by feasts to Brahmans, and by pilgrimages (*k*). A son too must assist his father in old age (*l*). These duties a Sudra's adopted son can perfectly well perform, and it is easy to understand how, as they are conspicuous, they should with many come to appear the most important. The desire to imitate the higher castes (*m*) has been gratified, and the impossibility of satisfying the ceremonial conditions has led to their sometimes being dispensed with (*n*), or regarded as not essential (*o*), not only in the case of Sudras but of the higher castes (*p*). Where there has been

---

(*e*) So 2 Str. H. L. 130.

(*f*) *Beharee Lall Mullick* v. *Indur Mohinee Chowdhrain*, 21 C. W. R. 285; S. C. L. R. 7 I. A. 24; S. C. I. L. R. 5 Cal. 776, P.C.

(*g*) Steele, L. C. 46.

(*h*) Vyav. May., Chap. IV., sec. I., para. 14.

(*i*) Ellis at 2 Str. H. L. 149, points out that the "twice-born" really means in the present age the Brahmans, and the Sastris in some of their replies say that the Kshatriyas and Vaisyas have disappeared as distinct castes. The application of the law of adoption thus restricted would be of comparatively very small extent.

(*k*) Steele, L. C. 42.

(*l*) *Ibid*. 181.

(*m*) See above, p. 403.

(*n*) Manu regarded the sraddhas apparently as not competent to Sudras, Manu IV. 223; but this need not prevent a laukika adoption, *i.e.* one for mundane purposes, unless the latter are to be deemed purely incidental. The customary law approves and requires the celebration of the sraddhas by nearly all castes, as may be seen by reference to Steele's L. C. 27, 42, 181, 380.

(*o*) See Ellis in 2 Str. H. L. 131.

(*p*) See Col. Dig., Book V., T. 273 Comm. The Sastris usually insist on the regular ceremonies as indispensable, but they do not define which was essential. See Steele, L. C. 184, and the section below on the METHOD OF ADOPTION. The castes annul irregular adoptions, Steele, L. C. 388. The Hindu authorities

a formal giving and acceptance the adoption is, for all classes in Bombay as in Madras, to be regarded as complete (q), as the

---

generally regard a boy defectively adopted as a das or slave of the highest class; see below, "CONSEQUENCES OF ADOPTION." *Tilak* v. *Tai Maharaj*, L. R. 42 I. A. 135.

(q) Steele, L. C. 184. See *V. Singamma* v. *Vinjamuri Venkatacharlu*, 4 Mad. H. C. R. 165. In *Kenchava* v. *Ningappa*, S. A. 645 of 1866, 10 Bom. H. C. R. 265, the parties were not Brahmans but apparently Lingayats. Jagannatha in Col. Dig., Book V., T. 273 Comm., dwells at great length, if not with invincible logic, on the oblation to fire as being not essential. In *Crastnarav* v. *Raghunath*, Perry O. C. 150, the safe opinion is expressed that where the essential ceremonies have been performed the omission of unessential ones does not invalidate an adoption. Colebrooke more definitely pronounces the sacrifice not essential, 2 Str. H. L. 126, 131. *Chiman Lal* v. *Ramchandra*, I. L. R. 24 Bom. 473; *Tilak* v. *Tai Maharaj*, L. R. 42 I. A. 135; *Valubai* v. *Govind*, I. L. R. 24 Bom. 218; *Govindayyar* v. *Dorasami*, I. L. R. 11 Mad. 5; *Ranganayakammav* v. *Alwar Setti*, I. L. R. 17 Mad. 219; *Atma Ram* v. *Madho Rao*, I. L. R. 6 All. 276, the case relates to the Dakhai Brahman.

In *Sree Narain Mitter* v. *Sreemuthy Kishen Soondory Dassee*, L. R. S. I. A. 157, the Judicial Committee say: "The most important issue in the cause was whether there was a formal gift of the child . . . whether there was an actual delivery of the child in addition to the execution of the deeds." That was a Bengal case, but the parties were Sudras; the decision is conclusive of the sufficiency of actual giving and receiving to constitute adoption in that caste in every province. Corporeal gift and acceptance are again pronounced necessary and sufficient in *Mahashoya Shosinath Ghose* v. *Srimati Soondari Dasi*, L. R. 7 I. A. 250. In *Bhagvandas* v. *Rajmal*, 10 Bom. H. C. R. 241, Sir M. Westropp, C. J., after pronouncing Jains subject generally to the Hindu law of inheritance, discusses an alleged adoption by gift to a man and his wife deceased. This his Lordship held to be impossible, but from what is said in the course of the judgment (see p. 257), it may be gathered that a gift accepted by the adoptive parents would have been thought enough.

Lakshman v. *Malu*, Bom. H. C. P. J. 1875, p. 186, was apparently a case between Marathas, and there it was decided that there must be strict proof of the gift as well as of the acceptance.

These last two cases, though they point to the general sufficiency of a gift accepted, in so far as they do not dwell on any distinction of caste, yet do not precisely establish the validity of an adoption amongst Brahmanas without the prescribed religious ceremonies. The Sastris generally insist on these as indispensable, but in one case at least, that of *Jagannatha* v. *Radhabai*, S. A. 165 of 1865, it seems to have been held by the High Court of Bombay that no particular religious ceremony is absolutely necessary even in the case of Brahmans. It will be seen that there is hardly authority for laying down a proposition as to this caste with perfect confidence. The ceremonies are by all Brahmans thought important, and in practice the omission of them would throw such suspicion on an alleged adoption as to impair very seriously the proof of an alleged giving and taking with the requisite expression of intent.

performance of the ceremony of the Datta-homam may be delegated to a priest or a relation (r).

The custom in some castes, as Jains and Talabda Kolis, of adoption without regard to the spiritual benefits to be obtained through the adopted son, forms a point of transition to a custom in other castes by which adoption is not recognized at all, or only under certain circumstances (s), and with incidents different from those of ordinary adoption. The mere "celebrity of the name" (t) of the adoptive father hardly affords a sufficient basis in the absence of the intimate spiritual connection for so important a part of the family law as adoption, and the lower castes have in many instances proceeded but a short way in their imitation of the Brahmanical institution. It seems probable, indeed, that such adoption as they recognize is of independent natural growth, and giving effect merely to an instinctive craving, stands on a principle quite apart from the adoption commanded by religion and primarily serving religious purposes. In the continued associations of the lower orders with the Brahmans their ideas on this as on other subjects have been coloured, sometimes quite changed, but in other cases they remain in substance what they have been from the first. Regarding such classes as dissenters from orthodox Hinduism, the recognition of their own customs as binding on themselves is still consistent with the Hindu Law (v).

It will have been noticed that in several cases in the earlier parts of this work rights were set up by men claiming as palaka-putras, or foster sons of one deceased. A similar instance occurs in

---

(r) *Lakshmibai* v. *Ramchandra*, I. L. R. 22 Bom. 590; *Subba* v. *Subba*, I. L. R. 21 Mad. 497; *Vadavalli* v. *Mangamma*, I. L. R. 27 Mad. 538, 539.

(s) In one case a thakur (a Rajput Raja) seeking to exclude from succession his half-brother (elder) and his brother (younger), devised his estate (called a raj) to his daughter-in-law. The Sastri pronounced this valid, and he said that the daughter-in-law could not adopt while the brothers of her deceased husband survived; MS. 281. This must have been an instance in which a son of an elder wife had taken precedence of an elder son by a junior wife, a modification accepted in some families of the rule favouring mere seniority of birth, see above, pp. 65, 74; Steele, L. C. 40, 60, 63, 178, 229. It is plain that the male kinsmen were opposed to the adoption, and that being so the case must probably be reduced to one in which a widow could not adopt for want of the requisite assent of the kinsmen, see Colebrooke in 2 Str. H. L. 92; Mit., Chap. I., sec. XI., para. 9, note. It does not appear that in the class in question the mere existence of male heirs makes adoption legally impossible.

(t) Datt. Mim., sec. I. 9.

(v) Above, p. 558.

Bhagvan v. *Kala Shankar* (*w*), and it seems likely that the case at 2 Str. H. L. 113 was one of the same kind (*x*). These instances point to a custom pretty widely prevalent amongst the lower castes by which a sonless householder assumed the guardianship of a boy, and either forthwith or afterwards declared him his heir, whereby without further ceremony he was vested with the rights of a son subject to partial defeasance only on the birth of a begotten son (*y*).

The replies of many castes in Gujarath to Borradaile's enquiries show that the foster son was as well recognized amongst them as the son by regular adoption. In many cases adoption was not at all practised (*z*), in some no foster son was taken. Especially where the remarriage of a widow was allowed it was said that no adoption or fostering by her was possible. "Yet," it was answered, "if the Sastras allow adoption we cannot presume to

---

(*w*) I. L. R. 1 Bom. 641.

(*x*) See also Sp. App., No. 74 of 1851, M. S. D. A. D. for 1852, p. 62, referred to in *V. Singamma* v. *Vinjamuri*, 4 Mad. H. C. R. 165.

(*y*) Steele, L. C. 184. The Palaka-Kanya amongst the dancers was an imitation which implied the pretty wide prevalence of the institution copied. See Steele, L. C. 186. In one case the Sastri said a foster son of a temple dancer was her heir to an allowance from the temple estate. A foster-son, he said, may be heir by custom, MS. 1707, though according to the case above, Q. 4, p. 339, he can ordinarily take even by gift from the foster-father only so much as may be becoming and usual where there is a real son.

The adoption of a person *sui juris* under the earlier Roman Law was a very solemn proceeding, to which effect could be given only by a decree of the people in the Centuria Curiata. (See Poste's Gaius, I. 107, Comm.) It was preceded by an enquiry and declaration of the Pontiffs that there was no religious objection, and being formally voted by the assembly after formal public questioning of the parties, was hence called "*Arrogatio*." (See Gaius I. 99.) It was accompanied by a formal renunciation of the sacra of the family of birth. These formalities were gradually disused, and at length adoption and arrogation were allowed by will as a mere means of constituting an heir who would preserve the testator's name. The adopted son retained his place in his family of birth while he acquired in that of his adoption merely a right of intestate succession to his adoptive father (Maynz, Dr., Rom. § 328). His position was thus very like that of the palaka-putra amongst many Indian castes.

(*z*) Thus adoption is not recognized amongst the Kumbhars at Surat (Borr. MSS. G. Koombhar 10). In some castes, as the Bhatele, the Sastri said adoption is not allowed while there is a male kinsman surviving, MS. 405 The non-recognition of adoption was found to prevail amongst some of the Dekhan castes also, see Steele, L. C. 181, 381. This might be regarded as a survival of the objection to giving or taking a son recorded by Apast., Pr. II., Khand. 13, para. 11; but the classes who reject adoption are probably for the most part non-Aryan in origin.

set them at naught" (a). This indicates how adoption of the Brahmanical type has gradually superseded the looser tie of mere fosterage (b). The latter had the advantage that the foster son did not lose his right of inheritance in his family of birth, and that it fitted the needs and habits of castes to whom the elaborate system of adoption could not be adapted without violent distortions of the institution itself and of the customs amongst which it was introduced (c). The foster son, however, has always been frowned on by the Sastris (d). He has failed to get recognition from the Courts (e), and the member of a lower caste who now desires to benefit a nephew or the son of a friend has to adopt him in order to give him rights which will avail after the adoptive father's death (f). The iron tie thus forged often becomes irksome to one

---

(a) Hujjam Kahnoomiya, Book F., p. 130. In the case of fifty-six castes at Poona it was said that ancient usage established by evidence and a vote of the caste constituted the law. But in cases of unusual difficulty Brahmans were called in and a decision made according to the Dharmasastra. It is obvious that as transactions and affairs grow more complicated this must give to the Sastras a continually widening influence as law. It is not thought necessary to conform to the Sastra in every particular, but submission to it is considered as at least proper and desirable. See Steele, L. C. 122, 126. A Sastri said that the different opinions held on the subject of adoption ought to be applied to any case according as they agree with the custom of the community, and in the case of a Brahman with the doctrines of the Shakha to which he belongs, MS. 405.

(b) The manasaputra in *Abhachari* v. *Ramchandrayya*, 1 Mad. H. C. R. 393, was probably taken with an idea derived from a similar kind of fosterage at one time recognized in Madras. The Pandits said that the manasaputra was not known to the Hindu Law, but the High Court held the *quasi*-father bound by the deed of general donation in favour of the manasaputra.

(c) Many classes called Ati-Sudras rank below the recognized Sudras themselves, who have been brought fairly within the Brahmanical system.

(d) A man having purchased or otherwise obtained a boy, brought him up as a foster-son, and bequeathed part of his property to him. The Sastri upheld the bequest, but held that the legatee's title did not extend any further as against the blood relatives of the testator, as there had not been a formal adoption, MS. 122.

In another case it was said that nephews, though separated, inherit before a mere foster-son, MS. 119.

(e) See *Nilmadhab Das* v. *Biswambar Das*, 3 B. L. R. 27, 32 P. C.

(f) An intermediate case in which the Brahmanical law of adoption has been partially accepted is that of the Talabda Kolis of Surat. The son is not taken for the same spiritual purposes as in the higher castes. His adoptive or foster father is to dispose of his property; but failing such disposition the foster son succeeds, and his rights in his family of birth are extinguished. Meanwhile

or both parties, but the easier connection has been so discredited that it cannot apparently be restored except by an act of the Legislature.

The adopted son, according to Manu's rule (Chap. IX. 168, 169), must be "sadrisam" (=adequate, alike). This Medhatithi in his commentary explained as meaning of appropriate family and character (*g*). But Yajnavalkya (Book II. v. 133) says the adopted or other subsidiary son must be of equal class with the father, and resting on this, Nilakantha adopts Kulluka's interpretation of Manu to the same effect. It was a natural process, as marriage of a wife of lower caste became unlawful (*h*), that adoption should be similarly restricted. It was part of the imitation of nature which has influenced the whole institution that when a Kshatriya son of a Brahman became impossible, or one of intermediate caste, the adoption of such a son should become impossible also. The different construction given to the text of Manu under these different circumstances is a good instance of a process to which the smritis have frequently been subjected in adapting their precepts to the needs of the age.

A boy bestowed in adoption is usually given before the tonsure (*i*), which amongst the twice-born takes place at three,

---

he does not take his adoptive father's name as a true adopted son should do. These particulars are gathered from the papers in Sp. App., No. 64 of 1874.

The influence of imitation and a desire to rank higher in the social and religious scale, strong as it is, has done less in late years towards the assimilation of the lower classes to the Brahmanical pattern than the action of the Courts. The law of the Dharmasastra being taken as the common law of the Hindus, exact proof has been required of deviations from it, and on such proof failing through the ignorance or misapprehension of those concerned, one rule after another of the Brahmanical Code has been established as the law of the lower castes. Bold generalizations, too, have been ventured on, which by ignoring the distinctions of caste tend to uniformity at the cost of usage. A good instance of this is the broad statement in *Pandaya Telaver* v. *Puli Telaver*, 1 Mad. H. C. R. 478, that connubium subsists amongst the sub-divisions of each of the four historical castes. This is manifestly incorrect, as shown above, p. 709, however desirable it may be to get rid of restrictions on the choice of a wife.

(*g*) See Col. Dig., Book V., T. 285, Comm. So under the Roman Law an adrogatio was allowed only after an inquiry "qua causa . . . sit adoptionis quae ratio generum ac dignitatis, quae sacrorum." Cic. Pro. Domo. XIII. 34; see Aul. Gell. V. 19; Willems, Dr. P., Rom., p. 84.

(*h*) Col. Dig., Book V., T. 173.

(*i*) As to the second birth of initiation see Vishnu XXVIII. 37—40; XXX. 44; Vasishtha XI. 49—51; II. 3; Baudh., Pr. I., Adh. 2, Kand. 3, 6, 12; Gaut. Chap. I., paras. 5—14; Manu II. 35, 36. The difference in status arising

four, or five years of age (*k*). The general opinion of Hindu lawyers is against the validity of an adoption after this ceremony into any other gotra than that of birth (*l*) and of dedication of the boy (*m*). Within the same gotra, using the same invocations, an adoption at a later age is deemed permissible (*n*). Amongst the lower castes the limitations resting on gotra relations in the stricter sense have no place (*o*). In these cases, as marriage is the only initiatory rite giving an advanced status to the Sudra (*p*), some lawyers would pronounce married men unfit for adoption (*q*). This opinion has not been generally accepted (*r*). Men of all ages up to fifty have been adopted when no change of gotra (*s*) was involved. Even this change has been held not to be an obstacle (*t*), as the tonsure and even investiture may be annulled (*v*), but it may be doubted whether this licence ought to be

---

from the performance of the earlier Samskaras is indicated by the funeral ceremonies and the ceremonial impurity provided for in Manu V. 67 ss.

(*k*) Steele, L. C. 43; Col. Dig., Book V., T. 182, 183, Comm. The genuineness of the text is doubted by Nilkantha, Vyav. May., Chap. IV., sec. V., para. 20, and some others.

(*l*) *P. Venkatesaiya* v. *M. Venkata Charlu*, 3 Mad. H. C. R. 28; 2 Str. H. L. 104, 109.

(*m*) Col. Dig., *loc. cit.* See the Smritis quoted above as to initiation. The Sudras are expressly excluded from it and from Vedic study, Apast., Pr. I., Pat. I., Khand. 1, paras. 5, 8, 20, 21.

(*n*) Vyav. May., Chap. IV., sec. V., para. 19; Steele, L. C. 44. *Sri Brijhookunjee Maharaj* v. *S. G. Maharaj*, 1 Borr. R. 202.

Under the Roman Law an adoption could not be attended with a "term" postponing its operation or with a condition making its existence insecure. (Maynz, Dr., Rom. § 328; above, p. 187.)

(*o*) Such relations as are contemplated in Vishnu XXII. 21—24 cannot now be found. *Quasi*-gotra, *i.e.* blood relationships, are recognized amongst the lower castes, though not to the same distance of connection as amongst the Brahmans.

(*p*) Col. Dig., Book V., T. 122; Rao Saheb V. N. Mandlik's Vyav. May., p. 431. As to women, Vishnu XXII. 32. Various ages are prescribed by caste custom, Steele, L. C. 182.

(*q*) 2 Str. H. L. 87; Steele, L. C. 44, 383, 384.

(*r*) *Raje Vyankatrao* v. *Jayavantrao Ranadive*, 4 Bom. H. C. R. 191 A. C. J.; *Nathaji Krishnaji* v. *Hari Jagoji*, 8 Bom. H. C. R. 67 A. C. J. See Steele, L. C. 384; *Dharma Ragu* v. *Ramkrishna*, I. L. R. 10 Bom. 80. Among Jains a married man may be adopted, *Asharfi* v. *Rup*, I. L. R. 30 All. 197.

(*s*) Steele, L. C. 43. Within the same gotra no ceremonies other than gift and acceptance are essential. Steele, L. C. 46. Comp. Col. Dig., Book V., T. 275, Comm.

(*t*) Datt. Chand., sec. II. 26 ss.

(*v*) Datt. Mim., sec. IV., 50—52.

recognized in Bombay (*w*). The Sastris are generally opposed to it: the High Court seems in one case to have looked on it with favour (*x*), but the case was one between Sudras, in whose case there could be no initiation by tonsure and investiture to undo (*y*).

In the case even of an adult the giving by his father or mother cannot be dispensed with (*z*). The adopted son's own assent is equally necessary when he has reached years of intelligence (*a*).

(*w*) See *Balvantrav* v. *Bayabai*, 6 Bom. H. C. R., at p. 85.

(*x*) *Lakshmappa* v. *Ramava*, 12 Bom. H. C. R. 364, 371.

(*y*) There is no Sraddha even, in the proper sense, for a Sudra. It involves ceremonies which the Sudra cannot perform. See above, pp. 790, 823.

(*z*) *Bashetiappa* v. *Shivalingappa*, 10 Bom. H. C. R., at p. 271; *Collector of Surat* v. *Dhirsingji Vaghbaji*, *ibid.* 235; *Subbaluvammal* v. *Ammakutti Ammal*, 2 M. H. C. R. 129; *Balvantrav* v. *Dayabai*, 6 Bom. H. C. R. 83 O. C. J. The formula pronounced by the giver is appropriate only to the father, see 2 Str. H. L. 218. Hence, as the cases decide, an orphan cannot be given by his brother. In Steele, L. C., p. 46, it is incidentally noticed that an elder may adopt a younger brother. This may have been established in some castes by custom, but instances of the custom have not occurred in the superior Courts, or have been so rare as to escape particular observation. It is opposed to the generally received principle of a possibility of union between the real mother and the adoptive father, but this principle is not regarded amongst Sudras.

A woman (widow) cannot adopt until she attains puberty and therefore could be a mother. Steele, L. C. 48. A man *ought* not to adopt prematurely. *Ibid.* 43.

Under the Roman Law the imitation of nature was held to prevent the adoption of any one who was not at least eighteen years younger than the adoptive father (Maynz, Dr., Rom. § 328). In case of arrogation of one *sui juris* the adoptive father was required to be sixty years of age. Fifty is the age prescribed in the French and the Italian Codes.

Gaius says it was still disputed in his time whether any one could adopt a person senior to himself; but this was afterwards settled so as to require a seniority of eighteen years in the adoptive father. (Poste's Gaius, I. 106, 107, and Comm.)

(*a*) Col. Dig., Book V., T. 275, Comm.

Under the Roman Law of the XII. Tables a father could transfer his child by manicipation (see Cod. Li. VIII. Ti. 48 l. x.), which in the case of a son given in adoption had to be performed thrice (Maynz, Dr., Rom. § 326), though for a *noxæ datio*, in which a son was given up to escape damages incurred on his account, a single ceremony was sufficient. Justinian replaced this ceremony by a declaration made before a public officer (*op. cit.* 328). In the case of a boy *sui juris* his "arrogation" or gift of himself had to be preceded by an enquiry whether this would be advantageous to him. (Gaius I. 102.) His express assent was required (Gaius, I. 99) as well as that of his guardian if he had one. An ordinary adoption could not be made against the consent of the boy adopted, but in the absence of protest the gift of his father or other person exercising the patria potestas was sufficient, and at the same time indispensable.

The son, though a man's own, is not a chattel to be given away without his own consent (*b*), and the rule of Baudhayana (*c*) which exacts this in the case of a Kritrima adoption is equally applicable to any case where the person adopted is old enough to have a will and judgment of his own (*d*). While he has no discrimination his father may part with him, but only, according to the religious law, under the pressure of some great exigency (*e*). Parents are to bestow their son with anxious care (*f*) on one to whom he has an affectionate feeling (*g*).

Jagannatha, relying on the fact that the Smriti texts speak only of the adoption of sons (*h*) denies altogether that a daughter can be adopted. The Datt. Mimamsa, sec. VII., has an elaborate argument to establish that an adoption of a daughter may be admitted by analogy to that of a son. The argument would have been needless had the sacred writings afforded any direct authority for Nanda Pandita's position. He supports it by several instances drawn from the Puranas, but whatever weight may be due to these they have not led to any general imitation which would constitute a custom. When we consider the main purpose and the history of adoption it is plain that the admission of a daughter within the scheme would be quite anomalous. Even the appointed daughter taking in her own person the place of a son was centuries ago found incongruous with the general Hindu system, and no local law seems to have preserved or invented such an exaggeration of a discarded rule as would be involved in recognizing a substitutionary daughter bound as a daughter to leave the family by marriage.

An "arrogation" was under the later law completed by a rescript under a petition to the Emperor. (Maynz, Dr., Rom. § 328.)

(*b*) Vyav. May., Chap. IV., sec. I., paras. 12, 13; Datt. Mim., sec. IV. 47.

(*c*) Col. Dig., Book V., T. 284.

(*d*) See Datt. Mim., sec. IV. 47; Balambhatta on Mit., Chap. I., sec. XI., para. 9.

(*e*) Mit., Chap. I., sec. XI., para. 10; Vyav. May., Chap. IV., sec. I., paras. 11, 12, 15; Chap. IX., para. 2.

(*f*) Vyav. May., Chap. IV., sec. V., para. 1.

(*g*) Manu IX. 168.

(*h*) Col. Dig., Book V., T. 420, Comm.

Women could not originally be adopted under the Roman Law, and it is obvious that they could not serve the intended purpose of maintaining the family sacra. But as this purpose was gradually superseded by considerations of another kind, the adoption of daughters as well as of sons was allowed. (Gaius, I. 101.)

It was said, indeed, that the adoption by a woman of a daughter given by her mother might be recognized if conformable to the caste rules (*i*), and there are no doubt several venerable legends which state or imply the giving of daughters. On these a system of female adoption might have been built, but it must have been the embodiment of a theory essentially distinct from that which has in fact prevailed in the law of adoption. The process must be looked on as merely imitative, and having no other jural efficacy than may be given to it by some special usage. It does not appear that any caste rules in the Bombay Presidency allow such an adoption, in the sense of giving a particular status to the adopted daughter (*k*). In *Gangabai* v. *Anant* (*l*), a case under the Vyav. May., it has been held that a Brahman cannot adopt a daughter conferring on her the status of a real daughter.

The relation of a Guru and his disciple is said to be similar in many respects to that of adoptive father and son (*m*). It is a relation recognized by the Sastras, but the connections subsisting amongst ascetics of the lower castes and their disciples are governed entirely by the custom of the class or of the institution to which they belong (*n*). Some gosavis buy boys to bring up as

---

(*i*) MS. 1681.

(*k*) See 2 Str. H. L. 217. In the case of an adoption by a Kalavantin (temple woman) the Sastri replied that no rules for such an adoption were to be found in the Sastras, MS. 1651. In Steele's Law of Caste, adoptions by dancing women are incidentally recognized as possible, p. 183. But the adopted girl is called a palak-kanya (foster-daughter), p. 186, and the (so-called) adoption may be annulled at the pleasure of the foster-mother, p. 185, while a true adoption cannot be annulled, p. 184. It is therefore merely an imitative institution which can be supported on the custom of the class only if the class are as such capable of making binding rules for their members. This is denied in the *Naikin's Case* (*Mathura* v. *Esu N.*, I. L. R. 4 Bom. 545) as opposed to public policy and to the general customary law of the Hindus as constituted by present usage. The purchase of children by dancing women was once common. Such children ranked as slaves, 2 Str. H. L. 225, 229. Ellis, at 2 Str. H. L. 128, says that women have no right to adopt even for the transmission of their separate property. "No spiritual benefit," he says, "results to a woman from adoption." But then sraddhas are performed by their sons, whether real or adopted. The incapacity must be placed on other grounds, such as those stated in the text.

The Roman Law seems not to have allowed an arrogation of a female prior to Justinian's legislation. Ort. Inst. § 140.

(*l*) I. L. R. 13 Bom. 690.

(*m*) Steele, L. C. 192, App. B., para. 12.

(*n*) 1 Str. H. L. 150; above, pp. 516 ss.; Steele, L. C., App. B. A Sastri replied in one case that all classes, gosavis included, can adopt with the due

their disciples and successors (*o*). More frequently they take them by gifts as pupils and spiritual sons without the ceremonies of adoption (*p*), the theory of which, indeed, is opposed to the ranking of such boys as adopted sons. It is the grihastha or householder (*q*) in the stage of life when he may properly attend to worldly affairs who is bound to provide a son for the continuation of the family (*r*). A man retired from the world has no such duty. The ascetic who renounces ordinary affairs (*s*) as a young man, ought to do so effectually, and look to spiritual fatherhood (*t*) as the only one open to him for the future (*v*). The relations of the gosavi and his disciple differ widely, as has been seen, from those of the ordinary father and son, and though some of the ceremonies of adoption are imitated in taking a *chela*, the latter does not in any practical sense become an adopted son (*w*).

The effect of adoption is to sever the boy adopted entirely from his family of birth (*x*). His proper residence is with his adoptive parents (*y*). He exchanges "the gotra" of his real father for that of the adoptive father as a woman enters her husband's gotra by marriage (*z*). He learns the sacred invocations in his family of adoption, and in the absence of a son by birth completely takes his place (*a*). His right of inheritance as the son of his real father

---

ceremonies. Gosavis, he said, must be considered Sudras, and in adopting omit the recitations from the Vedas, MS. 1678.

(*o*) Colebrooke points out that the practice of gosavis and sannyasis in this particular is analogous to adoption by purchase, which is itself obsolete, 2 Str. H. L. 133.

(*p*) *Op. cit.*, para. 26 ss.

(*q*) Vasishtha, VIII. 1, 11.

(*r*) Apast., Pr. I., Pat. I., Khand. 1, para. 19. He escapes this duty if he proceeds immediately from his studentship to a life of ascetic meditation. See Phil. of the Upanishads, Chap. IV.

(*s*) Vasishtha, Chap. X.

(*t*) Apast., Pr. II., Pat. 9, Khand. 21, paras. 8, 10, 19.

(*v*) See Mit., Chap. II., sec. VIII., paras. 2, 8; 2 Str. H. L. 248.

(*w*) See Steele, L. C., App. B.

(*x*) Datt. Chand., sec. II. 32, IV. 1 ss.; Vyav. May., Chap. IV., sec. V., para. 21; Steele, L. C. 47. An adoption once concluded is indefeasible. Amongst Brahmans the homa sacrifice marks the completion of the ceremony. Steele, L. C. 184. *Sreenarain Mitter* v. *Kishen Soondery Dassee*, 11 Beng. L. R. 171, P. C.; S. C. L. R. I. A. Supp. 149.

(*y*) *Lakshmibai* v. *Shridhar Vasudeo Takle*, I. L. R. 3 Bom. 1.

(*z*) Smr. Chand., Chap. X., paras. 13, 14.

(*a*) Vyav. May., Chap. IV., sec. V., para. 21. An adopted son fully represents his father in a partition of property after the father's death. Smr. Chand., Chap. X., para. 18.

perishes (*b*), at the same time that he acquires the same right as son of his adoptive father (*c*), and succeeds both lineally and collaterally (*d*) though his adoption does not have a retrospective effect (*e*). Yet in the latter capacity his right is so far defeasible that the birth of a son reduces him to one-fourth of a share (*f*), as compared with the full share taken by the begotten son (*g*) of the same father. An adopted son of a coparcener is entitled on partition to the same share as the natural son in competition with a son of another coparcener (*h*).

According to most of the authorities (*i*) the severance of the boy from his own family is effected according to the Hindu Law by the requisite ceremonies, even though on account of a difference of caste or some other insuperable obstacle he cannot be initiated in the family of adoption (*k*). In such a case he is regarded like a child uninitiated as being only of the rank of a dasa (slave) or a sudra (*l*). He is entitled to maintenance, but does not inherit (*m*). The caste customs are more liberal than the books to the boy defectively adopted. Where an adoption has failed, either through the unfitness of the persons or defect in the process, they simply annul the relation supposed to have been constituted, with the effect apparently of restoring the adopted son to his family of birth (*n*). It might be supposed that in some cases difficult

---

(*b*) Steele, L. C. 186; Smr. Chand., Chap. X., paras. 14, 15.

(*c*) Vyav. May., Chap. IV., sec. V. 21—23; Steele, L. C. 47, 407.

(*d*) *Kali Komul Mozoomdar* v. *Uma Shunkur*, L. R. 10 I. A. 138; *Pudma Coomari Debi* v. *Court of Wards*, L. R. 8 I. A. 229; *Sumbhoo Chunder Chowdhry* v. *Narain Dibeh*, 3 Knapp, 55.

(*e*) *Bhubaneswari Debi* v. *Nilkomal*, L. R. 12 I. A. 137.

(*f*) Vasishtha XV. 9; Vyav. May., Chap. IV., sec. V., para. 25; Steele, L. C. 47. The proportions vary according to caste custom, *ibid.* 186, 387.

(*g*) See above, p. 347. The begotten son takes precedence, and where primogeniture prevails is entitled to the advantages of the firstborn, Steele, L. C. 186, 387.

(*h*) *Nagindas Bhugwandas* v. *Bachoo Hurkissondas*, L. R. 43 I. A. 56; S. C. I. L. R. 40 Bom. 270.

(*i*) Vyav. May., Chap. IV., sec. V., para. 16.

(*k*) Steele, L. C. 46.

(*l*) Baudh. I. Khand. 3, 6, 12; Col. Dig., Book V., T. 182, 273, Comm. See below "CONSEQUENCES OF ADOPTION."

(*m*) Datt. Mim., sec. III. 3.

(*n*) Steele, L. C. 388.

According to the Roman Law an adopted son became a member of the group of agnates to which his adoptive father belonged. This was because agnation rested on a conceivable dependence on a single head of the family. Cognation,

questions would arise out of the legal relations that had intermediately grown up, but the records of the Courts do not show that these have in practice produced litigation of any importance.

---

on the other hand, rested essentially on connection by blood. Hence the adopted son retained his cognate relation to his family of birth and did not acquire such a relation to his family of adoption except the agnates. The husband was an *affinis* of his wife's cognates and she to his, but the cognates had no affinity *inter se*. The adopted son acquired no affinity to his adoptive family : much less, therefore, did he gain any such relation to the family of his adoptive mother. "In adoptionem datus, aut emancipatus, quascunque cognationes adfinitatesque habuit, retinet : adgnationis jura perdit. Sed in ea familia, ad quam per adoptionem venit, nemo est illi cognatus præter patrem eosque quibus adgnascitur : adfinis autem ei omnino in ea familia nemo est." Dig. Lib. XXXVIII. Tit. X. Fr. 4, § 10.

As the Roman wife married by the ancient forms came under the "manus" or full authority of her husband, she and her children were co-agnates. The free form of marriage was in the end the only one used, and then there was no agnation between her and her children; much less, therefore, between her and her adopted son. Mutual rights of inheritance between a mother and her children were established by special laws, and Justinian placed cognates on the same footing generally as agnates; but this did not extend the connection of the adopted son. Adoption indeed, as we have seen, was by the same legislator reduced almost to a form which left the adopted son still a member of his family of birth. (See Maynz, Dr., Rom. § 15, 304, 338.)

The influence of the Church made itself felt in this as in other spheres. It became customary to obtain a religious sanction to adoptions by a ceremony performed by a priest. This was supposed to induce such a relation that the impediments to marriage in the case of a real son were regarded as subsisting equally for the adopted son. This position was reached by successive steps like the other prohibitions which gained recognition in the early centuries of the Christian Church. The original significance of adoption was in the meantime continually declining, and at last Leo the Philosopher allowed even eunuchs and women to adopt at pleasure without the petition and endorsement which had previously been required. (See Zach. Jus. Græc. Rom. §§ 4, 23.) But when the former legal importance of adoption died out the old associations connected with it died out too, and it fell into comparative desuetude until reconstituted under altered conditions in recent times as a means for satisfying the parental instinct. Codice Civile, Lib. I. Tit. VII.; Code Nap. § 343 ss. Comp. Civ. Co. of New York, Chap. II.

The nomination of grandsons or others as heirs by such documents as the one preserved by Marculfus (see Canciani, Leg. Barb. v. II., p. 228) had little or no connection with the ancient law of adoption; and when the Feudal system was established, kings and over-lords naturally discountenanced adoptions which would deprive them of the advantages of reversion. In India adoption was too intimately connected with religion to be extinguished, but the ruling powers have usually insisted on their sanction being taken and on receiving reliefs in the form of nuzzarana or salami in return for recognition of the adopted heir. The right is recognized as belonging generally to grantors of inams. See Steele, L. C., pp. 182, 183, 386.

The blood connection of the adopted boy with his family of birth is still recognized for the purpose of prohibiting marriage with a relative within seven degrees (*o*). Some have maintained that the same restriction arises in the family of adoption (*p*), but the more general opinion perhaps is that this extends to only three degrees (*q*), though for purposes of inheritance a connection is recognized to seven degrees (*r*) or even as far as in the case of a begotten son (*s*). The adopted son takes that position relatively to the wife of his adoptive father as well as to the adoptive father himself (*t*). Whether a connection arises between him and his adoptive mother's family of birth such as to engender mutual rights of inheritance has been controverted. The prevailing opinion is in favour of the existence of such rights (*v*).

The change of status induced by adoption cannot be renounced (*w*). The adopted son may, if he will, give up his right of inheritance, and if he positively declines to fulfil the duties of a son, the widow, it was said, may adopt another in his place (*x*). But this does not restore him to his family of birth (*y*). A complete adoption amongst the twice-born implies initiation as the adoptive

---

(*o*) Datt. Chand., sec. IV. 7, 8, 9; Vyav. May., Chap. IV., sec. V., para. 29; Steele, L. C. 27, 47. The prohibition extends to his great-grandson. *Ibid.*

(*p*) Vyav. May., Chap. IV., sec. V., paras. 32, 35.

(*q*) Datt. Mim., sec. VI. 32.

(*r*) Vyav. May., Chap. IV., sec. V. 34.

(*s*) The Samskara Kaustubha and the Dharmasindhu limit the connection by the Samskaras performed in each family. A full connection to seven and five degrees exists where the upanayana plus the preliminary rites have been performed; where only the one or the other, a connection extending to but five and three degrees. See above, pp. 108, 109, and Rao Saheb V. N. Mandlik's Vyav. May., p. 352. A sister succeeds to her brother by adoption as to one by birth; *Mahantappa* v. *Nilgangawa*, Bom. H. C. P. J. 1879, p. 390.

(*t*) Datt. Mim., sec. VI. 53; Steele, L. C. 188.

(*v*) *Pudma Coomari Debi* v. *The Court of Wards*, L. R. 8 I. A. 229; where, however, the term "relations" may perhaps be confined to blood relatives through the adoptive father.

(*w*) *Ruvee Bhudr* v. *Roopshankar*, 2 Borr. 713, cited and approved by Sir M. Westropp, C.J., in *Lakshmappa* v. *Ramava*, 12 Bom. H. C. R., at p. 388; *Mahadu* v. *Bayaji*, I. L. R. 19 Bom. 239.

At Athens an adopted son was allowed to return to his family of birth, but only on condition of his leaving a son to represent him in the family of adoption. See Petit, Leges Atticæ, p. 141.

(*x*) *Verbadru* v. *Baee Ranee*, 2 Morr. 1, 3.

(*y*) Comp. Manu IX. 142; *Sreemutty Rajcoomaree Dosee* v. *Nobcoomar Mullick*, 2 Sevestre 641 n.

father's son (z) and a consequent severance from the sacra of the family of birth, which must devolve on the same person who takes the estate (a).

An adopted son, like a real son, may take a share or compound for it, and part from his adoptive father. He thus becomes separated, but he does not lose his rights of inheritance (b).

SECTION III.—THE CAPACITY TO ADOPT AND THE CIRCUMSTANCES UNDER WHICH IT MAY BE EXERCISED.

A. 1.—Adoption by Males.

The first duty of the married Hindu householder is to beget a son. The nature and the stringency of this obligation have been

(z) Col. Dig., Book V., T. 183 Comm.

(a) Vyav. May., Chap. IV., sec. V., para. 21.

(b) Steele, L. C. 185. See above, pp. 56—57, 324, 342.

We gain a more vivid conception of the extreme antiquity of the Vedas, and the social life of which they afford glimpses, by considering that the stages in the constitution of the family which they and even the post-vedic literature present as still existing facts, had already for the most part been passed through by the Greeks and Romans at the remote beginnings of their history. Adoption had then already superseded amongst them the other modes of continuing the family, which at a still earlier time they had no doubt shared with the Brahmanic branch of the race. In Sparta it is said that down to a comparatively late age the eldest brother taking the patrimony became lord of his brethren after the fashion commended by Manu, and sharing the scanty produce of a small estate with them, took one wife also for the whole group. (Polyb. Excerpt. Vat. XII. 6; Schöm, Ant. Gr., p. 214.) Sparta was the asylum of archaic traditions. Poverty was given as a reason for this custom, but the reason was probably one invented to account for what had existed from time immemorial, and which affords a mark by which to track the Greeks back to a time before the dispersion of the Aryan nations.

The legend of Draupadi is referred to in the Datt. Mim. sec. II. 49, to show that there is nothing anomalous in a boy's being the son at the same time of several fathers. This confirms the suggestion made above, p. 396 (x), which is also supported by such stories as the one recorded in Datt. Mim., sec. II. 45. The limited polyandry thus indicated was itself an amelioration of that implied in the female gentileship of Sudras asserted by Saunaka in Datt. Mim., sec. V. 18, and made a basis for the doctrine of the eligibility amongst the Sudras of a sister's or daughter's son for adoption.

The survival of the more primitive institution in Malabar is referred to by Ellis in 2 Str. H. L. 167. In Puffendorf's Law of Nature, Book VI., Chap. I., will be found several references on this subject to the early travellers in India.

discussed in the preceding Section (*c*). But failing a son by birth, adoption becomes a duty incumbent on all males except ascetics and members of those castes which, as to this institution, have remained without the pale of ordinary Hindu Law. The duty implies a capacity to adopt, and this is a general attribute of a Hindu, subject only to such qualifications and exceptions as arise from particular circumstances of mind, body, or estate, such as will presently be considered. The desire to make sure of a successor has led to several infringements of a purely logical development of the first principles of the law, and the faculty of adopting has been widened far beyond the religious need, for which its main purpose is to provide. Such irregularities occur in almost every system of law, and have to be dealt with in detail, as in the following paragraphs gathered from the native sources and the decisions of the Courts.

It has been observed (*d*) that the duty to adopt a son does not arise until the birth of a son becomes very improbable. It is not quite consistent with theory that the authority should exist without strict regard to the need, but custom has settled this point the other way, and it may be said that any sonless male, married or unmarried, if capable of legal acts, may adopt (*e*).

"In the ancient rule the adopter is spoken of only in the masculine (*f*). A woman cannot perform a ceremony prescribed by the Vedas, and adoption requires the recitation of hymns. The Samskara Kaustubha allows a woman to adopt (*g*), the Vyavahara Mayukha does not, except with the permission of her husband or of his relatives" (*h*).

"The different opinions held on the subject of adoption should be applied to any case as they agree with the custom of the community, and with the Sakha to which a Brahman belongs" (*i*).

(*c*) See above, p. 812.

(*d*) Above, p. 814.

(*e*) See above, p. 822. *Gopal* v. *Narayan*, I. L. R. 12 Bom. 329; *Hanmant Ramchandra* v. *Bhimacharya*, I. L. R. 12 Bom. 105.

(*f*) See above, p. 790. A husband putting away a worthy wife must endow her with one-third of his property, or if poor maintain her; but one element of her worth is that she have borne "an excellent son." Vyav. May., Chap. XX., para. 2.

(*g*) *See Bayabai* v. *Bala Venktesh Ramakant*, 7 Bom. H. C. R. xiii. App.; above, pp. 783, 795.

(*h*) MS. 405.

(*i*) MS. 405. From the same answer it appears that in some castes (the Bhatele) adoption is not allowed while there is a male kinsman surviving.

" A man may adopt a boy in his lifetime, or authorize his widow to do so after his death " (*k*).

Adoption is for the husband and not for the wife (*l*), except by delegation as shown below. Adoption is primarily resorted to for the sake of securing a performance of the funeral rites of a man having no male issue, and to perpetuate his name. Inheritance follows, but it is a secondary consideration (*m*). The religious obligation or the spiritual benefit raises a strong probability in an appropriate case in favour of an adoption (*n*). The celebrity or perpetuation of the family name of the adopter is, however, recognized as a sufficient motive for adoption, even though there be in the caste a disbelief regarding the spiritual motives for an adoption (*o*).

In one case it was ruled that an irregularly adopted son cannot adopt his wife's sister's son, so as to defeat the reversionary rights of a daughter and daughter-in-law of his adoptive father, who are alive. Otherwise it was said the adoption of such a relation may be made (*p*). The first adoption, however, being of a daughter's son, was invalid. The additional reason given that the adoptive father had a daughter was unfounded in law. His having a daughter-in-law would, according to some, indeed most, opinions, make an adoption by him improper if not impossible, even had there been no other objection. The pseudo-adopted son thus pretended to be taken into the family acquired no position in it, and an adoption made by him could not affect the devolution of the property. As a really adopted son he could undoubtedly have adopted so as to defeat the expectations of other heirs.

(*k*) *Huradhun Mookurjia* v. *Muthoranath Mookurjia*, 4 M. I. A. 414; S. C. 7 C. W. R. 71 P. C.

(*l*) *Chowdry Padom Singh* v. *Koer Udaya Singh*, 12 C. W. R. P. C. 1; S. C. 2 Beng. L. R. 101 P. C.; S. C. 12 M. I. A. 350; *Bykant Mony Roy* v. *Kristo Soondery Roy*, 7 C. W. R. 392; *R. V. Venkata Krishna Row* v. *Venkata Rama Lakshami Narsayya*, L. R. 4 I. A. 1; *Puttu Lal* v. *Parbati Kunwar*, L. R. 42 I. A. 155; *Jai Singh* v. *Bijai Pal*, I. L. R. 27 All. 417.

(*m*) *Rungamah* v. *Atchummah et al.*, 4 M. I. A. 1; S. C. 7 C. W. R. 57 P. C.

(*n*) *Huradhun Mookurjia* v. *Muthoranath Mookurjia*, 4 M. I. A. 414; S. C. 7 C. W. R. 71 P. C.

Extreme old age, a wife past child-bearing, the apparent adoption of a boy, his death in the family of adoptive father, the need of such a son in a religious point of view, are, it was said, considerations that tend, when evidence is conflicting, to prove the fact of adoption.

(*o*) *Bhala Nahana* v. *Parbhu Hari*, I. L. R. 2 Bom. 67; the parties in this case were of the *Talabda Koli* caste; Datt. Mim. I. 9; Datt. Chand. I. 3.

(*p*) *Baee Gunga* v. *Baee Sheoshunkur*, Bom. Sel. Rep. 73.

Adoption *pendente lite* is valid (*q*), though made to defeat a gift previously made. The adopter, it was held, was not under an obligation to the donee not to adopt. Even if a contract to this effect had been made, it was doubted whether such contract would affect the validity of the adoption (*r*).

Adoption by an unmarried person, even though he may be a minor (*s*), is not prohibited by Hindu Law (*t*).

" A Brahmachari (*v*) can adopt and transmit his heritable rights to his adopted son (*w*).

" An unmarried Brahman may adopt " (*x*).

" A sonless widower may adopt " (*y*).

The decisions of the Courts agree with this opinion. Thus it was ruled that an adoption by a widower is valid (*z*).

Conversion either to Islam (*a*) or to any other religion, *e.g.*, Brahma, has no effect upon the capacity of the convert to give his son in adoption (*b*).

A. 1. 2.—In Relation to Paternity.

A second son cannot be adopted during the life of the one first adopted (*c*) except by special custom (*d*), unless the son has

---

(*q*) *Lahiri* v. *Lahiri*, I. L. R. 11 Cal. 43.

(*r*) *Rambhat* v. *Lakshman*, I. L. R. 5 Bom. 631. This ruling is not inconsistent with the legal principle that no son can set aside a valid alienation made prior to his birth or adoption. The adopted son was held bound by the donation.

(*s*) *Jumoona Dassya* v. *Bamasoonderai Dassya*, L. R. 3 I. A. 72; S. C. I. L. R. 1 Cal. 289.

(*t*) *N. Chandvasekharuda* v. *N. B. Eahmana*, 4 Mad. H. C. R. 270. See above, p. 814, note (*d*). *Gopal* v. *Narayan*, I. L. R. 12 Bom. 329.

(*v*) A Brahmachari is a professed student of the sacred writings.

(*w*) *Gunnapa Deshpandee* v. *Sunkapa Deshpandee*, Bom. Sel. Rep. 202, 229 (2nd edn.); Suth. Syn. Note 4; Col. Dig., Book V., T. 273.

(*x*) MS. 1670. As to adoption by an unmarried man, see above, p. 922.

(*y*) MS. 1677. *Nagappa* v. *Subha*, 4 M. H. C. R. 367.

(*z*) *N. Chandvasekharuda* v. *N. B. Eahmana*, 4 Mad. H. C. R. 270; *Nagapa Udapa* v. *Subba Sastry*, 2 Mad. H. C. R. 367.

(*a*) *Sham* v. *Santa*, I. L. R. 25 Bom. 551.

(*b*) *Kusum* v. *Satya*, I. L. R. 30 Cal. 999.

(*c*) Datt. Mim., sec. I., para. 6; Steele, L. C. 45; 2 Macn. H. L. 200; 2 Str. H. L. 85; *Dace* v. *Motee*, 1 Borr. R. 75; *Yachereddy Chinna Basapa et al.* v. *Y. Gowdapa*, 5 C. W. R. 114 P. C.; *Rungama* v. *Atchama*, 4 M. I. A. 1; *Gopal Lall* v. *Musst Sree Chundraolee Buhoojee*, L. R. I. A. Supp. 131; *Surendra-*

been expelled from caste (*e*). The expulsion even of a begotten son is held to warrant an adoption in his place.

The following opinions of the Sastris fully recognize this principle.

"No one having a lawfully begotten son can adopt (*f*). Nor one having an adopted son living" (*g*).

The adoption of a son, while a son is living and retains the character of a son, is invalid (*h*).

In Madras, a person having adopted a son married a second wife, and in conjunction with her adopted a second son, the first adopted being still alive. The second adoption was held valid (*i*). But this cannot now be considered as law except where supported by special custom: the Judicial Committee, indeed, have said that it is settled law that a man having an adopted son living cannot adopt another (*k*).

The Dattaka Mimamsa, it is said, allows the adoption of a second son, the first living, with the consent of the first (*l*). But the author plainly disapproves the doctrine though he cannot deny the instances afforded by the Puranic writings, and it cannot now be considered part of the law.

---

keshav Roy v. *Doorgasundari Dassee*, I. L. R. 19 I. A. 108; *Mohesh Narain* v. *Taruck Nath*, L. R. 20 I. A. 30.

(*d*) Steele, L. C. 181, 183.

The Peshwa, it is said, received a present of some lakhs of rupees on one occasion for allowing a double adoption. *Ibid.*

The existence of a daughter makes no difference. See *ex. gr.* the appointment in *Sri Raghunadha* v. *Sri Brozo Kishore*, L. R. 3 I. A., p. 156.

(*e*) Steele, L. C. 42.

(*f*) MS. 1659.

(*g*) MS. 1637. As to the invalidity of a plurality of sons sought by adoption, see above, p. 821. Yet one or two castes allow an adopted son for each wife, and traces of the same custom are pretty widely spread. See note (*e*).

(*h*) *Joy Chundro Raee* v. *Bhyrub Chundro Raee*, 1 M. S. D. A. R. 1849, p. 461. A grandson obstructs adoption equally with a son. See above, pp. 814, 821, 822.

(*i*) *See Rungamah* v. *Atchummah et al.*, 4 M. I. A. 1; S. C. 7 C. W. R. 57 P. C.; Datt. Mim., sec. I., paras. 6, 12; Col. Dig., Book III., T. 295.

(*k*) *Gopeelal* v. *Musst. Chundraolee Buhajee*, L. R. I. A. Supp. 131; S. C. 11 B. L. R. 391 Pr. Co., 19 C. W. R. 12 C. R. approving *Rangamma* v. *Atchamma*, 4 M. I. A. 1. See above, p. 821. In 1 Str. H. L. 78 a second adoption is allowed, subsisting the first, but this is denied by Sutherland (2 Str. H. L. 85), though Jagannatha allows adopted sons of the several castes (various descriptions), Col. Dig., Book V., T. 308 Comm. *Mohesh Narain* v. *Taruck Nath*, L. R. 20 I. A. 30.

(*l*) MS. 1657. Passage not cited, but obviously Datt. Min., sec. I., para. 12.

The death of the son first adopted does not render the adoption of a second son made in his lifetime a valid one (*m*).

A second adoption on the death of the first adopted son without issue is good (*n*), as a son in the situation of the first adopted son could not exhaust the whole of the spiritual benefit which a son was capable of conferring on his deceased father (*o*).

A wife's pregnancy, though known, does not, it was said, prevent an adoption (*p*).

" A second son may be adopted in place of one whose adoption was illegal " (*q*).

A. 1. 3.—FICTITIOUS CESSER OF PATERNAL AND FILIAL RELATION.

" The insanity of a man's son enables him to adopt (*r*), or that of his adopted son " (*s*).

(*m*) *B. Camumah* v. *B. Chinna Venkatasa*, M. S. D. A. R. 1856, p. 20; *Veraprashyia* v. *Santanraja*, M. S. D. A. R. 1860, p. 168.

(*n*) *Rungamah* v. *Atchummah et al.*, 4 M. I. A. 1; S. C. 7 C. W. R. 57 P. C.; *Shamchunder* v. *Narayani Dibeh*, 1 C. S. D. A. R. 209; *Huradhun Mookurjia* v. *Muthoranath Mookurjia*, 4 M. I. A. 414; S. C. 7 C. W. R. 71 P. C.; *Musst. Bhoobyn Moyee Debia* v. *Ramkishore Acharjee*, 10 M. I. A. 279; S. C. 3 C. W. R. 15 P. C.; *Ramabai* v. *Raya*, I. L. R. 22 Bom. 482.

(*o*) *Ram Soondur Singh* v. *Surbanse Dossee*, 22 C. W. R. 121. The adopted son simply takes the place of the begotten son, and his death is attended with the same consequences as that of the begotten son.

(*p*) *Nagabhushanam* v. *Seshamma Garu*, I. L. R. 3 Mad. 180, contrary to *Narayana Reddi* v. *Vardachala Reddi*, M. S. D. A. R. for 1859, p. 97. This decision is opposed to the general principle of adoption being a merely supplementary process to provide against orbation, but practice, as will have been seen, has diverged from first principles in many instances. *Hanmant Ramchandra* v. *Bhimacharya*, I. L. R. 12 Bom. 105.

(*q*) MS. 1665. " Illegal " here means void. Comp. *Lakshmappa* v. *Ramava*, 12 Bom. H. C. R., at p. 393, 397.

(*r*) MS. 1654; comp. Manu IX. 169, and see above, pp. 814 ss.

(*s*) MS. 1702. The father is regarded as virtually sonless, seeing that the lunatic son cannot perform the requisite ceremonies for ensuring his repose in the other world, or satisfy the debt to the father's ancestors, see above, pp. 150, 544 ss. For the rules of the customary law as to the disqualifications of a son which justify adoption, see above, pp. 816, 817. It may perhaps be doubted whether under the present law expulsion from caste of itself causes such a moral death that the father of a man so expelled can adopt another, see above, p. 815; Steele, L. C. 185. The outcast may be restored, and unless there has been a formal and valid act of disinheritance (above, p. 549) he would claim the succession against the adopted son.

A. 1. 4.—EXISTENCE OF A WIDOW OF A SON OR GRANDSON.

" A father-in-law (son deceased) may adopt notwithstanding the existence of the daughter-in-law; but she cannot adopt without his permission (Brahman) " (*t*).

" A father-in-law is competent to adopt after his son's death notwithstanding the existence of his daughter-in-law, but the preferable course is to allow her to adopt " (*v*). " The son adopted by her, indeed even after an adoption by her father-in-law, succeeds to her property and that of her husband," though not apparently in the Sastri's opinion to that of the husband's father (*w*).

A. 1. 5.—CAPACITY IN RELATION TO AGE.

Though there is no exact restriction as to the adopter's age, it is inferred that he should not adopt until no hope remain of begetting a son (*x*). But this cannot be regarded now as more than a simply moral precept; the age is really unlimited by law (*y*), provided only it exceed that of the adopted son (*z*) in case of a male adopter (*a*), and the adopter has reached years of discretion (*b*). The last restriction is uncertain. In the *Mankar Case* (*c*) the Sastris were asked at what age a man hopeless of offspring might adopt. One says at sixteen, another at twenty. Others say no precise time is fixed by the Sastras, whence, probably, one replies that he may adopt when he pleases. Three of the nine sages insist strongly on all possible measures being first used to remove the disability, and one says that hope must

---

(*t*) MS. 1668. The daughter-in-law is obviously the proper person to adopt a son to her deceased husband and herself. According to the authorities which give her the right to adopt, the competence of her father-in-law would introduce rival claimants to succession and sacra. But her dependence makes the assent of her father-in-law necessary to her performance of a religious act, such as adoption. *Vithal* v. *Bapu*, I. L. R. 15 Bom. 110; *Collector of Madura* v. *Mootho Ramalinga*, 12 M. I. A. 396.

(*v*) MS. 1660. See below.

(*w*) MS. 1666. *Lakshmi* v. *Vishnu*, I. L. R. 29 Bom. 410.

(*x*) Steele, L. C. 43. See above, pp. 812, 813, 814.

(*y*) *Ibid*. 182, 383.

(*z*) *Ibid*. 384; compare Cic. Pro. Domo. Ch. 13. 14.

(*a*) *Gopal* v. *Vishnu*, I. L. R. 23 Bom. 250.

(*b*) See above, p. 814, note (*d*); *Jumoona Dassaya* v. *Bamasoonderi Dassaya*, L. R. 3 I. A. 72.

(*c*) 2 Borr. R., at p. 102.

not be abandoned or a son adopted until the proposed father has reached old age.

The principle stated above (*d*), as to the imitation of nature, should prevent the adoption of a son at any rate by a boy under puberty; but this can hardly be stated with certainty as a rule of the positive law. Mr. Shamacharn, in the Vyavastha Darpana, seems to think that an adoption by a child between 8 and 15 may be good for religious, but not for civil, purposes; but the proposed severance seems inconsistent with the principles of the law of inheritance. It is opposed too to the principle laid down by Holloway, J., and apparently approved by the Privy Council (*e*), that the validity of an adoption is to be deduced by spiritual rather than by temporal considerations, that the substitution of a son of the deceased for spiritual reasons is the essence of the thing, and the consequent distribution of property a mere accessory to it.

Bengal Reg. X. of 1793, § 33, says that an adoption shall not be competent to a minor (*f*) of whose estate possession has been taken by the Court of Wards. The Sadr Court of Bengal held that this prevented the minor equally from giving a power to adopt (*g*). In other cases the power to adopt may be given at the ordinary age of discretion (*h*). The judgment last referred to discusses the evidence as to minority but does not expressly say that adoption by a minor is generally incompetent. No provision on this subject is made by Act XX. of 1864, which provides for the care of minors and the administration of their property in the Presidency of Bombay. Act IX. of 1875, fixing the age of majority in ordinary cases at eighteen, but in that of wards at twenty-one, does not affect capacity in relation to marriage or adoption.

"A man aged twenty may adopt" (*i*).

(*d*) Page 798 (note).

(*e*) *Sri Viradi Pratapa Raghunada* v. *Sri Brozo Kishoro Patta Deo*, 7 Mad. H. C. R. 301; I. L. R. 1 Mad. 69; 25 C. W. R. 291 (C. R.); L. R. 3 I. A. 154, 193.

(*f*) Under 18, Reg. XXVI. of 1793, sec. 2.

(*g*) *Anandmoyee Chowdrain* v. *Sheebchandar Roy*, S. D. A. R. for 1855, p. 218.

(*h*) *Jumoona Dassya* v. *Bamasoonderi Dassya*, 25 C. W. R. 235, I. L. R. 1 Cal. 289 (P. C.); S. C. L. R. 3 I. A. 72, citing *Rajendro Narain* v. *Saroda Soondaree Debia*, 15 C. W. R. 548. Whether adoption by a minor without consent of the Court of Wards is wholly void is questioned in *Musst. Anundmoyee Chowdhoorayan* v. *Sheeb Chunder Roy*, 9 M. I. A. 287.

(*i*) MS. 1623. See above, p. 814, note (*d*).

A. 1. 6.—CAPACITY IN RELATION TO INTELLIGENCE.

An insane man may, it is said, adopt with the consent of his kinsmen. The adoption is generally made by his wife under an assumed authority sanctioned by the kinsmen or the caste (*k*).

An adoption by a person in a state of insensibility (*i.e.* disturbed mind) from dangerous illness, by verbal declaration, without performance of the prescribed ceremonies, was held invalid (*l*). The transactions of sick and dying men always call for close scrutiny, and the Judicial Committee have said that in a case of adoption or will by a dying man the jealous requisitions of the law as to the proof of acts of persons done *in extremis* are fully to be complied with (*m*).

" The adopter must be able to ask for the son, to accept him, and to smell his head " (*n*).

A. 1. 7.—CAPACITY IN RELATION TO BODILY STATE.

A person disqualified to inherit cannot adopt, and thus secure to a stranger the right to a share which is allowed to the natural-born son (*o*).

In case No. XX., under the head of Adoption in Macnaghten's Hindu Law (*p*), the Sastri says a leper is incompetent to adopt. In case No. XXI. the Sastri thinks competence may be regained by penance, and with this Macnaghten agrees; but unless leprosy is of a virulent form, it does not act as a disqualifying element either in inheritance (*q*) or in adoption (*r*). An impotent man it

---

(*k*) Steele, L. C. 43, 182, 382.

(*l*) *Bullubkant Chowdree* v. *Kishenprea Dassee*, 6 C. S. D. A. R. 219.

(*m*) *Tayammaul* v. *Sashachalla Naiker*, 10 M. I. A. 429, 437.

(*n*) MS. 1662. The authority for the last-mentioned ceremony is not quoted. In performance it resembles the uttering of a prayer or formula in a whisper. The smelling of the head (aghrana), however, is a mode of salutation used in receiving a child or younger brother after any prolonged absence. It is practised amongst some of the South-Sea Islanders. It may have become a part of the ceremony through a real or supposed capacity thus to distinguish a member of one's own gotra. As to the extreme olfactory sensibility of some races, see Tyler's Anthropology, pp. 2, 70, and Letourneau's Sociology, p. 75.

(*o*) Mit., Chap. 2, sec. 10, para. 11; above, p. 795.

(*p*) Vol. 2, p. 201.

(*q*) See above, pp. 541, 544.

(*r*) *Mohunt Bhagwan Ramanuj Das* v. *Das*, L. R. 22 I. A. 94.

is said cannot adopt, at least until his incapacity has been proved by marriage (*s*). His religious duty no doubt is to beget a son if he can; but the allowance of adoptions by bachelors and widowers shows that the religious obligation is not accompanied by a legal incapacity. A man who is blind, deaf, dumb, or diseased may adopt (*t*).

A. 1. 8.—Capacity in Relation to Religious State.

Adoption by one who has renounced the world and devoted himself to a life of study and asceticism ought not, according to theory, to be possible, but the restriction is now only speculative (*v*).

Pollution from the death of a relative incapacitates during its continuance for adoption (*w*).

"A person *in extremis* is not so affected with impurity by a death in the family as to be incompetent to adopt" (*x*).

A. 1. 9.—Capacity in Relation to Caste Connection or Exclusion.

A man degraded from caste cannot adopt (*y*) during his exclusion.

The Mitakshara denies the capacity to adopt generally to a man himself disqualified for inheritance (*z*), and specifies loss of caste in particular as a cause of disinherison. This extends equally to women as to men (*a*). The only persons who can take the father's place in such cases are the legitimate issue and the son begotten

---

(*s*) Steele, L. C. 43.

(*t*) Steele, L. C. 43.

(*v*) See above, pp. 524, 537, 835: Apast., Pr. II., Pat. 9, Kh. 21, para. 19, Kh. 23.

(*w*) *Ramalinga Pillai* v. *Sudasiva Pillai*, 1 C. W. R. 25 Pr. Co. The periods of pollution vary with the caste and the nearness of relationship, as noticed above, p. 478. For Brahmans the extreme time is 10 days, for Kshatriyas 12, for Vaisyas 16, for Sudras 30 days.

(*x*) MS. 1674.

(*y*) Steele, L. C. 43, 182, 382.

(*z*) Mit., Chap. II., sec. X., para. 11; see above, p. 880.

(*a*) *Loc. cit.*, paras. 8, 9.

on the wife by a kinsman (*b*). The latter is not now recognized, so that the man born blind or deaf is deprived of all resource. Loss of caste is now declared by statute not to involve loss of inheritance, and by analogy the out-cast ought perhaps to have power to adopt, but the whole position of the out-cast retaining his heritable rights is so anomalous that no very confident opinion can be offered on this subject (*c*). The questions that can arise out of it must be very few, as an out-cast could scarcely obtain a son in adoption.

A. 1. 10.—In the Case of Particular Castes.

In the case cited above, p. 827, the Sastri said that a daughter-in-law could not adopt while the brothers of her deceased husband's father survived (*d*).

A. 1. 11.—Vaisyas.

A Vaisya who has undergone the ceremony of *vibhut vida* is capable of adopting a son. The Hindu Law does not expressly prohibit it. A contrary custom is to be proved by satisfactory evidence (*e*).

A. 1. 12.—Sudras.

"An unmarried Sudra may adopt" (*f*).

A. 1. 13.—Jains.

The Jains generally submit to the Hindu law of adoption though denying important doctrines. Their capacity to adopt in the

---

(*b*) Col. Dig., Book V., T. 334.

(*c*) Comp. the remarks above, pp. 815, 816, and Manu. IX. 125, as to the precedence of the first-born son.

(*d*) MS. 281, but on this see the note *loc. cit.*

(*e*) *Mhalsabai* v. *Vithoba Khandappa*, 7 Bom. H. C. R. App. 26. "Vibhut vida" is a renunciation of worldly affairs and interests analogous to that prescribed by the Smritis for Brahmanas, see Manu VI.; Gaut. III.

(*f*) MS. 1653. See above, pp. 824-5.

absence of custom is therefore governed by the ordinary rules (*g*). They can, however, adopt a daughter's son, and their widows enjoy the right of adoption without the permission of their husbands or the consent of their heirs (*h*).

A. 1. 14.—BHATELES.

"The custom of the Bhatele caste prevents adoption when there is a kinsman in existence" (*i*).

A. 1. 15.—GARASIAS.

In the Hindu caste of Chudasama Gamati Garasias adoption is recognized (*k*).

A. 1. 16.—SANNYASIS AND GOSAVIS.

"All classes may adopt with due ceremonies, Gosavis included" (*l*).

A married Gosavi took a boy (Talabda Koli) in adoption, on a promise to settle property on him. This was carried out by his widow about thirty years after the husband's death, and was disputed by his relatives, but was held sufficient (*m*).

A. 2.—ADOPTION BY A MALE—BY DELEGATION.

A. 2. 1.—BY MEANS OF WIFE.

"A woman may adopt with her (living) husband's order (*n*).

(*g*) See above, p. 924, note (*h*); below, sec. III. A. 3. *Chotay Lall* v. *Chunnoo Lall*, L. R. 6 I. A. 15; *Amava* v. *Mahadgauda*, I. L. R. 22 Bom. 416; *Ambabai* v. *Govind*, I. L. R. 23 Bom. 257.

(*h*) *Sheo Singh Rai* v. *Musst. Dakho*, L. R. 5 I. A. 87; S. C. I. L. R. 1 All. 688.

(*i*) MS. 405.

(*k*) *Verabhai* v. *Bai Heraba*, I. L. R. 27 Bom. 492.

(*l*) MS. 1678. See 2 Str. H. L. 133. Instances will be found below of adoptions by Prabhus, by Lingayats, and others; and also above, p. 347 ss.

(*m*) *Bhala Nahana* v. *Parbhu Hari*, I. L. R. 2 Bom. 67.

(*n*) Reply of a Sastri in the *Mankar Case*, 2 Borr. R., at p. 102.

It is not lawful for her to do so without the permission of her husband" (o).

If the husband's death approaches the wife may obtain his permission and afterwards adopt as a widow (p).

A. 2. 2.—By Means of Widow.

If a man begins the ceremonies of adoption, and dies before completing them, his widow might complete them (q).

A. 2. 3.—By Means of Daughter-in-Law.

In case of lunacy of a husband the wife of the lunatic may adopt with her father-in-law's sanction (r).

The Sastri in one case held a "daughter-in-law bound by her father-in-law's engagement that she should adopt" a specified sapinda (s). This was after the father-in-law's death. It is not clear whether the adoption was to be to the promisor or to his deceased son. If to the former he could not properly thus deprive his dead son of his due sraddhas, and the delegation was altogether questionable if meant to operate during the father-in-law's life; equally questionable as an attempt to bind the widow of his son after his death.

(o) Reply of Sastris of the Sadr Court in *Sree Brijbhookunjee Maharaj* v. *Sree Gokoolootsaojee Maharaj*, 1 Borr. R., at p. 211. See the Viramitrodaya and the Dattakakaustubha to the same effect, quoted in *Narayan* v. *Nana*, 7 Bom. H. C. R., at p. 159, and Col. Dig., Book V., T. 273 Comm. Also Vasishtha XV. 5.

(p) 2 Str. H. L. 88; MS. 1661. Such cases as these, though sometimes regarded as instances of delegation, are more properly referred to implied authority to adopt given to the widow.

(q) 2 Str. H. L. 88; MS. 1661. Such cases as these, though sometimes regarded as instances of delegation, are more properly referred to implied authority to adopt given to the widow. *Lakshmibai* v. *Ramchandra*, I. L. R. 22 Bom. 590; *Subbaraya* v. *Subbammal*, I. L. R. 21 Mad. 497.

(r) See above, sec. III. A. 1. 6. As to adoption by a wife on behalf of a disqualified person, as an insane husband incapable of appointing her, see above, p. 817. She ought to adopt to her husband in the case in the text. Comp. *Ramjee Hurree* v. *Thukoo Baee*, 2 Borr. R. 485; *Vithoba* v. *Bapu*, I. L. R. 15 Bom. 110; *Lakshmibai* v. *Vishnu*, I. L. R. 29 Bom. 410.

(s) MS. 1682; *Y. Venka Reddi* v. *G. Soobha Reddi*, M. S. D. A. Dec. 1858, p. 204.

A. 3.—Restrictions on Adoption to Persons Deceased.

Spiritual benefits are not the only ground of adoption. The Jains recognize adoption though they do not practise the Sraddha or Paksha ceremonies (*t*). Adoption rests generally on the advantage of having a son to perform funeral rites, which the Jains deny. But though the Hindu law of succession is applicable to them, yet it cannot be further extended so as to allow adoption to dead parents or sanction the exercise of a power of adoption by another to dead persons (*v*) through a fictitious gift.

A son cannot, it was said, be adopted to the great-grandfather of the last taker after the lapse of several years, when all the spiritual purposes of a son, according to the largest construction of them, should have been satisfied (*w*). This, however, is the law in the Bombay Presidency. In the case of *Kannapalli* v. *Pucha Venkata* (*x*) the Judicial Committee have approved of the view expressed by Mitter, J., in *Ram* v. *Surbana* (*y*), that a married son did not exhaust all the spiritual benefit which a son could confer on his father.

A. 4.—Qualifications of the Power to Adopt Arising from Family and Political Relations.

A. 4. 1.—Consent of Wife.

A wife's consent to adoption by her husband is not indispensable to the validity thereof (*z*). Adoption is the act of the husband alone. The wife may join in it (*a*), and ought to do so for a full compliance with the religious law (*b*). Her association, however,

---

(*t*) See above, p. 533. *Sheo Singh Rai* v. *Musst. Dakho*, L. R. 5 I. A. 87.

(*v*) *Bhagvandas* v. *Rajmal*, 10 Bom. H. C. R. 241, 265.

(*w*) *Musst. Bhoobun Moyee Debia* v. *Ramkishore Acharjee*, 10 M. I. A. 279; S. C. 3 C. W. R. 15 P. C.; Beng. S. D. A. R. 1856, p. 122; *Ramkrishna* v. *Shamrao*, I. L. R. 26 Bom. 526. A narrower limitation exists as held in the case of Jains. See above.

(*x*) L. A. 33 I. A. 145, 154.

(*y*) 22 W. R. 121, 123.

(*z*) *Alank Manjari* v. *Fakir Chand*, 5 C. S. D. A. R. 356.

(*a*) *See Rungamah* v. *Atchummah et al.*, 4 M. I. A. 1; S. C. 7 C. W. R. 57 P. C.

(*b*) Colebrooke says that according to the Mitakshara, though the mother's consent may perhaps be essential to the gift, it is not to the taking of a son in adoption. Mit., Chap. I., sec. XI., para. 9, note. See below, sec. V., as to the gift.

is not indispensable, and an adoption is valid even when it takes place against her express wishes. After her husband's death, she can give her son in adoption provided there is no express prohibition by the husband (c).

The Poona Sastris replied in the *Mankar Case* (d) that the husband ought to consult his wife on a proposed adoption, but that the right belongs to him alone.

A. 4. 2.—Family Relations—Kindred.

The existence of brothers or other kinsmen does not affect a man's capacity to adopt. It is said, indeed, that in a few castes the parents or an undivided brother (e) may object to a particular adoption, and in many the assent of near relatives must be asked (f), but it is not provided that their disapproval shall invalidate the adoption (g). They must be invited to take part in the ceremony, and a son of a brother or other near relative is to be chosen by preference, but these obligations are of a simply religious character.

A. 4. 3.—Pupillage.

The sanction of the Court of Wards is necessary to an adoption by a minor under its care (h). Act XX. of 1864 makes no provision on this subject. It provides for the guardianship of a minor's person and the administration of his estate, but does not declare him generally incapable of jural acts. In the Bombay Presidency therefore a boy under guardianship, but capable of religious acts, may possibly adopt or marry, though he may not deal with his property (i).

(c) *Jogesh* v. *Nritya*, I. L. R. 30 Cal. 965.

(d) 2 Borr. R., at p. 102.

(e) Steele, L. C. 385, 386. The consent may be a necessary restriction when a minor proposes to adopt—especially the consent of his parents.

(f) Steele, L. C. 183, 385.

(g) Steele, L. C. 45.

(h) See above, sec. III. A. 1. 5, p. 845. *Jumoona Dassya* v. *Bamasoonderi Dassya*, L. R. 3 I. A. 72.

(i) See above, A. 1. 5; and below, B. 3.

A. 4. 4.—CONSENT OR ACQUIESCENCE OF THE SOVEREIGN.

"The writing of documents is insignificant (not essential). The Sastras do not require the permission of Government to be obtained for an adoption" (*k*). But "they enjoin that a proposed adoption should be notified to the Government" (*l*). "The object of applying to Government is that it may continue to the adopted son Watans, &c., held from it. When the seat of Government is distant intimation may be made to the local officer" (*m*). Even notice to the ruling power is not necessary to validate an adoption (*n*), but it is so usual that an omission of it in an important case casts suspicion on the transaction. A want of sanction by the ruling power is not sufficient to invalidate adoption duly made with sufficient ceremonies (*o*). The sanction of the ruling power to an adoption by a Kulkarni or his widow, or by a coparcener in Kulkarniship or his widow, is not necessary to give it validity, nor has Government a right to prohibit or otherwise intervene in such adoption (*p*).

In several cases it seems to have been supposed that the sanction of the Government was necessary to an adoption by a widow where it would not have been essential to an adoption by her deceased husband (*q*). The authorities, however, on which the widow's power rests impose no such condition on its exercise.

Bombay Act II. of 1863, sec. 6, cl. 2, as to the non-recognition of adoption by a Court relates only to a question of assessability of land when raised between Government and the claimant by adoption (*r*). It is not intended to regulate the enjoyment of an estate as amongst the heirs of the original grantee.

(*k*) MS. 1675.

(*l*) MS. 1677, 1683.

(*m*) MS. 1711; 2 Str. H. L. 87.

(*n*) *Sutroogun Sutputty* v. *Sabitra Dye*, 2 Knapp. p. 287; S. C. 5 C. W. R. P. C. 109.

(*o*) *Bhaskar Buchajee* v. *Narroo Ragonath*, Bom. Sel. R. 25.

(*p*) *Ramachandra Vasudev* v. *Nanaji Timaji*, 7 Bom. H. C. R. 26 A. C. J.; *Sree Brijbhookunjee Maharaj* v. *Sree Gokoolootsaojee Maharaj*, 1 Borr. 181, 202 (2nd ed.); *Narhar Govind* v. *Narayan Vithal*, I. L. R. 1 Bom. 607; *Huebutrao Mankur* v. *Govinrao Mankur*, 2 Borr. 75, 83 (2nd ed.); *Alank Manjari* v. *Fakir Chand*, 5 C. S. D. A. R. 356.

(*q*) See below, B. 3. 36.

(*r*) *Vasudeo Anant* v. *Ramkrishna*, I. L. R. 2 Bom. 529.

THE CAPACITY TO ADOPT AND ITS EXERCISE.

B.—Adoption by Females.

B. 1.—No Adoption by a Maiden.

The Hindu Law imposes on parents the duty of getting their daughters married. It does not contemplate children as necessary to women on their own account (*s*). Even a married woman or a widow adopts only for her husband, and herself takes but an incidental benefit save under the exceptional custom allowing a kritrima adoption to the woman alone in Maithila. For the unmarried woman there is no adoption; nor in strictness for any woman except to her husband.

B. 2.—Adoption by a Wife.

A wife only can receive authority to adopt (*t*) either as wife or as widow. *She can adopt only as the representative of her husband, and under a real or assumed authority from him.* This is generally admitted (*v*), and is established by the following cases.

B. 2. 1.—Adoption by a Wife under Express Delegation.

In *Thakoo Baee Bhide* v. *Ruma Baee Bhide* (*w*) the Sastris quote from Vasishtha—"A husband's commands to adopt are required for a married woman, but for a widow to adopt without such command the permission of the father, or if he be not alive then of the (jnati) relatives must be obtained."

The express authority of her husband is indispensable, if a wife adopts in his lifetime (*x*).

(*s*) See above, p. 790; below, B. 3. 13.

(*t*) *Bhagvandas* v. *Rajmal*, 10 Bom. H. C. R. 241.

(*v*) See *Ramji* v. *Ghamau*, I. L. R. 6 Bom., at p. 501; *Puttu Lall* v. *Parbati Kunwar*, L. R. 42 I. A. 155; *Jai Singh Pal* v. *Bijai Pal*, I. L. R. 27 All. 423.

(*w*) 2 Borr. R., at p. 492.

(*x*) *Narayan* v. *Nana*, 7 Bom. H. C. R. A. C. J. 153, 174; *Bayabai* v. *Bala Venkatesh*, 7 Bom. H. C. R. App. i.; *Rangubai* v. *Bhagirthibai*, I. L. R. 2 Bom., at p. 380; *Ramji* v. *Ghamau*, I. L. R. 6 Bom. 498.

B. 2. 2.—IMPLIED DELEGATION.

This arises in such cases as those of a husband beginning the ceremonies of adoption with the participation of his wife. In the event of his becoming helpless she may complete the adoption. Any unequivocal indication of his assent would probably be taken as equivalent to an express command. This may be gathered from the cases in the next sub-section.

B. 2. 3.—CONDITIONS OF EFFECTIVE DELEGATION.

The husband directing his wife to adopt must be in a condition with regard to freedom from loathsome disease, such that he could himself adopt. So also as to his relations to his caste. In case of insanity his assent or command is assumed by the rules of several castes, his place being taken by the kinsmen in controlling the choice made by the wife (*y*).

A husband may authorize his wife to adopt a particular child, named by him, or a child selected by her (*z*).

B. 3.—ADOPTION BY A WIDOW.

"The permission expressed or implied of her deceased husband is requisite to enable a widow to adopt. An implied permission arises from a known intention of the deceased to adopt. Failing this she must obtain the permission of her father-in-law or other relative" (*a*). This permission is merely substitutive in default of any intimation by the deceased husband of his wishes. When he has clearly signified his wishes, these prevail over the wishes either of the widow or of the relatives, as shown farther on.

The husband's sanction must have been given, according to the Mitakshara, as understood by Colebrooke (*b*), because otherwise the adoption could not benefit him. But Colebrooke says the sanction may be replaced by that of the husband's kindred (*c*).

(*y*) Steele, L. C. 43, 182.

(*z*) *Veerapermal Pillay* v. *Narrain Pillay*, 1 Str. R. 91; *Ry Sevagamy Nachiar* v. *Heraniah Gurbah*, 1 Mad. S. D. A. Dec. 101.

(*a*) MS. 1662.

(*b*) 2 Str. H. L. 91; so Ellis, *ibid.*

(*c*) *Ibid.*, and Mit., Chap. I., sec. XI., p. 9, notes.

Ellis thinks that the prior assent of the husband may not be necessary amongst Sudras; but it must be either expressed or presumed.

The capacity of a widow to adopt must thus, like that of a wife, be drawn from a real or an assumed authorization on the part of the husband. If he has intimated a wish that there should be no adoption none can be made (*d*). If he has left no direction at all, there can, according to the Bengal Law, be no adoption. According to the law of Bombay his assent may, in such a case, be assumed; but the widow's choice is controlled by the kinsmen, at least in a united family (*e*). The consent or authority of the husband has been pronounced indispensable to an adoption by a widow after his decease, in Bengal (*f*), in the N. W. Provinces (*g*), and in Madras (*h*), but in Madras it may now be replaced by the assent of the undivided members of the husband's family, as in Bombay (*i*). In Mithila the assent of the husband must be given at the time of the adoption, and therefore a widow cannot receive a son in adoption, according to the Dattaka form (*k*).

A Jain widow can adopt without her husband's authority or that of his kinsmen (*l*).

A widow in Bengal on the other hand cannot adopt without her

(*d*) *The Collector of Madura's Case*, 12 M. I. A., at p. 443; *Bayabai* v. *Bala Venktesh*, 7 Bom. H. C. R., at pp. xvii. ss. App.

(*e*) *Ramji* v. *Ghamau*, I. L. R. 6 Bom., at pp. 502, 503; *Collector of Madura's Case*, 12 M. I. A. 397, 442; *Patel* v. *Chunilal*, I. L. R. 15 Bom. 565.

(*f*) *Musst. Tara Munee Divia* v. *Dev Narayan et al.*, 3 C. S. D. A. R. 387; *Huradhun Mookurjia* v. *Muthoranath Mookurjia*, 4 M. I. A. 144; S. C. 7 C. W. R. 71 P. C.; *Sutroogun Sutputtee* v. *Savitra Dye*, 2 Knapp, 287; S. C. 5 C. W. R. P. C. 109; *Musst. Bhoobun Moyee Debia* v. *Ramkishore Acharjee*, 10 M. I. A. 279; S. C. 3 C. W. R. 15 P. C.; *Juggodumba Debea* v. *Moneruth Mookerjea* C. S. D. A. R. for 1858, p. 834; *Soorodhunnee Debea* v. *Doorgapersad Roy*, C. S. D. A. R. for 1858, p. 995; *Jummoona Dasya* v. *Bamasoondari D.*, I. L. R. 1 Cal. 289; *Musst. Sheboo Koeree* v. *Joogun Singh*, 8 C. W. R. 155 (a case of Kritrima adoption). See the Datt. Mim., sec. I., para. 15; Col. Dig., Book V., T. 273; 2 Str. H. L. 84, 92, 96; 1 Macn. H. L. 66; 2 Macn. H. L. 175, 182, 189; Macn. Con. H. L. 125, 155, 158.

(*g*) *R. Hasmun Chull Singh* v. *Koomer Gunsheam Sing*, 2 Knapp, 203; S. C. 5 C. W. R. P. C. 69; *Thakur Oomrao Singh* v. *Tha Mahtab Koonwar*, 2 Agra Rep. 103; *Jairam Dhama* v. *Musan Dhama*, 5 C. S. D. A. R. 3.

(*h*) *Veerapermal Pillay* v. *Narrain Pillay*, 1 Str. R. 91.

(*i*) *Shri Raghunadha* v. *Shri Brozo Kishore*, L. R. 3 I. A. 154, 191.

(*k*) *Collector of Madura* v. *Moottoo Ramlinga*, 12 M. I. A. 396.

(*l*) *Sheo Singh Rai* v. *Musst. Dakho*, L. R. 5 I. A. 87; *Asharfi* v. *Rup*, I. L. R. 30 All. 197.

husband's consent, even though his heirs consent to the adoption (*m*).

Similarly an adoption by a widow was set aside for want of proof of authority for the adoption given by her husband (*n*), in the N. W. Provinces. Adoption, without the husband's authority, gives to the adoptee, before or after the widow's death, no right to property inherited by her from her husband (*o*), where this law prevails.

Where a widow had adopted a boy without authority from her husband and the consent of the Sapinda had been obtained to an adoption purporting to be made in pursuance of an alleged authority and had been influenced by undue considerations, the adoption was held invalid for want of authority (*p*).

In the case of *Patel Vandrawan Jakosin* v. *Chunilal* (*q*) it has been held that in the Marhatta country, as well as in Gujrat, a widow was competent to adopt without the consent of her husband's kindred if she received her power *bona fide* for religious purposes, and in *Vithoba* v. *Bapu* (*r*) it has been laid down that the widow of a coparcener can make a valid adoption if permitted by the father-in-law irrespective of the consent of other coparceners.

The rule, however, as to an express authority is, as the Judicial Committee have shown, less exacting than the Dattaka Mimamsa declares (*s*).

The existence of brothers is not an obstacle to adoption under an authority from a deceased husband (*t*). A Hindu may execute an instrument giving authority to adopt when he has attained the

---

(*m*) *Raja Shumshere Mull* v. *Ranee Dilraj Konwar*, 2 C. S. D. A. R. 169.

(*n*) *Musst. Thakorain* v. *Mohun Lall*, N. W. P. S. D. R. N. S. Pt. I., 1863, p. 352.

(*o*) *Chowdry Padom Singh* v. *Koer Udaya Singh*, 12 C. W. R. P. C. 1; S. C. 2 Beng. L. R. 101, P. C.; S. C. 12 M. I. A. 350; *Musst. Oodey Koowur* v. *Musst. Ladoo*, 15 C. W. R. 16, P. C.

(*p*) *Karunabdhi Ganesa Ratnamaiyar* v. *Gopala*, L. R. 7 I. A. 173; *Venkamma* v. *Subrahmania*, L. R. 34 I. A. 22.

(*q*) I. L. R. 15 Bom. 565; *Rakhmabai* v. *Radhabai*, 5 B. H. C. R. 191, A. C. J.

(*r*) I. L. R. 15 Bom. 110.

(*s*) See below, B. 3. 1.

(*t*) 2 Macn. H. L., p. 180 (Chap. VI., Case 5); *Sri Raghunada's Case*, *supra*, p. 857 note (*i*); below, B. 3. 1. *Hurkisondas* v. *Mankorebai*, L. R. 34 I. A. 107; S. C. I. L. R. 29 Bom. 81.

ordinary age of discretion (*v*). This the Judicial Committee seem to have considered the age of majority by law, which would now be eighteen years (*w*). But if the capacity to give authority arises at the same time with the capacity to adopt, that would by some Hindu lawyers be fixed at the age when religious ceremonies in general can be fully performed (*x*).

It seems that a state of indivision between a son and his father does not affect the validity of an authority given by the former. In the case of *Gobind Soondaree Debia* v. *Juggodumba Debia* (*y*) the suit was on behalf of a son adopted on an alleged authority from a husband who had died nine years before his father. The authority was discredited, but the discussion shows that the Court thought that if genuine it would be valid. This has an important bearing on the right of the widow, where, as in Bombay, the assent of the deceased husband is presumed.

B. 3. 1.—ADOPTION BY A WIDOW UNDER EXPRESS AUTHORITY GIVEN BY ACT *Inter Vivos*.

An adoption thus authorized needs no sanction by the relatives (*z*). A widow may adopt with the consent of her husband obtained before his decease or with that of his relations thereafter (*a*).

An authority to adopt under the husband's hand, though not complete as a testamentary disposition, is yet evidence of a declaration of fact (*b*).

(*v*) *Jamoona Dasya* v. *Bamasoonderai Dasya Chowdhrani*, L. R. 3 I. A. 72, 78.

(*w*) Act IX. of 1875, sec. 3. The Act does not, however, affect adoption, see sec. 2.

(*x*) See *Rajendro Narain Lahoree* v. *Saroda Sundaree Dabee*, 15 C. W. R. 548. The attempt to postpone the son's capacity beyond his attainment of majority approved in *R. Huroosoondery* v. *Coomar Kristonath*, 1 Fult. 393, would not now be sustained.

(*y*) 3 C. W. R. 66; S. C. 15 *ibid.* 5 Pr. C.

(*z*) See *Dhasker Bhuchajee* v. *Naroo Ragoonath*, Bom. Sel. R., p. 24 (1st ed.); above, B. 3.

(*a*) *Ry Sevagamy Nachiar* v. *Heraniah Gurbah*, 1 Mad. S. D. A. R. 101; *Arundadi Ummal* v. *Kupumall*, 3 Mad. H. C. R. 283; *Collector of Madura* v. *Mutu Ramalinga Sathupatty*, 1 Beng. L. R. 1 P. C.; S. C. 12 M. I. A. 397; S. C. 2 Mad. H. C. R. 206; *Mutsaddi Lal* v. *Kundun Lal*, L. R. 33 I. A. 55.

(*b*) *Brojo Kishoree Dassee for Radhanath* v. *Sreenath Bose for Judonath*; 8 C. W. R. 241; S. C. 9 C. W. R. 463; *Mutsaddi Lal* v. *Kundun Lal*, *supra*.

Even in the case of the husband's long absence it was said by the castes in Poona and Khandesh that a wife could adopt only with the written authority of her husband. If the absence was so prolonged as to raise a presumption of death the wife might adopt as a widow (*c*).

Amongst the Poona Brahmans a widow, it was said, must have her husband's order, and must also consult his kinsmen. In other castes it was said the consent of the relatives and of the caste, in some that the consent of the relatives alone, would supply the place of the husband's order (*d*). The leading doctrines on the widow's substitutionary power of adoption have been thus stated by the Judicial Committee:— " Mr. Colebrooke's note on the Mitakshara (Chap. I., sec. XI., art. 9), which has been much discussed, clearly involves three propositions—First, that the widow's power to receive a son in adoption, subject to some conditions, is now admitted by all the schools of Hindu Law except that of Maithila; second, that the Bengal (or Gaura) school insists that the widow must have the formal permission of her husband in his lifetime; third, that some at least of the other schools admit the adoption to be valid, if made by the widow with the assent of her husband's kindred. The first two propositions are admitted; but it has been argued for the appellants that on the true construction of this note, Mr. Colebrooke's authority for the last proposition is limited to the Mahratta school, in which the treatise called the 'Mayukha' is the predominant authority. Balam Bhatta, however, whom he cites as an authority for a power of adoption in the widow, wider even than that expressed in the third proposition, was a commentator of the Benares school. And the several notes of Mr. Colebrooke at pp. 92, 96, and 115 of the second volume of Strange's Hindu Law seem to their Lordships to show conclusively that he considered the doctrine embodied in the third proposition to be common to the followers of the Mitakshara in the Benares as well as in the Mahratta school, and as such to be receivable as the law current in the Zillah Vizagapatam, which lies within the Northern or Andra Division of the Dravada Country."

" Again Sir Thomas Strange's statement of the law in his work,

---

(*c*) Steele, L. C. 187. A written authority does not seem legally indispensable, see below.

(*d*) Steele, L. C. 47, 187.

vol. I, p. 79, is clear and unambiguous. He says: ' Equally loose is the reason alleged against adoption by a widow, since the assent of the husband may be given, to take effect (like a will) after his death; and according to the doctrine of the Benares and Maharashtra schools, prevailing in the Peninsula, it may be supplied by that of his kindred, her natural guardians; but it is otherwise by the law that governs the Bengal Provinces " (*e*).

According to the Benares (Mitakshara) law it was said that the authority of a husband to a widow for adoption could not be replaced by that of his heirs after his death (*f*). The Dattaka Mimamsa, the Pandits declared, prevailed over the works which allow a substitutive authority (*g*). Macnaghten held the same view; but Colebrooke maintained the sufficiency of the kinsmen's sanction, and his doctrine was approved by the Judicial Committee in the *Collector of Madura's Case* (*h*).

There is no stereotyped form of authority to adopt (*i*). It may be given either orally or in writing (*k*).

A deed, containing no words of devise, nor intended by testator to contain any disposition of his estate, except so far as that results from adoption of a son under it, is only a deed of permission to adopt, and not of a testamentary character (*l*).

Defects in evidence relating to the execution of a deed authorizing adoption are less material than as to the disposition of a property by will (*m*).

B. 3. 2.—ADOPTION BY WIDOW UNDER AUTHORITY GIVEN BY WILL.

A will giving power is sufficient authority (*n*).

A will of a childless Hindu, giving power to adopt, though

(*e*) *The Collector of Madura* v. *Muttoo Ramalinga Sathupatty*, 12 M. I. A., pp. 432—33.

(*f*) *Raja Shumshere Mull* v. *Ranee Dilraj Koonwur*, 2 C. S. D. A. R. 169.

(*g*) See Datt. Mim., sec. I., para. 16; Viramitrodaya, Transl., p. 116.

(*h*) 12 M. I. A., at p. 432.

(*i*) *Pritima Soondaree Chowdrain* v. *Anund Coomar Chowdhry*, 6 C. W. R. 133 C. R.

(*k*) 2 Str. H. L. 95, 96; *Gudadhur Pershad Tewaree* v. *Soondur Koomaree Debea*, 4 C. W. R. 116 P. C.; *Mutasaddi Lal* v. *Kundun Lal*, L. R. 33 I. A. 55.

(*l*) *Musst. Bhoobun Moyee Debia* v. *Ramkishore Acharjee*, 10 M. I. A. 279; S. C. 3 C. W. R. 15 P. C.

(*m*) *Jumoona Dassya* v. *Bamasoondari Dassya*, 25 C. W. R. 235; S. C. L. R. 3 I. A. 72.

(*n*) *Sayamalal Dutt* v. *Soudamini Dasi*, 5 Beng. L. R. 362.

opposed to the interests of the widow or of the next reversionary heirs of the testator, is not inofficious (*o*).

A permission given for adoption of a boy as co-heir with a son cannot be converted into one for adoption after the death of the natural son (*p*). It is really void from the first (*q*).

B. 3. 3.—Positive Command to Adopt.

When a husband has given a positive command, the widow's capacity to adopt appears in its strongest form as opposed to the wishes or interests of the kinsmen who will be affected by the adoption (*r*). The only question that can be raised in such a case is that of whether adoption is compulsory. The duty does not seem to be doubted, but in recent times it has come to be regarded as one that the Courts cannot properly enforce or at least not within any particular time (*s*). A widow directed by her deceased husband to adopt is bound to give effect to his wishes before she can claim under the deed of permission framed chiefly for the benefit of the son she may adopt (*t*).

A direction cannot be carried out contrary to the law, as *ex. gr.* while a son of the husband is living (*v*).

B. 3. 4.—Choice Prescribed.

It is common for a husband authorizing an adoption to specify the child he wishes to be taken (*w*). Should that child die or be refused by his parents the authority would still be held to warrant the adoption of another child unless indeed he had said " such a

---

(*o*) *S. M. Sarroda Dossee* v. *Tin Cowry Nandy*, 1 Hyde R. 223.

(*p*) *Joy Chundro Raee* v. *Bhyrub Chundro Raee*, C. S. D. A. R. 1849, p. 461.

(*q*) *See Padma Coomari Debea* v. *Court of Wards*, L. R. 8 I. A. 229; and B. 3. 3. below.

(*r*) See above, B. 3. and 3. 1.

(*s*) See above, pp. 813, 814; and below, Omission of Adoption.

(*t*) *Musst. Subudra Chowdryen* v. *Goluknath Chowdry*, 7 C. S. D. A. R. 143. See above, p. 813; and below, B. 3. 15; B. 3. 37.

(*v*) 2 Macn. H. L., p. 199 (Chap. VI., Ca. 19); *Bhoobun Moyee's Case*, 10 M. I. A. 279.

(*w*) See above, pp. 813, 814.

child and no other." The presumption is that he desired an adoption, and by specifying the object merely indicated a preference (x).

A Hindu by will expresses a wish that his wife, after his death, should adopt the second son of a person, who had only one son born alive at testator's death. The widow is not bound to wait indefinitely till the person begets a second son, but may adopt a boy of her own choice under the power (y).

When a husband authorizes the adoption of a particular boy named by him, his widow or any of his widows (if there are more than one) cannot adopt any other boy so long as the boy thus designated is alive (z), unless his adoption cannot be carried out (a).

When authority has been given to a widow to adopt the son of a particular person it is exhausted by his adoption. If he die it will not warrant another adoption to replace him (b).

A Hindu cannot authorize any other person to adopt conjointly with the widow or by herself on widow's death. The widow has the right to adopt, but her selection of the boy may be restricted by the choice of others nominated by the husband in his will (c).

B. 3. 5.—AUTHORITY GIVING QUALIFIED DISCRETION.

The husband sometimes defines the class out of which the adopted son is to be taken, and failing such, names another class without prescribing the individual to be adopted. The same principles of construction would probably be applied in this as in the last case.

An instance of a qualified discretion is to be found in the deed of permission given in *Musst. Bhoobun Moyee Debia's Case* (d).

(x) *Kanuapalli Suryanarayana* v. *Pucha Venkata Ramana*, L. R. 33 I. A. 145.

(y) *Veerapermal Pillay* v. *Narrain Pillay*, 1 Str. R. 91. See above, p. 813, Note (t).

(z) *Ramchandra* v. *Bapu Khandu*, Bom. H. C. P. J. 1877, p. 42. We may add "and not given in adoption." See below, secs. IV. V.

(a) *Lakshmibai* v. *Rajaji*, I. L. R. 22 Bom. 996.

(b) *Purmanand Bhuttacharuj* v. *Oomakunt Lahoree and others*, 4 C. S. D. A. R. 318; *Gour Nath Choudhree* v. *Anopoorna Choudhoorain*, C. S. D. A. R. for 1852, p. 332.

(c) *Amrito Lal Dutt* v. *Surnomoye Dasi*, L. R. 27 I. A. 128.

(d) 10 M. I. A., at p. 281. The same permission is conditional on the death of the son by birth, and provides for successive adoptions.

In this the selection of a son is directed to be made by preference from the executant's own gotra, but alternatively from another gotra.

B. 3. 6.—AUTHORITY GIVING COMPLETE DISCRETION AS TO PERSON.

This is probably the most common form, and it has been held that under it the widow has a large discretion—or even an unlimited one—as to whom she will adopt or whether she will adopt at all (*e*).

Such an unfettered discretion as to the boy to be adopted was granted by the Anumati patra, or authority executed by the husband in the case of *Kashee Chundree Mustofee* (*f*). This is the case most analogous to the assumed permission under which a widow adopts in Bombay.

B. 3. 7.—AUTHORITY TO ADOPT WITH COMPLETE DISCRETION AS TO EXERCISE OF THE POWER.

When a mere permission is given to adopt, should the widow think fit, the authority is complete, but according to the cases no obligation rests on the widow beyond the religious one to further her husband's welfare in the other world (*g*). She cannot delegate this power to adopt to any other person (*h*).

B. 3. 8.—CONDITIONAL AUTHORITY.

According to the Hindu Law, a widow who has received from her deceased husband an express power to adopt a son in the event of his natural-born son dying under age and unmarried, may, on the happening of that event, make a valid adoption.

Thus an authority to adopt, in case the son dies, is valid, it was held, according to the law of Bengal (*i*), and the Judicial

---

(*e*) See above, pp. 813, 814.

(*f*) C. S. D. A. Part I. 13 Summ. Cases. The widow, it was directed, was to adopt on attaining maturity.

(*g*) See 2 Str. H. L. 97.

(*h*) *Lakshmibai* v. *Ramchandra*, I. L. R. 22 Bom. 590.

(*i*) *Musst. Solukhna* v. *Ramdolal Pande et al.*, 1 C. S. D. A. R. 324.

Committee have recently laid down in *Kanuapalli Suryanarayana* v. *Pucha Venkata Ramana* (*k*) that a widow without special power for a second adoption can adopt a second son upon the death of a son first adopted.

In *Purmanand Bhuttacharaj* v. *Oomakunt* (*l*) the authority was an alternative one between a boy named and a Brahman boy in case there was a bar to the adoption of the former, and the widow having adopted a boy under the power, the boy died. She then adopted another boy, not coming within the above description, and the adoption was held illegal, as there was no sanction for the second adoption.

An authority to adopt, in case the son and mother disagree, will not operate (*m*).

B. 3. 9.—Implied Authority.

This arises when a husband has begun an adoption but has been prevented from completing it by death. In Bombay any distinct intimation of his wish for an adoption would probably be held sufficient to support an adoption proper in itself, but the kinsmen have still a right, in an undivided family, to a controlling voice as to the choice of the boy to be adopted (*n*).

The adoption of a brother was begun by a husband, and completed by the widows. The widows were not permitted to question the adoption, nor the right of the adopted son to adopt his nephew as his heir after his death (*o*).

(*k*) L. R. 33 I. A. 145.

(*l*) 4 C. S. D. A. R. 318. The precise contingency specified must happen. *Mohundro Lall Mookerjee* v. *Rookminey Dabey*, Coryton's R. 42.

(*m*) *Musst. Solukhna* v. *Ramdolal Pande et al.*, 1 C. S. D. A. R. 324. Conditional grants are not favoured by Hindu Law, and here the contingency provided for is one that should not be anticipated.

(*n*) *Ramji* v. *Ghamau*, I. L. R. 6 Bom. 498.

(*o*) *Ranees Rathore et al.* v. *Q. Khosal Sing*, N. W. P. S. D. R., Pt. II. 1864, p. 465. In the cases quoted above, sec. III. A. 2. 1, p. 952, the widows proceeded to complete the adoptions on an implied authority from their husbands, with whom they had taken part in the initial ceremonies. *Subba* v. *Subbammal*, I. L. R. 21 Mad. 497; *Lakshmibai* v. *Ramchandra*, I. L. R. 22 Bom. 590.

B. 3. 11.—Adoption by a Widow—Authority Excluded by Prohibition or Dissent of the Husband.

Express Prohibition.

The Judicial Committee, recognizing the substitutionary character of the widow's function in adopting a son, have declared her exercise of it impossible whenever a prohibition was to be gathered from the husband's language or conduct.

"It appears to their Lordships that, inasmuch as the authorities in favour of the widow's power to adopt with the assent of her husband's kinsmen proceed in a great measure upon the assumption that his assent to this meritorious act is to be implied wherever he has not forbidden it, so the power cannot be inferred when a prohibition by the husband either has been directly expressed by him, or can be reasonably deduced from his disposition of his property, or the existence of a direct line competent to the full performance of religious duties, or from other circumstances of his family which afford no plea for a supersession of heirs on the ground of religious obligation to adopt a son in order to complete or fulfil defective religious rites" (*p*).

Hence where there is a positive prohibition by the husband a widow cannot adopt (*q*), nor where the husband's assent cannot be implied (*r*).

Such an adoption will not affect his testamentary disposition in favour of his brother (*s*).

(*p*) *Collector of Madura* v. *Mootoo Ramalinga*, 12 M. I. A., at p. 443. "Although some of the Maratha Schools may use the expression that the widow may adopt without the consent of the husband, this means simply without his express assent.' The foundation underlying every adoption amongst Hindus is the consent of the husband. The only difference between the Schools is that some require that it should be express, and that others are content with an implied assent, and are ready to imply it if he have neither said nor done anything inconsistent with such an implication." Per Westropp, J., in *Bayabai* v. *Bala Venkatesh*, 7 Bom. H. C. R. xviii. App.

(*q*) *Malgauda* v. *Dattu*, I. L. R. 37 Bom. 107; *Bayabai* v. *Bala Venkatesh*, 7 Bom. H. C. R. App. i.; *Lakshmibai* v. *Sarasvatibai*, I. L. R. 23 Bom. 789; *Patel Vandravan* v. *Chunilal*, I. L. R. 15 Bom. 565.

(*r*) *Narayen* v. *Nana*, 7 Bom. H. C. R. 173 A. C. J.; *Ramachandra* v. *Bapu Khandu*, Bom. H. C. P. J. 1877, p. 42. See the Sastri's opinion below, p. 867, note (*w*).

(*s*) *Janki Dibeh* v. *Sadasheo Rai*, 1 C. S. D. A. R. 197.

B. 3. 12.—Implied Prohibition or Dissent.

"The Maratha School of Hindu Law permits the widow to adopt . . . provided [the husband] has neither said nor done anything which can be regarded as a prohibition to her or a refusal by himself when *in articulo mortis* to adopt." The widow alone has the right to adopt, and a Hindu cannot authorize any other person to adopt for him with or without the widow's participation therein (*t*). She may adopt when her husband has not intimated his dissent, even without the consent of kinsmen, at least according to some of the authorities (*v*), but this is properly limited in Bombay to the case of a divided family (*w*).

Where a husband writes to the Collector that his daughters are his heirs, this may indicate a prohibition on the husband's part to adoption by the widow while the daughters live or their line continues (*x*).

B. 3. 13.—Adoption Under an Assumed Assent of the Husband.

From the preceding cases it will have been gathered that authority from the husband, either express or clearly implied, enables a widow to adopt. On the other hand his prohibition or

---

(*t*) Per Westropp, C.J., in *Bhagwandas* v. *Rajmal*, 10 Bom. H. C. R. 257; *Amrito Lal Dutt* v. *Surnomoye Dasi*, L. R. 27 I. A. 128.

(*v*) See above, pp. 783, 796; *Patel Vandravan* v. *Chunilal*, I. L. R. 15 Bom. 565.

(*w*) *Ramji* v. *Ghamau*, I. L. R. 6 Bom., at p. 503.

In the case of *Virubudru* v. *Baee Ranee*, Morris R., Pt. II., p. 1, a question was put to the Sastri of the Sadr Court as follows:

"Can a widow of the Nagar Brahman caste adopt a son without having obtained the permission of her husband?"

The answer was—"If the husband forbade the adoption of a son, the widow could not adopt; but if he did not prohibit it, it must be understood that he assented to it. For it is commanded in the Shastr that a person who has no male issue must adopt a son, and if the widow adopted under such circumstances, in the way required by the Shastr, her act would be valid. Some law-books deny this right to the widow, but the greater number allow it. To give publicity to the adoption, it should be made known to the ruler, though if this was not done the adoption would not be invalid, if otherwise in accordance with the Shastr." See also *Abajee Dinkur* v. *Gungadhur Vasudeo*, 3 Morr. R. 420.

(*x*) *Collector of Madura* v. *Mutu Ramalinga Satherpatty*, 10 C. W. R. 17 P. C.; S. C. 1 Beng. L. R. 1 P. C.; 12 M. I. A. 397; 2 Mad. H. C. R. 206.

dissent, however intimated, so it be decidedly intimated, makes an adoption impossible (*y*). The widow does not, except incidentally, adopt for herself, but for her husband (*z*). The Maratha doctrine of her capacity when no intimation of his will has been given by the husband rests on an assumption of his assent to what would be at once a duty and a benefit to him. The Sastris have in several cases placed the widow's capacity on this very ground (*a*). She continues subordinately the ideal religious existence of her husband (*b*), and when he has not expressed his wishes may express them for him (*c*), though owing to her dependence, subject to the approval and control of the surviving male members of the undivided family (*d*).

The Sastris, to a question put them by the Court in *Thukoo Baee* v. *Ruma Baee* (*e*), replied: "Katyayana also says—'A married woman (naree) certainly must not act without orders,' which we conceive to mean, those of a father, husband, and son. However, a widow has the power of adopting even without the orders of her husband. A widow destitute of all three legal protectors, is mistress in her own right of the power both of giving and receiving."

The Vyavahara Mayukha distinctly declares that the law of Yajnavalkya as to the dependence of women bears on the wife as essentially dependent on her husband and only during her coverture. As a widow she may adopt without the command to which she is subject only as a wife (*f*). In the *Mankars' Case* (*g*) the Sastris said a widow could adopt her husband's brother's son, but no one else, without her husband's authority. Of the nine

---

(*y*) See *Bhagvandas* v. *Rajmal*, 10 Bom. H. C. R., at p. 257; 2 Str. H. L. 91; *Chowdhry Padam Singh* v. *Koer Udaya Singh*, 2 Beng. L. R., at p. 104 P. C.

(*z*) *Ibid.* Her spiritual interests are fully recognized, but are considered as bound up in his.

(*a*) See above, p. 867, note (*w*).

(*b*) Above, pp. 82, 91.

(*c*) *Bhagvandas* v. *Rajmal*, 10 Bom. H. C. R., at p. 257.

(*d*) *Ramji* v. *Ghamau*, I. L. R. 6 Bom., at pp. 502, 503. The Viramitrodaya contends strongly for the necessity of assuming the husband's assent, while it recognizes that the assent must be had of the brethren on whom the widow is dependent. Transl., p. 116.

(*e*) 2 Borr. 488.

(*f*) Vyav. May., Chap. IV., pp. 17, 18.

(*g*) 2 Borr. R., p. 104.

Pandits consulted in the case (*h*) two say that the rule of the Dattaka Mimamsa requiring the husband's express consent is the one generally followed, but that the Samskarakaustubha and the Vyavahara Mayukha have established for the Marathas that a widow may adopt without her husband's order. Four say the order may be dispensed with. One says the adoption may be made with the consent of the husband's kindred and of the caste, or even without any order or consent at all. To this another adds "provided her husband did not say he wished to have no son adopted." In the two answers of the Sastris which follow, the same vacillation may be noticed.

"A widow without her husband's permission may adopt with the sanction of some senior member of the family" (*i*).

"An adoption by a widow is not invalidated by want of permission from the deceased husband or his brother" (*k*).

Where there is no prohibition, there is a permission on the husband's part for a widow to give but not to take in adoption, according to the Bengal Law (*l*).

The consent or authority of the husband is not indispensable to adoption by a widow :—

In the Dravida country, Madras (*m*).

In the Saraogi Agarvali caste of Jains (*n*).

The Sastras of the Jains authorize a widow to adopt without the sanction of her husband. The age for adoption extends to the 32nd year (*o*).

The Sastris in the Bombay Presidency have usually favoured the widow's unfettered power to adopt, as in the two following instances.

(*h*) 2 Borr. R., at p. 104.

(*i*) MS. 1674; Vithoba v. Bapu, I. L. R. 15 Bom. 110.

(*k*) MS. 1753. In this case the permission of the nearest relative, which in the previous answer was said to be necessary, is pronounced needless. *Lakshmibai* v. *Sarasvatibai*, I. L. R. 23 Bom. 789.

(*l*) *Tarini Charan* v. *Saroda Sundari Dasi*, 3 Beng. L. R. 145 A. C. J.; S. C. 11 C. W. R. 468; see Datt. Chand., sec. I., paras. 31, 32, and sec. V. below.

(*m*) *Collector of Madura* v. *Mutu Ramalinga Satherpatty*, 12 M. I. A. 397; S. C. 2 Mad. H. C. R. 206; see next page.

(*n*) *Sheo Singh Rav* v. *Musst. Dakho*, 6 N. W. P. H. C. R. 382; Mit., Chap. I., sec. XI. 9 note; 1 Str. H. L. 79; 2 Str. H. L. 92, 96, 115; Vyav. May., Chap. IV., sec. V. 17, 18.

(*o*) *Maharaja Govindnath Ray* v. *Gulalchund et al.*, 5 C. S. D. A. R. 276; *Sheo Singh Rai* v. *Musst. Dakho*, L. R. 5 I. A. 87.

"The widow of a member of an undivided family may adopt" (*p*).

"The widows of two brothers may severally adopt" (*q*).

The adoption by a widow under an authority by her husband is valid even though it takes place after the birth of a posthumous child to the other coparcener (*r*). Her authority is of course unfettered when she takes as widow of a separated coparcener (*s*).

"The daughter-in-law may adopt notwithstanding a prior adoption by her father-in-law" (*t*).

"A mother-in-law and then the daughter-in-law adopt different boys. The one adopted by the daughter-in-law is heir to her husband" (*v*).

"There being an adoptive mother and a widow of an adopted son, the former cannot adopt without special reason" (*w*).

In a joint family under the Mitakshara a widow may adopt with the permission of her husband, and so divest his coparceners to some extent of their estate by introducing another sharer (*x*).

Under the law which prevails in the Dravida country, a widow without any permission from her husband may, if duly authorized by his kinsmen, adopt a son to him in every case in which such an adoption would be valid if made by her under written authority from her husband (*y*). The requisite authority in the case of an undivided family must be sought within the family, even though

---

(*p*) MS. 1650. This means without sanction.

(*q*) MS. 1750.

(*r*) *Hurkisondas* v. *Mankorebai*, L. R. 34 I. A. 107; S. C. I. L. R. 29 Bom. 51.

(*s*) *Ramji* v. *Ghamau*, I. L. R. 6 Bom. 498, F. B. The previous cases are in this fully discussed. See below, 3, 23; 3, 25; 3, 33.

(*t*) MS. 1666; *i.e.* the widow may adopt to her own husband. But the son thus adopted would succeed only to his adoptive father's separate property. The adoptive father's interest in the joint estate merged on his death in his father's. Such at least is the doctrine favoured by the Courts. See references in note (*s*).

(*v*) MS. 1761. See below, sub-sec. 3, 23. *Pudma Coomari Debi* v. *Court of Wards*, L. R. 8 I. A. 229; *Tarachurn Chatterji* v. *Suresh Chunder*, L. R. 16 I. A. 166.

(*w*) Above, p. 384, Q. 22.

(*x*) *Surendra* v. *Sailaji*, I. L. R. 18 Cal. 385; *Bachoo* v. *Makorebai*, I. L. R. 31 Bom. 373, P. C.; *Vithoba* v. *Bapu*, I. L. R. 15 Bom. 110.

(*y*) *Rajah Vellanki Venkata Krishna Rav* v. *Venkatrama Lakshmi*, I. L. R. 1 Mad. 175; S. C. L. R. 4 I. A. 1.

the particular property devolving upon the adopted son is to be held in severalty and not in coparcenary (*z*).

B. 3. 14.—Adoption by a Widow, a Conscientious Obligation.

It follows from what has been said that the widow is bound in religion to adopt conscientiously with a view to the benefit of her deceased husband, not capriciously, or so as to spite the husband's family. If a suitable boy can be had she ought to adopt from the husband's gotra, as she is thus most likely to maintain the family sacra (*a*). This obligation is not precisely a legal one (*b*), but if the widow disregards it without reason and seeks to introduce an objectionable member into the family the kinsmen may interfere (*c*). On the other hand they cannot properly refuse their assent to the dependent widow who desires to free her conscience and further her husband's happiness by a fit adoption (*d*).

The obligation to adopt is one that cannot be legally and directly enforced even when an express authority or command has been given by the deceased husband, much less can it be enforced when no direction has been given. The widow is then left to the promptings of her own conscience and judgment alone (*e*).

If a widow in a divided family adopts in the proper and *bona fide* performance of a religious duty, and neither capriciously nor from a corrupt motive, the adoption is good in the Maratha country, as well as in Gujrat, though without permission of the husband or consent of his kindred (*f*), or even that of the co-widow (*g*).

(*z*) *Ramnad Case*, 12 M. I. A. 269; *Sri Raghunadha* v. *Sri Brozo Kishoro*, L. R. 3 I. A. 154.

(*a*) 2 Str. H. L. 98.

(*b*) See sec. IV.

(*c*) See *Ramji* v. *Ghamau*, I. L. R. 6 Bom. 498.

(*d*) See above, pp. 864, 881; Steele, L. C. 45; *Rakhmabai* v. *Radhabai*, 5 Bom. H. C. R. 181 A. C. J.

(*e*) See above, pp. 813, 814. *Mutasaddi Lal* v. *Kundun Lal*, L. R. 33 I. A. 55.

(*f*) *Bhagvandas* v. *Rajmal*, 10 Bom. H. C. R., at p. 257; *Ramji* v. *Ghamau*, I. L. R. 6 Bom., at p. 501; *Thuckoo Baee* v. *Ruma Baee*, 2 Borr. 488 (2nd ed.); *Patel Vandravan* v. *Chunilal*, I. L. R. 15 Bom. 565.

(*g*) *Rakhmabai* v. *Radhabai*, 5 Bom. H. C. R. 181 A. C. J.; *Rupchand Rakhmabai*, 8 Bom. H. C. R. 114 A. C. J. It is as incumbent on the sapindas

The widow adopting must be a free agent. Constraint or undue influence will vitiate the adoption (*h*).

The observations of the Judicial Committee in the *Ramnad* case to the effect " that there should be such evidence of the assent of kinsmen as suffices to show that the act [of adoption] is done by the widow in the proper and *bona fide* performance of a religious duty, and neither capriciously nor from a corrupt motive," were explained in the sense that " Nice questions are not to be entertained as to the motives of a widow making an adoption so long as they are not corrupt or capricious " (*i*).

B. 3. 15.—Time for Adoption by a Widow.

The religious obligation under which a widow is placed by a direction to adopt makes it an imperative duty to fulfil her husband's purpose as soon as possible. But though inordinate delay has in one or two cases been considered a cause for preventing widows from reserving to themselves benefits in which they were intended to have only an incidental share, yet it cannot generally be said that promptness in adopting is more than a pious duty. On the other hand the capacity to adopt is not barred by limitation; it may be exercised virtually at any time during the widow's life (*k*).

The sooner adoption is made after the husband's death the better (*l*). " A widow should adopt within a year of her husband's death " (*m*). The non-exercise, however, by a widow of the right of adoption for one year after her husband's death does not entitle his next heir to sue for his share, for during the widow's life he has no right to present possession (*n*).

An adoption, fifteen years after the husband's death, under his

---

to allow a widow to appease her husband's manes as it is on the co-widow to join in furthering this pious purpose.

(*h*) *Bayabai* v. *Bala Venktesh*, 7 Bom. H. C. R. 1 App.; *Somasekhara* v. *Subhadramaji*, I. L. R. 6 Bom. 524, 527.

(*i*) *Raja Vellanki* v. *Venkata Rama*, L. R. 4 I. A. 1.

(*k*) *Mutasaddi Lal* v. *Kundun Lal*, L. R. 33 I. A. 55.

(*l*) *Verapermal Pillay* v. *Narrain Pillay*, 1 Str. R. 91.

(*m*) MS. 1734.

(*n*) *Ramanamall* v. *Suban Annavi*, 2 Mad. H. C. R. 399.

authority, was held good (*o*), and even an adoption twenty years after the husband's death (*p*).

The presumption against adoption arising from neglect by a widow to adopt for six or seven years after the death of her husband (the Raja of Nattore) was considered not so great as the presumption in favour of the Raja's having given power to adopt (*q*).

B. 3. 16.—Adoption by Widow—Of Husband's Nephew or Other Sapinda.

Religious feeling usually prompts a husband in giving authority to adopt to designate a nephew or a member of his gotra either individually or by class as the person for adoption. He may, however, designate a stranger as he might adopt a stranger, or he may leave the choice to his widow's discretion. In the last case, and in what may in Bombay be deemed the similar case of no particular intimation of his wishes having been given by the husband, the widow, like the husband, ought to adopt from amongst nephews or near kinsmen (*r*). The Sastris, as has been seen, have been disposed to exempt her from control if she should take a nephew, but they have shrunk from pronouncing an adoption of a stranger duly celebrated invalid. The choice, therefore, though subject to control, cannot be deemed legally limited to any particular family so long as it is made within the caste, and outside the offspring of sisters and daughters of the husband (*s*). In *Srimati Uma Deyi* v. *Gokoolanand Das Mahapatra* (*t*) the Judicial Committee have held that the adoption of a very distant relation, not included within the *sapindas* of the adoptive father, made in violation of the preferential right of the son of a brother of the whole blood was valid. The texts which prescribe the preferential adoption of such son have not the force of law.

(*o*) East's Notes, Case 10, 2 Mor. Dig. 18.

(*p*) *Musst. Anundmoyee* v. *Sheeb Chunder Roy*, 9 M. I. A. 287; S. C. Beng. S. D. A. Rep. 1855, p. 218.

(*q*) *R. Chundernath Roy* v. *Kooer Gobindnath Roy*, 18 C. W. R. 221.

(*r*) Above, pp. 800, 818; sub-sec. 3. 13.

(*s*) See further on this subject in the next section.

(*t*) L. R. 5 I. A. 40; S. C. I. L. R. 3 Cal. 587.

B. 3. 17.—Adoption by Widow—Authority in the Case of Two or More Widows.

Where there are two widows the husband may authorize both to adopt. In *Venkata Narasimha Appa Row* v. *Parthasarathy Appo Row* (v) their Lordships of the Privy Council have held that the power given to two widows to adopt jointly cannot be exercised by only one, even though such an adoption has become impossible as by the death of one of them. In the absence of an order they ought both to concur in an adoption. But in case of difference the elder has the superior right; and the younger cannot, it would seem, adopt without her senior's authority, except in case of irregularity on the senior's part causing interference by the caste (w). Thus the Sastris say:

"The eldest of several widows has the right to adopt. On her death or disqualification the right passes to the next widow in order of marriage. She is disqualified by leprosy" (x).

"A man having directed an adoption, the elder widow may adopt against the wish of the junior" (y).

"The senior widow of a Sudra, though married by pat, has a preferential right to adopt over the second though married by 'lagna,' the one ceremony conferring in that caste the same rights as the other" (z).

"The elder of two widows may adopt though the younger has a daughter" (a).

A husband gave directions to each of his two wives to adopt. After his death they divided the property. The elder gave away her share and died. The younger then adopted a son. The Sastri said he might recover the aliened share from the donee (b). In this case if the two widows, as is sometimes supposed, took a joint estate inalienable and vesting on the death of one widow solely in

---

(v) L. R. 41 I. A. 51.

(w) Steele, L. C. 48, 187: *Rakhmabai* v. *Rakhabai*, 5 Bom. H. C. R. 181 A. C. J.; *Ramji* v. *Ghamau*, I. L. R. 6 Bom., at p. 503.

(x) MS. 1669. See above, p. 390, Q. 36.

(y) MS. 1656. An authority cannot be given to each of two widows to adopt so that there may be two adopted sons at once. See *Gosavi Shree Chundrarulee* v. *Girdharajee*, 4 N. W. P. R. 226.

(z) MS. 1655. See above, pp. 391, 394, 404.

(a) MS. 1734. The existence of a daughter does not in any case prevent an adoption.

(b) 2 Macn. H. L. 247, Case XL.

the other, the donee could not of course have taken anything as against the surviving widow (c). This does not, however, seem to have been the view of the Sastri. The performance of the Sraddhas ought in his opinion to be provided for by adoption, and the fulfilment of the duty which was incumbent from the beginning of widowhood defeated the gift made at a later time and subject to the duty (d).

Where the elder of two widows has assented to an adoption by the other she cannot herself adopt another boy (e).

B. 3. 18.—Adoption by Widow—Circumstances in which the Capacity may be Exercised.

These are generally the same as for the husband himself. The obstacles to adoption by the husband operate equally to prevent an adoption by the widow. For instance the existence of a son, either begotten or adopted, or the deceased husband's having died outcast. The circumstances which bar, or are supposed to bar, adoption by a widow are more particularly considered below. Where the elder of two widows has adopted a son the other cannot during his life adopt another (f). On the death of a son adopted by the senior widow under authority of her husband, the second widow may adopt a second son upon an independent authority from her husband (g). The authority to make successive adoptions is considered below.

B. 3. 19.—Adoption by Widow—Son Deceased Sonless.

An authority to adopt is frequently conditional on the death of a son. It provides sometimes for the event of a first or second

---

(c) Above, p. 95.

(d) The adoption of a son operates retrospectively as a renewal or continuance of the adoptive father's existence as to an estate held solely or jointly by the latter at the time of his death.

(e) *Ramchandra* v. *Bapu Khandu*, Bom. H. C. P. J. 1877, p. 43; *Surendrakeshav Roy* v. *Doorgasundari Dassee*, L. R. 19 I. A. 108.

(f) Steele, L. C. 48. See p. 874 (y); *Rungama* v. *Atchama*, 4 M. I. A. 1; *Mohesh Narain* v. *Taruck Nath*, L. R. 20 I. A. 30; *Ramabai* v. *Raya*, I. L. R. 22 Bom. 482.

(g) *Shama Chunder et al.* v. *Narain Debeah*, 1 C. S. D. A. R. 209; contra *Narainee Debeh* v. *Hurkishore Rai*, 1 C. S. D. A. R. 39.

adopted son's replacement in the event of his death. In such cases, it has to be borne in mind, the husband has by no means an unlimited power of future disposition. The son, whether begotten or adopted, by his birth or adoption and initiation, acquires rights and becomes a source of rights, which are regulated and guarded by the family law so as not to be subject to indefinite modification at the will of any individual. The authority to adopt cannot be made a means of upsetting the law on which it rests. Where the husband has given power to a widow to adopt, on the death of a natural son, an adopted son, or one adopted by her, the widow can exercise the authority only when the son dies unmarried, or leaving no child or widow (*h*).

B. 3. 21.—SUCCESSIVE ADOPTIONS BY A WIDOW.

Where the son dies unmarried and without having adopted, full effect can be given to the authority to adopt son after son without the embarrassment of competing rights, which must arise from a series of adopted sons leaving widows, each perhaps entitled to adopt. The difficulty that would arise in the latter case has been perceived by the Judicial Committee. In *R. V. Venkata Krishnarao* v. *Venkata Rama Lakshmi Narasaiyya* (*i*), Sir J. Colville says: "It is not necessary to consider in what way successive adoptions operate. It is sufficient to say that the law has established that they may take place." This right she can exercise despite the fact that the deceased son had attained ceremonial competence by marriage, investiture, or otherwise (*k*).

Where a widow adopted a second son, upon the death of an adopted son, the Court rejected the suit of the deceased owner's brother with reference to the uncertainty of the law, in respect of the right of the presumptive next taker after a Hindu widow, to a decree, declaring her adoption invalid (*l*).

(*h*) *Musst. Bhoobun Moyee Debia* v. *Ramkishore Acharjee*, 10 M. I. A. 279; S. C. 3 C. W. R. 15 P. C.; S. C. Beng. S. D. A. R. 1858, p. 122; *Thayammal* v. *Venkatarama Aiyan*, L. R. 14 I. A. 67; *Pudma Coomari Debi* v. *Court of Wards*, L. R. 8 I. A. 229; *Gavadappa* v. *Girimalla*, I. L. R. 19 Bom. 331.

(*i*) L. R. 4 I. A. 1; S. C. I. L. R. 1 Mad. 174.

(*k*) *Venkappa* v. *Jivaji Krishna*, I. L. R. 25 Bom. 306; *Gopal* v. *Vishnu*, I. L. R. 23 Bom. 250; *Payapa* v. *Appanna*, I. L. R. ibid. 327; *Kanuapalli* v. *Pucha Venkata*, L. R. 33 I. A. 145.

(*l*) *Ry Brohmo Moyee* v. *R. Anand Lall Roy*, 19 C. W. R. 419.

When not expressly prohibited, a widow may make a second adoption with the sanction of the kinsmen. If some kinsmen give sanction, and others withhold it from interested motives, and both these are equally related to the deceased, the widow can adopt, acting upon the sanction of those kinsmen who gave it (*m*).

A second adopted son takes the place of the first, but only if the first adopted died without issue (*n*). In an authority to adopt successively the condition "if necessary" must be understood. Where an authority had been given to a wife to adopt five sons in succession, and the son first adopted lived to perform all the sacra, it was held that on his death unmarried his mother could adopt to his father (*o*). This may perhaps be justified on the principle that there was no widow of the adopted son to take a jointure of the sacra, but the retrogression of the right to adopt could not be carried further without introducing confusion (*p*).

B. 3. 22.—Adoption by a Widow—Simultaneous Adoptions.

As the existence of one son makes the adoption of another illegal, the attempt to adopt two sons at once has been pronounced invalid as to both (*q*). It could indeed be no more regarded as generally possible than the simultaneous marriage of two or more wives under a law of monogamy.

(*m*) *Parasara Bhatar* v. *Rang Raja Whatar*, I. L. R. 2 Mad. 202; see also *Rakhmabai* v. *Radhabai*, 5 Bom. H. C. R., at p. 191. This shows that the authority to give or withhold sanction is not a right of property, but simply a part of the religious and family law.

(*n*) *Shama Chunder* v. *Narain Debeah*, 1 C. S. D. A. R. 209.

(*o*) *Ram Soondur Singh* v. *Surbanee Dossee*, 22 C. W. R. 121 C. R.

(*p*) See below, B. 3. 23; B. 3. 25.

(*q*) *Akhoy Chunder Bagchi* v. *Kalapahar Haji*, L. R. 12 I. A. 198; S. C. I. L. R. 12 Cal. 406; *Surendrakeshav Roy* v. *Doorgasunderi Dassee*, L. R. 19 I. A. 108; *Gyanendro Chunder Lahiri* v. *Kalla Pahar Hajee*, I. L. R. 9 Cal. 50; *Monemothonauth Day* v. *Ouauth Nauth Day*, Bourke's R. 189; *S. Siddesory Dosee* v. *Doorgachurn Sett*, Bourke 360; *Bhya Ram Singh* v. *Agur Singh*, 1 N. W. P. H. C. R. 203; *Senkol Tevan* v. *Aurlanada Ambalakaran*, M. S. D. A. R. for 1862, p. 27.

B. 3. 23.—Adoption by a Widow—Circumstances which Bar Adoption.

It follows from the delegated or substitutionary character of the widow's authority to adopt (r) that the impediments to adoption external to the husband which affect adoption by him equally affect adoption by the widow. And as she has to perform an act of intelligence of sacred import, she must in her own person satisfy the conditions requisite to make such an act effectual. The circumstances in which the power can or cannot be exercised have already been considered. Amongst these might have been placed the existence of vested interests as viewed from the negative side, but this recently developed doctrine having been usually discussed by the Courts with reférence to its positive operation as a bar to adoption or as depriving adoption of its usual consequences, will be here treated from the same point of view.

The principle now generally accepted by the Courts that a widow cannot adopt so as to defeat a vested interest (s) is not to be found in that form in the Hindu authorities (t). It has been taken in two senses: (1) that the adoption under such circumstances is void, and (2) that though not void its regular effects are limited so as not to divest the vested estate. There has been a difference of views also as to whether the husband's authority does or does not make the rule inapplicable. It is almost inevitable that an adoption by a widow should cause some loss to kinsmen or contingent reversioners, and the principle has again been varied so as to make the consent of the parties thus interested or of a majority or of some of them necessary (v). In Bengal the widow

---

(r) See 2 Str. H. L. 88, 91, 92, 94.

(s) *Tarachurn Chatterji* v. *Suresh Chunder Mookerji*, L. R. 16 I. A. 166; *Thayammal* v. *Venkatarama Aiyan*, L. R. 14 I. A. 67; *Gopal* v. *Vishnu*, I. L. R. 23 Bom. 250; *Bhimabai* v. *Murar Rao*, I. L. R. 37 Bom. 598; *Payapa* v. *Appanna*, I. L. R. 23 Bom. 327; *Rupchand* v. *Rakhmabai*, 8 Bom. H. C. R. 114.

(t) A mere descent cast makes no difference except when a son has taken the estate and left a widow. A right so devolved cannot be displaced by an adoption even under an express authority from the deceased son's father by his mother. See *Bhoobunmoyee Debia's Case*, 10 M. I. A. 279, quoted in *Rajah Vellanki Venkata Krishna Rao* v. *Venkata Rama Lakshmi Narsayya*, L. R. 4 I. A., at p. 9.

(v) See *The Collector of Madura* v. *Muttu Ramalinga Sadhupatty*, 12 M. I. A. 397; *Sri Raghunada* v. *Sri Brozo Kishoro*, L. R. 3 I. A. 154, 191, 192; *Ramji* v. *Ghamau*, I. L. R. 6 Bom. 498, 501.

takes a life estate though not more even in an undivided family. If she adopts under a licence from her husband she deprives his brethren of the succession. In Bombay she takes the succession only in a divided family, but an adoption by her defeats the estate which otherwise must go to the heirs next in succession at her death. She may have a daughter or a daughter's son taking, according to the prevailing theory, from her deceased husband. It is inconsistent with the theory of her position as not being a source whence succession is derived that she should have a power of defeating at her pleasure that succession which the law approves, but this has by the decisions been conceded to her.

The adoption of a son operates retrospectively (*w*). He is looked on in the light of a posthumous son, and though a widow cannot adopt with the consequence of giving effect to a fraud (*x*), yet there is nothing unreasonable in the loss of an estate divested by an adoption when the estate has from the first been subject to that kind of defeasance. The defeasance arises from what is in theory a deferred act of the deceased adoptive father, who could always have adopted had he lived, and whose spiritual life is continued by his widow.

In *Bhoobunmoyee Debia's Case* the divesting of an estate was put forward by Lord Kingsdown rather perhaps as an illustration of the inconvenience that would arise from adoptions creating new collateral heirs than as a thing in itself impossible under the Hindu Law (*y*). In other cases the inconvenience has been made a ground for a supposed prohibition (*z*). It is true that in many instances the supposed prohibition coincides in its operation with the actual principles of the Hindu Law as drawn from the Hindu sources, but in others it does not. It is desirable therefore that these principles and their bearing on the matter in question should, if possible, be

---

(*w*) The common statement has been adopted. Its proper sense is that an adopted son is regarded as a continuator of the adoptive father's personality as to his property and sacra whether separate or in a united family. The adoption is not retrospective for the purpose of enabling the son to take back a property which his father had not, and which between the father's death and the adoption has been given by the law to some other separated relative or branch of the original family.

(*x*) See above, pp. 348, 349.

(*y*) See also *Sri Raghunadas's Case*, L. R. 3 I. A., at p. 193.

(*z*) See *The Collector of Madura's Case*, 12 M. I. A. 397; *Rupchand* v. *Rakhmabai*, 8 Bom. H. C. R. 114; *Kally Prosono Ghose* v. *Gocoolchundra Mitter*, I. L. R. 2 Cal. 307.

ascertained and established. The sacra of a Hindu family are regarded as descending regularly with its estate from father to son for ever. The birth and the initiation of the son make him the joint or the sole depositary of this group of connected rights and obligations. He is bound to provide for his father's sraddhas: he is entitled to the due performance of his own. The proper celebrant is a son begotten or adopted; but if the estate passes to a remoter heir the duty goes with it. The last holder—though no ceremonies are so effectual as those performed by a son—yet receives such benefit as is possible from the actual successor to the property. Now by an adoption higher in the line this blessing is lost. The son adopted, for instance, by the mother of one deceased performs a father's sraddhas for his ceremonial father, but not for his ceremonial brother. The latter is thus, according to Hindu sentiment, placed in a worse position than if there had been no adoption at all. If the deceased have left a widow, it is she alone who, as partner during his life of his sacra, and capable of continuing them after his death, can in accordance with theory adopt a son. The son is her son as well as her husband's. Even in his life both ought to concur in an adoption. The books say nothing of a husband, even in his life, authorizing an adoption by anyone but his wife, and Sir M. Westropp was fully warranted in stating that there is no authority for anyone but the widow to adopt a son to her husband after his death (*a*). She only could legally have joined in procuring the son by birth who is replaced by the adopted son, and the imitation of nature thus points her out as solely endowed with the faculty of adoption when her husband can no longer exercise it.

There are thus strong reasons, though the Sastris seem in a few instances not to have sufficiently adverted to them (*b*), why adoption by a mother to her son should be disallowed (*c*), and why an adoption by her to her deceased husband should not be allowed to supersede the right of the deceased son's widow. The reasons do not at all rest on a devesting of the junior widow's estate, but the preservation of her estate is incident to her exclusive faculty of adoption. If the view here taken is correct, a mother succeeding to her son after the son's investiture (upanayana) is not the more

---

(*a*) *Bhagvandas* v. *Rajmal*, 10 Bom. H. C. R., at pp. 257, 258.

(*b*) See 2 Str. H. L. 93, 94, 95. See below, sub-sec. 3. 26.

(*c*) See above, sub-sec. 3. 13; *Krishnarav v. Shankar Rav*, I. L. R. 17 Bom. 164.

capable of adopting a son to him because she devests no estate but her own, but a case to the contrary is referred to below (*d*).

There are cases, however, in which an only son or an adopted son dies unmarried or married without leaving a widow or issue. She may then adopt a second and a third son, even though the first and the second might have attained ceremonial competence by marriage, investiture, or otherwise, provided she does not thereby derogate from any other right (*e*). To this qualification there are four exceptions, viz., (1) when a widow adopts to the detriment of her co-widow (*f*), (2) when a mother succeeds as heir to a son, legitimate or adopted, married but leaving neither a widow nor issue, or unmarried, (3) when an adoption takes place with the full assent of the party in whom the estate has vested by inheritance, *e.g.*, a daughter-in-law adopting with the consent of the father-in-law (*g*), and (4) when there has been ratification by conduct or acquiescence (*h*).

When the deceased husband has died as a member of an undivided family the faculty of adoption is still peculiar to the widow. But as a consequence of her general dependence she cannot exercise this faculty without the approval of the kinsmen (*i*), except where that approval is improperly withheld (*k*). The sanction is not necessary where the husband has given her authority to adopt, and especially where he has himself designated the boy for adoption. In such a case the vested interests of the kinsmen are displaced by the adoption, whether they approve it or not (*l*). This shows that the need of their sanction does not arise

---

(*d*) *Bykant Monee Roy* v. *Kisto Soonderee Roy*, 7 C. W. R. 392 C. R. See the remarks of Melvill, J., in *Rapchand* v. *Rakhmabai*, 8 Bom. H. C. R., at pp. 118, 123 A. C. J.

(*e*) *Venkappa* v. *Jivaji Krishna*, I. L. R. 25 Bom. 306; *Musst. Bhoobunmoyee Debia* v. *Ramkishore Acharji Chowdhry*, 10 M. I. A., at p. 310; *Rajah Vellanki Venkat Krishnarav* v. *Venkatrama Lakshmi Narsayya*, L. R. 4 I. A. 1; *Vasdeo* v. *Ramchandra*, I. L. R. 22 Bom. 551, F. B.

(*f*) *Bhimowa* v. *Sanjawa*, I. L. R. 22 Bom. 206.

(*g*) *Vithoba* v. *Bapu*, I. L. R. 15 Bom. 110.

(*h*) *Payapa* v. *Appanna*, I. L. R. 23 Bom. 327; *Gopal* v. *Vishnu*, I. L. R. 23 Bom. 250.

(*i*) *Shri Raghunadha* v. *Shri Brozo Kishore*, L. R. 3 I. A. 191.

(*k*) See *Rakhmabai* v. *Radhabai*, 5 Bom. H. C. R. 181, 188; above, pp. 783, 796.

(*l*) See *Sri Raghunada* v. *Sri Brozo Kishore*, L. R. 3 I. A. 154, 173; *Dinkar Sitaram Prabhu* v. *Ganesh Shivaram Prabhu*, I. L. R. 6 Bom. 505; *Govind Soondaree Debea* v. *Jugganunda Debea*, 3 C. W. R. 66; 15 I. A. 5.

from their rights in the property but from their family relation to the widow. Their authority may be likened to that sometimes given to a girl's guardian under the English Law to give or to withhold his sanction to her marriage. This, though its exercise may greatly affect his own fortune, is not a right of the guardian which he is at liberty to use for his personal enrichment. He is bound to use it conscientiously, and failing to do so he may be superseded. So the Hindu kinsmen must not withhold their assent to an unobjectionable adoption merely because it will introduce another sharer of the estate (*m*). The widow is bound (at least religiously) to seek a son within the family. When she does so the family is not in any way impoverished by the adoption, but if she is forced to go out of the family for a son the kinsmen have still not a right of property to exert or to forgo, but a faculty to exercise (*n*), which they must use to the advantage of the family at large, but especially of the deceased member. Such a sanction it has been held is sufficient as affords a reasonable guarantee that the widow has acted with moderate prudence and conscientiousness (*o*). If the sanction were a right resting on property the infant co-members would have to be consulted through their guardians, and might have a right to disapprove at a later period what had been improvidently allowed in their infancy, but no provisions to this effect are found in the law books.

The son united with his father may have died childless before him. His joint interest in the property and the sacra then reverts to the father, who may adopt a son and make him heir as he might have begotten a son. In such a case, as the deceased never had an independent right, being unseparated from his still living father, his widow cannot adopt without the sanction of her father-in-law. On the other hand the father-in-law, who has sanctioned an adoption by his son's widow, and thus given himself a grandson, cannot afterwards adopt a son. If he first adopts a son to himself he may still sanction an adoption to his deceased son. If he dies without either adoption having been made it might seem that the

---

where the inquiry into the fact of the authority would have been needless unless it would operate if proved. Steele, L. C. 176.

(*m*) Above, pp. 783, 795, 814, 871.

(*n*) See *The Collector of Madura* v. *Moottoo Ramalinga Satthupatty*, 12 M. I. A., at p. 442.

(*o*) See *Gopal* v. *Naro*, 7 Bom. H. C. R. xxiv. App.; and *Rakhmabhai's Case, supra*.

right would pass rather to his widow, should he leave one, than to his daughter-in-law. The replies of the Sastris, however, favour the right of the daughter-in-law even during the father-in-law's life, giving to her adopted son rights equal or superior to those of the son adopted by the father-in-law (*p*), according to the earlier or later adoption of the latter. On the death of the father-in-law without adoption they prefer to his widow the widow of his son, by whose adoption the manes of both father and son may be appeased (*q*). A daughter-in-law, the widow of a pre-deceased son, can make a valid adoption with the contemporaneous consent of her mother-in-law, in whom the estate of the last full owner has vested as her heir (*r*).

Where two or more united brothers have died in succession and sonless the household sacra in which they were jointly interested must have devolved solely on the one who survived the other. In such a case the widow of the last deceased as a sharer, though in a minor degree, of his ceremonial virtue, and having with him in his life a joint capacity to adopt, according to the religious view. is the proper person to adopt to her husband, and so devolve the family sacra centred in herself. The wife of the predeceased united member, however, had with him a joint interest in the family sacra, though this was never so developed by his separation as after his death to give efficacy to her substitutionary acts on account of a new family (*s*). The common sacra centre on the death of one in the surviving members of the united family: the widow is spiritually and temporally dependent, and cannot adopt without the assent of the brethren. If all have died, the widow of the last has succeeded, so far as a woman can, to the sacra of the family, but she has not a superiority corresponding to that of her husband over the widow of a predeceased member, and enabling her to approve or disapprove an adoption by that widow (*t*). Such an adoption is, according to one view, no longer feasible when no one is left to give the requisite sanction. Though a widow has the sole faculty of adopting to the deceased husband, this faculty

(*p*) See above, p. 354, Q. 13, to which the remarks in the text apply, and sub-section B. 3. 13 of the present section.

(*q*) See a decision to the same effect in sub-sec. 3. 26.

(*r*) *Siddappa* v. *Ningangavda*, I. L. R. 38 Bom. 724.

(*s*) See above, p. 338.

(*t*) That a widow is subject to control only by near male relatives appears from the answer in *Thukoo Baee's Case*, quoted above, p. 868.

cannot be exercised in a united family except with the assent of the male members. On their extinction the faculty is virtually gone.

According to the other and the approved view, the widow, by the death of her husband's former co-members of the family, is merely freed from a control which they might exercise for her good during their lives. She may then adopt at her own discretion, as no controlling power is attributed to the widow of one deceased member over the acts of another (*v*). Nor is she subject to the control of an infant member incapable of discrimination. This view is the one more consonant to the doctrines of the Nirnayasindhu, the Samskarakaustubha, and the Dharmasindhu, admitting that any sanction at all is necessary to adoption by a widow. The Vyavahara Mayukha recognizes the need of a sanction while there are qualified persons present to give or withhold it but not otherwise (*w*).

In a divided family the ties of mutual dependence and support are much less close than amongst united kinsmen. According to the doctrine of the Mitakshara the widow of a separated member takes his estate in full ownership, and becomes herself, though in her husband's family, a new source of inheritance (*x*). According to the now prevailing Bengal doctrine she takes only a life interest, but still during her life the estate is completely vested in her (*y*). Thus there are no immediate interests to impede her freedom as to adoption. But the division of the once united family has been necessarily attended with a separation in the performance of the daily sacrifices and the other periodical rites, community in which is the central point of family union (*z*). The husband who has once been a celebrant of the sacra for himself alone cannot have lost the capacity and the obligation except by the process of reunion. If as usual he has died separated his sacra pass to his son, and in default of a son to his widow (*a*), who in her turn may

---

(*v*) See the opinion of the Sastris in *Thukoo Baee* v. *Ruma Baee*, cited above in sub-sec. B. 3. 13.

(*w*) See *Bayabai* v. *Bala Venktesh Ramakant*, 7 Bom. H. C. R. App. xii.; Vyav. May., Chap. IV., sec. V., para. 18.

(*x*) See above, pp. 308, 309, 473, 484, 712.

(*y*) Above, p. 89.

(*z*) See above, pp. 638, 773; *Sri Raghunada's Case*, L. R. 3 I. A., at p. 191.

(*a*) Above, pp. 87, 250.

impart the requisite faculty by adoption. As no one shares the sacra there is no joint interest on which an interference with her discretion can properly be grounded (*b*). A tradition of the necessary dependence of women still exacts from the widow a decent regard for the interests and wishes of the family at large notwithstanding the partition that has taken place, but as on the one hand she cannot urge her connexion as a ground for a right to maintenance in distress (*c*), neither can the kinsmen on the other hand urge it as a ground for legal control of her faculty of adoption (*d*).

These considerations apply to the actual estate of the deceased husband, whether joint or separate. If the deceased husband had no ownership of an estate in question, either as being individually separate or as being a member of a branch separated from the one to which the estate belonged, it is obvious that he had no sacra which that estate was bound to sustain. He might, had he survived, possibly have come in as the nearest collateral on the extinction of the proprietary branch, but when in his absence another has succeeded, that other has assumed the whole of the sacra connected with the estate he has taken (*e*). No participation in them belongs to the widow of the predeceased which she can impart to a son by adoption. One separated collateral cannot therefore be ousted by an adoption made after his succession by another collateral's widow. Much less can any one representing the proprietary branch undivided in itself be thus superseded.

It accords with the views just stated that if a Hindu husband gives to his wife an instrument of permission to adopt, should she be left a widow, and if he has born to him a son, who survives him, and if this son dies leaving a widow in whom the estate is vested, the power of adoption given to the mother-in-law is incapable of execution and is at an end (*f*).

(*b*) See Viramitrodaya, Transl., p. 257.

(*c*) Above, pp. 230, 236.

(*d*) *Ramjee* v. *Ghamau*, I. L. R. 6 Bom., at pp. 502, 503.

(*e*) See the opinion in *Bamundass Mookerjia* v. *Mt. Tarinee*, 7 M. I. A., at p. 188; and above, pp. 63, 350, 554.

(*f*) *Padma Kumari Debi Chowdhrani et al.* v. *Jagatkishore Acharjia Chowdhri*, I. L. R. 8 Cal. 302 P. C.

B. 3. 24.—ADOPTION BY A WIDOW—CIRCUMSTANCES BARRING ADOPTION AS IN THE CASE OF A MALE.

" A widow cannot adopt while a previously adopted son is alive " (*g*).

A son by her co-wife prevents adoption by a widow equally with one born of herself (*h*).

" The widow cannot adopt two sons, because the adoption of the first creates an immediate change of the essential condition of sonlessness " (*i*).

The existence of an adopted son is a bar to another adoption (though under power from the husband), by a widow, as well as to one by a husband himself (*k*).

A husband abandoned his wife, who became a Moorlee. By his second wife he had a son. The first wife adopted a son. This was held invalid (*l*).

Adoption by a Hindu in concert with his senior wife, it was said, supersedes the original permission given by him to each of his two wives to adopt a son for each, unless after the adoption he expressly confirmed the permission to his junior wife to adopt (*m*).

B. 3. 25.—ADOPTION BY A WIDOW—NOT TO DEFEAT A VESTED ESTATE.

Though the Hindu authorities do not furnish such a rule, it must now be accepted perhaps as a principle established, or at least strongly favoured by the decisions, that adoption cannot be made to devest or defeat an inheritance already vested (*n*), except in

---

(*g*) MS. 1664. See above, sec. III. B. 3. 18; B. 3. 19.

(*h*) Above, p. 489.

(*i*) MS. 1671. *Mohesh Narain* v. *Taruck Nath*, L. R. 20 I. A., 30.

(*k*) *Gopee Lall* v. *Musst. Chundraolee Buhoojee*, 4 N. W. P. R. 226; S. C. in Appeal, L. R. Supp. I. A. 131, and 19 C. W. R. 12 C. R.

(*l*) MS. 113.

(*m*) *Goureepershad Raee* v. *Musst. Jymala*, 2 C. S. D. A. R. 136; Macn. Con. H. L. 181, 182; 2 Str. H. L. 61. The permission could not operate while the son actually adopted was alive.

(*n*) *Annammali* v. *Mabhu Bali Reddy*, 8 Mad. H. C. R. 108; *Kally Prosonno Ghose* v. *Gocool Chunder*, I. L. R. 2 Cal. 295; *Rupchand Hindumal* v. *Rakhmabai*, 8 Bom. H. C. R. 114 A. C. J. See the discussion above, sec. III. B. 3. 23; *Gayabai* v. *Shridharacharya*, Bom. H. C. P. J. 1881, p. 145; *Thayammal* v. *Venkatarama Aiyan*, L. R. 14 I. A. 67; *Tarachurn Chatterji* v. *Suresh Chunder Mookerji*, L. R. 16 I. A. 166.

four cases mentioned in *Payapa* v. *Appanna* (o) and *Gopal* v. *Vishnu* (p). The Hindu rule seems to be this, that when a deceased was an actual co-owner or sharer in interest in an estate in question, his son received in adoption, whether by himself or by his widow, takes his place. When he was separated and the law has given the estate of his deceased relative to some one else, the succession having passed by his line, cannot be recovered, because there is no authority for taking the estate from the hands into which it has fallen. The same principle is applied in the case of a blind or dumb man's son. Such a man cannot be an actual coparcener. There is a rule allowing his son to take his place in a partition, but when once the partition has been made, the son subsequently born or adopted is not remitted to a right which did not subsist in his father (q). The particular rule, like that giving an estate to the existing collaterals, is not accompanied by any proviso in favour of subsequently adopted sons. In a united family there is a remitter through the identification in interest of the son with his father who died a co-sharer.

A widow (having legal power to adopt from her husband) (r) cannot adopt so as to deprive or defeat an inheritance or interest already vested in a widow of a son, natural or adopted, who survived his father (s), or in the son of such a son (t), or in the heirs of the adoptee's grand-uncle by adoption, who had succeeded to the grand-uncle's property upon the death of his widow (v). Where the estate has come down to the widow of the last male survivor of the husband's family prior to the adoption (w), it might seem that an adoption by a widow of a previously deceased coparcener could not be made so as to defeat the vested estate. This, however, will depend on the different views discussed above (x). A new line cannot be substituted by adoption to take

(o) I. L. R. 23 Bom. 327.

(p) I. L. R. *ibid.* 250.

(q) See *Bapuji Lakshman* v. *Pandurang*, I. L. R. 6 Bom., at p. 620.

(r) *i.e.* where such power is essential.

(s) *Musst. Bhoobun Moyee Debia* v. *Ramkishore Acharjee*, 10 M. I. A. 279; S. C. 3 C. W. R. 15 P. C.; S. C. Beng. S. D. A. R. 1858, p. 122; *Krishnarav* v. *Shankar Rav*, I. L. R. 17 Bom. 164.

(t) *Thukoo Baee* v. *Ruma Baee*, 2 Borr. 488 (2nd ed.); *Ramkrishna* v. *Shamrao*, I. L. R. 26 Bom. 526.

(v) *Kally Prosonno Ghose* v. *Gocool Chunder*, I. L. R. 2 Cal. 295.

(w) *Gobind Soonduree Debia* v. *Juggodumba Debia*, 3 C. W. R. 66; S. C. 15 C. W. R. 5 P. C.

(x) Sec. III. B. 3. 23. And see above, p. 560.

what a natural-born son would not have taken (*y*); but there does not seem to be anything in the Hindu Law to prevent his taking what a natural-born son would have taken at the moment of his birth or of his father's death. In *Bhoobun Moyee Debia's Case* the adoption was in itself invalid, but if it had been made by the widow of one brother or cousin after the estate had descended to the widow of another the right of the former to adopt to her deceased husband, which had always subsisted, would not, according to the prevailing Hindu notions, be extinguished by failure of the male members. It would only be freed from a condition arising from the widow's dependence while they lived. The only theory on which the prohibitive right of the widow of the last full owner can be sustained seems to be that the sacra along with the estate centred in the widow's husband and have centred in her, so that she is religiously bound to continue the family by adoption, and to retain the estate for the benefit of the son to be adopted. His adoption operating retrospectively will make the estate devolve wholly upon him as his adoptive father's heir, and the adoption of a son by the widow of a predeceased member being made subject to the contingency of the adoption of a son to the last deceased may be deemed subject to the approval of the latter's adopted son as the male sapinda on whom she is dependent. The law books and the practice of the people do not, however, support such a theory as this: they rather allow and encourage an adoption by a widow duly authorized without sanction when there is no one to give or to withhold it, though such an adoption made by the widow of a separated collateral after the estate has passed to another collateral, will not serve to create for the adopted son an estate in possession in which his father had no more than a contingent interest. When it has passed to a collateral separated in interest it has passed for good as against a collateral who, when it passed, had no share or interest (*z*). There is in the last case a break in the succession as contrasted with the ideal continuity of interest amongst all the members of a united family (*a*). A right in possession is kept alive by the widow's constant capacity to adopt, so as to blend an additional element retrospectively with the united family, but a mere possibility once extinguished cannot be revived. Thus adoption

(*y*) See *Musst. Bhoobun Moyee Debia's Case*, 10 M. I. A., at p. 311.

(*z*) Comp. above, pp. 545, 554.

(*a*) Above, pp. 63, 561.

in a separated branch cannot divest the estate which the law gave to the then nearest collateral, and which has passed *unshared* to him who has it. But within a group of united brethren the widow of one may adopt so as to devest an estate wholly or in part (*b*). Much more, it would seem, may the widow of one united in interest with the last holder adopt so as to devest the estate that has passed to a mere collateral never united with the deceased (*c*). The latter will necessarily be much more completely represented by a son of a united brother than by a mere collateral, whose own right may be that of an adopted son or have descended through an adopted son. In one case it has been held that the adoption by a widow could not give to the adopted son the position of a co-sharer with a united brother of her deceased husband (*d*). The adoption would certainly need the sanction of the surviving brethren unless this should be improperly withheld (*e*). In the case cited as a precedent (*f*) a son had died before his father but leaving a widow who adopted a son thirty-five years after her father-in-law's death. She had recognized his nephews as members with him of an undivided family, and she could not adopt without their assent unless it were improperly withheld (*g*). On the death of the son before his father his proprietary right had wholly merged in his father's (*h*). He had never had separate sacra, and it might perhaps be contended that therefore the widow never had a right to adopt (*i*). The Sastris, however, recognizing the joint interest of the son in the estate and the sacra, and his claim to the due celebration of his Sraddhas by a son, favour this right of a predeceased son's widow. They do not think it excluded by the existence of a widow or a daughter of the father-in-law, much less by the existence of remoter heirs to whom the estate has passed away from the direct line of the deceased (*k*). In the case of co-sharers standing on an equal footing the Indian lawyers

(*b*) See *Sri Raghunadha's Case*, L. R. 3 I. A. 154. It is not regarded as devesting any more than a birth after a long gestation would be so regarded. *Hurkisondas* v. *Mankorebai*, L. R. 34 I. A. 107.

(*c*) This competition may arise in the case of a raj or a vatan.

(*d*) *Govind* v. *Lakshmibai*, Bom. H. C. P. J. 1882, p. 12.

(*e*) *Payapa* v. *Appanna*, I. L. R. 23 Bom. 327.

(*f*) *Gayabai* v. *Shridhara Charya*, Bom. H. C. P. J. 1881, p. 145.

(*g*) Above, sub-sec. 3. 13.

(*h*) *Udaram Sitaram* v. *Ranu Panduji*, 11 Bom. H. C. R., pp. 76, 86.

(*i*) See above, B. 3. 23.

(*k*) See above, B. 3. 13, pp. 867 ss.

certainly do not recognize any obstacle to adoption by the widow of one as arising from the estate on his death having vested in the other (*l*), nor apparently would the Judicial Committee (*m*) countenance such a doctrine.

Though a cousin cannot sue, as next heir, to set aside an adoption, he has a right to question it if he takes under a deed such an interest as may be affected by the adoption (*n*).

An estate being once vested cannot, it was said, be devested by a subsequent adoption in a collateral line (*o*) even when the adoption has been prevented by the fraud of him who has taken the estate through the absence of an adopted son.

B. 3. 26.—Adoption by a Widow—Her Capacity as Affected by Her Age.

Generally a widow cannot adopt until she has attained maturity (*p*). This is an instance of the imitation of nature which, however, is in some castes not closely adhered to (*q*). In these there may be an earlier taking, but the celebration is postponed until the time of possible maternity. It shows how adoption is regarded as almost exclusively the husband's affair, that under an authority from him an infant widow may adopt. "A widow of 10 years, unshorn, and not yet arrived at puberty, may, in pursuance of her husband's wish or assent, adopt from another gotra, though there be a non-assenting undivided brother of the

---

(*l*) See above. They regard death "without male issue" (see p. 560) as not having occurred until the death of the widow makes adoption impossible.

(*m*) See *Sri Raghunadha's Case, supra.*

(*n*) *Brojo Kishoree Dassee* v. *Sreenath Bose*, 9 C. W. R. 463; S. C. 8 C. W. R. 241.

(*o*) *Nilcomul Lahuri* v. *Jotendro Mohun Lahuri*, I. L. R. 7 Cal. 178, referring to *Keshuv Chunder Ghose* v. *Bishun Pershad Ghose*, C. S. D. A. R. 1860, Pt. II., p. 340; *Sreenarain Mitter* v. *Sreemutty Kishen Soondery Dassee*, 11 Beng. L. R. 171, P. C.; *Kally Prosonno Ghose* v. *Gocool Chunder Mitter*, I. L. R. 2 Cal. 295; above, pp. 349, 350; and *Sri Raghunadha's Case*, L. R. 3 I. A. 154. In the last case it will be noticed that subsequent adoption deprived of an estate an undivided brother in whom it had fully vested. See also sub-sec. 3. 26 below. *Shri Dharmidhar* v. *Chinto*, I. L. R. 20 Bom. 250.

(*p*) Steele, L. C. 48.

(*q*) Steele, L. C. 187.

husband surviving" (r). By the usages of the sect of Sarogees, adoption at the age of nine years is valid, and on the death of an adopted son without issue, during the lifetime of the adoptive mother, the father's right of adoption vests in the widow and not in the mother (s).

"A mother-in-law cannot legally compel her daughter-in-law under age to adopt against her will. If she has compelled an adoption by undue pressure the daughter-in-law can adopt again" (t). Undue influence indeed invalidates an adoption in every case (v).

B. 3. 27.—ADOPTION BY WIDOW—CAPACITY AS AFFECTED BY INTELLIGENCE.

Where the husband has given an express direction the cases immediately preceding seem to show that his wishes may be carried out by a child widow. When a discretion has to be exercised general principles would require that a certain degree of understanding should have been attained before the duty is performed, but it does not seem that any precise rule on this point has been laid down in the case of adoption. Where a mental capacity is attained for religious functions in general it seems to be gained for adoption. Such restrictions as are recognized may be referred rather to other grounds than mere defect of understanding unless this should amount to positive lunacy.

B. 3. 28.—ADOPTION BY A WIDOW—HER CAPACITY AS AFFECTED BY HER STATE AS TO BODY, MIND, RELIGION, AND CASTE.

"Leprosy of a virulent type disqualifies a widow for adopting though otherwise competent" (w).

(r) MS. 1648. A widow under age it was said might adopt under a direction from her husband, though his brothers survived; *Haradhan Roy* v. *Biswanath Roy*, 2 Macn. H. L. 180; *Gopal* v. *Vishnu*, I. L. R. 23 Bom. 250.

(s) *Musst. Chimnee Baee* v. *Musst. Guttoo Baee*, 8 N. W. P. S. D. R. 1853, p. 636.

(t) MS. 1675.

(v) *Somasekhara Raja* v. *Subhadramaji*, I. L. R. 6 Bom. 524, 527.

(w) See B. 3. 17, p. 874, as to misconduct. *Mohunt Bhagwan Ramamuj Das* v. *Das*, L. R. 22 I. A. 94.

A woman's want of chastity deprives her acts of all religious efficacy (*x*). An unchaste woman, pregnant in concubinage, is incompetent to adopt (*y*); but after removal of the sin by penance she can adopt (*z*).

A widow under puberty cannot adopt (*a*), except in some castes with the consent of her husband's kinsmen, or of the caste, or of both. But even when the adoption is made by an immature girl the ceremonies should be deferred till after her " shanee " (*b*) or attainment of puberty.

" Widows of Brahmans and of others amongst whom the custom obtains are deemed impure after the attainment of puberty until they undergo tonsure. They are, however, competent to adopt " (*c*).

" A widow who has attained puberty cannot perform any religious act and therefore cannot adopt until she has undergone tonsure " (*d*).

B. 3. 29.—Adoption by a Widow—Capacity Annulled by Her Re-marriage.

Re-marriage is not recognized amongst the higher castes (*e*). Any association called by such a name is a cause of impurity disabling the subject of it from performing religious acts. But even amongst Sudras re-marriage entirely severs the previous family connexion and prevents adoption by the widow who has formed a new alliance. Re-marriage as laid down by the Bombay High Court is no bar to a widow giving her son in adoption if authorized by her husband (*f*). In *Putlabai* v. *Mahadu* (*g*) she is held to have the power to adopt even without her husband's

---

(*x*) See *Moniram Kolita* v. *Kerry Kolitany*, L. R. 7 I. A., at p. 125.
(*y*) *Sayamalal Dutt* v. *Saudamini Dasi*, 5 B. L. R. 362.
(*z*) *Thukoo Baee* v. *Ruma Baee*, 2 Borr. 488 (2nd ed.).
(*a*) Steele, L. C. 48.
(*b*) *Ibid.* 187.
(*c*) *Lakshmibai* v. *Ramchandra*, I. L. R. 22 Bom. 590.
(*d*) MS. 1615.
(*e*) See Act XV. of 1856, already several times referred to.
(*f*) *Panchappa* v. *Sangambasawa*, I. L. R. 24 Bom. 39.
(*g*) I. L. R. 33 Bom. 107.

consent, as her power to adopt proceeds from her position as a mother, and re-marriage cannot deprive her of this right.

"A Sudra's widow having married another person cannot adopt a son to the deceased husband" (*h*).

B. 3. 31.—Adoption by a Widow—Consent Required.

The widow's right to adopt under an express authority from her husband is unqualified by any absolute necessity for the consent of relatives (*i*). In the absence of such authority she may, as a junior widow, require the consent of her co-widow, and as a member of her husband's family the consent of his near relatives, provided it be not improperly withheld (*k*).

B. 3. 32.—Consent of Co-Widow.

Where there are two widows they ought regularly to concur in an adoption. In case of disagreement the right belongs, as we have seen, to the elder (*l*). "But a second widow may adopt with the consent of the elder" (*m*). A co-widow, however, cannot make an adoption without the consent of the other co-widow in whom the whole estate of her son has vested by inheritance (*n*). In Bengal such an adoption by the junior widow has been held not to divest the estate vested in the senior widow in her capacity as a mother (*o*).

B. 3. 33.—Consent of Mother-in-Law.

The consent of a mother-in-law to an adoption by her adoptive son's widow seems to have been thought necessary, but was inferred from the absence of a prohibition in *Thukoo Baee Bhide* v.

(*h*) MS. 1749.

(*i*) See above, B. 3. 1 and B. 3. 2.

(*k*) See *Dinkar Sitaram Prabhu* v. *Ganesh Shrivram Prabhu*, I. L. R. 6 Bom. 505. *Padajirav* v. *Ramrav*, I. L. R. 13 Bom. 160; *Mandakini Dassee* v. *Adinath Day*, I. L. R. 18 Cal. 69.

(*l*) Sec. III. B. 3. 17. *Padaji* v. *Ramrav*, *supra*.

(*m*) MS. 1658. The assent was in one case pronounced unnecessary. MS. 1663. See 2 Str. H. L. 94.

(*n*) *Anandibai* v. *Rashibai*, I. L. R. 28 Bom. 461.

(*o*) *Faizuddin* v. *Tincowri*, I. L. R. 22 Cal. 565.

Ruma Baee Bhide (*p*). The necessity for this consent could not, probably, be maintained on the authorities. In *Siddappa* v. *Ningangavda* (*q*) it was held that the widow of a pre-deceased son could make a valid adoption with the consent of her mother-in-law, in whom the estate of the last full owner had vested, as an adoption by such a daughter-in-law during the lifetime of the father-in-law would not devest the estate vested in the mother-in-law (*r*).

B. 3. 34.—ADOPTION BY A WIDOW—CONSENT REQUIRED OF HUSBAND'S KINSMEN OR SAPINDAS.

This subject has been much discussed in the judgments in recent years. The law varies in Bengal, Madras and Bombay. It differs according as the deceased husband was undivided or separated from his brethren. In the former case the dependence of the widow and the necessity for the sanction of the kinsmen is recognized by all the systems; in the latter case the Bengal Law is still strict in requiring the husband's sanction (*s*), the Madras Law requires some sanction of the relatives, the Bombay Law practically dispenses with it (*t*).

"A woman cannot adopt without the consent of her husband. If the husband be dead he should have expressed his intentions which the widow may carry out. Failing this she must obtain his father's permission. Failing him she must obtain the assent of the relatives (or caste fellows). Without this the adoption is invalid. A deed transferring her property inherited from the husband to the adopted son is invalid unless countersigned by the relatives" (*v*). "A widow must have her husband's permission;

(*p*) 2 Borr. R. 488, 495. Perhaps the Sastris were influenced by the prevailing idea in Gujarath of the mother's superiority to the wife.

(*q*) I. L. R. 38 Bom. 724.

(*r*) *Gopal* v. *Vishnu*, I. L. R. 23 Bom. 250.

(*s*) *Raja Himun Chull Sing* v. *Koomer Gunsheam Sing*, 2 Kn. P. C. C. 203, 222. The case was one from Etawah in the N.W. Provinces.

(*t*) Jud. Cit., at p. 221. *Ramji* v. *Ghamau*, I. L. R. 6 Bom., at p. 502.

(*v*) MS. 1652. The law here enunciated does not give the widow unbounded discretion. It rather resembles the law prevailing in Madras. See *Appaniengar* v. *Alemalu Ammal*, M. S. D. A. R. for 1858, p. 5; Smr. Chand., Chap. I., paras. 31, 32; 2 Str. H. L. 92.

or that of her father-in-law; or of his widow her mother-in-law " (*w*). The Vyavahara Mayukha dispenses with the assent of the deceased husband of a widow on the ground that the text limiting a woman's power rests on her essential dependence during coverture, and expressly mentions only the assent of a husband to the act of the wife as necessary (*x*). From the same text the Dattaka Mimamsa deduces that the husband's express authority is indispensable. The middle doctrine of the assent of the kinsmen being necessary and sufficient is favoured by the Mayukha (*y*), and this may be considered to have prevailed over both the extremes (*z*), at least in the case of a united family. A Hindu widow, who has not the family estate vested in her, and whose husband was not separated at the time of his death, is not competent to adopt a son to her husband without his authority or the consent of his undivided coparceners (*a*).

As to what assent is sufficient, in default of authority from the husband, in case of adoptions in divided and undivided families, reference may be made to the cases below (*b*). In the first of these it was ruled that what constitutes the consent of kinsmen must depend on circumstances. In a united family a widow adopting without her husband's authority must have the permission of her father-in-law if he is alive; if he is dead the consent of all her husband's surviving brothers (*c*). Where, however, the

---

(*w*) MS. 1672. " Among the Brahmins &c. . . . the widow may adopt if ordered to do so by her husband before his death," even where on his decease his share is absorbed in the shares of his brothers. Steele, L. C. 176. *Vithoba* v. *Bapu*, I. L. R. 15 Bom. 110; *Siddappa* v. *Ningangavda*, I. L. R. 38 Bom. 724.

(*x*) Vyav. May., Chap. IV., sec. V., paras. 16—18.

(*y*) *Loc. cit.*, para. 17.

(*z*) See above, B. 3. 13.

(*a*) *Ramji* v. *Ghamau*, I. L. R. 6 Bom. 498; *Dinkar Sitaram Prabhu et al.* v. *Ganesh Shivram Prabhu*, I. L. R. 6 Bom. 505. Above, p. 891, note (*r*).

(*b*) *Collector of Madura* v. *Mutu Ramalinga Sathupatty*, 1 Beng. L. R. 1 P. C.; S. C. 12 M. I. A. 397; S. C. 2 Mad. H. C. R. 206; *Sri Varada Pratapa Sri Raghunadha* v. *Sri Brozo Kishoro Patta Deo*, 25 C. W. R. 291 C. R.; 7 Mad. H. C. R. 301; L. R. 3 I. A. 154; I. L. R. 1 Mad. 69; *Sooburnomonee Debia* v. *Petumber Dobey*, 1 Marsh. 221; *R. V. Venkata Krishna Row* v. *Venkata Rama Lakshmi Narasayya*, L. R. 4 I. A. 1; S. C. I. L. R. 1 Mad. 174. In this case it was said that limitation as against one disputing an adoption is to be computed from the time when he became aware of the adoption.

(*c*) " The authority of a father-in-law would probably be sufficient to a widow. It is not easy to lay down an inflexible rule for the case in which no father-in-law is in existence. Every such case must depend upon the circumstances of the family. All that can be said is that there should be such evidence of the

widow succeeds to her husband as owner of a separated estate the consent of her husband's nearest kinsmen is sufficient.

In the second case the High Court of Madras held that the assent of a single sapinda replaced what under the older law would have been a procreation by him (*d*), but from this the Judicial Committee dissent. The law of Madras, their Lordships say (*e*), "in this respect is something intermediate between the stricter law of Bengal and the wider law of Bombay," and by that law "a widow not having her husband's permission may adopt a son to him if duly authorized by his kindred." "The requisite authority," they thought, "is in the case of an undivided family to be sought within that family" (*f*). In the particular case the property was an impartible zamindary, and Holloway, J., having held that in such a case, though the family was undivided, the principles applicable to a divided family and a separated estate ought to govern succession and adoption, the Judicial Committee take occasion to intimate their doubt whether such a doctrine is tenable (*g*). It is obviously inconsistent with the principle that "the substitution of a son of the deceased for spiritual reasons is the essence of the thing and the consequent devolution of property a mere accessory to it."

The wider law of Bombay referred to by the Judicial Committee

---

assent of kinsmen as is sufficient to show that the act is done by the widow in the proper and *bona fide* performance of a religious duty and neither capriciously nor from a corrupt motive." Privy Council in the *Ramnad Case* (12 M. I. A. 442), on which Sir J. Colville observes (I. L. R. 1 Mad. 190):

"Their Lordships think it would be very dangerous to introduce into the consideration of these cases of adoption nice questions as to the particular motives operating on the mind of the widow, and that all which this Committee in the former case intended to lay down was, that there should be such proof of assent on the part of the sapindas as should be sufficient to support the inference that the adoption was made by the widow, not from capricious or corrupt motives, or in order to defeat the interest of this or that sapinda, but upon a fair consideration, by what may be called a family council, of the expediency of substituting an heir by adoption to the deceased husband."

(*d*) 7 Mad. H. C. R., at p. 305.

(*e*) L. R. 3 I. A., at p. 191.

(*f*) In earlier Madras cases it had been ruled that the relations whom a widow is to consult for adoption may be her father-in-law or other elders of the family (*Ramasashien* v. *Akyalandumal*, M. S. D. A. R. 1849, p. 115), or her husband's nephew (*Appaniengar* v. *Alemalu Ammal*, M. S. D. A. R. 1858, p. 5). The consent of his nephew as nearest male representative was held sufficient in *N. Chandvasekharuda* v. *N. B. Eahmana*, 4 Mad. H. C. R. 270.

(*g*) See L. R. 3 I. A., at pp. 191, 192.

is that allowing a widow of a Hindu separated from his family to adopt without the sanction of any one in any case in which the husband has not intimated a wish to the contrary (*h*).

In *Raja V.V. Krishnarao's Case* (*i*), reference is made to the *Ramad Case* (*k*) to show that where the deceased had been separate in estate such "assent of kinsmen suffices [as will] show that the act is done by the widow in the proper and *bona fide* performance of a religious duty, and neither capriciously nor from a corrupt motive." As to this "their Lordships think it would be very dangerous to introduce into the consideration of these cases of adoption nice questions as to the particular motives operating on the mind of the widow." Where, as in Bombay, the widow's authority in a divided family is greater, it would obviously be still more dangerous to scrutinize her motives too closely in the light cast on them by the suggestions of interested relatives. The difficulty is removed by dispensing with their sanction. The opinions of the Sastris on this subject have varied somewhat, according to the authorities on which they have relied, but the doctrine of the Samskara Kaustubha has generally prevailed (*l*).

The assent of separated kinsmen will by no means replace that of the deceased husband's undivided brother (*m*). Where the husband of a Hindu widow dies separated, and she herself is the heir, or she and a junior co-widow are the heirs, she may adopt without the sanction of her husband (if he have not, expressly or by implication, indicated his desire that she shall not do so) and without the sanction of his kindred (*n*).

In one Bombay case it was held that the consent of a single sapinda in a family apparently undivided was sufficient to validate an adoption by a widow (*o*), but this cannot now be considered as the received law (*p*). Where assent is needed it is the assent of the

---

(*h*) *Ramji* v. *Ghamau*, I. L. R. 6 Bom., at p. 503. See above, pp. 783, 796. *Lakshmibai* v. *Sarasvatibai*, I. L. R. 23 Bom. 789.

(*i*) L. R. 4 I. A. 1; S. C. I. L. R. 1 Mad. 174.

(*k*) 12 M. I. A. 397.

(*l*) See above, pp. 783, 796.

(*m*) *Sri V. P. Raghunadha* v. *Sri Brozo Kishore*, L. R. 3 I. A., at p. 189.

(*n*) *Rakhmabai* v. *Radhabai*, 5 Bom. H. C. R. 181 A. C. J.; *Ramji* v. *Ghamau*, I. L. R. 6 Bom. 498; *Mahableshwar* v. *Durgabai*, I. L. R. 22 Bom. 199; *Patel Vandravan* v. *Chunilal*, I. L. R. 15 Bom. 565.

(*o*) *Gopal Shridhar* v. *Naro Vinayak*, 7 Bom. H. C. R. App. xxiv., approved in *Rakhmabai's Case*, 5 Bom. H. C. R., at p. 190.

(*p*) See *Ramji* v. *Ghamau*, I. L. R. 6 Bom., at p. 503.

father or of all the male members of the undivided family. Still, however, the right to give or refuse assent cannot be regarded as absolute. "The assent of kinsmen seems to be required by reason of the presumed incapacity of women for independence, rather than the necessity of procuring the consent of all those whose possible and reversionary interest in the estate would be defeated by the adoption" (*q*). A widow refused permission without reasonable grounds might on Hindu principles properly apply to a Civil Court for a declaration of her right to adopt even against the will of one or more of the sapindas of the husband (*r*.)

B. 3. 35.—ADOPTION BY A WIDOW—WITH CONSENT OF THE CASTE.

A woman may adopt for her deceased husband if she has permission of the caste (*s*) according to some interpretations.

In *Sree Brijbhookunji's Case* (*t*) the Sastris are made to say that a widow not having a written permission from her husband may adopt with the sanction of the caste and the cognizance of the Government. The jnati are more properly the kinsmen, the gentile relatives, and so Colebrooke translates the word (*v*), but the Sastris insist on the approval of the caste unless indeed members of it be not within reach for consultation (*w*). They therefore must have taken "jnati" in the sense of caste fellows.

Many castes at Poona said a widow could adopt with the consent of the caste (*x*). They probably took the ambiguous "jnati" in a sense supporting this rule.

(*q*) *The Collector of Madura* v. *Mootoo Ramalinga Sathupathy*, 12 M. I. A., at p. 442. This agrees with the Nirnaya Sindhu and the Vyav. Mayukha.

(*r*) See above, sub-sec. B. 3. 26, p. 891, note (*r*).

(*s*) *Narayan* v. *Nana*, 7 Bom. H. C. R. 153 A. C. J.; Vyav. May., Chap. IV., sec. V. 17, 18; Steele, L. C. 48, 188; *Sree Brijbhookunjee Maharaj* v. *Sree Gakoolootsaojee Maharaj*, 1 Borr. 181, 202 (2nd ed.); *Thukoo Baee* v. *Ruma Baee*, 2 Borr. 488 (2nd ed.). See above, p. 868.

(*t*) 1 Borr. R., at p. 214.

(*v*) See Mit., Chap. I., sec. XI., para. 9, note.

(*w*) *Brijbhookkunjee's Case*, 1 Borr. 216.

(*x*) Steele, L. C. 187.

B. 3. 36.—Adoption by a Widow—Consent of Persons whose Interests are Affected by the Adoption.

It has been shown above, B. 3. 25, that according to some decisions a vested interest cannot generally be devested by means of an adoption. According to the same decisions, however, the person whose estate is to be devested may assent to the adoption and thus give it validity. This doctrine agrees with that of the Hindu lawyers in so far as it gives weight to an assent which must be disinterested. It is opposed to the Hindu Law if it is applied so as to make the widow's right to adopt absolutely dependent on the assent of one who is interested in refusing it. A separated relative on whom the widow is not spiritually dependent does not acquire a right to control her by taking the estate for which it is her religious duty to provide a better heir. The mother of the deceased is hardly less bound than his widow to secure his eternal peace; she can have no right to deprive him of it merely because she may have succeeded to the estate. The doctrine as thus far developed takes no account of the joint right even in the case of collateral succession according to some jurists (*y*) which the son of the man in whom the estate has vested has forthwith acquired in that estate. The sons' assent to an adoption, if the need for assent rests on proprietary right, ought to be as essential as their father's, but the law has not been pushed to this logical conclusion. Nor has the vested interest as yet been held to involve a right to defeat an express authority to adopt given by the deceased owner to his widow. Such an effect indeed would be entirely opposed to the decisions (*z*). But as the widow's capacity rests on a presumed assent there seems to be no good reason where this principle is admitted for allowing an interested relative merely on the ground of his interest to annul the presumed authority. The necessity for sanction is really a consequence of the widow's dependence (*a*). According to the Bombay Law she cannot adopt to take away an estate from collaterals without their assent except when she herself has a right superior to theirs. In

---

(*y*) See above, pp. 655—657.

(*z*) See above, B. 3. 13, B. 3. 23, B. 3. 25; above, p. 895.

(*a*) Above, B. 3. 23; pp. 224 ss., and 898.

It is inconsistent with the consent of relatives, being in them a right of property that, if they refuse it, it may generally be replaced by that of representative members of the caste. Steele, L. C. 394. A question which the caste cannot settle may be referred to the ordinary Courts. *Ibid.* 185, 186.

an undivided family she has to obtain their sanction; in a divided family she herself represents the line, failing other representatives, that would be represented by her adopted son (*b*). When she ends one collateral line she cannot take away the estate from another by adoption (*c*).

It is desirable that the actual decisions should, if possible, be brought into harmony with the principles thus deduced from the Hindu Law itself. These decisions are in themselves somewhat contradictory, and as the Courts in India have built on a few dicta of the Judicial Committee a theory which they seem too narrow to support, a return to the guidance of Indian authority may be the course attended with least disturbance of precedents.

In the Maratha country it was maintained by Sir R. Couch on a very complete review of the authorities that a conscientious adoption by a widow without the consent of kinsmen or co-widow may be legal (*d*). In a later case (*e*), this was qualified by a statement that the consent of a kinsman would be material if an interest in property is vested in him, and he would be devested of it by the adoption (*f*). This prohibitive power was even placed in the hands of a kinsman's widow. Thus a widow of the husband's brother who died in possession (*g*), or a widow of a son who died after his father (*h*), is not, it is said, to be devested by an adoption which would give to the adopted son a place prior to them in the line of inheritance. The deceased husband was the last full owner

---

(*b*) *See Lulloobhoy* v. *Cassibai*, L. R. 7 I. A. 212.

(*c*) See above, sub-secs. B. 3. 23, B. 3. 25, B. 3. 34. *Pudma Coomari Debi* v. *Court of Wards*, L. R. 8 I. A. 229; *Thayammal* v. *Venkatrama Aiyan*, L. R. 14 I. A. 67; *Tarachurun Chatterji* v. *Suresh Chunder Mookerji*, L. R. 16 I. A. 166.

(*d*) *Rakhmabai* v. *Radhabai*, 5 Bom. H. C. R. 181 A. C. J.

(*e*) *Rupchand Hindumal* v. *Rakhmabai*, 8 Bom. H. C. R. 114. In this case one of two co-widows it is said must submit to an adoption by another for her husband's beatitude, while to the widow of a united brother such an adoption would work "manifest injustice." But as the adoption could be made to the prejudice of the surviving brother, why not to the prejudice of his widow, who at most continues his existence? The widow of the first deceased similarly continues his existence, and the Hindu Law contemplates an adoption by the widow of each brother so as to reproduce the united family.

(*f*) *Annammali* v. *Mabhu Bali Reddy*, 8 Mad. H. C. R. 108; *Kally Prosono Ghose* v. *Gocool Chunder*, I. L. R. 2 Cal. 295.

(*g*) *Rupchand* v. *Rakhmabai*, 8 Bom. H. C. R. 114 A. C. J.

(*h*) *Musst. Bhoobun Moyee Debia* v. *Ramkishore Acharjee*, 10 M. I. A. 279; S. C. 3 C. W. R. 15 P. C.; Beng. S. D. A. R. 1858, p. 122.

in these cases. Where the deceased was a member of a joint family the widow of a predeceased coparcener may, on the principles above stated, adopt after the death of the last deceased as she could before it, and with a similar effect (*i*). Where he was separated no right can be acquired against his own line by adoption in another. Where on failure of his own line and of united coparceners the estate has passed to a separated branch it cannot be taken away by another by means of a subsequent adoption; but the failure of his own line is not definitive until his widow has died without adopting.

B. 3. 37.—Adoption by a Widow—Consent of Government.

It has been shown (A. 4. 4) that the consent or at least the acquiescence of the Government has sometimes been thought requisite to a valid adoption. The same idea has prevailed still more with respect to adoption by widows. It does not seem to be better founded in the one case than in the other. Some intimation to the Government might be desirable for publicity, and where an estate supporting a public office was to be taken there were obvious reasons why the sovereign should insist on adoptions being made only with his approval, but so far as the Hindu Law is concerned such a sanction was not needed any more for the adoption than for the procreation of a son (*k*). Each is in its place a religious duty, superior to the will of the temporal ruler. Yet according to the Sastri—

"The assent of relatives and of the Government is requisite to the validity of an adoption by a widow" (*l*).

(*i*) A partition and distribution after a coparcener's death seem to prevent a recovery by a son afterwards adopted by his widow. See below, sec. VII.

(*k*) "In contemplation of law such (adopted) child is begotten by the father . . . on behalf of whom he is adopted." *Per* Willes, J., in the *Tagore Case*, L. R. Supp. I. A., at p. 67.

(*l*) MS. 1644. The assent of the Government is not now deemed necessary, *Rangoobai* v. *Bhagirthibai*, I. L. R. 2 Bom. 377; *Narhar Govind Kulkarni* v. *Narayan Vithal*, I. L. R. 1 Bom. 607; 2 Str. H. L. 88.

"The sanction of Government is necessary to an adoption by a widow" (*m*).

Except when her husband is alive a woman may adopt (*n*) with the sanction of the ruling power (*o*).

When the Government has sanctioned and confirmed an adoption, gift, or bequest, the defectiveness thereof need not be inquired into (*p*). Its non-interference entitles the adopted son to succeed to a vatan (*q*).

(*m*) MS. 1644. But as to this see A. 4. 4. In the *Mankars' Case* the following replies were given by the Sastris :

1. "That a woman, whether Brahman or Shoodr, was permitted to adopt a son, without her husband's order, after his death."

2. "That the widow could adopt a son after her husband's death."

3. "A woman is permitted to take a son in adoption according to the Mayookha."

4. "From political motives Bajee Rao declared the adoption of a son by a widow, without the orders of her husband, to be illegal, though he permitted two or three exceptions."

5. "The widow is permitted by the Shastr to adopt any one as her son."

6. "An elderly widow is allowed, of her own accord, to do that which will insure her happiness in the next world, and as adopting a son is one means of attaining it, she may adopt a son."

(*n*) *Narayan* v. *Nana*, 7 Bom. H. C. R. 153 A. C. J.; Steele, L. C. 45, 47, 187.

(*o*) *Sree Brijbhookunjee Maharaj* v. *Gokolootsaojee Maharaj*, 1 Borr. 181, 202 (2nd ed.).

In this case the Sastri said : "A widow, notwithstanding she has no written permission from her husband, may, if she be desirous of adopting a son, do so legally by obtaining the sanction of the gentiles, and informing the ruling authorities."

"A woman . . . in the event of her receiving no order (from her deceased husband) must send for her relations . . . and after acquainting the ruling authorities, may adopt a son according to the ceremonies laid down in the Vedas."

(*p*) *Sree Brijbhookunjee Maharaj* v. *Sree Gokoolootsaojee Maharaj*, 1 Borr. 181, 202 (2nd ed.); *Rakhmabai* v. *Radhabai*, 5 Bom. H. C. R., at p. 187 A. C. J. The importance attached to confirmation by the sovereign where a public trust was concerned may be seen from pp. 206, 209 of the report of Borradaile.

(*q*) *Ramachandra Vasudev* v. *Nanajee Timajee*, 7 Bom. H. C. R. 26 A. C. J., in which references were made to *Bhasker Buchajee* v. *Narro Raghunath*, Select Cases, p. 25; *Virbudru Hurrybudru* v. *Baee Ranee*, Morris, Pt. II., p. 1; *Trimbak Baji Joshi* v. *Narayan Vinayak Joshi*, 3 Morris's S. D. A. R., p. 19; *Vishram Baboorow* v. *Narainrow Kassee*, 4 *ibid.* 26; *Chenbasawa* v. *Pampangowda*, S. A. No. 655 of 1864; *Rakhmabai* v. *Radhabai*, 5 Bom. H. C. R. A. C. J. 181.

B. 3. 38.—Adoption by a Widow—Omission or Postponement of Adoption.

Though it is a religious duty on the widow's part to give effect to any express direction left by her husband she cannot be constrained to perform it. Without goodwill indeed the reception could hardly be religiously perfect. The cases collected under B. 3. 15 will serve to illustrate this sub-division also along with those which follow.

The right of inheritance is not suspended by pregnancy or until adoption (*r*).

Authority to adopt, upon death of the natural son, does not prevent the widow from succeeding to the son, the authority not being imperative (*s*).

A widow having permission to adopt three sons in succession cannot be compelled to act on that permission before she is allowed to take her contingent estate on the death of the adopted son (*t*). A husband's express authorization, or even direction, to adopt, does not constitute a legal duty on the part of the widow to do so, and for all legal purposes it is absolutely non-existent till it is acted upon (*v*).

B. 3. 39.—Adoption by a Widow—Pretended Adoption.

Some instances of pretended adoption have occurred and have been dealt with by the Courts on the ordinary principle of avoiding fraudulent transactions. As a pretended adoption is not an adoption, the subject does not require detailed treatment.

(*r*) *Dukhina Dossee* v. *Rash Beharee Mojoomdar*, 6 C. W. R. 221.

(*s*) *Dino Moyee Chowdhrain*, v. *A. D. C. Rehling*, 2 C. W. R. 25 Mis. Rulings.

(*t*) *Deeno Moyee Dossee* v. *Doorgapershad Mitter*, 3 C. W. R. 6 Mis. App. See above, pp. 813, 814.

(*v*) *Uma Sunduri Dabee* v. *Sourobinee Dabee*, I. L. R. 7 Cal. 288; *Mutasaddi Lal* v. *Kundun Lal*, L. R. 33 I. A. 55.

B. 4.—Adoption by Females—Anomalous Adoptions.

As a husband and wife must be joint parents of the legitimate begotten son, and ought to join in adopting a boy to replace him, so the widow alone can in strictness be qualified to adopt after her husband's death a son who, becoming his son, becomes hers also. And so long as the widow exists it is quite opposed to principle that she should be supplanted in the performance of this duty by any one else. But in the case of boys dying as infants the right of the mother to adopt has gained recognition by a kind of necessity, and this right has in some instances been allowed an extension even to cases in which the deceased son had left a widow. Where a son has died before his father the sacra have never wholly devolved upon him, and adoption by the father may be conceived as not depriving the daughter-in-law of any distinct spiritual jointure; where she is ousted by her mother-in-law, it must rather be ascribed to confusion of thought or to the predominance allowed in many ways to a mother by caste custom, some instances of which have already been noticed (*w*).

B. 4. 1.—Anomalous Adoptions—Adoption by Mother.

A widow, after succeeding to her natural-born son as his heiress, *may adopt a boy to her own husband* (*x*), or, it is said, to the son himself (*y*), so as to devest her own interest.

" If a daughter-in-law has made an invalid adoption contrary to the wish of the mother-in-law the latter may adopt an eligible

---

(*w*) See above, pp. 91, 92, 152, 372.

(*x*) *Bykant Mony Roy* v. *Kristo Soondery Roy*, 7 C. W. R. 392; *Mondakini* v. *Adinath*, I. L. R. 18 Cal. 69.

(*y*) *R. V. Venkata Krishna Rao* v. *Venkata Rama Lakshmi Narsayya*, L. R. 4 I. A. 1; S. C. I. L. R. 1 Mad. 174.

" A widow succeeding as heir to her own son does not lose the right to exercise the power of adoption. By making an adoption she divests her own estate only." The adoption by a mother on account of her deceased son is questionable. It is impossible that the same boy should have been her son and her son's son. Her adoption should be of a son to her husband, in place of the one deceased without son or widow. See B. 3. 13; 2 Str. H. L. 94.

person " (*z*). " If she make an illegal adoption her mother-in-law may make one " (*a*).

A widow having, against the wish of her mother-in-law, who wanted a boy of her own gotra, adopted one of a different gotra, this was pronounced invalid. The mother-in-law adopted a boy of her gotra. The Sastri pronounced this, too, illegal, as the right vested in the daughter-in-law. But of the two the preference was, he said, to be given to the adopted of the mother-in-law as being of the same gotra (*b*).

In a case at 2 Str. H. L. 93 the Sastri said a mother directed to do so by her dying son could adopt for him. Mr. Ellis treated this as a case of delegation, and thought she might act as her son's deputy, as " the Hindu Law and religion allows of vicarious substitution in almost every possible case." The mother could not act as " deputy " for a son deceased, but during his life he might perhaps commission her to act for him, in a simply ceremonial act (*c*), though this is not certain. Colebrooke in the case in question seems to have thought that a mother might complete, on behalf of her son, an adoption begun by the latter but interrupted by his death. Sutherland thought that notwithstanding the son's request the mother could not, after his death, adopt for him (*d*). Adoption by a mother to her own husband after her son's death is, as we have seen, under some circumstances permissible. An adoption by her to her son cannot be regarded as otherwise than grossly anomalous. It is only his wife or his widow who can adopt for a man (*e*) and at the same time for herself, the adoption taking the place of procreation, in which a son and a mother could not possibly join (*f*).

(*z*) MS. 1672. But see 2 Str. H. L. 91 ss.

(*a*) MS. 1632.

(*b*) MS. 1744. See above, p. 92, note (*t*).

(*c*) See *Vijiarangam* v. *Lukshman*, 8 Bom. H. C. R., at p. 256 O. C. J.

(*d*) So *per* Westropp, C. J., in *Bhagvandas Tejmal* v. *Rajmal*, 10 Bom. H. C. R., at p. 265.

(*e*) *Bhagvandas* v. *Rajmal*, 10 Bom. H. C. R. 241.

(*f*) An adoption invalid on account of an intervening holder of an estate is not set up by the death of that person. See *Bykant Moonee Roy* v. *Kisto Soonder Roy*, 7 C. W. R. 392, as compared with the explanation of *Bhoobun Moyee's Case*, in *Pudma Coomari* v. *Court of Wards*, L. R. 8 I. A. 229.

B. 4. 2.—ANOMALOUS ADOPTIONS BY FEMALES—BY A DAUGHTER-IN-LAW.

The case discussed above under A. 2. 3 may, from one point of view, be regarded as falling under this section. The validity of such an adoption would hardly now be admitted (*g*).

B. 4. 3.—BY A GRANDMOTHER.

A grandmother who succeeds to an unmarried grandson cannot adopt (*h*).

C. 1.—*Quasi*-ADOPTIONS—BY MALES.

"Of the twelve enumerated sons two only—the lawfully begotten and the adopted—are allowed in the Kaliyuga (*i*).

The Kritrima adoption by a male to himself alone or by a husband and wife to both conjointly, is still recognized in Maithila (*k*), but it is of little or no importance for other districts.

The palak putra has no right as such (*l*).

"A foster-son may be heir by custom" (*m*). In such a case the "adoption" must, so far as is known, be made by the foster-father himself.

C. 2.—*Quasi*-ADOPTIONS BY FEMALES—KRITRIMA ADOPTIONS.

"In Maithila the widow is as of right at liberty to adopt without special authority for the purpose (a Kritrima son); the adopted in this case succeeding to her exclusive property only, not to that of her deceased husband to whom he is not considered in any way

---

(*g*) In *Dinkar Sitaram* v. *Ganesh Shivram Prabhu*, I. L. R. 6 Bom. 505, the authorization of a father-in-law seems to have been thought of some importance. But no part of the ultimate decision rests on this point. At p. 508, line 5, a seeming error is caused by the omission of the word "of" before "Krishna."

(*h*) *Ramkrishna* v. *Shamrao*, I. L. R. 26 Bom. 526.

(*i*) MS. 1633.

(*k*) See below, sec. VII

(*l*) Steele, L. C. 184. As to the palak putra, see above, p. 828.

(*m*) MS. 1707. As to the fosterage or *quasi*-adoption prevalent amongst the lower castes, see above, p. 827.

related" (*n*). He acquires no relationship save to the adopting mother (*o*).

In Maithila it appears that a wife may adopt to herself independently of her husband by the Kritrima form. The son thus taken succeeds only to her Stridhana (*p*).

The son thus adopted by a wife or a widow does not lose his place in his own family (*q*).

The consent of the person adopted is indispensable (*r*).

C. 2. 1.—*Quasi*-ADOPTIONS BY FEMALES—SUBJECT TO THE ALYA SANTANA LAW.

A female, where the Alya Santana law prevails, cannot adopt if she have male issue living (*s*).

C. 2. 2.—*Quasi*-ADOPTIONS BY FEMALES—BY KALWANTINS, NAIKINS, &C.

"The Sastras contain no rules applicable to adoption by Kalwantins" (*t*). A dancing girl can adopt, but only a daughter (*v*).

The Pandit of the Supreme Court at Calcutta when consulted on an adoption of a daughter by a courtesan answered that there was no such instance of the adoption of a daughter to inherit by the Hindu Law (*w*).

(*n*) 2 Str. H. L. 204, quoting Sutherland's Synopsis.

(*o*) *Boolee Singh* v. *Musst. Busunt Koveree*, 8 C. W. R. 155. With the Kritrima adoption may be compared that allowed in the later ages of the Roman Law. See above, pp. 814, 815.

(*p*) *Sree Narain Rai* v. *Bhya Jha*, 2 C. S. D. A. R. 23.

(*q*) *Collector of Tirhoot* v. *Hurroo Persad Mohunt*, 7 C. W. R. 500 C. R.

(*r*) *Luchman Lal* v. *Mohun Lal*, 16 C. W. R. 179 C. R. See above, pp. 814, 828, 833.

(*s*) *Cotay Hegady* v. *Manjoo Kumpty et al.*, M. S. D. A. R. 1859, p. 138. The Alya Santana succession is that of a nephew to his maternal uncle. See above, pp. 274, 276, 398.

(*t*) MS. 1651.

(*v*) *M. C. Alasani* v. *C. Ratnachellum*, 2 Mad. H. C. R. 56; *Manjamma* v. *Shishgirirao*, I. L. R. 26 Bom. 491. This is not a real adoption. See above, p. 835. The adoption (so called) of a Palak Kanya as a dancing-girl may be annulled at pleasure by the adopter, Steele, L. C. 185.

(*w*) *Doe dem Hencower Bye* v. *Hanscower Bye*, 2 Mor. Dig. 133.

SECTION IV.—FITNESS FOR ADOPTION.

When a substitutionary son is needed the man seeking him is not at liberty to adopt any child indiscriminately. There are conditions as to sex (*x*), caste, family and personal qualities, which must be satisfied in order to constitute a fit subject for adoption. Some of these afford no more than a ground of preference, but others are indispensable. They go to the root of the capacity to render the desired benefits, or rest on the duties due to the family of birth, which must not be thrown off even in the lower castes. The statement that "an adoption once made cannot be set aside" (*y*) cannot be sustained in the sense that a mere performance of the ceremonies gives validity to an adoption of a disqualified person (*z*), or one given by a person not competent to make the gift. Sir M. Westropp denied that the *factum valet* principle could be applied to such a case (*a*) where a widow without express authority had given an only son in adoption.

1.—Fitness for Adoption as Affected by Caste.

The rule which requires that a boy who is to be adopted shall be of equal class with the adoptive father has already been considered (*b*). It is implied in several of the texts quoted below. The instances of a breach or attempted breach of this rule are, as might be expected, very few. In two cases the following answers were given:

"No adoption is permitted from a different caste" (*c*).

(*x*) The ancient institution of the putrika-putra makes the mention of "sex" not superfluous. See Vyav. May., Chap. IV., sec. V., para. 6.

"The substituting of a daughter for a son is also prohibited, being included amongst those rejected in the Kaliyuga." 2 Str. H. L. 152.

(*y*) *Raje Vyankatrao* v. *Jayavantrao*, 4 Bom. H. C. R., at p. 195.

(*z*) *Lakshmappa* v. *Ramava*, 12 Bom. H. C. R., at p. 389, and the cases there quoted.

(*a*) *Ibid.*, p. 397. So Colebrooke at 2 Str. H. L. 178.

(*b*) Above, p. 830. See Vyav. May., Chap. IV., sec. V., para. 4.

(*c*) MS. 1637. An adoption is annulled if it be discovered that the boy adopted was of a lower caste than the adoptive father, Steele, L. C. 185. This means that the adoption is declared to have been null from the first. See Datt. Mim. II. 25, 27.

An adoption was pronounced illegal on the grounds that the adopted was of a different caste from the adopting widow, and was an only son (*d*).

---

2. 1.—Connexion in Family Generally.

By the birth of a son to one of several brothers, says the Smriti (*e*), all become fathers of male offspring. The probable origin of this notion has already been discussed (*f*). In the more recent developments of the law we have seen that a brother might properly be called in to supply a brother's failure to procure offspring (*g*). In this state of the scripture and of custom it was natural that as adoption gradually supplanted the other methods of recruiting a family the brother's son should seem the fittest for adoption. In his case there was a kind of sonship already, so much so that some writers contended against the necessity of any adoption at all when there was a brother's son (*h*). There could be no question in his case as to an effective change of gotra seeing that no change was needed. He would of necessity sacrifice to the same remote ancestors with the same formulas as would a begotten son of the adoptive father. Besides these considerations the preference of a brother's son found a natural basis in family affection (*i*), and when the brethren were united, as in early times they usually were, the interest of all, and of the children of those who had sons, were better preserved by adopting a son from amongst the necessary participators of the estate than by introducing a stranger who would take a part from all the other members of the family (*k*). Amongst remoter relatives these

---

(*d*) MS. 1750. It may seem strange that such a question should have arisen, but the Viramitrodaya, Tr. p. 117, admits a Sudra son by adoption to one of higher caste. See above, p. 830.

(*e*) Manu IX. 182; Mit., Chap. I., sec. XI., para. 36; Vyav. May., Chap. IV., sec. V., para. 19.

(*f*) Above, p. 396.

(*g*) Above, pp. 794, 795.

(*h*) See Datt. Mim., sec. II. 73.

(*i*) The Datt. Mim., sec. II. 29, says a half-brother's son is not to be taken while a whole brother's son is available. There is almost a repulsion between sons of rival wives. But see below, p. 913.

(*k*) The nearness which is generally understood as nearness of family connexion is by some construed as nearness in locality of residence. See

reasons could not operate with the same force. But it was inevitable that next to a brother's son, a cousin, or a cousin's son should be sought as the fittest for adoption, and that the order in point of proximity should become that of practical preference in selection (*l*). A man, Vasishtha says, is to adopt the son of the nearest relative who can and will give one (*m*); but of two persons equally nearly related, either is eligible (*n*). Genealogies carefully preserved indicated at once whence wives might not, and sons, if need were, might be had; the gotra invocations were the same; and the higher deities were worshipped under the same names and conceptions. It is not surprising that the limitation of choice which was thus induced in practice should have come to be regarded by many as necessitated by the law (*o*); but the sources do not afford any authority for such a restriction. What they exact is nearness and likeness, so far as these can be secured, identity of caste, according to the best interpretations, and also, but not indispensably, of family or gotra. Amongst the Sudras the distinctions of gotra in the Brahminical sense cannot exist (*p*). Their *quasi*-gotras mark the more distant family connexions, but there is no objection to a Sudra adopting from a gotra different from his own (*q*).

The question being as to the existence of a legal objection to the adoption of a son from a remote branch the Sastri answered only: "The Sastra is in favour of the adoption of a boy belonging to the near branch" (*r*). Colebrooke says that only a preference is

---

Viram. Tr. p. 117. This view seems to be favoured by the Mit., see Chap. I., sec. XI., paras. 13, 14, and notes. The Vyav. Mayukha says the nearest by blood is to be taken, see Chap. IV., sec. V., para. 19, and Datt. Mim. II. 16; V. 36, 38.

(*l*) See above, p. 819, as to the superior claims of the nearer relatives.

(*m*) Vasishtha, Chap. XV. 6.

(*n*) *Sree Brijbhookunjee Maharaj* v. *Sree Gokoolootsaojee Maharaj*, 1 Borr. 181, 202 (2nd ed.).

The Pandits said, "It is written in the Mayukha that it is necessary that the person to be adopted be of a virtuous disposition, learned, beloved by him who adopts him, and also be the nearest of kin to him, adding verbally, that if there were two persons equally near, Maharanee would be at liberty to adopt either." See Datt. Chand. I. 10; Vyav. May., Chap. IV., sec. IV., para. 19.

(*o*) See Mit., Chap. I., sec. XI., paras. 13, 36, note; Vyav. May., Chap. IV., sec. V., para. 19; Datt. Mim., sec. II., paras. 2, 13.

(*p*) See Datt. Mim. II. 5 ss. 80.

(*q*) *Rangamma* v. *Atchamma*, 4 M. I. A. 1.

(*r*) MS. 1640. See Datt. Mim. II. 18.

to be given to a brother's son, not so exclusive a preference as to shut out the exercise of discretion (*s*). The prohibition against an adoption of an asagotra is of a moral rather than legal character (*t*), and in one case a Sastri expressed the opinion that "if a Brahman cannot find a person fit for adoption in his own gotra he may adopt from another gotra a man of thirty having children" (*v*). In another case amongst Brahmans, a question having been put as to the adoption by a widow of a boy whose upanayana (*w*) had been performed, the answer was merely that if a boy of her own gotra could not be obtained she might take one of another gotra (*x*).

The general rule of propinquity giving a preference for adoption is illustrated by the following cases. A few of them admit the adoption of a younger by an elder brother. Balchandra Sastri gathered a support for this adoption by inference from the elder brother's being "in place of a father" (*y*), but the Smriti had in view merely the nurture and protection of the family by its head. The castes do not seem to have admitted this adoption, and it is opposed to the principle of imitating nature (*z*). It can hardly be regarded, therefore, as allowed by the law.

In *Brijbhukhan's Case* (*a*) the Sastris say that the person to be adopted must be the nearest of kin who can be obtained. But then they add that what has been done conformably to the Vedas cannot be undone, and that a son taken, not from amongst the gentiles, even by a widow, is not a mere dharm-putra but a datta-putra with the full rights of that relation (*b*). It follows that the preference of the nearest is not a matter of legal obligation.

A widow, on the death of her son, adopted a remoter kinsman than one who was available, and on his behalf applied for a certificate of guardianship, which was refused, as the adoption

---

(*s*) 2 Str. H. L. 103.

(*t*) *Durma Samoodhany Ummal* v. *Comara Venkatachella Redayar*, M. S. A. R. 1852, p. 111; 1 Str. H. L. 85; 2 *ibid.* 98, 103, 106; *Srimati Uma Deyi* v. *Gokoolanand Das Mahapatra*, L. R. 5 I. A. 40; S. C. I. L. R. 3 Cal. 587.

(*v*) MS. 1639.

(*w*) Thread ceremony.

(*x*) MS. 1617.

(*y*) Steele, L. C. 44.

(*z*) See Datt. Mim., Sec. III. 30.

(*a*) 1 Borr. R., at p. 214.

(*b*) 1 Borr. 218.

was prejudicial to rights of nearer heirs, and their consent was not shown to have been obtained to rebut the presumption of caprice arising from the facts. She was referred to a regular suit to establish a valid adoption, and directed to renew the application for guardianship under Act XX. of 1864 (*c*).

In the following case the Sastri in approving the adoption to a man of his brother by birth put the permission on the ground of a total severance of natural ties by the adoption of the deceased into another family (*d*). "Adoption," he said, "severs the connection with the natural relatives so completely that the adopted son's widow may adopt his younger brother (*e*). But consanguinity, according to the general opinion, is not to be overlooked in adoption any more than in marriage.

Though the adopting brother has been adopted into another family, several decisions have settled that he cannot adopt his natural brother, on the ground that consanguinity does not cease with adoption (*f*). Thus it has been ruled that a brother cannot adopt his brother in Maithila (*g*), or in the Andra country, Madras (*h*).

A Maratha, a widow, having adopted her husband's illegitimate son, his right to inherit was put on his position as a bastard son of a Sudra (*i*).

---

2. 2.—Relation Between the Boy to be Adopted and the Adoptive Father through the Natural Father.

This connexion affords, as we have seen, the strongest ground of preference, but it does not, according to the decisions, give to the nearer relatives a legal right to impose a son on a person about to adopt. This would indeed be inconsistent with the affectionate

---

(*c*) *Bhagubai* v. *Kalo Venkaji*, Bom. H. C. P. J. 1875, p. 45.

(*d*) Above, p. 834.

(*e*) MS. 1625.

(*f*) *Moottia Mudalli* v. *Uppon Venkatacharry*, M. S. D. A. Dec. 1858, p. 117. See below, sec. VIII.

(*g*) *B. Runjeet Singh* v. *Obhye Narain Singh*, 2 C. S. D. A. R. 245.

(*h*) *Ramanamall* v. *Suban Annavi*, 2 Mad. H. C. R. 399; *Muttusawmy Naidu* v. *Lutchmeedevumma*, M. S. D. A. Dec. 1852, p. 96; *Moottia Mudalli* v. *Uppon Venkatacharry*, M. S. D. A. Dec. 1858, p. 117. Not even his half-brother, see below, sub-sec. 2. 4

(*i*) MS. 1691.

relations which it is an object of the law to foster between those connected by adoption (*k*). The limitation of choice has been thought somewhat stricter in the case of a widow, and there are some obvious reasons why this should be so, but in a united family her necessary dependence secures the desired end, and it cannot be said that apart from this she is confined to the family or gotra of her husband by any strictly legal restraint (*l*).

A near relative of the same gotra, a nephew if possible (*m*), is the first choice. Failing such, a distant gotraja. Failing him, a bhinna gotra-sapinda (*n*). Failing him a non-sapinda of not more than five years, and whose tonsure (chaula, chuda) has not been performed. If such an one cannot be obtained then one of greater age may be taken (*o*). Steele gives the order of choice in adoption according to the customary law of the Dekhan as follows (*p*): Any brother's son should be the first selected for adoption; should there be none, or should the boy's parents, &c., refuse consent, his place is to be supplied by—(2nd), Any boy of the same gotra, and descended from a common ancestor within three generations (sanghit, sagotra, sapinda); (3rd) Any boy connected with the family by the female line of connexions, for whom funeral cakes are offered (usagotra sapinda), such are the mother's brother's son, or the father's sister's son; (4th) Any boy of the same gotra, descended from a common ancestor within seven generations, within which degree marriage is prohibited (wirudh sumbhand)—these relations are called the sagotra dushantil; (5th) Any boy of the same gotra, the genealogy of whose relationship is otherwise unknown (sagotramatra); (6th) A boy of a different gotra, but of the same caste (pargotra)—such are the sister's son and daughter's son, who are adoptible in default of the preceding. A paternal uncle cannot be adopted, being in place of his father. Nor a maternal uncle, for "an elder relation" (without regard to the relative age of the parties) "cannot be adopted."

The castes at Poona answered more simply (*q*):

(*k*) See the texts quoted below.

(*l*) *Srimati Uma Deyi* v. *Gokoolanand Das Mahpatra*, L. R. 5 I. A. 40.

(*m*) Datt. Mim. II. 67, 73.

(*n*) As to these terms, see above, pp. 107, 123.

(*o*) MS. 1672. In Punjab amongst many tribes there is no limit, but the adoption must preferably be from amongst near kinsmen and must be from the gotra or tribe. Punjab Customary Law II. 155.

(*p*) Steele, L. C. 44.

(*q*) Steele, L. C. 182.

The following relations are to be selected in order: 1, brother's son; 2, paternal first cousin; 3, paternal second cousin; 4, one of the same gotra; 5, one of the same caste, P. Should the party first in order be refused by his immediate family, the caste may advise, and if they fail to persuade the party, another boy is, with their concurrence, to be adopted.

From Khandesh a still simpler answer was received (*r*): "The son of the nearest relation is to be adopted; but should his father not consent, a stranger may be adopted with the consent of several respectable persons."

"The son of a half brother may be adopted in preference to the son of a full brother" (*s*).

The existence of a brother's son does not deprive the uncle of power to adopt another boy, the selection being a matter of conscience and not of absolute prescription (*t*).

"A man may adopt the son of a distant, instead of the son of a near, kinsman" (*v*).

"The widow . . . is enjoined to give preference to the nearest relation who is eligible. But the validity of an adoption actually made does not rest on the rigid observance of that rule of selection: the choice of him to be adopted being a matter of discretion" (*w*). The Sastris have expressed the rule more strictly. A husband's brother's son, they said, can be adopted by a widow, even without the injunction of the husband (*x*). When such nephew exists, she cannot adopt another without her husband's injunction (*y*).

(*r*) Steele, L. C. 182.

(*s*) MS. 1627. This is opposed to the Datt. Mim., sec. II. 29.

(*t*) *Gokoolanund Doss* v. *Musst. Wooma Daee*, 15 Beng. L. R. 405; S. C. 23 C. W. R. 340; S. C. in App. to P. C. L. R. 5 I. A. 40; *contra*, *Ooman Dutt* v. *Kunhia Singh*, 3 C. S. D. A. R. 144, on an adoption in the kritrima form. See Suth. Syn. Head II. and the comment by the Judicial Committee, L. R. 5 I. A., at p. 53; 1 Macn. H. L. 68; 1 Str. H. L. 85.

(*v*) MS. 1628.

(*w*) Colebrooke in 2 Str. H. L. 98. See above, p. 600, note (*a*).

(*x*) *Huebatrav Mankar* v. *Govindrav Mankar*, 2 Borr. 75 (83 2nd ed.). See Vyav. May., Chap. IV., sec. V., paras. 17, 18, 19; Datt. Mim., Chap. II., 29, 73; Datt. Chand., Chap. I. 20, 27, 28; Manu XI. 182; Mit., Chap. I., sec. XI., para. 36 ss.

(*y*) . . . "They (the Shastrees) said, a widow can, by her husband's injunction, adopt a son, but not without it, but the prohibition is meant against her taking any other person when the son of her husband's brother exists, whom she may adopt even without such injunction; for from the words (of Manu,

Even amongst the lower castes a Sastri said:

"The deceased husband's brother's son should be adopted by a Sudra widow. Failing him she may take any one of the caste junior to the adopter" (z).

"Though the deceased husband desired that the son of his brother should be adopted, and the brother is willing to give his son—which the Vyavahara Mayukha allows, though sinful (a)—yet the widow is not under such circumstances obliged to take such a son. In taking the son of some other relative, however, she must have the assent of the relatives" (b).

In one case the Sastri said that a widow cannot adopt her deceased husband's first cousin (c). But this was founded on his notion that the adoption of a brother's son was obligatory. In himself a first cousin of the deceased is a proper person to adopt in the absence of a nearer relative, *i.e.* a nephew (d). In Bengal it was said that whatever the preference due to a brother's son it did not prevent a resort elsewhere if that son were refused (e). The same is the law of several Poona castes (f).

---

2. 3.—Relation Between the Son to be Adopted and the Adoptive Father through the Son's Natural Mother.

Contrary to the rule by which the connexion with the adoptive through the natural father gives at least a religious claim to preference to the boy thus related, a near connexion through the boy's mother usually makes adoption impossible. The doctrine of the imitation of nature prevents a man's standing in the relation of adoptive father to a son whom he could not have begotten

---

Chap. 9th, v. 182, quoted by the Zillah Shastrees) found in the Mitakshara, book second, leaf 55th, page 1st, line 3rd, it appears, that even without the injunction of her husband, a widow may adopt the son, either of her husband's eldest, or youngest, brother." 2 Borr. 99.

(z) MS. 1675.

(a) *I.e.* the only or eldest son. It does not condemn the gift generally. See Vyav. May., Chap. IV., sec. V. 9, 19.

(b) MS. 1644.

(c) MS. 1703.

(d) MS. 1660.

(e) *Gokoolanund Doss* v. *Musst. Wooma Daee*, 15 B. L. R. 405, 416; S. C. 23 C. W. R. 340, 341; S. C. L. R. 5 I. A. 40.

(f) Steele, L. C. 189.

without incest according to the religious law. The prohibited degrees, however, though observed with strictness by the higher castes, have been little regarded by the Sudras. The unions of the latter have not been looked on as having any sacred character, and the means seldom exist amongst them of tracing *quasi*-gotra relationships to any considerable distance. The aboriginal custom of making a sister's son heir (*g*) was thus readily moulded to the needs of a system of adoption, while the daughter's son growing up in the grandfather's house naturally took the place of the appointed daughter's son and became recognized, when some inclusion within the law of adoption was felt necessary, as a fit subject for adoption (*h*).

The opinion of the Sastris in the case of *Haebut Rao Mankar* v. *Govindrao Bulwantrao Mankar* (*i*) declares a son of a daughter, a sister, or a mother ineligible for adoption, except amongst Sudras (*k*). Three at least of the nine Pandits consulted in the case (*l*) pronounce expressly against the adoption of a daughter's or a sister's son. The other six give no opinion on this particular point. A similar opinion to that of the three is expressed by the Sastri, above, p. 410, Q. 6.

The general principle recognized in many decisions of the Courts that adoption is prohibited where the adopter could not marry the mother of the boy proposed for adoption in her maiden state (*m*) is confined to specific instances of a daughter's son, a

---

(*g*) See above, pp. 276, 398, and the *Mankars' Case*, 2 Borr., at pp. 95, 96. 106, 107.

(*h*) "Adoption of a sister's son is strictly prohibited unless in the case of Sudras." Ellis, who refers to the Datta Kaustubha,—but this allows such an adoption in case of necessity, see below. He says the Datta Mimamsa of Sri Ram admits this in case of necessity, and that in practice it is not uncommon in all castes. 2 Str. H. L. 100, and Stokes's H. L. B. 553. "Not regarding the putrika-putra as a subsidiary son, his affiliation (it would not be unreasonable to infer) would be valid in the present age." Sutherland, 2 Str. H. L. 201. See also Sutherland's Syn., note I.

(*i*) 2 Borr. 106.

(*k*) Macn. Cons. H. L. 149, 154; 1 Str. H. L. 71; 2 *ibid.* 77. See above, pp. 800, 801. *Bhagwan Singh* v. *Bhagwan Singh*, L. R. 26 I. A. 153; *Ramchandra* v. *Gopal*, I. L. R. 32 Bom. 623; *Walbai* v. *Heerbai*, I. L. R. 34 Bom. 491; *Yamnava* v. *Lakshman Bhumoo*, I. L. R. 36 Bom. 533.

(*l*) 2 Borr. R., at p. 106.

(*m*) *Shrinivas Timaji* v. *Shintaman Shivaji*, S. A. 587 of 1866; *Jivanee Bhayee* v. *Jivu Bhayee*, 2 M. H. C. R. 462; *Sriramulu* v. *Ramayya*, I. L. R. 3 Mad. 15.

sister's son, and the mother's sister's son (*n*); and thus a widow has been held competent to adopt her brother's son in Bombay (*o*), Madras (*p*), and Allahabad (*q*). In *Puttu Lal* v. *Parbati Kunwar* (*r*) their Lordships of the Judicial Committee have held to the same effect, laying down that the gloss by Nanda Pandit or Dattaka Mimamsa must be accepted with caution. It has been recognized that the rule is not binding on Sudras. Thus it has been held that a Lingayat (as being a Sudra), or a Kayastha (*s*), may adopt a sister's or a daughter's son, but a member of a higher caste may not, in the absence of a special custom. The doctrine of *factum valet* does not validate such an adoption (*t*).

The adoption of a brother was disallowed in Madras (*v*).

The adoption of a sister's son is invalid, according to the decisions, as it imports incest not only among Brahmins (*w*), but generally in the three regenerate classes, except perhaps the Vaisyas (*x*); in the Dravida country (*y*); in the Andra country (*z*); in the North-West Provinces (*a*).

(*n*) *Ram Chandra* v. *Gopal*, I. L. R. 32 Bom. 623; *Walbai* v. *Heerbai*, I. L. R. 34 Bom. 491; *Yamnava* v. *Lakshman*, I. L. R. 36 Bom. 533; *Jai Singh Pal Singh* v. *Biji Pal*, I. L. R. 27 All. 417; *Bhagwan Singh* v. *Bhagwan Singh*, L. R. 26 I. A. 153.

(*o*) *Bai Nani* v. *Chuni Lal*, I. L. R. 22 Bom. 973.

(*p*) *Sriramulu* v. *Ramayya*, I. L. R. 3 Mad. 15; *Ragavendra Raw* v. *Jayaram*, I. L. R. 20 Mad. 283.

(*q*) *Jai Singh Pal* v. *Biji Pal*, I. L. R. 27 All. 417.

(*r*) L. R. 42 I. A. 155.

(*s*) *Rajcoomar Lall* v. *Vissessur Dyal*, I. L. R. 10 Cal. 688; Ramalinga *Pillai* v. *Sadasiva Pillai*, 9 M. I. A. 506.

(*t*) *Gopal N. Safray* v. *H. G. Safray*, I. L. R. 3 Bom. 273, 298.

(*v*) *Muthuswamy Naidu* v. *Latchmeedavamma*, M. S. D. A. R. for 1852, p. 96. See above, p. 865.

(*w*) Datt. Mim. II. 91-93; Datt. Chand. I. 17; 2 Str. H. L. 100; *Doe dem Kora Shunko Takoor* v. *Bebee Munnee*, East's Notes, Case 20; 2 Mor. Dig., p. 32; *Nursing Narain* v. *Bhutton Loll*, Sp. No. C. W. R. 194. This case pronounces against the legality of the putrika-putra in the present day.

(*x*) *Ramalinga Pillay* v. *Sadasiva Pillay*, 9 M. I. A. 506; S. C. 1 C. W. R. 25 P. C. The Vaisyas are only partially recognized. See Steele, L. C. 90.

(*y*) *Gopalayyan* v. *Raghupatiayyan*, 7 M. H. C. R. 250.

(*z*) *Narasammal* v. *Balaramacharloo*, 1 M. H. C. R. 420.

(*a*) *Luchmeenath Rav* v. *Musst. Bhima Baee*, 7 N. W. P. R. 441, 443.

In the Punjab the objection to sisters' or daughters' sons arises from their taking the property into another got. The consent of the male relatives, therefore, is required. Punjab Customary Law, II. 156.

"If a Prabhu cannot obtain a son of his own gotra he may take from another, except the son of a sister or daughter" (*b*).

The husband's brother's grandson (grand-nephew) may be adopted, as the adoptive father could have married the nephew's wife in her maiden state (*c*).

The adoption of a first cousin's daughter's son having been recognized for a long time, was upheld (*d*).

An adoption by a Brahman of his daughter's son was pronounced invalid, though it was strongly asserted in the particular case to be in accordance with the custom which prevailed among the caste. A few instances to the contrary, adduced to prove a special custom holding such adoptions valid, were set aside as insufficient by the Bombay High Court (*e*). A special custom, favouring adoption of a sister's son in the Dravida country by Brahmans, was similarly refused recognition by the Court (*f*). The subordination of particular usages to the general customary law is discussed in the *Naikins' Case* (*g*).

"A (Sudra) widow may adopt her husband's sister's son" (*h*), as the husband himself could have done.

A sister's son is incompetent to question an invalid or illegal adoption on the part of his maternal uncle in Benares (*i*) and in Maithila (*k*).

(*b*) MS. 1613. As to the Parbhus, see Steele, L. C. 89, 94.

(*c*) *Morun Moyee Debia* v. *Bejoykisto Gossamee*, Cal. F. B. R. 121.

(*d*) *Lakshmapya* v. *Ramapa*, Bom. H. C. P. J. F. for 1873, p. 59. This case, from the Southern Maratha Country, was disposed of conformably to the laxness of the law there as to prohibited degrees already noticed.

The legality of marriage between an uncle and niece was denied in *Ramanagavda* v. *Shivaji*, Bom. H. C. P. J. 1876, p. 73 (the parties being apparently Lingayats of the Southern Maratha country), but an application for review (*ibid.* p. 154) was dismissed on the ground that the suit was barred by limitation.

(*e*) *Gopal Narhar Safray* v. *Hanmant Ganesh Safray*, I. L. R. 6 Bom. 109. This case illustrates the difficulty of establishing a particular custom of a caste or sect diverging from the general law. It will be seen below that there is considerable authority for the practice.

(*f*) *Gopalayyan* v. *Raghupatiyyan*, 7 M. H. C. R. 250.

In the Panjab, it may be noticed, adoption may be made of a relative through a female. See Tupper, Panj. Customary Law, vol. II., p. 111.

(*g*) I. L. R. 4 Bom., at p. 557 ss.

(*h*) MSS. 1622, 1706. The parties, though the caste is not explicitly stated, must have been Sudras.

(*i*) *Thakoorain Saluba* v. *Mohun Lall*, 11 M. I. A. 386.

(*k*) *Musst. Mooneea* v. *Dhurma*, 11 M. I. A. 393.

As to the daughter's son the Sastris have said: "A Brahman cannot adopt his daughter's son" (*l*); and "The adoption of a daughter's son is invalid. Though Pandits differ, the texts do not differ" (*m*). Again, to a question whether a daughter's only son could be adopted by her father in pursuance of an agreement with her husband at the time of marriage, the Sastri says only "the adoption of a daughter's son is forbidden" (*n*).

On the other hand the Pandits of the Poona College on the authority of the Samskara Kaustubha and the Nirnaya Sindhu admitted the adoption of a daughter's or a sister's son in default of boys available within the adoptive father's own gotra (*o*).

In the South Maratha country the customary law allows the adoption of a daughter's son with the consent of the kindred of the adopter (*p*).

It is valid in Saraogi Agarvali caste, which is a sect of the Jains (*q*).

The son of a woman adopted by her paternal uncle was pronounced entitled to the management of business as Muttadar Patel, while the widow of the deceased nephew was pronounced heir to his property (*r*).

In *Somasekhara* v. *Subhadramaji* (*s*) the Court declined to express an opinion on the validity of an adoption of a son whose mother was second cousin of the adoptive father. As a marriage would have been impossible between the real mother and the adoptive father the adoption would be invalid judged by that test.

(*l*) MS. 1638; *Bhagwan Singh* v. *Bhagwan Singh*, L. R. 26 I. A. 153; *Ramchandra* v. *Gopal*, I. L. R. 32 Bom. 623; *Walbai* v. *Heerbai*, I. L. R. 34 Bom. 491; *Yamnava* v. *Lakshman Bhumoo* ,I. L. R. 36 Bom. 533.

(*m*) *Jivanee Bhayee* v. *Jivu Bhayee*, 2 M. H. C. R. 462; *Nursing Narain* v. *Bhutton Lall*, Sp. No. C. W. R. 194.

(*n*) MS. 1633. This question indicates a clinging to the ancient institution of the putrika-putra. See above, pp. 793, 800, 801.

(*o*) Steele, L. C. 44. See above, pp. 800-1; 2 Borr. 95, 96.

(*p*) Steele, L. C. 183.

The fitness of a daughter's son for adoption, where it is recognized by the higher castes, may be traced either to the institution of the appointed daughter (see above, pp. 800, 801) or to the imitation of their low caste neighbours at the prompting of natural affection.

(*q*) *Sheo Singh Rai* v. *Musst. Dakho*, N. W. P. H. C. R. 382; S. C. L. R. 5 I. A. 87; S. C. I. L. R. 1 All. 688.

(*r*) MS. 5. Nothing is said of the caste, or of division or non-division. Division and Sudra caste seem to be assumed. If the widow of the nephew had adopted a contest might have arisen such as is referred to at p. 889, note (*c*).

(*s*) I. L. R. 6 Bom. 524

Where the adoption of a sister's or a daughter's son is allowed the test seems inapplicable. In the South, whence the case came, marriage with a sister's daughter is common even amongst Brahmans, and custom is, to say the least, lax in restricting adoptions. It would seem therefore that the adoption in question was not open to objection on the ground of prior family connexion between the parties.

In one case (*t*) the opinion seemed to be held that a man could adopt his wife's sister's son, but that this had been invalid in the particular case as tending to deprive the heirs of their right of succession (*v*).

There is of course less objection to the adoption of a father's brother's son or a mother's brother's son than to adopting a father's sister's son or a mother's sister's son (*w*).

---

2. 4.—Relation Between the Son to be Adopted and the Adoptive Mother.

The principle of an imitation of nature operates, though less conspicuously, in the case of a blood connexion between the proposed adoptive mother and son as between the adoptive father and son.

In the earlier form of the law as the relation of the adopted son to his adoptive mother was merely incidental, the doctrine of a possibility of union between her and the real father seems not to have been developed. It grew up as natural feeling gradually gave to the adoptive mother, as compared with the adoptive father, a more and more important relation to the child whom they brought up as their own. Then as the condition was accepted of a possible union of the real mother with the ideal father to produce the adopted son, a corresponding notion was suggested of a similar necessary relation between the ideal mother and the real father (*x*).

(*t*) *Baee Gunga* v. *Baee Sheoshunkur*, Bom. Sel. R. 73; *Bai Nani* v. *Chuni Lal*, I. L. R. 22 Bom. 973.

(*v*) This case is discussed above, p. 841.

(*w*) *Shrinivas Timaji* v. *Chintaman Shivaji*, S. A. 587 of 1866. See Datt. Mim. II. 107, 108.

(*x*) See above, p. 796. In a footnote at 1 M. H. C. R. 427 to *Narsarammal* v. *Balarama Charlu*, *ibid.* 420, several cases are quoted to show that there must have been a possibility of legal union between the adoptive father and the real mother. One is cited from Macn. Cons. H. L. 170, to show the need of a similar relation between the adoptive mother and the real father.

Thus it came to be admitted, though not at all universally, that where the real father and the adoptive mother could not, without incest, have joined in procreating the boy, he is not a fit subject for adoption (*y*). Such at least is the rule followed by most of the authorities. Others are more indulgent. A deceased wife's connexion with the family whence the boy is to be taken is not recognized as an obstacle to his adoption. This may be taken as a sign of the imitative character of the doctrine. The relation of a deceased adoptive father to the real mother is an obstacle in the same cases as if he were alive, but on the other side the imitation has not proceeded beyond the relation of an adoptive mother still living.

In several instances the fitness for adoption has been pronounced on solely by reference to the connexion between the boy's real mother and his adoptive father, when the only question under the Hindu Law was whether the relation between the real father and the adoptive mother prevented a valid adoption. The Dharmad-vaitta Nirnaya allows the adoption of the wife's blood relatives, but this is opposed to the general sense of the authorities (*z*) as regards the higher castes. The two following cases will serve for further illustrations.

In the first it was ruled that the adoption of a wife's brother is valid (*a*), as the adopter could have legally married adoptee's mother in her maiden state (*b*).

In the second it was laid down that—

1. The son of a wife's brother may be adopted.
2. The rule of Hindu Law that a legal marriage must have been possible between the adopter and mother of the adoptee refers to relationship prior to marriage.
3. This rule has nothing to do with the case of a stepmother in her virgin state, accordingly a half-brother cannot be adopted (*c*).

When the connexion between the propositus and the intended adoptive mother arises through the boy's mother, such a relation

---

(*y*) Datt. Mim. sec. II. 32, 33. The living wife must (religiously) join in an adoption. As a widow she adopts to her husband, but he surviving does not adopt to her.

(*z*) See Datt. Mim., sec. II. 33, 34.

(*a*) *Runganaigum* v. *Namasevoya Pillai*, M. S. D. A. Dec. 1857, p. 94.

(*b*) *Kristniengar* v. *Venamamalai Jyengar*, M. S. D. A. Dec. 1856, p. 213.

(*c*) *Sriramulu* v. *Ramaya*, I. L. R. 3 Mad. 15. The sense of this is that though the particular restriction would not operate, another one does, which prevents an allowance of adoption which would otherwise follow

creates no obstacle to adoption. Two sisters or two female cousins could not possibly be parents of the same boy, so that the ceremonial relation does not in this case imitate anything legally impossible.

Thus a man may adopt his wife's sister's son (*d*).

" A widow may adopt her sister's son if this be consistent with the custom of the caste " (*e*).

A widow may adopt her brother's son (*f*).

---

2. 5.—Family Connexion with the Adoptive Parents Amongst Sudras.

It has been pointed out (*g*) that the practice of adoption amongst the lower castes is probably a mere graft of Brahmanical usage upon a primitive stem of a very different kind. The result shows signs of this composite origin. The aboriginal tribes had a family system of their own, which in some form they must retain. The marriage of first cousins, marriage of an uncle and niece, heirship of a sister's son, reception of a daughter's husband as *quasi*-son when there was no real son in the way; for all these and other customs room had to be found in the Brahmanical system before the uncivilized converts could be subdued to it (*h*). Similarly in the case of adoption the practice of succession of a sister's and of a daughter's son had to be admitted; it was brought within the general system by widening the gateway of adoption in the case of Sudras, who in their turn were so far influenced by the ideas of their more intellectual neighbours, that in most cases they gradually accepted adoption as necessary to fully constitute the heritable right (*i*). Concurrently with these changes vicarious sacrifices were allowed (*k*) for those who, under the antique scheme of religion, were wholly excluded from spiritual benefits (*l*). Adoption became ceremonial, yet not so essentially ceremonial but

---

(*d*) 2 Str. H. L. 106.

(*e*) MS. 1708.

(*f*) *Bai Nani* v. *Chunilal*, I. L. R. 22 Bom. 973.

(*g*) Above, p. 825 ss.

(*h*) See above, pp. 800, 801.

(*i*) Comp. p. 823.

(*k*) Comp. Manu X. 126, 127.

(*l*) Above, pp. 811, 823, 831; 2 Str. H. L. 263.

that a giving and taking might be effectual without symbolical acts, or sacrifices, or recitation of sacred formulas (*m*). The customs springing from natural loathing of incestuous unions were referred to the principle of the family and gotra as conceived by the twice-born; and even spiritual benefits, it became dimly recognized, might be secured through the proper ministers by the low-caste son for his low-caste father. Still the marriage and the adoption of a Sudra could never be regarded by the depositaries of the sacred traditions but with a kind of contempt. It was of little consequence in their eyes whether purity from physical or spiritual contamination was preserved amongst people who had no devolution of sacra as contemplated in the Veda (*n*), and with whom there was no association on the part of the higher classes that would not honour them. Thus the disdain inspired by caste feeling joined with the desire of gain and of importance to make the Brahmans admit Sudra adoption with the peculiarities that it still presents. Whether in those cases in which the Brahmans themselves follow usages generally peculiar to the lower castes this is to be ascribed to a special development of their own original system or to the mere influence of a majority rising gradually in the social scale (*o*) is a question which cannot at present be answered very decisively. It seems likely that in some cases at least there has been a mixture of classes and of customs which descendants aiming at a higher rank have set themselves to forget as completely as possible (*p*).

Some instances have already been given of the relaxation of the ordinary rules of adoption in favour of Sudras as contrasted with the higher castes. Several other points are brought out by the opinions and the decisions, the chief of which are the following:

(*m*) See above, p. 824 ss.

(*n*) Datt. Mim. II. 80.

(*o*) See above, p. 825.

(*p*) See above, p. 807. It is not a very unusual thing for a man of dubious caste position, who has got up in the world, to assume the sacred thread which he never wore before. A story is got up of his connexion with a regenerate caste much as a pedigree is made to order in Europe, and Brahmans are not wanting to perform the rites of investiture. It has sometimes even been a matter of discussion in a caste whether though hitherto uninvested they might not assume the thread and claim rank at least as Vaisyas. The expense of the ceremonies stands in the way. See further below, sec. VI. D. 1. 2.

Consanguinity does not invalidate an adoption where the parties involved do not belong to any of the three regenerate castes (*q*).

"A Sudra may adopt a sister's son" (*r*).

"A Sudra only may adopt a sister's or daughter's son" (*s*).

"A brother's or sister's son may be adopted by a sister or brother amongst Sudras only" (*t*).

"A Lingayat may adopt his daughter's son" (*v*).

In the Bombay presidency it might seem from the case quoted below that the adoption of a sister's son by a Vaisya was allowed (*w*), and the language of the judgment is so general as to extend to all classes, but the parties were in fact Lingayats, and Lingayats are Sudras (*x*), amongst whom no doubt the sister's or the daughter's son is the most proper for adoption (*y*). The Sudra is bound to adopt a daughter's or a sister's son according to the Mayukha if one is available (*z*). This obligation, however, cannot probably be ranked higher than the ordinary one to adopt the son of a near sapinda which has been pronounced to be merely religious or discretional (*a*).

In a Madras case it was said in argument before the Judicial Committee that the parties were Vaisyas (*b*). If they were the decision is an authority for the legality of a Vaisya's adopting a sister's son in that province, but it would be desirable to have had the caste more satisfactorily established.

It is allowed amongst Jains as a law of the caste (*c*).

The adoption of a sister's son allowed in Bengal in a case noted below (*d*) was afterwards pronounced invalid there (*e*) though allowed in Maithila (*f*).

(*q*) *Nunkoo Singh* v. *Purm Dhun Singh*, 12 C. W. R. 356.

(*r*) MS. 1749. (*s*) MS. 1636. (*t*) MS. 1672.

(*v*) MS. 1641. The Sastri quotes Vyav. May., Chap. IV., sec. V. 9, which relates to Sudras.

(*w*) See *Gunpatrao* v. *Vithoba*, 4 Bom. H. C. R. 130 A. C. J.

(*x*) See below, and I. L. R. 3 Bom. 273.

(*y*) Above, p. 824.

(*z*) Above, pp. 823, 824; Datt. Mim. II. 74 ss.

(*a*) Above, p. 800, note (*a*); Datt. Mim., sec. II.

(*b*) *Ramalinga* v. *Sadasiva Pillai*, 9 M. I. A. 506; S. C. 1 C. W. R. 25 P. C.

(*c*) *Hasan Ali* v. *Naga Mal*, I. L. R. 1 All. 288.

(*d*) Macn. Consid. H. L., p. 167.

(*e*) *Doe dem Kora Shunker* v. *Bebee Munnee*, East's Notes, Case XX.; 2 Mor. Dig., p. 32.

(*f*) *Chowdree Purmessur* v. *Hunooman Dutt*, 6 C. S. D. A. R. 192.

A Sudra's widow having adopted her daughter's illegitimate son, the latter was pronounced heir both as grandson and as adopted son (*g*).

" A Wani, being a Sudra, may adopt his sister's son " (*h*).

" Adoption of a first cousin is forbidden among Sudras " (there having been apparently a sister's or a daughter's son available) (*i*).

The adoption of a mother's sister's son is valid among Sudras (*k*).

Apart from the indulgence conceded as to the adoption of sons of female blood relatives, the rules of adoption amongst the Sudras as to the choice of a boy do not differ essentially from those of the other castes. The necessity, whether legal or religious, of taking the nearest relative in preference to the more remote, or to a stranger, is hardly dwelt on by the Sastris, and is treated in practice merely as a counsel of perfection, which may be followed or disregarded. Many castes, which are really sub-divisions of the Sudra class, decline to recognize this, and affect in some particulars the customs of the twice-born, as in the case of the closer relations which prevent adoption. The remoter relations are hardly recognized, but adoptions seem to be generally forbidden (*l*) which would involve a kind of absurdity, as *ex. gr.* the adoption of an uncle or one older than the adopter (*m*).

" A Mhar may adopt a cousin's son in preference to a brother's son " (*n*).

A Hindu may adopt an asagotra among the Sudras (*o*).

" A Sudra may adopt from an illegitimate branch of his family, though there be eligibles of a legitimate branch " (*p*).

(*g*) MS. 236.
(*h*) MS. 1624.
(*i*) MS. 1618.
(*k*) *Chinna Nagáyya* v. *Pedda Nagayya*, I. L. R. 1 Mad. 62.
(*l*) Steele, L. C. 184.
(*m*) *Op. cit.* 388.
(*n*) MS. 1630.
(*o*) *Rungamah* v. *Atchummah et al.*, 4 M. I. A. 1; S. C. 7 C. W. R. 57, P. C.; *Lakshmappa* v. *Ramava*, Bom. H. C. P. J. 1875, p. 394; S. C.; 12 Bom. H. C. R. 364. See above, p. 824, and 2 Str. H. L. 89.
(*p*) MS. 1646.

3.—Relation of the Son to be Adopted to his Family of Birth.

The cases of an only son (*q*), and of the eldest son (*r*) have already been dwelt on. The relation next to these in practical importance is that of the orphan (*s*). The svayamdatta or son self-given is, as we have seen (*t*), not recognized in the present age, and the Sastris have disallowed the adoption of a man otherwise eligible, because his parents having died there was no one who could give him in adoption (*v*). The giving by an eldest brother as head of the family, though there is some authority for it (*w*) amongst the castes, is not contemplated by the sacred formulas, and has been condemned by high authorities (*x*).

The ceremonies of adoption are equally unadapted to the gift of an adopted son, and such a gift is not contemplated by the Hindu Law. The adopted son must generally be an only son, but even when a son has been born there is no formula adapted to the purpose of transferring the adopted son (*y*) to another family. There is none even for restoring him to his family of birth (*z*).

---

3. 1.—Relation of Son to be Adopted to his Family of Birth—An Only Son.

In *Radha Mohun* v. *Hardai Bibi* (*a*) the Judicial Committee have laid down that an only son may be given and taken in adoption according to the Hindu Law.

An only son may be given as a dvyamushyayana (*b*).

In Madras such an adoption has been held valid (*c*), and also

---

(*q*) Above, p. 818.

(*r*) Above, p. 820.

(*s*) Above, p. 806.

(*t*) Above, p. 807.

(*v*) P. 832; *Balvantrao* v. *Bayabai*, 6 Bom. H. C. R. 83 O. C. J.; *Bashetiappa* v. *Shivalingappa*, 10 Bom. H. C. R. 268.

(*w*) *Veerapermal* v. *Narain Pillai*, 1 Str. R. 91.

(*x*) See p. 832. Macn. Cons. H. L. 207, 228; 1 Mor. Dig., p. 19.

(*y*) See above, p. 808.

(*z*) See above, p. 832, note (*z*), and below, sec. VII.

(*a*) L. R. 26 I. A. 113.

(*b*) *Raja Shumshere Mul* v. *Ranee Dilraj Koer*, 2 C. S. D. A. R. 169.

(*c*) *Chinna Gaundan* v. *Kumara Gaundan*, 1 Mad. H. C. R. 54.

in the North-West Provinces (*d*). The principle was applied in these cases of *factum valet* (*e*).

Among Sudras of the Lingayat caste, an only son can be given in adoption (*f*).

There have been a few cases in which the adoption of an only son has been recognized even in Bombay (*g*).

The doctrine of *factum valet* has been supposed to give efficacy even in Bengal (*h*) to the kind of adoption in question. The adoption of an only son, though criminal, cannot perhaps be set aside (*i*), it was said.

In Madras it was at one time held that it was not lawful for a brother to adopt the only son of a brother in preference to his uncle's son; but in the sense that such an adoption involves both the giver and the receiver in sin, not that it is legally invalid (*k*). In other cases it has been said that—

The adoption of an eldest or only son is sustainable if made by a paternal uncle (*l*). He would generally be taken as a dvyamushyayana.

A dvyamushyayana is not recognized in the present age (*m*), according to the late Sadr Court of Madras. The legality of the dvyamushyayana, however, has been recognized by the Judicial Committee (*n*), and, as the cases show, this form of adoption is not at all uncommon in some districts of the Bombay Presidency. The following are two instances—

(*d*) See above, p. 817.

(*e*) *Hanuman Tiwari* v. *Chirai et al.*, I. L. R. 2 All. 164.

(*f*) *Basava* v. *Lingangavda*, I. L. R. 19 Bom. 428.

(*g*) *Abaji Dinkar* v. *Gungadhur Wasoodeo*, 3 Morris S. D. A. R. 420, 423; *R. Vyankatrav* v. *Jayavantrav*, 4 Bom. H. C. R. 191 A. C. J.

(*h*) Col. Dig., Book V., T. 273 Com. *sub. init.*

(*i*) *Nundram et al.* v. *Kashee Pande et al.*, 3 C. S. D. A. R. 232; S. C. 4 C. S. D. A. R. 70; 1 Str. H. L. 87. The effect of the case is given as stated in *Chinna* v. *Kumara Gaundan*, 1 M. H. C. R., at p. 57, but the point was not really decided so as to support the decision in Fulton's Reports, I. 75.

(*k*) *Arnachellum Pillay* v. *Jyasami Pillay*, 1 M. S. D. A. R. 154.

(*l*) *Perumal Nayker* v. *Potteeammal*, M. S. D. A. Dec. 1851, p. 234; *Gocoolanund Doss* v. *Musst. Wooma Daee*, 15 Beng. L. R. 405; S. C. 23 C. W. R. 340; Chinna Gaundan v. Kumara Gaundan, 1 Mad. H. C. R. 54 (reviewing *Perumal Nayker* v. *Potteeammal*).

(*m*) *Annamala Auchy* v. *Mungalum*, M. S. D. A. R. 1859, p. 81.

(*n*) See above, pp. 808, 819.

" An agreement may be made at the time of adoption that the son shall represent both fathers, but without this he cannot succeed to his natural father's property " (*o*).

" If a Brahman adopts a boy of a different gotra the presumption is that he has taken him as a dvyamushyayana " (*p*).

The decisions seem to show that this kind of adoption is generally legal (*q*). Thus:

The only son of a brother may be adopted in Maithila (*r*).

The only son of a person may be adopted by another, on condition that he becomes a son of both of them (*s*). It is presumed from such an adoption (*t*) that the son became a dvyamushyayana.

---

3. 2.—Relation of Son to be Adopted to his Family of Birth—Eldest Son.

The grounds of distinction between the cases of the eldest son and the only son have been discussed in a preceding section (*v*). The Mitakshara is distinctly opposed to the gift of an eldest equally as to that of an only son (*w*), but the Dattaka Mimamsa (*x*) and Dattaka Chandrika (*y*), though they prohibit the gift of an only

---

(*o*) MS. 1692.

(*p*) MS. 1675. A similar presumption arises where an only son or eldest son has been given to his uncle. *Nilmadhab Dass* v. *Biswambhar Dass*, 13 M. I. A. 85, 101. See Datt. Mim., sec. IV. 32. In *Chinna Gaundan's Case*, 1 M. H. C. R., at p. 55, Scotland, C. J., refers to *Sy. Joymony Dossee's Case*, Fult. 75, as establishing that a condition of double sonship will be presumed after adoption in every case, but that could not be so where a dvyamushyayana is not admitted, see above, p. 809.

(*q*) See p. 927, note (*k*).

(*r*) 2 Macn. H. L. 197. The adoption was in the Kritrima form. As to which see below, and 7 C. W. R. 700.

(*s*) *R. Shumshere Mull* v. *Ry. Dilraj Konwar*, 2 C. S. D. A. R. 169.

(*t*) *Sy. Joymony Dossee* v. *Sy. Sibosoondry Dossee*, 1 Fult. 75; *Nilmadhab Dass* v. *Biswambhar Dass*, 12 C. W. R. P. C. 29; 3 Beng. L. R. P. C. 27; S. C. 13 M. I. A. 85. The presumption extended to cases other than those of adoption of a brother's son tends to nullify the general rule, but an only son can properly be given only to his uncle as a dvyamushyayana. See above, p. 808 ss.

(*v*) Above, pp. 819, 820.

(*w*) Mit., Chap. I., sec. XI., paras. 11, 12.

(*x*) Sec. IV.

(*y*) Sec. I.

son, are silent as to the eldest son. This may be taken as a tacit allowance of the adoption of such a son on the principle frequently repeated that "when there is no prohibition there is assent" (z).

The Vyavahara Mayukha (a) assumes that the Mitakshara allows the legality while it asserts the sinfulness of the gift of an only or an eldest son. It then goes on to refute the supposed permission and maintain that neither an only son nor an eldest son can be given (b). Now it is true no doubt that Vijnanesvara in his disquisition on the nature of property (c) dwells on its secular character and the possibility of acquiring it without reference to the ceremonial rules provided for spiritual purposes (d). But he does not admit that acquisition without regard to the means produces property (e). He regards what is unfit to be given as incapable of being taken by gift (f) and could not apparently (g), any more than Nilkantha himself, hold the adoption of an eldest son valid (h). The legal possibility of this adoption must rest on the absence of any distinct condemnation of it in the older sources of the law, and on the allowance, though a grudging allowance, of it by custom (i), and at least by implication in some writers of high authority. For the Bombay Presidency the matter may perhaps be considered closed by the case of *Kashibai* v. *Tatia* (k), which gave effect to the adoption of an eldest son.

(z) Datt. Chand., sec. I., para. 32; Vyav. May., Chap. IV., sec. V., para. 18.

(a) Chap. IV., sec. V., paras. 4, 5.

(b) Chap. IV., *loc. cit.*, and para. 36.

(c) Mit., Chap. I., sec. I., para. 8 ss.

(d) Comp. the Sarasvati Vilasa, sec. 472. And for the special character of religious gifts, Mit., Chap. I., sec. VIII., para. 8.

(e) *Loc cit.*, para. 11.

(f) 2 Str. H. L. 433; Colebrooke, *loc. cit.*, shows that the Smriti Chandrika and the Madhaviya agree with the Mitakshara in regarding a forbidden gift as invalid. Compare the passage quoted Vyav. May., Chap. IX., para. 3.

(g) The sin, he says, is the parents' who give without necessity; an only son or an eldest son is not to be given at all. See Mit., Chap. I., sec. XI., paras. 11, 12.

(h) The Viramitrodaya (Transl., pp. 115, 117) is opposed to the gift of an only and of an eldest son, but says nothing of the allowance of either by Vijnanesvara.

(i) See Steele, L. C. 183, where the gift of the eldest is disapproved, while the gift of the only son is forbidden.

(k) I. L. R. 7 Bom. 225. It was ruled that the adoption of an eldest son was permissible though not approved, the authorities against such an adoption

In *Bomlingappa's Case* it was held that the adoption of an eldest son was invalid in the southern Maratha country (*l*). The Subordinate Judge, after consulting the Sastri, had found this adoption good, as being that of a nephew, and this seems to have been approved by the Sadr Court in a later case (*m*).

In Bengal an adoption of the eldest of several sons is allowable (*n*).

The adoption of an only son being allowed (*o*) it follows *à fortiori* that an eldest son may be adopted (*p*). In Bombay the opinions of the Sastris have not been uniform. Thus it was said "an adoptive son should not be the only or the eldest son of his father" (*q*). "The eldest surviving son must not be given in adoption" (*r*). And again, "the giving of an eldest son is a sin: some hold that an only son can neither be given nor taken" (*s*). But on the other hand—" Though a man's eldest son be dead, the next may be given in adoption" (*t*). And "the eldest of several sons may be given in adoption" (*v*). In another case the Sastri said "the eldest son may be given in adoption to a widow" (*w*).

The case of *Mhalsabai* v. *Vithoba* (*x*), upholding the gift by a widow of her eldest son, was dissented from by Sir M. Westropp, C.J., in *Lakshmappa* v. *Ramava* (*y*). The adoption of an eldest son is undoubtedly disapproved by Hindu Law (*z*), but all that it

---

being much less numerous and emphatic than those condemning the adoption of an only son. This was followed in *Jamunabai* v. *Raychand*, *ibid*. 229; see 2 Str. H. L. 105.

(*l*) See 12 Bom. H. C. R., at p. 383.

(*m*) *Ibid*., pp. 387, 388.

(*n*) *Janokee Debea* v. *Gopaul Acharjea et al.*, I. L. R. 2 Cal. 365.

(*o*) *Radha Mohun* v. *Hardai Bibi*, L. R. 26 I. A. 113.

(*p*) See above, p. 927.

(*q*) MS. 1672.

(*r*) MS. 1647.

(*s*) MS. 1682.

(*t*) MS. 1685.

(*v*) MS. 1621.

(*w*) MS. 1612.

(*x*) 7 Bom. H. C. R. xxvi. App.

(*y*) 12 Bom. H. C. R., at p. 394.

(*z*) *Nilmadhab Dass* v. *Biswambhar Dass*, 12 C. W. R. P. C. 29; S. C. 3 Beng. L. R. P. C. 25; S. C. 13 M. I. A. 85; *Jugbundoo Run Sing* v. *Radasham Narendro*, C. S. D. A. R. for 1859, p. 1556. An eldest son cannot be given in adoption according to Mit., Chap. I., sec. XI., p. 21; Colebrooke, 2 Str. H. L. 105. So Ellis, *ibid*., who says some authorities make exceptions. The eldest son of a brother, however, may be adopted (1 Str. H. L. 85) as an adult.

seems safe to say on the authorities is that the adoption of an eldest son is improper, not that it is invalid (*a*), as is the adoption of an only son (*b*).

Even by those who object to the gift of an eldest son it is admitted that if a person has by his first wife a son, and by his second wife several sons, the eldest of the latter may be given or received in adoption (*c*). It is also recognized that the subsequent death of the elder son does not render invalid an adoption of a second son in the lifetime of the elder son (*d*).

---

3. 3.—Relation of Son to be Adopted to his Family of Birth—Youngest Son.

The Dakhan castes disapproved the gift of the youngest son out of three or more (*e*), and a doubt seems sometimes to have been felt as to the lawfulness of such a gift. It is not, however, condemned by any recognized authority. A Sastri's response on a case submitted to him was "The youngest son may properly be given in adoption to a man of a different gotra. The Sastras forbid giving an eldest but not a youngest son" (*f*).

---

3. 4.—Relation of the Son to be Adopted to his Family of Birth—Amongst Sudras.

Although the gotra relation in its stricter sense does not subsist amongst Sudras, yet propinquity is recognized as giving rise to

---

(*a*) *Debee Dial et al.*, v. *Hurhor Singh*, 4 C. S. D. A. R. 320; *Veerapermal Pillay* v. *Narain Pillay*, 1 Str. R. 91; Col. Dig., Book V., T. 273 Com.; Mit., Chap. I., sec. XI., para. 12; 2 Str. H. L. 81, 105; Vyav. May., Chap. IV., sec. V., para. 4.

(*b*) Datt. Mim., sec. IV. 1 ss.; Datt. Chand. sec. I. 29, sec. III. 17; Steele, L. C. 183; 2 Macn. H. L. 182, 195; Macn. Cons. H. L. 126, 146, 147; 2 Str. H. L. 105.

The references show a general condemnation of the giving of an eldest son, but less decisive and unanimous than in the case of an only son.

(*c*) *Veerapermal Pillay* v. *Narain Pillay*, 1 Str. R. 91.

(*d*) *Musst. Dullabh De* v. *Manee Bibi*, 5 C. S. D. A. R. 50; *Nilmadhab Dass* v. *Biswambhar Dass*, 12 C. W. R. P. C. 29; S. C. 3 Beng. L. R. P. C. 27; S. C. 13 M. I. A. 85.

(*e*) Steele, L. C. 183, 384.

(*f*) MS. 1677. In the *Mankars' Case*, 2 Borr. R., at p. 95, the Sastris say a father is bound to keep his eldest and youngest sons, but for the latter part of the rule no authority is cited.

certain connexions and restrictions which coincide in a measure with those that prevail amongst the higher castes (*g*). Through the gradual attraction and reception of the Sudras within the Brahminical religious system (*h*) the relation of a son to his father has with many come to be regarded as involving a position and duties analogous at least to those of the Brahman (*i*). The father being thus concerned in the rites to be celebrated by his son (*k*) the same rules which guard against the loss of these benefits amongst the other classes ought equally or almost equally to operate amongst Sudras (*l*). This may be thought to have been secured for Bombay by the following decision on the point. "There is not in the books any ground for drawing any distinction between Sudras and other classes on the question of the legality of the adoption of an eldest or only son" (*m*). The Sastris hold the same view.

The adoption by a Sudra of an only son as a karta putra is allowed by the Hindu Law (*n*) in Bengal. A similar view was taken in Bombay by Sir M. Sausse, C.J. (*o*), which has since been followed in *Basava* v. *Lingangauda* (*p*).

4.—Fitness for Adoption as Affected by Personal Qualities—Sex.

There is no instance in Hindu Law of an adoption of a daughter to inherit (*q*).

(*g*) Datt. Mim., sec. II., 80.

(*h*) Above, p. 827.

(*i*) See above, pp. 824, 825.

(*k*) See Steele, L. C. 225. The Jains do not celebrate the kriya ceremonies, and amongst them adoption must be referred to a different basis. See Steele, L. C. 416; above, pp. 825.

(*l*) See Steele, L. C. 413, 414.

(*m*) *Per* Sir M. Westropp, C.J., in *Lakshmappa* v. *Ramava*, 12 Bom. H. C. R., at p. 390.

(*n*) *Musst. Tikdey* v. *Lalla Hureelal*, Suth. R. for 1864, p. 133. The term karta putra is used as a synonym for kritrima putra.

(*o*) *Mhalsabai* v. *Vithoba*, 7 Bom. H. C. R. xxvi. App.

(*p*) I. L. R. 19 Bom. 428.

(*q*) *Doe dem Hencower Bye et. al.* v. *Hanscower Bye et al.*, East's Notes, Case 75. Daughters cannot be adopted, 2 Str. H. L. 217. See above, p. 906, C. 2. 2, as to a *quasi*-adoption by a dancer. *Gangabai* v. *Anant*, I. L. R. 13 Bom. 690.

In the Dattaka Mimamsa a section (VII.) is devoted to the attempt to establish the adoption of daughters as an institution of the Hindu Law. Great learning and ingenuity were expended on this effort, but it has failed to gain acceptance for the proposed doctrine (*r*). The Vyavahara Mayukha (*s*) rejects it, and no Sastri has maintained it except as a possible variance justified by caste custom. As when one said—" An adoption by a woman of a daughter given by her mother may be recognized if conformable to the caste rules " (*t*). The only custom allowing it is that of the dissolute women whose imitations of adoption have already been considered (*v*).

In *Hencower's Case* (*w*) the pandit denied that the adoption of a daughter was consistent with the Hindu Law. Yet in another case the adoption of a niece in order that she might become the mother of a putrika-putra was allowed (*x*). The adoption, it was said, should be prior to marriage. This decision seems never to have been followed, and like Nanda Panditta's doctrine stands outside the living law (*y*). The validity of any such adoption of a daughter must rest on a special custom.

The adoption of a sister, it was ruled, is illegal to the prejudice of legal heirs (*z*).

A sister's daughter, or her son, cannot become a putrika-putra (*a*). The institution is in fact no longer recognized (*b*), though in the case quoted below it was only questioned by the Judicial Committee whether the old rule of Hindu Law still exists, namely, whether a daughter may be specially appointed to raise a son, and the son of such daughter be preferred to more distant male relatives. If so, it was said, inasmuch as the rule breaks in upon general rules of succession whenever an heir claims to

---

(*r*) See above, pp. 790, 833.

(*s*) Chap. IV., sec. V., para. 6.

(*t*) MS. 1681.

(*v*) Above, pp. 833, 834. *Manjamma* v. *Sheshgirirao*, I. L. R. 26 Bom. 491.

(*w*) Above, p. 932 (*q*).

(*x*) *Nawab Rai* v. *Buggawuttee Koowur*, 6 C. S. D. A. R. 5.

(*y*) 1 Macn. H. L. 102.

(*z*) *Toolooviya Shetty* v. *Coraga Shellaty*, M. S. D. A. R. 1848, p. 75. The adoption of a sister is wholly illegal; she could not have been begotten by the adoptive father without incest.

(*a*) *Nursing Narain* v. *Bhutton Lall*, Sp. No. C. W. R. 194.

(*b*) See above, pp. 800, 803, 806.

succeed by virtue of that rule, he must bring himself very clearly within it (*c*).

---

4. 1.—Fitness for Adoption—Age.

The proper age of the son to be adopted is stated in widely different ways by different castes (*d*). It is generally agreed that the child ought to be young in order that he may become united by affection to his adoptive parents (*e*), but this is rather a maxim of prudence than of law. Some castes fix the limit of age at five years; many at twenty-five; a few at fifty. The last indeed do not recognize a legal limit of mere age, though, with the others they require that the adopted son should be younger than his adoptive father (*f*).

The proper age for adoption is not uniform even for the same district in every caste. A boy may generally be adopted from the twelfth day after birth to his upanayana, which is eight years for Brahmans, eleven years for Kshatriyas, twelve for Vaisyas. Sudras may be adopted till the sixteenth year (*g*). This is, however, simply the age of majority according to Hindu Law. The statement must be taken as rather of what is recognized as right than of what is obligatory.

The Hindu lawyers have written very elaborately on the subject of the boy's age as connected with his Samskaras. These views are considered below (*h*). In the North-West Provinces it was ruled, conformably to the Dattaka Mimamsa, that adoption in the Dattaka form ought to be within six years of age of the adoptee (*i*). In *Ganga* v. *Lekraj* (*k*) it was held that a boy upon whom the

---

(*c*) *Thakoor Jibnath Singh* v. *The Court of Wards*, 23 C. W. R. 409. For the law as now received, see above, pp. 800, 803, 807, 833; 1 Macn. H. L. 102.

(*d*) Steele, L. C. 383. See above, p. 831.

(*e*) See above, p. 833.

(*f*) Steele, L. C. 182.

(*g*) *Ry. Sevagamy Nachiar* v. *Heraniah Gurbah*, 1 Mad. S. D. A. R. 101. See 1 Mor. Dig., p. 22, notes 8 and 9. The authorities quoted in 2 Macn. H. L. 175, 178, give five years as the age within which a boy ought to be adopted. See Datt. Mim., sec. IV. 32, 33, 48, and the Datt. Chand., sec. II. 30, which gives eight years of age as the usual limit amongst Brahmans.

(*h*) Sub-sec. 4. 7.

(*i*) *Th. Oomrao Singh* v. *Th. Mahtab Koonwar*, 2 Agra Rep., p. 103.

(*k*) I. L. R. 9 All. 253

ceremony of the investiture with the sacred thread had not actually been performed, and if he be a Sudra, then before his marriage, may be adopted. In Bombay, as among the Jains (*l*), on the other hand, a person of whatever age is eligible for adoption (*m*). Even—

"A man of fifty and having children, may be adopted if he has parents to give him away, but not otherwise" (*n*).

"A fatherless person of thirty years of age," it was said, "may be adopted with the consent of his mother or elder brother" (*o*).

---

4. 2.—Juniority of Adopted Son to Adoptive Father.

It has been noticed that the son adopted must be junior to the adoptive father. He need not, however, be junior to his adoptive mother, when she, as a widow, adopts him (*p*).

---

4. 3.—Birth During Adoptive Father's Life.

The imitation of nature is not carried so far as to disqualify a boy who, from the time of his birth, could not have been begotten by a deceased adoptive father. When authority to adopt is given to a widow, she may adopt a boy not born at her husband's death (*q*).

---

4. 4.—Identity or Difference of Family or Gotra.

This subject has been considered in the preceding Section (*r*). When members of the lower castes are concerned, the term

---

(*l*) *Asharfi* v. *Rup*, I. L. R. 30 All. 197.

(*m*) *R. Vyankatrav* v. *Jayavantrav*, 4 Bom. H. C. R. 191 A. C. J.; *Mhalsabai* v. *Vithoba Khandappa*, 7 Bom. H. C. R. App. xxvi.

(*n*) MS. 1755. *Dharma* v. *Ramkrishna*, I. L. R. 10 Bom. 80.

(*o*) MS. 1645. The competence of the elder brother to give in adoption is denied. See above, p. 832, and below, sec. V.

(*p*) *Gopal* v. *Vishnu*, I. L. R. 23 Bom. 250; *Ranganaya* v. *Alwar*, I. L. R. 13 Mad. 214.

(*q*) East's Notes, Case 10; 2 Mor. Dig., p. 16.

(*r*) Above, p. 830 ss. and sub-sec. 2. 2. of the present section. In the *Mankars' Case*, 2 Borr., at p. 95, the Sastris say that a brother's or a daughter's son may be adopted without any ceremonies but an oral gift and acceptance.

" gotra " is used in a second intention, but though this part of the subject is rather obscure it would probably be held that the same degree of propinquity which makes mere age a matter of indifference in the higher castes has the same effect amongst Sudras (*s*). Whether the absence of a true gotraship enables a Sudra to adopt indiscriminately any son younger than himself is a point that still awaits determination. The opinions of the Sastris would probably be opposed to such a licence except on the grounds of the Sudras being below the operation of the religious family law, but no obstacle or preference probably would be recognized by the Courts as arising from consanguinity—none, that is, of an obligatory character. In case of difference of gotra the adoptee should be under five years of age; in case of identity the age of the adoptee is not restricted (*ss*).

Difference of gotra makes it important that the Samskaras should not have been performed in the family of birth. Identity of gotra makes this a matter of comparative indifference (*t*). Hence the following opinions:

" The person adopting may select whom he likes, without the

(*s*) See Datt. Mim. II. 5, 80.

(*ss*) Steele, L. C. 43. *Extract from the Dharmasindhu—Who may or may not be adopted* (see 12 Bom. H. C. R. 373):

Amongst Brahmans the son of a uterine brother, because preferable, is to be taken first.

In his absence any Sagotra-Sapinda, or the son of a half-brother.

In the absence of such, an Asagotra-Sapinda, one produced in the family of the maternal uncle or in that of the father's sister, &c.

In the absence of such, an Asapinda of the same gotra.

In the absence of such, even an Asapinda of a different gotra.

Of the Asagotra-Sapindas the sister's son and the daughter's son are prohibited. . . . But by a Sudra even a sister's son and a daughter's son are receivable. . . . The adopter having adopted should perform the ceremonies commencing with the jatakarma or those commencing with the chudakarana for the boy adopted. This is the preferable doctrine: but if a boy for whom they can be so performed is not procurable, then from amongst the Sagotra-sapindas, one whose upanayana ceremony has been performed, or even whose marriage has taken place, may become an adopted son; but in the latter case, only if he has not produced a son. So it seems to me. If adoption is to be (=can be) made from amongst Asapinda-Sagotras only he whose upanayana ceremony has been performed is to be (may be) taken. This appears also. As to a Bhinna-gotra (one of a different gotra), he whose upanayana has not been performed is alone to be received. Some authors, however, say that a Bhinna-gotra whose upanayana has been performed may also be received.

(*t*) Above, p. 830.

assent of his relatives. If of a different gotra the boy should be adopted before tonsure " (*tt*). On the other hand—

" A man of fifty, and having children, may be adopted if of the gotra of the adoptive father. The latter should invite his kinsmen, but their assent is not essential " (*v*).

A married sagotra may be adopted by a widow in the Dekhan (*vv*). A gift made by the widow, prior to the adoption, may be set aside by the adopted son, in this as in other cases (*w*).

Some decisions recognize that limitation of age becomes material if the adoptee is taken from a line of strangers (*ww*), agreeing with the Sastri, who says—

" The adoption of a boy of eight years old, belonging to another gotra, and whose chaul and munj have been performed, is invalid " (*x*), but this rigour cannot probably be maintained in the present day (*y*).

---

4. 5.—Bodily Qualities.

The same qualities are required in an adopted son as in a son who is to inherit. Thus leprosy of a virulent form (*z*) or congenital blindness would disqualify, as making it impossible that the sufferer should discharge the ceremonial obligations of a son to his ancestors (*a*).

(*tt*) MS. 1683. Before upanayana, 2 Str. H. L. 104.

Colebrooke says : " See Mitaksh. on Inh., Chap. I., sec. XI. 13 : A difference of opinion prevails in regard to adoption of adults, or persons for whom certain ceremonies termed Samskara (marriage of Sudras, and tonsure of the higher tribes) have been performed, the prevalent doctrine, in most parts of India, being adverse to it. The objections are less forcible in the instance of a relation of the male side than in the case of a stranger." 2 Str. H. L. 109.

(*v*) MS. 1634. See sub-sec. 4. 9.

(*vv*) *Dharma Dagu* v. *Ramkrishna*, I. L. R. 10 Bom. 80.

(*w*) *Nathaji* v. *Hari*, 8 Bom. H. C. R. 67 A. C. J., quoting—(1) *Raja Vyankatrav Anandrav Nimbalkar* v. *Jayavantrav bin Malharrav Ranadive*, 4 Bom. H. C. R. A. C. J. 191; (2) *Rakhmabai* v. *Radhabai*, 5 Bom. H. C. R. A. C. J. 181; (3) Steele, pp. 44, 182; (4) *Ranee Kishen* v. *Raj Oodwunt Singh et al.*, 3 C. S. D. A. R. 228; (5) *Bamundoss Mookerjea et al.* v. *Musst. Tarinee*, 7 M. I. A. 169.

(*ww*) *Verapermal Pillay* v. *Narrain Pillay*, 1 Str. R. 91.

(*x*) MS. 1629.

(*y*) See below, sub-sec. 4. 7.

(*z*) A cripple. Steele, L. C. 184. *Mohunt Bhagwan Ramanuj Das* v. *Das*, I. L. R. 22 I. A. 94.

(*a*) See above, p. 539 ss.

4. 6.—Mental Qualities.

Idiocy or insanity disqualifying for inheritance disqualifies for adoption also (*b*), and for the same reason. Cases are wanting, as in practice no one seeks to adopt a boy known to be disqualified. When the boy has reached a stage of intelligence his own assent must be obtained, which at an earlier stage may be replaced by that of his parents (*c*). Sadrisam (*d*), properly understood, includes a kindly feeling between the adoptive father and son, and a disposition to obedience on the part of the latter not amenable to strict legal rules (*e*).

---

4. 7.—Religious and Ceremonial Qualities.

Great differences of opinion are found amongst the authorities as to the precise stage of progress in the Samskaras or family sacra at which a boy becomes indissolubly united to his family of birth (*f*). Some maintain that a severance may be made at any stage such as to fit the subject for initiation in another family (*g*). The Dattaka Mimamsa seems to allow adoption after tonsure to six years of age (*h*). The Dattaka Chandrika gives eight years of age as the limit of age of a tonsured boy (*i*). But both seem to allow a dissolution of the filial bond even after initiation by a repetition of the ceremony of initiation (*k*). The Vyavahara Mayukha expressly allows the adoption of a married man (*l*), though marriage is the limit set forth by other authorities as that at which adoption even of a Sudra becomes impossible. It concurs with the Dattaka Chandrika in doubting the genuineness of a passage on which the limitation to five years of age is founded. Sutherland, in his Synopsis, gives it as "the most general and consistent rule that 'any person on whom the adopter may legally

---

(*b*) See above, p. 545 ss; Steele, L. C. 184.

(*c*) Above, p. 833; Datt. Mim., sec. IV. 47.

(*d*) Above, p. 830.

(*e*) Steele, L. C. 182.

(*f*) As to these, see the note Col. Dig., Book V., T. 134; Datt. Mim. IV. 23; and Manu II. 27—68.

(*g*) Above, p. 830 ss.

(*h*) Datt. Mim., sec. IV. 48—54.

(*i*) Datt. Chand., sec. II. 30.

(*k*) Datt. Chand., sec. II. 25—28; Datt. Mim., sec. IV. 51, 52.

(*l*) Vyav. May., Chap. IV., sec. V., para. 19.

perform the upanayana rite (*m*) is capable of being affiliated as a dattaka son' " (*n*). Macnaghten states very decidedly that no adoption is possible after the upanayana has united a boy to his family by a second birth (*o*).

The Nirnaya Sindhu, which is frequently followed by the Sastris, calls that son anitya datta who before adoption has proceeded in the Samskaras even so far as tonsure, but on this point the people have rather taken the Samskarakaustubha for their guide, which allows adoption after initiation (as the Vyavahara Mayukha allows it after marriage (*p*).

The authorities being so obscure and inconsistent, the guidance afforded by custom and by the Sastris becomes of peculiar importance. Here again, however, there are considerable differences, the caste rules being much more indulgent than the learned Brahmans.

In the opinion of the Sastri " the adopted boy should be under five years old, and his chuda (*q*) and other sacraments should be performed assigning him the adoptive father's gotra " (*r*). Some of the Hindu authorities moreover and several decisions allow that the effect of tonsure as barring adoption (*s*) may be undone by an appropriate sacrifice even in the case of an only son. But on the other hand however much the age of adoptee may be above five years, his adoption will be valid if tonsure was not performed in the natural family (*t*).

(*m*) Investiture with the sacred thread.

(*n*) Suth. Synops. Head II. *ad fin.* See Notes XI. and XII. to the same.

(*o*) 1 Macn. H. L. 73.

(*p*) See above, p. 808.

(*q*) Tonsure.

(*r*) MS. 1673. See above, p. 831.

(*s*) *Sy. Joymony Dossee* v. *Sy. Sibosoondry Dossee*, 1 Fult. 75, 28 March, 1837; 1 Macn. H. L. 72 ss.; 1 Col. Dig., Book V., T. 182, 183, 273; Macn. Con. H. L. 141, 146, 192, 205; 1 Str. H. L. 91; 2 Str. H. L. 87, where the Sastri gives the upanayana or marriage as the limit beyond which a transfer to another family becomes impossible. The caste laws do not in Bombay make tonsure a limitation, though they, in some cases, give this effect to investiture and marriage, Steele, L. C. 182. Even as to these the practice is lax. See sub-sec. 4. 9.

(*t*) *Veerapermal Pillay* v. *Narain Pillay*, 1 Str. R. 91; *Musst. Dullabh Dai* v. *Manee Bibi*, 5 C. S. D. A. R. 50; see Datt. Chand., sec. II. 20—33; Datt. Mim., sec. IV. 22—54, and the notes to the preceding case. At 2 Str. H. L. 123 Ellis says that a boy adopted after tonsure becomes an anitya datta, whose son belongs to the original family of his father. Colebrooke says the son belongs to the family of his father's munj (investiture).

Connexion in gotra makes a new initiation unimportant, and thus the adoption of (1) a sagotra, (2) or of one descended directly from a common male ancestor, (3) or of a near relative of adopter on the paternal side is good, though he is above five years in age and tonsure has been performed in his natural family (*v*).

---

4. 8.—Investiture with the Sacred Thread.

A boy ought to be adopted before the performance of his munj (*w*), or investiture with the sacred thread (*x*), according to the law of some few castes. The others do not appear to make a point of this. In many of course there is no upanayana ceremony; the fullest initiation of which a youth is capable is obtained by marriage, which in such castes takes the place to some extent of the investiture (*y*). The restriction, however, must in either case be understood as subsisting only as between strangers by family and gotra. Amongst persons nearly connected there is no barrier raised to adoption by final dedication to the same family or gentile divinities (*z*).

(*v*) *Tanjore Raja's Case*, 1 Str. R. 126; *Veerapermal Pillay* v. *Narrain Pillay*, 1 Str. R. 91.

(*w*) See above, p. 830 ss.; and 4. 8.

(*x*) Steele, L. C. 182, 383. For the proper ages of investiture see Datt. Chand., sec. II. 31, note.

(*y*) Datt. Chand., sec. II. 29, 32; Col. Dig., Book V., T. 121 Comm.

(*z*) *Extract from the Samskarakaustubha* (see 12 Bom. H. C. R. 374): "One may be adopted as a son whether the Samskaras commencing with tonsure have taken place or not, and whether he has passed his fifth year or not. As to the doctrine 'one whose Samskaras have not taken place is alone to be adopted,' and 'who has not completed his fifth year is alone to be adopted,' founded upon the Kalika Purana, that is wrong; because some say the passages are not genuine, as they are not to be found in many copies of the Kalika Purana; and others say that, even if they be genuine, the first three shlokas have reference to Asagotra adoption; that, therefore, the last shloka also must be taken to have reference to the same subject; and that hence the rule does not apply to a Sagotra adoption; and they lay down that even a married (man) may be adopted. But the truth is, that even in the case of Asagotras a general prohibition (or non-recognition) of adoption after the Samskaras ending with the upanayana have been performed is not possible upon the strength of the Purana passages, because the authority of the Vedas to overrule contrary passages from the Smritis (and Puranas) is well established by the rule of commentators to determine the relative authority of texts, and the above passages of the Purana are in opposition to the Bahvricha Brahmana. Thus it is indisputable that

It has indeed been said that there is not in strictness any authority for the adoption of a boy whose munj or upanayana has been performed (*a*). And also that—

"A boy (Brahman) cannot be adopted after his munj. The form of adoption gone through confers no right of heirship on him" (*b*).

In other cases the Sastris answered—

"A boy of a different gotra should not be married or have been invested with the thread" (*c*).

"A boy adopted from another gotra should be taken before his thread investiture and marriage. In the same gotra this is not essential. In the former case the adopted acquires no rights of inheritance" (*d*). A boy whose upanayana had been performed would in Madras become but temporarily attached to the adoptive family (*e*). In Bombay on the other hand the adoption by a Brahman of a boy of a different gotra, whose munj had been performed, was pronounced quite legal and effectual (*f*), and a similar answer was grounded on an instance of such an adoption said to be given in the Veda (*g*).

In *Lakshmappa* v. *Ramava* (*h*) it is laid down by Nanabhai Haridas, J., consistently with the replies just quoted, that the performance of the chudakarana (*i*) and the upanayana (*k*) in

---

the expression 'the son given and the rest' includes 'the son made and the rest.' Hence it follows that one on whom the Samskaras have been performed in his natural family cannot become a self-given son either. But in the Brahmana it is plainly stated that Shunashepa himself became the son of Vishvamitra, and it is not to be supposed his upanayana had not been performed in his natural family."

(*a*) *P. Venkatesaiya* v. *M. Venkata Charlu et al.*, 3 Mad. H. C. R. 28.

(*b*) MS. 1751. See above, pp. 809, 810.

(*c*) MS. 1616. The question was as to son of father's brother's daughter's son, who would be unfit for adoption on account of his mother's consanguinity with the adoptive father according to the stricter rules as to the prohibited degrees. See above, p. 837.

(*d*) MS. 1615.

(*e*) *P. Venkatesaiya* v. *M. Venkata Charlu*, 3 Mad. H. C. R. 28; 1 Str. H. L. 88, 89, 90. The anitya datta, whose son returns to the family of the father's original gotra, is nowhere recognized by the Bombay Sastris, see above, p. 810.

(*f*) MS. 1719.

(*g*) MS. 1717. The reference is to the story of Sanahsepa (above, p. 808) on which the Samskarakaustubha founds the doctrine here followed by the Sastri.

(*h*) 12 Bom. H. C. R., at p. 370.

(*i*) Tonsure.

(*k*) Investiture.

the family of his birth does not disqualify even a Brahman for adoption, as the effect of these ceremonies may be annulled.

In Bengal the adoption of a boy, eight years old, was held to prevail over a daughter's claim to inheritance, the boy not having been initiated in the natural father's family (*l*). But a contrary rule would prevail where even the chuda had been performed.

The father of a boy after agreeing to give him in adoption performed his tonsure under his own family name. Afterwards the adoption was carried out and the *homam* performed. The Pandit pronounced such an adoption invalid (*m*).

---

4. 9.—Fitness for Adoption—As Affected by Marriage.

Strange (*n*) gives marriage in the fourth class as a ceremony after which adoption becomes impossible. This is confirmed by a Madras Sastri (*o*), and the same appears to have been the opinion of Jagannatha (*p*).

"The Poona Sastris do not, however, recognize the necessity that adoption should precede munj and marriage. The passage so interpreting the law is said by the author of the Mayukha to be an interpolation" (*q*). It is only the question of marriage that could be raised in the majority of cases, as for Sudras there is no other (initiatory) ceremony but marriage (*r*). Thus it was answered:

"The son of a sister-in-law may be adopted by a Brahman. But a married man of the same gotra only can be adopted" (*s*).

(*l*) *Keerut Nuraen* v. *Musst. Bhobinsree*, 1 C. S. D. A. R. 161; *Sreenevassien* v. *Sashyummal*, M. S. D. A. Dec. 1859, p. 118; see 1 Str. H. L. 89, 90.

(*m*) 2 Macn. H. L. 181.

(*n*) 1 Str. H. L. 91.

(*o*) 2 Str. H. L. 87.

(*p*) Col. Dig., Book V., T. 183, 273 Comm. "The investiture and other ceremonies . . . concern men of the twice-born classes: marriage is the only sacrament for a man of the servile class." Col. Dig., Book V., T. 121 Comm. "A man of the servile class universally obtains marriage as his only sacrament (Samskara)" *Ibid.*, T. 122.

(*q*) Steele, L. C. 44. See above, p. 834.

(*r*) *Sy. Joymony Dossee* v. *Sy. Sibosoondry Dossee*, 1 Fult. 75; *Ganga* v. *Lekhraj*, I. L. R. 9 All. 253.

(*s*) MSS. 1642, 1643.

This condition being satisfied the adoption of a married man is admissible, though of the mature age of forty-five years, and though he has a family, and his natural father prohibited adoption (*t*).

The more recent decisions also say that the adoption of a married boy is admissible, if he is a sagotra, though he has children, amongst Sudras (*v*). And generally it may be said that by the law of Bombay the adoption of a married Sudra is not invalid (*w*), as in *Lakshmappa* v. *Ramava* (*x*) it is ruled that a married sagotra may be adopted, sagotra meaning one in a relation of natural propinquity.

Whether upanayana and marriage in the natural family are a bar to adoption in another family among Brahmans, was a question raised in the case referred to below (*y*). The Court refused to consider it, holding the defendant bound by estoppel from disputing the adoption as he had taken part in the ceremony. Elsewhere than in the Bombay Presidency a married man does not seem to be eligible for adoption, even amongst the lower castes. Thus in

---

(*t*) *Sree Brijbhookunjee Maharaj* v. *Sree Gokolootsaojee Maharaj*, 1 Borr. 181, 202 (2nd ed.); *Lakshmappa* v. *Ramava et al.*, 12 Bom. H. C. R. 364; Vyav. May., Chap. IV., sec. V. 19. The Sastris, in reply to a question put to them, said: In the commencement of the Shastr it is written, A woman who has lost her husband must obtain the sanction of her father previous to adopting a son, and if she have no father then that of the caste. Again it is written, that a woman who has reached years of discretion may of herself perform religious duties. So she may adopt a son without permission, if none of the caste are at the time to be found. It is also stated that a boy under five years of age should be adopted in order that he may be brought up in the religious tenets of his adoptive father. This relates to cases where no relationship subsists, but when a relation is to be adopted, no obstacle exists on account of his being of mature age, married, and having a family, provided he possess common ability, and is beloved by the person who adopts him. However, if the father of the person to be adopted be seriously averse to it, declaring that his son shall not be given in adoption, the ceremony cannot be performed, since the Shastr ordains that the free consent of the father is necessary to the adoption of his son by another person. *Dharma Dagu* v. *Ramkrishna*, I. L. R. 10 Bom. 80.

(*v*) *Nathaji* v. *Hari*, 8 Bom. H. C. R. 67 A. C. J.; *Lakshmappa* v. *Ramava*, Bom. H. C. J. F. for 1875, p. 394; Vyav. May., Chap. IV., sec. V. 19.

(*w*) *Lakshmappa* v. *Ramava*, Bom. H. C. J. F. for 1875, p. 394; *Mhalsabai* v. *Vithoba Khandappa*, 7 Bom. H. C. R. App. xxvi.

(*x*) 12 Bom. H. C. R., at pp. 372, 373; *Dharma Dagu* v. *Ramkrishna*, I. L. R. 10 Bom. 80.

(*y*) *Sadashiv Moreshwar* v. *Hari Moreshwar*, 11 Bom. H. C. R. 190.

Bengal the adoption of a Sudra, if otherwise eligible, is permissible at any age prior to marriage (*z*), not after it.

In Madras too the adoption of a married boy is illegal (*a*). It is illegal though the adopted is a Śudra (twenty-eight years old) (*b*).

---

4. 10.—Fitness for Adoption—Place in Caste of the Adopted Son.

According to the customary law of the Dekhan exclusion from caste annuls an adoption (*c*). It must *à fortiori* prevent it, as no benefit, or at least not the benefit chiefly regarded, can be had from an outcaste son.

5.—Fitness for Adoption—In Case of Anomalous Adoptions.

In the case of an adoption anomalous, as made by a mother instead of a widow, if such an adoption can be allowed, no variance, so far as is known, arises in the choice of the boy to be adopted. The dvyamushyayana has been considered under the head of "Only son" and of "Relation through the natural father" (*d*). As the connexion of a dvyamushyayana with his own family is not severed there is no fullness of the filial relation between him and his *quasi*-adoptive father; consequently the restrictions arising from ideal physical relations between the adoptive parents and the real ones do not apply to this case. In practice, however, the adoption of a sister's or a daughter's son as a dvyamushyayana is not known to occur. Where the adoption is allowed at all it is allowed in the fullest sense (*e*).

We have above seen one instance (*f*) in which a reminiscence of the ancient institution of the putrika putra seems to have been

---

(*z*) *Ry. Nitradaye* v. *Bholanath Doss*, Beng. S. D. A. R. 1853, p. 553; *Ganga* v. *Lekhraj*, I. L. R. 9 All. 253.

(*a*) *Ry. Sevagamy Nachiar* v. *Heraniah Gurbah*, 1 M. S. D. A. R. 101.

(*b*) *Virakumara Servai* v. *Gopalu Servai*, M. S. D. A. R. 1861, p. 147.

(*c*) Steele, L. C. 185; comp. above, pp. 843, 845.

(*d*) See pp. 808 ss., 913, 926.

(*e*) Above, p. 801.

(*f*) P. 919.

preserved in practice though opposed to the law of to-day (*g*). In such a case should the practice be authorized by caste custom, there can be no room for choice of the son (*h*).

According to usage in Malabar, adoption is necessary among the Chetty caste, to constitute the sons of daughters lawful heirs on failure of sons (*i*).

6.—FITNESS FOR ADOPTION—IN CASE OF *Quasi*-ADOPTIONS.

As to the kritrima form of adoption (*k*). No restriction seems to be placed on the choice of the son (*l*) adopted by a man or a woman. He must expressly consent to the adoption, and he contracts no family relation with the cognates of the adoptive father or mother (*m*). This is adoption with all the original significance taken out of it, as in the last stages of the Roman Law, or rather perhaps an inartistic inclusion within the law of adoption of an aboriginal local custom which could not be moulded exactly to the Brahminical scheme (*n*).

In the natural adoptions in use amongst the tribes in Gujarath (*o*) which from the orthodox Hindu standpoint must be regarded as mere *quasi*-adoptions, no restriction is known to exist on the choice of the boy. Nor is it known that a girl is recognized as a fit subject for adoption (*p*). The son of a near relative, male or female, is

(*g*) Above, pp. 793, 800.

(*h*) The putrika putra who in some lists (Yajnavalkya, Devala) stands second, has no place in Manu's list. This some explain by saying that he stands on exactly the same footing as an aurasa. By a laxity of expression the daughter herself might be called putrika putra, and being appointed by her father might perform his obsequies. Suth in 2 Str. H. L. 199. See above, pp. 793, 800, 801, 806.

(*i*) 1 Mad. S. D. A. R. 157.

(*k*) See above, p. 806.

(*l*) *Ooman Dutt* v. *Kunhia Singh*, 3 C. S. D. A. R. 144, is discredited by the observations in *Srimati Uma Deyi's Case*, L. R. 5 I. A., at pp. 51, 52.

(*m*) 1 Macn. H. L. 75, 76. Hence the adoption of an only son generally disallowed is lawful where the kritima adoption is recognized. *Musst. Tikdey* v. *Lalla Hurylal*, C. W. R. Sp. No., p. 133.

(*n*) See above, pp. 150, 787, 795, note (*d*), and 801.

(*o*) Above, p. 828.

(*p*) A foster-daughter is mentioned above, p. 427 Q. 1; but she is not recognized as a subject of any right of inheritance. The Gujarath castes who admit a foster-son do not allow him to be replaced by a daughter. *Gangabai* v. *Anant*, I. L. R. 13 Bom. 690.

taken as the foster son (palak putra) with such doubtful rights as have already been described.

The adoption of her own brother's daughter by a widow, governed by the Mitakshara, can be regarded only as an adoption in the popular not in the legal sense (*q*).

A man cannot be adopted into a family governed by Alya Santana law (*r*).

"Adoption amongst Kalavantins is to be governed entirely by the custom of the class. The Sastra gives no rules" (*s*). So far as an adoption can be recognized at all it seems to be a matter of the freest choice, as in the following case:—

A dancing woman brought up a son of her servant as her own. On her death his daughter was put into her place to draw the temple allowance. The Sastri declared the foster son heir by caste custom, not his daughter (*t*).

SECTION V.—THE CAPACITY TO GIVE IN ADOPTION AND THE CIRCUMSTANCES UNDER WHICH IT MAY BE EXERCISED.

THE CAPACITY LIMITED TO THE PARENTS.

It is plain that from the religious point of view the gift of a son in adoption ought not to be made without the concurrence of both his natural parents (*v*). Besides his first duty to his father, the son owes ceremonial services to his mother and her father (*w*). Even a step-mother shares the benefit of his sacrifices. In the sphere of positive law the natural connexion between the mother and her son has not been able to contend against the authority of the husband and father. The sources of the Hindu Law give, in some places, a rather uncertain sound, but the general result is

---

(*q*) *Musst. Thakoor Dayhee* v. *Rai Balack Ram*. 10 C. W. R. 3 P. C. See above, p. 834.

(*r*) *Munda Chetty* v. *Timmaju Hensu*, 1 Mad. H. C. R. 381 note.

(*s*) The case was one of a sister's son's son adopted by a Kalavantin. MS. 1651. As to the palak kanya of a dancer, see above, pp. 828, 906.

(*t*) MS. 1707.

(*v*) Above, p. 817. Datt. Mim., sec. IV. 14, 15.

(*w*) The subordinate character of the Sraddhas celebrated for a mother and her ancestors may be seen from the discussion. Datt. Chand. I. 24. See also Datt. Mim. II. 72, note.

that the mother has no real control over a proposed gift by her husband, and can herself act alone in giving away a son during her husband's life only on a real or assumed permission from him. This will be evident from the following examination of the authorities.

It will be seen, too, that the capacity of the widow to give in adoption without an authority from her husband is more generally recognized than her capacity to take in adoption, though even in giving she has not an unlimited right. The principal text is in Vasishtha, but with slight variances it is found in other Smritis.

" The father and mother may give, sell, or abandon their son. But an only son is not to be given or received, as he must continue the line of his ancestors. And a woman shall neither give nor receive a son except with her husband's permission."—Vasishtha XV. 2—5 (*x*).

The Dattaka Mimamsa says: " The capacity to give consists in having a plurality of sons, and the assent of the wife " and so forth (*y*). But the most perfect gift, from the religious point of view, must here have been intended, not one legally sufficient. At another place in the same work (*z*) it is laid down that " the husband singly even, and independent of his wife, is competent to give a son, for in the two passages cited (*a*) the father is mentioned singly and unassociated with the mother." The reason rests in part on a grammatical subtlety which it is hard to appreciate, both father and mother being mentioned apparently without any intention to assign a superiority to either (*b*); but reliance is placed also on the greater part of a father in his son (*c*), and on the generally subordinate place of the wife. Whatever may be thought of the reasoning the conclusion is perfectly clear. The Dattaka Mimamsa, however, allows the gift as it allows the

---

(*x*) Amongst the Saxons the right of a father to sell his children was recognized, and it continued for some time after they had embraced Christianity. —Kemble's Saxons in England, vol. I., p. 190.

The passages in the Smritis coupling gift with sale and limiting both to a time of distress point back to a stage at which the doctrine of adoption had not been developed to anything like the extent which now makes it so important. See above, p. 792; Col. Dig., Book II., Chap. IV., T. 7.

(*y*) Sec. V. 14.

(*z*) Sec. IV. 13.

(*a*) *I.e.*, Manu IX. 168; Yajnavalkya II. 130.

(*b*) Vasishtha *does* subordinate the mother as shown above.

(*c*) Above, p. 800.

acceptance of a son by a wife under a delegation from her husband still living (*d*). When he is dead his authority or assent can no longer be had, and an adoption is impossible, but the widow may give away her son under the authority of the Smriti, which says: "The father or the mother (both) may give" (*e*). While the husband is alive she must not give without his assent; when he is dead she may use her discretion in the exigencies which would warrant a gift by the father.

The Dattaka Chandrika, after quoting Manu and Atri to the effect that a man destitute of male offspring may adopt a son (*f*), cites the familiar text of Vasishtha, "Let not a woman either give or receive a son in adoption unless with the assent of her husband" (*g*). Hence he gathers that with this assent a woman may adopt. The case of adoption by a widow is not specifically dealt with, but a woman may give in adoption "with her husband's sanction if he be alive, or even without it if he be dead, or have emigrated or entered a religious order" (*h*). The author construes the passage of Yajnavalkya in its natural sense as giving authority to father and mother alike (*i*), a construction which obviously involves the competence of a widow to adopt also without special authority for the purpose from her deceased husband.

The Mitakshara limits the mother's authority to give thus (*k*): "He who is given by his mother with her husband's consent, while her husband is absent or after her husband's decease, or who is given by his father, or by both, being of the same class with the person to whom he is given, becomes his given son (dattaka). So Manu declares." Balambhat's commentary adds "incapable" to "absent," and "without his assent" to "decease," conformably to a general tendency to favour females found in this author. If the mother is present her assent is deemed as necessary it would seem as the father's (*l*). Caste custom, however, though it recognizes the mother's assent as desirable, does not regard it as indispensable (*m*).

(*d*) Datt. Mim., sec. I. 16, 17, 18.
(*e*) Datt. Mim., sec. IV. 10, 11, 12.
(*f*) Sec. I. 3.
(*g*) Sec. I. 7.
(*h*) Sec. I. 31.
(*i*) Sec. I. 32.
(*k*) Mit., Chap. I., sec. XI., para. 9.
(*l*) See Colebrooke's Note, *ad loc.*
(*m*) Steele, L. C. 183.

The Vyavahara Mayukha (*n*), referring to Manu, says that where both parents are alive the gift ought to be made by both, if the father be dead by the mother, if the mother be even absent by the father. The ceremonial prescribed in the same work (*o*) presupposes that the giver and receiver are both males. Vasishtha, however, is quoted as authorizing a woman's gift or acceptance of a son with the assent of her husband (*p*), and the necessity of assent being limited by inference to the woman under coverture, it is said that the widow's authority is unrestricted (*q*). The author had the taking of a boy in adoption more immediately in view (*r*), but his argument applies with at least equal force to giving.

The Viramitrodaya (*s*) says the mother may give with her husband's assent, the father on his own authority. It relies, like the other treatises, on Vasishtha, and maintains, contrary to the Dattaka Mimamsa and other works, not only that the assent of a living husband is unnecessary, but that no assent at all is necessary for a widow adopting. As to the giving of a son the Viramitrodaya is not explicit, and the reason given for allowing an adoption without the husband's assent, that otherwise his spiritual interest may suffer, does not apply to the gift of a son. When, however, there is no danger to these the widow's authority to give seems to be placed on the same level as her power to take: it is subject only in case of her dependence to the approval of the near relatives.

Questions relating to the capacity to give in adoption have naturally been far less frequent than those relating to the power to adopt. By a gift in adoption no one in the family of the child given loses anything, while the introduction of a child often takes away a succession or an estate from him who holds or expects it. The following responses show that a gift by the parents is essential to adoption but without drawing any distinction amongst the several cases of gift by the husband, the wife, and the widow.

"A boy cannot be given in adoption by any one except his parents," and this power cannot be relegated to another person (*t*).

"The father or mother should give a boy in adoption" (*v*).

(*n*) Chap. IV., sec. V., para. 1.
(*o*) Para. 8, 37 ss.
(*p*) Para. 16.
(*q*) Para. 18.
(*r*) See para. 36.
(*s*) Transl., p. 115.
(*t*) MS. 1643. *Lakshmibai* v. *Ramchandra*, I. L. R. 22 Bom. 590.
(*v*) MS. 1675.

The decisions of the Courts are to the same effect. No one but the natural father or mother can give in adoption (*w*). The grandfather, for instance (*x*), or the brother, has not the requisite authority (*y*).

An orphan cannot be adopted because there are no parents to make the requisite ceremonial gift (*z*). This principle excludes the svyamdatta or self-given (*a*).

Capacity to Give in Adoption.

A.—Gift by the Father.

A. 1.—Father's Personal Competence.

A leper, according to a Bengal case, can give his son in adoption (*b*) unless perhaps he has the disease in a severe and disabling form. Leprosy, as it disqualifies for the performance of religious acts (*c*), might, on that account, be held amongst the higher castes to prevent the gift by a father afflicted with it. The son in fact takes the place of a father thus disqualified in a Hindu family. In Bombay the gift, if made at all, would probably be made by the wife with the assent of relations (*d*).

A. 2.—Circumstances in which the Gift may be Made.

The Dattaka Mimamsa quotes Manu and Katyayana to prove that a gift of a son may be made only in a season of distress (*e*).

(*w*) *Lakshmappa* v. *Ramava*, 12 Bom. H. C. R., at p. 376, and cases there quoted.

(*x*) *The Collector of Surat* v. *Dhirsingji Vaghbaji*, 10 Bom. H. C. R. 235.

(*y*) *Bashettiappa* v. *Shivalingappa*, 10 Bom. H. C. R., at pp. 271, 272.

(*z*) *Balvantrao* v. *Bayabai*, 6 Bom. H. C. R. 83 O. C. J.; *Bashettiappa* v. *Shivalingappa*, 10 Bom. H. C. R. 268.

(*a*) So *Veerapermal* v. *Narain Pillay*, 2 Mad. H. C. R. 129; and *Muttusawmy Naidu* v. *Lutchmeedevumma*, M. S. D. A. R. Dec. 1852, p. 96.

(*b*) *Anund Mohun* v. *Gobind Chunder*, W. R. 1864, p. 173.

(*c*) See above, pp. 541, 544, 549; Viram. Transl. 256; Vyav. May., Chap. IV., sec. XI., para. 10; Daya Bhaga, Chap. IV., paras. 4, 18; Mit., Chap. II., sec. X., para. 10.

(*d*) See Steele, L. C. 182; Mit., Chap. I., sec. XI., para. 9, note.

(*e*) Sec. I. 7. The original passage of Manu (IX. 168) is quoted. I. L. R. 2 Bom., at p. 380; Katyayana at Col. Dig., Book II., Chap. IV., TT. 6, 7.

In famine a son may be given or even sold, and the stress of necessity justifies a widow in thus parting with her son (*f*). The author gives a strained interpretation to the passage by making it refer to the distress of him who has no son (*g*), but he cannot but accept the natural sense (*h*). The Mitakshara says the condition relates to the giver not to the taker (*i*). The Vyavahara Mayukha (*k*) finds fault with this doctrine of Vijnanesvara and contends that where the gift has not been justified by need, the desired religious state has not been induced by the form of adoption. This seems a rather cavilling objection; it is, at any rate, not one of any practical importance in the law. A gift made by a competent parent is universally admitted to be effectual, whether made under the pressure of want or not. Very few adoptions are made from pauper families, and the gifts or sales made during famine are not usually attended with any ceremonies of adoption.

A Sastri says—"Parents in indigent circumstances may give a son in adoption" (*l*), but no instance occurs of a gift pronounced invalid through want of a poverty qualification.

A. 3.—Qualifications of the Power.

The free consent of the mother is said to be necessary if she is living with her husband (*m*), but "desirable" would be the proper word (*n*) save in a quite exceptional instance. The restrictions arising from the condition of the boy as an only son or an eldest son have been discussed in the previous section. The only substantial qualification of the parents' power arises in the case of a boy sufficiently old to have intelligence and a will of his own. The assent of such a boy (or man) is necessary (*o*). Without

---

(*f*) Sec. IV. 12.

(*g*) Datt. Mim., sec. IV. 21.

(*h*) Datt. Mim., sec. I. 8; sec. IV. 18, 19.

(*i*) Chap. I., sec. XI., para. 10.

(*k*) Chap. IV., sec. V., para. 2. See above, p. 928.

(*l*) MS. 1683, but the condition is a purely moral one, and one that is very lightly regarded.

(*m*) Steele, L. C. 45.

(*n*) Steele, L. C. 183, 385.

(*o*) Steele, L. C. 385.

it the desired adaptation of character (*p*) is not in such a case to be hoped for, and the son is not a mere chattel (*q*). His assent may be safely inferred from his going through the ceremonies.

Relatives should be informed of an intended gift in adoption, but their consent and the consent of the caste are desirable rather than necessary. It is most nearly essential, where, owing to the refusal of near relatives to give a son, it becomes necessary to have recourse to distant connexions or to strangers (*r*).

The Poona castes seem to have thought, when questioned by Mr. Steele, that the consent of the Government was necessary in the case of Sarinjamdars and the like, not only to an adoption, but to the particular choice made in each instance (*s*).

B.—GIFT BY THE MOTHER.

B. 1.—AS A WIFE—BY EXPRESS PERMISSION OF THE HUSBAND.

The Dattaka Kaustubha prohibits the giving equally with the receiving of a son in adoption by a wife without her husband's permission (*t*).

The express permission of her husband is necessary to validate a gift in adoption by a wife of their son, though the Smriti Chandrika is not to be construed as placing adoption and giving in adoption by a wife on the same level (*v*).

B. 1. 2.—WITH IMPLIED ASSENT OF THE HUSBAND.

An express permission does not seem absolutely necessary. The law was stated thus. A wife is not competent to give her son in

---

(*p*) Above, p. 830.

(*q*) See above, pp. 832—833; Vayv. May., Chap. IV., sec. I., para. 11; Chap. IX., para. 2. The limitation of the right of disposal over children to the parents originated no doubt in religious feeling, but it has probably been maintained in a measure at least by a sense of its being a necessary safeguard for the children. Their interests were least likely to be sacrificed by their parents. The removal of the child from the class of mere chattels is important with respect to the illegality of giving in adoption subject to terms injurious to the child as a son in the family of adoption. Such terms the Sastris have in some instances pronounced void, as will be seen in the next section.

(*r*) Steele, L. C. 183.

(*s*) Steele, L. C. 182.

(*t*) Leaf 44, p. 1, l. 6 (Bom. Shaké 1783).

(*v*) *Narayen* v. *Nana*, 7 Bom. H. C. R. 153, 162, 167, 172; *Lakshmappa* v. *Ramava*, 12 Bom. H. C. R., at pp. 386, 397.

adoption against the will of her husband, expressed or implied, or gathered from the circumstances of the case (*w*).

It was held also that where the natural father permitted the adoption of his boy under certain conditions, one of which was imposed in consequence of a mistake as to the necessity of an assent of Government to an adoption, non-fulfilment of the condition rendered the adoption invalid (*x*).

When the father is insane and unable to give his consent, the mother alone can give her son in adoption (*y*).

B. 2.—Gift by the Mother—As a Widow.

Jagannatha says, a gift by the mother alone is void; by the father alone valid, though religiously defective (*z*). After the death of one of the parents he regards the father's power as complete, but the mother's as dependent on authority given by her husband (*a*), which will also validate a gift by a wife (*b*). He is thus less liberal to the widow than the authorities quoted in the beginning of this section. It would seem that the true view is that of a joint interest in the son with a discretional power of acting in the widow after her husband's death, except in cases plainly injurious to his spiritual welfare or opposed to his known wishes.

The Nirnaya Sindhu (*c*), quoting from Vatsa and Vyasa, "The son given by the father or the mother is a given son" (dattrima), maintains that the restrictions on the mother's capacity, either to give or to take, endure only while the father lives. The Smriti is obviously a much more direct authority for freedom in giving than in taking. "The Hindu Law clearly points to the mother as the person who can give in adoption when the natural father is dead" (*d*).

(*w*) *Rangubai* v. *Bhagirthibai*, I. L. R. 2 Bom. 377; *Lakshmappa* v. *Ramava*, 12 Bom. H. C. R., at p. 397.

(*x*) I. L. R. 2 Bom., at p. 383.

(*y*) *Hurosoondree Dossee* v. *Chundermoney Dossey*, Sev. R. 938. See above, sub-sec. A. 1.

(*z*) Col. Dig., Book V., T. 273, 274 Comm.

(*a*) *Ibid.*, T. 275 Comm.

(*b*) *Ibid.*

(*c*) Bom. Edn. Shaké 1784; Parichheda III. fol. 9, 1, ll. 3, 4.

(*d*) *The Collector of Surat* v. *Dhirsingji Vaghbaji*, 10 Bom. H. C. R., at p. 237.

The narrower view of the widow's capacity is illustrated by the following two cases, both in Bengal, where generally the widow's rights are most restricted.

Though the natural father consented to the adoption of his boy, he not having lived to make the gift, the adoption, it was held, could not be made (*e*). A mother indeed, it was said, cannot give her only son in adoption even as a dvyamushyayana without authority previously obtained from her deceased husband (*f*).

In a later Bengal case, however, it was said that the assent of the father to the gift of a son might be presumed where no dissent had been expressed, on the authority of the Datt. Chandrika (*g*), though this did not extend to the taking of a son in adoption (*h*).

The principle of the widow's dependence has been brought to bear in Madras as a means of controlling her right to give in adoption. It was ruled that in the absence of consent from her deceased husband, but with the consent of his father, brother, &c., a mother may give her younger son in adoption (*i*).

In Bombay on the other hand a Sastri said that "when either of the parents has given a son by pouring water on the hands the gift is complete. The parents need not consult their relatives" (*k*). The gift in the particular case, however, had been made by the father, and the Sastri did not probably contemplate the case of a gift by the mother without the consent of the father. Where a father has indicated that he does not wish his son to be given in adoption, his widow has not authority to make the gift. In any case in which he may probably have desired the retention of the son the gift is invalid if made without an express authority from him. Such authority is specially necessary where the gift will leave the deceased father spiritually destitute (*l*).

Even amongst the Lingayats, though they are Sudras (*m*), permission will not be presumed for a widow to give away an only

---

(*e*) *Gourbullab* v. *Jugernatpersaud Mitter*, Macn. Con. H. L. 217.

(*f*) *Debee Dial et al.* v. *Hurhor Singh*, 4 C. S. D. A. R. 320. His being the only son was material.

(*g*) Sec. I., paras. 31, 32.

(*h*) *Tarini Charan* v. *Saroda Sundari Dasi*, 3 B. L. R. 145 A. C. J.; S. C. 11 C. W. R. 468.

(*i*) *Arnachellum Pillay* v. *Jyasamy Pillay*, 1 Mad. S. D. A. R. 154; Col. Dig., Book V., TT. 273—275.

(*k*) MS. 1677.

(*l*) *Somasekhara Raja* v. *Subhadramaji*, I. L. R. 6 Bom. 524.

(*m*) *Gopal* v. *Hanmant*, I. L. R. 3 Bom. 373.

son or an eldest son in adoption (*n*). Where a mother, however, in pursuance of the promise of her deceased husband, allowed her son to be adopted, but did not herself (being ill) attend at the adoption ceremonies to give him in adoption, but commissioned her uncle to give the boy on her behalf, it was held that the adoption was not on that account invalid (*o*).

In one case at Madras it was held that the consent of a brother, as representing his deceased father, to the adoption of his brother, was sufficient. The mother not attending, her consent was presumed (*p*). But this ruling has not been approved. It is inconsistent with several subsequent cases (*q*), and though not entirely unsupported by Hindu authority (*r*) cannot be considered good law.

The concurrence of an eldest son may properly be required to the gift in adoption of a younger son by the widow (*s*). She is legally and religiously dependent on him as head of the family, and this authority may well be recognized where it can be exercised only in restraint of a parting with a brother (*t*).

C.—GIFT BY PERSONS INCOMPETENT.

C. 1.—BY ADOPTIVE PARENTS.

The texts do not warrant a gift by adoptive parents (*v*). The prescribed ceremonies imply a gift by the boy's real father to another taking him as his son (*w*).

(*n*) *Lakshmappa* v. *Ramava*, 12 Bom. H. C. R. 364; *Somasekhara* v. *Subhadramaji*, I. L. R. 6 Bom. 524.

(*o*) *Vijiarangam* v. *Lakshuman*, 8 Bom. H. C. R. O. C. J. 244; see 2 Str. H. L. 94 as to the delegation of ceremonial functions.

(*p*) *Veerapermal Pillay* v. *Narrain Pillay;* 1 Str. R. 91; see Macn. Cons. H. L., p. 220; Steele, L. C. 48, note.

(*q*) See *Bashettiappa's Case*, 10 Bom. H. C. R., at p. 272. Below, sub-sec. C. 3.

(*r*) See above, p. 817.

(*s*) Steele, L. C. 48.

(*t*) "A gift made by a dependent person without the consent of the principal owner (*i.e.* the 'head' or 'lord') is void." Col. Dig., Book V., T. 273 Comm.

(*v*) Above, p. 808; see 2 Str. H. L. 142. The Roman Law specially guarded against an adoptive father giving away his adopted son without good cause, while it allowed the son injured by adoption to claim emancipation on reaching his majority. Inst. Book I., T. XI. § 3, and Ortolan *ad. loc.*

(*w*) See 2 Str. H. L. 218; Datt. Chand. sec. II. 16; Datt. Mim. V. 13; Vyav. May., Chap. IV., sec. V., para. 8.

C. 2.—Persons Commissioned by the Parents.

The parents cannot delegate to any other person the authority to give in adoption after their decease (*x*), nor can they do so during their lifetime (*y*), excepting religious ceremonies to the Brahmans (*z*).

C. 3.—By Grandfather, Brother, &c.

When the father is dead, and the mother living, the grandfather cannot give away a boy in adoption (*a*).

The adoption of a boy, delivered by his brother, but not by either of the parents, and in which the adoptive mother did not obtain her husband's consent, was not upheld by the Court (*b*).

One brother cannot give another in adoption on account of their equality in position (*c*), more especially when the parents are dead; and even though the father had previously consented to such an adoption (*d*).

C. 4.—Self-Gift.

"The only son of one deceased cannot give himself in adoption" (*e*).

"The svyamdatta, or son self-given, is not to be recognized in the Kali yug" (*f*).

The kritrima or karta putra in the Maithila district is an exception. But this mode of adoption, as already noticed, is not allowed elsewhere.

(*x*) *Bashettiappa* v. *Shivalingappa*, 10 Bom. H. C. R. 268.

(*y*) *Amrito Lal Dutt* v. *Surnomoye Dasi*, L. R. 27 I. A. 128; *Lakshmibai* v. *Ramchandra*, I. L. R. 22 Bom. 590.

(*z*) *Ibid.*; *Santap* v. *Rangap*, I. L. R. 18 Mad. 397; *Vedavalli* v. *Mangamma*, I. L. R. 27 Mad. 538, 539.

(*a*) *Collector of Surat* v. *Dhirsungji Waghbaji*, 10 Bom. H. C. R. 235.

(*b*) *Musst. Tara Munee Dibea* v. *Deb Narain et al.*, 3 C. S. D. A. R. 387; Col. Dig., Book V., T. 275. Amongst some tribes in the Panjab a man may give his brother in adoption, but not his only son. Amongst some he may not give his eldest son. In some tribes he may give his only son to a brother or near relative. See Tupper, Panj. Cust. Law, vol. II., p. 155.

(*c*) *Muttusawmy Naidu* v. *Lutchmeedevamma*, M. S. D. A. Dec. 1852, p. 96.

(*d*) *Bashettiappa* v. *Shivlingappa*, 10 Bom. H. C. R. 268.

(*e*) MS. 1746. *Bashettiappa* v. *Shivalingappa*, 10 Bom. H. C. R. 268; *Lakshmappa* v. *Ramava*, 12 Bom. H. C. R., at p. 390.

(*f*) MS. 1755. See above, p. 807.

SECTION VI.—A.—THE ACT OF ADOPTION (g)—ITS CHARACTER AND ESSENTIALS.

Adoption amongst the Aryan Hindus, as it was amongst the Greeks and Romans, is essentially a religious act (h). Its purpose and the ideas connected with it have been discussed in sec. II. It follows almost necessarily from the view of the subject taken by the Brahmans and by those classes who have inherited or adopted Brahminical institutions that the sacrifices and invocations by which a boy is transferred from association with one line of names to another should be deemed indispensable to a true adoption (i). And as the rights of property are under the Brahminical system indissolubly connected with spiritual union (k) the succession to a member's place in the united family, or to the aggregate of rights and duties centred in him alone as the sole representative of a family, or as the source by separation of a new one (l), must needs pass to him who has the sacra. To the begotten son the sacra pass of right and of necessity (m); to the adopted son (n) they can pass only by means of the sacred rites supposed to be efficacious in bringing him under the same tutelary divinities as his adoptive father, and imparting to him the father's ceremonial virtue. Such ceremonies as the *putreshti*, and especially the *datta-homa*, are not therefore to be looked on as mere excrescences (o). In theory at least they are as important as the gift and acceptance, since without them the reception is defective and the spiritual end cannot be attained (p). Men of the mixed and lower castes, as they became imbued with the Brahminical doctrines (q), conceived that

---

(g) This section has once or twice been referred to under the title of the "METHOD OF ADOPTION," but on a review of the materials a more comprehensive title seemed preferable.

(h) Above, pp. 845, 846; Smith's Dict. Ant. Tit. Adoptio. Cic. Pro. Domo Sua, Chap. 13.

(i) See above, p. 832; Datt. Mim., sec. V. 56; Vyav. May., Chap. IV., sec. V., paras. 8, 37, 38.

(k) Manu IX. 126, 141, 142, 169.

(l) Above, p. 73.

(m) Comp. pp. 63, 790, 880, 889, above; Datt. Mim. IV. 27 ss.

(n) *Kali Komul Mozoomdar* v. *Uma Shunkur Moitra*, L. R. 10 I. A. 138; *Rungama* v. *Atchama*, 4 M. I. A. 1; *Gopee Lall* v. *Musst. Sree Chundraolee Buhoojee*, L. R. I. A. Supp. 131.

(o) Datt. Mim. V. 56.

(p) Datt. Mim. IV. 33, 36, 41.

(q) Above, pp. 827, 829.

for them too as for the pure twice-born, there might be a future of beatitude secured by religious services performed in this world by sons duly adopted (*r*), but this adoption, according to the same set of ideas, involved a dedication to the manes of the adoptive family, and the acquisition of spiritual fitness for its sacra. Thus amongst most of the classes aspiring to spiritual and social rank the religious ceremonies have grown to be regarded as at least religiously essential (*s*). It is a mark of inferiority and remoteness from Brahminical connexion that they should be superfluous or simply optional in any caste.

But while this continued extension of the Brahminical ceremonies has been favoured by caste ambition other causes have worked in the contrary direction. The excessive multiplication of ceremonies, natural to the sacerdotal class, made it impossible in many cases through poverty and other causes to fulfil them all (*t*), and as some had to be dispensed with, the idea gained ground that perhaps none were absolutely indispensable. The ancient and probably indigenous system of adoption or fosterage (*v*) required no more than a gift, where a capable giver existed, and a taking by the ceremonial parent (*w*). On this the Brahminical ritual was grafted to a varying extent. It could hardly be said with certainty what rites would by caste custom in any particular instance be deemed indispensable and which only desirable. Ignorance, haste, and other causes led to irregularities in adopting which it was highly desirable not to consider fatal to the affiliation. In some castes the spiritual purpose was disregarded, while the influence of example supported imitative ceremonies as a usual practice (*x*). Except amongst the Brahmanas perhaps nothing is precisely fixed and definite beyond a formal giving and receiving, and by a reflex action the religious ceremonies have become less essential even amongst the Brahmanas than in the earlier time when they were a more peculiar people, more markedly distinct from the other castes. The wish for a temporal heir and for an object of parental affection has grown in importance as the keen appreciation of the spiritual

(*r*) See above, p. 825.

(*s*) The state of things in Gujarath, where Brahminical influence of the Maratha and Benares schools is of quite recent introduction, is an exception that tends to prove the rule.

(*t*) Comp. Steele, L. C. 159.

(*v*) Above, pp. 823, 828; Norton, L. C., vol. I., p. 83.

(*w*) As amongst the Talabda Kolis and others, see above, p. 829.

(*x*) See above, p. 825.

need has declined, so that in Madras at least it has become an established doctrine that mere gift and acceptance will constitute adoption even amongst Brahmanas (*y*). In Bombay no Sastri, so far as can be discovered, has ever lent himself to this laxity of practice. The religious ceremonies are rigorously insisted on, at any rate for Brahmanas, though some indulgences in the actual performance of them have been countenanced. The definition of the essential ceremonies, however, is unsettled; the datta-homa is always prescribed in addition to the formal giving and taking, but beyond this it would be hard to say that any rite has been sufficiently pronounced indispensable. Even in the case of Brahmanas the Courts have shown a disposition to exact as little as possible of mere ritual (*z*), and the customary ceremonies enumerated by Steele (*a*) embrace all probably that would in any case be held essential. In some of the cases (*b*) reference is made to a supposed efficacy of the ceremony for civil, though not for religious, purposes (*c*). Even Sir T. Strange seems to have had a similar idea (*d*). It must be pronounced altogether foreign to the Hindu Law (*e*). It is in virtue of his religious capacity that the adopted takes the place of a born son (*f*).

A. 1.—The Act of Adoption—Its Character and Essentials as to the Gift.

A gift (*g*), which is attended with retention of ownership, even in part by the donor or subject to a condition precedent, is not by the Hindu Law regarded as valid (*h*). The considerations which apply to gifts in general are of more than usual force in the case of

---

(*y*) See also above, p. 825.

(*z*) See above, pp. 825, 826. *Lakshmibai* v. *Ramchandra*, I. L. R. 22 Bom. 590.

(*a*) See below, sub-sec. D. 1.

(*b*) See also above, p. 845.

(*c*) See *V. Singamma* v. *Ramanuja Charlu*, 4 M. H. C. R. 165, and the cases there referred to.

(*d*) 1 Str. H. L. 96.

(*e*) See *Rajendro N. Lahoree* v. *Saroda Soonduree Dabee*, 15 C. W. R. 548; L. R. 3 I. A., at p. 193.

(*f*) See above, p. 790.

(*g*) A gift in case of adoption, not a sale. See above, p. 806.

(*h*) See above, pp. 187, 415.

adoption. It is manifest that the intended purpose of adoption cannot be realized if the natural father's rights in the adopted son are retained. If the status of the son is subject to contingencies his position and that of the family he has joined are painfully uncertain (*i*). The solemn ceremonies prescribed for a complete adoption are intended to effect an immediate and complete transfer of the boy from the spiritual sphere of the natural to that of the adoptive family (*k*). As far as this point there is always a *locus pœnitentiæ*, but when once the gift is consummated no revocation is allowed (*l*); the capacity to give, which belonged to the natural parents, is not so acquired by the adoptive parents (*m*) that they can restore the son they have once taken.

It follows that a mere promise or engagement in *fieri* cannot constitute an adoption. There must be a present unqualified gift and acceptance, just as in the case of marriages, otherwise there is no adoption. The Judicial Committee have insisted on the necessity (*n*) of the actual transfer in several instances. Colebrooke had previously said: " A simple agreement to make an adoption, not carried into effect, will certainly not invalidate a subsequent adoption made with the requisite forms " (*o*), and again, " Be the mode of adoption what it might, this seemed indispensable; that, at whatever time it was contended to have taken place, it should be shown by the claimant, that the operative expressions had been used, indicative of the disposition to give, or to become adopted on one side, and to adopt on the other. The Hindu Law has not prescribed any particular expressions on the occasion; nor does it require that adoption should be by writing. But it has provided, that the intent shall be expressed at the time; and, if the transaction be by writing, its whole genius and course teaches us to look for it there " (*p*).

(*i*) See above, pp. 187, 831. Rights inherent in a status governed by the family law could not, under the Roman system, be affected by a contract. See Dig. Lib. II. Tit. XIV. Fr. 34 (Poth. Pand. § 41).

(*k*) See Datt. Mim. V. 34; Vyav. May., Chap. IV., sec. V., paras. 23, 29, 37, 38; and the formula 2 Str. H. L. 218.

(*l*) Steele, L. C. 184.

(*m*) Above, pp. 808, 821, 832. Under the Roman Law the patria potestas of the adoptive father was subject to severe restrictions if he desired to use it by getting rid of the adopted son. See Inst. Lib. I. Tit. XI. § 3.

(*n*) Above, p. 827.

(*o*) Colebrooke in 2 Str. H. L., p. 115.

(*p*) Colebrooke in 2 Str. H. L., pp. 143, 144.

In *The Collector of Surat* v. *Dhirsingji Vaghbaji* (q) Sir M. Westropp said: "It is clear Hindu Law that to constitute a valid adoption there must be a gift and acceptance," the gift after the father's death being competent only to the mother. It is only by reason of the gift indeed that the filial relation to the natural father is extinguished, or that the right of the son in the estate of the giver ceases. A mere deed or declaration by the alleged adoptive father that he has taken a boy as a foster son (palak putra) does not produce the effect of adoption (r). Hence, when the ceremonies of adoption had been performed, but no actual gift and acceptance of the child had taken place, the Judicial Committee held that the adoption was invalid (s).

The Judicial Committee have recognized the nullity as an adoption of a gift and acceptance still in a measure in *fieri*, though the contract was made by a deed registered and expressed in the present tense (t). It was not necessary for their Lordships positively to decide whether there could be "an adoption simply by deed," because in the particular case there was an intention to complete the adoption by the ordinary ceremonies, but a strong opinion on the subject is intimated. "They desire, however, to say that they are far from wishing to give any countenance to the notion that there can be such a giving and taking as is necessary to satisfy the law, even in a case of Sudras by mere deed without an actual delivery of the child by the father." The delivery accompanied by the requisite declaration of transfer of right makes a perfect gift forthwith. The adopted son must be given, not sold (v), as the Krita adoption is now disallowed. Hence an agreement by which the natural parents stipulated for an annuity to themselves as a consideration for giving their son in adoption was pronounced illegal (w). Similarly, it was held in *Bhaiya Rabidat Singh* v. *Maharani Indar Kunwar* (x) that an adoption otherwise valid was not prejudiced by an agreement

---

(q) 10 Bom. H. C. R. 235, referring to 1 Str. H. L. 95; Manu IX. 168; Mit., Chap. I., sec. XI., para. 1.

(r) *Nilmadhab Das* v. *Biswambhar Das*, 12 C. W. R. P. C. 29; S. C. 3 B. L. R. P. C. 27; S. C. 13 M. I. A. 85.

(s) *Bireswar Mookerji* v. *Ardha Chunder Roy Chowdhry*, L. R. 19 I. A. 101.

(t) *Mahashoya Shosinath Ghose et al.* v. *Srimati Krishna Soondari Dasi*, L. R. 7 I. A. 250.

(v) See further below, sub-sec. A. 6.

(w) *Eshan Kishor Acharjee* v. *Harischandra Chowdhry*, 13 B. L. R. 42 App.

(x) L. R. 16 I. A. 53.

between the adoptive mother and the natural father, that she should retain her husband's estate during her life, and that an agreement of this kind had no effect upon the rights of the son, nor did it render his adoption conditional. Nor will an agreement between two brothers, one of whom had a son, not to adopt "in case of failure of aurasa (self-begotten) male issue, bind the son or prevent that son's adoption from conferring title by inheritance" (*y*).

The gift must be expressly in adoption, as in the case of a wife the gift must be as in marriage. According to the Hindu Law a mere gift in either case without the attendant volition would be the bestowal merely of a slave (*z*). The religious ceremonies are important even where they are not regarded as essential, as in the case of adoption by a widow (*a*) or of a brother's son (*b*) or of a boy of the same gotra as the adoptive father (*c*), if only as marking clearly the specific nature of the gift and acceptance.

The assent of the mother, either natural or adoptive, is not absolutely necessary if her husband assents to the adoption. Without her assent "the mother's claim is not annulled by the donation" (*d*), but this claim is merely a moral one, making it expedient but not necessary to obtain a release from her as from the natural father of the son's filial duty (*e*). For jural purposes a gift by the natural father suffices: and as an adoption is made for the sake of the sonless man his acceptance of a son in adoption suffices without the assent of his wife, as shown in the previous section.

A. 2.—The Act of Adoption—Character and Essentials as to the Acceptance.

"Acceptance in a certain form is the efficient cause of

(*y*) *Sri Raja Rao Venkata Mahapati Surya Rao Bahadur* v. *Sri Raja Gangadhar Rama Rao Bahadur*, L. R. 13 I. A. 97.

(*z*) Col. Dig., Book V., T. 273; above, p. 836.

(*a*) *Lakshmibai* v. *Ramchandra*, I. L. R. 22 Bom. 590; *Chiman Lal* v. *Ramchandra*, I. L. R. 24 Bom. 473.

(*b*) *Valubai* v. *Govind Kassinath*, I. L. R. 24 Bom. 218. *Govindayyar* v. *Dorasami*, I. L. R. 11 Mad. 5; *Ranganayakamma* v. *Alwar Setti*, I. L. R. 17 Mad. 219; *Atma Ram* v. *Madho Rao*, I. L. R. 6 All. 276.

(*c*) *Balgangadhar Tilak* v. *Tai Maharaj*, L. R. 42 I. A. 135; S. C. I. L. R. 39 Bom. 441 P. C.

(*d*) Col. Dig., Book V., T. 273 Comm.; see 2 Str. H. L. 131.

(*e*) Col. Dig., Book V., T. 275 Comm.

filiation" (*f*). Hence there must be evidence of the taking as well as of the giving (*g*).

The free consent of the giving and receiving parents is indispensable (*h*). It is but rarely that a question on this point can arise when the giver and receiver were adult males, but in the case of women, and in that of minors, taking in adoption, should the practice be recognized (*i*) there is obviously room for abuses which ought to be guarded against. Fraud and cajolery practised on a widow, in inducing her to adopt, will be relieved against (*k*), and a Hindu female, acting unguided by disinterested advisers, ought not to be prejudiced by her acquiescence in an adoption or a will (*l*).

The gift and acceptance cannot be replaced by any other intimation of desire or consent. "Education and nurture do not constitute any relation entitling to inheritance" (*m*).

Although amongst Sudras no religious ceremony is necessary except in case of marriage (*n*), yet an adoption, even amongst Sudras, must be completed by corporeal gift and acceptance (*o*). A Sudra took a boy of four years old, intending to adopt him, and thenceforth supported him, but never actually adopted him, and in course of time had three begotten sons. The Pandit said this gave the boy no right as a son to share the estate, only a right to be settled in marriage (*p*).

(*f*) Col. Dig., Book V., T. 275 Comm. The salutation already noticed, p. 949, or the kissing of the boy's forehead, as it is described in Sutherland's translation of the Datt. Chand., sec. II. 7, is a solemn indication of acceptance. See, too, Vyav. May., Chap. IV., sec. V., para. 8.

(*g*) *Laxman bin Santaji* v. *Malu bin Ganu*, S. A. 550 of 1874.

(*h*) Steele, L. C. 385. *Somasekhara Raja* v. *Subhadramaji*, I. L. R. 6 Bom. 524; *Ranganayakamma* v. *Alwar Setti*, I. L. R. 13 Mad. 214.

(*i*) See above, p. 814, note (*w*).

(*k*) *Bayabai* v. *Bala Venkatesh*, 7 Bom. H. C. R. App. I. See *Somasekhara Raja* v. *Subhadramaji*, I. L. R. 6 Bom. 524; *Ranganayakamma* v. *Alwar Setti*, *supra*.

(*l*) *Tayammaul* v. *Sashachalla Naiker*, 10 M. I. A 429.

(*m*) Colebrooke in 2 Str. H. L. 111.

(*n*) *Sreemutty Joymoney Dossee* v. *Sreemutty Sibsoondaree Dossee*, Fult. R. 75, 76; 2 Str. H. L. 89.

(*o*) *Mahashoya Shosinath Ghose* v. *Srimati Krishna Soondari Dasi*, L. R. 7 I. A. 250.

(*p*) 2 Macn. H. L. 198; below, sec. VII.

A. 3.—The Act of Adoption—Assent of the Son.

Manu (*q*) prescribes that the son given shall be not only of the same class but "affectionately disposed." This implies an assent by the boy capable of discrimination (*r*) as a token of the requisite disposition. Accordingly Jagannatha prescribes that "no son must be given away against his will" (*s*).

A. 4.—The Act of Adoption—Contract of Adoption.

An agreement to adopt a child is not rendered void by the death of one of the parties, husband and wife, who executed it. If the husband at his death refers to the agreement, the wife is authorized to adopt the child mentioned in the agreement (*t*).

A mere agreement to adopt, however, is not itself an adoption, and will not invalidate a subsequent adoption made with the requisite forms (*v*). Nor probably would such an agreement be specifically enforced any more than a contract of betrothal (*w*).

Challa Papi Reddi v. *Challa Koti Reddi* (*x*) was a case in which a man A, adopted by his father-in-law according to the Illatam custom noticed elsewhere (*y*), associated another son-in-law B, with himself. This was not a case of adoption, but the son of A

(*q*) IX. 168.

(*r*) See Datt. Mim., sec. IV. 47.

(*s*) Col. Dig., Book V., T. 275 Comm. See above, pp. 832, 833. A child under eight years is considered as (dependent as) one unborn. Thence to sixteen he is called a bala or paganda (adolescent); after that he is of full age. Narada, quoted in Viv. Chint., Transl., p. 35. Hence the Sastris rule in favour of the widow's guardianship of a child under eight, at which age it is superseded by that of the paternal relatives. After eight years of age sufficient intelligence for religious acts is usually attributed to children, and the assent of a child so advanced is requisite to his adoption. It ought in strictness to be proved in contentious cases.

(*t*) *Ry. Sevagamy Nachiar* v. *Heraniah Gurbah*, 1 Mad. Sel. Dec. 101; see also *Bhala Nahana* v. *Parbhu Hari*, I. L. R. 2 Bom. 67, quoted below under sub-sec. A. 7.

(*v*) Colebrooke in 2 Str. H. L. 115, 135.

(*w*) See *Umed Kika* v. *Nagindas Narotamdas*, 7 Bom. H. C. R. 122 O. C. J. *In re Gunput Narain Singh*, I. L. R. 1 Cal. 74; Spec. Relief Act I. of 1877, secs. 12, 21, 22.

(*x*) 7 M. H. C. R. 25.

(*y*) Above, p. 398. For a similar institution, see Index "Gharjawahi," or Steele, L. C. 358.

was held bound by the engagement to B that he should share the estate with A.

A. 5.—The Act of Adoption—Proof of the Transaction.

The fact of an adoption having been made or attempted may be involved in varying degrees of doubt. The principles which govern the reception and appreciation of the evidence adduced in contested cases do not differ from those which operate in other departments of the law; but the special nature of the facts involved has given rise to many decisions which bear on the question of the sufficiency of particular acts and statements to constitute adoption. The same cases might properly be placed in section VIII. on the Litigation connected with Adoption; but it may be convenient to consider them here in close connexion with the legal essentials of gift, acceptance, and assent in the act of adoption (z).

The Courts have varied considerably in their views of the completeness of the proof of an adoption, which may properly be exacted before it is recognized in a contested case. No precise rules can be gathered from the decisions, except these, that the evidence must point to a real adoption, not to some connexion substituted for it, and that the religious ceremonies, even when not absolutely necessary, are in most castes so usual that the non-performance of them detracts much from the proof of a disputed adoption.

A. 5. 1.—Means of Proof.

In no case, it was laid down, should the rights of wives and daughters be transferred to strangers or remote relations, unless the fact of the adoption be proved by evidence free from suspicion of fraud, and so consistent and probable as to give no occasion for doubt of its truth (a).

The Court may exact but slight evidence of the performance of ceremonies on proof of the husband's permission to a widow to

---

(z) It will be seen below that the conduct of those interested has, in several instances, virtually been allowed to replace an act of adoption in constituting the legal relation. Occasionally even where an adoption was *primâ facie* impossible. See p. 969 (c).

(a) *Sootrugun Sutputty* v. *Sabitra Dye*, 2 Knapp, p. 287; S. C. 5 C. W. R. P. C. 109.

adopt. But from the mere observance of ritual forms no inference can be made of the permission (*b*).

For the validity of an adoption it is not sufficient to prove that the adoption was attempted *bonâ fide*, but satisfaction of the requirements of the Hindu Law must be proved (*c*). "Even a brother's son does not become adopted by the mere performance of other sacraments for him without the ceremonies of adoption" (*d*). A person, immediately on the death of his wife from cholera, asked his brother to give him his son in adoption. The brother assented, but urged the necessity of ceremonies, which were reserved for next day. The adopter also died from cholera the same day as the wife, and the ceremonies remained unperformed. The boy went through the funeral ceremonies of the deceased person. These facts were held not to constitute a valid adoption by gift and acceptance (*e*). Performance of funeral rites by an alleged adopted son and acquiescence of the adopter's widow will not sustain the validity of an adoption, unless it clearly appears that the act itself was performed under circumstances rendering adoption legal (*f*).

Long possession under an adoption will avail nothing if the adoption fails (*g*). "A man not regularly adopted, but who has lived as a member of an undivided family for twenty-five years, may be ejected from the joint property by the other members" (*h*).

Still less will mere residence and general recognition avail according to some of the cases. Thus it was held that in the absence of any formal adoption a sister's son residing in his uncle's house from childhood, and recognized and treated as his son, does not acquire the legal status of adopted son (*i*). And similarly that in the absence of any agreement mere residence with the family into which his aunt had married gives no right to any one to a share of the family property (*k*).

(*b*) 1 Hay. 311.

(*c*) *Teelok Chundur Raee* v. *Gyan Chundur Raee*, Beng. S. D. A. R. 1847, p. 554.

(*d*) MS. 585.

(*e*) *Kenchava* v. *Ningapa*, S. A. No. 645 of 1866, 10 Bom. H. C. R. 265.

(*f*) *Tayammaul* v. *Sashachalla Naiker*, 10 M. I. A. 429.

(*g*) *R. Haimun Chull Singh* v. *Koomer Gunsheam Singh*, 2 Knapp. 203; S. C. 5 C. W. R. P. C. 69. See above, p. 829 ss.

(*h*) MS. 123.

(*i*) *Bhagvan Dullabh* v. *Kala Shankar*, I. L. R. 1 Bom. 641.

(*k*) *Y. Venkata Reddi* v. *G. Soobba Reddi*, M. S. D. A. Dec. 1858, p. 204.

A man having bought or otherwise taken a boy and brought him up as a foster-child, bequeathed part of his property to him. The Sastri pronounced him disentitled to any more as against the blood relations in the absence of a formal adoption (*l*).

As to the nature of the evidence required no merely technical rules have been prescribed. Thus an adoption which took place sixty years ago may be proved by oral evidence (*m*). Ocular testimony may indood be dispensed with. The adoption of a son was held proved on strong circumstantial evidence, in the absence of direct proof of the performance of the necessary ceremonies (*n*).

A. 5. 2.—Presumption in Favour of Adoption.

Though a true adoption is impossible without the essential ceremonies (*o*), the Courts have in many instances given effect to adoptions of which the direct proof was insufficient. In some of the cases the proof entirely failed. The conduct of the members of the adoptive family it was thought had in such cases created an estoppel against their denying the adoption, or else there had been so long an acquiescence in the adoptive status that the son could not, without extreme hardship, be deprived of his sonship (*p*). To make them consistent with the general principle such cases ought to be referred, as generally they may be, consistently with the known facts, to a presumption of adoption arising from the circumstances. The position of an adopted son under such circumstances resembles that of an heir in whose favour, after long possession, every reasonable presumption will be made (*q*).

It depends upon the probabilities of each case under what circumstances an adoption may be recognized in the absence of the

---

(*l*) MS. 122. See above, p. 929; and p. 356, Q. 19.

(*m*) *Basappa* v. *Malan Gavda*, S. A. 229 of 1867. It will be seen that no writing is necessary to an adoption, though amongst some classes it is usual. Steele, L. C. 184.

(*n*) *Perkash Chunder Roy* v. *Dhunmonee Dassia*, Beng. S. D. A. R. for 1853, p. 96.

(*o*) *I.e.*, at least the transfer, and in the case of a Brahmana, the homa, according to nearly all opinions

(*p*) See *Bhala Nahana* v. *Parbhu Hari*, I. L. R. 2 Bom. 67.

(*q*) See *Rajendronath Holdar's Case* below, p. 969 (*z*). Where the question is of the due performance of ceremonies, the presumption arises that all was rightly done

original deed (*r*). There need not, however, be a deed: the Sastri says—"If one maintain another for a length of time, professing to have adopted him, and in fact committing all his affairs to his charge, having, upon his beginning to do so, invited and entertained his relations, acquainted the magistrate, and drunk manjanee, he cannot afterwards abandon the young man so adopted in favour of another; nor is the adopted compellable to renounce the connexion so formed. The relation of an adopted needs no writing for its support" (*s*).

A presumption arises that an adoption was duly made from the undisputed performance by the adopted in question of the kriya and paksha ceremonies for the members of the family of adoption (*t*). The decisions agree with this, as in the following instances: in the case of a brother's son recognized for many years and allowed by the family to perform the funeral rites of the deceased a presumption was admitted in favour of the adoption (*v*). So proof of the performance of ceremonies was dispensed with where the adoption was recognized for a series of years and the adoptee had possession of property (*w*), notwithstanding the continued residence of the adoptee with his natural parents (*x*).

A gift by a duly authorized person in adoption is to be presumed from an adoption which has been acquiesced in for thirty-three years (*y*). But a shorter time will suffice. An adopted son, whose adoption by a widow under a power from her husband with publicity and formality, was acted on and recognized for twenty-seven years by the family, died possessed of property. His adoption was held good until it should be rebutted by evidence of the strongest kind, after making due allowance for all imperfections of evidence on the side of the defendant arising from lapse of

---

(*r*) *Roopmonjooree* v. *Ramlall Sircar*, 1 C. W R. 145.

(*s*) 2 Str. H. L., p. 113.

(*t*) Steele, L. C. 184. Kriya = performance, obsequies; Paksha = fortnightly, periodical. See Steele, L. C. 27.

(*v*) *Veerapermal Pillay* v. *Narrain Pillay*, 1 Str. 91; *Behari Lal Mullick* v. *Indramani*, 13 B. L. R. F. B. 401; S. C. 21 C. W. R. 285; *Nittyanand Ghose* v. *Kishen Dyal Ghose*, 7 B. L. R. 1; S. C. 15 C. W. R. 300.

(*w*) *Sabo Bewa* v. *Nahagun Maiti*, 2 B. L. R. App. 51; S. C. 11 C. W. R. 380; *Rajendro Nath Holdar* v. *Jogendro Nath*, 14 M. I. A. 67; S. C. 15 C. W. R. 41 P. C.

(*x*) *Venkangavda* v. *Jakangavda*, Bom. H. C. R. P. J. 1875, p. 49.

(*y*) *Anandrav* v. *Ganesh Yeshwantrav*, S. A. 373 of 1863.

time; for otherwise the adoptee would be deprived of his estate in both families, natural and adoptive (z).

A plaintiff, suing for a declaration that an adoption is invalid, is even bound, it was said, to prove its invalidity (a), where an adoption took place long ago and has been acted on, and the defendants are in possession by virtue of the adoption (b).

The presumption has even been carried within the sphere of the law, where this was opposed to the adoption. Thus the adoption of a sister's son was upheld solely upon its having been recognized for a long time, and the impossibility of cancelling it without seriously affecting the rights of the adoptee (c).

A man having engaged that his daughter-in-law should adopt a person, and the latter having performed the promisor's funeral rites, the Sastri said that though no regular ceremony of adoption had been celebrated, yet the adoption, if the adopted was a sapinda of the deceased, might be considered valid (d). This opinion is not easy to reconcile with others or with the recognized authorities. What the Sastri meant probably was that a formal gift and acceptance might be presumed, and that this in the case of a sapinda would constitute an adoption.

A. 5. 3.—Estoppel.

The doctrine of presumption in favour of adoption (e) has been carried further, or else considerations not strictly applicable perhaps

---

(z) *Rajendro Nath Holdar* v. *Jogendro Nath*, 14 M. I. A. 67; S. C. 15 C. W. R. 41 P. C.; *Sayamalal Dutt* v. *Saudamini Dasi*, 5 B. L. R. 362; *C. Herasutoollah* v. *Brojo Soondur Roy*, 18 C. W. R. 77.

(a) *Brojo Kishoree Dassee* v. *Sreenath Bose*, 9 C. W. R. 463; S. C. 8 C. W. R. 241; *Hur Dyal Nag* v. *Roy Krishto Bhoomick*, 24 C. W. R. 107. See the cases in note (z).

(b) *Gooroo Prosunno Singh* v. *Nil Madhub Singh*, 21 C. W. R. 84.

(c) *Gopalayyan* v. *Raghupatiayyan*, 7 M. H. C. R. 250. The High Court, however, rejected the custom specially found by the District Court, and found "that communion had been created by the course of conduct of the plaintiff and his family." This illustrates note (c) to sub-section A. 5. above, p. 1091. The subsequent behaviour of the parties could not make that an adoption which really was not one. See the case cited below A. 5. 4. As far as the plaintiff was concerned the decision might have been placed on estoppel, but the one actually arrived at could be supported only on an absolute presumption against the rule of law as conceived by the Court.

(d) MS. 1682.

(e) See the cases under A. 5. 4.

to questions of status have been held to prevent the questioning even of an apparently invalid adoption by one who had countenanced it. In the case of an adoptive father, long recognition by one of another as his adopted son was said by the Sastri to make an attempted supersession by another adoption illegal. Colebrooke placed his assent to this on the ground that "the circumstances authorized the presumption" that an adoption had "been actually made" (*f*), but the Sastri considered the father bound as by estoppel.

An admission of the title of an adopted son was held strong evidence to uphold an adoption of a sister's son by a Vaisya (*g*). The admission has been made three times by the undivided brother of the deceased adopter. It was apparently held that the depositions were "decisive of the case" as "an admission of the whole title of the respondent both in fact and in law."

Active participation in the plaintiff's adoption by defendant's brother; acquiescence therein by many subsequent acts on the part of the defendant; letting the adoptive father die in the belief that the adoption was valid; concurrence in the performance of the funeral ceremonies by the plaintiff, were held to estop the defendant from disputing an adoption (*h*). Nor need the case be quite so strong. Though mere presence without raising an objection or protest at the ceremony is not consent (*i*), still presence at and acquiescence in an adoption and association with the adopted son as such in legal proceedings estop a person, it was held, from disputing the adoption (*k*). The Sadar Court of Madras went even so far as to say that the legality of an adoption cannot be challenged by one who has consented to it (*l*).

Where with full knowledge of the invalidity of the plaintiff's father's adoption, as declared by the Court, the defendants had admitted plaintiff to a share in the family estate and executed a

---

(*f*) 2 Str. H. L. 113.

(*g*) *Ramalinga Pillai* v. *Sadasiva Pillai*, 9 M. I. A. 506, 515; S. C. 1 C. W. R. 25 P. C. The effect of this must not be carried too far. It is limited by *Gopee Lall's Case*, below.

(*h*) *Sadashiv Moreshwar* v. *Hari Moreshwar*, 11 Bom. H. C. R. 190.

(*i*) *Vasdeo* v. *Ramchandra*, I. L. R. 22 Bom. 551, F. B.

(*k*) *Chintu* v. *Dhondu*, 11 Bom. H. C. R. 192A.

(*l*) *Pillari Setti Samudrala Nayudu* v. *Rama Lakshmana*, M. S. D. A. R. 1860, p. 91.

document to that effect, this was held binding on the defendants (*m*).

Admissions, however, or acquiescence caused by mistake will not create an estoppel, as when the Judicial Committee say: "It has been argued on the part of the appellant that the defendant in this case is estopped from setting up the true facts of the case, or even asserting the law in her favour, inasmuch as she has represented in former suits and in various ways, by letters and by her actions, that Luchmunjee was the adopted son of Damoodurjee, adopted by Damoodurjee's widow, his mother. But it appears to their Lordships that there is no estoppel in the case. There has been no misrepresentation on the part of Luchmunjee, or the defendant, on any matter of fact. She is alleged to have represented that Luchmunjee was adopted. The plaintiff's case is that Luchmunjee was in fact adopted. So far as the fact is concerned, there is no misrepresentation. It comes to no more than this, that she has arrived at a conclusion that the adoption which is admitted in fact was valid in law, a conclusion which in their Lordships' judgment is erroneous; but that creates no estoppel whatever between the parties" (*n*).

Thus too as to an alleged adoption by a dying man, it was said that acquiescence in the adoption by a widow who afterwards contested it, would not give it validity unless validity arose from the act itself and the circumstances under which it was performed (*o*).

In another case, however, of less authority, widows who after their husband's death had completed the ceremony of adopting a brother begun by him, were not allowed afterwards to question the validity of the adoption (*p*).

A. 5. 4.—Ratification.

A similar principle to that set forth in sub-section 5. 3, must, it seems, be applied to the case of a ratification of adoption by

---

(*m*) *Govind Balkrishna* v. *Mahadev Anant*, Bom. H. C. P. J. 1872, No. 31; P. J. 1873, No. 66.

(*n*) *Gopee Lall* v. *Musst. Sree Chundraolee Buhooeej*, 11 B. L. R. P. C. 391, 395; S. C. 19 C. W. R. 12 C. R.

(*o*) *Tayammaul* v. *Sashachalla Naiker*, 10 M. I. A. 429.

(*p*) Above, pp. 865, 917. The adoption must have been palpably void, unless warranted by a particular custom.

widows or male sapindas (*q*). The adoption must originally have been either valid or invalid, and in the latter case it could not really be ratified as being essentially null (*r*). The assent of the sapindas, when it is necessary at all, is necessary as a condition precedent to the efficacy of the widow's act. If the new status is not acquired the old one continues, with respect not only to the non-assenting sapinda but with respect to others (*s*). In such a case the doctrine of ratification is not properly applicable (*t*).

A. 5. 5.—LIMITATION.

The Limitation Act IX. of 1908, Sch. A, art. 118, prescribes six years after an adoption becomes known to a plaintiff, who may be a female (*v*) as the nearest reversioner (*w*), as the time within which he must sue for a declaration that it was invalid or never took place (*x*). The mere omission, however, by a particular person to sue cannot have the effect of validating a void adoption. The particular suit by the individual is barred, but otherwise the law, it is apprehended, operates as before (*y*.) Similar considerations apply to art. 119, which prescribes for a suit for a declaration of the validity of an adoption "six years from the time when the rights of the adopted son as such are interfered with." The status is not lost by forbearing to sue in a single instance.

(*q*) See *The Collector of Madura* v. *Ramalinga* (*Ramnad Case*), 2 M. H. C. R., at p. 233.

(*r*) Comp. *Rangamma* v. *Atchamma*, 4 M. I. A., at p. 103. *Vasdeo* v. *Ramchandra*, I. L. R. 22 Bom. 551, F. B.

(*s*) *Bawani Sankara Pandit* v. *Ambabay Ammal*, 1 Mad. H. C. R. 363.

(*t*) See *Rangubai* v. *Bhagirthibai*, I. L. R. 2 Bom. 377; *Bateman* v. *Davis*, 3 Madd. 98; 2 W. & T. L. C. 806 (3rd ed.); *Wiles* v. *Gresham*, 2 Drewry 258; S. C. 23 L. J. Ch. 667; Com. Dig. Confirmation (D 1); Shep. Touchst. 117, 311, 313, 314; *Armory* v. *Delamirie*, notes 1 Sm. L. C. 306 (5th ed.). "Ratification" is not a strictly correct term in relation to an act not done on behalf of those whose concurrent assent is needed to give validity to an act by another on her own behalf. Nor can ratification really change a state of facts, or touch the rights of third parties. See Maynz, Dr., Rom. Lib. I. § 34, 85.

(*v*) *Jumoona Dassya Chowdhrani* v. *Ramasoonderai Dasoya Chowdrani*, L. R. 3 I. A. 72.

(*w*) *Ramchandra* v. *Rangrav*, I. L. R. 19 Bom. 614; *Rani Anund* v. *Court of Wards*, L. R. 8 I. A. 22.

(*x*) *Mohesh Narain Moonshi* v. *Taruck Nath Moitra*, L. R. 20 I. A. 30.

(*y*) See below, sec. VIII.

A. 6.—Terms Annexed to Adoption.

It seems for the reasons already set forth that an adoption subject to a condition, whether precedent or a condition subsequent of defeasance, is impossible (*z*): a contract cannot be made that the validity of an adoption, any more than of a marriage, shall be contingent on a certain volition or event. Nor can it be postponed in operation; its effect is immediate or not at all (*a*). These rules spring from the nature of the institution (*b*), which equally prevents other terms being appended, such as liberty to give back the boy adopted or to adopt other sons which would involve the parties most concerned in perilous uncertainties (*c*). The disposal of the adoptive father's estate should, according to the older Hindu Law, be governed by rules as little subject to individual caprice as any within the system, but as separate property and freedom of disposal have grown up, even permitting the adoptive father to

---

(*z*) Above, p. 187. See, too, Di. Lib. 50, Tit. 17, Lex. 77.

(*a*) *Ibid.* The formula of gift imports this. *Balgangadhar Tilak* v. *Tai Maharaj*, L. R. 42 I. A. 135; *Bhaiya Rabidat Singh* v. *Maharani Indar Kunwar*, L. R. 16 I. A. 53.

(*b*) By the Roman Law, until a late period, mancipation was an essential part of adoption, and mancipation was a solemn public act. Like some other important jural acts, it could not be done subject to a condition or to a term postponing its effect to a future day. Such qualifications were abhorrent to the simplicity of primitive ideas, and too great a burden for the memory of the witnesses by whose recollection, in case of future dispute, the transaction would have to be proved. See Goudsm. Pand. p. 155; Maynz, Dr., Rom. III. 86, 87 (3rd ed.); Main, Anc. Law, p. 206 (3rd ed.). As society advanced the magistrate became of more and the witnesses of less importance, but in exercising a kind of voluntary jurisdiction he long preserved the old forms, and he had to guard the interests of the community as these became more clearly conceived. The considerations stated at p. 187 above then rose into manifest importance. Disastrous results must sometimes arise from its being a conditional matter, whether a certain man is, or is not, the husband of a certain woman, or the legal father of a certain other man. So, too, as to the celebration of the sacra by a person of doubtful competence. The family law consists for the most part of defined duties and rights annexed to mutual relations understood as absolute, and fixed once for all by birth, marriage, and other events of an invariable character, whoever may be the subject of them.

Some authentication of adoptions would prevent many lawsuits in India. As to the use of public authentications of transactions under the Roman and the Teutonic systems, see Meyer, Inst. Jud. Tom. I., p. 305 ss. The records of the Courts in England were originally the recollections of official witnesses. See Bigelow, Hist. Proc., pp. 318 ss.

(*c*) Comp. p. 84.

make a disposition by will (*d*), endeavours have been made to retain the spiritual advantages of adoption while avoiding the risks of handing over properties to the adopted sons. An agreement between the adoptive and the natural parent of the adoptee to the effect that the former will remain in possession of the property, or retain a certain portion in a certain eventuality, has been held binding upon the adoptee both by the Bombay (*e*) and Madras High Courts (*f*). The Judicial Committee have, however, held such an agreement to be invalid (*g*), though in an earlier case the question was left undecided (*h*).

By adoption a widow of a Hindu severed from his brethren deprives herself of her interest in the estate (*i*). The adopted son immediately displaces her as heir with a retroactive effect (*k*). In order to prevent this a widow sometimes endeavours to annex terms to the adoption by which she is secured a life interest in the estate and the management of it. Effect has been given to bargains of this kind both in Bombay (*e*) and Madras (*f*); but the Privy Council have held them as invalid (*g*), and they may be regarded probably as opposed to the strict Hindu Law of the Sastras. It has been said that as a father may even sell his son (*l*) much more may he part with him in adoption on such terms as he thinks reasonable. But the sale of a son (*m*) is allowed only as a last resource in a time of distress (*n*). The Krita adoption by purchase is distinctly forbidden (*o*), so that the *à fortiori* argument is met by a prohibition in a nearer case. The adopted son ranks as if born at his adoptive father's death: his mother could not appropriate to herself the estate of her child; nor could she as his guardian legally make a gain for herself at his cost out of a transaction in which she was bound to do the best for her ward.

(*d*) *Raja Venkata Surya Mahipati* v. *Court of Wards*, L. R. 26 I. A. 83.

(*e*) *Raoji Vinayakrav* v. *Laksmibai*, I. L. R. 11 Bom. 381, 398.

(*f*) *Visalakshi* v. *Sivaramisu*, I. L. R. 27 Mad. 577, 585, F. B.

(*g*) *Bhaiya Radibat Singh* v. *Indar Kunwar*, L. R. 16 I. A. 53, 59.

(*h*) *Ramasawmi* v. *Venkataramaiyan*, L. R. 6 I. A. 196.

(*i*) Steele, L. C. 47, 48, 185, 186, 188.

(*k*) 2 Str. H. L. 127; below, sec. VII. *Mondakini* v. *Adinath*, I. L. R. 18 Cal. 69.

(*l*) Col. Dig., Book III., Chap. I., T. 33 Comm.

(*m*) 2 Str. H. L. 224. See above, pp. 806, 808.

(*n*) Yajnavalkya prohibits it wholly. See Col. Dig., Book II., Chap. IV., TT. 7, 16. See below.

(*o*) 2 Str. H. L. 175 (Colebrooke).

The adoption invests the adopted with the estate as a support for the sacra; the widow took it but provisionally in her lower capacity for securing beatitude to her deceased husband (*p*), and this connexion being established by the law of the family is superior to a convention in which the adopted son himself takes no part. Where indeed he is of full age and assents to injurious terms it may be that he is bound to fulfil them, but it is as under a contract which cannot prevent the estate from passing to him the moment he becomes son to the deceased adoptive father. From the Hindu point of view indeed it is questionable whether in consenting to be adopted a man can lawfully accept terms which sever the estate, even temporarily, from the obligatory sacra; but as on acquiring the property he cannot be prohibited from dealing with it, the previous bargaining can hardly in practice be prevented in the case of an adult adopted son (*q*).

Even in the case of adoptions by males terms are sometimes made which alter the rights and obligations properly incident to the position of the adopted son as such. It is not possible perhaps to draw a precise dividing line between the bargains and settlements of this kind allowed and disallowed by the Hindu Law (*r*). The principles already stated apply to them, and all are subject to the control of the Court as representing the Sovereign according to Hindu principles in protecting the weak and helpless (*s*).

In the following case a contract was made which only expressed a right subsisting without it. A watandar's nephew adopted by him agreed to pay his daughter money in lieu of ornaments. On her death a balance remained due. Her daughter was pronounced entitled to claim it as "Saudayak stridhana" of her mother (*t*). The Sastri admits alternatively to the claim arising from family connexion that the son may have passed the agreement in

---

(*p*) See above, pp. 87, 789, 881.

(*q*) Such a case as that of *Tara Munee* v. *Deb Narayan Rai*, 3 B. S. D. A. R. 387, could hardly now be upheld. The declaration of the adopted son that in certain events his adoption should be null could not make it null. As to agnatic rights the case is expressly provided against by the Roman Law, Dig. Lib. 2, Tit. 14, Lex. 34.

(*r*) Under the Roman Law the terms had to be examined and approved by a judicial officer of rank. If prejudiced the adopted son could get himself set free. See Inst. Lib. I. Tit. XI. § 3; Di. Lib. I. Tit. VII. ff. 32, 33.

(*s*) Manu VIII. 27; Viv. Chint., Transl., p. 300; Col. Dig., Book V., T. 450 ss.; 2 Str. H. L. 80.

(*t*) MS. 1566.

consideration of the benefit he received by the adoption, but the case is but a weak one. The Sastris seem generally to have thought that limitations annexed to adoption by which the adopted son would be deprived of the usual advantages of his position could not be enforced. The decisions referred to above, p. 187, are on the whole to the same effect. In a case wherein a Lingayat of full age, about to be adopted by a widow, had agreed that she should retain the management of the estate, the Sastri said that nevertheless the adopted son was entitled to the management, as the widow by adopting had necessarily become dependent (*v*) except as to her stridhana and her right to maintenance (*w*). If the dependence of a widow having a son is regarded as a part of the public law (*x*) creating a relation not variable by the will of the individuals immediately concerned (*y*), this answer is correct, and such no doubt was the view of the Sastri. As a part of the family law resting on sacred texts it may well be supported, and the legal relations of the parties in other respects would, for the most part, be defined by the law (*z*), not left to the exercise of free volition.

In another case a similar agreement had been made with the adopting father and mother. On the death of the father the Sastri said the adopted son succeeded to his estate, but that it would be (morally) wrong for him to break his agreement and disobey his mother, unless she was wasting the property through ill-will towards the son (*a*). The Sastri, as in the case noted above, p. 187, must have thought the condition so repugnant to the status taken by adoption, that effect could not be given to it. In the case of a kritrima adoption, however (*b*), the Judicial Committee appear to have thought that such a condition might be annexed to the adoption, and in *Ramasawmi's Case* (*c*) it was held that an agreement by the real father in derogation of the rights as adopted son of his son whom he was giving in adoption "was not void, but was at the least capable of ratification when the son came of age."

(*v*) See Mit., Chap. II., sec. I., p. 25; Manu V. 147, 148.

(*w*) MS. 1743.

(*x*) See Col. Dig., Book IV., Chap I., T. 4, 5; Book II., Chap. IV., T. 55 Comm. *ad fin;* Book III., Chap. I., T. 52 Comm.; 2 Str. H. L. 96.

(*y*) See *In re Kahandas Narandas*, I. L. R. 5 Bom., at p. 164.

(*z*) See above, p. 349, note (*k*).

(*a*) MS. 1728.

(*b*) *Musst. Imrit Koonwar* v. *Roop Narain*, Pr. Co. 15th March, 1879; 6 Cal. R. 76.

(*c*) Above, p. 187.

But what requires ratification admits of repudiation, so that if ratification was necessary (which is not said) the son could not be prejudiced by such a transaction as the one in question. In *Bhaiya Rabidat Singh* v. *Maharani Indar Kunwar* (*d*) the Privy Council have laid down that an agreement between the adoptive and natural parent to the effect that the former should retain her husband's estate during her life was of no effect, and that the adoption otherwise valid was not rendered conditional in consequence. The Sastris' opinions therefore appear to have been set aside. Though an adopted son may resign his rights (*e*) it does not seem consistent with the older principles of the Hindu Law, as set forth in the Sastras, that a man, still less that a woman, adopting a son should be at liberty at the same time to disinherit him, and so sever the estate from the obligation to perform the sacra and maintain the helpless members of the family. Nor can the real father properly give his son on such terms. A father has not ownership in his son as in a chattel (*f*). This is obviously important with reference to the possibility of accepting conditions injurious to the son, such as might arise through arrangements of the kind recognized in *Vinayak Narayan Jog* v. *Govindrav Chintaman Jog* (*g*), *Chitko Raghunath* v. *Janaki* (*h*), *Radhabai* v. *Ganesh Tatya Gholap* (*i*), *Ravji Vinayakrav* v. *Laksmibai* (*k*), and in *Visalakshi* v. *Sivaramien* (*l*), however defensible in particular cases these may be on other grounds. The Bombay High Court has recently laid down that for such an agreement to be binding upon the adopted son, it must be reasonable (*m*) and not confer upon the widow powers to be exercised for the benefit of persons other than herself.

It would seem from the considerations that have been stated that the Sastris' view of this subject can hardly be contested on the ground which they have chosen. But it is certain that it is not allowed to govern the actual practice of the people; amongst

(*d*) L. R. 16 I. A. 53.

(*e*) See above, pp. 324, 341. *Mahadev Ganu* v. *Rayaji Sidu*, I. L. R. 19 Bom. 239.

(*f*) Vyav. May., Chap. IV., sec. I., paras. 11, 12, and sec. IX., para. 2.

(*g*) 6 Bom. H. C. R. 224.

(*h*) 11 Bom. H. C. R. 199.

(*i*) I. L. R. 3 Bom. 7.

(*k*) I. L. R. 11 Bom. 381, 398.

(*l*) I. L. R. 27 Mad. 577, 585, F. B.

(*m*) *Vyasacharya* v. *Venkubai*, I. L. R. 37 Bom. 251.

whom fair arrangements for the protection of the widow's interest, during her life, are commonly made, and are always supported by the authority of the caste (*n*). This is especially the case when the property was newly acquired by the father: it is generally felt as to such property that his wishes expressed or understood ought to prevail, and that his widow has an interest which ought to be protected (*o*). Sometimes the husband settles terms in an adoption made by himself. Sometimes he annexes to his will or to his permission to adopt specific terms as to the enjoyment of his sole or separate property. In some cases he leaves the whole or part of his property to relatives or to a charity, subject perhaps to a life interest of his widow or some other person. In other cases he gives no direction and dies intestate. Somewhat different questions arise under these different circumstances, and different views have been taken by the authorities.

In the case of an alleged adoption by a male of a nephew on condition or with a reserve to the wife of the adopter of a life enjoyment of the immovable property, and after her death of the self-acquired property to the adopter's daughters, the Judicial Committee said only that it would take very strong evidence to prove such an adoption, and held it had not been proved (*p*).

In *Vinayak* v. *Govindrao* (*q*) a direction was given to adopt a nephew by a will which greatly limited the estate to be taken by him as son. This was upheld on the ground that a sufficient provision was made for the adopted son and that he, after his adoption, had assented to the will and taken the benefit which it secured to him.

In a case, however, in which a will was thought effectual by the Pandits, they added: "If the testator had really given his wife verbal instructions to adopt a son in the event of her not bearing male issue, her compliance with those instructions would of course invalidate the will according to the Hindu Law, it being incompetent for the testator, who authorized the adoption of a son, to alienate the whole of his estate (*r*), and thereby injure the means of the maintenance of his would-be-heir" (*s*).

(*n*) The answers to Questions 3, p. 343, and 10, p. 352, above, were no doubt influenced by a sense of this. (*o*) Comp. above, p. 605, note (*v*).

(*p*) *Imrit Konwar* v. *Roop Narain Singh*, 6 Cal. R. 76, P. C.

(*q*) 6 Bom. H. C. R. 224 A. C. J.

(*r*) See above, pp. 212, 601, 694; Vyav. May., Chap. IX., para. 2.

(*s*) *Nagalutchmee Ummal* v. *Gopoo Nadaraja*, 6 M. I. A. 320. See above, pp. 209, 210, 214, 215.

In the case of an authority to adopt, unaccompanied by limitations of the property, the Judicial Committee said that—"A son adopted under a permission by a widow takes as such by inheritance from his adoptive father, not by devise" (*t*). If he takes without qualification as a son by inheritance it does not seem consistent with that, that he should be subjected to other terms by either adoptive parent than such as could be imposed on a son by birth. This was the view taken by the Sastri in the case referred to at p. 187. He pronounced the adopted son's right unaffected by stipulations imposed on him by the widow in her own interest.

The terms stated in the deed, where there is one, usually embody the notions of the parties as to the legal effect of the adoption (*v*). but this is by no means always the case. In *Chitko* v. *Janaki* (*w*) a widow adopted without, as appears, any direction from her husband. She contracted with the boy's father for his entire exclusion from any proprietary right, and for his heirship to her "subject" to these "conditions" or rather limitations. They could hardly be pronounced reasonable, but on account of the poverty of the boy's family they were upheld by the High Court. If the boy, however, immediately on the change in his status by adoption became heir to his adoptive father taking by inheritance an unqualified estate, the agreement must, it would seem, have been void. The widow's contract with the boy's father to the boy's detriment would no more stand than such bargains of hers with other persons.

When this ruling came under the observation of the Judicial Committee, their Lordships pronounced it a matter not unattended with difficulty (*x*). In the particular case they had at the time to deal with, their Lordships found that the bargain was one that could be and had been ratified by the adoptive son after he became of age.

It was dissented from by the High Court at Madras (*y*). Sir C.

(*t*) *Bhoobun Moyee's Case*, 10 M. I. A., at p. 311.

(*v*) As in the case at Steele, L. C., p. 188.

(*w*) 11 Bom. H. C. R. 199.

(*x*) *Ramasawmi* v. *Venkataramaiyan*, L. R. 6 I. A., at p. 208.

(*y*) In the judgment of the latter a compromise by the widow of claims set up by the members of her husband's family was upheld, though made with a view to adoption, and directly diminishing the estate. It was thought a fair arrangement in itself, and one therefore which was not affected by the subsequent adoption. (See above, p. 349.)

Turner, C.J., there said : " We are of opinion that a child taken in adoption cannot be bound by the assent of his natural father to terms imposed as a condition of the adoption, and that, like other agreements made on behalf of minors for other than necessary purposes, it would lie with the minor, when he came of age, to consent to or repudiate them (z). This we understand to be the effect of the ruling of the Judicial Committee in *Ramasawmi Aiyar* v. *Vencataramaiyan* " (a). In a later decision (b) the Madras High Court followed this view of the law, and laid down that no agreement in respect of curtailing the rights of an adopted son was valid. But in *Visalakshi* v. *Sivaramien* (c) a Full Bench of the same High Court decided that an agreement of this kind was valid provided it was fair and reasonable and " taken as part of the contract for the adoption, was for the minor's benefit, as being a condition on which alone the adoption would be made."

In Special Appeal No. 32 of 1871 (d) of the High Court of Bombay it was thought, however, following *Vinayak* v. *Govindrao* (e), to be at least possible that a widow adopting might reserve to herself a material part of the estate. In *Ravji Vinayakrav* v. *Lakshmibai* (f) the Bombay High Court approved of the view of the law taken in earlier decisions, and held an agreement of this nature to be valid. But in a subsequent decision (g) it qualified its former view of the law by laying down that an agreement to be valid must be reasonable and contain provisions for the benefit of the widow only, and not empower her to benefit others such as her daughter or brother.

The Judicial Committee, however, in *Bhaiya Rabidat Singh* v. *Maharani Indar Kunwar* (h) have held that an agreement between the two parents could not affect the rights of the son, which came into existence only after the adoption, nor could a condition attached to the adoption curtail his rights as the condition on grounds of equity would be void and adoption good.

(z) See *Bamundoss Mookerjea* v. *Musst. Tarinee*, 7 M. I. A. 169; *Nathajee* v. *Hari*, 8 Bom. H. C. R. 67 A. C. J.

(a) L. R. 6 I. A. 196; *Lakshmana Rau* v. *Lakshmi Ammal*, I. L. R. 4 Mad. 160, 163.

(b) *Jagannada* v. *Papamma*, I. L. R. 16 Mad. 400.

(c) I. L. R. 27 Mad. 577, 585, F. B.

(d) Decided 12th June, 1871.

(e) Above, p. 977, note (f).

(f) I. L. R. 11 Bom. 381, 398.

(g) *Vyasacharya* v. *Venkubai*, I. L. R. 37 Bom. 281.

(h) L. R. 16 I. A. 53.

A distinction may no doubt be taken between the widow adopting on a general authority or without authority, and one adopting under terms defined by the deceased husband. At Calcutta the husband's authority to limit at will the estate to be taken by his widow and by the son she was to adopt has been fully recognized (*i*). A power of adoption having been given by will to a wife, coupled with a direction that the widow should, during her life, retain all testator's property, ancestral as well as self-acquired, it was held that the widow after adopting had a life interest with remainder to the adopted son (*k*).

It does not seem possible to reconcile with this last decision the opinion of the Sastris given in the earlier case (*l*). In Bombay and the other provinces subject to the law of the Mitakshara a father's power of devise as against living sons is strictly limited (*m*), and the Sastris' opinion would substantially express the law. If the son adopted by a widow under a general power given by will takes even in Bengal otherwise than by inheritance, there is a difficulty on the decisions in conceiving how he can take at all. He may not have been born in the life of the testator (*n*), he could certainly not be ascertained at the moment of his death. No gift could be made to such a person nor consequently could a bequest (*o*). If, however, the adopted son takes by inheritance even the father's power of devise to his injury is very restricted. In *Baboo Beer Pertab Sahee* v. *Maharajah Rajender Pertab Sahee* (*p*) the Judicial Committee say: " A man

(*i*) The terms must, it seems, have been accepted by the boy's real father; otherwise a contention would have been raised on the ground of concealment of the limitations by the widow.

(*k*) *Bepin Behari Bundopadhya* v. *Brojo Nath Mookhopadhya*, I. L. R. 8 Cal. 357, following *Musst. Bhagbutti Daee* v. *Chowdhry Bholanath*, I. L. R. 2 I. A. 256. The latter was not a case of adoption but of a settlement by a man on his wife with the concurrence of his Kritrima son to whom was given a remainder on the wife's death.

(*l*) In a case where the widow was given " absolute control " and possession during her life, Sir R. Couch, C.J., refrained from saying whether she took more than a power of management for the proposed son in adoption. *Ramguttee Acharjee* v. *Kristo Soonduree Debia*, 20 C. W. R. 472 C. R.

(*m*) See above, pp. 206, 212, 214.

(*n*) Above, p. 1018.

(*o*) See the *Tagore Case*, L. R. S. I. A. 47, 67, 70; *Ramguttee Acharjee* v. *Kristo Soonduree Debia*, 20 C. W. R. 472 C. R.

(*p*) 12 M. I. A., at p. 38. *Hanmantapa* v. *Jivubai*, I. L. R. 24 Bom. 547; *Lakshman Dada Naik* v. *Ramchandra Dada Naik*, L. R. 7 I. A. 131; S. C. I. L. R. 5 Bom. 48.

(with male descendants) may dispose by will of his separate and self-acquired property . . . *if movable*, subject perhaps to the restriction that he cannot wholly disinherit any one of such descendants." The decision in *Rao Balwant Singh* v. *Rani Kishori* (q) gives the father of a family governed by the Mitakshara School full power of disposition over his self-acquired immovable property also. It follows therefore that he could devise his self-acquired immovables as well as movables. Adoption of a boy will not restrict his power in this respect, as there is no implied contract between the adoptive and the natural father that in consideration of the gift of his son, the former will not make a will (r) which would result in a loss to the adoptee.

The husband who authorizes a widow to adopt has not sons as coparceners to interfere with his disposal of his property, and an adoption by him after such a disposal could not affect it (s). But the case just referred to shows that a gift or devise, made after an adoption "could not prevail to any extent against the son" (t), so that if the adoption by the widow is absolutely retroactive a will in her favour being overcome by the son's survivorship cannot secure her against the ordinary risks of adoption. A mritya patra in a form not uncommon may be more effectual by giving her an immediate interest in the property subject to the life-use of the donor (v).

It is obviously somewhat inconsistent with the theory of a complete continuity of ideal existence between the son adopted by a widow and the predeceased adoptive father that the widow should be able to stipulate for terms other than those of the son's taking the whole estate with all its responsibilities (w). This

---

(q) L. R. 25 I. A. 54.

(r) *Raja Venkata Surya Mahipati* v. *Court of Wards*, L. R. 26 I. A. 83.

(s) *Rambhat* v. *Lakshman*, I. L. R. 5 Bom. 631, in which all the authorities have been reviewed.

(t) Jud. Cit., at p. 637, and cases there referred to.

(v) See above, pp. 213, note (n), 216. This form of will avoids the distinction drawn by the High Court of Madras between the gift and the will of an unseparated Hindu, unless the gift itself be deemed incomplete until separate possession of the property is given. See Col. Dig., Book II., Chap. IV., T. 56 Comm.; above, pp. 634, 642, 652, note (w); *Vitla Butten* v. *Yamenamma*, 8 M. H. C. R. 6.

(w) See above, p. 165. It is shown there that a Hindu inheritance is by native lawyers conceived as a *universitas*. The son takes it with all its burdens even though he should resign a part to the adoptive mother.

theory has in many cases been applied so as to annul the intermediate transactions of the widow (*x*), but withal it is not a thorough-going theory as is seen in the case of collateral succession between the decease and the adoption (*y*). The recognition of separate property, however, implies a right to dispose of it by the husband, and wills being allowed, he can give or bequeath to his widow as against an existing son (*z*), much more it may be said as against a son to be adopted (*a*). If dying sonless he makes no will, his widow takes his separate estate by inheritance (*b*), and even with respect to the immovable property, as she cannot be forced to adopt at all, it seems a necessary concession that she should be allowed to impose reasonable terms on an adoption for her own security (*c*). By avoiding any disposition her deceased husband has, under the law of Bombay, made her discretion virtually his own. If he has given particular directions these must probably be regarded as conditions, without compliance with which an adoption cannot be made in so far as they are conditions precedent (*d*), and which otherwise attend the adoption and govern the rights of property arising under it, so far as is consistent with the status induced by the adoption. The terms must, to satisfy in any degree the Hindu Law, be not grossly unfair to an infant adopted, and must be subject to control and revision by the Civil Court.

Though the Hindu Law, in its earlier form, strictly guarding the family estate, imposed rigorous limitations on gifts to females (*e*) it is inconsistent with its later development that they should not be capable of taking as large an estate as a donor is capable of

---

(*x*) Above, pp. 93, 349; *Rajkristo Roy* v. *Kishoree Mohun*, 3 C. W. R. 14; MS. 1716; 2 Str. H. L. 127.

(*y*) See, too, above, pp. 87, 89.

(*z*) Above, pp. 204, 205, 214. *Rao Balwant Singh* v. *Rani Kishori*, L. R. 26 I. A. 54.

(*a*) See above, p. 595. *Raja Venkata Surya Mahipati* v. *Court of Wards*, L. R. 26 I. A. 83.

(*b*) Above, pp. 82, 87, 94; Mit., Chap. II., sec. I., p. 39.

(*c*) Analogy would suggest a possible reserve of one-half as on a partition with her son she would take so much. See above, pp. 710, 714; Steele, L. C., 59. The Sastris' view of the proper extent of the mother's right was the same. See pp. 348, 352.

(*d*) Comp. *Rangubai* v. *Bhagirthibai*, I. L. R. 2 Bom. 377.

(*e*) Above, p. 262.

bestowing (*f*). The Mitakshara's doctrine of the widow's inheritance (*g*) implies that she may take the whole interest of her husband (*h*). The restrictions on her dealing with the immovable property (*i*) show that when they were set forth the law had not yet become fully unfolded. In the present age when individual right has taken a much higher place than formerly, and a man may dispose freely even of self-acquired lands (*k*), it seems to follow that he may bestow them by gift or devise on a wife or widow as well as on any one else. As regards movables no doubt can exist. The cases referred to above, pp. 205, 279, 299, show that an interest much larger than the technical widow's estate (*l*) may be given to a woman (*m*), and it has recently been expressly ruled (*n*) that a man owning separate property may devise it without limitation to his widows. The widows thus dowered might adopt a son, and the question would then arise of whether by doing so they must necessarily defeat their own estate by a retrospective operation of the adoption so as to nullify the will. The husband's gift to them of his separate property could not be defeated by his son, whether born or adopted, unless the son were thus reduced to indigence (*o*), and as in the particular case the wishes of the husband in favour of the widows have been strongly signified, there seems to be no valid reason why they should not be at liberty to make a reasonable reserve for themselves in settling the terms of an adoption. The assumed will of the deceased in favour of adoption may be supposed to have been thus conditioned, and the act of adoption to connect itself by relation with the purpose or permission that gives it effect (*p*).

(*f*) See above, pp. 205, 214, 279.

(*g*) Mit., Chap. II., sec. I., para. 39.

(*h*) Above, pp. 137, 281 ss.

(*i*) Above, p. 285 ss.

(*k*) Above, pp. 706, 739. *Rao Balwant Singh* v. *Rani Kishori*, L. R. 25 I. A. 54.

(*l*) Above, p. 87 ss.

(*m*) See above, p. 710.

(*n*) *Mulchand* v. *Bai Mancha*, Bom. H. C. P. J. 1883, p. 199; S. C. I. L. R. 7 Bom. 491, following *Jeewun Punda* v. *Musst. Sona*, N. W. P. H. C. R. 1869, p. 6. The father could not disinherit his son by will under the Mitakshara law, as in *Prosunno Coomar Ghose* v. *Tarracknath Sirkar*, 10 B. L. R. 267. See above, pp. 204, 205, 214, 347, 551; 2 Str. H. L. 19, 21. *Sri Braja Kishore* v. *Sri Kundana Devi*, L. R. 26 I. A. 66.

(*o*) Above, pp. 205, 212, 706.

(*p*) See Vin. Abrt. Tit. Relation

Where a deed of permission or a will has explicitly set forth the terms on which the deceased wished an adoption to be made, there should, it seems, be still less difficulty in giving effect to such terms wherever they are not wholly unreasonable. In the case of simple inheritance by a widow a transaction by which she defeats the rights of a *quasi*-posthumous son is certainly opposed to jural theory (*q*). Nor could a widow even claim a partition with her son so as to obtain an equal share (*r*). Her power to make stipulations in adopting must apparently be placed on the general subordination of merely pecuniary arrangements to the will of those concerned, on her faculty to adopt or not at pleasure, and on the benefit to be secured both to her husband and to the child of her choice (*s*) by not making the hazards of adoption too great. As it rests thus on considerations outside a strict construction of the law, it is peculiarly a subject for the equitable jurisdiction of the Courts, the exercise of which is most strongly called for where an infant is transferred from his family of birth and deprived of the rights annexed to his position there.

The older authorities, both textbooks and decisions, agree in a great measure with the strictness of the Sastris' view. It is only within a short time that a relaxation is to be noticed conformable to what has long been the usage in Bombay, and now perhaps going beyond it. As usual under such circumstances the decisions have not been quite consistent. In one case no such condition, it was said, as that of an adoption of a boy remaining good so long only as he was obedient to the mother was proved to have been imposed upon an adoptee at adoption, and even if it were, such a condition would be invalid (*t*). In some other cases, however, such a stipulation has been held not invalid, as in the one noted below, notwithstanding the widow's acknowledgment of the adoption and Government's having acted upon it without question (*v*). The Sastri, however, would not allow even the adoptive son by contract to divest himself of his estate. An

(*q*) Unless it can be maintained that in making no disposition the husband has intended her to be unlimited owner even of the immovable property. This is not admitted by the Courts. See the section on Stridhana.

(*r*) See above, pp. 605, 749.

(*s*) An analogy may be found in the marriage settlements arranged for minors by their parents under the English Law.

(*t*) *Ram Surun Doss* v. *Musst. Pran Koer*, N. W. P. R. for 1865, Pt. 1, 293.

(*v*) *Th. Oomrao Singh* v. *Th. Mahtab Koonwar*, 4 N. W. P. R. 103A.

adoptive mother (Koli) made an agreement with her son, whereby he resigned to her the bulk of the family property. This was pronounced by the Sastri illegal, and the adopted son, if capable, still entitled to inherit, subject to the duty of maintaining the mother (*w*).

The early cases are equally restrictive of the widow's right. The adoption, it was ruled, works retrospectively, notwithstanding that the adopting widow had declared in the adoption deed that the estate was to remain with her during her life (*x*). So also an attempt by a widow in adopting to reserve the estate to herself for life by a formal declaration in writing was pronounced of no avail (*y*).

The relative position of the adoptive mother and son are thus defined by Colebrooke: "Presuming the property here spoken of as the woman's to have been what devolved upon her by the death of her husband, and not to have been her proper stridhana, it ceased to be hers at the moment of a valid adoption made by her of a son to her husband and herself; in the same manner as property coming into the hands of a pregnant widow, by the same means, cannot be used by her as her own after the birth of a son. An adopted child is in most respects precisely similar to a posthumous son. From the moment of the adoption taking effect, the child became heir of the widow's husband; and the widow could have no other authority but that of mother and guardian" (*z*). Treating the interval before adoption like a time of gestation, the husband's bequests to his widow might take effect according to principles generally recognized. In the case of an intestacy recourse must be had it seems to popular usage, as a ground for an indulgence to the widow which is foreign to the system of the Sastras.

It was conformable to this, that in the case above where a widow had reserved to herself a portion of property at the adoption, it

---

(*w*) MS. 15.

(*x*) *Musst. Solukhna* v. *Ramdoolal Pande et al.*, 1 C. S. D. A. R., p. 324. In *Radhabai* v. *Damodar Krishnarao*, Bom. H. C. P. J. for 1878, p. 9, a document of somewhat doubtful import was construed as not intended to deprive an adopted son of his ordinary rights, and thus a discussion of *Chitko* v. *Janaki*, 11 Bom. H. C. R. 199, was avoided.

(*y*) *Musst. Sabitra Daee* v. *Suturjhun Sutputtee*, 2 C. S. D. A. R. 21.

(*z*) 2 Str. H. L., p. 127. *Ramakrishna* v. *Tripurabai*, I. L. R. 33 Bom. 88; *Lakshman* v. *Radhabai*, I. L. R. 11 Bom. 690; *Moro* v. *Balaji*, I. L. R. 19 Bom. 809.

was held she could sue in her own name in respect thereof (*a*). In *Srecramabai* v. *Kristamma* (*b*) the Madras High Court has, however, held that an adopted son could not challenge alienation by the adoptive mother made prior to the adoption during her lifetime.

A. 7.—Assent as a Valuable Consideration.

However restricted the capacity may be for varying the rights and duties annexed to the status of an adopted son, yet the boy whom it is proposed to give in adoption, and who has reached years of discretion, may exact terms from his family of birth. His assent to be given in adoption was held to be a good consideration for an agreement on the part of his brother, whose interest was necessarily augmented by the transaction, to give him a building site with a supply of water (*c*).

An engagement to adopt and to settle property on the adopted, in consequence of which parents actually give their son to the keeping of the promisor, is a contract that can be specifically enforced. It stands on a footing similar to that of a promise serving as an inducement to marriage, and the representative of the promisor may be compelled to make good the promised settlement. The estate which had passed to the promisor's widow was held bound by the contract to which she gave full effect by transferring the property thirty years after her husband's death (*d*).

Parents are not, however, allowed to annex to the gift of their son conditions in their own favour, exposing him to the risk of the adoption's being declared void (*e*). The Court refused to give effect to such a contract. Nor are the sapindas, whose assent may be needed, at liberty to sell their assent as if it were a right of property. As to such a (supposed) case the Judicial Committee said—" The rights of an adopted son are not prejudiced by any unauthorized alienation by the widow which precedes the adoption

---

(*a*) *Oomabai* v. *Sakatmal*, S. A. No. 32 of 1871.

(*b*) I. L. R. 26 Mad. 143.

(*c*) S. A. 433 of 1874; *Ramkrishna Moreshwar* v. *Shivram Dinkar*, Bom. H. C. P. J. 1875, p. 169. The elder brother executed a conveyance to the younger.

(*d*) *Bhala Nahana* v. *Parbhu Hari*, I. L. R. 2 Bom. 67.

(*e*) *E. K. Acharjee Chowdhry* v. *Hurischandra Chowdhry*, 13 B. L. R. 42, App. Reference is made to sec. 23 of the Indian Contract Act (IX. of 1872); S. C. 21 C. W. R. 381, 382; see above, p. 806, note (*r*).

which she makes; and though gifts improperly made to procure assent might be powerful evidence to show no adoption needed, they do not in themselves go to the root of the legality of an adoption " (*f*).

B.—The Act of Adoption—The Persons whose Participation is Required.

B. 1.—In Regular Adoptions.

The person who must attend at an adoption are—(1) Parents or survivors thereof on either side of the boy, or their representatives (*g*). (2) The boy to be adopted. (3) The officiating priest or priests in the castes in which sacrifices are thought indispensable.

Persons who may be invited to attend at adoption, but whose non-attendance does not affect validity of adoption, are (1) Near kinsmen (*h*). (2) Neighbouring gentry (*i*). (3) Visitors, standers by, who may become witnesses of adoption (*k*).

B. 1. 1.—The Parents Giving.

" The giver and receiver should both be present at the ceremony of adoption. It should take place at the adopter's house or other place free from impurity. The adopter must personally (not by deputy) take the child " (*l*).

(*f*) *The Collector of Madura* v. *Moottoo Ramalinga Sathupathy*, 12 M. I. A. 397, 443. See above, pp. 881 ss., 897.

(*g*) Sir F. Macn. Cons. H. L., p. 218; 2 Str. H. L., p. 87. Under the Roman Law " Is qui adoptat vindicat apud prætorem filium suum esse," Gaius I. § 134: after an " in jure cessio " by the natural father. The ancient form is given in the Digest (Lib. I. Tit. VII.) the giver saying " Mancipo tibi hunc filium qui meus est," and the receiver " Hunc ego hominem jure quiritium meum esse aio, isque mihi emptus est hoc ære æneaque libra." Poth. Pand. I. § VIII.

As usual in solemn ceremonies the personal presence of the parties was necessary. They had to make the prescribed declaration before a magistrate of high rank, whose authority then attached to the relation contracted in his presence; mere documents were ineffectual. *Ibid.* An irregular adoption could be confirmed after a judicial enquiry and hearing those who opposed it. *Ibid.*, § XV.

(*h*) *Alank Manjari* v. *Fakir Chand*, 5 C. S. D. A. R. 356.

(*i*) *Sootrugun Sutputty* v. *Sabitra Dye*; 2 Knapp, 387; S. C. 5 C. W. R. P. C. 109.

(*k*) *Veerapermal Pillay* v. *Narrain Pillay*, 1 Str. 91.

(*l*) MS. 1675. See above, p. 832.

The presence of the natural or the adoptive mother, it was held, is not necessary if the fathers be present (*m*). In the particular case the parties were Sudras, but the ceremonies imply the presence only of the fathers (when living) as indispensable even amongst the higher castes. In a case where proof of gift was wanting, either by the father or the mother of the boy, it was said that a deed executed only by the adoptive father was insufficient to establish an adoption (*n*).

Similarly in a case before the Judicial Committee it was laid down that the requisite declaration of gift can be made only by the parent (*o*) giving the boy. An instrument signed by the adopter and declaring the boy his representative is ineffectual for this purpose (*p*), and is needless. A Sastri says: "When either of the parents has given a son by pouring water on his hands the gift is complete." (The gift was in the question stated as made by the father) (*q*). "The parents need not consult their relatives" (*r*).

The corporeal gift of the boy to be adopted may be made by deputy as by a wife, or a brother of the real father, or as a deputy of a widow by her uncle when the request and assent have passed between the real and the adoptive parents (*s*).

B. 1. 2.—The Parents Taking.

"It is ordained that the husband and wife, among the Sudras, should be present, and that they should cause a Brahmin to make oblation to fire (*t*).

The wife, as we have seen above, Section III., may act under a delegation from her husband in giving or receiving a son in

---

(*m*) *Alvar Ammaul* v. *Ramasawmy Naiken*, 2 M. S. D. A. R. 67.

(*n*) *Lakshman* v. *Malu bin Ganu*, Bom. H. C. P. J. 1875, p. 186. See above, p. 817.

(*o*) See above, p. 808.

(*p*) *Nilmadhab Das* v. *Bishumbhar Das*, 3 B. L. R. 27 P. C.; S. C. 13 M. I. A. 85.

(*q*) MS. 1677.

(*r*) *Ibid.*

(*s*) *Vijiarangam* v. *Lakshuman*, 8 Bom. H. C. R., at pp. 256-7; *Rangubai* v. *Bhagirthibai*, I. L. R. 2 Bom. 377; *Jamnabai* v. *Raychand*, I. L. R. 7 Bom. 229.

(*t*) 2 Str. H. L., p. 130.

adoption. In such a case the husband's presence is of course dispensed with.

(1) Adoption by a wife of a son in her husband's lifetime; (2) carrying on a suit on his behalf and in his name; (3) non-denial of adoption, were held to be strong circumstantial evidence in favour of adoption with the husband's consent and with due ceremonies performed (*v*).

When one of the adoptive parents has died the other may accept in adoption subject to the conditions already considered. When both are dead, as the acceptance by either parent is impossible, the adoption itself becomes impossible also. The exceptions admitted in a few cases have been considered under Sec. III (*w*). The law was thus laid down by the High Court of Bombay: "There must be not only a giving but an acceptance manifested by some overt act to constitute an adoption according to Hindu Law (*x*). Here there is said to have been a giving, but to whom? to two dead persons, the only two who could have adopted a son to the man" (*y*).

B. 1. 3.—Presence of the Child Given.

The indispensable manual delivery and acceptance of the boy adopted (*z*) implies of necessity his presence at the ceremony. This gives him the opportunity, should he object to the transaction, of expressing his dissent (*a*).

B. 1. 4.—Presence of Relatives.

"The adopter's kinsmen ought to be convened, but their assent is not necessary" (*b*).

(*v*) *Tincowrie Chatterjee* v. *Denonath Banerjee*, W. R. 1864. p. 155.

(*w*) Above, p. 904.

(*x*) 1 Str. H. L. 95; Manu IX. 168.

(*y*) *Per* Westropp, C.J., *Bhagvandas Tejmal* v. *Rajmal*, 10 Bom. H. C. R. 265.

(*z*) Steele, L. C. 184.

(*a*) See above, A. 3.

(*b*) MSS. 1634, 1677. If the doctrine of the *Samskarakaustubha*, as to the widow's independence in adopting be taken as law for the Bombay Presidency, the presence of relatives cannot be necessary, as an intimation of a superfluous assent, see above, pp. 783, 795, 814; *Vasishtha*, XV. 6.

B. 2.—In Cases of Anomalous Adoptions.

In the *quasi*-adoptions in vogue amongst some castes of the Bombay Presidency (*c*) no forms appear to be used beyond those intimating assent on both sides, nor is the presence of relatives thought requisite.

In a kritrima adoption the consent of the party adopted is essential to the validity of it (*d*), and should be expressed simultaneously with the acceptance of the adopter.

In Macnaghten, H. L. vol. II., pp. 196 ss, will be found several cases of kritrima adoptions. Nothing seems essential but the assent of the parties and of the boy's parents if they are alive (*e*).

C.—External Conditions to be Satisfied.

C. 1.—As to Publicity.

To render adoption complete, there must be a public act of giving and receiving, accompanied by a performance of some religious ceremony (*f*).

"It is enjoined that notice of an adoption should be given to the relations within the (the circle of the) Sagotr Sapindas and to the Raja, though no provision appears in case of their disapprobation, even in adoptions by widows" (*g*).

This injunction bears less on the choice amongst different boys in the family than on the necessity or at least the desirableness of the countenance of all members of the family to the celebration of a religious ceremony. To show their assent and presence they ought to sign the deed when there is one (*h*).

"Intimation of an intended adoption should be given to a Mamlutdar or other Government officer of the vicinity, but the want of it does not vitiate an adoption otherwise made with due ceremony" (*i*).

(*c*) Above, p. 829.

(*d*) *Lachman Lall* v. *Mohun Lall*, 16 C. W. R. 179.

(*e*) Suth. Syn. notes xv. xvi.

(*f*) *S. Siddesory Dossee* v. *Doorgachurn Sett*, 1 Bourke, pp. 360, 361.

(*g*) Steele, L. C. 45. The object of the intimation to Government where its interests are concerned may be seen from the cases above, pp. 902—3, and the references at p. 838.

(*h*) *Ibid.* 183.

(*i*) MSS. 1677. 1711; *Vasishtha*, XV. 6.

Publicity is not absolutely essential to validity of adoption, yet it is always sought for on such occasions (*k*).

C. 2.—As to Time.

"A fortunate day ought to be selected for an adoption" (*l*).

"The Sankalpa or declaration of desire to adopt must be made by day. The remaining ceremonies may then take place by night. A formal acceptance is indispensable" (*m*).

C. 3.—As to Place.

It is not a ground for setting aside an adoption that it was celebrated not at the usual place of residence of the parties (*n*), though this is the proper course (*o*).

Sacrifice need not take place in the house of the adopter (*p*), but this is usual (*q*).

D. 1.—Ceremonies and Forms—Constitutive.

D. I. 1.—Amongst Brahmans.

(*a*)—*In adopting Strangers; and generally.*

(*b*).—*In adopting Sagotras.*

(*c*).—*In adopting Adults and Boys already tonsured or initiated.*

(*d*).—*In adopting as a Dvyamushyayana.*

D. I. 1 (*a*).—In Adopting Strangers; and Generally.

The ceremonies used in adoption are either regarded as essential to constitute the relation; as sacrificial; as auspicious; as

(*k*) *R. Vassereddi Ramanandha Baulu* v. *R. V. Jugganadha Baulu*, 1 M. S. D. A. Dec. 1832, p. 520; *Ranee Munmoheenee* v. *Jairnarain Bose*, C. S. D. A. R. 1857, p. 244; *Ranee Kishtomonee Debea* v. *Raja Anundnath Roy*, C. S. D. A. R. 1857, p. 1127.

(*l*) MS. 1677.

(*m*) MS. 1679.

(*n*) *Bhaskar Buchajee* v. *Naroo Ragonath*, Bom. Sel. Rep. 25.

(*o*) Datt. Chand., sec. II. 9.

(*p*) *Th. Oomrao Singh* v. *Th. Mahtab Koonwar*, 4 N. W. P. R., p. 103.

(*q*) Datt. Chand., sec. II. 16; Datt. Mim. V. 15, 21 ss.

authenticative; or as simply indicating joy and generosity. Amongst the Brahmanas, if the Sastris can be taken as faithful expositors of their law, the first two classes blend into one. But the second class is of very variable extent. At pp. 218 ss. of Strange's H. L. vol. II., there is a description of a very elaborate ceremonial, but at p. 87 this is cut down to a few simple particulars, the demand after invitations and notice to the authorities, the gift, the *datta homa*, followed after adoption by the upanayana to be celebrated by the adoptive father (*r*).

Jagannatha (*s*) insists on the datta homa and on the Samskaras (*t*) from tonsure onwards being performed in the adoptive family. The putreshti, he thinks, may be dispensed with, and this is so in Bombay (*v*).

The Vyavahara Mayukha (*w*) prescribes an elaborate ceremonial borrowed from Saunaka, the chief elements of which are those already indicated. That it was not deemed imperative in every particular may be gathered from Steele's Law of Caste, which describes the requisite ceremonies as follows:

"Of the numerous ceremonies enjoined in the Sastras, the following are the most essential:—1. Prutigruhu, the formal giving away of the boy by his parents, and acceptance by the other party, with the form of Julasunkulp, or pouring water on the hands. Presents may or may not be given. 2. Mustukawugrun (*x*), the placing the boy in the adopter's lap, the latter breathing on his head. 3. Hom, fire sacrifice performed by the Poorohit or others. This is said to be unnecessary in adoptions of a brother's or daughter's son, which are performed by Wakyudan, or verbal gift. Soodrus cannot perform any ceremonies requiring muntrus from the Veds (Vedokt-kurum). 4. Deepwarna, the revolution of a lamp, a ceremony at Pooja, or worship of the idol. 5. Brahmun Bhojun, alms of food, &c., to Brahmuns. Such of these ceremonies as require the repetition of muntrus, as the Mustukwugrun, &c., cannot be performed by a female adopter, personally; she must go

(*r*) See above, p. 838.

(*s*) Col. Dig., Book V., T. 275.

(*t*) A list of the Samskaras will be found in Col. Dig., Book V., TT. 133, 134, notes, and in Steele, L. C. 23. As the latter says, they are now much neglected, Steele, L. C. 159.

(*v*) Steele, L. C. 43.

(*w*) Chap. IV., sec. V., para. 8.

(*x*) See above, p. 847. The system of spelling followed by Steele differs from the one now usually followed.

through the essential form of taking the adoptee in her lap, and supply funds for Brahmun agency in other respects. After these ceremonies (Widhan) have been fully performed, an adoption cannot be annulled. Pending their performance, another may be chosen . . . they are not essential where the adoptee is of the same gotr. But in case of discovery that the boy, being of another gotr, was not adopted with those ceremonies, or that he was of another caste, the adoption is null, and the boy is to receive maintenance as a Das or slave " (*y*).

As the Sastris insist frequently on the necessity of the rites prescribed by the Sastra it may be pointed out that these are very simple as compared with the elaborate ritual which has been built up on them in later days. Thus Vasishtha says: " The adopter shall assemble his kinsmen, announce his intention to the ruler, make burnt offerings in the midst of his house, and recite the Vyahritis " (*z*).

As caste or local custom may regulate the forms of marriage (*a*) so it would seem may it regulate the forms of adoption. This being so, the Courts have naturally never insisted on proof of more than the minimum prescribed by the caste law (*b*). What this is has been differently estimated, but that all difficulties are to be got rid of by making mere gift and acceptance sufficient for adoption in all cases is a proposition that cannot be stated with confidence against the numerous opinions of the Sastris of the Bombay Courts (*c*).

Amongst Brahmanas of different gotras there may be a retraction until the datta homa has been celebrated, but not afterwards, and the last rule holds for all cases in which the fire sacrifice takes place (*d*). The homa is thus thought essential to a complete adoption (*e*). The celebration has no constitutive effect at all,

---

(*y*) Steele, L. C. 45, 46.

(*z*) Vasishtha XV. 6. The Vyahritis are mystic syllables pronounced in offering the fire oblations. See Bühler *ad loc.* The ritual described by Baudhayana is more elaborate. See Baudh. Parisishta, Pr. VII. Ad. 5; Datt. Mim., sec. V. 42; Datt. Chand., sec. II. 16.

(*a*) *Gatha Ram Mistree* v. *Moohita Kochin et al.*, 14 B. L. R. 298: *Rajkumar Nobodip Chundro Deb Burmun* v. *Rajah Bir Chundra Manikya Bahadoor*, 25 C. W. R. 404, 414. See above, p. 840.

(*b*) See above, pp. 824, 825.

(*c*) See above, pp. 825, 827.

(*d*) Steele, L. C. 184.

(*e*) Above, p. 835.

until, in its essential parts, it is completed, and a person is at liberty to change his mind and put aside a boy before full performance of the ceremony (*f*). This rule is subject to the qualification that in case of adoption of a brother's son (*g*) or of a boy of the same gotra (*h*) the performance of the ceremony of the datta homam is not essential for the validity of the adoption.

Jala Sunkalp, or the pouring of water on the hands, is deemed an essential part of the ceremony of giving a son (*i*).

In all the castes in which the Sastra ceremonies are observed at all the placing of the boy in the lap of the adopting parent is considered indispensable (*k*).

Steele says (*l*): "The Putreshta ceremony and the distinction of nitya and anitya adoptions are not recognized in Poona" (*m*).

The rule formerly announced by the Sadar Court of Bengal was that affiliation, established by sacrifice, is absolutely essential (*n*), and with this the opinions of the Bombay Sastris agree, at least as to the Brahmana caste. The following are instances:

"The only adoption to be recognized in the Kali Yug, is the 'Datt Vidhan,' with assent of parents and due ceremonies" (*o*).

"No adoption is valid unless made with the prescribed ceremonies. Mere declarations by the adoptive father will not constitute an adoption valid. Nor will the performance of funeral ceremonies for the adoptive father by the adopted son" (*p*).

"Sacrifices are to be made according to the Sastras" (*q*). "Adoption is a religious act. It requires a formal declaration of desire to take a son (Sankalp); a formal gift (Dan); and a ceremonious acceptance (pratigraha). There is an abbreviated form called Gampaksha for one *in extremis*. But in no case can the ceremonies be altogether dispensed with, even though the adopted be of the adopter's family. The contrary view of the

---

(*f*) *Daee* v. *Motee*, 1 Borr. R. 75.
(*g*) *Valubai* v. *Govind Kashinath*, I. L. R. 24 Bom. 218.
(*h*) *Tilak* v. *Tai Maharaj*, I. L. R. 39 Bom. 441, P. C.
(*i*) Steele, L. C. 42.
(*k*) Steele, L. C. 184.
(*l*) Steele, L. C. 48.
(*m*) See below, E. 1.
(*n*) *Alank Manjari* v. *Fakir Chand*, 5 C. S. D. A. R. 356.
(*o*) MS. 1755.
(*p*) MS. 1683.
(*q*) MS. 1675.

Dattaka Darpana is rejected" (r). "A person *in extremis*," another Sastri says, "may shorten the ceremony but cannot omit it (s), though the Dattaka Darpana says he may in adopting a relative" (t).

Steele speaks of adoption as "sometimes made by nuncupative will at the point of death" in the Southern Maratha Country (v). But by this he evidently means merely an adoption *in extremis* with ceremonies abridged to suit the exigency (w).

"No adoption," a Sastri again declares, "is valid without the prescribed ceremonies. The dispensation from ceremonies in the Samskar Ganpatti, supposing the passage genuine, extends only to daughters' and brothers' sons" (x), and another insists that, "Whatever is done contrary to the rules of the Sastras must be considered as null and void" (y). But the objections in the case went to the eligibility of the adopted and the adopting widow's capacity.

The age of the parties has not been thought to make any difference. An adoption of a married man was said to require for its validity the performance of the due ceremonies (z).

A man *in extremis* adopted a son without ceremonies. The adopted performed his funeral ceremonies. The Sastri said, this, according to the Mayukha, constituted the son only a priti-putra, not an heir (a).

(r) MS. 1714.

(s) MS. 1674.

(t) MS. 1675.

(v) Steele, L. C. 185.

(w) The reader will be reminded of the adoption by testament of Octavius by Cæsar, which, however, was, except in form, only the nomination of an heir, and had to be ratified by a vote of the people. This was not really an adoption; it was merely a mode of designating a successor, and preserving one's name which became common. (Maynz, Dr. R. § 328.) In a true adoption under the Hindu Law the adopted, except a dvyamushyayana, takes a new name and a patronymic from his adoptive father (see *Gangava* v. *Rangangavda*, Bom. H. C. P. J. 1881, p. 248), the palak-putra does not, nor does the kritrima son. An adoption by will is not allowed, only a permission to adopt, see above, sub-sec. III. B. 3.

(x) MS. 1686.

(y) MS. 1672.

(z) MS. 1643. This is the strongest mark of abandonment of right, and is properly used in such a solemn transaction as a gift or sale of land. See Mit., Chap. I., sec. I., para. 32; 2 Str. H. L. 426.

(a) MS. 1680. *Sayammaul v. Sashachaka Naiker*, 10 M. I. A. 429.

In the case of a son adopted without any rites by a man since deceased, the Sastri, not allowing that he was already sufficiently adopted, insisted on the elder widow's competence to adopt him as the person indicated by her husband, notwithstanding the opposition of the junior widow (*b*).

The required ceremonies need not be performed by the person adopting. They can be completed after his death so as to constitute a valid adoption (*c*). The Sastri answered that "a ceremony begun by a dying person, who does not live to complete it, may be completed by his widow" (*d*). She may, however, begin *de novo*, if she likes.

Jagannatha discusses at some length (*e*) the question of whether besides a gift the prescribed religious ceremonies and samskaras performed in the adoptive family are essential to adoption. His conclusion is that "should the oblation to fire be partly omitted through inability to complete it, the adoption is sometimes good." As to the samskaras he accepts the passage of the Kalika Purana which Nilkantha questions (*f*), and derives from it the rule that tonsure and the subsequent samskaras are at least requisite to the completion of sonship (*g*). Hence there can be no adoption of a boy whose tonsure has been performed (*h*). As there is no ceremonial tonsure as a samskara in the lower castes (*i*) the obstacle it would create does not exist amongst them (*k*), nor has any rite to be performed in order to complete an adoption beyond a gift and acceptance distinctly for that purpose.

Colebrooke too says—"Adopted sons being duly initiated by the adopter under his own family name become the sons of the adoptive parent. The upanayana (thread ceremony) . . . must be performed in the name of the adopter's gotra" (*l*).

(*b*) MS. 1649.

(*c*) *Lakshmibai* v. *Ramchandra*, I. L. R. 22 Bom. 590; *Vedavelli* v. *Mangamma*, I. L. R. 27 Mad. 538, 539.

(*d*) MS. 1661. *Subbarayar* v. *Subbammal*, I. L. R. 21 Mad. 497.

(*e*) Col. Dig., Book V., T. 273 ss.

(*f*) Vyav. May., Chap. IV., sec. V., para. 20.

(*g*) Col. Dig., Book V., T. 183 Comm.

(*h*) Col. Dig., Book V., T. 273 Comm. See 2 Str. H. L. 109.

(*i*) Col. Dig., Book V., T. 134, note. There is in most a tonsure, but without the sacramental significance.

(*k*) Col. Dig., Book V., T. 275 Comm. *sub fin.*

(*l*) Col. in 2 Str. H. L. 111. See above, p. 838.

The performance of the sacred ceremonies is not competent to a woman or a man of low caste, since the utterance of the Vedic formulas is forbidden to them (*m*). The difficulty is removed by a vicarious performance of these rites. "Like the consecration and dismissal of a bull, the adoption of a son may be completed by an oblation to fire performed through the intervention of a Brahmana" (*n*). The Brahmana incurs guilt, but the spiritual purpose is none the less achieved (*o*).

In Madras the mere gift and acceptance as in adoption constitute adoption even amongst Brahmanas (*p*). Proof of the datta homam is not necessary there. The Madras High Court quoted with approval Sir T. Strange's statement:

"There must be gift and acceptance manifested by some overt act. Beyond this, legally speaking, it does not appear that anything is absolutely necessary, for as to notice to the Rajah and invitation to kinsmen, they are agreed not to be so, being merely intended to give greater notoriety to the thing, so as to obviate doubt regarding the right of succession, and even with regard to the sacrifice of fire, important as it may be deemed, in a spiritual point of view, it is so with regard to the Brahmin only; according to a constant distinction in the texts and glosses, upon matters of ritual observance, between those who keep consecrated and holy fire, and those who do not keep such fires, *i.e.*, between Brahmins and the other classes, it being by the former only that

---

(*m*) Vyav. May., Chap. IV., sec. V., paras. 12—15.

(*n*) Col. Dig., Book V., T. 275 Comm.

(*o*) Vyav. May., Chap. IV., sec. V., para. 14; 2 Str. H. L. 89.

(*p*) *V. Singamma* v. *Ramanuja Charlu*, 4 M. H. C. R. 165. On this doctrine the Judicial Committee has observed : "Then it has been more recently decided in the Madras High Court that even in the case of an adoption by a Brahmini woman the ceremony is not necessary. Their Lordships intend to follow the example of the High Court in this case in not considering to what extent the Madras decision is correct, and how far the ceremonies may be omitted in the case of adoption by a Brahmini woman. They may, however, observe that the reasoning of the Madras Court applies even *à fortiori* to Sudras. The other Indian decisions which have been cited, and particularly those of the late Suddur Dewanny Adawlut, clearly show that the present question has long been treated as an open and vexed one by Pandits as well as Judges. It was so treated in a case before their Lordships in 1872, *Sree Narain Mitter* v. *Sreemutty Kishen Soondory Dassee*, L. R. I. A. Supp. 149, but was not then decided, the suit being dismissed upon another ground." *Indromoni Chowdhrain* v. *Behari Lal Mullick*, L. R. 7 I. A. 36. *Subbarayar* v. *Subbammal*, I. L. R. 21 Mad. 497; *Vedavelli* v. *Mangamma*, I. L. R. 27 Mad. 538.

the datta homam with holy texts from the Veda can properly be performed, as was held in the case of the Rajah of Nobkissen by the Supreme Court at Bengal. . . ." (q).

Even in Bombay and amongst the classes who imitate the Brahmanas in their ceremonies proof of the homa has not in all cases been thought essential (r) by the Courts.

In one case it seems to have been held that the religious ceremonies might be dispensed with even in the case of Brahmanas (s), while in *Tilak* v. *Tai Maharaj* it has been held that (t) no datta homam is necessary in case of adoption of a son of the same gotra. So in *Valubai* v. *Govind Kashinath* (v) the adoption of a brother's son without the homam was held valid.

In one instance a Sastri pronounced an adoption without sacrifice valid for a Brahmana. An adoption publicly made by a Brahmana without the homa was, he said, valid on the authority of the Logakshi Bhaskar (w.)

D. 1. 1.—Ceremonies and Forms.

(b). In Adopting Sagotras.

The homa sacrifice or burnt offering deemed religiously indispensable in other cases is by custom pronounced unnecessary in the adoption of a brother's or daughter's son (or a younger brother) (x). In these cases the mere verbal gift and acceptance are said to suffice (y). As a daughter's son can be adopted only by a Sudra, and no Sudra can pronounce a mantra from the Veda (z), the homa must in strictness be dispensed with in his case, though a vicarious offering and recitation by a Brahmana may according to the Vyav. May. Chap. IV. sec. V. para. 13, and

---

(q) *V. Singamma et al.* v. *Ramanuja Charlu*, 4 Mad. H. C. R. 167.

(r) *Crastnarao* v. *Raghunath*, Perry, O. C. 150; *Lakshmibai* v. *Ramchandra*, I. L. R. 22 Bom. 890.

(s) *Jagannatha* v. *Radhabai*, S. A. 165 of 1865.

(t) I. L. R. 39 Bom. 441, P. C.

(v) I. L. R. 24 Bom. 218.

(w) MS. 1688. See above, p. 825. The authority is not generally admitted.

(x) Steele, L. C. 46; Comp. Col. Dig., Book V., T. 275 Comm. *Valubai* v. *Govind Kashinath*, I. L. R. 24 Bom. 218.

(y) See above, p. 832.

(z) Datt. Mim., sec. I. 26.

by custom answer the purpose (*a*). In the case of a brother's son there is no need for a discharge from the gotra of birth and an admission to that of adoption, as both are the same, so that the main purpose of the fire sacrifice not existing, the sacrifice itself becomes needless (*b*).

The adoption of a nephew by word of mouth without burnt sacrifice is valid (*c*). The Sastri, however, said in another case: "The prescribed forms cannot be dispensed with even in the case of the adoption of a member of the adopter's family" (*d*). But again, as in the following case, the ceremonies may be excused: "An uncle must perform the ceremony even to adopt his nephew. But if he has accepted a gift of the nephew and performed his munj the boy is thus affiliated without the (regular) ceremonies" (*e*).

In Bengal the adoption of a kinsman may be made by verbal declaration, in presence of witnesses, but without any religious ceremony (*f*).

D. 1. 1.—Ceremonies and Forms—Constitutive.

(*c*). In Adopting after Tonsure.

It has been seen (*g*) that in the case of an adult the gift by his parents is as indispensable as in the case of a child (*h*). The formal acceptance is equally indispensable, though the placing of an adult son in the lap of the acceptor (*i*) may not be regarded as essential. Where burnt offerings are requisite they are not less, but if possible more, necessary in the case of one who, by

---

(*a*) Comp. Datt. Mim., sec. I. 27. *Valubai* v. *Govind Kashinath*, *supra*.

(*b*) 2 Str. H. L. 89, 104, 107, 123, 220.

(*c*) *Huebatrao Mankur* v. *Govindrao Mankur*, 2 Borr. 83, 95. Yama says: "It is not expressly required that burnt sacrifice and other ceremonies should be performed on adopting the son of a daughter or of a brother, for it is accomplished in those cases by word of mouth alone." (Wak Danu, a verbal gift.)

(*d*) MS. 1673. The Sastri is supported by this, that the Smritis which contemplate adoption from within the gotra still prescribe the homa sacrifice. See *ex. gr.* Vasishtha XV.

(*e*) MS. 1690.

(*f*) *Kullean Singh* v. *Kripa Singh*, 1 C. S. D. A. R. 9.

(*g*) See p. 832.

(*h*) See pp. 817, 832.

(*i*) Steele, L. C. 184.

the successive samskars has become more firmly knitted to his family of birth and its sacra (*l*). If adoption is at all regarded by a caste as involving a change of religious dedication it is not easy to conceive how it can take place when the samskaras have been completed even in the case of a man of one of the lower castes (*m*); but where the adoption is within the same gotra or *quasi*-gotra, no change of invocation is required, and the formal transfer should suffice.

In the case of untonsured children (*n*) mere irregularities in forms used in adopting are said to be cured by means of the performance of the sacrifices and samskaras by the adoptive father (*p*). The following is an instance:

"When a man has received a son in adoption, whether regularly or not, and has performed sacrifices for him as included in the adoptive father's gotra, he must be recognized as an adopted son. The adoption is not affected by the natural father's subsequently performing the boy's munj" (*q*).

Sacrifice to fire will undo the effects of tonsure in the natural family (*r*).

D. 1. 1.—Ceremonies and Forms—Constitutive.

(*d*). In the Case of a Dvyamushyayana.

The ceremonial in the adoption of a son as a dvyamushyayana does not differ from that of the ordinary adoption except by the variance in the formula of gift. "He shall belong to us both" (*s*).

(*l*) See above, p. 809.

(*m*) *I.e.* not twice-born. See above, p. 825, note (*i*).

(*n*) See Datt. Mim., sec. IV. 33.

(*p*) See Datt. Mim., sec. IV. 69.

(*q*) MS. 1677. See Col. Dig., Book V., T. 183 Comm.; Datt. Mim., sec. IV., 33 ss.

(*r*) *Sy Joymony Dossee* v. *Sy Sybosoondry Dossee*, 1 Fult. 75. See Datt. Mim., sec. IV. 51, 52. The author insists on a restriction to five years of age—not observed in Bombay—in order that the boy's investiture may take place in the adoptive family. The Datt. Chand. extends the age to eight years, sec. II. 23, 27, 30. This authority also insists on investiture not having taken place as a condition of fitness not apparently to be replaced by any ceremonies. In the case of a Sudra marriage there is the same obstacle as investiture in the case of a twice-born. (*Ibid.*, para. 32.)

(*s*) Vyav. May., Chap. IV., sec. V., para. 21.

D. 1.—Ceremonies and Forms—Constitutive.

D. 1. 2.—Amongst the Lower Castes.

The sacrifice of fire is important with regard to Brahmanas only (*t*).

" It is held that, if a lad be adopted into a family, even where it is not the custom to perform homam (sacrifice of adoption), he cannot be turned out of it at will " (*v*).

" It has been held that, in the case of Sudras, no ceremonies, except the giving and taking of the child, are necessary to an adoption." " The giving and taking in such an adoption ought to take place by the father handing over the child to the adoptive mother, the latter intimating her acceptance of the child in adoption " (*w*).

" As the Sastras do not recognize Kshatriyas as existing in the Kali age, those who call themselves so should follow the ceremonies prescribed for Sudras " (*x*).

(*t*) *Nobkissen Raja's Case*, 1 Str. H. L. 96; *Th. Oomrao Singh* v. *Th. Mahtab Koonwar*, 4 N. W. P. R. 103. The needlessness of the datta-homam ceremony amongst Sudras is placed by Ellis on the ground of their having no gotra (in the stricter sense). See above, pp. 831, 836. The transfer from the care of one to another set of tutelary deities being impossible, the rite by which it is consummated is superfluous. See above, pp. 823—829. It is plain that the central idea of adoption according to the Brahmanical conception must be entirely wanting in the case of Sudras. The indigenous natural adoption of the latter has been wrought into a kind of harmony with the former only by the accommodations shown in the preceding pages. Sraddhas are now looked on as appropriate to nearly all castes. See above, p. 825.

(*v*) 2 Str. H. L. 126. The following case rules only that no other ceremonies are necessary in Bengal : " It is admitted that whatever may be the force of the words ' so forth ' in the case of Brahmins, or members of the other superior classes, the only religious ceremony that is essential to an adoption by a Sudra is the *datta homam*, or burnt sacrifice, which it is said he, though as incompetent to perform that for himself as he is to repeat the prescribed texts of the Vedas, may perform by the intervention of a Brahmin priest." *Indromoni Chowdhrain* v. *Behari Lall Mullick*, L. R. 7 I. A. 35.

(*w*) *Shoshinath Ghose et al.* v. *Krishna Sunderi Dasi*, I. L. R. 6 Cal. P. C. 381.

(*x*) MS. 1675. . . . " The word Dvijate (twice-born) which in former ages included Brahmins, Kshatriyas, and Vaisyas, in the present is generally understood to be confined to Brahmins, these only performing the upanayanum, or ceremony of tying on the sacrificial cord; whence the second birth, with the texts of the Veda." 2 Str. H. L. 149; *ibid.* 263. Pure Kshatriyas and Vaisyas are not now recognized, Steele, L. C. 89, 90. In 2 Str. H. L. 263, Ellis gives an instance of a considerable conversion of Lingayats who thereon assumed the sacred thread as Vaisyas. Such cases are not very uncommon, and they justify the distrust with which the Brahmanas look on pretensions to the twice-born caste rank.

"An oral adoption is effected by the ceremony of giving and accepting" (*y*).

An overt act of adoption is sufficient to prove an adoption, unaccompanied by religious ceremonies. But evidence of the giving and receiving is indispensable, and is easily procured where there has really been an adoption in a family of any local consequence (*z*).

"The Sastras give no rules of adoption applicable to Lingayats. If the caste rules prescribe any particular ceremonies, these should be observed" (*a*).

But even of a Simpi it was said: "No one (not even a brother's grandson) can be adopted without the ceremony of homa or burnt offering" (*b*). The Sastri must, in this case, be considered to have stated the law too stringently.

A dying widow put sugar in the mouth of a child of one of her relatives and called him her son. The Sastri said there was nothing in the Sastras to give validity to this as an adoption (*c*).

"The Sudras cannot recite the Vedic texts, but they can adopt, confining themselves to the ceremonies proper to their caste" (*d*).

In a Sudra adoption the ceremony of "pootreshto jog" is not essential, yet it is conformable to law and religion; and if performed, is the best proof of real intention of adoption (*e*). It has been pronounced essential when the adoption is in the dattaka form (*f*). But it is not necessary in Bombay (*g*).

Among the Sikhs proof of datta homam does not seem to be essential (*h*).

Whether in Bengal religious ceremonies are generally necessary to make valid adoptions among Sudras might seem uncertain (*i*).

(*y*) MS. 1655. (Sudras.)

(*z*) *Premji Dayal* v. *Collector of Surat*, R. A. 54 of 1870; Bom. H. C. P. J. for 1873, No. 12.

(*a*) MS. 1677.

(*b*) MS. 1689. The Simpi ranks as an Atisudra, *i.e.* below the recognized Sudra. See Steele, L. C. 107.

(*c*) MS. 1687.

(*d*) MS. 1675. See above, p. 998 (*o*).

(*e*) *Hurrosoondree Dassee* v. *Chundermohinee Dassee*, Sev. 938.

(*f*) *Luchmun Lall* v. *Mohun Lall*, 16 C. W. R. 179.

(*g*) See above, pp. 1002—3.

(*h*) *Deo dem Kissen Chundershaw* v. *Baidam Bebee*, East's Notes, Case 14.

(*i*) *Sri Narayen Mitter* v. *Sy Krishna Soonduri Dossee*, 11 C. W. R. 196; S. C. 2 B. L. R. 279 A. C. J.; *Nittianand Ghose* v. *Kishen Dyal Ghose*, 7 B. L. R. 1; S. C. 15 C. W. R. 300.

The performance of the datta homam was once held essential there to the adoption even of a Sudra (*k*), but this was afterwards overruled (*l*) by a Full Bench, no further ceremony, it was said, being necessary than gift and acceptance (*m*).

D. 1.—Ceremonies and Forms—Constitutive.

D. 1. 3.—Subsidiary Forms.

Amongst these are the expressions of assent by the relatives and the representative of the Government. Additional prayers and sacrifices fall into the same class. But the chief subsidiary form is that of reducing the declaration of transfer to a formal instrument signed by the parents and attested by the relatives and other principal persons present. Where any particular settlement is made, varying in any way the rights and obligations of the parties within the limits allowed by their law, a written instrument should be deemed indispensable. For the adoption itself no writing is necessary; but in every case it may probably be useful to authenticate the transaction. Macnaghten says:

"There is no law requiring the execution of a written instrument on the occasion of receiving a boy in adoption, though the practice of resorting to writing is prevalent" (*n*). And the Judicial Committee ruled that neither registration of adoption, nor any written evidence, is essential to validity of adoption (*o*):

No stereotyped form of adoption is requisite; absence of registration or of a stamp may raise suspicion but cannot invalidate the deed (*p*). The language of the Privy Council in the case lately quoted is important. "According to the Hindu Law, neither registration of the act of adoption, nor any written evidence of that act, having been completed, is essential to its validity. It is to be lamented, that an irrevocable act, which

---

(*k*) *Bhairabnath Sye* v. *Maheschandra Bhaduri*, 4 B. L. R. 162 A. C.; S. C. 13 C. W. R. 169.

(*l*) *Behari Lal Mullick* v. *Indramani Chowdhrain*, 13 B. L. R. 401; S. C. 21 C. W. R. 285.

(*m*) *Nittianand Ghose* v. *Krishna Dyal Ghose*, 7 B. L. R. 1.

(*n*) 2 Macn. H. L. 176.

(*o*) *Sootrugun Sutputty* v. *Sabitra Dye*, 2 Knapp, p. 287; *Pritima Soonduree* v. *Anund Coomar*, 6 C. W. R. 133; 2 Wyman, 135.

(*p*) *Pritima Soonduree* v. *Anund Coomar*, 6 C. W. R. 133.

defeats the just expectations of the relations of deceased persons, may, at any distance of time after it is supposed to have been done, be proved by verbal testimony. It would certainly contribute much to the security of property and the happiness of Hindu families, if, in a country where the religious obligation of an oath is unfortunately so little felt, and documents are so readily fabricated, adoptions and all other important acts were required to be perfected in the presence of some magistrate and recorded in some Court."

"But although neither written acknowledgments, nor the performance of any religious ceremonial, are essential to the validity of adoptions, such acknowledgments are usually given, and such ceremonies observed, and notices given of the times when adoptions are to take place, in all families of distinction, as those of zemindars or opulent Brahmans, that wherever these have been omitted, it behoves this Court to regard with extreme suspicion the proof offered in support of an adoption. I would say, that in no case should the rights of wives and daughters be transferred to strangers, or more remote relations, unless the proof of adoption, by which that transfer is effected, be proved by evidence free from all suspicion of fraud, and so consistent and probable as to give no occasion for doubt of its truth" (*q*).

The execution of deeds, without actual gift and acceptance, is not sufficient (*r*) to constitute an adoption. A mere constructive giving and receiving cannot be relied on. A suit to set aside deeds giving and receiving in adoption, where no son was given according to the deeds, is not maintainable (*s*). [For without gift and acceptance there can be no valid adoption, and cancellation does not avail anything.] Where a deed was executed, signifying an intention, if a certain approval was obtained, to take a boy in adoption, and the boy was not given or accepted, the adoption was held incomplete, the deed being provisional and intended to be acted upon during the life of the executing party, who had not capacity to make a testamentary disposition (*t*).

(*q*) Lord Wynford in *Sootrugun Sutputty* v. *Sabitra Dye*, Knapp's P. C. pp. 290, 291.

(*r*) *Siddesory Dossee* v. *Doorga Churn Sett*, 2 I. J. N. S. 22; *Sri Narayan Mitter* v. *Sy Krishna Sundari Dasi*, 11 C. W. R. 196; S. C. 2 B. L. R. 279 A. C. J.

(*s*) *Sri Narayan Mitter* v. *Sy Krishna Sundari Dasi*, 11 C. W. R. 196; S. C. 2 B. L. R. 279 A. C. J.

(*t*) *B. Banee Pershad* v. *M. Syad Abdool Hye*, 25 C. W. R. 192.

An adoption of a daughter's son was held invalid for want of a writing or deed of adoption, and for want of proof that religious ceremonies were performed (*v*). This decision cannot be considered very satisfactory. If the parties were Brahmanas the adoption of a daughter's son was invalid. If they were Sudras religious formalities were unnecessary.

D. 1.—Ceremonies and Forms—Constitutive.

D. 1. 4.—Informalities.

According to the Poona castes—" Any irregularity or defective performance in the adoption of customary rule, . . . is a cause of its annulment " (*w*).

It is not easy to gather from the cases what informalities are to be regarded as vitiating an adoption and what do not affect its validity. The chief authorities tend, it will be seen, to the sufficiency of a gift and acceptance authenticated by *some* religious rites, especially the homa (*x*). The others cannot be regarded as so important that the omission of some of them is a cause even for grave suspicion. Colebrooke says: "An inadvertent omission of an unessential part as sacrifice does not vitiate adoption " (*y*). . . . " The essence of the adoption of a son given . . . is the gift on the one side, and the formal acceptance of the child as a son on the other . . . the rest of the ceremonies prescribed . . . may be completed in pursuance of the adopter's intention, by others for him, if he should die prematurely. The unintentioned omission of some part of them by the adopter would hardly invalidate the adoption; though the wilful omission of the whole by him might have that effect, since the performance of the ceremony of tonsure, and other rites, in the family of the adopter, is indispensable to the completion of the adoption " (*z*).

" However defective the ceremony," Ellis said, " and however small in consequence the spiritual benefit, the act of adoption

---

(*v*) *Baee Gunga* v. *Baee Sheokoovur*, Bom. Sel. Rep. 80.

(*w*) Steele, L. C., App., p. 388.

(*x*) See above, p. 836 ss. The Sastris, as we have seen, are more exacting.

(*y*) 2 Str. H. L. 126.

(*z*) Colebrooke in 2 Str. H. L. 155

cannot be set aside on any account whatever; *à fortiori*, not on account of any informality " (*a*). And Colebrooke on the same case, " The adoption being complete, it cannot be annulled. An adopted son may be disinherited for like reasons as the legitimate son (Mitakshara on Inheritance, Chap. II., sec. X.), but he cannot forfeit the relation of son " (*b*). " The meaning of that passage is, that a lawful adoption, actually made, is not to be set aside for some informality which may have attended it; not that an unlawful adoption shall be maintained " (*c*).

In one case Sir E. Perry expressed himself thus:

" Wassadeo Wittaji expressed a strong desire in his will that a son should be adopted to him; and as we find it indisputably proved that the widow did in fact solemnly adopt the infant plaintiff in the presence of a great many Brahmins, Purvoes, and relatives; that all the more important ceremonies were observed the Ganputty Puja, or worship of the god Ganput, the Puja Wachan, or reverence to the Ganges, the Hom or sacrifice of fire,—we were inclined to think that even if other observances had been disregarded, still, the essence of the ceremony having been adhered to, the adoption was good for every legal purpose " (*d*).

The non-observance, however, of the ceremonies, other than those held to be indispensable, though it does not render an adoption invalid, yet will afford presumptive evidence against the adoption where the situation in life of parties renders such forms usual (*e*).

In Madras " if the performance of the datta homam be established, the adoption is established; but, if otherwise, the converse does not hold good. Further evidence may be adduced. In no case can the omission of the ceremony affect an adoption in other respects valid. If not performed, when the adoption is from another gotram, it would seem, from analogy, that the son so adopted must be anitya datta " (*f*).

(*a*) Ellis in 2 Str. H. L. 126.

(*b*) Colebrooke in 2 Str. H. L. 126.

(*c*) 2 Str. H. L. 178, 179.

(*d*) *Crastnarao Wassadewji* v. *Raghunath Harichandarji et al.*, Perry's Or. Cases, pp. 150, 151.

(*e*) *Sutrugun Sutputty* v. *Sabitra Dye*, 2 Knapp, 287; 1 C. S. D. A. R. 15.

(*f*) 2 Str. H. L. 220.

D. 2.—Ceremonies and Forms—Collateral.

2. 1.—Inducing Good Fortune.

"Donations are to be given to Brahman mendicants" (*g*).

D. 2. 2.—Indicating Joy and Generosity.

"Some clothes and ornaments are to be presented to the adopted child" (*h*).

D. 2. 3.—Authenticative.

The instruments described above under sub-section D. 1. 3. might properly be placed under this head also. But in some few castes they are thought essential, and in all they serve to make the declaration explicit. A reference here seems enough. The assembly of relations and neighbours is another and the usual means of record of the transaction.

"At an adoption a festival is held, to which are invited relations, friends, and leading men of the caste. Presents are distributed among the head men of the caste, village officers, relations and guests. The fact of distribution of sugar, cocoanut, and pan is evidence of an adoption" (*i*).

E.—Variations—In the Case of *Quasi*-Adoptions.

E. 1.—Disapproved Adoptions.

A distinction was taken by a Pandit in Madras between a permanent (nitya) adoption accomplished by a ceremony including the homam and a temporary (anitya) one, where the homam had been dispensed with. In the latter case it was said the son of the man thus adopted might be initiated in either gotra. Ellis recognizes this (*k*), but the anitya adoption is not allowed in Bombay. The boy is wholly adopted or not at all.

(*g*) MS. 1675.

(*h*) MS. 1675.

(*i*) Steele, L. C., p. 184. "Pan" is the betel-leaf.

(*k*) 2 Str. H. L. 121, 123.

The krita son, it is said, must be received from the hand of the father or of the mother as his agent (*l*). This mode of adoption is no longer allowed (*m*), except in the modified form used by ascetics (*n*), who buy children to maintain a spiritual succession (*o*). A Sastri thought the ordinary forms should be used. " Sudras in adopting (and Gosavis are Sudras) are to omit the recitations from the Vedas " (*p*).

" In the kindred case of the kritrima, or son made, the mode of adoption as practised in those of our provinces in which it prevails is very simple, being completed by the declaration and consent of the parties without any religious ceremonies." The Datt. Mim., however, makes the religious rites indispensable alike to the Dattaka and Kritrima, and hence Colebrooke says they must, when the krita form is allowed, be essential to that also (*q*).

As to Bombay, adoption after payment of a price is not, it is said, recognized there in the Kali yuga (*r*), but one or two of the Gujarath castes adhere to the practice, and " with some castes in Madras the mode of adoption is uniformly by purchase " (*s*). Amongst them it may be allowed on the ground of class usage, which must also govern the ceremonies in any particular instance (*t*). The krita adoption [*i.e.* by purchase] is really obsolete, unless on the ground of local usage (*v*) even in Madras.

VARIATIONS IN THE CASE OF *Quasi*-ADOPTIONS.

E. 2.—CONNEXIONS RESEMBLING ADOPTION.

In the case of a palak putra a mere assent of the parties openly expressed is all that custom requires.

(*l*) Col. Dig., Book V., T. 281 ss.; see 2 Str. H. L. 138, 143.

(*m*) Above, p. 806, note (*r*).

(*n*) 2 Str. H. L. 133.

(*o*) See above, p. 516 ss.

(*p*) MS. 1678. See above, pp. 834, 835.

(*q*) Colebrooke 2 Str. H. L. 155. The consent of the person adopted by the kritrima form is indispensable. See above, p. 907.

(*r*) *Eshan Kishor Acharjee* v. *Harischandra*, 13 B. L. R. App. 42; S. C. 21 C. W. R. 381; see 2 Str. H. L. 156.

(*s*) 2 Str. H. L. 148.

(*t*) Above, p. 2.

(*v*) *Gooroovummal* v. *Mooncasamy*, 1 Str H. L. 102, 103; 1 Str. Notes of Cases, p. 61.

The Roman adoption *per æs et libram* approached most nearly amongst the Hindu forms, probably, to the krita. There was a real or fictitious sale by the paterfamilias of the person adopted.

In one case, noted above (*w*), the Sastri was of opinion that by mere nurture and recognition an Agarvali (*x*) had given to a boy the status of an heir. But this, as shown in the remark, is opposed to the general Hindu Law; it could be sustained only on the ground of caste custom.

Recognition of dancing girls as daughters suffices, it was said, to constitute adoption without any formal act (*y*).

SECTION VII.—CONSEQUENCES OF ADOPTION.

I.—Governed by the Ordinary Law.

I. 1.—Perfect Adoption.

A.—General Consequences.

A. 1.—Change of Status.

" Adoption causes an immediate change of status " (*z*).

" The relationship of the son to his family of birth ceases " (*a*).

" The theory of adoption depends upon the principle of a complete severance of the child adopted from the family in which he is born, both in respect to the paternal and the maternal line, and his complete substitution into the adopter's family as if he were born in it " (*b*). An adopted son ceases to be the son of his natural parents, and becomes the son of the adoptive father to all purposes (*c*).

(*w*) P. 356, Q. 18.

(*x*) See Steele, L. C. 97.

(*y*) *Vencatachellum* v. *Venkalasamy*, M. S. D. A. Dec. 1856, p. 65.

(*z*) MS. 1671. " Adoption alone constitutes affiliation; but the ceremony of tonsure performed by the family, to which he originally belonged, renders it essentially invalid. . . . But this affiliation once effected, is not cancelled by his naming his former family in performing a sacrifice, or in consecrating a pool. Birth caused by male seed and uterine blood is one ground of filiation, the second birth, by investiture and other ceremonies, is equally a ground of filiation, by whomsoever performed. When he who has procreated a son gives him to another, and that child is born again by the rites of initiation, then his relation to the giver ceases, and a relation to the adopter commences : this birth cannot afterwards become null by his erroneously reverting to his original family." (Col. Dig., Book V., T. 183 Comm.)

(*a*) MS. 1760.

(*b*) *Uma Sankar Moitro* v. *Kali Komul Mozumdar et al.*, I. L. R. 6 Cal. 259.

(*c*) *Gopeymohun Thakoor* v. *Sebun Koer et al.*, East's Notes, Case 64; 2 Mor. Dig., p. 105; *Appaniengar* v. *Alemaloo Ammal*, M. S. D. A. R. for 1858, p. 5; *Narasammal* v. *Balaramacharlu*, 1 M. H. C. R., p. 420. The statement must be slightly qualified. See below.

The adopted takes generally the rights and the duties of a begotten son (*d*).

"If it is once conceded that the adoption is valid, all the legal consequences attached to it must follow as a matter of course" (*e*).

It follows that "only one adopted son can subsist at one time" (*f*).

When a Hindu gives his son in adoption, his power, it was said, more resembles that of a proprietor than that of guardian (*g*). This is true in so far as a guardian could not possibly give away his ward. The father has power to annihilate his own paternal rights, and does so by giving in adoption.

The chief purpose, and originally it seems the only purpose, of adoption having been the maintenance of the adoptive father's sacra (*h*), it is said, "A son given is therefore the child, not of his adoptive mother, but of his adoptive father only" (*i*). The interest of the adoptive mother and her ancestors in the adopted son and the religious duties to be performed by him is an idea of later growth and less definitely settled. It may now be accepted, however, that "if a son be adopted by the husband, the wife has a secondary claim to that child, because property is common to

---

(*d*) Above, p. 349. "Adoption is as if the adoptive father had begotten the son." *Per* Willes, J., in the *Tagore Case*, I. L. R. I. A. Supp., pp. 47, 67. *Kali Komul Mozoomdar* v. *Uma Shunkur Moitra*, L. R. 10 I. A. 138.

(*e*) *Per* D. Mitter, J., in *N. Rajendro N. Lahoree* v. *Saroda Soonduree Dabee*, 15 C. W. R. 548. *Sreenarain Mitter* v. *Sreemutty Kishensoondery Dassee*, 11 Beng. L. R. 171 P. C.; S. C. L. R. I. A. Supp. 149.

(*f*) Steele, L. C., p. 45. *Gopee Lall* v. *Musst. Sree Chundraolee Buhoojee*. L. R. I. A. Supp. 131; *Mohesh Narain* v. *Taruck Nath*, L. R. 20 I. A. 30.

(*g*) *Chitko* v. *Janaki*, 11 Bom. H. C. R. 199. He is bound, however, to guard the interests of his son (see above, sec. VI. A. 6). Under the Roman Law down to a late time a child could be disposed of like goods, and therefore let on hire or pawned. This was forbidden except in cases of extreme necessity, such as justify a sale under the Hindu Law, and at last wholly prohibited by Justinian. See Maynz, Dr., Rom. sec. 410; Vyav. May., Chap. IV., sec. I., paras. 11, 12, sec. IV., para. 41, sec. V., para. 2, Chap. IX., paras. 2, 3, compared with Manu IX. 174, Vasishtha XV. 2; XVII. 31, 32. Apastamba forbids the sale, Pr. II., Pat. 6, Kh. 13, para. 11. So, too, does Yajnavalkya. Katyayana allows it in extreme necessity, Col. Dig., Book II., Chap. IV., TT. 6, 7, 16. Above, p. 806.

(*h*) Above, p. 789 ss.

(*i*) Col. Dig., Book V., T. 273 Comm. See H. H. Wilson, Works, vol. V., p. 57.

the married pair (*k*), and the line of the maternal grandfather is the ancestry of the adopter's father-in-law " (*l*).

I. 1. A. 2.—Change of Sacra.

The change of sacra, that is of connexion with the manes of ancestors, of obligations to them, and of the peculiar family rites and formulas, is the most important element of adoption to the orthodox Hindu. The supreme importance of initiation as completing this connexion is much dwelt on in the Sastras (*m*), and the due celebration of sraddhas occupies the chief place in the religious books (*n*). For their effectual performance the son adopted must be qualified by a complete reception into the family (*o*).

When a son has been adopted, and has gone through the samskaras, it must be inferred that, as in the case of a son by birth, a deliverance from *put* of the ancestors by adoption has by this fulfilment of duty been effected (*p*). In the event therefore of his death, no further adoption is necessary for the fulfilment of religious duty.

(*k*) See above, p. 86; Col. Dig., Book II., Chap. IV., T. 18.

(*l*) Col. Dig., Book V., Chap. IV., T. 275 Comm. The expression is in English very awkward. The son being commanded to honour his maternal grandfather, this is an interpretation of the command for the case of an adopted son. In the event of an adoption during a son's exclusion from caste, followed by the son's re-admission, the position of the adopted son on a reconciliation between the one he has replaced and his father seems not to have been settled. (See above, pp. 814, 815.) The adopted son would probably be reduced to a share of one-fourth.

(*m*) See above, pp. 789, 811 ss.

(*n*) Comp. Vyav. May., Chap. IV., sec. VII., 29 ss.

(*o*) See Vasishtha II. 4, 5; XI. 49; H. H. Wilson, Works, vol. V., p. 45, compared with the statement above, p. 880.

" Sraddha ceremonies are performed on the anniversary of a father's death. The Paksha ceremonies are performed subsequent to the first year after a father's death, at some time during the month Bahadrapad. There are also daily and monthly offerings for the benefit of a father and ancestors deceased." Steele, L. C., p. 26 (note); Col. Dig., Book V., T. 399 (note), enumerates sixteen Sraddhas that must be performed for a Brahmana recently deceased. See Col. Dig., Book V., T. 276 Comm.; above, pp. 418, 421, 795, 808; and Comp. Ortolan. Instituts, Tom. II., §§ 129, 132, on the corresponding institution at Rome.

(*p*) Col. Dig., Book IV., T. 155 Comm.; above, p. 789.

The ceremonial impurity arising from births and deaths in the family of his birth no longer affects the person who has been transferred to another by adoption. He presents no oblations to his natural father and his ancestors, but "distinct oblations" to the adopted father and his ancestors (*q*).

I. 1. A. 3.—ADOPTION TRANSFERS THE OFFSPRING.

"A man having a son is adopted and then dies. His son takes his place as heir in the adoptive family" (*r*).

"This is so though another son is born (to the adopted) after the adoption" (*s*).

"The son born before his father's adoption not only is heir to the adoptive grandfather's estate, but is answerable for a debt of the grandfather admitted by his father" (*t*).

By Act XXI. of 1870, § 6, the word "son" in the Indian Succession Act (X. of 1865) is in many places made to extend to an adopted son, and "grandson" to a grandson by adoption. The following sections of the Succession Act must be so construed, §§ 62, 63, 92, 96, 98, 99, 100, 101, 102, 103, 182.

I. 1. A. 4.—ADOPTION IN THE ADOPTIVE FATHER'S LIFE IS PROSPECTIVE.

The general effect of adoption is as if a son had been born, though the rights thus acquired are subject to total (*v*) or partial defeasance by the birth of a real son. Thus, it has been said, it is competent to an adopted son to claim a partition of ancestral property (*w*) where a begotten son could do so. The adoption is in this sense tantamount to the birth of a son to the adopter (*x*); consequently there cannot be two adopted sons (*y*). But neither

---

(*q*) Datt. Chand. IV. 2.

(*r*) MSS. 1730, 1742.

(*s*) MS. 1738.

(*t*) MS. 1737. See above, p. 76.

(*v*) As in the case of a Raj impartible. The right to maintenance must be excepted.

(*w*) MS. 1731.

(*x*) *Heera Singh* v. *Burzar Singh*, 1 Agra H. C. R., p. 256.

(*y*) Steele, L. C., App., p. 393; above, p. 821. *Gopee Lall* v. *Musst. Sree Chundraolee Buhoojee*, L. R. I. A. Supp. 131.

does the adoption any more than the birth of a son affect bygone transactions of the father which were valid when entered into (*z*). An adoption during the pendency of a suit affecting the ancestral property, does not affect a previously completed gift by the adoptive father though accompanied by a trust in his own favour (*a*).

I. 1. A. 5.—ADOPTION AFTER THE ADOPTIVE FATHER'S DEATH IS RETROSPECTIVE.

"As soon as a son is adopted by a widow he succeeds to her husband's estate. Her independent rights and those of her mother-in-law forthwith cease" (*b*). The widow succeeds to her separated husband, but her estate is subject to immediate defeasance on her adopting a son. Her right is reduced to a legal claim to maintenance.

Adoption works retrospectively and relates back to the death of the husband of the adoptive mother, invalidating a gift or sale, unless it was made for preservation of the estate from foreclosure under a prior conditional sale by the husband (*c*), or other necessary purpose. In the following cases the retroactive effect is expressed most strongly:—

"In *Ranee Kishenmunee* v. *Rajah Oodwunt Singh* (*d*) it was held that according to the Hindu Law, a boy adopted by a widow, with the permission of her late husband, has all the rights of a posthumous son, so that a sale by her, to his prejudice, of her late husband's property, even before the adoption, will not be valid, unless made under circumstances of inevitable necessity" (*e*).

(*z*) Even in the case of a partition the right of an after-born son to share in divided property depends on whether he was begotten at the time of the partition (*Yekeyamian* v. *Agniswarian et al.*, 4 Mad. H. C. R. 307, 310.) If begotten before it, he would take a share; if after it, he would share only with his father in the latter's share.

(*a*) *Rambhat* v. *Lakshman Chintaman Mayalay*, I. L. R. 5 Bom., at p. 635.

(*b*) MS. 1716.

(*c*) *Prannath Rai* v. *R. Govind Chandra Rai*, 5 C. S. D. A. R. 37; *Moro* v. *Balaji*, I. L. R. 19 Bom. 809; *Bijoy Gopal* v. *Nilratan*, I. L. R. 30 Cal. 990. "An adopted son is in most respects precisely similar to a posthumous son." Colebrooke in 2 Str. H. L. 127.

(*d*) 3 Beng. S. D. A. R. 228.

(*e*) *Nathaji Krishnaji* v. *Hari Jagoji*, 8 Bom. H. C. R. 73 A. C. J.

"In *Bamundoss Mookerjea* v. *Musst. Tarinee* (*f*) (in which the decision of the Bengal Sadr Divani Adalat was adopted without qualification by the Privy Council) the Judges, referring to that case, said:—'In that case the son, when adopted, became the undoubted heir, and it was of course the correct doctrine that no sale made by a widow, who possesses only a very restricted life-interest in the estate, could have been good against any ultimate heir, whether an adopted son or otherwise, unless made under circumstances of strict necessity" (*g*).

Yet in the case last quoted it was laid down that an adopted son has an absolute vested interest and a right of action only from date of actual adoption (*h*), and that the power of adoption in a widow does not, *per se*, divest her of her life interest. Her position in the meantime is such as has already been described (*i*), and as she is certainly a manager in possession, and represents the estate, her transactions with respect to it must, for the benefit of the estate itself, be upheld (*k*) where they have not been palpably detrimental or in excess of her limited powers of dealing with immovable property inherited from her husband (*l*).

In the case of a dispute between a widow and her husband's sapindas it was lately said by the High Court of Madras: ". . . Where *bona fide* claims are made which call for adjustment, where the existence of the husband's consent to the adoption is in question, we consider that the powers of the widow and reversioners may not improperly be exercised to effect a settlement of the claims before an adoption is made, and that their exercise is not affected by the circumstance that the dispute as to the direction or consent conveyed to the widow was at the same time set to rest, and that the arrangements affecting the estate were made in contemplation of the adoption. The widow, although she may have received an express direction to adopt, could not have been compelled to act upon it, and she might have persisted in her denial that she had received authority to adopt, had the reversioners declined to allow her to retain possession of the jewels" (*m*).

(*f*) 7 M. I. A. 169. (*g*) *Nathaji* v. *Hari*, *supra*.

(*h*) *Musst. Tarinee* v. *Bamundoss Mookerjea*, 7 C. S. D. A. R. 533.

(*i*) Above, pp. 87, 349.

(*k*) H. H. Wilson contends for the widow's full power of disposal. Works, vol. V., p. 66. Above, p. 291 ss.

(*l*) See above, pp. 349, 350.

(*m*) *Lakshmana Rau* v. *Lakshmi Ammal*, I. L. R. 4 Mad. 160, 165.

The right of inheritance then vests in an adopted son from the time of his adoption only (*n*) in this sense, that until the adoption by a widow, she fully represents the estate, though with limited powers, and may maintain suits concerning it. Such a suit continued in her own name after an adoption was held to have been maintained by the widow as guardian of the adopted son (*o*). For other purposes the adoption reacts as from the moment of the adoptive father's death.

The continuity of existence with the deceased does not affect rights and interests which were not his in his life or which are not a mere development of these (*p*). Thus where a new grant had been made, it was ruled that the absolute ownership of Government in the interval from the death of the Rajah until the act of State by which a transfer of territory was made to his widows and daughters was fatal to the claim of a defendant, in preference to the widow, as lineal heir to the Rajah, by right of adoption, though the adoption was valid (in all other respects) (*q*).

I. 1. A. 6.—Adoption is Irrevocable and Irrenounceable.

Adoption once really made is indefeasible (*r*). Accordingly the Sastris say:—"An adoption made with due ceremonies and followed by the chaul cannot be set aside" (*s*). "It is held that, if a lad be adopted into a family, even where it is not the custom to perform homam (sacrifice of adoption), he cannot be turned out of it at will" (*t*).

(*n*) *Bhubaneswari Debi* v. *Nilkomul Lahiri*, L. R. 12 I. A. 137.

(*o*) *Dhurm Das Pandey* v. *Musst. Shama Soondri Dibiah*, 3 M. I. A. 229; S. C. 6 C. W. R. P. C. 43; 2 Str. H L. 127.

(*p*) See below, sub-sec. B. 2. 6 (*b*).

(*q*) *Jijoyiamba Bayi* v. *Kamakshi Bai*, 3 M. H. C. R. 424.

(*r*) 2 Str. H. L. 142. See above, pp. 347, 838. "An adoption concluded agreeably to the Sastras is not annullable. It is not retractable among Brahmans after the Hom ceremony has been performed, nor among the lower castes." Steele, L. C., p. 184. *Sreenarain Mitter* v. *Sreemutty Kishen Soondery Dassee*, 11 Beng. L. R. 171, P. C.; S. C. L. R. I. A. Supp. 149.

(*s*) MS. 1752. "The inadvertent omission of an unessential part, as sacrifice is, even where it is enjoined, does not vitiate an adoption." Col. Dig., Book V., T. 273 Comm.

"The adoption being complete, it cannot be annulled. An adopted son may be disinherited for like reasons as the legitimate son (Mitaksh. on Inheritance, Chap. II., sec. X.), but he cannot forfeit the relation of son." Colebrooke in 2 Str. H. L. 126.

(*t*) 2 Str. H. L. 126.

When a widow sought to violate this rule the Court said—"Nor can we admit that the facts and the validity of the joint adoption (by two widows) being unquestionable, she is singly competent to set aside or annul in any degree an act which must be assumed to have been performed in obedience to the injunctions of her deceased husband" (v).

An adopted son cannot renounce his family of adoption and the consequent obligations to which he is subject. He can but resign his rights in that family (w). A Sastri declared that "an adoption cannot be annulled except on sufficient grounds (*i.e.* not by mere agreement)" (x), and the decisions rule that the status created by adoption cannot be given up by the adopted son (y) or dissolved by the parties immediately concerned.

Where a woman sought to disclaim an adoption made by her by a deed purporting to convey her property to her illegitimate son, this was pronounced illegal, though the upanayana of the adopted had been performed (after adoption) in his real father's house. "The adoption," Colebrooke said, "being once completely and validly made it cannot be recalled" (z).

In one case of an adoption of doubtful validity it was indeed ruled that—If after becoming of age an adopted son execute an agreement acknowledging the validity of his right to depend on his performance of certain conditions, his infraction of these will nullify his right (a). But the soundness of this judgment seems open to doubt (b). A man must belong to the one family or the other, it cannot rest on the mere option of another person (c).

I. 1. A. 7.—No Return to the Family of Birth.

This follows from the principles already laid down. According to the Sastri, "The son given in adoption cannot be reclaimed" (d).

(v) *Ry. Roop Koour* v. *Ry. Bishen Koour*, N. W. P. S. D. R. N. S., Pt. II. 1864, p. 655.

(w) Above, p. 838. Comp. pp. 924, 729. *Mahador Ganu* v. *Rayaji Sidu*, I. L. R. 19 Bom. 239.

(x) MS. 1741. See *Mohapattur* v. *Bonomallee*, Marsh, R. 317.

(y) *Ruvee Bhudr* v. *Roopshunkar*, 2 Borr. 713.

(z) 8 Str. H. L. 111.

(a) *Musst. Tara Munee Dibia* v. *Deo Narayan et al.*, 3 C. S. D. A. R. 387.

(b) See *Balkrishna Trimbak Tendulkar* v. *Savitribai*, I. L. R. 3 Bom. 54.

(c) See *In re Kahandas Narandas*, I. L. R. 5 Bom., at p. 164. Above, 187, and sec. VI. A. 6 of this Book.

(d) MS. 1748.

To a question put to the Sastris by the Court in another case they replied:—

"If any one about to adopt should receive from one not related to himself in the male line that person's son, and should perform his adoption according to the ceremonies of the Veda, and after that cause his regeneration by performance of the choora and oopanayana samskar, &c. (tonsure at three years of age; investiture with the string at five or eight years; and the remaining regenerating ceremonies) in the name of his own gotra, or paternal line, that son so invested with the lineage and estate of the adopter has no right to keep up connexion with the other lineage, that is, he cannot return to his own . . . " (e).

In Bengal as in Bombay the adopted son cannot return to his family of birth (f).

I. 1. A. 8.—The Connexion by Blood with the Family of Birth is not Extinguished.

Although there is a complete severance in religious and secular interests from the family of birth, the artificial status is not allowed to make marriage possible between an adopted son and his real mother or sister. It is only the religious and ceremonial connexion with the family of birth that is extinguished, and as the Datt. Mim. VI. 10 says, adoption does not remove the bar of consanguinity operating against intermarriage within the prohibited degrees (g).

I. 1. A. 9.—Terms and Conditions.

The incongruity of an adoption the operation or abiding validity of which is to be subject to a term or condition has already been noticed (h). In a case of this kind the Court said—

(e) *Ruvee Bhudr* v. *Roopshunkar*, 2 Borr. 656.

(f) *Sreemutty Rajcomaree Dossee* v. *Nobcoomar Mullick*, 2 Sevestre, 641 note.

(g) *Moottia Moodelli* v. *Uppon Venkatacharry*, M. S. D. A. R. for 1858, p 117; *Narasammal* v. *Balaramacharloo*, 1 M. H. C. R. 420. See above, p. 912.

(h) Above, p. 187, note (b). Under the Roman Law there could be no "adoptio ad diem" or "sub conditione," as mancipation by which it was originally effected was a solemn public act not susceptible of qualification. See Maynz, Cours. de Dr., Rom. sec. 412; Goudsm. Pand., p. 155; Maine, Anc. Law, p. 206 (3rd ed.).

"We . . . cannot find that the Hindu Law recognizes a conditional adoption, which appears to leave unsecured, and in jeopardy, the objects contemplated by the adopting, and to involve an element of injustice to the adopted party. . . . Insubordination to the widow of the deceased adopting father being an insufficient [reason] . . . we hold that he could not legally do so (*i*) and that the entry of such condition in the *wajib-ool-urz* (*k*) is worthless and ineffective. Nor do we admit that any value or efficacy would accrue to the entry, or that any validity would be given to the condition, even if the defendant, . . . when still very young, whether he were legally of age or not, authenticated the *wajib-ool-urz*, *pro forma* with the view of curing the ostensible defect of its having been authenticated by his father after his decease. It would be extremely inequitable to hold that he thereby deliberately intended to express his assent to the conditions . . . of which it is quite possible, and not at all unlikely, that he was ignorant. Even if he were aware of it, and ignorantly supposed himself to be bound by it, we are not prepared to admit that he is for that reason bound by it" (*l*).

In discussing under the preceding section (*m*) the legal possibility of making an adoption subject to terms differing from those annexed to it by the law, the effects of agreements and of adoptions thus made have been to some extent considered. It would seem that of the several cases which occur in practice, that of the adoptive father's stipulations for preserving the estate and securing his widow against destitution could not be refused effect by the Courts, so far at any rate as they bear on his separate or sole property. But if a man adopting for himself may do so on terms varying the usual rights of the son, it is but a slight extension of the principle when wills are once admitted to say that he may by a power or will allow his widow to impose such terms. And when a widow takes the whole estate without any will or direction to adopt, but with an assumed licence from her husband, it may be conceived that he, knowing an adoption was probable, but entirely at the option of the widow, has given her a tacit authority

---

(*i*) *I.e.* prescribe such a condition.

(*k*) A petition, memorial.

(*l*) *Per Curiam* in *Ram Surun Das* v. *Musst. Pran Kooer*, N. W. P. S. D. R. Pt. I., 1865, p. 293. Comp. the remarks of the Judicial Committee above, sec. VI. A. 6

(*m*) Sec. VI. A. 6.

to make her own terms. This logical development of the principles involved in the allowance of a will seems to be contained in the following two cases.

Where a power of adoption had been given by will to a wife coupled with a direction that the widow should during her life retain the whole of the testator's property, ancestral as well as self-acquired, it was held that the widow, after adopting, had a life interest with remainder to the adopted son (*n*).

In *Ramasami Aiyan* v. *Venkataramaiyan* (*o*) where the natural father of a boy, whom the widow of a deceased Hindu proposed to adopt as a son to her husband, entered into a written agreement with her to the effect that the boy should inherit only a third of the property of his adoptive father, the Privy Council held that the agreement was not void, but was at least capable of ratification when the adopted son became of age. *Chitko* v. *Janaki* (*p*) was referred to doubtingly. The stipulation that the boy adopted as a son should obtain that status without the corresponding rights was one, no doubt, unwarranted by the Hindu Law of the Sastras, and was subject to challenge by the son until he had ratified it on becoming *sui juris*. The Pandits consulted in Bengal on this point had said that an instrument by which a widow adopting a son reserved the property to herself for life was not lawful. The adopted son, they said, in spite of such an instrument, was entitled to the estate (*q*). In a somewhat similar case in Bombay, an adoptive mother (Koli) made an agreement with her son, whereby he resigned to her the bulk of the family property. This was pronounced by the Sastri illegal, and the adopted son, if capable, was, he declared, still entitled to inherit, subject to the duty of maintaining the mother (*r*). But wills also are not allowed by the Sastras, and yet in one form or another they have grown up to meet social needs, even within the sphere of the Hindu Law. So too the customary law has approved reasonable arrangements for

---

(*n*) *Bepin Behari Bundopadhya* v. *Brojo Nath Mookhopadhya*, I. L. R. 8 Cal. 357, following *Musst. Bhagbutti Daee* v. *Chowdry Bholanath Thakoor et al.*, L. R. 2 I. A. 256. The latter is not a case of adoption, but of a settlement by a man on his wife with the concurrence of his kritrima son, to whom was given a remainder on the wife's death.

(*o*) I. L. R. 2 Mad. 91.

(*p*) 11 Bom. H. C. R. 199.

(*q*) *Musst. Soolukhna* v. *Ram Doolal Pandeh*, 1 C. S. D. A. R. 324 (1st ed.). Above, p. 178 (*h*).

(*r*) MS. 15.

the adopting mother's security. It seems impossible now to say that this advance will not be maintained (*s*).

Cases such as that of *Ramguttee Acharjee* v. *Kristo Soondurec Debia*, referred to above at p. 981 note (*l*), must raise questions as to whether by the disposition the adopted son takes a vested estate forthwith on his adoption, although his enjoyment or actual possession be deferred, or whether his estate is wholly contingent or future. Such questions will probably be dealt with according to the analogies furnished by the English cases. A gift subject to a condition precedent could hardly be made under the Hindu Law (*t*), though one deferred, or by way of remainder, would not be inconsistent with it, the ascertained interest being created from the first. Such an estate, immediate in interest though deferred in enjoyment, must have been contemplated by the Court in the following remarks:—" Whatever directions an adoptive father may have given in regard to the time when the son was to get into the management and enjoyment of the estate, still he was the son and heir from the time of his adoption, and by his death apparently the mother would succeed him " (*v*). The Judicial Committee have held that a condition attached to the adoption is void, though the adoption is good (*w*). The law in Bombay and Madras, as already noticed, appears to be in favour of the validity of a condition attached to a valid adoption, if it is fair and reasonable and solely for the benefit of the adoptive widow.

(*s*) Any interest that a widow allows an adopted son to take in possession during her own life must so far be a detriment to her own estate, seeing that she is owner of the whole, and cannot, according to the Sastris, be deprived of this which they regard as a jointure by any testamentary disposition made by her husband. In the case of *Musst. Goolab* v. *Musst. Phool* (1 Borr. 173) the Zilla Judge proposed to the Sastris a question—Can a man separated in interest from his brother, and whose wife is alive, bequeath his property to his brother's son? The answer, resting on the Mitakshara, was—" The wife . . . has a right to inherit her husband's estate, and a will made by the husband . . . in favour of his brother's son is not valid " (pp. 175, 176). This was confirmed by the Pandit of the Sadr Court (p. 180). The theory of a power of bequest equal to the power of gift was not accepted by the law officers in these cases, and the widow was regarded as taking by a kind of survivorship, though no doubt with a restricted interest or faculty of disposal.

(*t*) See above, pp. 186 ss.

(*v*) *Per* L. Jackson, J., in *Gobindo Nath Roy* v. *Ram Kanay Chowdhry*, 24 C. W. R. 183.

(*w*) *Bhaiya Rabidat Singh* v. *Maharani Indar Kunwar*, L. R. 26 I. A. 53.

I. 1. B.—Specific Effects.

B. 1.—As to the Relations between the Adopted and his Family of Birth.

B. 1. 1.—Between the Natural Parents and the Son—Immediate Personal Relations.

(a) Parents the Active Subjects.

"When a father has given his son in adoption, his status and rights as father are extinguished" (x). Accordingly it was ruled that the adoptive parents have a right to the guardianship and society of the adopted son superior to that of the natural parents (y). The boy is often left for a longer or shorter time with his family of birth, but "though an infant after adoption be brought up by his natural parents, they must on demand surrender him to the widow who adopted him (z). "The natural father need not incur the expense of getting the boy married; it devolves properly on the adoptive mother. She cannot recover from his father the expenses of his adoption and investiture. She cannot restore the boy, nor can the father reclaim him on the ground of having got him married" (a).

"Tonsure performed in the family of the natural father, after gift, has no vitiating effect" (b).

(b).—Son the Active Subject.

"A boy severed by adoption from his own family and incorporated in the adoptive family is not affected in status by

---

(x) MS. 1759. *Sreenarain Mitter* v. *Sreemutty Kishen Soondery Dassee*, 11 Beng. L. R. 171 P. C.

(y) *Lakshmibai* v. *Shridhar Vasudev Takle*, I. L. R. 3 Bom. 1.

(z) In the *Mankars' Case* the Sastris, in the opinion quoted above, p. 901, recognize a widow's direct interest in adoption for securing her own future happiness. See, too, p. 838.

(a) MS. 1754.

(b) *Musst. Doolubh Dai* v. *Manee Beebee*, 5 C. S. D. A. R. 50. "The adoption of a child . . . for whom tonsure and other ceremonies were afterwards performed under the family-name of his natural father, would be nevertheless valid : for the ceremony of tonsure performed under the family name of his natural father is void, because he did not then belong to that family; and because the ceremony is performed by one who had no right to do so, since he truly became son of the adopter, and certainly belonged to his family, not having already initiated under the family-name of his natural father when the adoption took place." Col. Dig., Book V., T. 273 Comm.

performing the funeral ceremonies of his natural father and mother " (*c*).

" An adoptee performs the ceremonies of Kreea and Puksh for his [natural] father and relations, only in case his natural father should die without any other son or near relation, when he would perform them as a Dharmaputra. An adopted performs Sutak (*d*) for his natural family according to their adoptive relationship " (*e*).

" Since it is not a fit practice for a son given to perform the obsequies of his former mother, it is proper to take for adoption a boy whose mother is living, and who is given both by her and by her husband " (*f*).

" In case of being adopted by his father's brother, the adoptee is enjoined to perform the Sraddha both for his natural and adoptive fathers, inheriting the property of the former, however, only in default of heirs in order of succession before brothers' sons " (*g*).

An adopted son is considered in the nature of a purchaser for valuable consideration, which is his loss of inheritance in his natural family (*h*).

I. 1. B. 1. 2.—Relations as to Property.

" An adopted son forfeits all right of inheritance in his natural family " (*i*). " He (the adopted son) cannot, after being adopted, claim the family and estate of his natural father, which follow the funeral oblations; nor is he liable to pay his natural father's debts " (*k*). " He (an adopted son) can only inherit from his

---

(*c*) MS. 1673.

(*d*) Sutaka—Impurity; here ceremonies for its removal.

(*e*) Steele, L. C., p. 185

(*f*) Col. Dig., Book V., T. 275 Comm. The conception is that without a positive resignation the mother's claim to the son's religious services may continue.

(*g*) Steele, L. C., p. 47. He ranks as a brother's son. *Krishna* v. *Paramshri*, I. L. R. 25 Bom. 537.

(*h*) *Gopeymohun Deb* v. *Rajah Ray Kissen*, cited in *Doe Dem Hencower Bye* v. *Hanscower Bye*. East's Notes, Case 75; 2 Mor. Dig., p. 133. See above, sec. VI. A. 7.

(*i*) *Appaniengar* v. *Alemalu Ammal*, M. S. D. A. Dec. 1858, p. 5; *Chandra Kunwar* v. *Chaudhri Narpat Singh*, L. R. 34 I. A. 27; S. C. I. L. R. 29 All. 184.

(*k*) Steele, L. C., p. 47; Mit., Chap. I., sec. XI., para. 32; above, p. 347; Col. Dig., Book V., T. 181; Manu IX. 142. The term " funeral oblation "

natural father, in default of other heirs in previous order of succession . . . in virtue of his adoptive, not his original, relationship" (*l*). Even where the sacrificial idea is absent, "a Jain adopted by his uncle ceases to be heir as son to his natural father" (*m*). The Sastri added that "what he had acquired before adoption by using the capital of his natural father belonged to the latter" (*n*). The natural relation was in fact jurally annulled, and his father would no more inherit from him than he from his father (*o*). But in an emergency the Sastri says—"Should the natural parents have no other heir, the son they gave in adoption may perform their Sraddhas and take their property also" (*p*). Among the Gyawals in Gaya adoption does not deprive the adoptee of his rights in the family of his birth (*q*).

The Calcutta and the Madras High Courts have laid down that what had solely and absolutely vested in the adoptee remains unaffected by his adoption (*r*). This point is, however, unsettled, there being a difference of opinion thereon.

After adoption, the person adopted cannot mortgage property belonging to his natural family, nor can his widow do so after his death (*s*).

I. 1. B. 1. 3.—Relations as to Obligations.

The natural father is not responsible for the debt of a son given in adoption (*t*). Nor conversely is the son liable (*v*). Thus the Sastri says:—"A son given in adoption must pay his natural

---

intends that which is made for a father. *Pranvullubh* v. *Deocristin*, Bom. Sel. Rep. 4; *Kasheepershad* v. *Bunseedhur*, 4 N. W. P. S. D. 343.

(*l*) Steele, L. C., p. 186.

(*m*) MS. 1757.

(*n*) MS. 1756.

(*o*) Colebrooke in 2 Str. H. L. 129. *Muthayya* v. *Ninakshi*, I. L. R. 25 Mad. 394.

(*p*) MS. 1761.

(*q*) *Luchman Lal* v. *Kanhya Lal*, L. R. 22 I. A. 51; S. C. I. L. R. 22 Cal. 609.

(*r*) *Venkata Narasimha Appa Row* v. *Rangayya Appa Row*, I. L. R. 29 Mad. 437.

(*s*) *Yesubai kom Daji* v. *Joti*, Bom. H. C. P. J. 1875, p. 16.

(*t*) 2 Str. H. L. 125; see *Udaram Sitaram* v. *Ranu*, 11 Bom. H. C. R. 76, 84, 86.

(*v*) *Pranvullubh* v. *Deocristin*, Bom. S. D. A. Sel. Rep. 4.

father's debts only if he has inherited property from the natural father" (*w*), and in the case of a suit it was ruled that an adopted son is not liable for debts of his natural father who died in jail in execution of a decree for debt against him (*x*).

I. 1. B. 1. 4.—Relations Between the Adopted and the Other Members of his Family by Birth—Immediate Personal Relations.

An adopted son is to be considered as one actually begotten by the adoptive father in all respects except an incapacity to contract a marriage in his family of birth (*y*).

"Adoption does not remove the bar of consanguinity operating against intermarriage within the prohibited degrees" (*z*).

"An adopted son is restricted from intermarrying with any girl of either his natural or adoptive families within the prohibited degrees, and his descendants are under a similar restriction with regard to the former family to the third generation, viz., so long as remembrance may continue of the adoption" (*a*). "He cannot intermarry with either his natural or adoptive gotr" (*b*).

A Sastri said in one case, that "adoption severs the connexion with the natural relatives so completely that the adopted son's widow may adopt his younger brother" (*c*). We have seen that there is some authority for this kind of adoption (*d*), but the better opinion appears to be that embodied in the ruling that an adopted son cannot adopt as his son his brother by birth (*e*).

I. 1. B. 1. 5.—Relations as to Property.

"A son (an only son) who, having been given in adoption has passed out of his family of birth, has no longer any claim to the

---

(*w*) MS. 1758. See above, p. 347.

(*x*) *Pranvullubh Gokul* v. *Deokristen Tooljaram*, Bom. Sel. Rep., p. 4.

(*y*) *Narasammal* v. *Balaramcharlu*, 1 M. H. C. R. 420. The same case pronounces strongly against the adoption of a sister's son in the Andhra or Telingana country. *Kali Komul Mozoomdar* v. *Uma Shunker*, L. R. 10 I. A. 138.

(*z*) *Moottia Moodelli* v. *Uppon Vencatacharry*, M. S. D. A. Dec. 1858, p. 117.

(*a*) Steele, L. C., p. 47. Above, pp. 837, 838.

(*b*) Steele, L. C., p. 186.

(*c*) MS. 1625.

(*d*) Above, p. 911.

(*e*) *Moottia Moodelli* v. *Uppon Vencatacharry*, M. S. D. A. R. 1858, p. 117.

property of that family" (*f*), and reciprocally, a member of a Hindu family cannot as such inherit the property of one taken out of that family by adoption. His severance is so complete that no mutual rights as to succession to property can arise between him and his relations of the natural family (*g*). Hence it was said, that on an adopted son dying without issue, his property reverts to his adoptive family, his introduction into the new family causing his severance from his natural kindred, and they forfeiting all claims to succeed to his estate (*h*).

I. 1. B. 2.—CONSEQUENCES AS CREATING RELATIONS IN THE FAMILY OF ADOPTION.

B. 2. 1.—BETWEEN THE PARENTS AND ASCENDANTS, AND THE SON AND DESCENDANTS—IMMEDIATE PERSONAL RELATIONS.

(*a*) PARENTS THE ACTIVE SUBJECTS.

"An adoptive father is entitled to the custody of the person of the adopted son" (*i*). It follows that the proper residence of an adopted son is with his adoptive parents (*k*). The only exception is in case of cruelty or incapacity. Thus it was ruled that the adoptive parents, if willing, have a better right to act as guardians of their adopted sons than the natural parents, in the absence of proof of ill-treatment towards the boy or incompetency on their part to take care of him; the boy's residence with the adoptive family being part of the consideration for adoption (*l*).

An adopted son can claim maintenance from his father until put into possession of his share of the ancestral estate (*m*).

(*f*) MS. 1756.

(*g*) *Narasammal* v. *Balaramacharlu*, 1 M. H. C. R., p. 420; *Rayan Krishnamachariyar* v. *Kuppannayyangar*, 1 M. H. C. R., p. 180; *Srinivasa Ayyangar* v. *Kuppan Ayyangar*, 1 M. H. C. R., p. 180.

(*h*) *T. M. M. Narraina Numboodripad* v. *P. M. Trivicrama Numboodripad*, M. S. D. A. R. for 1855, p. 125.

(*i*) MS. 1677.

(*k*) *Lakshmibai* v. *Shridhar Vasudev Takle*, I. L. R. 3 Bom. 1.

(*l*) *Lakshmibai* v. *Shridhar Vassudev*, Bom. H. C. P. J. for 1878, p. 7: S. C. I. L. R. 3 Bom. 1; *Sheo Singh Rai* v. *Musst. Dakho et al.*, 6 N. W. P. R. 382.

(*m*) *Ayyavu Muppanar* v. *Niladatchi Ammal*, 1 M. H. C. R., p. 45.

"An adopted son's widow must be supported by her mother-in-law, who has got possession of the deceased's vatan" (*n*).

The chaul and munj of the adoptive son should be performed by the adopting widow (though but ten years old) (*o*).

The adoptive parents' authority, as we have seen (*p*), does not extend to giving away their son in adoption.

I. 1. B. 2. 1.—Immediate Personal Relations.

(*b*) Son the Active Subject.

"Adoption is . . . (1) to secure his (the adoptive father's) happiness in the future state by the adopted son's or his descendants' performance of funeral rites (kreea), mourning (sootak), and annual oblations of rice (sraddh sapindadan); and (2) to preserve the adopting parents' good name in the present world by the practice of alms-giving, feeding Brahmans, pilgrimages and other Hindu virtues" (*q*).

"The forefathers of the adoptive mother only are also the maternal grandsires of sons given, and the rest, for the rule regarding the paternal is equally applicable to the maternal grandsires (of adopted sons)" (*r*).

(*n*) MS. 1928. The widow of a predeceased adopted son has of course the same right to maintenance as if he had been a son by birth. (Above, p. 239 ss.: *Dilraj Koonwar* v. *Sooltan Koonwar*, N. W. P. S. D. A. R. for 1862, p. 240.)

(*o*) MS. 1648. See Steele, L. C. 187. Above, p. 891. The ceremonies ought to be completed on the widow's attaining maturity.

(*p*) Above, p. 926.

(*q*) Steele, L. C., p. 42. In *Ram Soonder Singh* v. *Surbanee Dasi*, 22 C. W. R. 121, Mitter, J., says the prescribed repetition of the Sraddhas implies a power of repeated adoption by the widow though a son should have attained maturity and passed through all the Samskaras. There does not seem to be any authority for this, but at any rate the duty would be that of the widow of the son should there be one. (See above, p. 87, and sub-sec. I. 1. A. 2 of the present section, p. 1012.)

(*r*) *Uma Sankar Moitro* v. *Kali Komul Mozumdar et al.*, I. L. R. 6 Cal. 261. According to Datt. Mim., VI., para. 50, the manes of the adoptive mother's ancestors benefit by the Sraddhas celebrated by the adopted son. "In the double set of oblations, it is indispensably necessary that the son should perform the Sraddha for the paternal line, not for the line of his maternal grandfather: but it is simply reprehensible in one who performs the Sraddha for the paternal ancestors, not to perform it also for the maternal grandfather and his progenitors. Consequently, since the Sraddha may be performed without

"Though the adoption be not annulled, yet should the adoptee not perform his filial duties, he separates from his adoptive father, receiving some share of the property" (*s*).

An adopted son succeeds to the adoptive father's property, subject to the right of maintaining the widow (*t*).

"There being a born son and an adopted son, they are jointly and severally responsible, according to their means, for the support of their parents" (*v*).

"A daughter-in-law adopts a son, and as his guardian manages the estate. The mother-in-law can claim maintenance from her" (*w*).

A widow of an adoptive father being refused maintenance by the adopted son sold part of the estate in her possession. The Sastri said the adopted son could recover it only on payment of the purchase money and interest (*x*).

I. 1. B. 2. 2.—Relations between the Parents and the Son with Respect to Property.

(*a*) Between the Adoptive Father and Son.

An adopted son has all the rights of a son born (*y*).

---

noticing the maternal grandfather's line in a subordinate double set of oblations, and the like, the Sraddha for the maternal ancestors is not requisite to the completion of the obsequies performed in the dark fortnight of Aswina." Col. Dig., Book V., T. 273 Comm.

(*s*) Steele, L. C., p. 185; above, p. 839. As to a second adoption on the refusal or incapacity of the first adopted to fulfil his duties, see above, pp. 549, 551, 838, 845.

(*t*) *Rungama* v. *Atchama*, 4 M. I. A., p. 1; S. C. 7 C. W. R. 57 P. C. See above, p. 241. "The adoptee is bound to provide the widow in necessaries." Steele, L. C., p. 188.

(*v*) MS. 1842.

(*w*) MS. 1831.

(*x*) MS. 16. See above, pp. 245, 605, 698; below, sub-sec. B. 2. 2 (*b*). Provision may be made for a widow's maintenance before rejecting her. (See above, p. 605.)

(*y*) Steele, L. C. 47; *Maharajah Juggurnath Sahaie* v. *Musst. Mukhun Kunwur*, 3 C. W. R. C. R. 24; *Teencowree Chatterjee* v. *Dinonath Banerjee*, 3 C. W. R. C. R. 49; *Ry. Kishenmunee* v. *Raj Oodwunt Singh*, 3 C. S. D. A. R. 228; *Srinivasa Ayyangar* v. *Kuppan Ayyangar*, 1 M. H. C. R. 180; *N. Chandvasekharudu* v. *N. Bramhanna*, 4 M. H. C. R. 270; *R. Vyankatrav* v. *Jayavantrav*, 4 Bom. H. C. R. A. C. J. 191; *Trimbuk Bajee* v. *Narain Venaik*, 3 Morris 19; *Rayan Krishnamachariyar* v. *Kuppannayyangar*. 1 M. H. C. R., p. 180; *Sree Narain Rai* v. *Bhya Jha*, 2 C. S. D. A. S. 27.

An interest vests in the adopted immediately on his adoption (*z*), though he be a minor, and he is entitled to the profits after his adoption (*a*), as also to immovable property purchased with money derived from ancestral estate, which property continued to exist at his adoption (*b*).

" A man who has adopted cannot alienate immovable property without good reason. With reason he may, especially what he has himself acquired " (*c*). The older cases agree with this opinion, as when the Judicial Committee ruled that by adoption a person divests himself of his right to dispose of immovable property without the consent of the son adopted (*d*). Adoption, however, it has been ruled, is not a valuable consideration proceeding from the boy adopted in such a sense as to bind the adoptive father against an alienation of his self-acquired property (*e*). The adopted stands in this respect on precisely the same footing as a son by birth (*f*). The case might have been dealt with on the ground that

---

(*z*) *Sudanund Mohapattur* v. *Sorjo Monee Debee*, 8 C. W. R. 455; S. C. 11 C. W. R. 436; reversed, 20 C. W. R. 377, by the Judicial Committee on the ground that the validity of the will questioned by the adopted son had been adjudged in a previous suit by him.

(*a*) *Sreemutty Deeno Moyee Dossee* v. *Doorga Pershad Mitter*, 3 C. W. R. Misc. 6.

(*b*) *Sudanand* v. *Bonomalee*, 6 C. W. R. 256.

(*c*) MS. 1725.

(*d*) *Rungama* v. *Atchama*, 4 M. I. A. 1; S. C. 7 C. W. R. P. C. 57. See above, pp. 572, 205 ss.

(*e*) *Purshotam Shenvi* v. *Vasudev Shenvi*, 8 Bom. H. C. R. 196 O. C. J.

(*f*) The case of *Mohapattur* v. *Bonomallee* (see above, p. 666) was relied on, because as in it the first adopted son suing as heir did not dispute the father's disposal of his self-acquired property, it was thought apparently that it could not be disputed. But that was a Bengal case, and in Bengal the relations of father and son as to property are different from what they are in Bombay (see Dayabhaga, Chap. II., 8, 17, 18, 28—30; 2 Str. H. L., 437, 444; Mit., Chap. I., sec. I., para. 27; above, p. 618; 12 M. I. A., at p. 38, there referred to; 2 Str. H. L. 449). Under the Mitakshara the son has a joint interest in the immovable property acquired by the father. He must submit to his father's dealings with such property on account of his subordination and the father's freedom from control (self-government) as manager (see above, pp. 207, 601), but this subjection cannot last beyond the father's life. The father's right is one of joint ownership plus *svatantrata*, unshared control (see 2 Str. H. L. 443). On his death the son's right by survivorship makes him complete owner, and the father's will cannot operate against him, although it would be effectual against others, not co-owners, only successors. (See above, p. 551.) The right to sell is not identical with the right to give, nor is the right to give identical with the right to devise (see above, p. 214). This is manifest from what the

where no more was engaged for, the adoption gave to the adopted only the ordinary advantages of a son. Had a contract been made or property settled on the son, there seems to be no doubt that on the principle of the cases referred to in sec. VI. A. 6 and 7, his becoming an adopted son would be a consideration (*g*) such as would make the transaction binding.

The right of interdiction has been recognized by the Sastris as acquired by adoption as in the following instance—" An adopted son can claim from his father property that the father is making away with in order to deprive the son of it (*h*), as an alienation made in order to deprive a son or brother may be rescinded by the State."

A Joshi having an adopted son, 15½ years old, executed a deed of gift of part of his vatan to his daughter's children. This was endorsed with an assent by the natural father of the adopted son. Such signature was pronounced useless. But the adopted son was pronounced answerable to make good a gift of part only of the vatan (*i*).

" A gift of a house made by a Brahman to his mistress does not enable her to dispose of it to the detriment of his subsequently adopted son, though she may retain it for life if she behaves becomingly to her master " (*i.e.* apparently the son) (*k*).

" An adopted son may claim a division of ancestral property from his father, but not of his father's own acquisitions " (*l*).

Judicial Committee say in *Lakshman Dada Naik's Case* (I. L. R. 5 Bom., at pp. 61, 62); and though the law of wills follows the analogy of the law of gifts it need not go so far. It is plain that it does not; and the power of a father to devise his acquired lands away from his son cannot apparently be rested on the recognized authorities (see Vyav. May., Chap. IV., sec. I., paras. 4, 5; Colebrooke in 2 Str. H. L. 435, 436). In the cost of *Musst. Goolab and Phool* (above, sub-sec. A. 9), the Sastris and the Courts refused effect to a will which went to deprive widows of their right of inheritance, though undoubtedly the wives could not have interfered with their husband's dealings during his life. Ellis at 2 Str. H. L. 428 expresses a similar opinion. Colebrooke differed only because he thought the power followed from wills ranking as gifts. The right of a son is as co-owner, that of the wife altogether dependent (see *Narbadabai* v. *Mahadev Narayan*, I. L. R. 5 Bom. 99).

(*g*) *See Bhala Nahana* v. *Parbhu Hari*, I. L. R. 2 Bom. 67.

(*h*) MS. 1735.

(*i*) MS. 711. See above, p. 193.

(*k*) MS. 712. See above, pp. 697, 698. The donor could by an explicit grant give her a larger interest. See above, pp. 205, 279, and sec. VI. A. 6 of this book.

(*l*) MS. 1731. In answer to Q. 1704, it is said, he cannot claim a partition (nature of property not specified).

"An assignment of a village for maintenance to an adopted son cannot be revoked" (*m*).

An adopted son can sell his right, title, and interest in his share of undivided family property (*n*).

"An adopted son's son can claim a share of the grandfather's (former) property though his father be alive, unless the property having been mortgaged or alienated the father has recovered it" (*o*).

An adopted son becomes heir to the whole of the adoptive father's property, and is excluded from inheritance in his own family (*p*).

A son, adopted by a widow under her husband's authority, supersedes all other heirs (*q*).

A son, adopted by a widow of a predeceased son, succeeds to his grandfather's estate as well as to that of his own adoptive father, whether the adoption took place in the grandfather's lifetime or not (*r*). If the adoption was made with the consent of the grandfather, his subsequent disposition or the birth of a son to his daughter in wedlock will not invalidate the adoption (*s*).

(*m*) MS. 790. This was probably understood as a case of partition. See above, pp. 648, 839.

(*n*) *Rutoo bin Bapooji* v. *Pandoorangacharya*, Bom. H. C. P. J. 1873, p. 176. The son was tenant of the whole property, and his interest was sold in execution. The purchaser was pronounced liable to the adoptive father for a moiety of the rent, he having been put into possession of the whole. See above, p. 615.

(*o*) MS. 1736. See above, p. 665.

(*p*) *Bhasker Buchajee* v. *Narro Ragoonath*, Bom. Sel. Rep., p. 25; *Duttnaraen Singh* v. *Ajeet Singh et al.*, 1 C. S. D. A. R., p. 20; *Gopeymohun Deb* v. *Raja Ray Kissen*, see East's Notes, Case 75; *Ranee Bhuwanee Dibeh* v. *Ranee Sooruj Munee*, 1 C. S. D. A. R., p. 135; *Srinath Serma* v. *Radhakaunt*, 1 C. S. D. A. R., p. 15; *Appaniengar* v. *Alemaloo Ammal*, M. S. D. A. R. for 1858, p. 5; *Raje Vyankatrav* v. *Jayavantrav*, 4 Bom. H. C. R. A. C. J., p. 191.

(*q*) *Veerapermal Pillay* v. *Narain Pillay*, 1 Str. 91; *Nundkomar Rai* v. *Rajindernaraen*, 1 C. S. D. A. R., p. 261. "Such child may be provided for as a person whom the law recognizes as in existence at the death of the testator, or to whom by way of exception, not by way of rule, it gives the capacity of inheriting or otherwise taking from the testator as if he had existed at the time of the testator's death, having been actually begotten by him." Willes, J., in the *Tagore Case*, L. R. Supp. I. A., at p. 67. See above, p. 879.

(*r*) *Gourbullab* v. *Juggernotpersaud Mitter*, Macn. Con. H. L. 217.

(*s*) *Ramkishen Surkheyl* v. *Musst. Sri Mutee Dibea et al.*, 3 C. S. D. A. R. 367. The assent of the grandfather was necessary on the principles stated in sec. III. B. 3. 33.

An adopted son takes by inheritance and not by devise (*t*) in the case of his adoption by a widow under an instrument providing for the boy only as an adopted son and successor.

An adopted son, though separated from his adoptive father, succeeds to the residue of the latter's estate, undisposed of by him by gift or will, in preference to the widow, in case he dies leaving no unseparated son surviving him (*v*).

On an adopted son's dying without issue his adoptive father's property goes, it was said, to his natural heirs (*w*). This would depend on whether the son died before or after the father.

In a suit by an adopted son to set aside a will, the will was held of no effect as a valid devise of property. At the father's death the right of survivorship was in conflict with the right by devise. Then the former, being the prior title, took precedence (*x*).

As an adopted son has no more rights than a natural son would have, so the adopter is at liberty to dispose by will of immovable property acquired by him, to any one he pleases (*y*).

If an elder adopted son takes the whole of the ancestral property, which the father could not dispose of without his consent, he must give up for the benefit of the second adopted son the whole property included in the devise, to the disposition of which his consent was not necessary (*z*).

A Hindu cannot disinherit a duly adopted son, even for bad character, nor can he adopt another (*a*). It is only in an extreme

---

(*t*) *Musst. Bhoobum Moyee Debia* v. *Ram Kishore Acharj Chowdhry et al.*, 10 M. I. A., p. 279, 309; S. C. 3 C. W. R. P. C. 15; Beng. S. D. A. R. for 1856, p. 122. See above, sec. VI. A. 6.

(*v*) *Balkrishna Trimback* v. *Savitribai*, I. L. R. 3 Bom. 54. See above, p. 342.

(*w*) *Sabrahmaniya Mudali* v. *Parvati Ammal*, M. S. D. A. R. for 1859, p. 265.

(*x*) *Vitla Butten* v. *Yamenamma*, 8 M. H. C. R. 6.

(*y*) *Purushotam* v. *Vasudev*, 8 Bom. H. C. R. 196 O. C. J. See above, pp. 205 ss., 595, 706. *Rao Balwunt Singh* v. *Rani Kishori*, L. R. 25 I. A. 54; *Raja Venkata Surya Mahipati* v. *Court of Wards*, L. R. 26 I. A. 83.

(*z*) *Rungama* v. *Atchama*, 4 M. I. A. 1; S. C. 7 C. W. R. P. C. 57. The right of the second adopted son rested wholly on the devise, his adoption being invalid.

(*a*) *Dace* v. *Motee*, 1 Borr. 84. "It is declared that, if culpable, even a son of the body does not take the heritage, hence vicious sons, whether begotten in lawful wedlock or the like, or adopted as sons given and the rest, are excluded from participation; sons so adopted, being void of good qualities, shall have a maintenance: but such sons, being virtuous, shall take the inheritance of a father, or of his kinsman," Col. Dig., Book V., T. 278 Comm. See above,

case of violation of duty that a son's rights are lost, or that a father can disinherit an adopted son. Both stand on the same footing (*b*).

Renunciation by an adopted son of his right in his adoptive father's property, though permissible, does not free him from adoption. If he resigns the right, the adoptive mother succeeds to the separate property of her husband (*c*).

An adopted son may for money relinquish his share in the adoptive father's family. This puts him into the position of a separated son. It does not disinherit him. If he be disinherited for adequate cause his son takes his place as heir (*d*).

On the death of an adopted son before that of the father his joint proprietary right, like that of the son by birth, is of course absorbed in that of the father (*e*), and his widow, should he leave one, is entitled to maintenance in the family of adoption (*f*).

I. 1. B. 2. 2. (*b*).—BETWEEN THE ADOPTIVE MOTHER AND SON.

"As soon as a son is adopted by a widow, he succeeds to her husband's estate. Her independent rights and those of her mother-in-law forthwith cease" (*g*).

---

pp. 539, 549, 551. A person cannot disinherit his son by will, *Gopeymohun Deb* v. *R. Raykissen*, East's Notes, Case 75; *Pranvullubh Gokul* v. *Deocristen Tooljaram*, Bom. Sel. Rep. 4.

(*b*) *Sadanund Mohaputtee* v. *Bonomallee*, C. S. D. A. R. 1863, p. 205. See above, p. 1011. In Khandesh, it was stated in answer to Steele's inquiries, that exclusion from caste does not cause a forfeiture of property or of the right of inheritance. Steele, L. C. 152. See above, p. 816. But the holder of any religious office peculiar to Hindus naturally forfeits it by change of religion. *Ibid.* Answer from Satara.

(*c*) *Ruvee Bhudr* v. *Roopshunker*, 2 Borr. 656; *Mahader Ganu* v. *Rayaji Sidu*, I. L. R. 19 Bom. 239. On his resigning, the right descends to the next in succession. This might be his son, who would take in preference to the mother.

(*d*) *Balkrishna* v. *Sabitribai*, I. L. R. 3 Bom. 54. See above, p. 354.

(*e*) *Udaram Sitaram* v. *Ranu Panduji*, 11 Bom. H. C. R. 76, 86.

(*f*) 2 Str. H. L. 235. See above, pp. 256 ss., 694.

(*g*) MS. 1716. See Steele, L. C. 48, 49. "Presuming the property here spoken of as the woman's to have been what devolved upon her by the death of her husband, and not to have been her proper stridhana, it ceased to be hers at the moment of a valid adoption made by her of a son to her husband and herself; in the same manner as property coming into the hands of a pregnant widow by the same means cannot be used by her as her own after the birth of a son. An adopted child is in most respects precisely similar to a posthumous

"The possession of authority to adopt a son by a widow in Bengal does not destroy or supersede her personal rights as widow, which continue until the adoption is actually made. . . . The property is in the widow from the death of the husband until the power of adoption is exercised. . . . It is only an alienation by the widow improper as against the subsequent heirs generally, that the adopted son can get rescinded" (*h*). The authorization in fact is as if non-existent until it is acted on by the widow (*i*).

An adopted son becomes son of both father and mother, and performs funeral rites to both (*k*). He is heir to the adoptive father, and, in the absence of a daughter, to the mother's stridhana (*l*). "In the lower castes a partition sometimes occurs, but the adoptee is heir to his adoptive mother, and generally manager during her life" (*m*).

Adoption by a widow in Bengal, under her husband's permission, deprives her of her widow's estate (*n*), and entitles her to maintenance (*o*). The same is the result even when the adoption is valid without the husband's permission, as amongst the Agarvali Jains (*p*). It follows from this that a Hindu widow, after adopting a son, cannot mortgage the family property as her own, nor can such a transaction be validated by the son's ratification (*q*).

---

son. From the moment of the adoption taking effect, the child became heir of the widow's husband; and the widow could have no other authority but that of mother and guardian." Colebrooke in 2 Str. H. L. 127.

(*h*) *Bamundoss Mookerjea* v. *Musst. Tarinee*, 7 M. I. A. 178, 180, 185, 206.

(*i*) *Uma Sunduri Dabee* v. *Sourobinee Dabee*, I. L. R. 7 Cal. 288. See above, p. 813.

(*k*) *Teencowree Chatterjee* v. *Dinonath Banerjee*, 3 C. W. R. 49. "An adopted son," the judgment says, "has all the rights and privileges of a son born." Datt. Mim., sec. I., para. 22. "Women have legally no right to adopt for the transmission even of their separate property but . . . such a custom may obtain in the caste." Ellis in 2 Str. H. L. 128.

(*l*) Above, p. 480. *Tincowri* v. *Denonath*, 3 W. R. 49; *Pudma Coomari Debi* v. *Court of Wards*, L. R. 8 I. A. 229.

(*m*) Steele, L. C., p. 186.

(*n*) *Nundkomar Rai* v. *Rajindurnaraen*, 1 C. S. D. A. R. 261; *Musst. Solukhna* v. *Ramdolal Pande et al.*, 1 C. S. D. A. R. 324; *Durma Samoodhany Ummal* v. *Coomara Venkatachella Reddyar*, M. S. D. A. R. for 1852, p. 111; *Radhabai* v. *Damodar Krishnarav*, Bom. H. C. P. J. for 1878, p. 9; *Mondakini* v. *Adinath*, I. L R. 18 Cal. 69.

(*o*) *Musst. Rutna Dobain* v. *Purladh Dobey*, 7 C. W. R. 450.

(*p*) *Sheo Singh Rai* v. *Musst. Dakho*, L. R. 5 I. A. 87.

(*q*) *Siddheshvar* v. *Ramchandrarao*, I. L. R. 6 Bom. 463.

An adoption works retrospectively and relates back to the death of the husband of the adoptive mother. It invalidates a gift or sale, unless it was effected under inevitable necessity, and entitles the adopted son to succeed to his estate as the same stood at the death of his adoptive father (*r*). In *Rajah Vyankatrao's Case* the adoption was made by the widow about seventy years after her husband's death (*s*). It follows from the widow's limited power that, as the Judicial Committee said, the rights of an adopted son are not prejudiced by any unauthorized alienation by the widow which precedes the adoption which she makes (and though gifts improperly made to procure assent might be powerful evidence to show no adoption needed, they do not in themselves go to the root of the legality of an adoption) (*t*). In the case, however, of an adopted son succeeding collaterally, his right, it is said, vests only from the adoption. At least he cannot retrospectively take away what passed to another collateral through his own non-existence, when the succession opened (*v*).

An adopted son, moreover, though he is competent to question his mother's acts during his minority or before his adoption, cannot question a sale effected by her with consent of all the legal heirs then existing and ratified by the Civil Courts (*w*).

A woman's religious gift of a house as her own which belonged to the family estate was pronounced invalid as against the adopted son. "There is no merit in a Krishnarpana made without the consent of the son" (*x*).

First there was permission given to adopt, then a sale by a Court of the property, then after twelve years there was actual adoption

---

(*r*) *Rajah Vyankatrav* v. *Jayavantrav*, 4 Bom. H. C. R. A. C. J. 191; *Nathaji* v. *Hari*, 8 Bom. H. C. R. A. C. J. 67; *Ranee Kishenmunee* v. *Rajah Oodwunt Singh*, 3 C. S. D. A. R. 228; *Bamundoss Mookerjea* v. *Musst. Tarinee*, 7 M. I. A. 169.

(*s*) See above, sec. III. B. 3. 23; 3. 34.

(*t*) *The Collector of Madura* v. *Mooltoo Ramalinga Sathupathy*, 12 M. I. A. 443.

(*v*) *Bamundoss Mookerjea* v. *Musst. Tarinee Dibia*, Beng. S. D. A. R. for 1850, p. 533; S. C. 7 M. I. A. 169; *Musst. Bhoobun Moyee Debia* v. *Ramkishore Acharj*, 10 M. I. A. 279; S. C. 3 C. W. R. 15 P. C.; Beng. S. D. A. R. for 1856, p 122; *Bhubaneswari Debi* v. *Nilkomul Lahiri*, L. R. 12 I. A. 137. On this subject see above, sec. III. B. 3. 23; 3. 25; 3. 34; 3. 35; and below, B. 2. 5.

(*w*) *Rajkristo Roy* v. *Kishoree Mohun Mojoomdar*, 3 C. W. R. 14; *Pilu* v. *Babaji*, 34 Bom. 165; *Vinayak* v. *Govind*, I. L. R. 25 Bom. 129; *Bijrangi Singh* v. *Manokranika Bakhsh*, I. L. R. 30 All. 1. See above, p. 349.

(*x*) MS. 714. For Krishnarpana, see pp. 91, 449.

under the permission. It was held, that what was sold was not merely the widow's interest, as the proceeds of the sale were applied to debts for which the property was liable. The purchaser was held not subject to eviction by the adopted son, after the death of the widow, who had enjoyed a life estate under the deed of permission to adopt (*y*).

"Under pressure of absolute necessity only an adoptive mother, living apart from her son, may sell the immovable family estate" (*z*).

A Sudra widow after adopting a son bought a field in her own name. It was held that she could give this to her daughter against the wish of her daughter-in-law, though she could not alienate the common property (*a*). As regards the patrimony the case would be different; the adopted son transmits to his widow a succession which excludes his mother (*b*).

In the event of successive adoptions the relations of the parties are determined by the following decisions. In the first it was said—

"The first adopted son became his father's heir. On the death of that son the widow became the heir, not of her late husband, but of the adopted son" (*c*).

Through adoption a widow, it was said, divests her own estate only, and by succeeding to her son as heir, she does not lose the right to exercise the power of adoption (*d*). The correctness of this depends on the principles considered in Sec. III. (*e*). She would, it seems, lose the right by the adopted son's leaving a widow (*f*). In other cases of adoption by a mother it has been said that a widow who has succeeded to her son, and who after-

---

(*y*) *Rajah Debendro Narain Roy* v. *Coomar Chundernath Roy*, 20 C. W. R. 30 C. R. (P. C.). It may be questioned whether, on strict principle, the permission could thus cut down the adopted son's interest. See above, sec. VI. A. 6. As to the widow's authority, see pp. 87, 349.

(*z*) MS. 14. This implies that the son is inaccessible, or else when applied to refuses sustenance. See above, pp. 605, 698. But the right is questionable in any case. She should sue the son. See pp. 238 ss., 605.

(*a*) MS. 1577. See above, pp. 298, 299, 475.

(*b*) *Vencata Soobamal* v. *Vencumal*, 1 Mad. S. D. A. R. 210.

(*c*) Privy Council in *Ramasawmy Aiyan* v. *Venkataramaiyan*, L. R. 6 I. A., p. 208.

(*d*) *Bykant Monee Roy* v. *Kisto Soonderee Roy*, 7 C. W. R. 392.

(*e*) Sub-secs. B. 3. 23; 3. 25; 3. 35.

(*f*) See *Musst. Bhoobun Moyee Debia* v. *Ram Kishore Acharj Chowdhry*, 10 M. I. A., at p. 310. Above, pp. 789, 1013.

wards adopts a son, thereby divests herself of the estate (*g*). Regarded as an unseparated brother of the deceased the adopted son would take precedence of the mother. As a separated brother he would not; but in adopting a son the widow must perhaps be considered as replacing the one deceased with all his rights. The transaction is so anomalous (*h*) that any determination of these must be in a great measure arbitrary. In similar circumstances the Judicial Committee hesitated to give a final decision, saying only "whether by the act of adopting another son, she in point of law divested herself of that estate in favour of the second son, may be a question of some nicety, on which their Lordships give no opinion" (*i*). In *Kannepalli Suryanarayan* v. *Pucha Venkata* (*k*) it has been held that a widow on the death of the first adopted son can validly adopt a second son if the power given to her to adopt was without any specific limitation. It follows that the rights and the duties of such a son must be those of an adopted son. The case of *Venkappa* v. *Jivaji Krishna* (*l*) is an authority for the proposition that a second son after the death of the first adopted son may be adopted.

A second adoption does not nullify an intermediate alienation by a widow after the death of the first adopted son (*m*).

A son adopted by the widow of a Hindu is legal representative of the deceased, and can maintain a suit under Act XIII. of 1855 for the benefit of persons entitled to compensation under the Act; but he is not entitled to any portion of the compensation awarded. Whether he would have been if adopted by the deceased himself is a question (*n*).

A widow cannot sue as representative of her husband so long as

---

(*g*) *Vellanki V. Krishna* v. *Venkata Rama Lakshmi*, I. L. R. 1 Mad. 174; *Jamnabai* v. *Raychand*, I. L. R. 7 Bom. 225.

(*h*) See above, p. 904.

(*i*) *Ramasawmy Aiyan* v. *Vencataramaiyan*, L. R. 6 I. A., at p. 208.

(*k*) L. R. 33 I. A. 145; *Lakshmibai* v. *Rajaji*, I. L. R. 22 Bom. 996.

(*l*) I. L. R. 25 Bom. 306.

(*m*) *Gobindo Nath Roy* v. *Ram Kanay*, 24 C. W. R. 183.

The widow succeeded the first adopted son, who seems to have died in childhood. Her power of alienation would then be governed by the estate she took. See above, pp. 102, 314, 349, 422, 424. She would not be allowed to make a second adoption a means of fraud. See above, p. 348 ss. Supposing the deceased son had sold or incumbered without reason, the anomaly of a second adoption acting retrospectively would be very manifest.

(*n*) *Vinayak Raghunath* v. *G. I. P. R. Co.*, 7 Bom. H. C. R. O. C. J. 113.

her adopted son is alive (*o*), nor can she prefer an appeal. A mere disclaimer by sons, and therefore by an adopted son, in the absence of proof of the widow's being herself the next reversioner after the sons (*p*) will not enable her to sue as owner. There must be a distinct assignment.

Where, pending a suit for partition by a widow in an undivided family, she adopts, though the suit is prosecuted in her own name, she is considered as guardian and trustee and accountable to her son for the profits of the property decreed (*q*).

An adoptive son like a real son will not, where there are dissensions, and a probability of waste, be allowed to take the estate out of his adoptive mother's hands without providing for her maintenance (*r*). Nor can he, by selling the family dwelling, deprive her of her right to residence (*s*).

As to the property more especially regarded as stridhana the relations are thus stated:—

The adoptive mother "retains, during life, the right over her own property, but the adoptee is heir to his adoptive mother" (*t*). "A son adopted by a widow," the Sastri said, even "without her deceased husband's permission, inherits her property" (*v*).

The son adopted by a daughter-in-law after an adoption by her father-in-law succeeds to her and her husband's property (*w*). The property taken in inheritance by a daughter is stridhana according to the Mitakshara (*x*). Hence an adopted son succeeds

---

(*o*) *Ram Kannye Gossamee* v. *Meernomoyee Dossee*, 2 C. W. R. 49; *Jannobee* v. *Dwarkanath*, 7 C. W. R. 455; *Narsava* alias *Gangava* v. *Ramangavda*, A. D. 1868.

The widow must proceed in the adopted son's name after obtaining a certificate of administration under Act XX. of 1864 unless the property is of a trivial value, falling under sec. 2 of the Act.

(*p*) *Ram Kannye Gossamee* v. *Meernomoyee Dossee*, 2 C. W. R. 49; *Jannobee* v. *Dwarkanath*, 7 C. W. R. 455.

(*q*) *Dhurm Das* v. *Musst. Shama Soondri*, 3 M. I. A. 229; S. C. 6 C. W. R. P. C. 43. In Bombay she could not claim a partition. See above, p. 627.

(*r*) *Jamnabai* v. *Raychand*, I. L. R. 7 Bom. 225. See above, pp. 256, 605, and as to the circumstances justifying a demand on the mother's part for a separate assignment of property, *Venkatammal* v. *Andyappa*, I. L. R. 6 Mad. 130.

(*s*) See above, pp. 674, 675, 751.

(*t*) Steele, L. C., p. 188.

(*v*) MS. 1710. This is not true in the Bombay Presidency, if without permission means contrary to his wish; see above, pp. 970 ss.; 2 Str. H. L. 91.

(*w*) MS. 1666. See above, pp. 353, 845.

(*x*) Above, pp. 138, 139, 319.

to the property which his adoptive mother inherited from her father (*y*), but not as first heir. An adopted son succeeds to his mother's stridhana in the absence of daughters (*z*).

As to the reciprocal succession to the son the decisions are:— A widow succeeds to her adopted son as to her son by birth (*a*), and takes a life-interest upon the death of the adopted son under age (*b*).

I. 1. B. 2. 2. (*c*).—Relations Between Adoptive Step-Mother and Son.

"The adopted son succeeds to all his step-mothers" (*c*).

Where a widow had adopted a son under authority of her husband, on the death of the widow and the boy, the other co-widow was allowed to succeed to a moiety of the estate in her own right, not in that of a son adopted by her with due authority from her husband (*d*). This decision is questioned, and it is obvious the widow had no right except to maintenance. The boy adopted by her, if validly adopted, was entitled to the whole estate (*e*).

On the death of one, adopted as son of one of two co-widows, the property does not descend to the other widow, but, it was said, to the next legal heir who was nephew of the original

---

(*y*) *Sham Kuar* v. *Gaya Din*, I. L. R. 1 All. 255. See, too, Col. Dig., Book V., TT. 273—275, Comm.

(*z*) *Teencowree Chatterjee* v. *Dinonath Banerjee*, 3 C. W. R., p. 49. See above, pp. 140, 308.

(*a*) 2 Str. H. L. 129.

(*b*) *Soondur Koomaree* v. *G. Pershad Tewarree*, 7 M. I. A. 54; S. C. 4 C. W. R. P. C. 116. See above, pp. 102, 422.

(*c*) MS. 1658. See above, p. 489. "If a son be adopted by a man married to two wives, he would have two maternal grandfathers, and would claim as maternal ancestry both their lines of forefathers. This seeming difficulty is thus reconciled: although there be two sets of maternal ancestors, they should be jointly considered as manes of ancestors, and they should be thus named in performing the Sraddha, 'Such a one, maternal grandfather, sprung from such a primitive stock! to thee (to each of you) this funeral cake is offered,' and so forth, as is done by the son of the wife considered as a son of two fathers. Thus some reconcile the difficulty." Col. Dig., Book V., T. 273, Comm.

(*d*) *Narainee Dibeh* v. *Hirkishor Rai*, 1 C. S. D. A. R. 39.

(*e*) *Mondakini* v. *Adinath*, I. L. R. 18 Cal. 69; *Bai Motivahu* v. *Bai Mamubai*, L. R. 24 I. A. 93.

proprietor or adoptive father (*f*). The succession being to the son, his step-mother's position would be determined by the rules given above, pp. 102, 441 ss.

A son adopted by one wife may succeed to the stridhana of another co-wife (*g*) in Bengal. In another case in that province the reciprocal right was denied. According to the Mitakshara, it was said, a step-mother cannot succeed to the estate of her step-son, or a step-grandmother to the estate of her step-grandson (*h*). According to the principles admitted in *Lullobhoy* v. *Cassibai* (*i*), the step-mother ought to come next in succession to the father's mother, and the analogy of the law of partition is in her favour (above, pp. 605, 606, 627).

The importance of the right to adopt as between two or more widows becomes evident when it is borne in mind that the one taking the place of mother succeeds first to her son on his death without a child or widow (*k*). The step-mother is comparatively a remote successor. H. H. Wilson (*l*) discusses in rather caustic terms a Bengal case of a contest amongst three widows (*m*). The youngest as mother of a posthumous son, who died, was entitled as his or as her husband's heir. The husband, however, had left directions for an adoption by his eldest or his youngest widow with the assent of the middle one. No concurrence proving possible, the master was ordered to report on a fit boy. He reported in favour of one named by the second widow, and son of her father's brother. This relation led the Court to order his adoption, not by the second widow but by the eldest. Thus the widow who had resisted his adoption became his mother and heir, while the one who had proposed him and the one in whom the estate had vested were reduced to the position of step-mothers. The property having been mostly ancestral, the learned author contends that the father could not by his will make a valid disposition which would affect the complete title of his posthumous son, and the estate taken by that son's mother as his heir (*mm*). This, while it goes further,

---

(*f*) *Kasheeshuree Debia* v. *Greesh Chunder*, C. W. R. Sp. No. 71.

(*g*) *Teencowree Chatterjee* v. *Dinonath Banerjee*, 3 C. W. R., p. 49.

(*h*) *Lala Joti Lal* v. *Musst. Durani Kower*, B. L. R. F. B. 67. See above, p. 443.

(*i*) L. R. 7 I. A. 212.

(*k*) *Annapurni* v. *Forbes*, L. R. 26 I. A. 246

(*l*) Works, vol. V., p. 58 ss.

(*m*) Sir F. Macn. Cons. on H. L. 168.

(*mm*) H. H. Wilson, Works, pp. 61, 62.

agrees in principle with the decisions of the Judicial Committee (*n*) against the capacity of a mother-in-law to adopt under a power so as to divest her daughter-in-law of the estate taken by the latter in succession to her husband.

I. 1. B. 2. 2. (*d*).—Relations between Adopted Son and Grandparents.

In *Siddappa* v. *Ningangavda* (*o*) it was held that the widow of a predeceased son was competent to make a valid adoption with the contemporaneous consent of her mother-in-law in whom the estate of the last full owner had vested as heir.

I. 1. B. 2. 3.—Relations with Respect to Obligations.

(*a*) Between the Father (and Grandfather) and the Son as to Debts and Claims.

"An adopted son like another is responsible independently of assets received for the debt of the grandfather by adoption though not incurred for the family" (*p*). Jagannatha agrees with the Sastri. The adopted son's liability for his father's debts, he says, like that of the son by birth, arises at the father's death, and is independent of assets (*q*). A previous partition even only throws the burden first upon those sons who remained in union with the father.

An adopted son is liable for his father's debts to the extent of the inheritance received by him, and if he waives or does not obtain the inheritance, his self-acquisition is not liable for the debts (*r*).

A son adopted in pursuance of an *unoomoti puttro*, some time after the death of his adoptive father, does not require, and is not entitled to obtain, a certificate under Act XXVII. of 1860, to

---

(*n*) *Bhoobun Moyee's Case*, 10 M. I. A. 278; *Pudma Coomari Debi* v. *The Court of Wards*, L. R 8 I. A. 229, 245; *Venkappa* v. *Jivaji Krishna*, I. L. R. 25 Bom. 306.

(*o*) I. L. R. 38 Bom. 724; *Payapa* v. *Appamma*, I. L. R. 23 Bom. 327.

(*p*) MS. 979. See above, pp. 75, 160.

(*q*) See Col. Dig., Book I., TT. 167—170, Comm.

(*r*) *Jummal Ali* v. *Tirbhee Lall Doss*, 12 C. W. R. 41. The adoption was that of a brother, but it was not a point in issue.

enable him to collect debts in respect of the properties left by his adoptive father, which accrued due while they were under the management of his adoptive mother. The estate of the adoptive father, if the adoption is a good one, vests immediately on the adoption in the adopted son, and debts to it, if they accrued due after the death of the adoptive father, are debts recoverable by the adopted son in his own right, and not as representative of his adoptive father (*s*).

I. 1. B. 2. 3. (*b*).—BETWEEN THE ADOPTIVE MOTHER AND SON.

A mortgage [before adoption] by a widow to pay off her husband's debts was upheld as against a boy subsequently adopted (*t*). On a similar ground of benefit received by the son, a bond executed by a widow in possession was held binding on the adopted son of the last zamindar, the bond having been given for debts which the adopted son as zamindar had by his acts admitted his liability to pay (*v*).

The widow's authority as manager makes the son liable for necessary debts. "A son adopted by a widow is responsible for a debt incurred by her for the family during his minority" (*w*). But he has once or twice been thought answerable merely as son for his mother. Thus an adopted son was pronounced liable for the mother's debt incurred for purposes not ascertained, he having taken her property, and as generally answerable apart from that for parents' debts (*x*).

In one case the High Court of Bengal seems to have thought that a second adopted son was liable in his estate for all debts, without distinction, incurred by the mother between the death of the first and the adoption of the second son (*y*). For this the case of *Bhoobun Moyee Debia* (*z*) is referred to, but it does not

---

(*s*) *Narain Mal* v. *Kooer Narain Mytee*, I. L. R. 5 Cal. 251.

(*t*) *Satra Khumaji* v. *Tatia Hanmantrav*, Bom. H. C. P. J. 1878, p. 121.

(*v*) *Chetty Colum Coomara Vencatachella* v. *Rajah Rungasawmy Jyengar*, 4 C. W. R. P. C. 71. The Judicial Committee say—"Unless those moneys so advanced to the widow personally were advanced to pay subsisting charges on the estate or otherwise, for its advantage, they, of course, could constitute no charge on the zemindary."

(*w*) MS. 1678.

(*x*) MS. 943. See above, pp. 164, 165.

(*y*) *Gobindo Nath Roy* v. *Ram Kanay Chowdhry*, 24 C. W. R. 183.

(*z*) 10 M. I. A. 279.

seem to deal with any such point. It views with some doubt the possibility of an adoption where a previous son had reached an age to fulfil the ceremonial duties (*a*), but nothing as to the liabilities arising should a second adoption be admitted (*b*).

It was said to be a nice question: What is the effect of admission of the adopter as binding on a subsequently adopted person (*c*)? It would seem that such admissions made by a widow would be subject to objection if prejudicial to the adopted son or the estate (*d*).

During the minority of a boy, adopted by a widow, she squandered her husband's property, contracted debts, and refused to render accounts to her son. It was held that as the son was liable to pay the *bonâ fide* debts of the mother, she was liable to account to him for her management, or to pay the damages claimed (*e*).

An adopted son's estate is not liable for personal debts of the adoptive mother (*f*), but a sale of part by the adoptive mother, a widow, to recoup co-sharers' payments of Government land revenue, was upheld as a lawful exercise of discretion by a guardian.

The adoptive mother is the legal representative of her son, and entitled to a certificate under Act XXVII. of 1860 (*g*).

I. 1. B. 2. 4.—Relations between Son by Adoption and Children by Birth.

(*a*) Immediate Personal Relations.

The adopted son gives place to a son by birth, should there be one in the performance of the kriya and the sraddhas. The

---

(*a*) See above, sec. III. B. 3. 25.

(*b*) It is an additional argument against an adoption by a mother after the death of an adult son, that the hazard to which creditors would be exposed would greatly impede her good management of the estate.

(*c*) *Brojendro Coomar Roy* v. *The Chairman of the Dacca Municipality*, 20 C. W. R. 223.

(*d*) The adopted son takes by a right paramount to that of the widow and will be bound by her acts and admissions only so far as these can be ascribed to her as manager or agent. See above, p. 349.

(*e*) *Nurhur Shamrao* v. *Yeshodabaee*, Bellasis, Rep. 65.

(*f*) *Roopmonjooree* v. *Ramlall Sirkar*, 1 C. W. R., p. 145.

(*g*) *Sreemutty Deeno Moyee Dossee* v. *Doorga Pershad Mitter*, 3 C. W. R. Misc. 6.

adopted son takes a minor part in some celebrations which it is needless to give in detail (*h*).

As the adopted son becomes a member of the adoptive family, the restrictions on marriage between him and female members of the family may be deemed the same as if he had been born into the place he occupies. This at least is so to three degrees from the stem, so that a woman may not be married to her first cousin by adoption (*i*). Whether the prohibitions extend further is uncertain; questions on the subject are very infrequent owing to the general prejudice against the marriage of near relatives.

Should an adopted son or his widow desire to adopt, the same grounds of preference and the same general principles would apply as if he had been born in the family of adoption (*k*).

(*b*) Relations with Respect to Property.

The relative rights of children by birth and by adoption in the matter of inheritance to the family estate have been discussed in *The Digest of Vyavasthas* (*l*). In relation to the adoptive mother's property as well to that of the father, the adoptive son takes a right (*m*) subject by analogy to a partial defeasance in competition with a son by birth.

"The share of an adopted son is one-fourth of the share of a son born to the adoptive father after the adoption" (*n*).

The heirs of a deceased Hindu in Shahabad being a real and an adopted son, the adopted son takes one-fourth, and the real son three-fourths of his property (*o*).

"If after the adoption of a boy, a son be legally begotten and

---

(*h*) See Datt. Chand, sec. II.

(*i*) See above, pp. 837, 838.

(*k*) See sec. III. and sec. IV.

(*l*) Above, pp. 351, 354 ss.

(*m*) Above, p. 480.

(*n*) *Ayyavu Muppanar* v. *Niladatchi Ammal et al.*, 1 M. H. C. R., p. 45; *Giriapa* v. *Ningapa*, I. L. R. 17 Bom. 100; *Ruklal* v. *Amrushet*, I. L. R. 16 Bom. 347. As to the proportion of the adopted son see Col. Dig., Book V., T. 301, Comm.; above, pp. 347, 354, 355. The begotten son cuts down the adopted to one-fourth according to Vasishtha XV. 9. In Bengal the ratio is one-third, Tag. Lec. 1880, p. 539. In the Punjab he takes equally, Cust. Law, II. 158.

(*o*) *Preag Singh* v. *Ajoodya Singh*, 4 C. S. D. A. R. 96.

born in marriage, the latter will inherit three-fourths of the father's property, the former one-fourth. The Kaustubh gives the adoptee one-third or even one-half" (*p*).

"After the adoption of a son, one is born to the adopter. The latter succeeds to his father's watan" (*q*). The precedence of the legitimate son by birth over the son by adoption is secured by several texts (*r*).

The Dattaka Chandrika, which says that the illegitimate son of a Sudra in competition with any heir down to the daughter's son takes but half a share (*s*), gives to the adopted son of a Sudra an equal share in a partition made during the father's life, and half a share in a partition after his death (*t*).

A woman's illegitimate son, it was said, takes nothing by inheritance from her in competition with her adopted son. Even her conveyance of her property to the former was pronounced invalid as against the heritable right of the latter (*v*). This could hardly be maintained unless the property was that of the deceased husband; of her separate estate the widow could dispose (*w*).

In one case an adoption had been contested. The adopted son took the estate and then died. It was sought to exclude from

---

(*p*) Steele, L. C., p. 47. "In some places, the two boys (the begotten and adopted) share all property equally; in others, the former takes two-thirds; in others, three-fourths; in others, the father, on the birth of his begotten son, gives the adoptee a present according to his ability, and separates him from the family, and in consequence he takes no share; in others, the adoptee obtains nothing without a complaint to the Sirkar. The former is entitled to management of hereditary property, and if an Enamdar or Wuttundar to the Dastkhat (right of signature), Sikka (seal), Naonagar (mark, or signature of a Patel), and other privileges of eldership." Steele, L. C., pp. 186, 187. See above, pp. 65, 678.

(*q*) MS. 1739. The watan is regarded as going by preference to the head of the family, see above, pp. 65, 180, 676, 836; Steele, L. C. 218, 229; and as an impartible estate, so far as it supports the office, see above, pp. 175, 676; *Purshotam* v. *Mudakangavda*, Bom. H. C. P. J. 1883, p. 228.

(*r*) See Datt. Mim. IV. 26.

(*s*) See above, pp. 79, 712.

(*t*) Sec. V. 30. As a Sudra father may give to his illegitimate son an equal share with his legitimate sons (see above, p. 708), it seems to follow that he should be able to do as much for his adopted son, though this is not provided for in the sacred writings, which do not indeed contemplate adoption by Sudras. Strange says, that "among Sudras . . . the after-born son and the adopted share equally the parental estate." 1 Str. H. L. 99.

(*v*) 2 Str. H. L. 110.

(*w*) Above, pp. 301, 319, 352, 353, 656; 2 Str. H. L. 127.

succession the son of him who had formerly denied the adoption; but the Court said:—" *Deendial's* denial [formerly] of *Munnoo's* adoption *de jure*, cannot, therefore, estop his son from claiming the right of succession to Munnoo's property unquestionably acquired by him *de facto* by adoption and by no other title " (*x*).

A sister succeeds to the brother by adoption as to one by birth (*y*).

Relations between the Adopted Son and Remoter Connexions by Blood.

I. 1. B. 2. 5.—Of the Adopted Father.

The adopted son becomes impure through deaths and births in the family of adoption, but for a shorter time than a son by birth (*z*). The son adopted into a united family becomes a participator in the family sacra celebrated by the head of the family (*a*). In the event of a partition after his adoption the sacra becomes dispersed, and he thenceforth offers sacrifices separately. If his father, being separated, had sacra of his own, the adopted son will naturally continue them, as even in a united family there are some services to the father's manes which devolve necessarily on the son. But if a member of an undivided family having no separate sacred fire of his own has died sonless, and then a partition has taken place causing a dispersion of the general family sacra amongst the parceners (*b*), the son afterwards adopted by the widow has no share in these. He honours his adoptive father's spirit, but cannot draw back the common sacrifices (*c*). The connexion of the estate with the sacra makes this consideration important for the law of property. There is no failure of the family sacrifices while the state of union continues. Every member joins in them directly or vicariously. On a partition it

---

(*x*) *Sheo Sohai Misser* v. *Musst. Billasee*, N. W. P. S. D. R. N. S. Pt. I. 1864, p. 504.

(*y*) *Mahantapa* v. *Nilgangowa*, Bom. H. C. P. J. for 1879, p. 390.

(*z*) Datt. Chand. IV. 1—5.

(*a*) Vyav. May. Chap. IV. sec. VII., para. 28.

(*b*) It is a general maxim that what was prevented at its proper season may not be taken up afterwards. See Colebrooke L. and Essays, vol. II. 138.

(*c*) The religious duties of separated brethren are necessarily divided. See Vyav. May., Chap. IV., sec. VII., pp. 28, 29; Manu III. 69; Narada XIII. 37, 41, 383; Mit., Chap. II., sec. XII., para. 3.

were sacrilege to let them sink into abeyance, and once separately appropriated they cannot, without sacrilege, be given up.

The adopted son, though he may be partially superseded by a begotten son, yet, in the absence of such a son, takes the whole share of his adoptive father in a partition of the joint estate (*d*). Nor do the Hindu authorities draw any distinction in this respect between a son adopted before and one adopted after the death of the adoptive father. Each member of a united family is replaced in the family by his son down to a partition of the inheritance (*e*). From the moment of partition the son fully replaces him only in the new family thus set on foot (*f*). The son adopted by a widow, ranking as posthumous, blends with the united family and takes his ideal father's interest in the estate (*g*), nor can this be prevented by the existence of other joint interests which the intruder impairs by sharing them (*h*). The control of the widow by the surviving brethren is an attribute of their guardianship, not of their ownership, and is itself subject to control if unfairly used according to Hindu notions. But if a partition has been made after the death of a sonless coparcener, and a provision has been made for his widow and daughter (*i*), it seems that a subsequent adoption will not enable the adopted to reclaim his ideal father's share from those amongst whom it has been dispersed. The texts say that a proposed partition must be postponed until the result of a widow's pregnancy is seen (*k*). They also provide for a redistribution in favour of an actually posthumous son (*l*). But they do not say that the parceners must await a widow's election to adopt or not, or that a share must be made up for the son subsequently adopted (*m*). As, therefore, there is a general

(*d*) Above, p. 836. *Tara Mohun Bhuttacharjee* v. *Kripa Moyee Debia*, 9 C. W. R. 423.

(*e*) *I.e.*, so far as the great-grandson of one in actual participation. See above, pp. 61, 62, 324, 711.

(*f*) Above, p. 338.

(*g*) Above, p. 348.

(*h*) See above, pp. 856, 859, 861.

(*i*) See above, pp. 694, 709, 712.

(*k*) Above, pp. 72, 608, 770, 847; Mit., Chap. I., sec. VI., para. 12.

(*l*) Above, p. 722.

(*m*) The Sastris in one case declared that—"Inspired legislators had made provision for the custody of the estate of minors, but neither they, nor any writer, had provided for the charge of the estate of the unborn during an indefinite time; therefore the unborn could have no property." *Bamundoss Mookerjea* v. *Musst. Tarinee*, 7 M. I. A. 188. See above, pp. 63, 554. The joint estate supporting

rule allowing partition at the will of the existing members and explicit exceptions for two particular cases, it would be opposed to the Hindu principles of construction to admit a claim in a third case on which there is no express authority for taking the property back from its separate owners (*n*).

The fact, again, of property held by one descendant or group of descendants from the same stock unshared by other descendants implies partition or separate acquisition. By an extinction of the united proprietary group the continuity and unity of ownership are destroyed. The principles of partition rather than of inheritance, as conceived by the Hindu lawyers (*o*), come into play, and the law distributes the property once for all to those who are at that moment entitled, by a distinct transfer and a creation of new interests incompatible with any continuance of the old. The revival of an interest once extinguished is nowhere contemplated. The law as laid down in cases of adoption subsequent to a partition following the adoptive father's death, or to the opening of a collateral succession, seems thus quite in accordance with Hindu principles. In the two cases immediately to be cited it does not appear that the distinction between the divided and the undivided family was kept quite clearly in view. In these there had not been a partition, and the family still admitted of increase by adoption. An adoption made by a widow will not, it was said, devest the surviving joint sharers with her late husband's father of any part of the property, nor when his father was separated will it devest the deceased husband's sisters of their succession to their father, unless made in either case with the assent of the persons entitled (*p*). Property vested in one of two united brothers by the death of the other, it was said in *Govind Purshotam* v *Lakshmibai* (*q*), cannot be devested by the subsequent adoption of a son to the deceased. In the absence of a partition it would seem that the adopted son must take his father's place, as in *Sri Raghunada's Case*.

---

common sacra remains accessible to an adopted son of an undivided member until it has been divided. After this there is no authority for recovering any portion.

(*n*) See above, pp. 552, 554.

(*o*) See above, p. 561.

(*p*) *Ramchandracharya* v. *Shridharacharya*, Bom. H. C. P. J. 1881, p. 145. See above, p. 889.

(*q*) Bom. H. C. P. J. 1882, p. 12; *Bhubaneswari Debi* v. *Nilkomul Lahiri*, L. R. 12 I. A. 137.

An adopted son succeeds collaterally as well as lineally (*r*) to ancestral property (*s*). But though an adopted son succeeds collaterally as well as lineally (*t*), his right, it is said, vests for this purpose only from the adoption (*v*), *i.e.* the widow till then can sue in her own right. Nor can he retrospectively take away what passed to another through his non-existence or non-adoption when the succession opened (*w*).

In a leading case the Judicial Committee said :—

" Their Lordships think, therefore, looking at these authorities (*x*), and the weight that is due to them, that an adopted son succeeds not only lineally but collaterally to the inheritance of his relations, and, if so, these appellants are not in a condition to succeed, because they have distinctly admitted in their own pleadings, and by the answer of their own pleaders given to the Court, that an adopted son of the brother by the whole-blood was in existence at the time of their suit being commenced. If an adopted son of the whole-blood is in the same situation as the natural son of the whole-blood, then the only remaining question is whether the son of the brother of the whole-blood succeeds in preference to the sons of the brother by the half-blood; and upon that point there is no dispute, for the authorities are uniform " (*y*).

That an adopted son of a whole-brother is preferred to a natural son of half-brother (*z*), follows from the principles stated in the

---

(*r*) *Sham Chunder et al.* v. *Nurainee Dibeh*, 1 C. S. D. A. R., p. 209; *Sumboochunder Chowdry* v. *Naraini Dibeh*, 3 Knapp, p. 55; S. C. 5 C. W. R., p. 100 P. C.; *Gour Hurrie Kubraj* v. *Musst. Rutnasuree Debia et al.*, 6 C. S. D. A. R., p. 203; *Tara Mohun Bhuttacharjee* v. *Kripa Moyee Debia*, 9 C. W. R. 423; *Lokenath Roy et al.* v. *Shamsoonduree*, Beng. S. D. A. R. for 1858, p. 1863.

(*s*) *Gokul Chund* v. *Narain Dass*, N. W. P. R. 1862, Pt. I., p. 47.

(*t*) *Sumboochunder Chowdry* v. *Naraini Dibeh*, 3 Knapp, 55.

(*v*) *Bamundoss Mookerjea* v. *Musst. Tarinee*, 7 M. I. A. 169. See above, A. 5.

(*w*) *Musst. Bhoobun Moyee Debia* v. *Ram Kishore Acharj*, 10 M. I. A. 279; *Bhubaneswari Debi* v. *Nilkomul Lahiri*, L. R. 12 I. A. 137.

(*x*) See Mit., Chap. I., sec. XI., pp. 30, 31; Suth. Syn. Head IV., Col. Dig., Book V., TT. 184, 217, Comm.

(*y*) *Sumboochunder Chowdry* v. *Naraini Dibeh*, 3 Knapp, Pr. Co. 61—62. See Mitakshara, Chap. II., sec. IV., paras. 5 and 7; Daya-Bhaga, Chap. XI., sec. VI., para. 2. " Can a son given be heir to a kinsman, or not? . . . A text of Manu shows that a son given, being endowed with every virtue, shall take the heritage." Col. Dig., Book V., T. 277, Comm.

(*z*) See above, pp. 103, 104, 354. The Mitakshara gives the succession to the half-brother in preference to the whole brother's son, but still the latter precedes the son of a half-brother. The Judicial Committee placed the right

earlier part of this work. It will be noticed too that in a case between separated brothers and their sons, the latter do not represent their predeceased father in succession to his post-deceased brother, or take so long as another brother survives. Much less, therefore, would an adopted son take back any part of the succession thus disposed of before he was adopted. In the case of a daughter's son, as he is not by his birth, nor therefore by his adoption, a co-owner with his maternal grandfather whose proprietary personality could thus be conceived as persisting in him, he cannot take back the estate from those to whom the law before his existence has given it. This is the application of the general principle made by the Sastris at 7 M. I. A. p. 188. In Bombay the daughter herself would succeed in the case supposed, and then supposing her father had had an undivided brother predeceased, the question would arise of whether the daughter's existence was a bar to adoption by the widow of the first deceased brother, or to the succession of the son thus taken. There is not the slightest Hindu authority for saying that the adoption could not be made; and when made it would react so as to put the boy adopted in the place held by his adoptive father in the undivided family. A daughter, though she inherits, does not continue the estate and the sacra as a son or a widow does (a). Her existence is no bar to adoption, and in the case supposed the right to adopt a fit person would subsist though she were a son.

In the case of collaterals generally, the nearest or those who are equally the nearest of the nearest kin succeed. Amongst them too there is no waiting for the possible birth of a posthumous son, who, if already born, would precede those in existence (b). The widow of a gotraja sapinda under the Bombay Law intercepts the estate for her unborn child, but amongst the Bandhus the principle of interpretation adopted by the Vyavahara Mayukha (c) would shut out a child from succession, though when born, the nearest to the propositus, if his birth followed instead of preceding the opening of the succession. Similarly in the case of a son adopted: he can retroactively continue an estate, but cannot recover one given to others prior to his adoptive existence. If his mother has

---

of the adopted son on his becoming "for all purposes the son of the [adoptive] father." See Rep., p. 60.

(a) See above, pp. 87, 120, 121, 789.

(b) Comp. p. 542, Q. 2, Rem. 2; p. 546, Q. 8, Rem. 1.

(c) Above, p. 460.

succeeded as representative of her husband's line, he as son can supersede her: if she has not, he cannot supersede others whose personality is not identified with his adoptive father's (*d*).

That the estate which has once passed away to a separated collateral cannot be affected even in part by a subsequent adoption is strongly shown by the case of *Nilcomul* v. *Jotendro Mohun Lahuree* (*e*), where even a postponement of adoption procured by fraud was allowed to prevent the adopted boy, as a collateral, from defeating the intermediate collateral succession of the guilty party.

In the case of collateral succession to the property of separated branches or members of a family, there is no rule reducing the share of an adopted son in competition with a son by birth. The rule applies in terms only to the patrimony in which interests are acquired by birth and by adoption, not to an estate passing through default of co-sharers to a collateral line. The adopted son is a sapinda (*f*), equally with the son by birth, and the analogy of the equality of the half-blood with the full-blood in the case of sapindas not specifically provided for (*g*), may fairly be extended to the adopted son. As the collaterals in the adoptive family inherit equally from him as from a son by birth, so should he inherit from them equally with a son by birth.

An adopted son of a coparcener excluded on account of blindness, &c., from a share in a partition is, according to the Dattaka Chandrika, entitled to maintenance (*h*).

A niece's son adopted by her paternal uncle was pronounced entitled to the management of business as managing Patel, while the widow of the deceased nephew was pronounced heir to his property (*i*). (Nothing is said of the caste or of division or non-division. Division and Sudra caste seem to be assumed.)

" An adopted son is not precluded from inheriting the estate

(*d*) In the event of a property falling in collaterally to a branch united in itself, this inheritance would be taken by the then existing members to the exclusion of a son afterwards adopted by a widow of a predeceased member of the group. Such at least is the view that seems most conformable to principle for the reasons set forth above, pp. 648, 659; but the matter as shown there is one of controversy amongst the Hindu lawyers.

(*e*) Above, pp. 350, 890. I. L. R. 7 Cal. 178. Affd. *Bhubaneswari Debi* v. *Nilkomul Lahiri*, L. R. 12 I. A. 137; S. C. I. L. R. 12 Cal. 18.

(*f*) Above, pp. 107, 108, 435.

(*g*) Above, p. 116.

(*h*) Sec. VI. 1.

(*i*) MS. 5.

of one related lineally, though at a distance of more than three generations from the common ancestor." "The rights of an adopted son, except in a few instances precisely defined in the Dattaka Chandrika and the Dattaka Mimamsa by express texts, are in every respect similar to those of a natural-born son. The adopted son succeeds to the sapinda kinsmen of his father, and as regards the sapinda relationship, there is no difference between the adopted and natural-born son" (*k*).

In Bengal, it has been held that an adopted son succeeds to the property of a son of his sister by adoption (*l*).

One adopted succeeds another as nearest collateral relative (*m*).

RELATIONS BETWEEN THE ADOPTED SON AND REMOTER CONNEXIONS BY BLOOD.

I. 1. B. 2. 6.—OF THE ADOPTIVE MOTHER.

As to the succession of an adopted son to property in right of a connexion through his mother with her family of birth (*n*) the decisions have differed (*o*). In *Chinnaramakristna Ayya* v.

(*k*) *Puddo Kumaree* v. *Juggut Kishore*, I. L. R. 5 Cal. 615; in appeal S. C. L. R. 8 I. A. 229; *Mokundo Lall Roy* v. *Bykunt Nath Roy*, I. L. R. 6 Cal. 289, quoting *Tara Mohun Bhuttacharjee* v. *Kripa Moyee*, 9 C. W. R. 423; *Kali Komul Mozoomdar* v. *Uma Shankar Moitra*, L. R. 10 I. A. 138. See above, p. 838. Sutherland, 2 Str. H. L. 116, says, he (the adopted son) inherits collaterally as well as lineally according to the Mitakshara, notwithstanding passages in Datt. Mimamsa and Datt. Chandrika limiting his sapindaship to three degrees.

(*l*) *Puddo Kumaree Debee* v. *Juggut Kishore Acharjee*, I. L. R. 5 Cal. 615; S. C. L. R. 8 I. A. 229.

(*m*) *Gour Hurrie Kubraj* v. *Musst. Rutnasuree*, 6 C. S. D. A. R. 203; *Sham Chunder et al.* v. *Naraiani Dibeh*, 1 C. S. D. A. R. 209.

(*n*) See above, p. 456 ss. "In a case where the right is not dubious, the funeral cake shall be offered by a daughter's son to his maternal grandfather, although he do not claim the estate and family." Col. Dig., Book V., T. 276, Comm.

(*o*) Under the Roman Law an adoption did not make the adopted a cognate of his father's cognates; the mutual rights of inheritance were restricted to those connected as agnates. With the adoptive mother's family he had no connexion to form a basis for mutual rights. (See Willems, Dr., Pub. Rom., p. 87; above, p. 836.) Justinian's rule under which the adopted son remained in the family of his birth corresponded to the preference long established by practice of the marriage without "Manus" to that accompanied by "Manus." The Roman wife in the later ages remained a member of her father's family.

Minnatchi Ammal (*p*) he was refused the place of a daughter's son as heir to her father's property. The P. Sadr Amin had decided in his favour on the authority of the Dattaka Mimamsa, but the High Court set him aside in favour of the grandson of a brother of the adoptive mother's father. The latter is by the Madras High Court ranked as a Bandhu. According to the Mitakshara he is a gotraja sapinda of the propositus, but would still rank after the daughter's son; but the Madras decision denies to the adopted son any right at all as a grandson to his mother's father.

In the North-West Provinces on the other hand it was held, in *Sham Kuar* v. *Gaya Din* (*q*) that the adopted son succeeds to the property inherited by his adoptive mother from her father, and as the doctrine of a mere life estate being taken by a female heir prevails there (*r*), the adopted son must have been thought a competent heir to his maternal adoptive grandfather.

In Bengal a decision precisely the reverse had been given in *Gunga Mya* v. *Kishen Kishore Chowdry* (*s*). In *Teencowree Chatterjee* v. *Dinonath Banerjee* (*t*) it was ruled, that to his adoptive mother's stridhan the adopted son succeeds in the absence of daughters. It had previously been held that *Gunga Mya's Case* was not conclusive, and that where an adopted son was the propositus, the maternal relatives inherited from him as from a son by birth (*v*). This would seem to establish a reciprocal connexion by which the adopted son ought in his turn to benefit, but such a doctrine was denied in *Moun Moyee Debeah* v. *Bejoy Kishto Gosave* (*w*), and it was by this case that the Madras Court was governed in that of *Chinnarama* v. *Kristna Ayya.* The text of Manu is very explicit in giving the right only to a son begotten

---

She did not become a member of her husband's family. It was, therefore, most natural that her husband's adopted son whose connexion even with the adoptive father's family was limited to the agnates should have none at all with hers. The mutual rights of succession between mother and child rested on special laws. See Ortolan, Inst. § 152. Willems, Dr., Pub. Rom., p. 77.

(*p*) 7 M. H. C. R. 245.

(*q*) I. L. R. 1 All. 255.

(*r*) See above, p. 316.

(*s*) 3 C. S. D. A. R. 128.

(*t*) 3 C. W. R. 49.

(*v*) *Gangapersad Roy* v. *Brijessurree Chowdhrain*, 15 S. D. A. R. 1091. See above, p. 454 ss.

(*w*) W. R. F. B. 121. See 1 Hay, 260.

by the daughter's husband (*x*), and the "daughter's son" in Vishnu (*y*) probably had no other in view. But as the adopted son now makes oblations to his adoptive mother's male ancestors (*z*) the connexion may logically be attended with mutual rights of inheritance, as in the case of a daughter's son by birth (*a*).

The question came before the Judicial Committee in *Rani Anand Kunwar* v. *The Court of Wards* (*b*), but their Lordships did not pronounce upon it. The High Court of Bengal, however, has held that, according to Hindu Law, an adopted son takes by inheritance from the relatives (father and brother) of his adoptive mother in the same way as a legitimate son (*c*). A similar opinion has more recently been expressed by the Judicial Committee in *Kali Komul Mozoomdar* v. *Uma Sunkar Moitro* (*d*). Their Lordships say:—"As to the second question, their Lordships have held in *Pudma Coomari Debi* v. *The Court of Wards* (*e*), that an adopted son succeeds not only lineally, but collaterally, to the inheritance of his relatives by adoption. In that case the claimant was the adopted son of the maternal grandfather of the deceased, and it was argued for the appellant that it was distinguishable from this case. But their Lordships laid down that an adopted son occupies the same position in the family of the adopter as a natural-born son, except in a few instances, which are accurately defined both in the Dattaka Chandrika and Dattaka Mimamsa. That this is the Hindu law is shown by the careful examination of the authorities by the learned native Judge who delivered the judgment

(*x*) Above, p. 421.

(*y*) Above, p. 420.

(*z*) See Col. Dig., Book V., T. 275, Comm.

(*a*) Above, pp. 418, 460.

(*b*) I. L. R. 6 Cal. 764; S. C. L. R. 8 I. A. 14.

(*c*) *Uma Sunker Moitro* v. *Kali Komul*, I. L. R. 6 Cal. 256. "It is, therefore, clear, that the adopted son confers the same spiritual benefit upon the relatives of his adoptive mother as a legitimate son does, and that he is cut off from the inheritance of the relatives of his original mother. That being so, it would accord with the dictates of natural justice, as well as with the principles upon which the Law of Inheritance in the Bengal School is based, to hold that an adopted son succeeds to the property of the relatives of his adoptive mother in the same way as a legitimate son." (Jud. Cit., p. 262.) This is approved and followed in *Surjokant Nundi* v. *Mohesh Chunder Dutt Mojoomdar*, I. L. R. 9 Cal. 70.

(*d*) L. R. 10 I. A. 138.

(*e*) L. R. 8 I. A. 229.

of the Full Bench of the High Court, which is the subject of this appeal. The respondent claims to succeed as being the daughter's son, and consequently the heir of his maternal grandfather at the death of his widow, which he would be if he were a natural-born son, and as an adopted son he is in the same position. This is clear from the Dattaka Mimamsa, sect. 6, p. 50, where it is said, 'The forefathers of the adoptive mother only are also the maternal grandsires of sons given and the rest, for the rule regarding paternal is equally applicable to maternal grandsires (of adopted sons).' Their Lordships are, therefore, of opinion that the decree of the High Court in favour of the respondent is right."

I. 2.—Imperfect Adoption under the Ordinary Law (*f*).

The law of the Sastras, or what was supposed to be so (*g*), has practically been superseded by the customary law and the decisions of the Courts as to the status of a boy defectively adopted. These decisions are of course authoritative so far as they extend. Still it may be useful to consider what the Hindu lawyers have said as to the consequences of an imperfect adoption as affecting the relations between the adopted and the family of birth and the family of adoption, and the view taken of his relations as a grantee of public lands or endowments.

The customary law is thus stated:—

"Adoptions may be annulled if made contrary to caste custom. Several of the caste enquire into the irregularity complained of, and their decision is carried into effect (whether declaring the validity or annulment of the adoption)" (*h*).

"In such case the separating adopted son might take a small share (one-tenth) without being chargeable with the payment of his adoptive father's debts" (*i*).

I. 2. A.—Relations to the Family of Birth.

An adoption may have been imperfect in the sense of not constituting the proposed relation or, in having failed merely in

(*f*) See sec. VI. A. 5. Should no adoption be attempted the estate descends as if none were intended. See sec. VIII. and 2 Str. H. L. 90.

(*g*) Above, pp. 835, 836.

(*h*) Steele, L. C. App., p. 388.

(*i*) Steele, L. C. App., pp. 389, 390.

some unessential particular not impairing its jural effect. The Hindu lawyers recognize an intermediate result, where the gift has been so far completed as to sever the child from his family of birth, but the acceptance in adoption has not been so made as to make him a member of the adoptive family (*k*). This status of the adopted is of only theoretical interest; both the castes and the Courts, as we have seen, refuse to acknowledge a parting from the one family without a union to the new one.

The rights of a man in his family of birth remain unaffected when his adoption has been invalid (*l*).

I. 2. B.—Relations to Family of Adoption.

To disqualify for sharing in a partition leprosy of a virulent form (*m*) or the like defect must have arisen previous to division; but if succession is once vested exclusively in the others, it is not devested by adoption (*n*) on the part of the disqualified man whose share has been appropriated. It seems that such persons cannot themselves adopt, but that sons already adopted are entitled to a provision for their maintenance (*o*). Custom sometimes allows a vicarious adoption (*p*).

When an adoption of a son has once been absolutely made and acted on, it cannot be declared invalid or set aside at the suit of the adoptive father. A cancellation of adoption might, it was ruled, be based upon the grounds—(1) The adoption was not in

---

(*k*) The gift alone severs connexion with the family of birth, even if the rites are insufficient to establish a connexion with the family of adoption. (Datt. Chand. II. 19, 20; see 2 Str. H. L. 122.)

(*l*) *Bhawani Sankara Pandit* v. *Ambabay Ammal*, 1 M. H. C. R. 363, 365; above, p. 836. "Examples of irregularities justifying annulment are: adoption of a father's brother or sister's son, or an elder than the adopter, or of a boy without the necessary consent, or of a boy who is a cripple, or disabled in senses or understanding." Steele, L. C. App., p. 388. As to a defective gift being null, 2 Str. H. L. 433; H. H. Wilson, Works, vol. V., p. 73.

(*m*) *Mohunt Bhagwan Ramanuj Das* v. *Das*, L. R. 22 I. A. 94.

(*n*) *Sevachetumbara Pillay* v. *Parasucty*, M. S. D. A. R. for 1857, p. 210; 1 Str. H. L 163. Above, p. 886.

(*o*) See above, sub-sec. I. 1 B. 2. 5, and pp. 544, 551, 689, 690, 795. The son adopted when the adopter was competent, as before he was afflicted with leprosy, ought on general principles to take his father's place as though the father had died. See above, pp. 149, 542.

(*p*) See above, p. 546.

the manner and according to the ceremonies required by Hindu Law; (2) The boy was not a fit and proper person to perform the plaintiff's obsequies or to make offerings for the benefit of the souls of the plaintiff's ancestors, being devoid of education and religious knowledge and principles, and the associate of thieves, gamblers, and women of immoral character; (3) He failed to perform his part of an agreement or compromise in writing entered into by him with the plaintiff (*q*).

An absolute disqualification of the boy, the performance of the ceremonies of adoption on a boy of a different caste, or the omission of them in adopting a boy of a different gotra (*r*), is variously said to make the adoption null, while severing the boy from his family of birth or to constitute an adoption of an inferior kind. According to either view the boy defectively adopted is entitled to maintenance on the footing of a das or slave (*s*). The gift alone is supposed to sever him completely from his family of birth (*t*). The authority last cited makes the performance of the ceremonies by the adoptive father effectual to release even a tonsured son from connexion with his family of birth, and to raise him from the servile rank to that of a son to the adoptive father (*v*). It would now probably be held that there must be the proposed change of status or none at all, and that failing a complete adoption, the boy must remain a member of his family of birth (*w*). The gift or sale, which formerly gave a good title to the purchaser as owner of a slave, can no longer operate since the passing of Act V. of 1843 (*x*). The doctrine of a complete gift and acceptance as son being sufficient, and the attendant ceremonies only incidental, not absolutely essential, gets rid of many difficulties arising from the precepts just considered (*y*). That there cannot be a complete gift without complete acceptance, *see* the Viram. Transl. pp. 33, 35, and comp. Datt. Mim. sec. IV. 3. The work

---

(*q*) *Sukhbasi Lal* v. *Guman Singh*, I. L. R. 2 All. 366. Above, pp. 843, 845.

(*r*) Datt. Mim. V. 56.

(*s*) See Steele, L. C. 46, 184; Datt. Mim., sec. III. 2, 3; sec. IV., 40 ss.; Col. Dig., Book III., Chap. I., T. 29, 33, Comm.; Book V., T. 182, 273, 275, Comm.

(*t*) Datt. Chand., sec. II. 19.

(*v*) See *ibid.*, para. 27.

(*w*) See Colebrooke in 2 Str. H. L. 223; Steele, L. C. 386. Comp. Just. Inst., Book I., T. XI. 2; and Ortolan, § 138.

(*x*) See 2 Str. H. L. 221, 224.

(*y*) See Col. Dig., Book V., T. 273, Comm.

last cited specifies a gift, acceptance, and burnt offering as indispensable (z), and with this, as to Brahmanas, custom seems to agree (a). Colebrooke explains the slavery incurred by the *quasi*-adopted as servitude only of that highest kind from which a man frees himself by resigning his right to subsistence (b). The servitude indeed could not be more than nominal, seeing that though the son irregularly adopted was not entitled to succeed or to share the patrimony, his adoptive father was bound to get him married, and so set him up as a householder (c).

If one of a different caste has been adopted, the authorities exclude him from any share in the patrimony, but declare him entitled to maintenance (d), a right which arises in every case of severance from the family of birth without complete acceptance into that of adoption. Thus "in case of discovery that the boy being of another gotra, was not adopted with [the regular] ceremonies, or that he was of another caste, the adoption is null and the boy is to receive maintenance as a das or slave" (e). A Smriti passage frequently repeated says: "If a doubt arises as to a remote kinsman (adopted), *i.e.* as to his qualifications, the adopter shall set him apart like a Sudra" (f).

The decisions recognizing the particular status we are now considering have been very few. In one it was held that a Hindu invalidly adopted is entitled to maintenance in the adoptive family (g). In another case it was ruled that the adopted son of one whose adoption has been held invalid, cannot claim through the right of his adoptive father to be maintained by the alleged adoptive grandfather (h).

(z) See sec. V. 56.

(a) Steele, L. C. 184.

(b) As to this, see Col. Dig., Book III., Chap. I., T. 29, 48; 2 Str. H. L. 223, 226, 228.

(c) Datt. Mim., sec. V. 45, 46; Datt. Chand. sec. II. 18; sec. VI. 3, 4; MS. 1744. The earlier Roman Law required both a *mancipatio* to transfer the son from his family of birth, and a *vindicatio* or claim to him by the adoptive father as son to make a complete adoption. This *vindicatio* had to take place before a judicial officer, whereby formality and publicity were secured. See Ortolan, Inst. § 133 note, § 140. Later the requisite sanction was derived either from an imperial rescript for the case of one *sui juris* or an order of a judge for one *alieni juris*. *Ibid.*, §§ 136, 137.

(d) Datt. Mim., sec. III. 1—3.

(e) Steele, L. C., p. 46.

(f) Vas. XX. 7.

(g) *Ayyavu Muppanar* v. *Niladatchi Ammal*, 1 M. H. C. R. 45.

(h) *Bawani Sankara* v. *Ambabay Ammal*, 1 M. H. C. R. 363. The adopted father's adoption had been pronounced invalid on the ground that the widow adopting had not authority from her husband.

The Sastris treat this semi-adoption as a living institution, as in the following answers:—" A son illegally adopted had," it was said, " a right to maintenance and marriage expenses " (*i*). " A boy adopted after his chuda and other sacraments becomes a das entitled only to such property as may be conferred on him by gift " (*k*).

The British Courts, rejecting generally any distinction except that of belonging to the one or the other family, regard an essentially defective adoption as no adoption. Thus it was said, an authority to adopt " must be strictly pursued, and, as the adoption is for the husband's benefit, so the child must be adopted to him and not to the widow alone. Nor would an adoption by the widow alone for any purpose required by the Hindu Law give to the adopted child, even after her death, any right to the property inherited by her from her husband " (*l*). An attempt was made in one case to establish the principle, that an adoption incompetent to the person who made it through the existence of a representative of the family and estate might, on the removal of this person by death, acquire the validity it would have had in the absence of the obstacle at the time when it was made (*m*). In *Bhoobun Moyee's Case* (*n*) it was ruled, that a power to adopt could not be exercised after the death of the natural son leaving a widow. This in a later case (*o*) was interpreted as meaning that the adoption was absolutely invalid, not merely ineffectual to deprive the son's widow of her estate by succession to the deceased son her

(*i*) MS. 1744. See above, p. 836. He is put on an equal footing with an illegitimate, and " the father is obliged to support his natural son, he performing the duties of a servant." Steele, L. C., p. 179.

(*k*) MS. 1674. The Sastri, 2 Str. Hindu Law, 121, speaks of a Nitya Datta or permanent adoption, and an Anitya Datta or temporary one, and this, as he explains, depends on the performance or non-performance of the upanayana before adoption. Colebrooke says, the son of such a dvyamushyayana belongs to the family of his father's upanayana (and consequent gotraship).

(*l*) *Chowdry Pudum Singh* v. *Koer Oodey Singh*, 12 M. I. A. 350, 356.

(*m*) The nearest analogy, perhaps, would be the setting up of a bigamous marriage amongst Christians, as validated by the subsequent death of the obstructive spouse. The adoption of a son in the lifetime of another is not validated by the death of the latter. See above, p. 844.

(*n*) 10 M. I. A. 279.

(*o*) *Pudma Coomari Debea* v. *The Court of Wards*, L. R. 8 I. A. 229; *Chandra* v. *Gojrabai*, I. L. R. 14 Bom. 463; *Payapa* v. *Appanna*, I. L. R. 23 Bom. 327; *Sidappa* v. *Ningangavda*, I. L. R. 38 Bom. 224.

husband (*p*). The argument of the High Court of Calcutta that the adoption, though ineffectual as against the son's widow, became effectual on her death, and made the adopted son, then a brother by adoption of her deceased husband, was rejected by the Judicial Committee. The elder widow could not indeed give effect by acquiescence or ratification to that which was absolutely void; and the so-called adopted son was held not to have taken any rights (*q*). In Bombay the son's widow would, unless he had intimated his dissent, have had a right to adopt to him as a separated Hindu (*r*), and with his authority, or the sanction of his father (*s*), or when the father is dead with the consent of his united brethren, if he was unseparated (*t*). But as in Bengal the mother armed with authority from her deceased husband could not adopt (*v*) after the estate and the sacra had wholly centred in her son by the completion of his samskaras (*w*), neither in Bombay could she by such an authority, or by a mere implied authority drawn from her son, adopt so as to withdraw the son's property from him to whom the law had intermediately given it (*x*). It is the widow and she only who continues her husband's spiritual existence (*y*), and can replace him at any moment by an adopted son (*z*), subject in a united family to the assent of the surviving male members on account of her religious subordination to

---

(*p*) An opinion of Colebrooke to precisely the same effect, even where the adopted was a nephew of the deceased adoptive father, is given at 2 Str. H. L. 93.

(*q*) L. R. 8 I. A. 229.

(*r*) Above, pp. 868, 880, 885. *Lakshmibai* v. *Sarasvatibai*, I. L. R. 23 Bom. 789.

(*s*) *Vithoba* v. *Bapu*, I. L. R. 15 Bom. 110.

(*t*) Above, p. 881.

(*v*) This seems to be the correct doctrine. See above, p. 880 ss. Comp. *V. V. Krishnarao* v. *Venkatrama Laxmi*, I. L. R. 1 Mad., at p. 187.

(*w*) As to the theory advanced in *Ram Soonder Singh* v. *Surbanee Dossee*, 22 C. W. R. 121, see above, sub-sec. I. 1. B. 2. 2. No adoption is approved by the Hindu Law over an initiated man's head, even when he has migrated to the other world. Even a single adoption may be replaced by a widow's sacrifices and austerities. See above, pp. 790, 1012, and Col. Dig., Book IV., Chap. III., sec. II.

(*x*) Above, p. 880. Sutherland, in 2 Str. H. L. 94, denies that a mother can adopt for a son. *Gopal* v. *Vishnu*, I. L. R. 23 Bom. 250; *Payappa* v. *Appanna* I. L. R. 23 Bom. 327.

(*y*) Above, pp. 86, 397.

(*z*) Above, pp. 869, 880.

them (*a*). However, a mother succeeding to her deceased son who has left no widow nor issue is competent to adopt (*b*); but it has been held in *Krishnarav* v. *Shankar Rav* (*c*) that her power to adopt is exhausted if she succeeds as heir to her son on his decease as well as that of his widow. According to this decision her power to adopt once postponed cannot be revived; but in Bengal it has been laid down that when the estate is once more vested in her (*d*) her right to adopt revives.

I. 2. C.—Relation as a Grantee.

It may be gathered from what is said of the customary law in Steele, L. C. 183, that under the native system an adoption would not in general be recognized by a sovereign or the grantor of an estate as imparting a right of succession to it without the superior's consent being gained (*e*).

An adopted son can succeed to his father's jagir, but if he rests his title to succeed on a confirmative sanad, he is bound, it was said, to prove it (*f*).

II.—Consequences of Adoption or *Quasi*-Adoption not Governed by the Ordinary Law.

II. A.—Validity Recognized.

A. 1.—Without Limitation (save by an Exceptional Law).

" By agreement at the time of adoption or by the operation of law when the adoptee is a brother's son (*g*) a boy may represent both fathers. But without this he cannot succeed to his natural father's property " (*h*).

(*a*) Above, p. 881.

(*b*) *Venkappa* v. *Jivaji Krishna*, I. L. R. 25 Bom. 306.

(*c*) I. L. R. 17 Bom. 164.

(*d*) *Manikchand* v. *Jagattsettani*, I. L. R. 17 Cal. 518.

(*e*) See above, pp. 853, 901. Comp. Blackst. Comm. Book II. Chap. 4, as to the feudal succession, recognition, and relief.

(*f*) *Maharajah Juggurnath Sahaie et al.* v. *Musst. Mukhun Koonwur*, 3 C. W. R. 24 C. R.

(*g*) *Krishna* v. *Paramshri*, I. L. R. 25 Bom. 537.

(*h*) MS. 1692. See above, p. 808 ss. *Behari Lal* v. *Shib Lal*, I. L. R. 26 All. 472; *Krishna* v. *Paramshiri*, I. L. R. 25 Bom. 537. As to this form of adoption among the Lingayats see *Chenava* v. *Basangavda*, I. L. R. 21 Bom. 105.

"If a Brahman adopts a son of a different gotra the boy is to be regarded as a dvyamushyayana, not as a legal son of the adopter. If the boy's chaul and munj have been performed he becomes a das entitled only to maintenance. But he may perform the adoptive father's Sraddha and succeeds in the absence of [a begotten] son, widow, and other near relatives" (*i*).

"A boy adopted from a different gotra after his munj becomes a dvyamushyayana," which the Sastri describes as one "bound to observe the prohibitions as to marriage applicable to both families" (*k*).

A dvyamushyayana does not take the name of his adoptive father (*l*).

When an only son is adopted he succeeds to his natural as well as to his adoptive parents (*m*) if taken as a dvyamushyayana. The effect by the Hindu Law of an adoption as a dvyamushyayana (son of two fathers) is not to deprive the adopted son of his lineage to his natural father, or to bar him of his right of inheritance to his father's estate (*n*). But in Bombay he does not inherit from his real father except in the absence of other sons (*o*).

II. A.—Validity Recognized.

A. 2.—With Local Limits.

A kritrima son adopted by a male inherits, it was said, in both families (*p*); and similarly it was said that "one adopted by the

---

(*i*) MS. 1675.

(*k*) MS. 1674. The boy would generally be dvyamushyayana merely because he could not properly be given except as a dvyamushyayana.

(*l*) *Musst. Edul Koonwar* v. *Koonwar Debee Singh*, 5 N. W. P. Dec. 341.

(*m*) *Nilmadhub Doss* v. *Biswambar Doss*, 12 C. W. R., p. 29 P. C.; S. C. 3 Beng. L. R., p. 27 P. C.; S. C. 13 M. I. A. 85. The Judicial Committee say—"Again, if there is, on the one hand, a presumption that Gooroproshad Doss would perform the religious duty of adopting a son, there is, on the other, at least as strong a presumption that Purmanund would not break the law by giving in adoption an eldest or only son, or allowing him to be adopted otherwise than as a dvyamushyayana, or son to both his uncle and his natural father."

(*n*) *Nilmadhub Doss* v. *Biswambar Doss et al.*, 13 M. I. A. 85. See above, p. 810.

(*o*) See above. p. 809.

(*p*) *Musst. Deepoo* v. *Gowreeshunkur*, 3 C. S. D. A. R. 307. See above,

kritrima form, which is in use in Behar, Tirhoot, &c., takes the inheritance both in his own family and in that of his adoptive father" (*q*).

With regard to kritrima adoptions it has further been ruled that a person adopted by the husband stands to him in the relation of a son, and is heir to his estate; but does not become the adopted son of the adoptive wife, nor succeed to her peculiar property (*r*).

Nor does the person adopted by the wife, as her son, become the adopted son of her husband, or succeed to his property, even by the Maithila shasters, though the adoption should have been permitted by the husband. But, as her son, he will succeed to her property (*s*). But if the husband and wife jointly appoint an adopted son, he stands in the relation of a son to both, and is heir to the estate of both (*t*).

When an adoption has been made in the kritrima form, the sons of the adopted have no right to set aside alienations which the adoptive father of the adoptee made of his self-acquired property for alleged illegitimate purposes (*v*).

A son, adopted by a widow without her husband's permission, has no right to her property until her death (*w*).

II. A.—VALIDITY RECOGNIZED.

3.—AMONGST CERTAIN CLASSES.

Among the Talabda Kolis of Surat, the son adopted according to their fashion celebrates his adoptive father's obsequies with a feast, and succeeds him. His adoptive father may dispose

---

p. 906. The kritrima adoption like that of a palak putra bears a pretty close resemblance to the Roman adoption in its latest stage. See above, pp. 827, 828.

(*q*) *Srinath Serma* v. *Radhakaunt*, 1 C. S. D. A. R. 15.

(*r*) *Srinarain Rai et al.* v. *Bhya Jha*, 2 C. S. D. A. R. 27.

(*s*) *Ibid.*

(*t*) *Ibid. Collector of Tirhoot* v. *Huropershad Mohunt*, 7 C. W. R. 500.

(*v*) *Baboo Banee Pershad* v. *Moonshee Syud Abdool Hye*, 25 C. W. R. 192.

(*w*) 2 Hay, 410. This, of course, implies where she has a right, otherwise the adoption would be invalid for all purposes. See above, I. 2 B.; 2 Str. H. L. 91

of his property as he pleases, but failing this the adopted son succeeds (*x*).

An adoptive father may, according to the custom of the Talabda Koli caste, repudiate an adopted son for such reasons as would justify a natural father in disinheriting his son (*y*).

II. B.—Validity not Recognized.

1.—Obsolete.

A person cannot succeed as adopted son of a daughter who has brothers alive, and who cannot be an appointed daughter if she had brothers when she married, nor can he succeed as claiming under a bought son (*z*).

One sold or given by his parents or by himself ranks as a slave according to Manu quoted by Jagannatha in Coleb. Dig. Bk. III. chap. I. sec. I. T. 33 and Commentary. Attempts to procure a son in this way are thus made abortive in the present age.

B. 2.—Adoption Partly Assimilated to that under the Ordinary Law.

Two brothers attempting to adopt the same sons declared—"According to our Sastras the said two adopted sons will perform our obsequies, and shall become successors of our ancestral and self-acquired property." Though this showed an intention to make and take a gift, yet it was pronounced inoperative if the persons did not fulfil the character of adopted sons (*a*).

"A person taken as pupil by a Gosavi cannot on his natural father's death claim a debt due to the latter" (*b*).

(*x*) *Bhala Nahana* v. *Parbhu Hari*, I. L. R. 2 Bom. 67.

(*y*) *Bhala Nahana* v. *Parbhu Hari*, I. L. R. 2 Bom. 67, 70.

(*z*) *Yachereddy Chinna Bassavapa* v. *Yachereddy Gowdapa*, 5 W. R. P. C. 114.

(*a*) *S. Siddesory Dossee* v. *Doorgachurn Sett*, 1 Bourke, 360. The Datt. Mim., sec. I. 30, says the same person cannot be adopted by two, but caste custom seems to have recognized it in a few instances in Central India. And the Datt. Mim. II. 47, 49, allows the adoption of one son (a nephew) by several united brothers, on the principle that the son of one is in a sense the son of all.

(*b*) MS. 1248.

B. 3.—Merely Analogous.

A son-in-law having been adopted succeeded to the estate. It was attached for the debt of the adoptive father. The Sastri said that the adopted son's son by a wife not his adoptive father's daughter had no claim to raise the attachment (*c*).

The Hindu Law does not recognize any legal status for the foster-son, either in the matter of performing ceremonies or of inheritance (*d*). "Nephews, though separated, inherit before a mere foster-son" (*e*).

"A palak putra is not entitled to share in any property *de jure* (*f*) generally in the Dakkhan; but in a few cases, such as the one above, p. 356, Q. 18, the Sastris have been more indulgent. In the case at 2 Str. H. L. 426, the Sastri so far assimilates the foster-son to an ordinary son, that he says a gift may be made to him in his absence without delivery of possession (*g*).

(*c*) MS. 31. If there was a true adoption, the son-in-law would transmit to his son the same rights as if he had been a son by birth. Probably the case was one like an Illatam adoption in Madras, see above, p. 398. Amongst the Motati Kapus, a low caste in Madras, an affiliation is allowed of a son-in-law in the absence of a begotten son. He takes the place of such a son in succession, and shares equally with one born after his affiliation. The question of his resembling an adopted son in other respects than for the purpose of succession was not decided, *Hanumantamma* v. *Rami Reddi*, I. L. R. 4 Mad. 272, 274. Similar customs are recognized by some of the Bombay castes; thus—"Should a man have a daughter and no son, he may give her in marriage to a gharjawahee, who is invested with the management of the house and property, but who becomes proprietor only of such property as his father-in-law gives him at his marriage, or with the consent of his other relations." Steele, L. C. App., p. 358.

(*d*) *Bhimana Gaudu* v. *Tayappa*, M. S. D. A. R. 1861, p. 124; *Samy Josyen* v. *Ramien*, M. S. D. A. R. 1852, p. 60; *Nilmadhub Doss* v. *Biswambhar Doss*, 12 C. W. R. P. C. 29; S. C. 3 B. L. R. P. C. 27; S. C. 13 M. I. A. 85; *Kalee Chunder* v. *Sheeb Chunder*, 2 C. W. R. 281. See above, p. 828.

(*e*) MS. 119. The Sastri, above, p. 906 (*m*), allowed that a foster-son might be heir by custom; and amongst Sudras he was in one instance given a place in the family. See above, p. 362, Q. 10.

(*f*) Steele, L. C., p. 184.

(*g*) See above, pp. 180, 634. The passages cited by H. H. Wilson, Works, vol. V., p. 90, show that while some change of possession is necessary in general to complete a title, yet a partial possession may, when rightly taken, be extended to the whole, and may be dispensed with where the deed is incontrovertible. As to the distinction taken by the Sastri between the ceremonies necessary for the transfer of immovable and of movable property, see the Mit., Chap. I., sec. I., para. 31; Col. Dig., Book II., Chap. IV., T. 33 Comm.; Book V., T. 390, Comm.

The Oudich (Kaletiya) Brahmanas of Broach answered Borradaile that either a foster-son or an adopted son might be taken. He would share *equally* with an after-born son, and he might, failing any other son of his real father, take both estates (like a dvyamushyayana) (*h*).

Adoption (so-called) amongst Naikins does not create any legal rights similar to those arising from a true adoption (*i*).

(*h*) MS. Book A., p. 63. The place given to the foster-son in this section is assigned to him only in deference to the uniform effect of the decisions of the Courts. See above, p. 829. Since that page was printed, the present writer has re-examined in the Borradaile MS. Collection the accounts given of their usages by 51 castes and sub-castes in Gujarath. Of these 38 reject both the adopted and the foster-son; of this number are Brahmanas of various classes. Two castes allow either kind of son. Ten allow only the foster-son. Two allow adoption only, but limited to a brother's son. In one caste (Vaghirs) the only recognized affiliation is by purchase. Four or five allow a dharma-putra to perform the parents' obsequies. Wherever the palak-putra is allowed, his heritable right to his foster-father is recognized, and, with a couple of exceptions, a right in relation to his real father, like that of a dvyamushyayana. In one caste (Surya Vamshi Kshatris of Broach) the foster-son takes only the self-acquired property of the foster-father, not the ancestral estate. In another (Guduja Machi) " one may take a boy and give him a little." One (Surathiya Mali) expressly excludes him from collateral succession in his new family. In most cases the foster-son is allowed to share equally with an after-born son: in others he is reduced to one-third or one-half as much. The relative shares are in a couple of instances subject to control by the father. A widow may take a foster-son from her husband's family, except (in some castes) when there is a nephew. The sanction of the family is required to her taking from her own family or a stranger, if there is property left by the husband (Surya Vamshi Kshatris). Liberty to re-marry disqualifies a widow for taking a foster-son (Kahnumiya Hajjam). No rites are prescribed for taking as a foster-son beyond an expression of consent by the parties concerned.

It may be gathered that adoption is generally disallowed or unknown as a usage in Gujarath, though, should any one take it on himself to adopt, the castes would find it hard to contend against the Sastra; and it is supposed that in such a case the ceremonies would be governed by the scripture rules. Where a substitutionary son is allowed, it is, considering the relative members in the castes, in at least nine cases out of ten, a foster-son. The actual usage of the people thus seems to be quite opposed on this subject to the opinions of the Sastris, and the decisions of the Courts influenced by those opinions. The difference is the more important, as from many of the answers of the castes it appears they were by the Government of the day promised the maintenance of their customary law when thus ascertained.

(*i*) *Mathura Naikin* v. *Esu Naikin*, I. L. R. 4 Bom. 545. The mere nurture and recognition by a temple woman of a man as her son was apparently thought sufficient by the Sastri to make him her heir. (See sec. IV. *ad fin.* Above, p. 945.)

SECTION VIII.—SUITS AND PROCEEDINGS CONNECTED WITH ADOPTION.

The principal decisions bearing on the substantive law of Adoption have been considered in the preceding sections (*k*). In the present section it is proposed to supplement them with a certain number illustrating the questions that arise in litigation, and the way in which these have been dealt with by the Courts The decisions will be distributed with reference mainly to the object of the litigation. Such a classification, though wanting in scientific precision, seems the most convenient for the practical purposes at which the present section aims.

The exercise of jurisdiction by the Sovereign in this class of cases is fully recognized by the Hindu Law (*l*). The source of the rights and duties that come in question is in the religious law, but the relations themselves are of a kind on which the Civil Courts are bound to adjudicate. According to the customary law—"The caste is competent to decide on the question of a legal adoption. If unsettled by them, it may be referred to the Sirkar" (*m*).

1.—Suits and Proceedings Arising out of Non-Adoption.

"A man cannot cancel his agreement to adopt by entering into a different one" (*n*).

No suit can be maintained for an order directing a minor widow to adopt, nor, it was said, was this a case in which a decree could be made declaring the validity of a direction (*o*) to adopt.

Where a will says—"I declare that I give my property to K., whom I have adopted. My wives shall perform the ceremonies and bring him up. . . . Should he die, and my younger brother

---

(*k*) The cases of adoption in the Bombay Presidency "may be taken to be governed by the Mayukha." (*The Collector of Madura* v. *Moottoo Ramalinga Sathupathy*, 12 M. I. A. 397, 439.)

(*l*) Compare what is said on matrimonial law by the Judicial Committee in *Ardaseer* v. *Perozeboye*, 6 M. I. A., at p. 391.

(*m*) Steele, L. C., pp. 185, 186. As to the jurisdiction of the caste and the appellate jurisdiction of the Courts of the King recognized, in all cases, see Ellis in 2 Str. H. L. 267—268; Yajnavalkya, Chap. II. 5, and the commentary of Vijnanesvara, 1 Macn. H. L., pp. 133, 141 ss.

(*n*) MS. 1745.

(*o*) *Musst. Pearee Dayee* v. *Musst. Hurbunsee Kooer*, 19 C. W. R. 127; *Mutasaddi Lal* v. *Kundun Lal*, L. R. 33 I. A. 55. See above, pp. 891, 902.

have more than one son, my wives shall adopt a son of his"—the gift to K, is absolute. So long as he is alive, no other can be adopted, nor can his right as devisee be defeated, whether the widows perform or decline to perform the ceremonies (*p*).

Where a person made a will to the effect that two sons should be adopted in case his pregnant widow should bear a daughter, and no child was born, and one of the two to be adopted died, and the other was not adopted, the latter was held not entitled to take any property as adopted son or legatee under the will (*q*).

A suit to declare void certain deeds of gift and acceptance of a child in adoption, brought by the donee against the donor,—the child not being a party to the suit,—was held not to be maintainable. The deeds, it was held, were not necessary to a valid adoption, and if the deeds were set aside, the adoption, if it had taken place, might be proved *aliunde*. If the deeds operated merely as an agreement to give and take in adoption, and a breach thereof had occurred, such breach, it was held, would not render the deeds void, or constitute any ground for setting them aside, or for declaring them void (*r*).

2.—Suits as to Rights and Duties of Widow Prior to Adoption.

A suit to obtain a declaration that a widow is heir of her deceased husband will lie, though she had authority to adopt. She does not forfeit her right by her omission or refusal to adopt (*s*). It seems she cannot be forced to adopt. Where no adoption is made "under an authority for the purpose," the widows having equal rights in the estate may no doubt share it, making due provision for the maintenance of "the mother and sister of the deceased husband" (*t*).

"In the interval then between the death of her husband and the exercise of the power, the widow's estate is neither greater

---

(*p*) *Nidhoomoni Debya* v. *Saroda Pershad Mookerjee*, L. R. 3 I. A. 253.

(*q*) *Abhai Charan* v. *Dasmani Dasi*, 6 Beng. L. R. 623.

(*r*) *Sree Narain Mitter* v. *Sreemutty Kishen Soondory Dassee*, L. R. Supp. I. A. 149.

(*s*) *Bamundoss Mookerjea* v. *Musst. Tarinee Dibbeah*, B. S. D. A. R. for 1850, p. 533; S. C. 7 M. I. A. 169; and *Prasannamayi Dasi* v. *Kadambini Dasi*, 3 B. L. R. O. C. J. 85; *Mutasaddi Lal* v. *Kundun Lal*, L. R. 33 I. A. 55.

(*t*) Colebrooke in 2 Str. H. L. 91. See above, pp. 95, 241.

nor less than it would be if she enjoyed no such power or died without making an adoption. She has the same power, no greater and no less, to deal with the estate. Such acts of hers as are authorized and would be effective against reversioners will bind the son taken in adoption. Such acts as are unauthorized and in excess of her powers may be challenged by the son adopted or by any other successor to the estate" (v).

An adopted son is at liberty to question alienations made by the widow, the adoptive mother, before his adoption. But a presumption exists in favour of her transactions assented to by the persons next in succession when they took place (w).

A Hindu widow claimed a share of ancestral property (under an anumatti patra, or deed of permission to adopt a son, alleged to have been executed by her husband) on behalf of the son whom she might adopt. It was held by the Sudder Dewanny Adawlut, that, until the adoption was made, no action would lie, and that the expression of any opinion as to the authenticity of the deed was in the present action uncalled for (x).

The possession of a widow (who has authority to adopt) previous to the adoption is not that of a trustee for the son to be adopted, so as to prevent limitation (y) from operating. A widow in Bengal adopted a boy under a power from her deceased husband in the course of a suit by her against his unseparated brother. This was held competent to her, and also the continuance of the suit in her own name, as that had not been objected to, and she might take the estate as trustee for her son (z).

A widow does not incur a penalty of absolute forfeiture by an attempt at a false adoption of a son (a).

If a widow succeeds to her adopted son, and then adopts

(v) *Lakshmana Rau* v. *Lakshmi Ammal*, I. L. R. 4 Mad. 160, 164.

(w) *Jadomoney Dabee* v. *Sarodaprosunno Mookerjee*, 1 Bouln. 120; *Rajkristo Roy* v. *Kishoree Mohun*, 3 C. W. R. 14, in which many earlier cases are referred to; *Ramakrishna* v. *Tripurabai*, I. L. R. 33 Bom. 88.

(x) *Musst. Subudra Chowdhryn* v. *Goluknath Chowdree et al.*, 7 C. S. D. A. R. 143.

(y) *Gobin Chandra* v. *Anand Mohan*, 2 B. L. R. A. C. J. 313. See above, pp. 87, 88.

(z) *Dhurm Das Pandey* v. *Musst. Shama Soondri Debiah*, 6 C. W. R. 43, Pr. Co.

(a) *Komul Monee Dossee* v. *Alhadmonee Dassee*, 1 C. W. R. 256.

again (*b*) her intermediate alienation is not affected by such adoption (*c*).

3.—Suits to Establish Adoption.

A party claiming in Bengal as a son adopted by a widow must establish by evidence—(1) authority given by the husband to adopt; (2) his actual adoption by the widow as her husband's son (*d*).

A plaintiff who desires, as an adopted son, to recover property, must sue for it, not for a mere declaration of his status as adopted son (*e*).

A vatandar in possession of vatan property may, as such, sue for a declaration of his adoption, preliminary to his application to the Collector for recognition of his right to officiate as a vatandar (under Bom. Act III. of 1874) (*f*).

An adopted son, who is afterwards discarded, may maintain a suit to establish his rights. According to the Hindu Law the suit may be brought on his behalf by any kinsman or friend (*g*). This would now be subject to the provisions of the Code of Civil Procedure (Act V. of 1908, O. XXXII., rr. 1, 2 and 3) and to the ruling of the Judicial Committee in *Doorga Persad's Case* (*h*).

On an estate descending to an adopted son, and from him to his widow, a further power to adopt given by the adoptive father to his widow becomes incapable of execution (*i*), [except Bengal, where on the death of the daughter-in-law, the widow's right to adopt revives (*k*)]. An adoption under it is void. It does not give

---

(*b*) *Venkappa* v. *Jiraji Krishna*, I. L. R. 25 Bom. 306.

(*c*) *Gobindo Nath Roy* v. *Ram Kanay Chowdhry*, 24 C. W. R. 183. See above, p. 349.

(*d*) *Chowdhry Pudum Singh* v. *Koer Oodey Singh*, 12 C. W. R. P. C. 1; S. C. 2 B. L. R. P. C. 101.

(*e*) *Ramchandra Narayan* v. *Krishnaji Moreshwar*, Bom. H. C. P. J. 1881. p. 288.

(*f*) *Ramchandra* v. *Radhabai*, Bom. H. C. P. J. 1880. p. 160.

(*g*) 2 Str. H. L. 79.

(*h*) L. R. 9 I. A. 27. See above, p. 701.

(*i*) *Pudma Coomari Debi* v. *The Court of Wards*, L. R. 8 I. A. 229; *Krishnarav* v. *Shankar Rav*, I. L. R. 17 Bom. 164. See above, sec. VII. I. 2 B., and pp. 870, 878.

(*k*) *Manikchand* v. *Jagatsettani*, I. L. R. 17 Cal. 518.

to the adopted a right ripening into that of a duly adopted son when the elder widow succeeds to the property (*l*).

Where a widow adopts under authority of her husband, the authority must be strictly proved (*m*). If the husband's authority to adopt is verbal, it must be proved by witnesses, the widow's testimony alone being insufficient (*n*).

If the husband's authority is in writing, and his handwriting is proved, the signature of witnesses is unnecessary. Otherwise it must be proved by witnesses (*o*).

In a case of inconsistent evidence as to the fact of adoption, the non-designation of the adopted in a public document as son of the adoptive father decided the Court against the alleged adoption (*p*).

In *Gangava* v. *Rangangavda* (*q*), the following facts were held inconsistent with an alleged adoption:

(1) The adoptive mother's name continued in Government records for lands belonging to her husband, after the alleged adoption. (2) The adopted acted as deputy under the adoptive mother. (3) The adoptee assumed his natural father's name after the date of his alleged adoption (*r*).

A presumption arises against the genuineness of a deed of permission to adopt from its not being acted on for seventeen years after the husband's death (*s*).

The omission of the usual intimations and ceremonies is a ground for strong suspicion as to the genuineness of an alleged adoption (*t*).

The registration of deeds giving power to the widow to adopt was recommended. When such a deed is not registered, the

---

(*l*) See above, sec. VII. I. 2 B. "Relation shall never make an act good which was void for defect of power." Vin. Abrt. Tit. Relation (H) 4; *Butler and Baker's Case*, 3 Rep. 29A. See, too, *Hawkins* v. *Kemp*, 2 Es. 410.

(*m*) *Chowdhry Pudum Singh* v. *Koer Oodey Singh*, 12 C. W. R. P. C. 1; 2 B. L. R. 101 P. C.; 12 M. I. A. 350.

(*n*) *Musst. Tara Munee Dibia* v. *Dev Narayun Rai et al.* 3 C. S. D. A. R. 387; *Ry Sevagamy Nachiar* v. *Heraniah Gurbah*, 1 Mad. Dec. 101; 2 Macn. H. L. 183.

(*o*) *Ry. Sevagamy Nachiar* v. *Heraniah Gurbah*, 1 Mad. S. D. A. Dec. 101.

(*p*) *Musst. Sabitree Daee* v. *Sutur Ghun Sutputtee*, 2 C. S. D. A. R. 21.

(*q*) Bom. H. C. P. J. 1881, p. 248.

(*r*) See above, p. 1062.

(*s*) *Chundermonee Debia Chowdhoorayn* v. *Munmoheenee Debia*, 8 M. I. A. 477.

(*t*) *Sootrugun Sutputty* v. *Sabitra Daee*, 2 Knapp, 287.

weight of evidence for or against an alleged adoption has to be compared (*v*). In the particular case it removed suspicion.

In the absence of strong documentary evidence for an alleged adoption, the Privy Council preferred the judgment of the lower Appellate Court to that of the High Court, as it had a better opportunity of testing the probabilities of the case (*w*).

Evidence is not necessary of the execution of a permission to adopt according to the exactness required in the case of a will (*x*).

When the Court is satisfied of the power comparatively slight evidence of the ceremonies will suffice (*y*).

The identity of a deed of permission to adopt was held sufficiently established by a reference to it in a subsequent proved deed (*z*).

The probabilities are in favour of an alleged adoption, where the document authorizing the widow to adopt bears the genuine signature of the deceased husband, and the next heir who disputes the document is shown to be on bad terms with the deceased (*a*).

In some cases upon a disputed question of adoption, though the Courts in India held the evidence not sufficient to prove the adoption, the Privy Council has reversed the decision and decreed in favour of the adoption (*b*). Thus the Privy Council decided in favour of adoption, upon a conflict of evidence as to whether it took place during pollution or not (*c*).

A bequest to two persons as adopted sons was held to fail through the simultaneous double adoption being void (*d*).

Where the plaintiff claims the full rights arising under

(*v*) *Chundernath Roy* v. *Kooar Gobindnath; The Collector of Moorshedabad* v. *Ry Shibessuree Dabea*, 11 B. L. R. 86.

(*w*) *Nilmadhub Das* v. *Biswambhar Das*, 12 C. W. R. P. C. 29; S. C. 3 B. L. R. P. C. 27; S. C. 13 M. I. A. 85.

(*x*) See above, pp. 859, 862.

(*y*) *Mohendrolal* v. *Rookiney Dabey*, Coryt. R. 42.

(*z*) *Kishen Shunker Dutt* v. *Moha Mya Dossee*, C. W. R. Sp. No. 210.

(*a*) *Sri Virada Pratapa Raghunada* v. *Sri Brozo Kishoro Patta Deo*, 25 C. W. R. P. C. 291; S. C. I. L. R. 1 Mad. 69; S. C. 7 M. H. C. R. 301.

(*b*) *Huradhun Mookurjia* v. *Muthooranath Mookurjia*, 4 M. I. A. 414; S. C. 7 C. W. R. P. C. 71; *Rungama* v. *Atchama et al.*, 4 M. I. A. 1; S. C. 7 C. W. R. P. C. 57.

(*c*) *Ramalinga Pillay* v. *Sadasiva Pillay*, 9 M. I. A. 506; S. C. 1 C. W. R. 25 P. C.

(*d*) *Siddesory Dossee* v. *Durgachurn Sett*, Bourke, 360. Above, p. 877.

an ordinary adoption, a different form of adoption (*i.e.*, dvyamushyayana) cannot be set up (*e*).

Persons claiming as adopted sons of a widow must prove their own adoption, and that the widow had possession in her own right (*f*); so too where plaintiff sues as adopted son of the owner himself (*g*); but the plaintiff need not in the former case prove how the widow came into possession (*h*). A suit to establish adoption independently of any claim to property can be maintained upon an institution fee of rupees ten, provided the plaintiff shows distinctly that he has a cause of action and a right to consequential relief (*i*).

A certificate cannot be refused to administer an adopted minor's estate, though his adoption has never been recognized, for such a certificate is necessary to clothe any administrator with authority to sue for such recognition of the adoption of the minor (*k*).

A certificate of guardianship under Act XL. of 1858 will not entitle a minor or his guardian, until the adoption is proved, to interfere with the possession of the estate by the widow of the deceased who denies the adoption (*l*).

4.—Suits to Set Aside Adoption.

The Legislature has by Acts VII. of 1870 and IX. of 1871 and XV. of 1877 and Act IX. of 1908 recognized the right to bring a suit to set aside an adoption independently of any claim to property (*m*).

The *onus probandi* lies on the adopted son, though defendant, to prove the validity of the adoption, and not on the plaintiff suing as heir to prove its invalidity, even though he alleges fraud, and adduces no evidence in support of it (*n*).

(*e*) *Musst. Edul Koonwar* v. *Koonwar Dabee Singh*, 5 Dec. N. W. P. 341.

(*f*) *Chutturdharee Lall* v. *Musst. Parbutty Kowar*, 12 C. W. R. 120.

(*g*) *Bhairabnath Sye* v. *Maheschandra*, 4 B. L. R. A. C. J. 162; *Ishur Panday* v. *Musst. Buskeela Koonwar*, B. S. D. A. R. for 1858, p. 471.

(*h*) *Chutturdharee Lall* v. *Musst. Parbutty Kowar*, 12 C. W. R. 120.

(*i*) *Baji Balvant* v. *Raghunath Vithal*, Bom. H. C. P. J. for 1876, p. 142.

(*k*) *Chintaman* v. *Sitaram*, Bom. H. C. P. J. 1879, p. 566.

(*l*) *Panch Cowree Mundul* v. *Bhugobutty Dossia*, 6 C. W. R. Misc. 47.

(*m*) *Kalova* v. *Padapa*, I. L. R. 1 Bom. 248, *per* Westropp, C.J. In the same case the points for consideration on a question of adverse possession by a widow, and on one of the validity of an adoption, are set forth with a reference on the latter point to earlier cases.

(*n*) *Tarini Charan* v. *Saroda Sundari Dasi*, 3 B. L. R. A. C. J. 145; S. C. 11 C. W. R. 468; *Roopmonjooree* v. *Ramlall Sircar*, 1 C. W. R. 145; *Kripa*

The presence of a brother of the adoptive father at an adoption and his associating the adopted son as such with him in a suit prevents his sons from afterwards denying the adoption (*o*).

The following grounds have been held insufficient for setting aside an adoption, once effected:—

(1) Its not having taken place at the usual residence of parties (*p*); (2) Its having taken place long after the death of adoptive father (*q*); (3) Want of permission from Government (*r*); (4) Tonsure having been performed in the family of birth after gift and acceptance but before fire sacrifice (*s*); (5) Existence of a nearer relation than adoptee available for adoption (*t*); (6) Want of presence of the mother (natural or adoptive), of burnt offerings, or of drinking saffron water by other than adoptive father, amongst Sudras (*v*).

A has two sons *B* and *C*. *B* marries *D* and dies before *A*. *C* dies unmarried after *A*. *E*, as widow of *A*, relinquishes her rights in favour of *D* and her adopted son *F*. This being sufficiently proved, *E* cannot question *F's* adoption (*w*).

A stranger having no interest in the matter has no right, even with the consent of the presumptive reversionary heirs, to sue for a declaration that an adoption made by a widow is invalid (*x*).

Although a suit, to contest an adoption, made by a Hindu widow of a son to her deceased husband, may be brought by a contingent

---

Moyee Debia v. *Goluck Chunder Roy*, 4 C. W. R. 78; *Bissessur Chuckerbutty* v. *Ram Joy Mojoomdar*, 2 C. W. R. 326; *Lal Kunwar* v. *Chiranji Lal*, L. R. 37 I. A. 1; S. C. I. L. R. 32 All. 104; *Chandra Kunwar* v. *Narpat Singh*, L. R. 34 I. A. 27; S. C. I. L. R. 29 All. 184. See above, sec. VI. A. 5.

(*o*) *Nidhoomoni Debya* v. *Saroda Pershad Bookerjee*, L. R. 3 I. A., at pp. 253, 256; *Chintu* v. *Dhondu*, 11 Bom. H. C. R. 192. The principle of estoppel was followed in the similar case, *Sadashiv* v. *Hari*, *ibid.* 190. See above, sec. VI. A. 5.

(*p*) *Bhasker Buchajee* v. *Narro Ragoonath*, Bom. Sel. R. 24.

(*q*) *Ibid.*

(*r*) *Ibid.*

(*s*) *Musst. Dullabh De* v. *Manu Bibi*, 5 C. S. D. A. R. 50.

(*t*) *Gocoolanund Dass* v. *Wooma Daee*, 15 B. L. R. 405; S. C. 23 C. W. R. 340; *Sree Brijbhookunjee Maharaj* v. *Sree Gokoolootsaojee Maharaj*, 1 Borr. 181, 202 (2nd ed.).

(*v*) *Alvar Ammal* v. *Ramasawmy Naiken*, 2 M. S. D. A. R. for 1867; *Sootrugun Sutputty* v. *Sabitra Dye*, 2 Knapp 287; S. C. 5 C. W. R. P. C. 109.

(*w*) *Musst. Ladoo* v. *Musst. Oodey Kowree*, N. W. P. S. D. R., Pt. II. 1864. p. 365.

(*x*) *Brojo Kishoree Dassee* v. *Sreenath Bose*, 9 C. W. R. 463; S. C. 8 C. W. R. 241.

reversionary heir, yet it is not the law that any one who may have a possibility of succeeding to the estate of inheritance held by the widow for her life is competent to bring such a suit. The right to sue must be limited. As a general rule, the suit must be brought by the presumptive reversionary heir—that is to say, by the person who would succeed to the estate if the widow were to die at the time of the suit. But it may be brought by a more distant heir, if those nearer in the line of succession are in collusion with the widow, or have precluded themselves from interfering.

If the nearest heir had refused, without sufficient cause, to institute proceedings, or if he had precluded himself by his own act or conduct from suing, or had colluded with the widow, or had concurred in the act alleged to be wrongful, the next presumable heir would be, in respect of his interest, competent to sue. In such a case, upon a plaint stating the circumstances under which the more distant heir claimed to sue, a Court would exercise a judicial discretion in determining whether he was or was not competent, in that respect, to sue, and whether it was requisite or not that any nearer heir should be made a party to the suit.

In a suit to have an alleged adoption set aside, the plaintiff, a minor, through his guardian, claimed to sue, on the strength of being the adopted son of (the husband of) a daughter of a brother of the father of the deceased, under whose authority the adoption was alleged to have been made by the widow, the defendant. The Judicial Committee, without deciding that as an adopted son this minor had the same rights as a natural-born son, and without deciding that he would have been entitled, in default of nearer relations, to succeed to the estate of inheritance, after the death of the widow, pointed out, that he could only have succeeded as a distant bandhu (*y*), and that he had not a vested, but at most a contingent, interest. Their Lordships held, that there being, in fact, heirs nearer in the line of succession than this minor, the grounds of his competence to sue in respect of his interest, assuming that interest to exist, should have been made out in the manner above indicated (*z*). The conclusions in the suit referred to were, that a suit to set aside an adoption by a widow may be brought—(1) by a presumptive reversionary heir; (2) by an heir a little more distant, in case the former act in collusion

(*y*) See above, pp. 458, 466.

(*z*) *Rani Anand Kunwar et al.* v. *The Court of Wards*, I. L. R. 6 Cal. P. C. 764. See above, p. 466.

with the widow; possibly (3) by an adopted son of a deceased brother's daughter's son, as a bandhu (*a*).

An obscure association of a boy as adopted son of a deceased person, in a suit brought by his widows to recover the husband's share in joint property, was held not conclusive of the boy's adoption. A reversioner was allowed to prove its not having taken place (*b*).

In a suit on a ground of existing right of inheritance and for possession and mesne profits in which the claims to relief are abandoned, the Court will not allow a change of claim and declare an adoption invalid (*c*).

A power to adopt imposed the condition of the consent of the husband's mother. A suit was brought against the adopted son, but the objection of non-fulfilment of the condition precedent of consent was not raised until the case was taken in appeal to the Privy Council. It was held then too late (*d*).

Ignorantia legis non excusat, it was said, is a maxim applicable to the Hindu law of adoption (*e*). There may, however, be an excusable ignorance, as when the Judicial Committee said:—" The concurrence of the widow, and the various acts of acquiescence attributed to her, would be important if they were brought to bear upon a question which depended upon the preponderance of evidence; but if the facts are once ascertained, presumptions arising from conduct cannot establish a right which the facts themselves disprove. The appellant is a Hindu female. So long as she is acting without the guidance of a disinterested adviser her acquiescence in an alleged adoption or will ought not to prejudice her. In such a case as the present it was hardly to be expected that she would be capable of distinguishing between an adoption in fact and a legal adoption, or between a will in fact and a valid will. The acts attributed to her are really no confirmation of the

---

(*a*) *Ibid.*

(*b*) *B. Sheo Manog Singh* v. *B. Ram Prakas Singh*, 5 C. S. D. A. R. 145.

(*c*) *Ry Rajessuree Koonwar* v. *Maharanee Indurjeet Koonwar*, 6 C. W. R. 1.

(*d*) *Rajendronath Holdar* v. *Jagendronath Banerjee*, 14 M. I. A. 67; so also *Musst. Mulleh* v. *Purmanund*, 4 Dec. N. W. P. 201.

(*e*) *Radhakissen* v. *Sreekissen*, 1 C. W. R. 62. Ignorance of the law does not relieve from a liability, but it operates no further. See *per* Blackburn, J., in *Reg.* v. *Mayor of Tewkesbury*, L. R. 3 Q. B., pp. 629, 635. See also *per* Lord Westbury in *Cooper* v. *Phibbs*, L. R. 2 E. and I. A., at p. 170. Jagannatha in Col. Dig., Book II., Chap. IV., T. 54, and the judgment of the Judicial Committee in *Periasami* v. *Periasami*, L. R. 5 I. A. 61, 76.

respondent's case, as every one of them upon which reliance is placed might equally have been done with respect to a legal or an avoidable adoption" (*f*).

An acquiescence arising from ignorance is not binding, though the ignorance is of the law applicable to the particular case (*g*). So too consent given by the first adopted son to an arrangement of his father under which the second adopted son was allotted certain property would not, it was ruled, be binding on the first adopted son, if he gave the consent in ignorance of his right, or if the father departed from the arrangement to the complete disinherison of the first son himself (*h*).

An assent obtained by a widow on a representation of an authority from her husband will not avail as against the sapinda heirs. The assent, too, being moved by self-interest, was held insufficient (*i*).

5.—SUITS IN WHICH ADOPTION IS AN INCIDENTAL QUESTION.

An adoption *de facto* must be supposed to be valid until set aside (*k*). An objection that an adoptee was the eldest son of his natural father was rejected in special appeal, because though raised it was not pressed in the lower Courts, nor taken specially in the petition of special appeal (*l*).

A case in which a conveyance was absolute, unless the grantor should adopt a son, but in that case to be subject to redemption, was held a sale subject to conversion into a mortgage during the vendor's life, but to become irredeemable on his death (*m*).

A widow may resist an ejectment brought by a person whom she has recognized as adopted son on the ground of the invalidity

(*f*) *Tayammaul* v. *Sashachalla Naiker*, 10 M. I. A. 429.

(*g*) See *Rangamma* v. *Atchamma*, 4 M. I. A. 1; *Beauchamp* v. *Winn*, L. R. 6 E. and I. A. 223; *Thomson* v. *Eastwood*, L. R. 2 A. C. 215, and *per* Sir G. Jessel, M.R., in *Lacey* v. *Hill*, L. R. 4 Ch. D., at p. 546.

(*h*) *Sudanund Mohapattur* v. *Bonomallee*, Marshall, 317.

(*i*) *Karunabdhi* v. *Gopala*, I. L. R. 7 I. A. 173, 177. Savigny denies the generally nullifying effect of error. See his System, vol. 3, App. VIII., and in the same sense Colebrooke, Book II., Ch. IV., T. 54 Comm.

(*k*) *Nunkoo Singh* v. *Purm Dhun Singh*, 12 C. W. R. 356.

(*l*) *Joy Tara Dossee* v. *Roy Chunder Ghose*, 1 C. W. R. 136. See above, sub-sec. IV.

(*m*) *Subhabhat* v. *Vasudevbhat*, I. L. R. 2 Bom. 113.

of the adoption, though her acknowledgment has been acted on by the authorities (*n*).

A plaintiff sued as widow of an adopted son for property of the adoptive father, and also on the ground of devise to the son. The adoption was held invalid according to Hindu Law, yet the High Court held that as the language of the testator sufficiently indicated the person who was to be the object of his bounty, that person was entitled to the property, although the testator conceived him to possess a character which, in point of law, could not be sustained (*o*). In a similar case it was held by the Judicial Committee that according to the true construction of the testator's will there was a gift of property to a designated person, independently of the performance of ceremonies (*p*).

6.—Suits and Proceedings Consequent on Adoption.

In granting a certificate under Act XXVII. of 1860 to an adopted son, a nephew of the deceased, the Judge ought to look into the fitness as well as the propinquity of the adoptee (*q*).

After adoption, the father had a son born to him. In a partition he gave the adopted boy a larger share than he was by law entitled to receive. The father then married a second wife, and had by her several children. These, it was held, could not contest the above disposition in favour of the adoptee (*r*).

Documents of the like tenor were executed by a man and his adopted son by which the property of the former was made over to his wife for life, without power of alienation, and a succession was secured to the adopted son. This was construed as a family settlement, giving to the son an estate in remainder, not as giving to the wife as a widow such an estate as if there had been no son (*s*).

The title of a second (invalidly) adopted son could not be maintained, it was held, on the ground of acquiescence by the

---

(*n*) *Thakoor Oomrao Singh* v. *Thakooranee Mahtab Koonwar*, 2 Agra Rep. 103. See above, sub-sec. 4, p. 1076.

(*o*) *Jivanee Bhayee* v. *Jivu Bhayee*, 2 M. H. C. R. 462.

(*p*) *Nidhoomoni Debya* v. *Saroda Pershad*, L. R. 3 I. A. 253.

(*q*) *Nunkoo Singh* v. *Purm Dhun Singh*, 12 C. W. R. 356.

(*r*) *Yekeyamian* v. *Agniswarian et al.* 4 M. H. C. R. 307. See above, pp. 73, 648, 709.

(*s*) *Musst. Bhagbuttee Daee* v. *Chowdry Bholanath Thakoor*, L. R. 2 I. A. 256.

first, as this had proceeded on an assertion by the father of the second son's right. Whether the first son's ratification would have the effect in such a case of previous consent was thought doubtful; but at any rate there had not been the knowledge which would make it binding (*t*). The first adopted son, however, was allowed to retain all he could claim against the father's disposition only on condition of giving up to the second all over which the father had unfettered power.

An adoptee, like a natural-born son, cannot claim to have a specific share declared and defined, but is only entitled to a decree declaring that the property is ancestral (*v*). A suit by the son of a first adopted son having been brought as heir of the second adopted son, the plaintiff cannot in appeal change his ground of action, treat the second adopted son as trespasser, and seek to recover property as belonging to his ancestor (*w*).

A son adopted *pendente lite*, to be bound by a pending suit affecting his adoptive father's ancestral property, must be made a party to the suit (*x*).

A representation made by one party for the purpose of influencing the conduct of the other party (as to marriage, giving in adoption, &c.), and acted on by him will in general be sufficient to entitle him to the assistance of the Court for the purpose of realizing such representation (*y*).

After the death of an adopted son, a widow alienated part of the property and subsequently adopted again. It was held that the second adopted son took subject to the alienation (*z*).

(*t*) *Rangamma* v. *Atchamma*, 4 M. I. A. 1, 103. On the doctrine of Acquiescence see *Beauchamp* v. *Winn*, L. R. 6 E. & I. App. 233. On Election, see *per* James, L.J., in *Codrington* v. *Lindsay*, L. R. 8 Ch. A., pp. 578, 592.

(*v*) *Heera Singh* v. *Burzar Singh*, 1 Agra H. C. R. 256. He cannot claim definition without partition, as the shares may vary through births and deaths, &c.

(*w*) *Gopee Lall* v. *Musst. Chandraolee Buhoojee*, 11 B. L. R. P. C. 391; S. C. 19 C. W. R. P. C. 12. The adoption here of the second son was invalid according to Hindu Law, as the first had left a son. See above, p. 843.

(*x*) *Rambhat* v. *Lakshman Chintaman Mayala*, I. L. R. 5 Bom. A. C. J., p. 630.

(*y*) *Bhala Nahana* v. *Parbhu Hari*, I. L. R. 2 Bom. 67.

(*z*) *Gobindo Nath Roy* v. *Ram Kanay Chowdhry* 24 C. W. R. 183. Reference is made to *Bhoobun Moyee's Case*, 10 M. I. A. 165; see *Sreemutty Deeno Moyee Dossee* v. *Doorga Pershad Mitter*, 3 C. W. R. 6 Misc. R. Above, p. 349.

A widow redeems a mortgage of her husband and sells the property at a profit. She then adopts a boy, and in the deed of adoption agrees to let the boy have the property "when released." The purchaser is said to have attested the deed of adoption. It was held that the attestation does not bind the purchaser either as to an agreement of resale or as to the price for which the property was to be sold (*a*).

When a widow applies under Act XL. of 1858 for a certificate in respect of an estate alleged to belong to an adopted son, the questions for inquiry are: (1) minority of the boy; (2) fitness of the petitioner for management (*b*). A certificate under Act. XL. of 1858 is rightly given to the guardian, where there is no doubt of the fact of adoption, the objector, who does not claim to be the guardian, having no *locus standi* (*c*). A certificate of guardianship was refused when the validity of the adoption was disputed (*d*).

An adoptive mother, as next heir, was held entitled to the management of a lunatic's estate in preference to a uterine brother (*e*).

A lady who has adopted a son may, as his guardian, be served with an order of foreclosure under the Bengal Law (*f*).

"In a Nuggur Panchaet case . . . in which both parties and Panch were Brahmans and Kulkarnis, the widow of an adoptee obtained a decree for the possession of a vatan given to him by the adopter (by the deed of adoption), in opposition to a claim set up by the nephew of the latter according to blood" (*g*).

A widow has not really such an interest in the appeal or such a *locus standi* as entitles her to insist that an appeal should go on, though the minor party, her adopted son, in whose name the suit was brought, after coming of age, wishes to withdraw from it (*h*).

A widow, claiming under the will of her husband, is the proper

---

(*a*) *Rambhat* v. *Ramchandra*, Bom. H. C. P. J. 1879, p. 426.

(*b*) *Brohmo Moyee* v. *Chettur Monee*, 8 C. W. R. 25.

(*c*) *Kisto Kishore Roy* v. *Issur Chunder Roy*, 15 C. W. R. 166.

(*d*) Above, pp. 911—12.

(*e*) *Huree Kishore Bhya* v. *Nullita Soonduree Goopta*, 18 C. W. R. 340.

(*f*) *Ras Muni Dibiah* v. *Pran Kishen Das*, 4 M. I. A. 392. See now above, p 624.

(*g*) Steele, L. C., p. 188.

(*h*) *Ry Bistoopria Putmadaye* v. *Nund Dhull*, 13 M. I. A. 602.

person to obtain a certificate under Act XXVII. of 1860, notwithstanding the objection of a person alleged to be the adopted son of deceased (*i*).

A, alleging himself to be an adopted son, opposed the application for the grant of certificate under Act XXVII. of 1860 to *B*, who, irrespective of the alleged adoption, would be the legal lineal heir of the deceased; the Court before which the application was made refused to grant the certificate on the ground that sufficient *primâ facie* evidence existed establishing the validity of the adoption. On appeal it was held that the Appellate Court, concurring with the opinion expressed by the Court of first instance in respect of the *factum* of the adoption, would not be justified in setting aside the decision on the ground that such Court was wrong in entering into and deciding the question as to the validity of the adoption. It was laid down that on an application for the grant of certificate under Act XXVII. of 1860, opposed by a party alleging a preferential title to it, the Courts should adjudicate the question of title with a view to determine which party has the preferential right to the certificate (*k*).

A permission to adopt during the life of the son cannot have effect given to it (*l*).

A widow, by virtue of the authority given by her husband's will, adopted a son and afterwards discarded him for misbehaviour. The boy, on attaining maturity, applied for the withdrawal of the certificate and for the grant of one to him. The validity of the will, it was said, could only form the subject-matter of a regular suit. It could not be contested in a summary proceeding (*m*).

Where a will gave the testator's widow permission to adopt and made provision for the adopted son entering into possession only after her death, providing further that if the adopted son died unmarried the estate should pass to the testator's nearest *sapinda*

(*i*) *Bissumbhur Shaha* v. *Sy Phool Mala*, 21 C. W. R. 31; *i.e.*, until he establishes his adoption.

(*k*) *Sheetanath Mookerjee* v. *Promothonath Mookerjee*, I. L. R. 6 Cal. 303. Reference was made to *Kali Coomar Chatterjee* v. *Tara Prosunno Mookerjee*, 5 Cal. L. R. 517; *Musst. Anundee Kooer* v. *Bachoo Sing*, 20 C. W. R. 476; *In re Oodoychurn Mitter*, I. L. R. 4 Cal. 411; *Koonj Behary Chowdhry* v. *Gocool Chunder Chowdhry*, I. L. R. 3 Cal. 616.

(*l*) See above, p. 865.

(*m*) *Issur Chunder* v. *Pooruna Beebee*, 4 C. W. R. Misc. 16. It would be hard to find any authority for a widow's "discarding" a son really adopted. She is dependent on him, not he on her. See above, pp. 1017, 1033.

gnyati, it was held that the gift or bequest was, according to the doctrine laid down in the case of *Tagore* v. *Tagore*, void and of none effect, because the nearest sapinda was a person who might not be in existence at the death of the testator, and one who could not be ascertained at that time (*n*).

"The case of *Baijnath Sahai* v. *Desputty Singh* (*o*) was this. A Hindu testator died, leaving *B*, alleged to be his adopted son, and *C*, who would be his heir in default of adoption, and made a will of which *B* applied for probate, and it was held under the Succession Act and Hindu Wills Act that creditors of *C* were not parties having any interest in the estate of the deceased, and were therefore not entitled to oppose the grant of probate. Their Lordships think this was a right decision" (*p*).

7.—Judgments and Evidence in Previous Cases.

A decision by a competent Court upon a question of adoption is not a judgment *in rem* or binding upon strangers, nor is a decree in such a case admissible as evidence against strangers (*q*), nor is it binding on any reversionary heir not a party to the suit, nor upon an adoptee in a suit by a reversionary not a party to the former suit (*r*).

The plaintiff's adoption, it was said, having been in issue in a former suit, though the defendant was not a party to it, and decided in the plaintiff's favour, was to be held good against the defendant until he got proof against the adoption (*s*) or could prove fraud or collusion (*t*). But in *Padma Coomari Debea's Case* (*v*) it was held that a former judgment against the validity of an adoption was not *res judicata* when the parties had been changed,

(*n*) *Ramguttee Acharjee* v. *Kristo Soonduree Debia*, 20 C. W. R. 472. See above, p. 212.

(*o*) L. R. 2 Cal. 208.

(*p*) *Rajah Nilmoni Singh Deo Bahadoor* v. *Umanath Mookerjee*, L. R. 10 I. A., pp. 80, 86.

(*q*) *Kanhya Lall* v. *Radha Churn*, 7 C. W. R. 338; *Lal Kunwar* v. *Chiranji Lal*, L. R. 37 I. A. 1; *Chandra Kunwar* v. *Narpat Singh*, L. R. 34 I. A. 27.

(*r*) *Jumoona Dassya* v. *Bamasoondari Dassya*, 25 C. W. R. 235; S. C. L. R. 3 I. A. 72. There is not in fact a recognized process by which an adoption can be established or set aside as to all persons.

(*s*) *Seetaram* v. *Juggobundoo Bose*, 2 C. W. R. 168.

(*t*) *Rijkristo Roy* v. *Kishoree Mohun Mojoomdar*, 3 C. W. R. 14.

(*v*) L. R. 8 I. A. 229.

but that the decision of the point of law on which the judgment had turned was binding as a precedent. A suit to set aside the adoption of the defendant, in which the adoptive mother was made a party, was held barred by Section 2 Act VIII. of 1859, because the same issue as to the validity of the adoption had been tried substantially in a former suit between the same parties as to a portion of the property now at issue (*w*). A plaintiff suing for property belonging to a Hindu widow on the ground of his being an adopted son of her husband's brother is not barred by a decision, in respect of other property, that he was not such (*x*).

In a suit between the adopted son of a landlord and the adopted son of his tenant, the decree being in favour of plaintiff by a competent Court, an appeal to the Privy Council or an omission to take rent for many years or to eject defendant, did not, it was held, alter the relationship of landlord and tenant between the parties (*y*).

The denial by *A* in an enquiry under Bombay Regulation VIII. of 1827 that *B* was adopted son of *C*, does not absolutely estop *A* from asserting in a subsequent suit that *C* adopted *B* (*z*).

A deposition of a plaintiff, in a suit against defendant, a widow (managing for her minor first adopted son), is not admissible in evidence under Sec. 33 of the Evidence Act in a subsequent suit by the defendant widow as mother and guardian of a second adopted son, as that son is not a representative in interest of the widow who was party to the former suit, but sues in his own right (*a*).

(*w*) *Kristo Beharee Roy* v. *Bunwaree Loll Roy*, 19 C. W. R. 62. See now Act V. of 1908, sec. 11.

(*x*) *Kripa Ram* v. *Bhugwan Doss*, 10 C. W. R. 100. The parties having been the same would be bound by a prior adjudication on the same question of right or jural relation between them, though the physical objects of their contention were different, see Act V. of 1908, sec. 11; *Krishna Behari Roy* v. *Musst. Brojeshwari Chowdhrani*, L. R. 2 I. A. 285. A question of limitation decided in a suit as to one piece of property was disallowed in a suit as to another in *Maharaja Rajender Kishen Sing* v. *Raja Saheb Pershad Sein*. P. C. 21, May, 1874.

(*y*) *Huronath Roy* v. *Golucknath Chowdhry*, 19 C. W. R. 18. Limitation is computed from the determination of the tenancy, and the time is twelve years. Act. IX. of 1908, Sched. I., Art. 139.

(*z*) *Pandurang Ballal* v. *Dhondo Ballal*, Bom. H. C. P. J. 1876, p. 209.

(*a*) *Mrinmoyee Dabea* v. *Bhoobunmoyee Dabea*, 15 B. L. R. 1; S. C. 23 C. W. R. 42. The decision may be questioned on the ground that there must be a continuity of the estate and of representation of it. The other party must, of course, be the same in both suits to make his deposition admissible.

A certificate may be granted to a widow, as guardian of her minor son, to collect her husband's debts, notwithstanding that her husband's adoption has been set aside (*b*).

8.—Limitation.

The limitation prescribed for a suit for a declaration of the validity of an adoption is six years from an interference with the rights of the adopted son as such (*c*). The Bombay (*d*) and the Madras (*e*) High Courts hold that Art. 119 of the Limitations Acts (now Act IX. of 1908, Sch. I.) would apply even though the suit be for the recovery of real property and not for a declaration of the validity of the adoption provided the plaintiff in order to succeed had no other title but the establishment of his adoption. The Calcutta (*f*) and the Allahabad (*g*) High Courts, on the other hand, lay down that Art. 119 does not apply where the suit is for possession of land, although the consideration of the validity of an adoption is involved. In a suit for a declaration that an adoption was not made or was not valid, the same period of limitation runs from "when the alleged adoption becomes known to the plaintiff" (*h*). The Judicial Committee have held that an omission to bring a suit within the time prescribed by Art. 118 for a declaration that an alleged adoption was invalid, or never, in fact, took place is no bar to a suit for recovery of the property (*i*). The Calcutta (*k*) Allahabad (*l*) and Madras (*m*) High Courts take

---

(*b*) *Nitto Kallee Debee* v. *Obhoy Gobind*, 5 C. W. R. Misc. F 10.

(*c*) Act IX. of 1908, Sched. I., Art. 119. The intention must, it seems, be to bar a suit on the ground of adoption in respect of the rights interfered with. An adoption cannot be cancelled by a mere seizure of an insignificant piece of property on a denial of adoption which remains unchallenged only because it is not worth while to challenge it.

(*d*) *Gangabai* v. *Tarabai*, I. L. R. 26 Bom. 720.

(*e*) *Ratnamasari* v. *Akilandammal*, I. L. R. 26 Mad. 291.

(*f*) *Jagannath Prasad* v. *Ranjit Singh*, I. L. R. 25 Cal. 354.

(*g*) *Lali* v. *Murledhar*, I. L. R. 24 All. 195; *Chandania* v. *Salig Ram*, I. L. R. 26 All. 40.

(*h*) *Ibid.*, Art. 118. See above, p. 895, note (*b*).

(*i*) *Thakur Tirbhurwan* v. *Raja Rameshar*, L. R. 33 I. A. 156; *Muhamed Umer Khan* v. *Muhamed Niazuddin Khan*, L. R. 39 I. A. 19.

(*k*) *Ramchandra Mukerjee* v. *Ranjit Singh*, I. L. R. 27 Cal. 242; *Parbhu Lal* v. *Mylne*, I. L. R. 14 Cal. 401.

(*l*) *Natthu Singh* v. *Gulab Singh*, I. L. R. 17 All. 167.

(*m*) *Velaga Mangamma* v. *Bandlamudi*, I. L. R. 30 Mad. 308.

the same view; but the Bombay High Court (*n*) is of opinion that a suit for possession of the property in question under the circumstances would be barred.

Where a widow, after the death of her son, adopts a boy under an alleged will of her husband, and a sister of the natural son sues for the inheritance on behalf of her son, disputing the will and the adoption, the cause of action arises on the death of the widow, not on the date of the adoption. An acknowledgment of the sister, previous to the birth of her son, admitting the adoption, does not bar the son's right (*o*); and he may sue within three years from attaining his majority. A reversioner's right to sue for possession by setting aside an adoption by a widow accrues on the death of the widow and not on the date of an adoption (*p*). Possession by strangers as adopted sons of a widow is not adverse against the reversioners so long as she is alive (*q*). As against an adopted son, suing for his share in the ancestral estate, limitation begins on demand and refusal (*r*). The time now runs from when a person excluded is aware of the exclusion (*s*).

(*n*) *Strinivasa* v. *Hanmant*, I. L. R. 24 Bom. 260, 266, F. B.; *Laxman* v. *Ramappa*, I. L. R. 32 Bom. 7; *Srinivasa Sargerav* v. *Balwant Venkatesh*, I. L. R. 37 Bom. 513

(*o*) *Tarini Charan* v. *Saroda Sundari Dasi*, 3 B. L. R. A. C. J. 145; S. C. 11 C. W. R. 468. See note (*h*). In Bombay the daughter would have to sue in her own right, which precedes that of her son. See above, pp. 96, 99.

(*p*) *Srinath Gangopadhya* v. *Mahes Chandra Roy*, 4 B. L. R. 3 F. B.; *Musst. Raj Koonwar* v. *Musst. Inderjeet Koonwar*, 13 C. W. R. 52; *Tarini Charan* v. *Saroda Sundari Dasi*, 3 B. L. R. A. C. J. 145; S. C. 11 C. W. R. 468. Comp. note (*h*), p. 1084.

(*q*) *Srinath Gangopadhya* v. *Mahes Chandra*, 4 B. L. R. 3, F. B.

(*r*) *Ayyavu Muppanar* v. *Niladatchi Ammal*, 1 M. H. C. R. 45; 3 M. H. C. R. 99.

(*s*) *Hari* v. *Maruti*, I. L. R. 6 Bom. 741; Act IX. of 1908, Sched. I., Art. 127.

APPENDIX.

Translations of Yajnavalkya, II. 47, 50, and 175, with the Commentary on these verses of the Mitakshara. BY DR. A. FUHRER.

Yajnavalkya, II. 47 (*a*).

"A son need not pay, in this world, money due by his father for spirituous liquors, for lustful pleasures, for losses at play; nor what remains unpaid of a fine or toll; nor anything idly promised."

Vijnanesvara's Commentary.

A debt incurred by a drinker of spirituous liquors, or under the influence of lust for the sake of enjoying a woman, or caused by losses at play, what remains due of a fine or toll (*b*), and money idly promised, that is, promised to impostors, bards, wrestlers, or the rest; for it is declared in a *Smriti*: "Fruitless is a present given to an impostor, a bard, a wrestler, a quack, a knave, a fortune-teller, a spy, or a robber"; all such debts incurred by the father, his son or other heir need not pay to the vintner and the rest. In the above clause, it is mentioned that the remaining portion of a fine or toll should not be paid; by that is not to understand that he has to pay the whole sum, if it is to be paid. For *Usanas* says in his Smriti: "The son need not pay the fine or the balance of a fine, a toll or the balance of a toll, or [any debt of the father] which is not proper" (*c*). Also *Gautama* [XII., 41] says: "Money due by a surety, a commercial debt, a toll, debts contracted for spirituous liquors, a loss at play, and a fine shall not involve the sons, that is, they shall not be paid by the sons [of the debtors]." In this way it has been mentioned which kinds of debts should not be paid.

(*a*) See above, p. 582.

(*b*) Haradatta in his Commentary on Gautama, XII. 41, explains sulka "fee due to the parents of the bride." The same does Jagannatha, see Col. Dig., I., 202.

(*c*) According to Viramitrodaya, l. 106, p. 1, debts for wines and spirits are improper debts.

Yajnavalkya, II. 50 (*d*).

"The father being gone to a foreign country, or deceased [naturally or civilly], or afflicted with an incurable disease, the sons or their sons must pay his debt, but, if disputed, it must be proved by witnesses."

Vijnanesvara's Commentary.

If the father is dead [naturally deceased, or having become a religious anchorite], or has gone to a distant abode in a foreign country, before having paid the due debts, or if he be afflicted with an incurable disease, the debts contracted by him must be paid by the sons and grandsons, even if he has left no property, on account of their being his sons and grandsons. The order of paying is this: In the absence of the father the son, in the absence of the son the grandson; but if the son or the grandson were to deny, that which has been proved by witnesses and the rest [*i.e.* documents] should be discharged. In the first clause, it is said that the debt should be paid off in case the father has gone to a foreign country; but as to the question when it should be paid off, the date fixed by Narada is to be admitted. For *Narada* says in his Smriti [I. 3, 14]: "The father, paternal uncle, or elder brother, having travelled to a foreign country, the son [or nephew, or younger brother even] shall not be forced to discharge the debt, until twenty years have elapsed." After the death of the father, the son if he be apraptavyavahara [*i.e.* if he has not yet reached full age], is not bound to pay the debt: otherwise, if he be fully grown up, he is to discharge it. The time has also been fixed by *Narada*, for he says [I. 3, 37, 38*a*]: "A child is comparable to an embryo up to his eighth year; a boy is called youth (pauganda) up to his sixteenth year. Afterwards he is of age and independent, in case his parents be dead." He is not bound to pay the debt, even after the death of his parents, though he be independent, being still a boy. For it is said in a *Smriti*: "If he have not yet reached full age—apraptavyavahara—and be independent, he is not bound to pay the debt, because the independence depends on his age, and that age is to be counted by qualifications and the years." The term apraptavyavahara includes also those that are forbidden to proclaim and to summon (before a court of law). For a *Smriti* says: "Apraptavyavaharas, messengers, those that are ready to give alms, ascetics, or those immersed in difficulties should not be proclaimed to or summoned by the king." Therefore it is declared in another *Smriti*: "When the son has reached his full age—praptavyavahara—he should, not caring for his own interest, discharge the debt in such a way that he may not go to hell." As regards the performance of funeral rites (Sraddha), even a boy is admitted. For *Gautama* [II. 5] says: "Except the religious performances in honour of the deceased father, the boy is not allowed to recite Vedic texts anywhere." By the plurality of sons and grandsons spoken of in the first clause it is to be understood, that if there are many, they should discharge the debt each in proportion to his own share, if living separated. And if living united,

---

(*d*) See above, p. 582.

the head of them all should pay it from the common stock in the proportion of the different debts (gunapradhana). For *Narada* [I. 3, 2] says: "After the death of the father, the sons, living separated, shall discharge the debt according to their respective shares, and if living united, he who has taken the burden [of a paterfamilias] upon himself, shall pay it." Though, in the first clause, it is said in general that the sons and grandsons shall discharge the debt of the father, still it should be paid by sons with the interest as the father does; the difference being that the grandson should only pay the principal and not the interest. For *Brihaspati* says: "The sons must pay the debts of their father, when proved, as if it were their own [*i.e.* with interest]; the grandson has to pay only the principal, while the great-grandson shall not be compelled to pay anything unless he have assets." When proved, signifies when established by the testimony of witnesses. Thus has been shown the liability for debts of the debtor, his son, and his grandson, and to whom it belongs to pay when they exist together.

Vijnanesvara's Commentary on Yajnavalkya, II. 175 (*e*).

On the Resumption of Gifts. Now, according to the lawful and unlawful way, I mention at large the chapters on law (vyavahara) styled "Non-Resumption of Gifts" (dattanapakarma) and "Resumption of Gifts" (dattapradanika). *Narada* [II. 4, 1] thus mentions the form of dattapradanika: "When a man, having unduly given a thing, desires to recover it, it is called "Resumption of Gift," which is a title of judicial procedure. Resumption of gifts is that title of administrative justice according to which a man wishes to take back a gift which has not been made in a due form [that is, in a prohibited mode] *i.e.* that title of law by which a gift is withdrawn which has been made unduly. That title of law is styled "Non-Resumption of Gifts" (dattanapakarma) by which a gift cannot be taken back when once given by ways sanctioned by laws. Gifts are four-fold; for *Narada* [II. 4, 2] says: "In civil affairs, the law of gift is four-fold: what may be given (deya), or what may not be given (adeya); and what is a valid gift (datta), or what is not a valid gift (adatta)." An alienable gift is that which is fitting the danakriya (the action of giving gifts), and which is sanctioned by law. An unalienable gift is that which cannot be given as a gift either because one cannot own it or because its giving is not sanctioned by law. An alienated gift is that which is given away and cannot be taken back because of its being given by one when in a sane state. An unalienated gift is that which can be taken back though once given. Now I mention briefly the four-fold gifts. *Yajnavalkya* [II. 175] says: "Without injuring the family estate, personal property may be given away, except a wife or a son; but not the whole of a man's estate, if he have issue living; nor what he has promised to another." That may be given away which is one's self-acquired property and which has been left after the expenses for the maintenance of the family have been defrayed, because the support of the family is necessary. For *Manu* [VIII. 35] says: "Aged parents, an honourable

(*e*) See above, p. 695.

wife, an infant child must be maintained even by means of a hundred trespasses." Thereupon it has been stated that alienable gifts are of one kind only, namely, as regards personal property. What is bailed for delivery, what is let for use, a pledge, joint property, and a deposit; these five have been proved, on the contrary supposition, to be unalienable gifts. For *Narada* [II. 4. 4, 5] mentions eight unalienable things: "An article bailed for delivery, a thing borrowed for use, a pledge, joint property, a deposit, a son, a wife, the whole estate of a man who has issue living, and [of course] what has been promised to another: the sages have declared unalienable even by a man oppressed with grievous calamities." By saying "these five things are unalienable" is not to be understood that we have only a (mere) claim on these things, since a wife, son, and what has been promised are included in the term "personal property"; but that personal property may be given away, excepting a wife, or a son. If then a son, or grandson, or the like survive, the whole property shall not be given away. For it is said in a *Smriti*: "He who has begotten a son and performed his tonsure shall provide for his sustenance." If he has promised a golden piece or the like to somebody, he is not allowed to keep his promise (at the cost of privation to his offspring).

INDEX.

ABDUCTION
gives no marital right, 793*n*

ABEYANCE
of an estate not tolerated, 179

ABSENCE,
what constitutes, 626
of a coparcener does not bar partition, 626, 742
of a co-sharer, sale during, 627*b*
gift possible during, 635*k*
in case of partition, 626
See ABSENTEE; EMIGRATION

ABSENT HUSBAND,
his wife's competence in adoption. See ADOPTION V., 948

ABSENTEE,
partition not postponed for the return of, 627
share of —— must be set apart on partition, and may be deposited with his son if fit to take care of it, 626, 730, 731, 742
returning, may claim repartition, 626
his share made up by deductions, 722
descendants of —— may claim to the seventh degree, 70, 627, 753*f*
represented is bound by partition, 627
See PARTITION; DISTRIBUTION OF PROPERTY

ACCEPTANCE,
indications of, in cases of adoption, 962
See ADOPTION II., 825, 826*q*; IV., 947, 949; VI., 957, 958, 960, 961, 963, 994, 998, 1011

ACCRETION,
made with aid of ancestral property becomes ancestral property, 654
ancestral property, recovered by coparcener, is generally an —— and partible, 662

ACCUMULATIONS,
how dealt with on partition, 665
by father, when ranked as his separate property and when not, 665, 666, 667

ACCUMULATIONS—*continued.*
out of allotments in a Zamindari are separate property of allottee and not rendered joint property by Kulachara, 153, 154, 682
by a widow, 298, 299
property purchased by widow out of —— from her husband's property goes along with the property, except where there is an intention to appropriate separately, and in Mithila, 299, 300, 301
See SAVINGS, 154; WIDOW

ACHARA, 30

ACHARYA. See PRECEPTOR, 128, 134, 451, 468
inherits from pupil, 658

ACKNOWLEDGMENT
of debt, 94
See ADOPTION VIII, 1084; MANAGER, 571

ACQUIESCENCE
of coparceners in alienation by manager binds them, 678, 688
immovable property recovered with —— of coparceners ranks as ancestral property, 662
in partition is conclusive, exceptions, 649*a*, *b*
in holding a lease from a single sharer is presumed after some years from partition, 712
long —— in possession by a mortgagee from father binds son, 576
in adoption by female, 963
See ADOPTION VIII. 1077
in Will by female unadvised, through misrepresentation or ignorance, 963, 1077, 1079
See IGNORANCE; ESTOPPEL

ACQUIRER. See ACQUISITION, 173; PROPERTY, 664, 666
other than manager entitled to a double share, 668*q*

ACQUISITION
of ownership, means of, 173
wife's —— belongs to her husband, 85, 278, 286
wife's —— by prostitution belongs to her husband, 483
by father and grandfather inherited by the son alone, 324
See SON
by members of joint family, presumed to be joint property, 663
separate ——s. See PROPERTY, SEPARATE AND SELF-ACQUIRED, 660*g*, 664
See BURDEN OF PROOF; DISTRIBUTION OF PROPERTY

ACTION. See CAUSE OF ACTION, 585*g*
Suit

ACTS
pointing to dissolution of union, but not conclusive, 636, 637

ACTS *IN EXTREMIS*,
closely scrutinized. See ADOPTION III. 847.

ADHIVEDANIKA, 258*p*, 259, 277
is a kind of Stridhana, 352, 353
a woman may eject her husband from a house given to her by him as ——, 287*x*

ADHYAGNIKA, 277
is a kind of Stridhana, 257, 352, 353

ADHYAVAHANIKA, 277
is a kind of Stridhana, 258

ADMINISTRATION OF MINOR'S ESTATE, 622*f*, 624*h*
See MANAGER; WIDOW; GUARDIAN; MINOR; ADOPTION VIII., 1073, 1080, 1081

ADMINISTRATOR,
suing, to set forth his qualification, 221p
had formerly no title against heir, 220*l*
estate now vests in ——, 220
See EXECUTOR

ADMISSIONS,
effect of (Adoption), 1076
cannot be taken advantage of by stranger to agreement, 189*n*

ADOPTED GRANDSON See GRANDSON BY ADOPTION.

ADOPTED GREAT-GRANDSON,
succession of ——, 67, 604

ADOPTED SON. See ADOPTION; DESCENDANTS
of father and of (begotten) son, their relative rights, 354
See ADOPTION VII.
and begotten son, their relative rights, 67*l*, 355, 368
See ADOPTION VII.

ADOPTION,
I. *Sources of the law of* ——, 779*ss*
comparative unimportance of —— in early ages, 779
the Veda of little importance as a direct source, 779
origin of ——, 792
importance of custom as a source, 787
II. *Its Nature and Place in the Hindu System*
has attained importance by slow degrees, disallowed in many castes, 789, 803, 1065
fosterage preferred to —— in several castes, 828, 1065
amongst lower castes recent and but partially allowed, 823, 828, 1065

ADOPTION—*continued.*
motive for ——, 789, 792, 807, 811, 812, 825, 841, 957, 974, 975
a single —— is a fulfilment of religious duty where the Samskaras are performed, 1012
no kriya amongst Jains, reason, 932*k*
is for husband not for wife, 489, 841
place of —— formerly filled by levirate and the appointment of a daughter, 790*w*, 793, 833, 834
the adopted is a "reflexion of a begotten son," who must be born of one whom the adoptive father could have married. Rule confined to daughter's son, sister's son, mother's sister's son, who cannot be adopted except by Sudras, 410, 800, 801, 801*k*, 823, 841, 916, 919, 957
orphans cannot be adopted, 806*p*, 832*z*
a parent alone may give in —— and to a father or his wife, 807*x*
an adopted son cannot be given in ——, 807*x*
effect of —— by uncle, 809
law of —— in China, 810*q*
in Rome, 814*w*, 820*g*, 828*y*
at Athens, 821*i*, 838*w*
effect of —— after investure (below IV., VII.), 810*n*
filial connexion depends on the Samskaras, 838*s*
reasons why —— not more common, 812*h*
recommended but not enjoined, in Bombay and Madras, widow may adopt without express power, but cannot be compelled to do so, and does not forfeit her right by her refusal, 813, 814, 372
coparceners cannot be compelled to assent to an ——, their assent necessary according to some authorities, the High Courts, 814, 814*w*, 895
widow must adopt the boy designated by her husband, proper only when the birth of a son becomes very improbable, not indispensable to the attainment of salvation, 813*t*, 862, 814, 832*z*, 840, 814*a*
age for making —— is that of discretion or capacity, 841*d*, 845
personal defects (except blindness or dumbness) of the son born may justify, so does insanity, 816, 817, 944
wife of a disqualified person may adopt, by custom, though not by the stricter law, 545, 817
of an only son is valid, 818, 819, 926, 927
the doctrine of *factum valet* in ——, 818, 927
once complete is indefeasible (below VII.), 835*x*
both parents ought to concur in giving in ——, in some instances, the head of the family may perhaps give as such, 817, 818
mother's assent not indispensable, 817*d*, 946*ss*
of the eldest son valid (below IV.), 820
while an adopted son exists invalid, valid according to Sir T. Strange, 820, 821, 822, 842
See below III.
simultaneous —— of two sons void, 822, 877
Sudra's capacity to adopt discussed, 823

ADOPTION—*continued.*

is (perhaps) complete by gift and acceptance, for all classes (below VI.), essential ceremonies in ——, laukika ——, irregular ——, a boy defectively adopted is regarded as a das or slave (below VII.), 825, 825*n*, *p*, 826, 826*q*, 827, 836

difference between —— customary and religious, 827

by dancing women and real, 834*k*

Homa sacrifice marks the completion of ——, 835*x*

severs the boy entirely from his family of birth, other effects of ——, 835*ss*, 836

See below VII.

begotten son takes precedence over adopted, 836*g*

second —— when adopted son declines to fulfil his duties, 838

sanction of Government and grantors of inams, to ——, 836*n*, 854

blood-connexion of the adopted son, 838

Roman ——. Influence of the church on ——, 836*n*

III. *Capacity to adopt and its exercise*

duty to adopt, 839, 1012

all males may adopt, exceptions, 840

different opinions as to —— by women without authorization, *ib.*

for husband, not for wife, 841, 855

funeral rites are objects of ——, and inheritance only a secondary consideration, 840, 841, 854

of wife's sister's son allowed, 841

proof of —— (see below VI.), 841*k*

pendente lite, 842

by unmarried persons, in South Maratha country, by a Brahmachari, a sonless widower, a convert, 814*w*, 822, 823, 828, 842, 842*x*

alienation before birth or —— cannot be set aside, 843*r*

in life of son or grandson is invalid, exceptions, 814, 815, 816, 821, 842, 843, 843*d*, 844

double —— exceptionally allowed, 843*g*

during wife's pregnancy allowed, 844

adopted son takes place of begotten one, 844*o*

See VII.

a supplementary process, 844*p*

insanity of the son enables father to adopt, other disqualifications, 844

by daughter-in-law, 326, 354, 845

by father-in-law, 845

quære, whether expulsion from caste of a son justifies a second ——, 842, 843, 844*s*, 844

Capacity in relation to age, 845, 935

minor's capacity to adopt, 823, 846

Capacity in relation to intelligence, 847, 848

Capacity as affected by bodily state, 847, 848

Capacity as affected by the religious state

by asceticism, pollution, according to statute, expulsion from caste of no effect, persons disqualified for inheritance cannot adopt, though allowed by some castes, 847, 848, 849, 546*o*

ADOPTION—*continued.*
Rules of particular castes, 849
by Nagar Brahmanas, 867*w*
Vaisyas, 849
Sudras, *ib.*
Jains, 849, 857, 869
Sarogees, 969, 891, 919
Bhateles, 787, 850
Talabda Kolis, 829*f*, 841*o*
Garasias, 850
Sannyasis and Gosavis, 850
Prabhus, 850*l*, 918
Lingayats, 917, 918
by *delegation*, by means of wife, widow, daughter-in-law, wife of a lunatic, 850, 851
to the great-grandfather, 852
As to assent and permission
wife's consent to —— not indispensable, *ib.*
as to assent of parents and brothers to an ——, 853
assent moved by self-interest deemed insufficient, 1077
sanction of the Court of Wards, 853
permission of Government not essential, only intimation necessary, 854
as affecting assessability of land, *ib.*
Adoption by Females
maidens cannot adopt, 855
or be adopted. See DAUGHTER, 790*w*, 833, 834
a wife or widow only can adopt for husband, 855, 859, 861, 862, 867
a wife only with distinct authority from husband, or under implied delegation, 855
conditions of effective delegation, 856
Adoption by a Widow
permission of husband necessary, real or assumed, how replaced, 856, 857, 860, 861, 867, 894, 895, 943*t*, 946, 1037
amongst Sudras, 856
in Bengal, 857
Madras, *ib.*
Mathila, 857
the N. W. Provinces, 857, 858
Age of capacity to authorize an ——, 858, 859
not affected by Act IX. of 1875, Sec. 3, 859*w*
postponement by will of capacity beyond majority, questionable, 859*x*
son united with father may authorize ——, 859
under authority needs no sanction of relatives; but without authority needs it in undivided family, 859, 867, 870
father-in-law's sanction sufficient, 859
authority good though insufficient as a will, 859
during husband's absence, *ib.*
authority and assent requisite to such ——, amongst the Poona Brahmanas, according to the Bengal law, the Mithila law, the Benares and Maratha school, 860, 861

ADOPTION—*continued.*

forms of authority variable, deeds of —— how construed, evidence of execution, express authority sufficient and binding, 861, 862

Positive command to adopt, duty to adopt, claim under the deed to follow the ——, directions contrary to law inoperative, and permission to adopt one as co-heir void, 862

when choice is prescribed, 862

rule in Bombay and Bengal, of a boy unborn, when he is named, when person adopted dies, 863, 865

Qualified discretion, 863

when the authority prescribes classes alternatively, *ib.*

Complete discretion as to person, widow's duty, 864

Conditional authority, *ib.*

according to the law of Bengal, *ib.*

in Madras, 865

Implied authority, 850, 865

Express or implied dissent of husband, positive prohibition, implied prohibition, assent assumed where not excluded, its necessity affirmed and denied, 866, 867, 868, 869

the Maratha doctrine as to widow's authority, unfettered power of a widow of a divided member, doctrine of the Viramitrodaya, assumed permission only to give in Bengal, express authority of husband not needed, in the Dravida country, and among the Jains, 867, 868, 869, 870, 871, 872, 895, 868*d*

son adopted by mother-in-law yields to one adopted by daughter-in-law, 870

a conscientious obligation of the widow, 871

her choice in —— limited, 871, 872, 1012

obligation not enforceable, 872, 903

from religious motives valid, 871

duty of Sapindas of husband, 871*g*, 895

adopting widow must be a free agent, 972, 890, 891

Time for —— by a widow, 871, 872

not precisely limited, 862, 867

preference for —— of husband's Sapindas, 873

of strangers not invalid, *ib.*

Authority in case of two or more widows, 874

the eldest has a prior right, unless disqualified, or she has resigned to the younger, 390, 874, 875

when each has a direction to adopt, 874

Circumstances in which a widow may adopt, 874, 875

Successive adoptions, 876, 881

authority to adopt on death of son limited, 875, 876, 1061, 1037

"if necessary" to be understood, 877

with consent of kinsmen, 877, 881, 884, 894

a presumptive heir not allowed to challenge a second ——, 876

Simultaneous ——s invalid, 822, 877

by woman having step-son is void, 489, 874*y*, 875

Circumstances barring adoptions by widow

as in the case of the husband, 878, 886

ADOPTION—*continued.*

can an —— *defeat a vested interest?* Question discussed, 350, 878, 879

exceptions, 881

principles of Hindu law as to perpetuation of the *sacra*, 879, 880, 883, 884

opposed to —— by a mother to her son, except on death of son an infant, need of the sanction of unseparated kinsmen, 880, 881—884

case where a united son dies childless before his father, when father-in-law can and cannot adopt, on his death this right passes to his son's widow, widow of the last coparcener may adopt, but cannot control other widows, male relatives only have control, this is the doctrine of the Nirnayasindhu, the Samskarakaustubha, the Dharmasindhu, the Vyavahara Mayukha, 882, 883, 883*t*, 884, 888

authority inoperative against son's successor, 885, 886, 887

the right co-exists with union of family, 889

ruling to the contrary, *ib.*

by predeceased son's widow, though his sister survives, *ib.*, 1041

Widow's capacity as affected by age, 890

maturity generally necessary, ceremony at least after maturity, by infant widow when directed by husband, 832*z*, 890, 891

amongst Sarogees, 891

under pressure invalid, *ib.*

Capacity affected by personal conditions, *ib.*

intelligence required as for other religious acts, 891, 943*t*

widow disqualified by leprosy and unchastity, 891, 892

by widow under puberty exceptional, *ib.*

none by untonsured widows of Brahmanas, *ib.*

Capacity annulled by remarriage, 892

Consent, when and when not required, *ib.*

none where there is express authority, 892, 894

in case of two widows, 893

consent of mother-in-law not necessary, 894

consent of husband's kinsmen when necessary, 894, 895

law in Bengal, 894, 895, 896

Madras, 894, 895, 896

Bombay, 871, 872, 883, 896, 897, 901

Dattaka Mimamsa exacts living husband's authority, 895

what assent suffices, 896, 897

effect of kinsmen's dissent not absolute, 898

Consent of the caste to ——, 898, 899, 943*t*

meaning of jnati, 898

Assent of persons affected in interest by an ——, 899

its necessity results from widow's dependence, 898, 899

not a right of property, 899*a*

Consent of Government to ——, 901—902

its confirmation cures defects, 902

Omission or postponement of ——, 903

ADOPTION—*continued.*
widow not constrained to adopt, 872, 903
pregnancy or right to adopt does not postpone inheritance, 903
pretended ——s how dealt with, *ib.*
Anomalous adoptions, 904
by mother succeeding her son, 904, 905
superseding an illegal —— by daughter-in-law? 905
by daughter-in-law, 905, 906
by daughter-in-law in preference to mother, 92*t*, 384, 880, 904, 905
by grandmother succeeding her grandson, 906
Quasi-adoptions, 906
by Gosavis, 824, 834—835
the Kritrima ——, 907
palak-putra, 906, 1065
according to Alya Santana law, 907
by Kalvantins, 834*k*, 907
by dancing girls, 907
by courtesans, *ib.*
IV. *Fitness for* ——, 908
As affected by caste, ib.
adopted to be of equal caste with the adopter, 830, 908, 909
of a Sudra son allowed by the Viramitrodaya, 909*d*
Connexion in family, 909
a brother's son supplies failure of offspring, *ib.*
proximity to be regarded in ——, 909, 910
meaning of proximity, 909*k*
illustrations, 911
proximity recommended, not obligatory, 910, 911, 913
when two persons are equally related, *ib.*
use of genealogies, *ib.*
the gotra invocations, *ib.*
worship of the deities, *ib.*
the Sastras in —— require nearness, identity of caste and gotra, *ib.*
Sudras can adopt from different gotras, *ib.*
as to —— by an elder of a younger brother, 832*z*
such —— not allowed, 912, 917
not even of a half-brother, 912*h*, 921
of an illegitimate son, 912
Relation through the natural father, 912
in case of a widow adopting, 913
order of choice in Punjab, the Dekhan, Poona, Khandesh, 913, 913*o*, 914
son of a half-brother may be chosen, uncle not limited in —— to nephew, preference a matter of discretion, but not allowed by Sastris to widow, except in case of injunction by husband, or assent of husband's relatives, 914, 915
by Sudra widow, 915
when nephew refused, *ib.*
Relation through the son's natural mother
usually makes adoption impossible, except among Sudras, but allowed in case of necessity, 916*h*, 919

ADOPTION—*continued.*
in case of a putrika-putra (see above II.), 916
son of a daughter, sister, or mother ineligible for —— (see above II.), 916, 918, 919
contra, 919
and son of a mother whom adopter could not marry, 800, 916
but only in the higher castes, 917
factum valet not applicable, *ib.*
son of a sister-in-law may be adopted by a Brahmana, 942
of sister's son invalid, 916*h*, 917
son of father's brother's daughter unfit for ——, 941*c*
sister's son unfit in the Dravida and Andra country, N. W. Provinces, Punjab, Maithila, and among Prabhus, 917, 917*a*, 918
of husband's brother's grandson valid, 918
of first cousin's daughter's son upheld, *ib.*
of husband's sister's son? *ib.*
invalid —— not to be questioned by a sister's son, *ib.*
of daughter's son in South Maratha country, 919
amongst Jains, *ib.*
of son of niece, 926
the son of second cousin, of wife's sister's son, of first cousin, paternal or maternal, 917, 919, 920
Relation between the son to be adopted and the adoptive mother
restrictions imitative, 920
the doctrine of a possibility of union between adoptive mother and real father, *ib.*
by widow, of her brother's son valid, 922
of her uncle's son not valid, 921
of wife's brother allowed, 921
a half-brother cannot be adopted, 922
connexion between real and adoptive mothers no obstacle to ——, *ib.*
Family connexion amongst Sudras
among the lower castes, influenced by the practice amongst the Brahmanas, the Sudras strictly have no sacra, relaxation in favour of Sudras, consanguinity no obstacle, 922, 923, 924
a brother's or sister's or daughter's son eligible for ——, 410, 924, 925
of one of the last two a duty, 924, 925
amongst Vaisyas (Madras), Jains, Lingayats, 924
of sister's son by Wanis, 925
invalid in Bengal, 924
allowed in Maithila, *ib.*
of daughter's illegitimate son, of mother's sister's son valid among Sudras, of sons of female blood relatives, of nearest relatives not obligatory, of uncle or an elder forbidden, by a Mhar of cousin's son, of Asagotras, from illegitimate branch of the family, 925
Relation of the son to his family of birth
of only son, eldest son, an orphan, son self-given, 806*p*. 807, 818, 820, 926, 947
giving in —— by an elder brother condemned, 832, 926

ADOPTION—*continued.*
no formula for transferring an adopted son, 926
of an only son by paternal uncle or his widow, 808, 927
in the N. W. Provinces, Madras, 818, 926, 927
principle of *factum valet* applied, 927
and occasionally in Bengal, in Bombay, 927, 818, 926
under special caste custom, *ib.*
sole remaining son deemed an only son, *ib.*
among the Lingayats, 927
only *the giving* of an eldest son is prohibited, *ib.*
of only son of a brother in Maithila, 928
as a dvyamushyayana, 926, 927
an agreement at —— necessary to constitute a dvyamushyayana, *ib.*
presumption of this in —— by a Brahmana from a different gotra, 928
similarly in —— of an only or eldest son, 928*p*
the presumption in such ——s, *ib.*
nullifies the rule that an only son can be given only to his uncle, 928*t*

Eldest son
case of *eldest* distinguished from that of an *only* son, gift of either opposed by the Mitakshare and the Vyavahara Mayukha, the Datt. Mimamsa and the Datt. Chandrika silent as to eldest, his —— allowed in Bombay, Bengal, Madras, the opinions of the Bombay Sastris, 819, 820, 928, 929, 930, 931
of a second son not invalidated by the death of elder, 930
gift of *youngest* son disapproved in the Dakhan, but not condemned by any authority, *ib.*
gift of youngest son even to a man of a different gotra is not forbidden, 931

Family of birth—amongst Sudras
propinquity gives rise to restrictions, *ib.*
of an only son among Sudras allowed, 932
the Lingayats allowed, 927
by a Sudra in Bengal, 932

Fitness as affected by Personal Qualities—Sex
daughters are not to be adopted, 932
except by special caste rules, 933
of a sister, illegal, 933*z*
a sister's daughter or son cannot become a putrika-putra, 933

Fitness for Adoption—Age
opinions vary as to the proper age of the boy to be adopted, 934, 937
so do caste rules, 934
he should be young, *ib.*
amongst Brahmanas, Kshatriyas, Vaisyas, Sudras, *ib.*
age of majority, *ib.*
the native lawyers as to the age of ——, *ib.*
the rule in the N. W. Provinces, Bombay, 934, 935

Juniority of Adopted Son to Adoptive Father

ADOPTION—*continued.*
the adoptee should be junior to the adoptive father, but not to the adopted mother, 935
Birth after Adoptive Father's Death
a boy not born in the life-time of adoptive father can still be adopted by his widow, *ib.*
Identity or Difference of Family or Gotra
sense of "gotra" when used in connexion with the lower castes, *ib.*
in ——s by Sudras no obstacle or preference arises from consanguinity, 936
when gotras differ, *ib.*
when they are the same, *ib.*
the order of preference amongst Brahmanas, 936*ss*
the son of a uterine brother, any sagotra-sapinda, asagotra sapinda, a sapinda of the same gotra, of a different gotra, *ib.*
the ceremonies of *jatakarma* and *chudakarana*, *ib.*
a *bhinna gotraja* to be adopted before his *upanayana*. *Contra*, *ib.*
the *samskaras* not to have been performed in —— from a different gotra, 936, 937
of a married sagotra in the Dekhan allowed, 937
limitation of age necessary in case of —— of a stranger, *ib.*
Fitness as affected by Bodily Qualities
leprosy, lameness, or blindness disqualifies for ——, 937, 937*z*
Mental Qualities
idiotcy or insanity disqualifies for ——, 938
Religious and Ceremonial Qualities
inseparableness from family of birth discussed, 937, 938
whether a married man adoptable, 938, 939*s*, 941, 943
exception, 944
upanayana an obstacle to ——, 938, 939*s*, 941, 943
exception, Bombay, 943
should be before tonsure, 830
except within the same gotra, 831
after tonsure, 939
tonsure no obstacle in Bombay, 939*s*
nor initiation, 938
Sastris' views in cases of ——, 938
to be before the boy is five years old, *ib.*
reason, 943*t*
effect of tonsure barring —— how undone? 939
after five years when valid, 943*t*
a sagotra may be adopted even after five years of age and tonsure, 940
Investiture with the Sacred Thread
to take place before boy's *munj*, 940, 942
when gotra differs, 940
a Brahmana boy cannot be adopted after *munj*, 941
except from sagotras, 941, 943
such an —— confers no heirship, 941
rule in Madras, *ib.*

ADOPTION—*continued.*

a Brahmana, after *chudakarna* and the *upanayana* not disqualified for —— in Bombay, 941, 943
of a boy eight years old and before initiation held valid in Bengal, 942
so when the *chuda* was performed, *ib.*
contra notwithstanding an agreement, *ib.*

Fitness—as affected by Marriage
after marriage impossible, 942, 943
contra according to the Poona Sastris, 942, 943
in case of a sagotra, 943
the rule in Bengal, Madras, 944
a married man of the same gotra only can be adopted, 943
of such a married man having a family admissible, 942, 943*t*
married men generally fit for —— amongst Sudras, 831
but not among other castes, *ib.*
the rule in Bombay, Bengal, Madras, 943, 944

Fitness—Place in Caste of the Adopted Son
exclusion from caste prevents an —— in the Dekhan, *ib.*

Fitness—In case of Anomalous Adoptions
no variance in the choice of the boy, *ib.*
defective filial relation between dvyamushyayana and his adoptive father, *ib.*
of a sister's or a daughter's son as a dvyamushyayana, *ib.*
in the Chetty caste —— is necessary to constitute the sons of daughters lawful heirs, 945

Fitness—In case of Quasi-adoptions
in the *kritrima* form of ——, *ib.*
no restrictions on the choice of the son, *ib.*
his express consent necessary, *ib.*
of an only son is lawful as a kritrima, 445*m*
no restriction on the choice of the boy in ——s in use in Gujarat, 945
of a daughter or foster daughter not recognized, 945
no —— in families governed by the Alya Santana law, 946
amongst kalavantins a matter of free choice, *ib.*

V.—*Who may give in Adoption and when*
The capacity limited to the Parents, 946—950
even in case of an adult, 832
concurrence of both parents necessary to gift of a son in ——, 943*t*, 946
after father's death mother competent to give in ——, 961
mother has no control over the gift by husband in ——, 947
widow's capacity to give in ——, 947, 948
recognized by Vasishta and other Smritis, 947, 949
husband singly may give in ——, 947
wife under husband's delegation may give in ——, *ib.*
and a widow without his authority, 948
doctrine of the Mitakshara, *ib.*
Balambhatta favours the right of females, *ib.*
mother's assent desirable not indispensable, *ib.*
the rule laid down by the Vyavahara Mayukha, 949

ADOPTION—*continued.*
Vasishtha authorizes woman's independent acceptance of a son, *ib.*
and a gift by her, *ib.*
the view of the Viramitrodaya, *ib.*
widow's authority conditioned by husband's spiritual interests, 950
grandfather or brother cannot give in ——, *ib.*
orphan cannot be adopted, *ib.*
Gift by the Father.—Father's personal competence
leper (in Bengal) can give in ——, *ib.*
the practice in Bombay, *ib.*
Circumstances in which the Gift may be made
a gift of a son morally objectionable unless made in distress, *ib.*
but a gift in —— by a competent parent always effectual, 951
a gift is not invalid through absence of poverty, *ib.*
grounds of the limitation of authority to give, 952*q*
Qualifications of the Power
consent of mother desirable, 451
intelligent boy's assent to —— necessary, 951
inferred from his submission, 952
information to relatives necessary, *ib.*
their consent and that of caste merely desirable, *ib.*
consent of Government thought necessary to ——s by Saranjamdars, &c., *ib.*
Gift by the Mother—as a Wife—by express permission of Husband
wife's giving and taking in —— without husband's permission prohibited, *ib.*
his *express* permission thought necessary for a gift, *ib.*
Husband's implied assent
husband's express permission probably not indispensable, 952
but no gift against his express or implied will, *ib.*
conditional assent, 953
assent of an insane husband needless, *ib.*
Gift by Widow
after father's death mother's power to give dependent on authority from him, *ib.*
or a discretion subject to his will, *ib.*
the narrower view of widow's capacity illustrated, 954
widow's rights most restricted in Bengal, ib.
assent of father to *a gift* presumed there when there is no dissent, *ib.*
and in Bombay except where he would be spiritually prejudiced, *ib.*
in Madras assent of relatives replaces that of deceased husband, *ib.*
assent of elder son desirable and once thought sufficient, 955
the widow being spiritually dependent on elder son, *ib.*
Gift by persons incompetent—By Adoptive Parents
gift by adoptive parents not warranted, *ib.*
such a gift guarded against by Roman Law, 455*v*
gift by real parents implied in prescribed ceremonies, *ib.*
Persons commissioned by the Parents
parents can neither authorize gift after their decease, nor can they

ADOPTION—*continued.*
during their lifetime except religious ceremonies to Brahmans, 857, 956
By Grandfather, Brother, &c.
grandfather cannot give when the boy's father is dead and mother living, *ib.*
gift by brother alone not upheld, 935*o*, 956
the practice in the Punjab, 956*b*
a brother cannot give in —— even with father's consent, 956
Self-Gift
the only son of one deceased cannot give himself in ——, *ib.*
the Svyamdatta not to be recognized in the kaliyug, *ib.*
the kritrima or karta putra an exception, *ib.*
such ——s allowed only in Maithila, *ib.*
VI. *The Act of Adoption—Its Character and Essentials*
is essentially a religious act, 957
the rights of property connected with sacra, *ib.*
ceremonies of *putreshti* and *datta homa* important, *ib.*
among the mixed and lower castes, *ib.*
no purely religious rite absolutely indispensable, 958
formerly gift and acceptance alone requisite, *ib.*
and still sufficient even amongst Brahmanas in Madras, 959
in Bombay essential ceremonies insisted on, *ib.*
essential ceremonies enumerated, 959, 993, 994
sacrifice not essential, 826, 826*q*
omission of ceremonies a cause of suspicion, *ib.*
The Act of Adoption—as to the Gift
gift of boy with any reserve not valid, 959
the ceremonies are intended to effect a complete transfer, 960
the *patria potestas* of adoptive father restricted under the Roman Law, 960*m*
mere engagement does not constitute ——, 960, 964
nor invalidate a subsequent —— ceremonially made, 960, 964
gift and acceptance essential, 960, 961, 962, 967
actual transfer necessary, 960
particular formula not prescribed, *ib.*
nor that it should be in writing, *ib.*
expressed intent to give and take only necessary, *ib.*
declaration only by the adoptive father ineffectual, 961
delivery with requisite declaration completes ——, *ib.*
gift must be expressly *in adoption*, 962
adopted son to be given, not sold, 961
assent of natural father legally necessary, 962
but mother's only morally necessary, *ib.*
assent of adoptive father alone suffices, *ib.*
salutation as an indication of acceptance, 847, 963*f*
The Act of Adoption—as to the acceptance
acceptance a cause of filiation, 962
evidence of giving and taking necessary, 963
free consent of giving and receiving parents indispensable, *ib.*

ADOPTION—*continued.*
gift and acceptance not to be replaced, *ex. gr.* by education and nurture, even among Sudras, *ib.*
The Act of Adoption—Assent of the Son
adopted to be of the same class and affectionately disposed, 964
never taken against his will, 832, 964
Contract of Adoption
agreement to adopt survives the parties, 964
husband's reference to it authorizes wife to adopt, *ib.*
such agreements not specifically enforced, *ib.*
association by adopted son of another with himself does not constitute, *ib.*
Proof of the transaction
principles of evidence of ——, 965
strong evidence necessary to displace widow or daughter, *ib.*
writing not necessary, 854, 968
husband's permission being proved slight proof of ceremonies required, 965
not so conversely, 966
satisfaction of requirements of Hindu law must be proved, *ib.*
performance of extraneous sacraments not sufficient, *ib.*
nor mere acquiescence of widow, *ib.*
proof of actual —— failing, long possession of no avail, *ib.*
so as to mere residence and general recognition, *ib.*
nurture as a foster-child is not adoption, 967
requirements as to proof not technical, *ib.*
Presumption in favour of Adoption
presumption in favour of —— when arises, 967, 968, 969
performance of ceremonies to be presumed, 968
presumption when —— is opposed to law, 969
subsequent conduct does not make that an —— which was not one, 969c
of sapinda without ceremonies pronounced valid, 969
brother preferred to sister's son acknowledged without ceremonies, 512
Estoppel
presumption in favour of an invalid —— when countenanced, 969, 970
recognition by one of another as his son creates estoppel, 970
and admission of the title of an adopted son, *ib.*
so do acts inducing adoptive father to believe in the validity of an ——, *ib.*
acquiescence in an —— and association with the boy deemed sufficient, *ib.*
in Madras mere consent to an —— held an estoppel, *ib.*
acquiescence in an —— through mistake no estoppel, 971
and cannot validate an invalid ——, *ib.*
widows completing an act of —— held bound by it, *ib.*
Ratification
ratification of —— by widow or male sapindas, *ib.*
cannot set up a void ——, 972

ADOPTION—*continued.*
doctrine of ratification not applicable to such a case, 972*t*
Limitation
to suit for declaring an —— invalid, 972
omission to sue does not validate a void ——, *ib.*
status not lost by particular omission to sue, *ib.*
Terms annexed to Adoption
rights by —— how far variable, 187*b*
subject to condition of defeasance impossible, 973
so as to mancipation under the Roman Law, 973*b*
but terms as to property are annexed to ——, 974
commonly by widows adopting, *ib.*
Terms, how far binding on the adopted son, effect given to them in Bombay and Madras, must be reasonable, disapproved by Sastris, held invalid by Privy Council, son adopted as an adult bound to fulfil accepted terms, assent of adopted son to contingent defeasance void, terms made in ——s by males, Roman law as to such terms, limitations annexed to ——s considered null by the Sastris, as *ex. gr.* that adopting widow should have management, son bound only morally; and not in case of waste, such terms annexed in kritrima ——s, and capable of ratification by son at majority, usage sanctions terms for protection of widows, husband may annex terms to his permission to adopt, or make dispositions which affect an ——, with reserve for wife and daughter, under a will limiting the boy's estate, 974, 975, 975*q*, 975*r*, 976, 977, 978, 980, 984
by widow with husband's instructions thought to invalidate his will, 978
the adopted takes by inheritance, not devise, 979
accompanying terms written or oral, *ib.*
terms held binding in Madras, 980
a compromise of sapindas' claims upheld, 979*y*
widow (in Bombay) may reserve part, 980
husband's limitations of estate of widow and adopted son recognized in Calcutta, 981
if accepted by boy's real father, 981*i*
they may give the widow a life interest, 981
analogous to settlement, 981*k*
opinions of the Sastris, 981
"absolute control" may mean only management for the son, 981*l*
questions arising from uncertainty as to the person to be adopted, 981
by a sonless man does not affect previous disposal of property, 596*g*, 982
but limits testamentary power, though not in respect of self-acquired property, 981, 982
use of a mrityu-patra, 982
adopted son should on theory take estate as an aggregate, 982, 985
but widow may impose protective terms, 983, 984
whether dowered widows adopting must necessarily defeat their own estate, 984

ADOPTION—*continued.*
grounds of the capacity discussed, 984, 985
the older authorities agree with the Sastris, 985
the recent ones agree with the usage in Bombay, *ib.*
cases discussed, 985, 986
Colebrooke's opinion, 986
Assent as a valuable consideration
assent of boy to be given is a valuable consideration, 907, 987
as against giving family, 987
receiver, *ib.*
natural parents not to contract for their own benefit, *ib.*
nor can sapindas, *ib.*
persons who must attend at an —— enumerated, 988
analogous practice in Rome, 988*g*
persons to be invited at an —— enumerated, 988
Persons taking part in the act—The Parents giving
the giver and receiver to be present, adopter must personally take the boy, mother's presence not indispensable, deed insufficient to constitute ——, declaration of gift can be made by the giving parent only, parents need not consult relatives, corporeal delivery of boy may be made by deputy, 988, 989
The Parents taking
husband and wife should be present, and a Brahmana to make oblation to fire, 989
or wife alone under delegation, *ib.*
facts indicating delegation, 990
when one of the adoptive parents is dead, *ib.*
no —— when both are dead, *ib.*
Presence of the Child given necessary, *ib.*
he may dissent, *ib.*
Presence of Relatives
to be sought but not indispensable, 990 and note *ib.*
Anomalous Adoptions
in *quasi* ——s no forms necessary except expressed assent, 991
in *kritrima* ——s consent of the boy essential, *ib.*
and of boy's parents, *ib.*
External conditions—Publicity
public transfer and religious rites requisite to ——, *ib.*
notice of —— to sagotra-sapindas and to the Raja or chief local officer enjoined, *ib.*
deed to be signed by the relations, *ib.*
such intimation and publicity not absolutely essential, 992
Time for Adoption
an auspicious day, *ib.*
declaration by daylight, *ib.*
Place for Adoption
usual place of residence desirable, not necessary, *ib.*
so of sacrifice in adopter's house, *ib.*
Ceremonies constitutive—Amongst Brahmanas
demand, invitations, notice, gift, sacrifice, investiture, *ib.*

ADOPTION—*continued.*
putreshti not essential to ——, 993, 995
rites prescribed by Vyav. Mayukha, 993
simple forms ordained by Vasishtha, 994
forms regulated by custom, *ib.*
economy of forms favoured by the Courts, *ib.*
whether mere gift and acceptance enough not certain, *ib.*
datta homa thought essential, 852, 994, 995
not in case of adoption of brother's son or of a boy of same gotra, 995, 999
not amongst classes imitating the Brahmanas, 999
isolated exceptions amongst Brahmanas, *ib.*
Jala Sankalpa, 989, 995
placing in adopter's lap, 847*n*, 995
sniffing the head, Aghrana, 847*n*
mere declarations pronounced insufficient, 995
so of performance of obsequies, *ib.*
Abridged Ceremony for one in extremis, 995, 996
no —— by will, 861, 996*w*
ceremonies exacted in case of adults, 996
ceremonies begun by dying husband completed by widow, 996, 997
Jagannatha's views, 997
investiture in adoptive family thought essential by Colebrooke, 997
vicarious ceremonies in lower castes, 998
mere gift and acceptance enough in Madras, *ib.*
observations of Judicial Committee, 998*p*
exceptional dispensations in Bombay, 999
In adopting Sagotras
sacrifices may be omitted, 831*s*, 999, 1000
though religiously prescribed, 999
Adoption after tonsure
ceremonies necessary, 1000
sacrifice annuls effects of tonsure (Datt. Mim), 1001*r*
In adopting as Dvyamushyayana
additional formula used, 1001
Ceremonies constitutive—Amongst the lower castes
sacrifice not needed, 824, 825, 1002, 1002*v*
but desirable, 1003
except perhaps in Bengal, 1002*v*, 1003
all castes below Brahmanas placed on the same level, 1002*x*
a Gosavi to adopt without Vedic rites, 824
cases of —— without sacred rites, 1003
Subsidiary Forms, 1004
writing needless, 1004
but usual, 1005, 1006
insufficient by itself, 1005, 1006
no invariable form, 1005, 1006
clear evidence to be insisted on, 1005, 1006
mere *intention* insufficient, 1005, 1006
case of invalidity for defect of forms, 1005, 1006

ADOPTION—*continued.*
Informalities, 1006
a cause of invalidity, *ib.*
in Madras immaterial, 1007
unintentional omission not fatal, 1006, 1007
except perhaps of all ceremonies, 1006, 1007
defect of forms but not of essence remediable, 1006, 1007
omission raises presumption against —— 1006, 1007
Ceremonies—Collateral, 1008
donations to Brahmanas, *ib.*
presents to the child, *ib.*
Authentication, *ib.*
instruments thought indispensable by some castes, *ib.*
distribution of sweetmeats, &c., 1008
Ceremonies—Variations in Quasi-Adoptions
nitya and anitya —— in Madras, *ib.*
krita ——s disallowed, 1009, 1011
imitated by ascetics, 1009
and in Gujarat, *ib.*
comparison of Roman law, 1001*g*
kritrima —— mere gift and acceptance, 1009
mere assent makes a foster son, *ib.*
mere nurture held to make an heir, 1010
and recognition in case of a dancer, *ib.*
VII.—*Consequences of Adoption—Perfect, General Effects, Change of Status*, 1010
effect of complete —— amongst the twice-born, 838
gift in —— extinguishes filial and paternal relations, 347*e*, 961
relation to family of birth annulled, 1010
causes complete severance from family of birth, 347*e*
whether consanguinity ceases with —— discussed, 912
law in Maithila, *ib.*
the Andra country, *ib.*
relation to adoptive family completed by initation, 1010*z*
confers right to inherit, 56
adopted becomes like a begotten son, 349*k*, 1010,68, 69
rights subject to partial defeasance, 1013
adopted son does not replace disqualified father?, 542, 545
not to be disinherited, 549
only one ——allowed at a time, 1011
except on refusal or incapacity of adopted son to fulfil duties, 1028
adoptive mother's interests gradually developed, 1011
her ancestor's interest, 1012
son includes adopted son in Succession Act, 1013
Change of Sacra, 1012
the most important result of ——, *ib.*
deliverance from *Put* effected by single ——, *ib.*
no ceremonial impurity from family of birth, 1013
Transfer of Offspring, *ib.*
son goes with father into adoptive family, *ib.*

ADOPTION—*continued.*
Adoption by Male prospective, ib.
by male does not affect bygone transactions, 596*g*, 1014
affect a completed gift, *ib.*
Adoption by Widow retrospective.
"operates retrospectively" how construed, 349, 879, 886, 888, 1014
not retrospective amongst competing collaterals, 888
even when postponed by fraud, 890
son by —— ranks as posthumous, 1014
by widow of the last male survivor of family, 887
widow's ownership ceases, 1013, 1014
her past transactions subject to rescission, 1015
upheld when they were necessary or beneficial, 1014, 1015
rights of action and vested interest arise at ——, 1014, 1016
but extend only to interests actually vested in deceased adoptive father, 884, 885, 1016
not to a raj re-granted to a widow, 1016
nor to collateral succession taken before actual ——, 1035
Adoption final, 1016
cannot be set aside, 348, 822*y*, 838, 960, 1017
or renounced, 1017
boy duly adopted not to be abandoned or disinherited, 324, 549, 968, 977, 1032
rights may be renounced, 1033
or made subject to conditions by agreement, 1017
no return to family of birth, 1017, 1018
Connexion with Family of Birth—As to prohibited degrees, 1018
a male, though given in —— cannot marry within seven degrees in family of birth, 837, 1018
Conditions and terms annexed to Adoption, 1018
not allowed to affect the status, 1019
conditions accepted in ignorance not binding, *ib.*
life interest retained by widow adopting under will, 1020
under agreement with natural father held ratifiable, *ib.*
contrary view of Sastris, *ib.*
allowed by customary law, *ib.*
nature of adopted son's interest under wills, &c., in favour of widow, *ib.*
Specific effects.—Relations to Family of Birth, 1022
natural must give up to adoptive parents, *ib.*
not subject to expenses of the boy's samskaras, *ib.*
tonsure wrongly performed by natural father void, *ib.*
obsequies performed for natural father ineffectual, *ib.*
adopted son should not preform obsequies for natural mother, 1023
no inheritance in family of birth, *ib.*
except in default of other heirs, 1024
among Gyawals, *ib.*
in what absolutely and solely vested in adoptee according to Calcutta and Madras High Courts, 1024
no obligation to pay natural father's debts, *ib.*

ADOPTION—*continued.*
the incapacity for marriage in family of birth continues, 1025
of younger brother by birth disapproved, *ib.*
relatives by birth do not inherit from boy given in ——, 1026

Relations to Family of Adoption
adopted son cannot marry within three degrees, 838, 1025
the adoptive father is entitled to custody of son, 1026
who should reside with him, *ib.*
adopted son entitled to maintenance, *ib.*
and his widow, 1027
his samskaras to be performed, *ib.*
objects of —— set forth, *ib.*
relation to adoptive mother's ancestors, *ib.*
succession to adoptive father's estate, 1028, 1031
bound to maintain widow, 1028
similar duty of daughter-in-law adopting, *ib.*
rights of son arise forthwith on ——, 1029
the ordinary right, *ib.*
alienation by father restricted, *ib.*
except of self-acquired property, 1029, 1032
different relations of father and son as to property in Bengal and Bombay, 1029*f*
interdiction open to adopted son, 1030
cases of an adopted son's rights, 1030, 1031
rights vest in son adopted by daughter-in-law, 1030, 1038, 1041
not annulled by subsequent disposition, 1031
or birth of daughter's son (Bengal), *ib.*
adopted son succeeds though separated, 1032
takes by survivorship, *ib.*
disinherison of adopted son, *ib.*
his renunciation and relinquishment of rights, 838, 1032
he is not thereby restored to his family of birth, 838
his widow entitled to maintenance, 1033
son not prejudiced by widow's unauthorized alienation, 349, 1035
may get such alienations rescinded, 349, 1034
but not those properly made, 1035, 1042, 1043
adopted son divests widow's estate, 349
cannot defeat or divest an estate, except in four cases, 886—887
cannot divest inheritance vested in son's widow, *ib.*
widow's right reduced to that of mother and guardian, 1033*g*, 1038
except in cases of necessity?, 1036
adopted son heir in turn to adoptive mother's stridhana, 480, 1034, 1038
alienation by widow after —— not ratifiable, 1034
her religious gift invalid, 1035
she may give her separate property, 1036
sale for husband's debts good, *ib.*
under necessity valid? *ib.*
rights in case of successive ——s by mother, 1036, 1037

ADOPTION—*continued.*
as to alienations between death of first adopted son and second ——, 1037, 1039, 1042
adopted son representative for suits, *ib.*
pending suit by widow, 1038
widow's right to maintenance against adopted son, 1037, 1038
and to residence, 1038
adoptive mother succeeds to son, 1039
adopted son succeeds to step-mothers, 1039, 1040
connexion in sacrifices, 1039*c*
succession of adoptive step-mother, 1039, 1040
importance of right to adopt as between co-widows, 1040
adopted son liable for adoptive father and grandfather's debts, 1041
and those properly incurred by widow, 1042
he recovers debts in his own right, *ib.*
adopted son pronounced liable as such for mother's debts? 1042, 1043
admissions by widow as manager as affecting adopted son, 1043
widow bound to account to adopted son, *ib.*
adoptive mother legal representative of adopted son, *ib.*
adopted son yields religious precedence to one by birth, *ib.*
marriage in adoptive family prohibited to three degrees, 1044
adopted son regarded as of the adoptive family for further ——s, *ib.*
adopted son competing with son by birth takes one-fourth, 347*e*, 354, 355, 707, 836, 1044
so in mother's property, 1044
exceptions (especially amongst Sudras), 1044*n*, 1045
son by birth takes vatan or impartible estate, 1045
adopted son excludes an illegitimate as heir to mother, *ib.*
sister succeeds to adoptive brother, 1046
Collateral Succession through Adoptive Father, *ib.*
adopted son shares sacra of the family, *ib.*
unless adopted after partition, 1046, 1047
partition excludes boy subsequently adopted, 901*i*
adopted son is a sapinda, 1051
he takes his father's share in a partition, 835*c*, 1047
or in a collateral succession, 1050
replaces him in united family, 1047
two cases *contra*, 1047, 1048
adopted son may compound for his share, 839
coparceners need not wait for an ——, 1048
adopted son takes collaterally only where succession opens after ——, 1049, 1050, 1052
he continues an estate but does not recover it once distributed, 1050
adopted son of whole brother preferred to natural son of half-brother, 1049
collateral inheritance by a group and subsequent ——, 1051*a*
collaterals inherit from adopted son, 1051
adopted son may separate from adoptive father, 839
but does not thereby lose his rights of inheritance, *ib.*
adopted sons succeed *inter se*, 1053

ADOPTION--*continued.*
adopted son succeeds to sister's adopted son, 1052
Collateral Succession through Adoptive Mother, ib.
comparison of the Roman Law, 1052*o*
cases discussed, 1053, 1054
conclusion that the adopted son takes collaterally through adoptive mother like son by birth, 838, 1054
Manu gives heritage of maternal grandfather only to begotten son, 420
Imperfect Adoption, 1055
comparison of the Roman law, 1058*c*
adoptions contrary to caste laws annulled by caste, 1055
a small share given in such cases, *ib.*
rights in family of birth unaffected by invalid ——, 1056
succession or participation to the exclusion of a person disqualified not divested by ——, *ib.*
sons already adopted take subsistence, *ib.*
or replace the father, 1056*o*
a vicarious —— allowed by custom, 1056
conditions of cancelling ——, *ib.*
invalidity, 1057
invalid —— transmits no right, 1058
right of maintenance arises in case of severance from family of birth, *ib.*
invalid —— not set up by subsequent change in family, 1059
no —— over the head of a man fully initiated even after his death, 1060*w*
or by other substitute than a widow? 1060
Case of a Grantee, ib.
the sovereign's or superior's consent required under native system for succession to the tenure, *ib.*
a confirmatory sanad relied on to be proved, *ib.*
Effects of Adoption as Dvyamushyayana, 1062
the boy inherits from his natural father in default of other sons, *ib.*
Other Irregular Adoptions.
kritrima son inherits in both families, *ib.*
contracts no family relation with the adoptive father's or mother's cognates, 945
kritrima son adopted by one parent succeeds to that one only, 1063
does not affect a Talabda Koli's right of disposal, *ib.*
similar law in some other castes, 1065
the adopted son may be replaced where a begotten son could be disinherited, 1064
no succession as son of adopted daughter, she having brothers, *ib.*
or under a bought son, *ib.*
plurality of adopters and adopted, *ib.*
a gosavi's pupil does not succeed to him as father, *ib.*
quasi —— of son-in-law not recognized, 1065
his rights under customary law, 1065*c*
foster-son not recognized by the Sastras as a successor, 1065, 1066

ADOPTION—*continued.*
but recognized by custom, 1066
as successor in both families, *ib.*
widely recognized by the castes in Gujarat, 1066*h*
adoptions generally disallowed there, *ib.*
quasi —— by Naikins ineffectual, 1066
exception, 1065*g*
VIII. *Suits and Proceedings connected with Adoptions*
jurisdiction recognized by Hindu law, 1067
In case of Non-adoption.
agreement to adopt binding, *ib.*
no suit to compel a widow to adopt, 1067, 1068
bequest to specified person not defeated by non-adoption, 1068
direction to adopt not equivalent to bequest, *ib.*
breach of a written agreement as to —— does not avoid it, *ib.*
Position of Widow before Adoption.
she may obtain a declaration of her heirship, 1068
authority to adopt no obstacle, *ib.*
two widows authorized may divide the property, *ib.*
a son adopted may dispute widow's prior transactions, 1069
presumption in favour of them if approved by heirs, *ib.*
declaration in favour of son still to be adopted cannot be made, *ib.*
widow is not a trustee for son to be adopted, 1069
widow continuing suit after —— may be regarded as trustee, *ib.*
no forfeiture for attempted false ——, *ib.*
alienation by widow before second —— not affected by it, 1070
Suits to establish Adoption.
a claimant in Bengal must prove authority and actual ——, *ib.*
must sue for property when it is sought, *ib.*
but may sue for declaration for use before another authority, *ib.*
an adopted son discarded may sue to establish his right, *ib.*
second —— under power invalidated by existence of widow of first adopted, 1071
authority where required must be strictly proved, *ib.*
evidence of ceremonies, 1072
facts deemed significant, 1071
presumption, 1071, 1072
registration of deeds of —— recommended, 1071
in a suit as adopted son a right as dvyamushyayana not to be set up, 1073
conditions of suit for declaration, *ib.*
institution fee, *ib.*
certificate of administration may be claimed to estate of one whose —— is disputed, *ib.*
certificate of guardianship does not give a right against a widow disputing the ——, *ib.*
Suits to set aside Adoption.
person interested may question an ——, 889
suit competent apart from claim to property, 1073
but not to a stranger, 1074

ADOPTION—*continued.*
adopted must prove ——, 1073
estoppel against one who has admitted —— by conduct, 1073, 1074
grounds deemed insufficient for setting aside ——, 1074
for establishing it, 1076
suit competent only to nearest heir unless this is impracticable, 1075
suit for possession as heir must not be changed into one for declaration against an ——, 1076
objection of consent not obtained held too late when raised before Judicial Committee, *ib.*
objection not pressed below disallowed in second appeal, 1077
admissions, as binding or not, discussed, 1075, 1076*ss*
acquiescence or consent through ignorance not binding, 1077
nor if got by misrepresentation, 1077, 1078

Adoption an incidental question
in fact presumed valid, 1077
case of conveyance convertible into mortgage on ——, *ib.*
devise to adopted son as *persona designata* upheld though —— invalid, 1077, 1078
Proceedings consequent on Adoption, 1078
under Act XXVII. of 1860, 1078; 1081
gift to adopted son not affected by birth of sons, 1078
settlement on widow with concurrence of adopted son upheld, *ib.*
son cannot demand a declaration of right to specified undivided share, 1079
son adopted *pendente lite* to be made a party, *ib.*
representation acted on to be made good, *ib.*
attestation of a deed of —— does not bind to a statement therein, 1080
certificate of administration to estate of adopted child, *ib.*
adoptive mother preferred as guardian, *ib.*
certificate of guardianship when to be given to a widow, 911, 912
widow cannot continue a suit against wish of adopted son after he has attained full age, 1080
she is entitled to certificate of administration to deceased husband's estate as against an alleged adopted son, 1081
the questions of title and of adoption to be adjudicated, *ib.*
in case of application for certificate of administration resisted, *ib.*
a contest between widow and adopted son as to validity of will should be the subject of a regular suit, 1081
effect refused to permission to adopt during adopted son's life, *ib.*
bequest contingent on death of proposed adopted son unmarried invalid, *ib.*
grant of probate to alleged adopted son cannot be resisted by creditors of next heir, 1082
Judgments and Evidence in previous cases, *ib.*
no process for establishing or avoiding —— as to all the world, 1082*r*
judgment on —— is not *in rem*, 1082
decree not evidence in litigation with third parties, *ib.*
nor binding between adopted and a different heir, *ib.*
not *res judicata* when parties changed, *ib.*

ADOPTION—*continued.*
but between the same parties *res judicata*, though for a different portion of the property, 1083
different decision in case of other property, *ib.*
denied in a summary inquiry may be asserted in a suit, *ib.*
deposition of plaintiff in suit against one adopted son not admissible in suit for a second? *ib.*
a certificate may be granted as guardian to a son whose father's —— has been set aside, 1084
Limitation, 972, 1084
to suit for declaration of adoption six years from act contradicting it, 1084
for declaration against —— six years from knowledge, *ib.*
limitation computed from death of widow who had adopted after her son's death, 1084, 1085
acknowledgment by sister of deceased held not to bind her son, 1085
limitation in a suit for a share by one as adopted son computed from knowledge of exclusion, *ib.*

ADULTEROUS MOTHER
must be maintained, 555

ADULTEROUS WIFE
must be maintained by husband, *ib.*
not by his brethren, *ib.*
to be kept apart, *ib.*
her husband inherits her earnings by adultery, 483
See UNCHASTITY; MAINTENANCE; WIFE

ADULTERY,
an offence under the Indian Penal Code, 556
disqualifies a widow from succeeding, 83, 149, 406, 422, 552—557
but —— does not divest property already vested, 83, 554
revokes wife's authority to deal with husband's property, 86*s*
amongst the lower classes punishable as involving injury to caste rather than loss of chastity, 401
one begotten in —— has no right of inheritance, 368, 546*r*
but of maintenance only, 546*r*
reason why —— was denounced, 798*r*
entails only a penance when connexion was not with a man of a lower caste, 401
with a low-caste man punished with divorce, *ib.*
atoned at husband's will, *ib.*
See DISQUALIFICATION; UNCHASTITY; WIFE

ADVANCEMENT,
no presumption of —— from purchase by a Hindu father in son's name, 568, 665

ADYAM,
explanation of, 308*k*, 353

AGARVALI CASTE, 356

AGE
of Vijnanesvara, 17
the Dharmasastras, 30, 35
of majority fixed at eighteen, 846
this does not affect adoption, 859*w*
of competence for religious acts, 964*s*
child how designated at different times, *ib.*
See ADOPTION II., 814d, 831; III., 845, 858, 859, 869, 890; VIII., 1081
Boy.

AGHRANA. See ADOPTION III., 847*n*

AGNIHOTRA, 744

AGREEMENT,
private cannot alter the course of devolution 4, 151*m*, 178
not allowed to control customary law, 84
between adopted son and mother pronounced void, 178*l*, 187*b*
how far valid, 985, 1020
to divide after a certain event does not sever interests, 633
See ADOPTION VI., 960, 964; VII., 1017, 1020; VIII., 1067, 1068; EVIDENCE OF PARTITION; DISTRIBUTION; PARTITION; PARTNERSHIP.

ALIENATION,
power of —— dependent on circumstances, 169
limited by Hindu law, 186
by adoption, 738*w*
its growth in Europe, 735*q*
by absolute owner now unrestricted, 76, 215, 982
family estate once deemed inalienable, 672*k*
how the family estate became gradually alienable, *ib.*
generally disapproved in ancient laws, 714
of sacred property usually disallowed, 681
religious endowment alienable only to one in the line of succession, 200, 716*m*
otherwise indivisible and inalienable, 717
exceptions, *ib.*
interest of a temple servant alienable, 716*m*
vatan property cannot leave the family, 769
of self-acquired property limited to surplus over family needs, 601*x*, 695, 1215
impartibility consistent with alienability, 154, 378, 681*f*
but checks incumbrance, 162
inalienability a question of family custom, 154
raj not necessarily inalienable, 681*f*
widow's right to maintenance in alienable, 698

ALIENATION—*continued.*
Alienation by Coparcener
a coparcener may alienate for value his share without consent of others in Bombay and Madras; (but not in Bengal, Behar and N. W. P.,) 565, 616, 687*m*, 203, 215
not by gift, 447, 568, 616, 651, 203
or by devise, 616, 651, 203
except for pious purposes, 816
he cannot dispose of joint property without consent of the others (Mitakshara), 448, 478, 562*h*, 564*s*, 651
restrictions on —— by caste custom, 684*d*
made under necessity valid by custom, 688*t*
Alienation by Father.
of patrimony subject to control of descendants unseparated, 206, 593*l*, 739, 740*e*, *h*, 587
without assent of heirs invalid by custom, 599*o*
son may prevent improper ——, 193*a*, 594
or annul it unless made before his birth or adoption, 596*g*, 732, 1013
care for child unborn, 208*q*
of immoveable property, though self-acquired, said to be invalid? 705, 739
father has full power over property self-acquired, 705, 733, 982
by will invalid against a united son, 740*h*
subject to provision for family, 727
depriving a widow or family of subsistence invalid, 210, 234
for purposes not immoral binding on son, 340, 581, 582, 587, 987
immoral purpose affecting but a trivial portion does not invalidate it, 8
Alienation by Grandfather
with son's assent not disputable by that son's son, 731
Alienation by Mahant
fraudulent —— set aside, 187*b*, 199
See TRUST, *ib.*
Alienation by Manager, 592*k*, 701
acquiesced in by coparcener is binding on him, 688*s*
Alienation by Mistress
mistress not to alienate a house given to her by her patron, 193*y*
Alienation by Son
requires father's consent, 740
Alienation by Uncle
without assent of nephews, 740*e*
Alienation by Widow
dependent by caste usage on non-existence of male relatives of her husband, 714*b*
not to prejudice subsequently adopted son, 1033
See WIDOW
Pilgrimage, 306
Alienation by Wife
in case of paraphernalia under English law, 186*s*
See OWNERSHIP; MANAGER; PROPERTY SELF-ACQUIRED; ADOPTION VII., 1029, 1034, 1035, 1036, 1041, 1043; VIII., 1069

ALAMANNI,
laws of the, 798*p*

ALLOWANCES,
temple, are hereditary and divisible, 681
Chirde, 425
Desaigiri, *ib.*
Muglai, *ib.*
Sirpava, *ib.*
Vazifa, *ib.*
from Government, arrears of are Stridhana, 491

ALYA SANTANA LAW. See ADOPTION III., 907; IV., 946

ANALOGY OF HINDU LAW
followed in succession to principalities, &c., 677
a means of construction, 100
See INTERPRETATION

ANANTADEVA,
author of Samskarakaustubha, 25

ANCESTOR-WORSHIP, 270
See SRADDHAS

ANCESTRAL LANDS,
lands once held by common ancestor, 657*t*

ANCESTRAL PROPERTY. See PROPERTY ANCESTRAL; SUCCESSION; PARTITION; ALIENATION

ANIMAL SACRIFICE,
formerly prevalent, 811*x*

ANITYA ADOPTION. See ADOPTION, 1008, 1058

ANITYA DATTA, 810*n*
who is —— son? 98*l*, 939*t*
son of —— son, 939*t*

ANNUITY. See INVESTMENT; NIBANDHA; PROPERTY

ANOMALOUS ADOPTION. See ADOPTION

ANVADHEYA,
is a gift subsequent to marriage, 135, 277, 486
is a kind of stridhana, 485, 486
is shared by sons and unmarried daughters equally, 135, 309, 486*k*

APARIBHASHIKA STRIDHANA, 485, 496

APARADITYADEVA
is another name for Apararka, 19

APARARKA,
the author of Yajnavalkyadharmasastranibandha, *ib.*
Apararka's doctrine as to Stridhana, 19, 712

APASTAMBA SUTRA, 32

APASTAMBA OR APASTAMBHA,
school of, 36

APOSTASY,
(mere) does not free from the Hindu marriage law, 559*a*

APPANAGE
of juniors in case of primogeniture, 256
when it reverts, *ib.*
in India and Germany, 677*a*
See MAINTENANCE; ZAMINDARI, 682

APPEAL
suspends effect of decree for partition, 615, 633

APPOINTMENT
of daughter, place of —— in Hindu law, 800
daughter by —— is ranked third amongst subsidiary sons by Vasishtha, 801
no longer recognized, 800
not recognized by Apastamba, 802
nor by Gautama, *ib.*
nor by Baudhayana, 803
of daughter conceived in two ways, 801
traces of —— in the existing law, 800
relative position of —— and her son, 803
analogue amongst the Greeks, *ib.*
See ADOPTION—PUTRIKA-PUTRA

APRATIBANDHA DAYA, 63
See INHERITANCE UNOBSTRUCTED

APSARASES, 798*r*

ARROGATION,
origin of the term, 828*y*, 830*g*
Roman, limited to those who had attained years of discretion, 805*k*
age of the adopter in an —— of one *sui juris*, 832*a*
safeguards for sons taken in ——, 820
of women not allowed before Justinian's legislation, 834*k*

ARSHA, 265, 481, 484, 486
See MARRIAGE

ARYAN HINDUS. See HINDUS, ARYAN

ASAGOTRA SAPINDA. See BANDHUS; BHINNAGOTRA SAPINDAS; ADOPTION IV., 872

ASAHAYA, 44

ASCETICS,
orders of ——, 17, 18
succession to, based on personal association 521*w*
relations between —— and their disciples governed by custom, 834
cannot alter succession to an endowment, 521*w*
cannot impose restrictions on successors contrary to custom, *ib.*
See MAHANT; ADOPTION III., 839; VI., 1008

ASCETICISM. See ADOPTION III., 848

ASRAMAS, 61

ASSENT
of sons deemed necessary to alienation by father, 599*o*, 601*x*
See ALIENATION
signified by attestation, 593*l*
as once in Europe, 191*n*, 218
requisite to a gift, 191*k*
of members of family is necessary to expensive sacrifices, performed by one of them, 564*s*
to gifts at mother's obsequies, *ib.*
not necessary to resigning holding by Government occupant, *ib.*
of brethren to adoption essential on account of widow's dependence, 868*d*, 871, 889, 901*l*
of brethren ought not to be refused except for special cause, 871*g*, 876, 895—898
by —— property dedicated to service of family idol may be disposed of, 716*m*
but not that dedicated to public temple, *ib.*
coparcener, desiring to limit his responsibility for liabilities [maintenances of relatives, &c.] may secure himself by —— of interested parties, 719, 720
of co-sharers to charges binds them, 688
to adoption implied from non-prohibition, 867*w*, 869*k*, 869
See ACQUIESCENCE; ADOPTION, *passim*

ASSESSMENT. See ADOPTION III., 854

ASSETS
taken are accompanied by liability for debts of one deceased, 165, 168, 602*z*
the responsibility of a son is not by Hindu law dependent on ——, 165, 1088
but so limited by statute, 76*i*, 686
See DEBT; FATHER; INHERITANCE

ASSIGNMENT,
none of a right to maintenance, 191, 246, 250, 253, 288
of debts to a parcener on partition, 718
possible, of part-ownership in a physically indivisible property, 757
of obligations, 685e

ASSOCIATION
capable of creating a law for itself? 559
See CUSTOM

ASTROLOGER, 180
astrologer's relation to those who take his services governed by custom, 388, 389
See JOSHI

ASURA MARRIAGE. See MARRIAGE

ASVALAYANA DHARMASASTRAS, 46

ATHENIAN LAW
compared with Hindu law, 177b, 838w

ATTACHMENT
of property for debts discussed, 161
and sale of family land unknown to Hindu law books, 602
not properly directed against undivided share? 579d
of whole undivided property may be made for debt of one coparcener, 615f
subject to rights of sons, &c. 616
of undivided share creates a charge on undivided interest, 566y, 567
effect of —— of impartible zamindari, 161
whether purchaser in execution of manager's share can be ousted? 567d

ATTACHMENT BY GOVERNMENT, 763

ATTESTATION
under Hindu law intended to be of the transaction, 218
See ASSENT
is a mark of assent, 593l, 673, 710, 771
according to decisions —— does not bind to contents, 1080
in case of wills, 217ss
See WILLS

ATTICA,
laws of —— against alienation and sub-division, 210
compared with Hindu law, 210, 271, 395

ATTORNMENT,
equivalent to possession, 643

AUNT (Paternal),
not a gotraja sapinda even in Gujarat, 122p

AUNT—*continued.*
but is entitled to rank as a bandhu, 122*p*, 458
when —— succeeds, 453
See SAPINDA
(paternal)——'s son is a bandhu, 123, 457, 461
case of exclusion of —— by sister's son, 463
is excluded by great grandson of fifth ancestor of the deceased, 456
(maternal) ——'s son is a bandhu, 123, 457, 461
excluded by sister's son, 463

AURASA SON. See SON, 804, 805

AUSTERITIES,
may replace adoption, 790, 1013, 1060

AUTHENTICATION,
public—of transactions, 973
records originally recollections, *ib.*
See ADOPTIONS VI., 1007

AUTHORITIES
on Hindu law enumerated, 9
(See separate list)
their relative weight considered, 9—54

AWARD,
stranger to an—cannot rely on admissions in it, 189*n*

BALAMBHATTA, 18
See ADOPTION V., 948

BALAMBHATTATIKA,
written by Lakshmidevi, 18
otherwise called Lakshmi Vyakhyana, *ib.*
is a commentary on the Mitakshara, *ib.*
gives the widest interpretation to the text of Yajnavalkya, 18

BANDHAVAS,
include maternal uncle, 125

BANDHUS,
Vijnanesvara's conception of ——, 124, 443, 458
defined, 124, 457, 458, 464
enumeration of ——, 123, 457
the enumeration of —— is not exhaustive, 124, 126, 458
limit of bandhu relation, 457, 463
origin of this, 457
includes all relatives within the degrees expressed, 458, 459, 461
See SAPINDA
among unenumerated ——, nearer succeed before remote, 460

BANDHUS—*continued.*
mentioned in law books, 461
not mentioned in law books, males, 462, 127
females, 465
order of succession, 124, 324, 456, 460, 461, 463
Sapindas and Samanodakas are preferred to ——, 123, 458
postponed to Gotraja Sapindas, 460*n*
in Bengal, —— succeed before remoter Sapindas, 108*y*, 457*b*
aunt's sons preferred in N. W. Provinces to cousin's widow? 454

BANTS. See TRIBES, 272*w*

BANYA, 390

BARRENNESS,
not an impediment to inheritance in Bombay, 474

BASTARDS,
inherited under Irish and Welsh law, 77*n*
See ILLEGITIMATE

BAUDHAYANA,
on female inheritance, 117*ss*
See LIST OF HINDU AUTHORITIES

BENAMI SYSTEM,
may be traced to union of Hindu family, or law of agency in the Mohammedan law, 157, 562*h*
transaction, presumption in a, 665*e*, 158
principle of, *ib.*, 158
purchase in son or daughter's name, 158, 665
purchase in wife's name who is found in possession, 158
purchase by manager in his own name, 158
purchase from or mortgage by benamdar holding himself out as real owner with or without notice, with the acquiescence of beneficial owner, 159

BENAMDAR
may sue or be sued in his own name, 160

BENEFITS,
spiritual. See ADOPTION IV., 922, 944; VI., 987

BEQUEST
of property acquired by partition good against remote heirs, 129
of undivided share invalid, 588, 616
merely for Dharma ineffectual, 223
tying up the corpus is invalid, 224
by a coparcener singly is inoperative, 564
by husband to wife treated as a gift, 297*c*

BEQUEST—*continued.*
to one son to the prejudice of others invalid, 205, 206, 705, 736
See GIFT, 564 ; DEVISE; WILL ; TESTAMENTARY POWER ; PERPETUITY; WIFE; WIDOW; ADOPTION VIII., 1068, 1081

BERADA CASTE, 405

BETROTHAL AND MARRIAGE,
sometimes confounded, 266

BHACHA,
nephew through a sister on one side, 511

BHAGADARI LANDS,
male preferred to female in succession to ——, 407
in —— holdings, sub-division is prohibited, 684
and also separation of the house from the holding, *ib.*
sale of part of a bhag is void though made by a Court *

BHAGDARI VATAN, 435*b*

BHAGAVANTA BHASKARA,
consists of twelve divisions, 20
enumeration of these, *ib.*

BHANGA SALI CASTE, 406

BHARADVAJA SMRITI, 47

BHARTHI SECT, 530

BHATELE CASTE, 787, 850

BHATT VAIRAGI,
a mere grihastha, 536

BHATT VRITTI, 671*e*

BHAVIN,
a votary of Rawalnatha, 494*v*

BHILS. See TRIBES, 276

BHOOTEAH. See TRIBES, *ib.*

BHINNAGOTRA SAPINDA,
daughters of descendant and collaterals within six degrees are ——s, 127
descendants of daughters are ——s, 127, 400*n*

---

* *Collector of Broach* v. *Rajaram Laldas*, I. L. R. 7 Bom. 542.

BHINNAGOTRA SAPINDA—*continued.*
maternal relations within four degrees are ——s, 127
sister's son is a ——, 459
grand-daughter's grandson is a ——, 127
but her great-grandson is not a ——, *ib.*
sapindas extend to mother's great-grandfather and his fifth descendant, 459
not so in Madras, 460*n*
seventh descendant through daughter is a —— according to one opinion, *ib.*
admission of more than one female link in connexion giving heritable right questionable, 460*n*
succession of ——s, 459*ss*
daughter's husband's —— to Stridhana of his wife, 503—505

BHRATARAH, 121*n*

BIRTH
actual —— necessary to the full constitution of right as son, 63, 596*g*, 732
at once confers on the son the right to participate in property, 665, 732, 740
See ADOPTION VII., 1021, 1025, 1031, 1043, 1044, 1045, 1054, 1056, 1057; VIII., 1078
Son

BLIND; BLINDNESS,
who is blind? 541
blindness does not prevent disposal of property, 542
disqualifies for inheritance, 141, 541—543
if congenital, 150
not partial, 543
disqualifies for taking under partition, 747
persons married and having families inherit in some castes, 150
sons of —— persons are not excluded, 541
disqualifies a widow, *ib.*
men must be maintained, *ib.*
of the son born does not justify adoption, 817
See ADOPTION III., 848; DISQUALIFICATION, 541; MAINTENANCE

BLOOD-RELATIONSHIP,
recognized amongst the lower castes, 831*o*
gives a right to inherit, 56
not jurally extinguished by adoption, 1024
See ADOPTION VII.

BOOK,
land in England originally pious grants, 191*n*

BOOKS
when indivisible and when not, 671, 675
to be kept by coparceners having them, 717

BOROUGH—English, 338

BOY
a —— may not recite Vedic formulas except for obsequies, 1089
See AGE

BRAHMA MARRIAGE
See MARRIAGE, 481, 484, 486, 494

BRAHMACHARI,
divided into Upakurvana and Naishthika, 56, 60
meaning of Upakurvana and Naishthika ——, 469o, p
succession to Upakurvana ——, 56, 73, 468
Naishthika ——, 133
See ADOPTION III., 842v

BRAHMIN COMMUNITY,
when —— inherits, 128

BRAHMANA, 61, 434
is born under three obligations, 789
he only is born under three obligations, 823
Brahmanas may become Sannyasis, 518
Nagar, 867
See ADOPTION III.
widow, 921, 941, 942, 943
See ADOPTION IV.
Brahmanas have a spiritual title to all things, 128f
succession of learned ——s on failure of blood relations to the property of a ——, 125, 128
See SROTRIYA
this succession of ——s not recognized by English Courts, 128
See ADOPTION III., 860, 891; VI., 958, 889, 998, 1002x, 1007

BRETHREN,
a grant to united —— constitutes a Hindu joint tenancy, 72

BRIDE-CAPTURE,
See CAPTURE, 797

BRIDE-PRICE, 263, 267
discussed, 355
common amongst the wild tribes, 270
and low castes, 358
institution of —— existed among Hindus for a time among all classes, 264
came to be looked on with abhorrence by the Brahmanical community in later times, 265
became peculiar to Vaisyas and Sudras, *ib.*
though in the Arsha form of marriage gift of bull or cow was still preserved, *ib.*

BRIDE-PRICE—*continued.*
practice extending in Sub-Himalayan districts, 270
sales still not unusual in Gujarat, *ib.*
Sulka and ——, 265—268
amongst the Jews, 266*w*
Germans, *ib.*
connexion with *dos legitima* and *morgengabe*, 266, 267
Roman *co-emptio*, 266
in China, 267
Stridhana had a pre-historic origin in the ——, 263
goes to the mother or the brother, 265, 266
father in the Huzara district, 265*g*
See SULKA; STRIDHANA

BRIDE-PURCHASE. See BRIDE-PRICE, 264

BRIHASPATI SMRITI, 43
its age, 44

BRIHAT SAUNAKA, 46

BROTHERS,
are the coparceners specified by Mit. and May., 69, 70
include more remote relations according to the opinions of the Sastris, 70, 71
sons of the same concubine are ranked as full, 74, 369
succession of ——, 102, 324, 379, 404, 411, 426, 432, 438, 497
under Mit. full and half —— rank equally in undivided families, 72
but in divided families full —— are preferred to half ——, 772
in Bengal full —— take before half —— in undivided families, and undivided or reunited half —— take equally with separated full ——, 71, 429
when —— and nephews succeed simultaneously, 71, 100, 103
exclude foster-daughter, 426
reunited half —— take equally with separated full ——, 130
reunited full —— exclude reunited half ——, 131
half —— acquire the right of inheritance by reunion, 71
succession of —— of half-blood, 104, 334, 383, 410, 427, 429, 430, 438
according to Mit. and Vyav. May., 104
half —— postponed to full sister by Vyav. May., 430
succession of, to full sister, 436, 439
separated —— postponed to father, 427
by birth take precedence of one previously adopted, 900*g*
half —— postponed to full sister, 104
divided —— preferred to first cousin's widow, 427
sister's son, 512
succession of —— to unmarried females, 134, 470
to Stridhana of females married by approved rites, 507, 509
by blamed rites, 488, 494
take Sulka Stridhana, 266, 268, 269, 311, 486*m*
succession of half —— to Stridhana of married females, 510

BROTHERS—*continued.*
succession of illegitimate —— to legitimate, 364
whether illegitimate and legitimate half —— form a united family, *ib.*
partition between ——, 741—747
may demand partition at any time, 611
take equal shares on partition, 345, 710, 742
and divide debts equally, 344, 718
elder —— takes management with consent of others, 272*w*, 568
younger —— not to precede the elder in marriage, 820*b*
elder —— enjoyed a superior position in ancient times, 270*m*
ancient authority of —— in disposing of sisters, 269
a —— may interdict dealings with heritage by another to the prejudice of his right, 279*f*
initiatory and marriage expenses of unmarried —— a charge on joint estate, 714*a*, 742, 746
brother's share is liable for sister's marriage if her share is insufficient, 714*a*
elder —— takes right side of house by custom, 748
western ——, *ib.*
brother's power to mortgage joint property, 746
widow of the last deceased —— takes the property, 328
See ADOPTION V. 949, 954, 955, 956; VII., 1046, 1050; NEPHEW; PRIMOGENITURE; RENUNCIATION

BROTHER-IN-LAW,
succeeds to a widow, 492
is preferred to the widow's brother, 494

BROTHER'S DAUGHTERS,
are bandhus, 465
to be married at the expense of the family estate, 747
succession of ——, 465
take equally, 431
preferred to brother's daughter's son, 465
postponed to first cousin once removed, *ib.*

BROTHER'S DAUGHTER'S GRANDSON, *ib.*

BROTHER'S DAUGHTER'S SON,
excluded and admitted in Bengal, *ib.*

BROTHER'S GRANDSON,
preferred to daughter's grandson, 449

BROTHER'S SON,
can be adopted, 924
succession of ——, 104
sons succeed *per capita*, 431
succeeds to an interest vested in his father before his death, 101
excluded by brothers, *ib.*

BROTHER'S SON—*continued.*
sons (unseparated) exclude widow, 431*t*
of the whole and half blood, 427, 431
(half) succession of, 104
See ADOPTION IV., 908, 913, 914, 921
Nephew

BROTHER'S WIFE, 395

BURDEN OF PROOF :—
acquisition since partition to be proved by party asserting it, 636
after partition —— lies on party questioning it, to show that particular parts of the property were not included, 649*b*
separate acquisition to be proved by party asserting it, 669
sons, seeking cancellation of sale by father, to prove that the charge was one they were not answerable for 686
incumbrancers to show good reasons for holding son's property liable to pay off father's debts, 687
incumbrancer to scrutinize a transaction by widow, 93, 94*d*
gross inequality of partition by father between sons to be proved by party asserting it, 737
of indivision on plaintiff when he has had separate possession of part for 16 years, 642
See ESCHEAT, 129

BURGUNDIAN LAW,
compared with Hindu law, 82*w*

BURUDA. See under CASTE, 378

CACHARIS. See TRIBES, 270

CANON LAW,
compared with Hindu law, 235*h*

CAPTURE IN MARRIAGE, 269*i*
once common, 797*n*
still observed in form by some tribes, 269, 400
of the bridegroom amongst the Garoos, 274*f*

CARMINA,
metrical form of early laws, 49*b*

CASTE.
its influence on the descent of property, 61
was thought of much more than chastity in early times, 399, 798*r*
except Brahmanas, all placed on the same ceremonial level, 1002*x*
expression of will of ——, 520, 561
law of —— subordinated to general Hindu law, 84
decisions subject to the King's courts, 560*c*

CASTE—*continued.*
questions excluded from the cognizance of civil courts, 560*c*
incidentally cognizable, 561
temple, 520
expulsion from —— extinguished share in property by disabling for religious rites, 551, 552, 553, 689*z*
but was not a ground for retraction, 552, 553
exclusion from —— a bar to adoption, 848
loss of —— is now not a disqualification warranting the adoption of a substitute? 816
does not affect inheritance, 403, 541*y*, 610
comparison of Roman laws as to heretics, 541*y*
non-forfeiture of rights by loss of ——, 553
exclusion from —— not a cause of forfeiture in Khandesh, 1033*b*
two degrees of loss of —— recognized by the Viramitrodaya, 56*c*
restoration to —— by means of penance, 56*c*, 553

CASTES AND CLASSES, 613, 614
Agarvali, 355
Bants (Canara), 272*w*
Berada, 405
Bhanga Sali, 406
Bharthi, 530
Bhata, 375*w*
Bhavin, 494*v*
Buruda, 378
Chambhar or Chambar, 738
Charana, 375
Chetti, 945
Dorik, 553
Durgee Meerasee Soorti, 401*o*
Gavali, 385
Giri, 530
Goojar Talabda, 249*p*
Gosavi, 518, 513
Gujar, 447
Gurava, 410*t*
Jains, 152, 533, 812*h*, 826q, 932*k*
See ADOPTION III., 849, 850; IV., 924
Jangams (Lingayat priests), 532
Jati, 533
Jogtin, 494
Kanoji, 331
Kanphatta—Gosavi, 528
Khalpa Khumbatta, 241*p*, 249*p*
Khatri, 546*r*, 1065
Kolambi, 375*x*
Koli, 356
Koombhars, 241*p*, 249
Kunabi, 339, 342, 393, 404, 471, 483, 531, 767

CASTES AND CLASSES—*continued.*
Lingayat, 342, 394, 477, 954, 1003
Lohar Sootar, 249*p*
Lohar Surati, *ib.*
Machee Gudrya, 241*p*
Mahar, 339, 353, 416
Mali, 361, 493
(Moghrelia), 516*a*
Malri, 535
Manabhau, 535, 536
Maratha, 460, 493
Marwadi, 359, 428, 434
Mochi, 249*p*
Murali, 416, 471, 489, 494*v*
Naigama, 519
Nanakshahi, 535
Paradesi Sutar, 249*p*, 360*p*, 427, 508, 550, 738
Parit, 422
Pashandas, 519
Prabhu or Parbhu, 488, 850*l*, 918*b*
Puri, 530
Rajput, 366, 430
Ramavat, 539
Rangari, 342
Salvees, 689*y*
Sikh, 1003
Simpi (Tailor), 583, 1003
Sonar, 473
Sonis, 689*y*
Sravak, 534
Sutar, 249*p*
Tapodhana, 410
Taulkiya Audichya, *ib.*
Vaghree, 241*p*
Vairagi, 537, 538, 539, 552
Vandi, 375
Vani, 389, 476, 490
Yati, 56, 133, 533, 534
Yogi, 728
See Adoption, *passim*; Tribes
Custom, 516*ss*

CASTE CONNEXION. See Adoption III., 848, 849, 854

CASTE PROPERTY,
jurisdiction declined in suits relating to —— ? 559*b*

CAUSE OF ACTION,
usually exhausted by a suit, 585*h*
but not so in particular cases, *ib.*
comparison of the English, Hindu, and Roman law, *ib.*

CELTIC LAW,
compared with Hindu law, 77

CEREMONIAL. See ADOPTION V., 949
gift, *ib.*

CEREMONIAL SERVICES,
son owes —— to his father, mother, and step-mother, 946

CEREMONIES,
questions on ——, 13
essential. See ADOPTION VI., 958, 959
no particular —— essential to complete adoption, 825
no initiatory —— for Sudras except marriage, 942, 963
vicarious celebration in the case of Sudras and women, 824
joint performance of —— implies union of interests, 775z
separate performance of —— not conclusive of partition, 637, 638
a stranger not to perform religious ——, 185
See ADOPTION, passim.
Sacra

CHALUKYA DYNASTY, 17, 18

CHAMBHAR OR CHAMBAR CASTE, 738

CHANCE. See GAINS, 666

CHARANA
(juggler), 375

CHARANAS
(the schools), 30, 31, 48
the origin of intellectual life, 30

CHARGE ON LAND,
sense of, 706, 707

CHARGE,
on inheritance, 155ss
enumeration of ——s, 684, 685
created by decree and attachment of undivided share, 588, 652—653
a joint trade loan is a —— on joint family property, 324
for payment of debts of the deceased owner, 155
non-liability of property in hands of *bonâ fide* purchaser, 73
promises made by the father, 161
debts by father, contracted not for immoral or illegal purposes are —— though not incurred for benefit of family, 72, 73, 162, 164, 167, 661, 685, 719, 729, 740
so are father's directions as to charities, 686g
husband's just debts are ——, 299

CHARGE—*continued.*
separate debts of deceased coparcener are not charges on undivided property, 72, 718, 720
maintenance of those entitled thereto ranks as ——, 685
as *ex. gr.* the maintenance of a widow, 163
and —— concubine and her children, 164
marriage expenses of unmarried brothers and sisters are ——, 713, 742, 746
what ——s may be on the manager's share, 699t
incurred by the manager when binding, 687
enforcible against holder of part of the property, 721

CHARITABLE USES
purposes beneficial to the public, 198
enumerated, 204*l*
moulded to modern needs, 204*l*, 224*k*
superstitious —— not disallowed, 211*f*

CHARITY-IES,
common —— enumerated, 203
cy près doctrine admitted by Hindu Law, 224
dying directions as to —— must be fulfilled, 686*g*
See ALIENATION; DHARMA; ENDOWMENT; GIFT; WILL, 221

CHASTITY
less regarded than caste in early times, 401, 798*r*

CHATTEL See SON, 833, 951

CHELA,
purchase of —— recognized in some cases, 525
not regarded as adoption, *ib.*
must be nominated by his guru and confirmed by mahants, 520, 522
bound to maintain his guru in distress, 723*g*
chela's succession to guru, 520
succession of a —— among Sravaks, 522
chelas joint succession of two, *ib.*
See DISCIPLE

CHIEFSHIP,
succession to ——. See PRINCIPALITY; RAJ.

CHINA. See ADOPTION, 92, 810*q*

CHINESE LAWS AND CUSTOMS
compared with Hindu, 262*w*

CHIRDE RIGHTS. See ALLOWANCES, 425

CHRISTIANS,
native, not free to adhere to Hindu law since the passing of Indian Succession Act, 4

CHUDA
ceremony to be performed in adoptive father's family, 939
See ADOPTION IV. 957

CHUDAKARANA,
tonsure, 936*ss*
See ADOPTION, 941; CHUDA

CHUNDAVAND, 399
See PATNIBHAG

CIVIL DEATH
of a person results from his entering religious order, 56
from a woman's being expelled from caste by *Ghatasphota*, *ib.*
but since Act XXI. of 1850, by loss of caste a person does not lose his civil rights, 610

CLOTHES IN USE
to be kept by those having use of them, 717, 756
when indivisible, and when not, 670, 673
how divided, 717

COCHIN. See POLYANDRY, 272

COGNATES. See BANDHUS; BHINNAGOTRA-SAPINDAS; ADOPTION, IV., 945

COLLATERALS
in partition take *per stirpes*, 710
subject to allowance for prior partial partition, *ib.*
See ADOPTION, III. 888; BANDHUS

COLLATERAL SUCCESSION. See SUCCESSION

COLLUSION BY CO-SHARER. See FRAUD, 570*s*

CO-MEMBERSHIP OF COMMUNITY.
gives right to inherit, 56

COMMENSALITY,
cesser of —— is evidence of partition, 637, 751
in case of —— property presumed to be joint until contrary shown, 663

COMMENTATORS,
Hindu, 16*p*
use other Smritis to supplement the one commented, 49

COMMENTARIES,
Sanskrit, 18

COMMON PROPERTY
Classified, 654

COMMON STOCK. See PROPERTY

COMPENSATION
for land withdrawn from general partition, 711
in case of partition of interests, without one *in specie*, 710
when one divided coparcener loses his share through the wrong of another, 788

COMMUNITY,
change of —— frees from the operation of the customary law of inheritance, 3
community's right of ownership still asserted, 174*e*

COMPOUND
is divisible under ordinary circumstances, 757

CONCEALMENT. See REPARTITION

CONCUBINAGE
allowed amongst Gosavis by custom, 518
in low castes not disgraceful, 401

CONCUBINE
regarded as a dasi or slave, 81, 365
pat-wife having first husband alive is a ——, 392
remarried widow was regarded as a —— before Act XV. of 1856, 391
keeping a low-caste —— entails penance only, 401
can take bequests, 359
entitled to maintenance, 76, 164, 193, 366, [illegible] 546, 556, 654*w*
investment may be made for her maintenance, 392
must be provided with maintenance before she is deprived of property in her possession, 691
of the late owner entitled to maintenance from heir, 393
See SARANJAM
sons of a —— are regarded as brothers of the whole blood *inter se*, 78, 364
See ILLEGITIMATE SON
daughter of a —— entitled to a provision, 164

CONDITIONS
in some cases not allowed, 187*b*
running with land, 189
cannot be annexed to status of son or to marriage, 187*b*, 959
subsequent void if repugnant, 187
in cases of adoption, 1018
See GIFT, 186, 187, 416; GRANT, 188; ADOPTION, VI., VII.

CONFIRMATION
of adoption by the soverign deemed important, 902*b*

CONSANGUINITY
the foundation of the right of succession, 59, 143, 689
duty of sacrifice annexed to ——, 689*y*
See ADOPTION, IV. 923

CONSENT. See ASSENT; ADOPTION IV. 945; V. 948, 951, 952, VI. 990; VII. 1061; VIII. 1075, 1076

CONSTITUTUM POSSESSORIUM, 214*v*

CONSTRUCTION OF GRANTS, 377, 435
See INTERPRETATION

CONSTRUCTION OF LAWS. See INTERPRETATION

CONTINGENCY. See GIFT, 212; CONDITION

CONTINGENT REMAINDER. See REMAINDER

CONTRACT
Hindu law superseded by Statute, 7
between Hindus and other classes, 6
law of defendant applicable to ——s, *ib.*
contracts of the father pass to the heir, 75
of betrothal not to be specifically enforced, 964
for gain by giving in adoption illegal, 961

CONVERSION,
effect of—on capacity to give in adoption, 842
—on status, 4, 5, 153

COOKING,
separate —— evidence of partition, 775

CO-OWNERSHIP, 189

COPARCENER,
who are ——s, 70 71
who are not ——s, 435
males only can be ——s, 605
coparcener's possession is primâ facie possession of all ——s, 589*e*
coparcenership continues though some members separate, 617
difference between joint tenant and ——, 562*h*
purchaser of undivided share becomes tenant in common with other ——s, 566
Powers of Coparceners, 567
in case of urgent need may dispose of joint property, 588, 747

COPARCENER—*continued.*
may dispose of undivided share for value but not by way of gift or devise, 565, 587. 616
consent of all ——s requisite to any gift (Panjab), 747*l*
See ALIENATION; REPRESENTATION
in Bengal incapable of dealing with his share, 581
may redeem from mortgage and claim contribution, 720
separated ——s must contribute in case of share taken to satisfy a common liability, 760
not entitled to redeem his share alone, 720
undivided ——s may take separate interests, 192
and though divided may take jointly, *ib.*
a —— cannot by giving costly ornaments to his wife deprive the others of their share in his acquisitions, 205, 280
may resign his share for a trifle, 611, 752, 762
cannot be compelled to assent to an adoption by a widow, 783, 796, 814
not generally entitled to an account from another ——, 700*c*
no ownership of any definite share is predicable of a particular —— while united, 635
notice of enhancement of rent by some ——s held sufficient in Bengal, 567*d*
comparison of English Law, *ib.*
adult —— bound by the transactions of manager when he takes the benefit, 575, 576
a —— cannot singly oust a family tenant or enhance rent, 567
in Bombay a person holding with the assent of one —— regarded as if put in possession by him, 567*d*
some ——s only not allowed to take advantage of a condition of re-entry, *ib.*
Partition between Coparceners, 741—754
each ——'s whole property supposed to belong to common stock, 653
a —— may demand partition at any time, 617
coparcener's prior engagement *inter se* bind in partition, 761, 762
coparceners in existence only entitled to a share on partition, 722
a —— is not liable at partition to make up what he has expended in excess of his own share, 700
except in cases of dishonest waste, 760
a —— takes on partition what he has expended in excess of his own share of debts, 345
absence of some ——s does not bar partition, 626, 742
after-born ——s share only their father's share, 722
fraud does not disqualify a —— from receiving a share at partition, 629, 630, 760
but the fraudulent —— may be made to restore property sought to be withheld, 629, 630, 700, 703, 760
purchaser of undivided share has to work out his right by partition, 566
Succession to Coparceners, 61, 70, 131, 323—337
a —— dying without issue his share goes to his undivided ——s, 329
Suits by and against Coparceners
all ——s must join as plaintiffs in a suit on a joint claim, 573

COPARCENER—*continued.*
except when one sues in a representative capacity, *ib.*
a —— cannot alone sue to set aside a charge created by another, 568
some only allowed to eject an intruder contrary to wish of another, 567*d*
a —— cannot recover his fractional share in joint property from stranger, 567, 568
a —— is liable after partition for shares of debts, 720
coparceners are not generally entitled to account from manager for transactions prior to demand, 760
payment to one of several ——s frees the tenant
coparceners not answerable for separate debts, 588
unless incurred for family necessity, *ib.*
Suits by and against Coparcener
coparceners who have colluded with a tenant to defraud a co-sharer may be sued by him in common with the tenant, 570
creditor of one —— may attach undivided property, 652
See MORTGAGE, 747

COPARCENER REUNITED, 56, 58, 60, 129, 327
coparceners —— of equal degree share equally, 131
succession to ——, 130, 131
See FAMILY, JOINT; INTERDICTION, 652*w*

COSHARER. See COPARCENER
Property, 1089

COURT OF WARDS. See ADOPTION III, 853

COURTYARD,
division of a —— refused, 832

COURTS, HINDU, 233

COURTESANS,
ornaments of —— exempted from seizure, 798*r*
ranked as members of a business association, *ib.*
See ADOPTION III., 907

COUSIN
used in a general sense for collateral, 452
united —— inherits in preference to the widow, 334
first ——, 126
See ADOPTION IV., 913, 922
second —— excludes a third, 447
of five removes inherits, 412
distant —— if united preferred to widow and daughter-in-law, 553
husband's —— excludes husband's sister's son, 496, 497
separated first —— postponed to united half-brother, 334
though separated is preferred to illegitimate son, 444
(= nephew) —————————— sister-in-law, 452

COUSIN—*continued.*
maternal aunt's son postponed to samanodaka, 456
succeeding to a female (Sudra), 511
female ——. See ADOPTION IV., 921
first ——'s son an heir, 460*n*
See ADOPTION IV. 915

COUSIN'S DAUGHTER'S SON. See ADOPTION IV., 918

COUSIN'S SON
prefered to sister's son, 332
See BROTHER'S GRANDSON

COUSIN'S WIDOW, 454
her succession, 454, 455
See STRIDHANA

COUSIN'S WIFE. See WIDOW OF COUSIN

COVERTURE. See HUSBAND; WIFE; FEMALES; STRIDHANA; ADOPTION V., 949

CO-WIDOW. See ADOPTION VII.; SUCCESSION, 1040, 141, 893

CO-WIFE,
son of —— as heir, 489. See ADOPTION III.

CREDITOR,
when bound to inquiry, 94*d*, 165, 168, 687
when a minor's interests are touched —— must prove good faith, 687
of the father must establish his claim, 595*d*, 1089
a joint —— cannot sue alone, but can give an effectual discharge, 570*s*
of an undivided coparcener may enforce partition, 582, 615, 652, 686, 720
creditor's assent should be obtained by parcener on partition to secure himself against further claims, 719
in partition enforced by —— share of wife must be provided for, 693
creditor's fraudulent transactions may be rescinded by a coparcener, 688
See ADOPTION VIII. 1081; DEBT; MINOR; PARTITION

CUSTOM; CUSTOMARY LAW,
Its Origin, 559
regarded as based on lost Smritis, 517
the basis of Hindu Law*, 1
duty of conquerors to maintain ——, 2
to be upheld by the king, 519
cannot be made by one family, 682
but upheld when found, *ib.*

---

* On the recognition of custom as a source of law by the Hindu authorities, *see* R. S. V. N. Mandlik's Vyav. Mayukha, Introd. p. xliv. ss.

CUSTOM, CUSTOMARY LAW—*continued.*
raj regranted after 20 years governed by former law of succession, 153
when an estate is by family —— impartible the ordinary law is so far only superseded, *ib.*
family —— excluding partition, 675, 683z
pronounced a question of fact*
In case of Sacred property
governs succession to temple emoluments, &c., 151, 178
See BELOW
Effect of —— its relation to the general law. See above, 85, 150
has the force of law, 785, 786, 788f
may preserve or alter the law of the family, 516, 517
as a means of interpretation, 516
controls the received construction of texts, 197d, 787
replaces the Veda, when the precept of the latter is not decisive, 786, 787
construction of documents showing family ——, 682r
governs marriage relations, 84, 151m
and the parties, ceremonies, &c., in adoption, 927, 939, 945, 994
governs devolution of sacred property, 199
mode of proof, 218
of a matha or religious community governs succession to its property, 517, 519
if not injurious, 519
governs the relations within a sect or class, 519, 535, 559
of the particular institution makes its law in absence of evidence of the nature of the foundation, 526
of succession to gurus, 533
regulating property in offerings, 389
gives to widows a power of disposal over husband's property subject or not to conditions, 714b
makes son liable for family debts, 729
See ELDERSHIP
family —— determines succession to principalities, 677—679
may exclude females, 151
Contests as to ——
proof of ——, 4, 787, 788
Court to take notice of general ——, 788
divergence of —— from the ordinary law to be proved, 151
unless already recognized, *ib.*
difficulty of this. See ADOPTION, 918e
refused recognition. See ADOPTION, 918
the action of the Courts tends to extinguish special usages, 829b
See ADOPTION, 994, 1017, 1056, 1065; ASCETICS; JAINS; KHOJAS; SRADDHA; USAGE, 825.

DADU, 537

---

* *Burjore Bhavani Pershad* v. *Musst Bhagana*, L. R. 11 I. A. 7. The family custom was of a patnibhag, of exclusion of daughters, and of limitation of a widow's adoption to sons of near sapindas of the husband.

DAIVA MARRIAGE, 481, 484, 486

DAMAGES. See COMPENSATION, 761

DAMDUPAT,
Rule of —— when applicable, 718*v*
not abrogated by Act XXVIII. of 1855, *ib.*
to whom applicable, *ib.*
See INTEREST

DAMSEL. See MAIDEN, 470

DANA. See GIFT

DANCER. See ADOPTION VI., 1009

DANCING WOMEN,
association of —— not foreign to Hindu system, 798*r*
adoption by —— ——, 960
See COURTESANS, 798*r*; ADOPTION II., 834*k*; III., 907, 945

DAIVA. See MARRIAGE, 481, 484, 486

DAS. See ADOPTION II., 825, 836
Marriage, 81

DASI, 364, 483
connexion with —— innocent according to Narada, 798*r*
See CONCUBINE

DASI-PUTRA. See ILLEGITIMATE SON

DASNAMAH
elects a successor, 722

DATTA HOMA. See ADOPTION, 835; VI. 957, 958, 994, 995, 827

DATTAKA SON. See ADOPTED SON
alone now recognized as substitute for a son, 806
See ADOPTION IV.; V. 948

DATTAKA CHANDRIKA,
an authority on Western India, 9, 23
its weight as authority, 13
See ADOPTION, 953

DATTAKA KAUSTUBHA. See ADOPTION V., 952
and separate List of Hindu Authorities

DATTAKA MIMAMSA,
an authority on Western India, 9, 23
its weight as authority, 13
See ADOPTION IV., 947, 949, 950
and separate List of Hindu Authorities

DATTRIMA,
meaning of, 853

DAUGHTER,
Her Status
her position generally inferior to widow's according to Privy Council, 97
contra in Bombay, 97, 98
position of —— in undivided family is the same as that of sister, 333
by marriage passes into husband's family, 120
hence does not share father's exclusion from caste, 121
not named as representative of collateral line by Vyav. Mayukha, 441
Her Relation to Father and his Estate
inherits from her father, 96, 261
daughter's claim to inherit inferior to adopted son's, 942
succession to her separated father's property, 82, 96, 406*ss*, 428, 432, 437, 438, 470, 497, 554
origin of the right of succession of ——, 97, 397
it is still postponed to that of male collaterals in some castes, 684*d*
gradual recognition of —— as heir, 803
daughter's portion, 691*i*
daughters of the same condition inherit equally, 97, 417
cannot inherit in an undivided family, 332, 333, 335, 413
inherits in a divided family, 96, 406
excluded in some Narvadari villages, 406
succeeds on failure of widow, 260
preferred as heir to a daughter-in-law, 119*g*, 409, 411
to step-mother, 409
to separated brother, 411
brothers exclude foster ——s, 427
excluded by brethren in some castes, 684*d*, 722*a*
is excluded by brother and nephew of deceased in undivided family, 470*g*
daughters married preferred according to their indigence, 134, 417
daughters unmarried preferred to marired, 96, 97, 134, 308, 309, 417, 476
reason of this, 97
daughters unendowed preferred to endowed, 134, 308, 417, 418, 476
unmarried in undivided family takes a quarter share, 333
daughters excluded at first as unmarried succeed in preference to their sister's heirs (Bengal and Madras), 319*a*
in Bengal a married —— having or likely to have a son succeeds, 474
childless widow excluded in Bengal, 417
her right not extinguished by her becoming such, *ib.*
Bengal law compared with that of Bombay, *ib.*
barrenness of a —— not a cause of exclusion, 99
and illegitimate son of a Sudra take equally, 97, 472

DAUGHTER—*continued.*
unchaste —— does not succeed to her parents according to Macnaghten, 149*z*
step —— inherits, 502
Estate taken by Daughter
in the Panjab generally transmits no right, 406
in the Panjab usually excluded, 407
lands not given to ——s by the Rajputs beyond a life-interest, 301*e*
growth of father's power to provide for —— out of tribal lands and to take her husabnd into the family, 407
takes limited interest in property inherited from father in Bengal, 407
in Madras and Bengal her estate assimilated to that of widow, 139, 407
Maithila law, 316
but in Bombay a —— takes it as Stridhana, 407, 408
daughters take separately, excluding survivorship, 98
two or more ——s divide, 417
this view is held by Vyav. Mayukha, 101
in Madras ——s take as a class with survivorship, 100
takes in Bombay an absolute estate transmissible to her own heirs, 98, 100, 294, 311, 407
not a mere life-tenancy, 91
different view of the Privy Council, 408
daughters are entitled to shares in a partition according to the Viramitrodaya, 288
daughter's share being one-fourth of a son's, 629
takes property on partition as Stridhana, 216, 284
enitled to maintenance and residence, 64
and marriage expenses, 413, 470*q*, 691, 748
of a deceased coparcener must be maintained, 227, 241, 691*e*
of a reunited coparcener must be provided for, 133, 413
of a predeceased son entitled to maintenance, 690
and a marriage portion, *ib.*
of a concubine entitled to a provision, 164
reasonable provision for —— must be made good by son, 205, 333
Relation to Mother and her Estate
daughter's succession to her mother, 134, 139, 258, 295, 310, 311, 471, 478
preferred to son in succession to mother, 514
daughter's son, 473
daughter-in-law, 451
takes mother's property after payment of her debts, 438, 472
unmarried ——s share equally with sons Anvadheya and Pritidatta Stridhana, 135, 259, 486*k*
unmarried ——s alone succeed to Yautaka Stridhana, 309, 311, 486*k*
has full power over Stridhana devolved from her mother, 288
Succession to her
in Bengal on the death of —— property goes to her father's heirs, 407
she cannot alienate it to their detriment, *ib.*
devolution of property taken by ——s, 316, 319, 418, 419
As to Adoption
not to be adopted, 790, 833, 834

DAUGHTER—*continued.*
existence of —— no bar to adoption, 778, 1050
See ADOPTION, 842, 867, 978, 985; SISTER'S DAUGHTER; SISTER; BROTHER

DAUGHTER, ILLEGITIMATE,
cannot inherit, 408
whether —— —— of a Sudra can inherit is a question, *ib.*
is entitled to maintenance and marriage expenses, 408

DAUGHTER'S DAUGHTER,
daughters receive a trifle when there are daughters, 139
daughters receive a trifle in Anvadheya and Pritidatta Stridhana at division, 135
not an heir to a male, 447
her right admitted to Balambhatta, 121*n*
succession of —— —— to Stridhana, 139
next to daughter in succession to grandmother, 478

DAUGHTER'S GRANDSON
inherits to a woman, 503
postponed to brother's grandson, 450

DAUGHTER'S HUSBAND. See ADOPTION IV., 922

DAUGHTER'S SON
of an ascendant an heir in Bengal, 462
daughter's sons take *per capita*, 101, 419
precedes grandson's widow, 419
excluded by a great-grandson in the male line, 371
and illegitimate son of a Sudra take equally, 99
inherits separate property of a united coparcener, 99
inherits to a separate grihastha, 99, 141, 409
takes as full owner, 419
inherits to a married female, 140
daughter's sons preferred to son's sons, 479
excluded by a daughter, 140, 409, 419
when —— —— shares the inheritance with his aunt, 409
step —— —— inherits, 502
Sudras may adopt —— ——, 924
Lingayats may adopt —— ——, *ib.*
See ADOPTION, 800, 801, 841, 918, 919, 944, 945, 1031, 1051

DAUGHTER-IN-LAW
may take gift or legacy from her father-in-law if not prejudicial to others' rights, 281
succession of ——, 451, 452, 495
Balambhatta and the Viramitrodaya on ——'s right to inherit, 496
preferred to mother-in-law as heir to her deceased husband, 387
to son's daughter, 495

DAUGHTER-IN-LAW—*continued.*
to first cousin's widow, 452
excludes distant cousins, *ib.*
is excluded by brother, 408, 427, 452
brother's son, 431, 452
daughter, 409, 452
daughter's son, 419
entitled to maintenance, 239, 240, 244, 692, 696*d*, 697
daughter-in-law's claim on father-in-law as such denied, 694*z*
does —— forfeit her right to maintenance by residing with her father? 694
has a better claim than her father-in-law to adopt to her husband, 352
See ADOPTION III.
has a better claim than her mother-in-law, 384
See ADOPTION III.; VII., 1031, 1038, 1041; WIDOW

DAUHITRA, 81, 121*n*

DAYA
compared with inheritance, 55, 63, 232, 561, 629, 656
participation by birth is the typical form of ——, 321
widow has independent power over ——, 288

DAYA APRATIBANDHA. See APRATIBANDHA DAYA

DAYABHAGA,
succession under the, 142—148

DAYADA, 125

DAYAVIBHAGA
defined, 55
includes rules for the division of an estate, 55
of Jumuta Vahana, see separate List of Hindu Authorities

DEAF; DEAFNESS
disqualifies for inheritance, 141, 541
See ADOPTION III., 848; DISQUALIFICATION, 541

DEATH. See CIVIL DEATH; PRESUMPTION

DEBT,
Joint Family's
contracted by the manager *bonâ fide* presumed to be for the common benefit, 687
and binding on other members, 688
a first charge on joint estate, 689
incurred by a member under pressure of distress is binding on all, 588, 688
family ——s to be discharged (but this not indispensable) before partition), 718

DEBT—*continued.*
debts of a joint business must be paid before profits are distributed, *ib.*
debts how distributed on partition, 717*ss*
when ——s are distributed creditors' assent should be obtained, 719
Separate—
personal —— of a deceased member not a charge on the joint estate, unless his interest was attached or vested in official assignee before his death, 161
not even for family, if no necessity, *ib.*
Father's and Grandfather's
son bound to pay father's and grand-father's ——s, 75, 161, 164, 165, 551, 567*d*, 568, 596, 685*f*, 686
not during their life, 597*ss*, 728
the Hindu Law insists strongly on payment of father's ——s, 572
son's liability according to Yajnavalkya and the Mitakshara, 1087*ss*
obligation to pay father's ——s a part of the inheritance, 163, 166, 168
estate taken by son is assets for paying father's ——s, 566*y*
obligation to pay father's ——s depends on their nature, 73, 164, 192
son liable to pay independently of assets? 1041
liability to pay father's ——s limited to those incurred for the family? 685, 686
impartible estate liable to pay father's ——s, 163*y*
ancestral estate in the hands of a son liable for father's ——s, 76, 166, 192, 597
translation of this into power of the father to encumber in his life, 572
a son must pay father's ——s even in his life? 572, 581, 582
hence a sale of family property to pay these binds son, 579
liability to pay father's ——s after his death and in his life distinct, 685*f*
son's liability to pay father's ——s incurred before partition, 720*g*
son liable by custom for all ——s properly incurred for family, 729
father's ——s not prodigally contracted may be charged on the inheritance, 165, 168, 192
comparison of English Law, 578*a*
several sons liable according to their shares, 719*e*
separated sons not liable for father's ——s, 165, 720
property not hypothecated to pay father's ——s, 73, 161, 193, 685*f*
community of obligation amongst successors not recognized by Hindu Law except in joint family, 570
unsecured ——s not a charge on the estate, 192, 193, 685
son not directly responsible for unsecured ——s except after father's death, 164, 582
securities created by father unless profligate bind sons, 73, 164, 572
responsibility of son according to Hindu Law arises only at his majority, 164, 578, 582, 1088
minor bound to discharge on attaining majority, 164, 1089
decree-holder for father's ——s preferred to one for owner's ——s, 688*s*
Son's—
father not to pay son's ——s, 550
must pay ——s necessarily incurred by sons living with him, 729
Husband's—

DEBT—*continued.*
widow bound to discharge husband's ——s, 94
not if barred by limitation, *ib.*
Coparcener's—
undivided property not answerable for separate ——'s ——, 72, 164, 718, 720
of a member to the common estate set off though barred by limitation, 689
apportionment of ——s amongst sons and successors, 570, 703
Annexed to Estate taken
obligation to pay ——s dependent on taking property, 76*i*, 160
is limited by Bombay Act VII. of 1866, 76*i*, 165, 686, 718
income liable to pay ——s if property descends as hereditary, 161, 166
brother answerable for brother's ——s only to extent of assets, 667*o*
See ADOPTION VII., 1024, 1036, 1041, 1042; CHARGE; COPARCENER; DECREE 585; DAYA; FAMILY PARTITION 703; OBLIGATION

DEBTOR
one of several joint ——s may represent all in paying, but not in resisting payment, 570*s*
agriculturist under Native Governments, 717

DECISIONS OF COURTS.
weight to be given to, 789

DECREE
may award arrears and future payments, 253, 693*r*
awarding separate interests destroys joint estate, 633, 634, 765
comparison of English Law, 634*d*
right to partition under —— lost by non-execution, 615*e*
effect suspended by appeal, 566*b*, 615, 642
for partition of land paying revenue to be executed by the Collector, 723
for maintenance a charge on estate, 693*r*
against a member of joint family as affecting other members, 577*ss*, 583*r*
against representative member on a joint debt may be executed against the family property, 574
law as laid down in N. W. Provinces, 575
in Madras, 585
against manager only, binds the whole estate, 591
against a father a charge on property, 686
not to be satisfied out of his share at his death? 585
Judicial Comimttee's decision *contra*, 168, 585
effect of the execution of a —— for father's debts against ancestral property, 166
against a widow for arrears as a charge; only her estate passes, 592*d*
against the widow; when it binds the reversioner, 89*v*
See ADOPTION VIII., 1082

DEDICATION
understood in grants to Brahmanas, 128*f*
to religious uses, 156, 160

DEDICATION—*continued.*
to religion inalienable under most systems of law, 156, 185o, 523
the first exception to inalienability of patrimony, 191n, 195
connected with the growth of individual ownership over wastes, 195s
to an idol creates a trust, 156
See ENDOWMENT, 155, 522

DEDUCTION
in partition in favour of eldest son, 733, 735
disallowed, 734
See PARTITION; DISTRIBUTION

DEED
of partition not essential to partition, 631s, 771
constitutes separation, 765
required by some castes, 631s
held inoperative as not acted on (Madras), *ib.*
See REGISTRATION
of adoption not necessary. See ADOPTION VI., 961, 989, 991

DEFECT
of son warranting adoption. See ADOPTION III., 817
of organ. See DISQUALIFICATION, 541

DEFENDANT,
law of —— when it prevails, 5, 6, 7

DEGREES
of affinity obstructing marriage, 837, 916
prohibited extend to great-grandson of one given in adoption, 838s
under the Canon Law, 236
See ADOPTION II., 837, 838; IV., 912, 916; VII., 1017, 1018; VIII.

DELEGATION
by husband. See ADOPTION III., 855, 856, 946, 947; VI., 889

DEMANDANT,
partition confined to the ——, 617

DERANGEMENT
presumed from prodigal alienations, 204
See LUNATIC; ADOPTION III.

DESAI, DESAIGIRI. See VATAN; ALLOWANCES, 425

DESCENDANT
what ——s form a united family, 603
which ——s take the inheritance by representation, 61, 62
such ——s extend to third generation, 604

DESCENDANT—*continued.*
rights on partition between the ancestor and his first three ——s, 704, 705
first three ——s of a separated person take *per stirpes*, 74
descendants of an absentee may claim down to the seventh degree, 627

DESCENT,
law of —— is not regarded as inherent in land, 683z
law of —— is determined by personal status, 4, 683z
or by family custom, 4, 151, 675
Zamindari or Vatan aliened or divided is freed from special rule of ——, 683z
comparison of English Law, *ib.*
See DEVOLUTION; VATAN

DESGAT VATAN. See VATAN

DEVASTHAN
does not revert, 681*f*
See DEDICATION 176*o*; GRANT; ENDOWMENT, RELIGIOUS

DEVISE
is on the same footing as a gift *inter vivos*, 280
merely for "Dharma" ineffectual, 224
executory —— (remote) not recognized by Hindu Law, 90, 180, 184
not to be regulated by English Law, 90*f*
to several sons with cross remainders is good under Hindu Law, *ib.*
of inam village to widows against son, 734
alienating ancestral property void against a son unseparated, 740*h*
to a *persona designata* as adopted son effectuated, 1077
of land once inoperative in England without assent of heir, 214*w*
See ADOPTION VI. 979; VIII. 1077, 1078; BEQUEST; WILL 734, 740

DEVOLUTION,
course of —— cannot be altered by private agreeemnt, 4, 151*m*, 178, 549
prescribed by law, 179, 184*f*, 549
of jagirs and other public grants governed by the intent of sovereign, 180
See VATAN

DHARMA,
the rule of law, 233
what it comprises, 30
a devise merely to —— ineffectual, 224
engagements against ruler's —— do not give a right to enforcement, 188
See DEVISE

DHARMA-PATNI,
alone inherits, 82
who is a ——, *ib.*

DHARMA-PUTRA, 804*c*, 1022, 1065

DHARMASASTRAS, 30
their divisions, 31
of Usanas, 34
of Sankha, 37
of Manu and Yajnavalkya, 40, 41
Asvalayana, 46

DHARMASINDHU,
an authority in Western India, 12
Dharmasindhu's weight as authority, 13
compiled by Kasinatha, 25

DHARMASUTRA, 31
Gautama, 32
Vasishtha, *ib.*
materials of which ——s are constructed, 34
Dharmasutras existed in the time of Patanjali, 36
four of them composed in the South of India; the fifth probably in the North, 37

DIKPRADARSANA, 100, 257*k*, 607
indication of a principle to be followed, 71

DIKSHA,
meaning of, 532*q*
Jangama, *ib.*
Triordha, 533

DINARA, 44, 45

DINING APART,
a sign of partition, 637
but —— not conclusive of partition, *ib.*

DISCIPLE,
natural son may become, 524
ceremonies at the nomination of ——, 523
succession of —— to Guru, 468, 520
who deserts his Guru forfeits succession, 537
takes equally with a united Gurubhau, 522
succeeds to a Gosavi, 521
disciple's disciple inherits, 527
succession of female —— to a Gosavi, 526
See FELLOW-DISCIPLE, 527

DISEASE, INCURABLE,
sufferers from —— disqualified to inherit, 149

DISINHERITANCE,
by father of son by birth or adoption for adequate reasons, 549
of adopted only as of begotten son, 1016, 1032

DISINHERITANCE—*continued.*
son disinherited may be restored, 549
no —— by will, 549, 984*n*
comparison of Roman and Athenian laws, 549*x*
See ADOPTION III., 844; VII., 1032, 1033

DISOBEDIENCE,
simple —— does not disable the wife from inheriting, 406

DISPOSITION,
power of —— limited by Hindu law, 194, 366
See ADOPTION VI., 978, 984; VII., 1031; FAMILY; FATHER; GIFT; MAINTENANCE

DISQUALIFICATION,
persons disqualified to inherit, 141, 539*ss*
arising from :—
insanity, 141, 541, 545
subsequent insanity no ——, 545
incurable blindness, *ib.*
but only congenital, 150
lameness, 541, 543
leprosy of a virulent type, 149, 526, 544
deafness and dumbness, 141, 544, 545
enmity to father, 547
addiction to vice, 550
adultery and incontinence, 552
by loss of caste cured by penance, 56*c*
loss of caste now no ——, 149*y*, 403, 539, 610, 816
son of disqualified father may take his father's place down to the partition of the inheritance, 549, 817, 149
disqualified father replaced only by begotten son (or Kshetraja), 542
not by one born or adopted after succession or partition, 542, 545, 553, 689, 722, 848
simple disobedience of wife no ——, 406
under the Mitakshara and the Mayukha barrenness in a daughter no ——, 474
to inherit from defect arising after inheritance or partition does not cause forfeiture, 417
as *ex. gr.* in case of lunacy, 545
the rule of exclusion qualified by custom, 150, 689*z*
for inheritance to be scrutinized by Courts, 550
for sharing under customary law, 689*z*
to inherit excludes from a share on partition, 629
and from right to demand partition, *ib.*
but this right to exclude might be waived, 690
disqualified father not entitled to a share on partition, 629, 749
disqualified persons entitled to maintenance, 241, 689*y*
wife of a disqualified person may adopt, 817, 846
by custom, not by the Sastra, 545, 546*o*
See ADOPTION III., 844, 847, 848

DISTRESS,
warrants alienation of common property by coparcener, 588, 728
in —— husband may deal with wife's Stridhana, 86, 264, 283, 294*m*, 303
season of —— justifies gift of a son—see ADOPTION V., 590
See COPARCENER, 746; DEBT, 588, 688

DISTRIBUTION,
capricious or inhumane —— of property not allowed, 205, 206
of property naturally indivisible to be equitable, 673
of property amongst the Jews, 735*q*
unequal —— when valid, 705, 706, 738
subject to control by the Courts, 737
not to be effected by will? 705*s*, 740
allowed by custom, 706*v*
has regard to property as it actually subsists, 698
by division of proceeds, 642
of liabilities, 684, 721
in specie when takes place, 704
is equal on a partition of ancestral property between an ancestor and his descendants to three generations, *ib.*
on a partition between brothers, 710
on a partition between reunited coparceners, 715
on a partition between collaterals —— is *per stirpes*, 710
partial —— on a former occasion how taken into account, 645, 710
of rents and profits is not conclusive of partition, 717
of debts, 717, 718, 719
by marshalling in favour of creditor in possession, 589, 710
See DIVISION; PARTITION

DIVISION,
none between husband and wife, 85, 131
cannot be partial, 613, 646, 717
except by consent, 767
of a religious fund or dedication by turns of office and emoluments, 716*m*
patrimonial lands not divisible according to the Smritis, 672*k*
See PROPERTY, SACRED
may be made of upadhyapana by custom, 716*m*
not completed creates no separate interests, 635
unequal when good, 738, 763
of rents and profits a permissible partition, 641, 717
of income for convenience does not amount to a separation, 641
of the profits of a Vatandari village, 717
agreement to make a —— does not sever interests, 634
will Courts ever refuse to decree a ——? 626
See FAMILY; PARTITION; SEPARATION

DIVISION OF PROCEEDS,
a mode of joint enjoyment, 643
of partition, 641

DIVORCE,
by Ghatasphota, 552
by Soda chiti, 555
at husband's will, 491o, 492
by agreement in some castes, 490
seldom occurs, 492
allowed amongst the lower classes, 490
not in the higher ones, *ib.*
disentitles a woman to maintenance, 556v

DOCUMENTS. See ADOPTION III., 853

DONATIO MORTIS CAUSA,
recognized by Hindu law, 214

DORIK. See under CASTES, 553

DOS LEGITIMA, 303l

DOWER (ENGLISH LAW), 303l, 376
capable of release not of alienation, 287x
See PALLA, 395h

DRAUPADI,
legend of, 270

DRAVIDA COUNTRY. See ADOPTION II., 869, 870

DUHITRA-SUTA, 79

DUMB, DUMBNESS,
congenital —— disqualifies for inheritance, 141, 150
of the son born does not justify adoption, 817
See ADOPTION III., 848; DISQUALIFICATION, 544

DUPLAS. See TRIBES, 275

DUTY,
of a Hindu depends on his personal law, 7
indispensable; discharge of —— a ground for alienation by single coparcener, 688t

DVAITA NIRNAYA,
is a work by Sankara, 21
necessary to explain some parts of the Mayukha, *ib.*

DVYAMUSHYAYANA, 808, 819
of the original type not now recognized, 818
in what sense now recognized, *ib.*
not unusual in the Southern Districts of Bombay, 809

DVYAMUSHYAYANA—*continued.*
status of the son of ——, 810
celebrates the Sraddhas of both fathers, but his son those of the grandfather by adoption only, *ib.*
form in adopting a ——, 1001
Dvyamushyayana's right of inheritance, 1061, 1062
not to be set up in a suit on ordinary adoption, 1072
See ADOPTION IV., 927, 944; V., 953; VII., 1062; VIII., 1072

DWELLING. See HOUSE

EARNINGS,
are at the disposal of the woman according to Jimuta Vahana, 286
of a woman belong to her husband, 279
by prostitution belong to husband, 483
See STRIDHANA

EAST INDIA COMPANY'S
power to legislate, 1

EATING,
separate —— evidence of partition, 774*ss*

ECCENTRICITY,
implying injustice ascribed to derangement, 194

EGYPT, 92*s*

EJECTMENT,
by wife against her husband, 287*x*

ELDER BRANCH,
succession of —— by custom, 682, 683

ELDER; ELDERSHIP,
advantage allowed to —— by custom, 716
gives precedence, 669, 671*e*
and preference for office, 684
precedence allowed by some family laws to son of elder wife, 827*s*
gives title to the right or western side of family house in partition, 749
gives a perference as to custody of family idols, 716*m*
supremacy annexed to —— connected with the sacra, 669
the —— brother has precedence in sacrifices and marriage, 820*b*
stil of consequence, 676*v*
transition from —— to single succession, 669, 672*k*
the mode of establishing —— a source of disputes in India and Europe, 676*v*
See BROTHER; MANAGER; PRECEDENCE; PRIMOGENITURE; RAJ

ELECTION, 1079*t*

EMANCIPATION,
under Roman law son injured by adoption claimed ——, 955v

EMIGRANT HEIR,
descendants of ——, 70
See ABSENTEE

EMIGRATION,
does not alter the law of inheritance, 3

ENDOWMENT,
creation of ——s, 198, 155
interest of the State in religious ——s, 211
gift for religious —— by coparcener approved, 616
no restriction on creation of religious —— by grant, 185o
religious —— not allowed to cover a private perpetuity, 618
consent of whole family may annul a rivate religious ——, 743
charitable ——s are inalienable according to Madras and Bombay High Courts, but alienable for benefit of endowment according to Calcutta and Allahabad High Courts, 176, 199, 523, 744
and irresumable, 199
endownments never revert, 681f
endownments frequently confined to a single family, 199
property given to a purohit is in the nature of an ——, 198
usually impartible, 199
succession to be governed by custom, 199
See VRITTI, 671e
may be temporarily pledged for necessary purposes, 523
succession to an —— determined by custom, 198
holder of an —— cannot impose rules on successors, 199
or alter succession, 74, 521w
succession to religious —— is *per formam doni*, 198k
See ALIENATION; ASCETICS, 521w; TRUST; TRUSTEE

ENEMY OF HIS FATHER,
defined, 547, 548
is especially one from whom religious benefits are not obtainable, 549, 551
is disqualified from inheriting and sharing in partition, 149, 548, 629, 689

ENGAGEMENTS,
Hindu law enforces, 8

ENGLISH LAW,
operation of —— in a presidency town, 3

EQUITY,
aids Hindu law, 8
decides when Smritis conflict, 13
rules of —— decide questions of partition, 757
See ADOPTION; HINDU LAW; INTERPRETATION; JURISDICTION; PARTITION

ERROR. See ACQUIESCENCE; ADOPTION VIII., 1078; IGNORANCE, 1077, 1078; MISREPRESENTATION

ESCHEAT,
State takes by —— on failure of heirs proved, 129
and with incumbrances, 664*b*

ESTATE,
one cannot create a new form of ——, 179*r*, 192, 183
solely *in futuro* not allowed by Hindu law, 212
not to be in abeyance, 179
deferred in enjoyment, 1022
right of father and son are equal in ancestral ——, 71
mortgaged property until recovered continues to be a joint ——, 633
family —— once inalienable, divisible only for use, 672*k*
connexion with this of the right of pre-emption, *ib.*
how the family —— became alienable, *ib.*
and partible, *ib.*
ancestral —— in the hands of sons liable for father's debts, 76, 163, 168
may be encumbered by any coparcener in an emergency, 747
separate —— liable for debts in the hands of the heir, 660
See ADOPTION VI., 978, 980, 981, 982, 983, 984; VII., 1045, 1050; VIII., 1080; ALIENATION; DEBTS; DESCENT; DEVOLUTION; FATHER; GRANT, 664*b*; PROPERTY; STRIDHANA; VATAN

ESTOPPEL,
fed by subsequently acquired interest a doubtful principle under Hindu law, 190*z*
in case of adoption, 969*ss*, 1073
where adoption has been admitted by conduct, 1074
does not arise from denial of adoption, 1083
against reversioner who concurred in an alienation by a widow, 710*f*
against a mortgagee who has sold, 720
See ACQUIESCENCE; ADOPTION IV., 943; VI., 969; VIII., 1073, 1074

ETHICS,
relation of —— to Hindu Law, 8

EUNUCHS
entitled to maintenance only, 690*a*

EVIDENCE
of caste custom. See CUSTOM
of family custom by declaration. See CUSTOM, FAMILY, 151*m*
Of Partition, not peculiar, 631
conduct and oral testimony are ——, 631, 637
is a question of intention, 631, 632
signs according to the Hindu Law, 636*ss*
circumstantial —— sufficient to prove partition, 638
of separation is on a matter of fact, 638

EVIDENCE—*continued.*
separate possession of portions of the property, once joint, raises a presumption of separation, 640
false statements made for the common benefit are not —— of partition, 641
exclusive possession for thirty years affords conclusive —— of partition, 643
separation for fifty years was pronounced ——, 639*a*
taking profits in certain defined shares is not conclusive ——, 641, 642
living and dining apart is not conclusive ——, 637
separate performance of religious rites is not conclusive ——, *ib.*
proof of instrument by single witness by assent, 218
admissions not to be used by strangers, 189*n*
burden of proof in case of separate acquisition disputed, 669*ss*
of adoption, 965, 1072
decree on a contested adoption is not —— when there is a change of parties, 1082
See ADOPTION VI., 964, 1005, 1007; VIII., 1072, 1082; BURDEN OF PROOF; PRESUMPTION; STRANGER

EXCLUSION
from caste, 944
from caste extends to sons born after but not to those born before the expulsion, 121, 549
sons born after expulsion from caste take the outcast father's place, 549
daughters are not excluded with their father, *ib.*
from inheritance and partition on account of vice, 689*y*
under customary law, *ib.*
for twelve years extinguishes the right, 635, 645
persons excluded from shares are entitled to maintenance, 241, 629, 689, 709
See DISQUALIFICATION; LIMITATION; POSSESSION, 650*d*

EXECUTION
against one coparcener affects only his share, 615*f*
liability of the son's share in —— against the father discussed, 576*ss*
a "reversioner's" contingent right cannot be sold in ——, 89
See DEBT; DECREE; SALE

EXECUTOR,
under Act V. of 1881, 220, 221*p*
may pay a barred debt, 572
in mofussil may sue without probate, 221
executors are the representatives of the testator, 162
executor's legal position discussed, 220
takes a qualified "universitas" in personal estate (English Law), 209
takes subject to survivorship, 220

EXECUTORY DEVISE. See DEVISE, 90

EXPECTANT HEIRS
not to be prejudiced by widow, 306

EXPECTANT INTEREST
probably not saleable, 190*z*, 246*v*

EXPENDITURE; EXPENSES
of united family defrayed out of the family estate, 749
authority of the wife as to household ——, 86*s*
of a coparcener. See PARTITION, 760
previous inequalities of —— not taken into account in case of partition, 698, 761
unless fraudulent, 760
marriage —— of children to be provided for on partition, 691*i*, 713
of a daughter of deceased member must be provided for, 470*q*
funeral ——of father a charge on the common property, 686*h*
See ASSENT, 564*s*

EXPRESSIONS,
operative —— for adoption, 960

EXPULSION
from caste. See EXCLUSION

EXTRA SHARE. See DISTRIBUTION (unequal); PARTITION

"FACTUM VALET"
discussed, 208, 234, 737, 818

FADERFIUM, 269*d*

FAMILIA, 164*o*

FAMILY ARRANGEMENT,
given effect to, 631, 646

FAMILY CUSTOM,
how proved, 4, 156*m*
See CUSTOM

FAMILY DWELLING
divisible? 717
belonged to eldest son under old English law, 734*o*
but by custom to the youngest, 675*n*

FAMILY, HINDU,
the cherished institution of the Hindus, 231
father's duty to provide for ——, 601
no transaction approved which tends to indigence of ——, 593
Adoptive, 957, 1010
Divided. See ADOPTION III., 267, 896, 897
succession in —— ——, 73—82, 96—107, 123—126, 338—466
See INHERITANCE; PARTITION

FAMILY, HINDU—*continued.*
Joint or United ——
normal state of a Hindu —— is one of union, 562
described, 603
how constituted, 561
is of two kinds, undivided or reunited, 603
characteristics of —— ——, 563
Hindu —— —— regarded as continuous, 561
extends to great-grandson in existence, 616, 607
in a —— —— presumption of all property being joint, 666*m*, 670*b*
son cannot demand a declaration of his right to specified undivided share, 1079
not a partnership, 560*c*
usually represented by a manager, 568
compared with joint tenants under English Law, 562*h*
principle of the —— —— and gotra adopted by the Sudras to govern adoption, 922
Sudras illegitimate sons may *inter se* form a —— ——, 604
and probably also with legitimate half-brothers, *ib.*
may be formed by prostitutes or dancing girls, 562*h*
how regarded as to mutual responsibilities, 700, 869, 896, 897
reciprocal rights and obligations, 562
members jointly liable for common debts, 570
powers of a member of a —— ——, 567, 688*s*
rights of coparceners in —— ——, 568
gift to —— —— is joint property, 605
acquisitions of members accede to joint estate, 699
including manager's gains, 703*f*
where one member has disappeared the rest may deal with common property in good faith, 567
transactions of —— —— require unanimity according to the older authorities, 564, 565, 567
view of the Viramitrodaya, 564*s*
alienation of undivided share now allowed. See COPARCENER, 565
origin of this, 565
rights of a grantee from one member subject to rights of coparceners, 647
suits by —— ——, 567, 568
when a —— —— carries on trade all members must join as plaintiffs in a suit, 573
suit by one member followed by common suit, 565
suits against —— ——, 575, 576
where there is effectual representation, all may be bound, though not immediately made parties, 573
liability of sons for father's acts and suits put on the ground of representation, 574, 575, 578
where interests are common one member of a —— —— sometimes taken to represent all in a suit, 574
contra, 596
infants held liable though manager had had no right to defend in their name, 573

FAMILY, HINDU—*continued.*
sale or incumbrance by a single member valid in case of urgent need, 688*t*, 747
grantee from one member may enforce partition, 651
a decree against the father may be executed against the family property, 574, 575
inheritance in a —— ——, 61, 321
separation of a —— ——, 607, 725
See ADOPTION *passim*; ALIENATION; COPARCENER; DEBT, 688; EXPENDITURE, 747; ILLEGITIMATE SON; LIABILITY; MANAGER; PRESUMPTION; PROPERTY; SACRA
Family Reunited, described, 607
formed only by those who were before united, 607

FAMILY NECESSITY,
cases showing what is a —— ——, 569*n*
a ground for alienation by any coparcener, 688*t*, 747

FAMINE,
a reason for giving away a son, 951
See ADOPTION

FARIKHAT, 762
or deed of release in case of partition, 771
See PARTITION

FATHER
once supreme over family estate, 657
growth of restraints on his authority, *ib.*
in case of father's incapacity his son takes his place, 594, 610*v*
has uncontrolled power before birth or adoption of a son, 596*g*
son given equal rights with —— in grandfather's estate come to the father, 657
gradual development of this right, *ib.*
hence a right of interdiction, 193
owner of ancestral estate in same sense as sons, 595
as manager is by Hindu Law in the same position as any other manager (see BELOW), 594
father's relation to son as joint owner and sole manager, 1029*f*
and representative, 574, 653
may deal with share of infant but not of adult son? 578
father's power in distributing ancestral and self-acquired property, 704—706, 727, 733*ss*, 740
may alien or incumber ancestral estate in certain cases, 168, 169, 192, 594, 595, 687
effect of decrees against —— as regards the sons, 578, 652, 653
can alienate patrimony without the consent of his sons, 203, 568, 577, 578, 601*x*, 739
shown by their attestations, 593*l*
may dispose of ancestral estate on failure of sons or separation from them, 73

FAMILY, HINDU—*continued*.
rulings of the courts extend his powers, 165, 168, 593, 595, 687
making excessive alienation presumed deranged, 203
father's limited power over property a general rule of jurispdudence, 705*n*
father's power of distributing at pleasure recognized by Jagannatha, 233
contrary to Mitakshara, *ib*.
father's power of distribution amongst sons, 705*n*, 733*ss*, 740
cannot make a gift or bequest to one son to the prejudice of others, or of a grandson, 205, 206, 705, 736, 737
except of self-acquired property, 205, 207, 703, 733
may dispose of self-acquired property, 703, 733, 739, 760
is free to deal with his own share, 168
subject perhaps to subsistence of family, 192, 193, 694, 1089
may make religious gifts within moderate limits, 203
gift by —— to adopted son not affected by subsequent birth of sons, 1078
cannot wholly disinherit a descendant, 740
except for adequate reasons, 549, 551, 739, 815
As Manager, 568, 576*ss*, 594
the care of the family especially incumbent on ——, 594
is naturally manager of the joint family estate, 568
as manager can be superseded for incapacity by his son, 594
in same position as mother, 685
presumption in favour of his transactions, 592, 593
allowed disposal in ways opposed to good management, 595
not liable to pay his son's debts, 550
unless incurred for indispensable duty, 588
father's transactions plainly detrimental whether binding on the family estate, 593
may charge the whole estate with debts not prodigally contracted, 168, 192, 597, 653
purchaser or incumbrancer from —— bound to inquiry, 168, 595
son bound to pay debts of ——, 75, 164, 597
son in Bracton's time bound to pay father's debts out of inheritance in England, 165
his contracts and obligations pass to the heir, 75
his promises morally binding, 203
and sacred, 686*g*, 1087—1090
as also his donations to charities, 686*g*
instruments made under distracting influence void by Hindu Law, 193*a*, 597
son suing to upset father's transactions bound to prove his non-liability, 595
suit against —— does not affect sons not joined, 596
liability of the son's share in execution against the —— discussed, 169, 576*ss*, 587, 652
decree against the —— alone will not ordinarily bind his sons as to ancestral property, 167, 596
but will where decree is against —— as representative, 653
effect of a sale in execution of the interest of the —— in ancestral property, 167, 575, 596, 653

FAMILY, HINDU—*continued.*
separated from brethren is the origin of a new line of succession, 73, 1046
when —— inherits, 102, 324, 346, 379, 426
when —— succeeds to his daughter, 134, 309, 470, 481, 484
separated preferred to brother separated, 427
preferred to mother as heir by the Mayukha, 102, 422
or ascendant may separate from his descendants at any time, 609
cannot, it seems, separate sons *inter se* against their will, 617*ss*
cannot make an unfair partition, 645, 733
may reserve a double share of self-acquired property, 729
or alienate it at his pleasure, 705
held answerable in partition for personal debts, 597
in Punjab a father's division revisable at his death, 617
when —— is entitled to maintenance, 255, 603, 723, 1028
bound to support indigent son, 723
See Adoption IV., 913, 941, 944; V. *passim*; Charges; Debts; Decree, 166, 686; Liability; Patria-Potestas; Property; Securities; Suits

FATHER'S BROTHER'S DAUGHTER'S SON. See Adoption IV., 941*c*

FATHER'S MATERNAL AUNT'S SONS
are Bandhus, 123, 457

FATHER'S MATERNAL UNCLE
is a Bandhu, 458*e*

FATHER'S MATERNAL UNCLE'S SONS
are Bandhus, 123, 457

FATHER'S PATERNAL AUNT'S SONS
are Bandhus, *ib.*, *ib.*

FATHER'S SECOND COUSIN
is postponed to paternal aunt in a divided family? 453

FATHER'S SISTER'S SON
is a Bandhu, 461

FATHER-IN-LAW. See Adoption III., 844, 851, 882, 895*ss*

FEE,
gratuity of a woman, 139
goes to her husband, *ib.*
See Sulka; Stridhana

FELLOW-STUDENT,
when inherits, 126, 326, 451, 468, 539
fellow-student's disciple, 539

FELLOW-DISCIPLE
inherits, 527
of a Guru, inherits, 528

FEMALE GENTILESHIP, 272ss
not necessarily indicated by the use of a "matronymic," 399n
traces of —— —— in the law of succession, 274, 399
sister's son heir to uncle among original tribes, 801k
in Malabar, 608h
amongst Garos, 398
Khasyas, *ib.*
Koches, *ib.*
Nayars, *ib.*
in Travancore, *ib.*

FEMALE,
position of females in early times, 261, 270, 275, 290ss, 793, 797, 800
females regarded as chattels in some tribes, 397
under tutelage and generally dependent, 284
female's consequent incapacities, 246w
regarded as necessarily dependent by the Teutonic laws and in China, 262w
gradual recognition of the capacity of females to hold property, 259, 263ss
favoured by Balambhatta. See ADOPTION V., 943
females may succeed to some priestly emoluments appointing substitutes 389
females may become Gosavis, 526, 531
Vairagis, 537
females may be excluded by family custom from inheritance, 673
females not excluded from succession to inam property, 407
females could inherit *book land* in England, 82w
females in the Punjab do not transmit inheritance, 177
females cannot form a joint family, 364
cannot generally transfer her right as wife, widow, or mother, 246w, 287w
possible exception, 287w
a gift to females may be accompanied with power to alien, 297c
so as to a devise, 984
comparison of the English Law, 246w
females generally incapable of inheriting in Bengal and Madras, unless named by special texts, 117
so in Benares? *ib.*
so in Eastern and Southern India, 118
but not in Western India where the Mitakshara prevails, 118, 119
female's incapacity still recognized in Sialkot, 261m
cannot be a Karnam (Madras), 329
females cannot become Sannyasis, 519
married females are subject to husband's guardianship, 506
failing him and his family to that of their parents and their kinsmen, *ib.*
what females are Gotraja Sapindas, 121

FEMALE—*continued.*
a license to —— use ornaments not a gift of them, 186
females can succeed to a vatan, 326*i*
property given to —— for maintenance confers only a life estate, 215
their succession regarded as inheritance, 606*x*
females have inchoate rights of participation which become effective when separation takes place, 605
their rights distinguished from those of males, 607
females' share in partition, 629
their right arises on a partition either voluntary or enforced, 627*c*
females cannot claim partition though entitled to shares, 627
a grandmother in Bengal may sue to sever her share along with dividing parceners', 627*d*
widow of a coparcener in Bengal may sue to sever her share, 629
others are entitled to maintenance only, 689
heirs to females, 134*ss*, 470*ss*
unmarried females, 134
married females leaving issue, 134—140
no issue, 140—141
remote succession to females governed by same rules as to a male, 308*m*
descent through females in Malabar, 608*h*
connexion for succession limited to a single —— link in same line, 466
involving several links not admitted, 460*n*
See Adoption; Daughter; Gotra; Maintenance; Manager; Mother; Partition; Priest; Sister; Stridhana; Succession; Widow; Wife; Woman
See Inheritance; Raj; Vatan

FICTIONS
become law by adoption, 796*l*

FINDER. See Treasure Trove, 797

FIRST COUSIN. See Cousin, 125

FIRST COUSIN'S WIDOW
succeeds in competition with her daughter-in-law, 454

FORFEITURE OF RIGHTS
refusal to adopt not a ground for ——, 372, 814, 1068
incurred by widow remarrying, 102, 403, 406, 430, 553
not by unchastity subsequent to succession, 83, 554
subsequent insanity does not cause —— —— ——, 545
of inheritance by a Guru through fornication, 535
See Adoption VIII., 1069; Maintenance; Unchastity; Widow

FORMS OF ADOPTION, 960, 964
Roman ——, 1018*h*
See Adoption VI., 994, 1003—1006

FORMULAS
of ceremonial law, 48
sacred, 33, 43
their coercive force, 791
See ADOPTION IV., 922; VI., 992ss; INHERITANCE; SRADDHA

FORNICATION,
a ground of disinheritance in case of a Guru, 534
girls encouraged by Smritis to —— with men of higher caste, 798r
See FORFEITURE, 534

FOSTER DAUGHTER,
amongst dancers, 828y
foster daughter's heritable right not recognized, 427
is excluded by a brother, ib.
See ADOPTION IV., 945p

FOSTER SON,
rights of a ——, 340
not recognized as an heir, 356, 362, 829
recognized by some castes, 828, 1065
may be heir by custom according to a Sastri's opinion, 828y
advantage of —— over adopted son, 828, 829
See ADOPTION VII., 1065

FRAUD,
repugnant to Hindu Law, 8, 650, 764
to be prevented, 188, 244
a cause of rescission, 591
of manager's transactions, 688s
a ground of action against a coparcener, 570s
and in suit by one, 688s
as affecting right to share in partition, 629, 630, 763
vitiates a partition, 650
and is a ground for suit, 649a, 652
co-sharer answerable for ——, 700c, 760
does not deprive him of his right to share, 760
compensation taken, 630
vitiates an adoption, 963
preventing adoption successful in Bengal, 651
a ground of action by a widow for maintenance against vendee, 693r
against creditors, &c., not allowed to be effected by partition, 650
See ADOPTION III., 890; COPARCENER; MANAGER; MINOR; PARTITION, 703; PURCHASER

FULL-BLOOD. See BROTHERS; SUCCESSION

FUNERAL CEREMONIES,
all sons liable for —— ——, 686h
responsibilty for —— —— of a married female, 507n
performance or non-performance does not affect heritable right, 689
See ADOPTION II., 700; III., 840; VII., 1022; KRIYA; SRADDHAS

FUNERAL EXPENSES,
a charge, 685, 720*g*, 728
See Charges on Inheritance, 686*p*

FURNITURE,
generally indivisible, 671
articles, if numerous, may be sold and the proceeds divided, 673
may be kept by coparceners using them, 717

GAINS OF CHANCE, OF SCIENCE, AND OF VALOUR,
when self-acquired and when joint property, 667, 668, 669
See Property, Separate and Self-Acquired

GAINS OF SCIENCE,
"science" means the particular profession, not elementary education, 669
right of acquirer to —— —— ——, 700
are separate property, 666*ss*
See Property, Separate and Self-Acquired

GAINS OF VALOUR
are separate property, *ib.*

GANDHARVA. See Marriage, 481, 484, 486

GHARBARI. See Gosavi, 529

GAROO. See Tribes, 274, 275, 398

GAUTAMA DHARMASUTRA, 32

GAVALI. See Caste, 385

GENEALOGIES,
preservation of —— by purohits (family priests), 235*h*

GENTILES. See Gotrajas, 120

GENTOOS, 6

GHARJAWAHEE, 1065

GHATASPHOTA, 56, 552
See Divorce

GHATWAH TENURE, 177

GIRI. See Gosavi, 530

GIFT
much discussed by Hindu lawyers, 189
law of —— governs wills, 740

GIFT—*continued.*
sale had formerly to take the form of ——, 191
inter vivos can confer only interests recognized by law, 183
with reserve of ownership invalid, 180, 187, 415, 959
a mere license to a woman to use ornaments on particular occasions not a ——, 186, 280
of jewels under English Law, 186*s*
to persons unborn cannot take effect, 180, 182
reasonable —— from parent to be respected, 205, 738
resumable if improperly made, 1088
as a contract, 189
essentials of ——, *ib.*
transfer of possession generally necessary, 190, 216, 416
not perhaps amongst near relatives, 190, 1065
void unless completed by delivery, 180, 204, 634, 642
as against subsequent transferee, 416
of inalienable property void, 1089
cannot, according to the Mitakshara law, be made of an undivided share, 217*p*, 564, 565, 588, 616
except for pious purposes (see below), 616
nor of ancestral immoveable property? 447
unless attested by sons, 592*k*
as assenting, *ib.*
of whole estate subject to provision for wife, 191
limited to self-acquired property minus subsistence fund of family, 695, 1089
and sale of child forbidden by Apastamba, 792*n*
of girl to be expressly in marriage, 960
religious gifts in India and Europe compared, 191, 203, 204
nature of —— to religous uses, 20, 195, 198
moderate religious —— may be made by a father, 203
religious —— inalienable and irrevocable, 195
in Krishnarpana, 91, 190
every —— is accompanied under Hindu Law by a tacit condition of recovation, 187
or defeasance, 187, 416
not cancelled under present law, 416
conditional —— is invalid according to Viramitrodaya, 186
so also under the Mitakshara, *ib.*
but not necessarily according to Narada, *ib.*
contingent —— inoperative save as a promise, 212, 181
condition precedent may invalidate a ——, 187, 212, 961
subsequent invalid if repugnant to law, 187
limitation to male descendants only is bad, 182
valid though donor retain life-interest, 188, 190
cannot be made subject to fantastic directions and limitations, 194, 664*b*
may be accompanied by a trust, 188, 200*ss*, 416
trust now enforced, 416
comparison of the Roman Law, 416
by coparcener. See ALIENATION, 385, 568

GIFT—*continued.*
whether valid against coparceners, 191
religious —— not to be used for other purposes, 743
to child, wife, or concubine binding, 193
to one son upheld against another, 738
unequal —— to a son not generally allowed, 205, 206, 735, 738
of moderate amount to a separated son allowed, 723, 735
by father to adopted son not affected by birth of begotten son, 1078
to illegitimate son valid, 547
to a daughter, 205
valid if provision is made for widow's maintenance, 392
of affectionate kindred to wife, 86
to a wife by her husband not invalidated by joint interest of sons, 204
to wife of heritable interest, 297*c*
to future wife, 280
See FEMALE
of whole property to wife (excluding sons) void, 759
See ALIENATION; FATHER
as a token of affection. See PRITIDATTA
at the bridal altar (or nuptial fire). See ADHYAGNIKA
at marriage. See YAUTAKA
for maintenance, is a kind of stridhana, 259
by a son, 287*x*
a sum of money given in lieu of maintenance is stridhana, 295
from the brother, a kind of stridhana, 259, 352, 353
is valid, if not fraudulent, 279, 281
from the father, a kind of stridhana, 257, 352, 353
gifts from kinsmen, 486*m*
from the mother, a kind of stridhana, 259, 352, 353
from a son, a kind of stridhana, 352, 353
in the bridal procession. See ADHYAVAHANIKA
on supersession. See ADHIVEDANIKA
subsequent. See ANVADHEYA
See ADOPTION II., 825; V. *passim*; VI., 957, 960, 961, 989; VIII., 1078; ENDOWMENT; FATHER; ORNAMENTS; PRESENT, 509; STRIDHANA

GIRASIA, 421, 850

GIRASI HAKKS. See HAKKS, *ib.*

GIRL,
not adoptable. See ADOPTION IV., 942

GIVER IN ADOPTION. See ADOPTION II.; V., 817

GONDS. See TRIBES, 270

GOOD FAITH
protects an alienee from the widow or mother as manager, 570
See ALIENATION; CREDITOR; DEBTS, 687; FATHER; MANAGER; MINOR; WIDOW

GOSAVI,
ceremonies at initiation of Gosavis, 523
position of Gosavis in the community, 519
Sudras and women may become ——, 519, 835*ss*
Gosavis are either Puri, Giri, or Bharathi, 530
Gosavis Kanphata, 527
Gosavis are not Sannyasis, 518
difference between Sannyasis and Gosavis, 519
some Gosavis engage in trade, *ib.*
Bharathi sect of Gosavis marry, 525
married Gosavis are eligible to mahantship, *ib.*
Gosavis marry in some other cases, 519, 525
Gharbari Gosavis, 529, 530
concubinage allowed by custom of Gosavis, 519
Gosavis for what actions out-casted, 523
adoptions by Gosavis, 834, 835
mode in which Gosavis get their chelas, 835
relation between —— and his disciple differs from true adoption, *ib.*
(male) heirs to a ——, 521, 529
natural sons of —— may become disciples and inherit, 525
not the offspring of an adulterous connexion, *ib.*
(female) heirs to a ——, 531
See Adoption II., 825; III., 849; VII., 1065; Ascetics; Vairagis, 539

GOSAVINI,
= a female Gosavi, 531
See Gosavi

GOTRA,
sense of —— among lower castes, 935
imitation of —— relations by the Sudras, 922
a woman by marriage enters her husband's ——, 120, 121
identity or difference of —— as affecting adoption, 935*ss*
See Adoption IV., 910, 913; Gotraja

GOTRAJA,
according to Smriti Chandrika means sprung from the family, 121*n*
according to Vyav. Mayukha means born in the family, 121

GOTRAJA SAMANODAKAS, 123
See Samanodakas

GOTRAJA SAPINDAS,
who are included in the term, 107—122, 435*ss*, 503
table of —— ——, 115*s*
enumeration of —— —— given by Vijnanesvara not exhaustive, 110, 111, 114
meaning of —— —— according to the Mitakshara, 120
Vyav. Mayukha, 121
division of —— ——, 108
Samanagotra the same as —— ——, 120

GOTRAJA SAPINDAS—*continued.*
distinguished from Bhinnagotra Sapindas, 497
what females are —— ——, 121
order of —— ——, 108, 109, 435*ss*, 449
inherit according to their nearness to the deceased, 107
succession of —— ——, 443*ss*, 44
collateral succession of —— —— stops with grandson of the ascendant in Madras, 115
in Bengal with great-grandson of the ascendant, *ib.*

GOVERNMENT. See ADOPTION III., 853, 901—902

GRAND-AUNT, PATERNAL,
entitled to maintenance, 336

GRAND-DAUGHTER
is a Bandhu, 465
cannot inherit in an undivided family, *ib.*
may inherit in a divided family, *ib.*
grand-daughter's succession to a female, 477
is heir to her grandmother, 139, 477

GRAND-DAUGHTER'S SON, 465
See BANDHU; SAPINDA

GRANDCHILDREN,
not entitled to maintenance, 694*z*
entitled according to Mitakshara, *ib.*, 1089

GRANDFATHER
is a gotraja, 108
may separate from his descendants at any time, 611
grandson bound to pay debts of ——, 75, 1088
when —— succeeds, 108, 433, 443
See ADOPTION V., 949, 1081; VII., 1041; DEBTS; GRANDSON

GRANDFATHER'S (PATERNAL) BROTHERS
are gotrajas, 109

GRANDFATHER'S (PATERNAL) BROTHER'S SONS
are gotrajas, *ib.*
when inherit, 449, 450

GRANDMOTHER (PATERNAL),
cannot demand partition, 627
but may in Bengal (see FEMALES), 627*d*
but on partition is entitled to a share, 712, 750*r*
when succeeds, 105, 433, 443
has a special place assigned to her, 105
special ground for her succession according to Smriti Chandrika, 121*n*
preferred to step-mother, 442

GRAND-NEPHEW. See ADOPTION IV., 918

GRAND-NIECE (MATERNAL),
takes with the same power of alienation as a daughter or sister, 467

GRANDSON
entitled to maintenance? 694*z*, 1089
cannot control grandfather's alienation with his father's consent, 732
grandson's right of inheritance, 64, 74, 323, 370
may separate by agreement, 611
grandson's right to partition with grandfather not directly recognized, 729, 730
it arises only after his father's death*, 610, 730
grandsons take a share equal together to their father's, 611
takes his father's place on the exclusion of the father, 815*l*
takes mother's share by representation when mother dies between death of her father and actual partition, 103
not to be defrauded by grandfather's gift to a son, 737
of the maternal uncle of the mother may inherit, 467
of a sister, *ib.*
See ADOPTION II., 814, 821; III., 842, 843, 844

GRANDSON BY ADOPTION,
succession of —— in undivided family, 67, 603
succession of —— in divided family, 76, 370

GRANDSON, ILLEGITIMATE,
succession of —— of a Sudra, 69
legitimate son of illegitimate son takes half-share of his father among Sudras, 77, 371

GRAND-UNCLE See GRANDFATHER'S (PATERNAL) BROTHERS

GRAND-UNCLE'S GRANDSON is a Gotraja Sapinda, 451

GRAND-UNCLE'S GRANDSON. See GRANDFATHER'S (PATERNAL) BROTHERS SONS

GRANT,
construed so as to be effectual, 183
the words "aulad aflad" in a —— how construed, 184*f*
to be preserved for designated purpose, 184
a village taken by —— to one is self-acquired property, 664, 667*o*
religious —— favoured by Hindu Law, 211*f*
cannot be alienated, 681*f*
a —— may be impartible, 683
by the sovereign may make an estate impartible, 180, 197

---

* See Mitakshara, Chap. I. Sec. V. para. 3 note; Vyavahara Mayukha Chap. IV. Sec. II. para. 2.

GRANT—*continued.*
treated as separate property disposable by grantee, 734
a condition against alienation is generally void, 188
the extent of estate conferred by a —— in Bombay, 664*b*
tenure of —— to support an office, 683
not divisible to prejudice of service, 681
cannot be resumed, 195, 378
not voidable by the executive, 665
binds grantee to its terms, *ib.*
he cannot enclose pasture-lands appendant to village holdings, *ib.*
not liable to debts of holder after his death, 679
except in case of confiscation, *ib.*
grantee's mortgage upheld against an escheat, 665
holder of a jagir or saranjam can make a —— for his own life, 664*b*
succession to —— governed by its nature, 681
srotriyam is descendible to grantee's sons only, 667*o*
grants public devolve according to special terms prescribed, 180
distinguished from private, *ib.*
to a man, his children, and grandchildren confers an absolute estate, 485, 664
to united brethren constitutes a joint tenancy, 73, 654
by a father to his illegitimate son for his maintenance is valid, 360, 547
in favour of persons not in existence fails with the estates dependent on it, 182
to mistress. See SARANJAM, 698*r*
See ADOPTION VIII., 1081; BROTHERS; ENDOWMENT; INAM; INTERPRETATION; SROTRIYAM

GRANTEE
adopting should obtain consent of grantor, 1061
See ADOPTION VII., GRANT

GREAT-GRANDFATHER, 109, 444
may separate from his descendants at will, 609
See ADOPTION III., 852

GREAT-GRANDMOTHER, 109, 111, 443
entitled to inherit according to Mitakshara, 119

GREAT-GRANDSON
great-grandsons through different sons are Gotraja Sapindas, 451
position of —— in a partition, 622
when he inherits, 60, 61, 74, 129
in the male line precedes a daughter's son, 370
of the fifth ancestor succeeds before his father's sister's son, 456

GREAT-GRANDSON BY ADOPTION,
succession of ——, 67, 603

GREAT-GRANDSON'S SON
is not entitled to any share, 622*e*
does not take share, 606

GREAT-GREAT-GRANDSON
is not entitled to any share, 622e
does not take share, 606
but —— —— succeeds as a Gotraja Sapinda, 607

GREEK CUSTOM,
as to exposure of infants, 209e

GREEKS. See ADOPTION VI., 957

GRIHASTHA AVIBHAKTA, 56

GRIHASTHA VIBHAKTA, *ib.*

GUARDIAN,
till eight years of age the mother is ——, 409
under Maithila law mother preferred to father as ——, 338
adoptive mother preferred as —— to adopted son, 1080
so in case of a widow, 353
natural father is not —— while adopted parents live, 622f
a near relative has the best right to guardianship of a minor, 380
a paternal relation preferred, 413, 624h
guardianship of female sought by husband, she denying the marriage, 507
over a female is vested after marriage in the husband, his sons, and his sapindas, 306, 507
nature of this guardianship, 227
husband's family being extinct, parents and their kinsmen are the guardians of a woman, 228, 507
on failure of both the king is ——, *ib.*
a person cannot be appointed —— or administrator against his will, 622f
ad litem may be appointed when there is no administrator, *ib.*
an officer of the Court may be appointed ——, *ib.*
may demand partition for the minor, 624
sell to maintain a suit for the minor's benefit, 622f
alienation by an unauthorized ——, 350
See ADOPTION VII., 1033, 1037; VIII., 1080; AGE; FEMALE, 506; MINOR

GUDHAJA, 805

GUJAR. See CASTE, 446

GUJARAT,
peculiarities of the law in ——, 13
See ADOPTION II., VII.; CUSTOM; FATHER; MOTHER; SISTER; WIDOW

GURAVA,
interest of a —— in the temple land is alienable, 717
See CASTES AND CLASSES

GURU,
position of —— in a temple or matha, 520, 521
relation of —— and his disciple somewhat resembles adoption, 834
bound to maintain his chela in distress, 723*g*
succeeds to a Vairagi by custom, 539
disciple, 469
nominates a chela as successor, 522
succession of disciples to ——, 520, 533
succession to —— limited to one disciple, 467

GURU BAHINA, 536

GURU'S FELLOW DISCIPLE, 528

GURUBHAU
is heir to a Vairagi, 539
See FELLOW-DISCIPLE

GURU-SISHYAS, 535

HAKKS, 323
are immovable property, 706*x*

HALF-BLOOD. See BROTHER

HALF-BROTHER. See BROTHER

HALF-BROTHER'S SON
is a sapinda according to Vyav. May., 106
succeeds to his aunt, 511
See ADOPTION IV., 913

HALF-SISTER
is a gotraja sapinda, 535
may be included in "bhagini," 534
preferred to step-mother, 441
uncle's widow, *ib.*
doctrine of Viv. Chintamani and Vyav. Mayukha, *ib.*

HARITA, 37

HEIR,
meaning of —— under English Law and Hindu Law compared, 601
See DAYA
expectant. See REVERSIONER, 89*ss*
presumptive, cannot sue for declaration of his right, 371
See FEMALE

HEMADRI, 9

HEREDITARY OFFICES,
now regulated by enactments, 684
how divided, 716
must not leave the family of the office holder, 684
See VATAN

HERES NECESSARIUS, 196

HERITABLE RIGHT
of the widow discussed, 84
See BIRTH; INHERITANCE; WIDOW

HERITAGE
rests on positive law, 8
under Hindu Law implies ownership, 425
woman's —— ranked as Stridhana, 134
See DAYA; HEIR; INHERITANCE; STRIDHANA

HINDU LAW,
operation of —— ——, 1*ss*
application of —— —— authorized by the legislature, 1
assisted by equity, 7, 8
conflict of laws of different communities, 5
when law of defendant prevails, 5, 6, 7
its connexion with religion and ethics, 8
religious element preponderates in —— ——, 233
scope of ancient —— —— purely religious, 49*b*
rather personal than provincial, 3
sources of —— —— of a sacred character, 9, 940
based on the Smritis, 54*ss*
authorities on —— ——, 9
conflict between —— —— books, 14*k*
criticism of —— —— necessary, 8, 9
often turned into verse, 49*b*
custom, basis of —— ——, 1
tends to conformity with written —— ——, 9
schools of, 12—54
(1) Maharastra, 12
(2) Dravida, 51
(3) Benares, 52
(4) Mithila, *ib.*
(5) Gauriya or Bengal, 53
allows all classes of Hindus to be governed by their own customs, 559*a*, 788
general —— superseded by particular custom, 2
modified by custom, 150
but —— regulates all beyond, 2
customary law of inheritance may be changed, 3
capable of development, 516*a*
analogy to the English law, *ib.*
history of ——, 8, 50

HINDU LAW—*continued.*
developed under the control of religious ideas, 48, 49*b*
of the Sastras extends in operation with the increased complexity of affairs, 829*a*
binds the Jains in the absence of special custom, 152
binds the Khojas in the absence of special custom, *ib.*
undoes what is done fraudulently, 8, 9
every important duty prescribed by a Smriti legally enforceable under ——, 233, 235
distinction between religious and legal obligations not clearly drawn, 233
See ADOPTION I., 780*ss*; V., 953; VI., 959, 960, 961, 962; VII., 1052, 1058; VIII., 1067; APOSTASY, 559; EQUITY; INTERPRETATION; SMRITIS

HINDU LAW OFFICER. See LAW OFFICER

HINDU WILLS ACTS—
XXI. of 1870, 219, 1081
V. of 1881, 220
See separate List at the beginning

HINDUS, ARYAN, 957

HIRANYAKESI SUTRA, 32

HOMA SACRIFICE. See ADOPTION II.; IV.; VI.

HOUSE
built on ancestral land by coparcener with his separate funds is not subject to partition, 710, 711
why family dwelling was considered indivisible property, 672, 717
See RESIDENCE

HOUSEHOLD GODS,
custody of, 716*m*
See IDOL

HUSBAND,
authority of—see ADOPTION V., 946, 947, 948
is guardian of his wife, 306, 506
takes gifts made to his wife by strangers, 279, 281
takes his wife's earnings, 279
even those by prostitution, 483
deserting wife must maintain her to the extent of one-third of his property, 556*w*
inherits, failing children, 140, 480—483, 508
wife's Stridhana if married according to the approved forms, 309*ss*, 484, 494
of "Pat" wife when inherits, 482
alienation by —— depriving his family or widow of subsistence is invalid, 235*g*, 1089

HUSBAND—*continued.*
so as to devise, 1021*s*
husband's brother's succession, 494
sapindas succeed to a female, 484*ss*

HUSBAND AND WIFE,
not generally capable of mutual contracts, 246*w*
See MARRIAGE

HUSBAND'S BHINNAGOTRA SAPINDAS. See SAPINDAS

HUSBAND'S BROTHER. See BROTHER-IN-LAW, 492, 494

HUSBAND'S BROTHER'S SON
inherits, 496
See ADOPTION IV., 914

HUSBAND'S BROTHER'S WIDOW, 497

HUSBAND'S COUSIN, 497, 498
excludes husband's sister's son, 499, 502
excludes husband's sister and son-in-law, 498

HUSBAND'S DISTANT KINSMEN, 500

HUSBAND'S HALF-BROTHER
inherits, 492, 495

HUSBAND'S INJUNCTION,
a widow may adopt husband's brother's son without ——, 914
See ADOPTION I.

HUSBAND'S PATERNAL UNCLE'S GREAT-GRANDSON, 499

HUSBAND'S PATERNAL UNCLE'S SON, 497, 499

HUSBAND'S RELATIVES,
as heirs to a woman, 493*ss*
extent of recognized connexion (Bengal), 505*f*
See STRIDHANA

HUSBAND'S SAPINDAS. See SAPINDAS OF THE HUSBAND, 141
See ADOPTION III.; FEMALE; WIDOW

HUSBAND'S SISTER
preferred to distant cousins, 503
inherits as a Sapinda, 504

HUSBAND'S SISTER-IN-LAW, 497

HUSBAND'S SISTER'S SON, 504
is excluded by husband's cousin, 498

HUSBAND'S SISTER'S SON'S SON, 504

HUSBAND'S UNCLE'S GREAT-GRANDSON, 499

HUSBAND'S UNCLE'S SON, 497

HYPOTHECATION. See ALIENATION; COPARCENER; DEBT; FATHER; MORTGAGE; WIDOW

IDIOT,
disqualified for inheritance, 141, 541, 544
when his idiotcy is congenital, 150
not disqualified for taking by conveyance, 748
See DISQUALIFICATION

IDOL,
ideal personality of —— recognized, 185*o*, 198
endowments of ——, 198
property dedicated to an ——, 160, 717
property subject to trust for —— partible, 681
custom as to distribution of ——s, 755
family ——s generally remain with the eldest, 716*m*
refusal to give up an —— for worship a cause of action, *ib.*
See CHARITY; ELDERSHIP; ENDOWMENT; PERPETUITY; PROPERTY; SACRED

IGNORANCE,
deprives acquiescence or consent of usual effect, 1076
inducing mistake in partition a ground for suit, 649*a*

IGNORANTIA LEGIS NON EXCUSAT,
discussed, 1075*ss*

ILLATAM, 398*h*, 399
See SON-IN-LAW

ILLEGAL DIRECTIONS AND TERMS (VOID).
See ADOPTION III., VI., VII.; GRANT; PARTITION; WILL

ILLEGITIMACY
is a disqualification to inherit among higher castes, but not among Sudras, 61, 69, 76, 129
See ILLEGITIMATE SON

ILLEGITIMATE BRAHMANA
takes only what his father gives to him, 444

ILLEGITIMATE BROTHERS. See BROTHERS

ILLEGITIMATE CHILDREN, 546, 547

ILLEGITIMATE DAUGHTER. See DAUGHTER, ILLEGITIMATE

ILLEGITIMATE GRANDSON. See GRANDSON, ILLEGITIMATE

ILLEGITIMATE GREAT-GRANDSON,
succession of —— of a Sudra, 69

ILLEGITIMATE SON,
sons of a European not a joint family, 4
of higher castes cannot claim inheritance, 149, 547
son superseded by adopted son, 1045
excluded from succession to a raj, 153
excluded from succession under Lombard law, 77*n*, 361*s*
once favoured by English law, 359*n*
of higher castes can claim maintenance only, 77, 193, 254, 369, 547
of higher castes can claim maintenance, but not as a charge on the property, 256
of a brother awarded maintenance, 546*r*
in higher castes a father may make a grant to ——, 256, 360, 547
irrevocable by after-born legitimate son, 547
Of Sudras
inherits, 69, 76, 77, 369, 392, 421
inherits collaterally by custom, 78
position of —— —— when recognized by his father, 78, 392
supposed to take equally with legitimates, 364
this questioned, *ib.*
inherits half a share if legitimates living, 76, 362
takes precedence of legitimate son's daughter, 361
assigned equal share with daughter, 472
takes the whole estate on failure of daughter's sons, 69, 362
a Sudra's right to disinherit —— limited, 366
illegitimate sons joint *inter se*, 364, 603
illegitimate sons may form a united family with legitimate half-brothers, 79, 364
son is entitled to half a share on partition, 712
to a full share at his father's choice, 362, 708
but not greater than a legitimate son's share, 362
See SON

IMAGE. See IDOL

IMITATION
of higher by lower castes, 402
of nature—see ADOPTION III., 845; IV., 920

IMMORALITY
of debt of father as affecting son's liability, 577*ss*, 595
son required to prove ——, 580, 596*l*

IMPARTIBILITY
not identical with inalienability, 154
principle excluding division on death applies to division by alienation, 154, 378
no ground for succession as to separate estate, 680
See ALIENATION, 681*f*

IMPARTIBLE PROPERTY. See PROPERTY, IMPARTIBLE

IMPEDIMENTS TO SUCCESSION. See DISQUALIFICATION

IMPLEMENTS. See TOOLS AND IMPLEMENTS

IMPOTENCE,
disqualifies for inheritance, 141, 541, 544, 551
as affecting capacity to adopt—see ADOPTION III., 848; DISQUALIFICATION, 541

IMPROVIDENCE,
of father, 581
See DEBT, 191, 656; INTERDICTION

IN EXTREMIS. See ADOPTION III., 847, 848

INALIENABILITY. See ALIENATION; ESTATE; IMPARTIBILITY; OWNERSHIP

INAM, 180
ranks generally as ordinary ancestral property, 377
is self-acquired property of individual grantee, 664, 666*l*, 667*o*
resumed and rebestowed held separate property, 666*l*
is generally partible, 377, 754
re-imposition of land-tax does not change estate, 666*l*
held subject to ordinary rules of succession, 765
inheritance and partition of an —— determined by the grant, 677*z*
settlement of —— on wife to exclusion of son? 734
See ESCHEAT; GRANT, 734; INTERPRETATION

INAMDAR
may have different rights under the same grant, 377
subject to rights previously created, 378
Inamdar's relation to tenants, 377

INCEST,
became revolting in Vedic times, 270*l*
child by —— has no right of inheritance, 546*r*
theoretical —— a bar to adoption, 920
See ADOPTION IV., 922

INCONTINENCE
annuls right to maintenance except of the wife and the mother, 555, 556
a ground of disinheritance in case of a widow, 553, 554

INCONTINENCE—*continued.*
but not for retraction, 554
of widow not a cause of forfeiture in Bengal, 249
effect of —— on the succession of mother, 554
of daughter, *ib.*
comparison of the English law, 554*f*
See FAMILY; UNCHASTITY, 554

INCONVENIENCE
of division *in specie* at partition considered, 626, 755, 757

INCREASE
of share effected by death of coparcener during pendency of suit for partition, 633
before partition, 633*z*
after partition, 632, 649*a*

INCUMBRANCE. See ALIENATION, 162; DEBT; ESTATE; FATHER; MORTGAGE; TRUST, 188; TRUSTEE, 521

INCURABLE DISEASE
is a disqualification to inherit, 149, 541
persons afflicted with —— must be maintained, 543

INDIGENCE
revives the claims of father and son to subsistence after partition, 723
of family to be guarded against in alienation, 1089
See ALIENATION; MAINTENANCE, 723

INDIVISIBLE PROPERTY. See PROPERTY, INDIVISIBLE

INFANTS,
exposure of —— in Greece and Rome, 209*s*
See AGE; GUARDIAN; MINOR

INFIRMITY
in body or mind disqualifies a person to inherit, 141, 142

INHERITANCE,
definition of ——, 51
customary law of —— may be changed, 3
law of —— not affected by emigration, *ib.*
determined by the law of the defendant, 5
as a source of property, 57
above individual will, 56, 178, 179
course of devolution not alterable by private agreement, 178
direction of a line of descent unknown to the law, inoperative, *ib.*
once regarded as impartible and inalienable, 261
and partition as viewed by Hindu lawyers, 561
distinguished from partition, 57

INHERITANCE—*continued.*
historical development of the law of ——, *ib.*
special rules of ——, 150*ss*
in tail male not known to Hindu law, 58
law of —— in what sense regulated by funeral oblations, 59
heir takes estate as a "universitas," 162
under Hindu law heir continues the person and family with which he has been identified, 56, 62*y*
under the Roman law, *ib.*
according to Vyav. May. is an inseparable aggregate of rights and obligations, 162, 164*o*
the rules of —— under Mitakshara come into operation only as to separate estate, 429
not postponed by pregnancy, 902
right to —— not extinguished by separation, 340
sub-divisions of the law of ——, 56, 57
obstructed and unobstructed, 60, 561, 656
right of succession arises as in partition on the death of propositus, 64
coparceners of the deceased; when they inherit, 70
no property of male to pass from family while a member survives, 487
by females. See CUSTOM; DAUGHTER; MOTHER; SISTER; STRIDHANA; WIDOW
collateral. See ADOPTION II., 838; VII.
disqualifications for —— enumerated, 541, 548, 549, 551
See DISQUALIFICATION
son previously adopted by one becoming disqualified to be provided for, 1056
in cases of inalienability, 297
to Bhagdari and Narvadari lands governed by Hindu law and custom, 686
in Gujarat males preferred to females, 407
burdens on ——, 160*ss*
through females, 608*h*
See FEMALE GENTILESHIP
debts not prodigally contracted, 192
to Females
sister preferred to husband's sister, 312
son by first husband preferred to second husband's family, 312, 313
Mitakshara to be harmonised in the island of Bombay, 13
to Ascetics. See ASCETIC; PRECEPTOR
See ADOPTION III., 840, 845, 848, 887, 902; VI., 963, 979; VII., 1023, 1050, 1062; BRAHMACHARI; BROTHER; DESCENT; DEVOLUTION; EMIGRATION, 3; NAISHTHIKA; SUCCESSION

INITIATION, 830*i*
of a Jangama, 532
in relation to adoption, 1010*z*, 1060*w*
to be provided for out of joint property, 691*i*, 747
See MARRIAGE, 940

INSANE, INSANITY,
does not necessarily prevent marriage, 817
of the son born with respect to adoption, *ib.*

INSANE, INSANITY—*continued.*
disqualifies for inheriting, 141, 541, 544, 545
and for share in partition, 626
but does not cause forfeiture, 545
See ADOPTION III., 844, 846, 847, 856; V., 953; DISQUALIFICATION 541, 545

INSENSIBLE. See ADOPTION III., 846, 847

INSTRUMENTS
executed under disturbing influences void by Hindu law, 595, 597
See ADOPTION; DEED, 630; DOCUMENTS, 1007; GRANT; INTERPRETATION; REGISTRATION; WILL

INTELLIGENCE. See ADOPTION III., 846, 847

INTENTION,
unequivocal, of partition constitutes partition, 765, 776

INTERDICTION
son's right of —— against waste, 193*a*, 594, 658*w*, 737
by adopted son, 1030
by coparcener against sale by another allowed in Madras? 652*w*

INTEREST,
compound —— not disapproved by Hindu law, 685*e*
utmost —— recoverable = the principal (damdupat), *ib.*
rule of damdupat applies to some mortgages, 718*v*
when the defendant is a Hindu, 718
may be turned into principal by a new account, 685*e*
vested. See ADOPTION III., 898

INTERPRETATION,
principles of ——, 6, 13, 257*k*, 707
to be consistent with texts, 16*p*
of texts, 197*d*
governed by custom, 787
every text must be given effect to if possible, 116
when different objects are included in a class by different Smritis the class is to embrace all, 260*i*
of texts influenced by philosophical systems, 8, 116, 257*k*
rules of ——, 16*p*, 184
etymological preferred to technical, 137
equitable —— approved, 756
according to the reason of the law, 702
"Dikpradarsana" or extension of a rule to analogous cases, 100, 505, 785
strained analogies to be avoided, 197*d*
contradictions in Hindu law books, how settled, 14*k*
discrepancies in sacred writings must be reconciled, 781*i*, 759*g*
inference by reasoning to be preferred to the assumption of a plurality of revelations, 781*i*

INTERPRETATION—*continued.*
of a special rule when a general one exists, 759*g*
Smritis are construed by reference to the one taken as a subject of commentary, 260*i*
where a particular purpose is assigned as a ground for a permission this implies a prohibition where the purpose is already attained, 815*e*
of Mitakshara, 19
meaning of half-a-share, 69
rules of —— by the Courts, 788
governed by decisions, 789
to be drawn from within the Hindu law, 197*d*
of private documents, 435
actual notions of Hindus to be adverted to, 620
according to the situation of the parties, 713*x*
extensive —— of document showing family custom of succession, 682
words indicating males may include females, 620
repugnant provisions void, 696
and those imposing restrictions disapproved by the law, *ib.*
See AGREEMENT; PARTITION; PROPERTY
instruments are construed so as to express something legal according to Hindu law, 183, 184
of a deed allotting money, &c., to a widow according to situation of parties, 713*x*
of gift by husband to wife, 185, 287*w*, 297*c*, 305*q*, 984
of gift to sister with words of limitation, 184
of grant to a widow and other heirs, 285*q*
of the words "aulad aflad," 184*f*
of wills and testamentary instruments, 183, 184, 219, 222, 223, 618*x*
will construed as a family settlement, 184
of "putra paotradi krame," 224, 620
of "mrityu patras," 217
See CUSTOM, FAMILY, 690; EQUITY; GRANT, 184f, 435, 664; HINDU LAW; SMRITI; TEXT; WILL

INTERPRETERS,
of ceremonial law, 48

INVESTITURE,
age of, 940*z*
rites of ——, 942*p*
See ADOPTION III., 810*n*; IV., 921; VI. 992, 997, 998

INVESTMENT,
to be made to secure maintenance of widow, 697
of concubine, 698*r*

INVOCATION. See ADOPTION IV., 910; VI., 957

IRISH LAW, ANCIENT,
as to property retained undivided in partition, 671*d*

IZAFATDAR,
not a proprietor, 664*b*

JAGIR, 175, 180
jagirs are grants of the revenues, 175
are impartible, *ib.*, 683*z*
holder of —— can make a grant for his own life, 664*b*
resumable at pleasure of the sovereign, 175
an exception to the rule of devolution, 180
devolves according to the character of the grant, 677*z*
succession to a —— by primogeniture, 683*z*
See SARANJAM, 683

JAINS,
divided into Yatis, devotees, and Sravakas, 533
deny the authority of Vedas, *ib.*
are Pashandas, *ib.*
have no kriya ceremonies, 932*k*
sraddha or paksha ceremonies, 812*h*
are subject to Hindu law of inheritance in the absence of special custom, 152, 827
See ADOPTION III., 850, 869; IV., 925

JALA SANKALPA, 989, 995

JANGAMA,
Jangamas are Lingayat priests, 532
are married in some mathas, 533
heirs to a ——, 532
the head —— appoints his successor, 533

JANGAMA-DIKSHA, 532

JATAKARMA
= birth ceremony, 936*ss*

JATI,
heirs to——, 533
See YATI

JATS. See TRIBES, 270*l*, 394, 400*z*

JEWELS,
possession of —— does not affect widow's right to maintenance, 692*m*
See ORNAMENTS; PARTITION, 204, 294*m*

JNATI. See ADOPTION III., 898

JOGTIN, 494

JOINDER,
all interested in pressing a claim must be joined in a suit, 567*g*
and in a demand, *ib.*
comparison of English law, 570*s*

JOINT FAMILY. See FAMILY

JOINT LESSORS
must jointly re-enter, 567*g*

JOINT OBLIGATIONS
are indivisible, 672

JOINT TENANCY (ENGLISH),
difference between —— and Hindu joint estate, 562*h*
See BRETHREN; COPARCENERS

JOINT-TENANT
severs by sale, 651*h*
See TENANT, JOINT, 621*a*

JOSHI VATAN. See VATAN, 556

JOSHI VATANDAR,
may recover damages from an intruder, 377
presumed to be entitled to officiate in a particular family, 378
may be compelled to perform his duties, *ib.*

JUDGMENT,
on a contested adoption not *in rem*, 1082
not evidence where parties are different, *ib.*
See ADOPTION VIII. 1082; RES JUDICATA

JUDGMENT-CREDITOR
of coparcener can demand partition, 565, 609, 615
See BROTHER; COPARCENER; CREDITOR

JURISDICTION, 233, 234
of the Courts is recognized over any question that the caste cannot settle, 899*a*
See ADOPTION VIII., 1067; HINDU LAW; OBLIGATION, 813

KABIR, 537

KALAVANTIN. See ADOPTION II., 834k; III., 907; IV., 945

KALIYUG. See ADOPTION V., 956

KAMALAKARA,
author of the Nirnayasindhu, 23
in what estimation his writings are held, *ib.*

KAMALAKARA—*continued.*
his parentage, *ib.*
his writings and date, 24

KANAM MORTGAGE, 272*w*

KANARA,
mortgage in ——, 672*k*
assent of the village community formerly taken to a grant in ——, 672*k*

KANGRA DISTRICT. See TRIBES, 358
extra share of eldest son in ——, 733*g*

KANINA, 805

KANOJI CASTE, 330

KANPHATA GOSAVI, 527

KARNAVAM. See MANAGER, 569*p*

KARTA,
position of ——, 701
alienation by —— on whom binding, 592*k*
See MANAGER

KARTA PUTRA
= Kritrima son, 956
See ADOPTION V., 956; KRITRIMA

KASINATHA,
author of the Dharmasindhu, 25

KATHIS. See TRIBES, 269*i*

KATYAYANA, 950
Smriti of ——, 44

KEPT WOMAN. See CONCUBINE, 365

KHALSAT LAND, 764

KHANDOBA, 489*p*

KHASIAS. See TRIBES, 274*f*, 276*m*, 398

KHOJAS,
governed by the Hindu law of inheritance unless special custom proved, 152, 153, 559*a*

KHOLLS. See TRIBES, 269*i*, 270*n*

KHONDS. See TRIBES, 358

KHOT,
managing, limit of his powers, 571

KHOTI ESTATE,
normal condition of, 641
usually enjoyed in parts without partition, *ib.*
does not imply ownership of village lands, 664*b*

KINDRED. See KINSMEN; FEMALE-GENTLESHIP

KING,
the ultimate guardian of infants, 506
when inherits as *ultimus heres*, 125, 129, 359, 390, 532, 546
must show failure of heirs, 129, 507
must support females and pay funeral charges, 359, 507
See ESCHEAT

KINSMEN,
kinsmen's gifts to a woman, 486*m*
consent of —— validating alienation by a widow, 90
assent of —— necessary to adoption by a widow, 827*s*, 871, 896
remote —— postponed to sisters, 430, 436
See ADOPTION III., 852, 870, 881, 895*ss*

KOCHES. See TRIBES, 269*i*, 398; FEMALE-GENTILESHIP

KOLAMBI CASTE, 375*x*

KOSHA ORDEAL
not resorted to at the present day, 703

KRISHNARPANA,
gift in ——, 91, 285*n*, 327
by mother without consent of son invalid, 1035

KRITA
= the son bought, 805, 807*w*, 1064
adoption now disallowed, 807, 961
See ADOPTION VI., 1008, 1046

KRITRIMA
= orphan taken with his own consent, 805
son = karta putra, 956
still recognized in Maithila, 806
See ADOPTION III., 907; IV., 945; VI., 990, 1008, 1011*d*; VII., 1062; KARTA-PUTRA; SON, 805

KRIYA. See JAINS, 932*k*; FUNERAL CEREMONY
all sons liable for father's ——, 686*h*

KSHATRIYAS,
a division of Hindus, 61
said to have disappeared, 825*i*
Gandharva form of marriage lawful for ——, 481
may become Sannyasis, 518
See ADOPTION IV., 934; VI., 1002*x*

KSHETRAJA
= son begotten by an appointed kinsman, 691*d*, 805
placed by Yajn. next to appointed daughter's son, 396
still recognized by custom in Orissa, 516*a*, 786
See SON, 893

KULACHARA
= family custom, 151*o*, 699
operation of ——, 153, 679
See CUSTOM, FAMILY

KULADHARMA
= worship of the tutelary deity, 773*x*

KULKARNI. See VATAN, 336, 413, 456, 477

KUNABI CASTE, 338, 342, 393, 403, 471, 483, 498, 530, 767

LABHA, 259, 279

LAGNA WIFE. See WIFE

LAKSHMIDEVI. See BALAMBHATTATIKA

LAMENESS
disqualifies for inheritance, 141, 541
taking on partition, 747
gives a title to maintenance, 543

LAND,
property in —— and modes of holding it discussed, 169*ss*, 672*ss*

LANDLORD AND TENANT,
relation of —— not altered by omission to take rent, 1083
occupier and superior not always in this relation, 643, 644

LAPSE. See GRANT; FORFEITURE, 83, 102, 404, 406, 430, 535, 542, 545, 553, 554

LAUGAKSHI SMRITI, 45

LAVAJIMA OR LAJIMA ALLOWANCE, 323

LAW,
power of Mohammedans to convey not measured by Hindu law, 6
applicable dependent on personal status, 4
the Greeks and the Romans regarded their ——s as of divine origin, 49*b*
See HINDU LAW

LAW, CEREMONIAL, *ib.*

LAW, CUSTOMARY. See ADOPTION I., 792; IV., 944; CUSTOM

LAW OF DEFENDANT, 7

LAW, ETHICAL, 49*b*

LAW, FAMILY,
annexes defined duties to fixed relations, 973*b*
does not leave them to free volition, 976
basis of right to support. See MAINTENANCE
See CUSTOM, FAMILY

LAW, HINDU. See HINDU LAW

LAW, MOSAIC, 49*a*
See MOSAIC LAW

LAW, MUNICIPAL,
its source in the religious law, *ib.*

LAW, ROMAN. See ADOPTION V., 955*e*; VII., 1052*e*, 1058*c*; ROMAN LAW

LAW, SOCIAL, 49*a*

LAW-OFFICERS,
importance of their opinions, 2, 3, 785
their testimony with respect to the authorities of the Hindu law, 13
See PANDITS; SASTRIS

LEGALITY OF PARTITION, 760—767
See PARTITION

LEPROSY,
disqualifies for performance of religious acts, 950
for inheriting, 149, 526, 544
for partition, 629
See ADOPTION III., 847, 891; V. 950; DISQUALIFICATION

LESSEE,
rights of —— under a member holding in severalty, 711
from the manager not discharged by receipt from another member, 569
See TENANT

LEVIRATE,
once general in India, 394
but now forbidden, 395
sprang from polyandry, 396
reason of its prevalence, 792
still practised by some Brahmanas, 396*v*
in the North of India, 399
and amongst some of the lower castes and in Orissa, 807
Thiyens, 397*z*
in Spiti, *ib.*
in Rohtak, *ib.*
gradual disappearance of ——, 794
traces of the former prevalence of ——, 795
amongst the Jews, 397

LEX LOCI,
want of —— replaced in cases of succession by that of the person, 4

LEX VOCONIA, 435*b*

LIABILITY—IES
on inheritance how distributed, 684, 721
distribution of debts in partition, 718
includes common debts, 684
provision for the maintenance of relations of a deceased coparcener, 721, 685
liabilities distributable on partition, 684, 698
liability in partition for assets does not arise till they are realized, 699*t*
of ancestral property for debts not affected by birth of a son, 166
of impartible zamindari for payment of father's debts, 163*y*
so as to an hereditary polliam, 166
of the heir under a decree against the last holder, 163
for contribution, 718*x*
See PARTITION, 721

LIFE-INTEREST. See ADOPTION VI., 981; VII., 1020; FEMALE; STRIDHANA; WIDOW

LIMITATION,
under Hindu law, 640*d*, 645
comparison of Roman Law, 644*z*
an executor may pay a barred debt, 572*l*
a representative not bound to plead —— whenever he can do so, 572
barred debts may be set off against claims on an estate, 572*l*, 689
does not operate on a part reserved in partition, 648
effect of —— on the right to claim partition, 644, 650*d*
to suit for partition under Act XIV. of 1859, 642
under Act IX. of 1871, 631*t*, 650*d*
under Act XV. of 1877, 636*n*, 6, 642*t*, 644, 650*d*
under Act IX. of 1908, 645, 972, 1073

LIMITATION—*continued.*
in case of partition account limited to three years before suit, 699*v*
exclusive enjoyment for 12 years bars a suit, 642
period of attachment by Government excluded, 642*r*
where property is not available for partition —— does not operate except through exclusive possession subsequently, 648
in case of maintenance, time computed from refusal, 698
as to Malikana and Hakks, 706
in cases of adoption, 672, 1084
a suit barred as to some necessary parties is barred as to all, 573
though instituted by others within time, *ib.*
See ADOPTION VIII., 1084, 1085; POSSESSION, 644*z*

LIMITATION ACTS,
The Indian —— XV. of 1859, IX. of 1871, XV. of 1877, IX. of 1908, see separate List

LIMITATIONS OF PROPERTY, 169*ss*
repugnant —— disallowed, 182
See PROPERTY

LINGAYATS, 342, 394, 477
transformed to Vaisyas, 1002*x*
may adopt sister's or daughter's son, 917, 924
See ADOPTION III., 8501; IV., 916, 927, 932; JANGAMAS, 532

LIS PENDENS, 635*k*

LITIGATION,
application of Hindu law to ——, 1
between Hindus and others in the Supreme Court governed by Stat. XXI. Geo. III. c. 70, 5

LIVING APART,
a sign of separation, 603*ss*, 636, 637

LOCUS PŒNITENTIÆ,
in adoption, 960

LOMBARD LAW,
compared with Hindu law, 77*n*, 361

LOSS OF CASTE,
disqualifies for inheriting, 149, 541, 544, 551
for partition, 629
See DISQUALIFICATION; EXCLUSION; OUTCAST

LUNACY. See ADOPTION III., 844, 851, 890, 891; DISQUALIFICATION; INSANITY, 194, 544*ss*

MADNESS,
disqualifies for inheritance, 141, 541
See DISQUALIFICATION, 541; INSANE

MAGNA CHARTA,
provision in favour of infant heir as to debts, 578a
preference of dower to debts, 685f

MAHANT, 519
cannot say who shall succeed his own successor, 179r
there cannot be two existing ——s, 524

MAHANTSHIP,
succession to ——, 521w
not disposable by way of reversion, 521w, 524
obtained sometimes by wandering chelas, 537s
See GOSAVIS, 525; ASCETIC; MANAGER

MAHAR CASTE, 339, 353, 416

MOHAMMEDAN RULE
effect of —— on Hindu law, 196

MAIDEN. See ADOPTION III., 854, 855
succession to her stridhana, 470, 471
See MARRIAGE; SISTER; STRIDHANA

MAINTENANCE,
the obligation rests according to Hindu law on relationship, 231, 241
not on contract, 402p
but springs from jural relations of the parties, 237, 254, 402p
originally contemplated only as subsistence in the family (see below), 231, 248
not dependent on ancestral estate, 237, 238, 243
a different view held by the Smriti Chandrika, 242
modified only by property, 232, 237, 247
the right to —— is not strictly an interest in the estate, 246, 250, 251, 693
or a charge on it? 244, 245, 254
duty of —— annexed to the estate wrongly taken, 242, 243o,
the right to —— cannot be attached, 251, 287x
nor assigned, or released, or defeated, 191, 246, 250, 254, 287x
of family must be provided for, 215, 240, 242, 244, 1089
discussion as to mode, 215
head of family bound to afford —— to the members, 225, 229, 237, 243, 244, 255, 603, 694z
where primogeniture prevails junior members entitled to ——, 65, 66, 254.
See APPANAGE
of wife by husband, 225, 553ss
claim of mother or wife to —— not extinguished by allotment to her of a share, 723

MAINTENANCE—*continued.*
a wife deserting her husband not entitled to separate ——, 401, 554, 555
divorced woman not entitled to ——, 554, 556*v*
of dependants not to be evaded by disposal of property, 244, 245, 254, 594
of family to be provided for before alienation, 601*x*, 1089
gift of whole estate is subject to ——, 191, 254, 373
wife not to be deprived of —— by husband's alienation, 254, 372
nor by his devise, 242, 244, 254, 1021*s*
children, grandchildren, widow and concubine entitled to —— against terms of a will, 193
purchaser with notice of widow's right to —— bound, 75
right and duty co-extensive with (united) family, 239—241
including widow and daughters of pre-deceased son, 239, 240, 242, 690, 693*r*, 696
ruled *contra* in N. W. Provinces, 243
of son's widow a claim arising from family relation, 240, 242, 694*t*
widow of adopted son entitled to ——, 1063
Bombay law discussed, 694*t*
one member of a joint family not entitled to —— at the hands of others, 603
his right to —— arises through disability to inherit, 603, 689*ss*
necessary —— exceeding the share of the person to be made up by relatives, 544
persons excluded from inheritance and partition entitled to ——, 241, 543*ss*, 629
adopted son of one who becomes disqualified entitled to —— if not to a share, 1056
of a widow, 163, 712*w*
widow entitled to — from her husband's family, 64, 75, 191, 227, 228, 250 606*w*
but not if living apart without sufficient cause, 225, 237, 255, 555*t*, 694
of a widow preferred by Sastris to other claims, 685*f*
but not by the Courts, *ib.*
comparison of English law, *ib.*
widow's right to —— is a personal right, 250, 287
it is a mere inchoate right, 191
usually provided for by allotment, 694
sum may be invested to produce ——, 75
a sum given to a widow in lieu of —— is at her disposal, 295
widow's right to —— taken away by partition, 230, 689
how satisfied, 247, 697
not impaired by her withdrawal from the family, 252, 694
not to be reduced on account of vexatious defence, 697*l*
cannot be attached or sold in execution, 251, 287*r*, 697
arrears of widow's —— may be awarded, 253, 697
proper amount of —— of widow, 254
may be awarded for the future, *ib.*, 693*r*
is subject to variation if necessary, *ib.*, 257, 692
decree for —— of widow may be made a charge, *ib.*, 545
separate —— to widow when allowed, 248, 252, 693
widow's right to —— not subject to an agreement with her husband, 75, 191

MAINTENANCE—*continued.*
may be awarded in a suit for a share, 256
unchaste widow not entitled to ——, 555
allowance assigned for —— of widow resumable in case of unchastity, *ib.*
concubine is entitled to ——, 75, 164, 193, 392, 556, 606*w*, 690
but not out of a saranjam, 698*r*
woman marrying without divorce and without first husband's consent entitled to —— as concubine, 556
son entitled to —— where father holds impartible property, 603
adult son entitled to —— only in extreme want, 255, 1089
illegitimate children entitled to ——, 75, 255
of higher castes entitled to ——, 77
daughter entitled to ——, 64
withdrawing without cause not entitled to ——, 556
parents and children mutually entitled to ——, 255, 303
of father to be first provided for, 603
of step-mothers, 229
of sister incumbent on brother, 238
till her marriage, 412
right to —— of children of deceased relatives in Punjab, 694*t*
right to —— of relatives disqualified and females, 689, 690
of wives and widows of the former, 690
of eunuchs, 690*a*
of lunatics, &c., *ib.*
limitation for a claim to ——, 252
time computed from demand and refusal of ——, 698
See ADOPTION VII., 1026, 1027, 1028, 1033, 1038, 1058; ALIENATION; ASSIGNMENT; FAMILY; WIDOW; WIFE, 193

MAJORITY,
general age of —— now eighteen, 76*i*
See ADOPTION III. 846, 859*x*; VI., 976; AGE.

MALE,
males have alone full coparcenery rights, 605
male offspring a restraint on alienation, 740*h*
male's rights arise immediately on birth, 607
or adoption, 1010*ss*
succession to ——s, 56*ss*

MALI CASTE, 360, 361, 493

MALRI CASTE, 535

MANBHAU, 531, 536

MANBHAVINI, 536

MANAGER,
joint family usually represented in external transactions by a managing member, 568

MANAGER—*continued.*
right of —— rests on the consent of the members, 568, 701
father is naturally the —— of a joint family, 568, 593
during his life and capacity for affairs, *ib.*
afterwards the eldest member qualified, *ib.*
elder brother may take the management unless others dissent, *ib.*
widow —— for an infant, 570
See MINOR.
position of a ——, 568, 701
power of a ——, 169
may discharge the religious obligation of the family out of its estate, 572
can bind the estate and family by transactions for the benefit of the family, 568, 574, 590, 592*k*
or with assent, 591, 688
or for what the creditor reasonably thinks to be for its benefit, 606
may deal with the capital of family firm, 592*k*
may enter into partnership with a stranger, 571
may carry on family business for its benefit, 691
may mortgage common property for common benefit, 590
may incumber or sell for necessities, 570, 687
can pledge property for the ordinary purposes of ancestral trade, 571
his gains and losses fall on joint estate, 703*f*
authority of —— to acknowledge a debt, 94, 571
not at liberty to pay out of the estate father's debts barred by limitation? 571
nor can he revive a claim against family barred by limitation?, *ib.*, 572
presumption in favour of his transactions, 592
especially in case of a father, 593
general liability of members for his acts (Bombay), 574, 591, 688*s*
transactions with a member only supposed to be a manager acting for the common interest upheld, 570, 591
transactions of —— bind one who consciously takes the benefit, 568, 575, 592*k*
lessee from —— not discharged by a receipt for rent passed to him by another member, 569
authority of —— to be liberally construed, 168, 173, 590
limitations on the authority of a ——, 570*ss*, 590
in Bombay, 593
a managing Khot has not authority to give up important rights vested in the members generally, 571
manager's act obviously prejudicial invalid, 593
fraudulent contracts by —— rescindible, 572, 591
alienee from —— bound to reasonable care and inquiry, 591, 688*s*
of minor's estate, 574, 590*o*
bound to guard interests of infants, 579*a*, 591
not a trustee? 701
powers of widow and mother as ——, 570, 571, 572
payment to mother as —— held to bind the son, *ib.*, 575
manager's liability to account limited, 592*k*, 699*t*
his liability for assets does not arise before realization, 699*t*

MANAGER—*continued.*
cannot claim for disbursements in excess of his proper share, 592*k*
in suits represents the whole family, 573, 591, 688*s*
in suits exceptionally another member perhaps may represent the whole family, 591
to bind minor co-sharer in a suit must, it seems, have a certificate of administration*, 625, 701*e*
decree and sale against —— alone affects only his own share, 574, 583*v*, 591, 651, 652
deceased ——'s interest not assets for satisfaction of a decree against him, 585
Karnavam (or manager) of a Malabar Tarwad, 569*p*
certificate to collect debts refused to him if a debtor of the deceased, *ib.*
of an endowment cannot impose rules on his successor, 199
See ADMINISTRATOR; COPARCENER; FAMILY; JOINT; FATHER; MOTHER; WIDOW.

MANASAPUTRA, 829*b*

MANAVA DHARMASASTRA, 29, 36

MANES OF ANCESTORS, 957, 958

MANNER AND LEGALITY OF PARTITION, 754—770

MANTRAS, 33, 43*r*, 791c

MANU. See SEPARATE LIST OF THE HINDU AUTHORITIES.

MANU SMRITI, 32
its age, 42

MARATHA CASTE, 480, 493

MARRIAGE,
is a Samskara strongly enjoined, 790*y*
of a girl a duty of the father, 747
age of ——, 790*y*
is the only sacrament for a man of the servile class, 942*p*
the prevailing idea of ——, 403*v*
governed by customary law, 84
mere apostasy does not free from the Hindu law of ——? 226, 559*a*
is the origin of special rights and duties, 403
not susceptible of a condition of nullity, 187*b*
not prevented by insanity, 817
of Hindu children is a contract made by their parents, *ib.*

---

* Administrator as next friend or guardian. On this subject see *Murlidhar and Vasudev* v. *Supdu and Balkrishna*, I. L. R. 3 Bom. 149; and *Jadow Mulji* v. *Chhagan Raichand*, I. L. R. 5 Bom. 306.

MARRIAGE—*continued.*
between persons of different castes possible only by caste laws, 403*t*
unequal —— possible according to Viramitrodaya, 77*n*
jus connubii between many pairs of castes, 403*t*
laxity of —— amongst Sudras, 401*l*
its ill effects the same as amongst the Romans, *ib*
contract (purchase) in China, 266*w*
of Sudras remote from Brahmanical conception, 401
looked upon as licensed concubinage, 81
treated with contempt, 922
and easily dissolved, 400, 922
not governed by Smriti law, 401
relations amongst the wild tribes and low castes discussed, 357*ss*
in some tribes not attended with change of family, 272
Roman *matrimonium sine conventione*, 272*v*
prohibited degrees of —— on father's side to 7th, on mother's to 5th, 459*i*
with maternal uncle's daughter allowed by custom in the Dekhan, &c., 786, 801
with sister's daughter common in the South, 919
out of the tribe entails expulsion in Punjab, 399*l*
gift and acceptance necessary to ——, 960
higher forms of —— formerly not allowed to Sudras, 80
Asura —— makes the wife only a dasi or concubine, 81
per verba de præsenti compared with the Gandharva, 266*w*
forms of —— as affecting succession, 503, 505
Arsha, 265, 481, 484, 486
Asura, 266, 268, 269, 273, 274, 481, 484, 486, 494, 503
Brahma, 481, 484, 486, 494
Daiva, *ib.*
Gandharva, *ib.*
Kshatra, 269*h*
Paisacha, 484
Prajapatya, 481, 484, 486
Rakshasa, 269, *ib.*
Svayamvara, 271
customs, 268, 269, 272
is the fullest initiation, 940
initiates wife in husband's family, 85, 120, 225
wife's legal existence is absorbed in husband's, 86
effect of —— by approved rites on the woman, 140
by —— property acquired by wife becomes her husband's, 85
exceptions—see STRIDHANA
effect of —— on wife's property in Germany and England, 284*f*
ceremony cannot be dissolved by contract, 402
effect of —— between relatives or persons of different castes, 790*y*
effect of omission to recite the mantras properly on ——, *ib.*
possibility of legal —— between the adopter and the mother of the adopted necessary, 921
See ADOPTION IV., 941, 942, 943; VII., 1025, 1043; DEGREES PROHIBITED; EARNINGS; EXPENDITURE, 691*i*, 713; HUSBAND;

MARRIAGE—*continued.*
MAINTENANCE; REMARRIAGE; RIGHTS, CONJUGAL; WIFE; WIDOW

MARRIAGE EXPENSES. See PARTITION, 713
of brothers and sisters to be provided for in partition, 713, 714, 747
the Smriti Chandrika imposes the charge independently of estate, 714*a*

MARRIAGE PORTION,
provision for —— —— on partition, 685, 689
daughters of deceased coparceners entitled to —— ——, 470*q*, 690, 691
share given to a sister in a partition is only a —— ——, 288

MARRIAGE SETTLEMENT, 372
of land on daughter in the Punjab, 271*q*
trousseau in the S. M. Country, 277*o*
See MARRIAGE PORTION; PALLA

MARRIED FEMALES,
having issue. See FEMALES
without issue. See FEMALES

MARWADI CASTE, 358, 428, 434

MATERNAL AUNT. See AUNT, MATERNAL

MATERNAL AUNT'S SON. See AUNT'S (MATERNAL) SON

MATERNAL UNCLE. See UNCLE, MATERNAL

MATERNAL UNCLE'S SON, 192, 457, 462
heir to married female, 512, 513

MATHA,
origin of ——s discussed, 523
custom regulates matters concerning ——s, 517, 523
should pass to disciple nominated by Guru, 522

MEMONS (CUTCHI),
governed by the Mahomedan law, 4, 5, 597*a*
but as to inheritance generally by Hindu law, *ib.*

MENTAL INCAPACITY. See FATHER, 193*a*, 203; IDIOT; INSANE

MERCHANT,
succession to a ——, 125, 126, 128, 129

MINOR, MINORITY
now ceases at 18 years by Act IX. of 1875, 622*f*
not answerable for father's debts during minority, 719*e*

MINOR, MINORITY—*continued.*
uninitiated may perform funeral rites, 1088
but not otherwise recite Vedic formulas (Manu II. 172), *ib.*
See Age.
position of a —— in partition analogous to that of absentee, 623
minor's rights in partition, 622*ss*
his assent to a partition is not necessary, 623
guardian of a —— cannot enforce partition against the will of the adult coparceners, 624, 741
except to prevent jeopardy to the minor's interests, 624
represented by guardian in partition, 622
bound by such partition, 741
minor's interests to be respected by manager and those dealing with him, 591
interests of—— to be protected by the sovereign, 623
the Minors Act for Bombay is Act XX. of 1864, 622*f*
See too Act IX. of 1861
this not superseded by the provisions of the Civil Procedure Code, *ib.*
whether property of a —— in an undivided family is subject to the provisions of the Minors Act (XX. of 1864), *ib.*, 624
not generally subject to separate administration, any one may come forward as a next friend to a ——*, 624*h*
a relative to be preferred, *ib.*
administrators of ——'s estate, 622*f*
bound by guardian's beneficial transactions, 622*f*
and by a suit brought by or against a legally representative member of joint family†, 591
remedy of a —— against manager, 702
unfairly used in a partition may repudiate it on attaing majority, 625
See Family; Father; Guardian; Manager; Representation, 653*y*

MIRAS, MIRASDAR, 177, 178, 672*k*

MIRAS, MIRASDARS,
could in theory reclaim their lands at any time, 177
their present position, 178

MIRAS, MIRASDAS',
assent formerly necessary for admission to ownership within their village, 672*k*

MIRAS TENURE,
compared with customary tenancies in England, 178*f*

MISREPRESENTATION,
deprives consent of usual effect, 1076, 1078

* *Kalidas Ravidat* v *Pranshankar Jibhai*, Bom. H. C. P. J. 1884, p. 8.
† *Gan Savant* v. *Narayan Dhond Savant*, I. L. R. 7 Bom. 467

MISTAKE. See IGNORANCE, 1075

MITAKSHARA,
where paramount, 12
is the commentary of Vijnanesvara on Yajnavalkya, 15
on payment of father's debts, 1087*ss*
on power of alienation of a paterfamilias, 1088
See ADOPTION *passim*; separate List of Hindu Authorities

MITRAMISRA,
the author of Viramitrodaya, 22

MOHANT. See MAHANT

MOHATUR WIDOW, 361

MONEY LENDING,
inter se by coparceners conclusive of partition? 636

MORAL DEFICIENCIES,
persons labouring under —— disqualified from inheriting, 149

MORGENGABE, 267, 268*z*
confused with dower, 268*a*

MORTGAGE,
not sale —— allowed by ancient law, 195, 672
accompanied by possession, *ib.*
requires assent of all coparceners, 747
except those absent and in case of emergency, 588, 672, 747
See COPARCENER; ALIENATION
by son is subject to maintenance of mother and marriage expenses of sister, 752*b*
coparceners liable *inter se* in proportion to shares, 720
a single coparcener may redeem the whole, *ib.*
and hold —— as security for contribution, *ib.*
all sharers to be served with notice, *ib.*
mortgagee's remedy lies against any share, 721
a sale in execution of a decree on a —— must embrace the whole interest, 720
attachment and sale not necessary to give effect to the lien, 584*a*
by father in Madras: all sons must be joined in suit, 584
in Kanara, 672*k*
See KANARA
redeemable for ever, *ib.*
so (formerly) in Norway, *ib.*

MORTGAGEE,
may refuse redemption of part, 720
must serve all co-sharers with notice of foreclosure, *ib.*

MORTGAGEE—*continued.*
in execution must sell the mortgagor's and his own interest, *ib*
See ALIENATION; MORTGAGE, 721

MOSAIC LAW,
mixed up things spiritual and temporal, 49*b*
compared with the Hindu law, *ib.*

MOTHER,
does not include step-mother, 102
never outcast to son, 555
preferred as guardian to father, 338, 413
See GUARDIAN
as manager cannot alienate without necessity, 570
must be maintained, 556*w*
is entitled to maintenance out of the family property, 751
mother's claim to separate maintenance when allowed, 1038*r*
claim of —— to support not extinguished by allotment to her of a share, 723
whether deprived of her right to residence by a sale of the family house, 674, 751
when inherits, 101, 421*ss*, 425, 428
though separate, 422
postponed to father by the Vyav. May. in Gujarat, 102, 421
succeeds to her daughter, 508, 509
inheriting from son takes absolutely? may not alien, 287*w*, 295, 296, 424
takes precedence over widow amongst Khojas, 152
and by custom in Gujarat, 152, 372, 383
but not allowed to dispose of the estate, 152
of a Girasia is entitled to the Girasi hakks by succession, 421
postponed to son in collateral line, 463*w*
but not in a succession devolving through her, *ib.*
mother's estate, 439
similar to that taken by a widow, 102, 287*w*, 422, 424
devolution of property inherited by ——, 436
property inherited through —— by a son once held to devolve in her line? 463
inheritance to —— is rather by succession than survivorship, 656*n*
in Punjab among some tribes property inherited through —— excluded from partition, *ib.*
not so among others, *ib.*
See PROPERTY, SEPARATE AND SELF-ACQUIRED, 656
son regarded by Vyav. Mayukha perhaps as having an unobstructed right of inheritance to his ——'s Aparibhashika Stridhana, 285*n*
but not said to be joint-owner by birth, 656*n*
whether such property taken by him is ancestral, 658
the Mitakshara does not recognize a joint ownership of mother and son, 135, 285*n*, 656*n*
nor does the Smriti Chandrika, 285*n*
children cannot demand partition of ——'s property in her life, 749
mother's assent to partition required by several castes, 605*t*, 612, 614*q*

MOTHER—*continued.*
cannot demand partition, 710*g*, 749
except as guardian for her son, 755
is entitled to a share in a partition, 710, 741, 749*ss*
mother's right to specific allotment arises when partition is made, 605*t*
limitation of her share, 606*x*
under what conditions —— takes a share, 386, 605*v*, 709*d*
mother's share equal to a son's in partition, 709*b*, 714, 745*b*, 749
share taken by —— in a partition is only a means of subsistence (Smr. Chand.), 288, 715
mother's power of disposal over share given her on partition, 713*x*, 749, 1036
cannot, by adoption, divest her son's widow's estate, 92, 880
remarriage of —— as affecting her right of succession, 102, 426, 440
See ADOPTION II., 817, 832; III., 880; IV., 944, 945; V. *passim*; STRIDHANA

MOTHER-IN-LAW
is the guardian of her daughter-in-law, 385
direct —— has preference over step ——, 490
postponed to her daughter-in-law as heir to her son, 386
succeeds to her daughter-in-law, 485, 489
See ADOPTION III., 870, 893

MOTHER'S COUSIN'S GRANDSON
is heir according to Bengal law, 460*n*

MOTHER'S FATHER'S BROTHER'S GRANDSON
is heir according to Bengal law, 460*n*

MOTHER'S (MATERNAL) AUNT'S SONS, 123, 457

MOTHER'S (MATERNAL) UNCLE'S SONS, *ib.*, *ib.*

MOTHER'S (PATERNAL) AUNT'S SONS, *ib.*, *ib.*

MRITYU PATRA, 197
is a conveyance operating after grantor's death, 216
common under Hindu law, 216, 217
how construed, 217
See ADOPTION VI., 982; WILL

MUGLAI HAKKS, 425
See ALLOWANCE

MUNDIUM, 797*n*

MUNJ,
meaning of, 939*t*
See ADOPTION IV., 941, 942; UPANAYANA, 941

MURALI CASTE, 416, 471, 489, 494v

NAIGAMA SECT. See CASTE, 519

NAIKINS. See ADOPTION VII., 1066

NAIRS OR NAYARS. See TRIBES, 272w, 396x
polyandry amongst ——, 272w
decay of polyandry amongst ——, 402q
female gentileship amongst ——, 398
women of —— not allowed to marry a man of a lower caste, 401e
marriage with brother's wife disallowed, 402q
two husbands discreditable, *ib.*
marriage of —— dissoluble at will, *ib.*

NAISHTHIKA BRAHMACHARI,
successor of Guru, 486
succession to —— ——, 133

NAIVEDYA
= food offering to gods, 764
separate offering of —— is a sign of partition, 637

NANAK-SHAHI SECT. See CASTE, 535
heirs to a ——, *ib.*

NANDA PANDIT, 917

NARADA SMRITI, 43
its age, 44

NARVADARI HOLDINGS,
sub-division of —— —— not allowed, 684
nor separation of the house from the holding, *ib.*
daughter excluded from succession to —— —— by custom in some places, 406

NATRA. See REMARRIAGE, 435b

NEARNESS OF KIN
to a deceased raja preferred to survivorship, 71

NECESSITY. See FAMILY, 588, 688t, 747

NEGATIVE ELEMENT
of combined will the stronger, 568i

NEPHEW,
(father deceased) and uncle have equal rights on partition, 71, 72
represents his father in undivided family, 333

NEPHEW—*continued.*
when —— succeeds, 103, 104, 424, 444
nephews take *per capita*, 424, 433
preferred to half-brothers by Vyav. May., 430*q*
when excluded by surviving uncles, 103, 429
excludes a sons' widow, 431*t*
succeeds to his aunt, 510
to be preferred by widow in adoption, 914
nephews held to be sufficiently represented by their uncle, 574
sister's son preferred to maternal aunt's son, 460*n*
postponed to cousin, 444
sister, 463
contra in Madras, 463*w*
to samanodaka, 456
See ADOPTION II., 809; BHACHA

NEPHEW'S DAUGHTER
not an heir in Bengal, 467

NEXT FRIEND OF INFANT,
any one may come forward as ——, 624*i*
a relative preferred, *ib.*
See MINOR

NIBANDHA,
ranked as immoveable property, 176*p*, 706*x*
whether of necessity "immoveable property" in statutes, 706*x*
widow excluded from succession to —— by Brihaspati, 261

NIECE
takes a share with her brother? 431
sister's daughter not an heir, 444
See ADOPTION IV., 919; BROTHER'S DAUGHTER, 465

NIECE'S GRANDSON,
his succession, 465

NIECE'S SON,
his succession, *ib.*
See ADOPTION IV., 919

NILAKANTHA
is the author of Vyav. May., 20
life of ——, 21

NIMBADITYA, 537

NIRDHANA,
meaning of ——, 262

NIRNAYASINDHU,
authority of ——, 13
is the work of Kamalakara, 23
See SEPARATE LIST OF HINDU AUTHORITIES

NITYA ADOPTION. See ADOPTION VI., 1008

NIYOGA,
in Orissa, 516*a*
makes the Kshetraja legitimate, *ib.*

NOMINATION
of a successor to a Guru, 521

NOTICE,
doctrine of ——, 8*p*
binding taker of property, 188
of foreclosure, 570*s*
See ADOPTION III., 693; VI., 991; IGNORANCE; MORTGAGE; REGISTRATION

NULLITY. See INSTRUMENT, 595

NUNCUPATIVE WILL. See WILL, 618, 740

NUPTIAL GIFT
constitutes separate property, 324, 666, 773

NUZZARANA
usually taken by Hindu rulers for recognizing an adoption, 836*n*

NYAYADHISH, 234

OBLATIONS,
funeral ——, 20, 59
performance of —— important, 62
See FUNERAL CEREMONY; INHERITANCE, 59; SRADDHA

OBLIGATION,
a Brahmana is born under three ——s, 789, 823
merely religious ——s will not be enforced by Civil Courts, 813
obligations of the father pass to the heir, 75, 1088
to pay father's debts is a part of the inheritance, 160
for debts dependent on taking property, 76*i*
limited by Act VII. of 1866, *ib.*
to pay father's debts does not extend to those of other members, 193
father's securities bind sons unless they are for profligate purposes, 73
assignment of ——s, 685*e*
See ADOPTION III., 870, 871; VII.; DEBTS; FATHER; PROMISE, 193, 203

OBSEQUIES. See ADOPTION VI., 995*o*; VII., 1022, 1023, 1027; FUNERAL CEREMONY

OCCUPANCY. See PRESCRIPTION

OCCUPATION,
of waste is under Hindu law a natural right, 174
mere —— does not confer ownership (Mit.), 361

OFFICE. See ELDERSHIP; HEREDITARY OFFICE, 715; VATAN, 684

OFFSPRING,
of concubine entitled to support, 75
(Sudra) of a casual connexion inherits if recognized, 78

OPPRESSION,
of debtors under British and Native rule, 718*v*

ORAONS. See TRIBES, 269*c*

ORDEAL, KOSHA, 703

ORDERS. See ASRAMAS, 61

ORGAN,
defect of, a cause of disqualification, 117, 141, 541

ORISSA, 516*a*, 786

ORNAMENTS,
commonly worn by a woman not subject to partition, 205, 674, 675*p*
unless given in fraud of coparceners, 205, 675
given for ordinary wear are Stridhana, 205, 294*m*
license to use —— on particular occasions not a gift of them, 186, 281*r*
of courtesans exempt from seizure, 798*r*
given to concubine inherited by her husband, 482
or her patron? *ib.*
See GIFT; JEWELS; PARTITION

ORPHAN. See ADOPTION II., 806*p*, 832*z*; V., 949

OTTI MORTGAGE, 273

OUDICH BRAHMANAS, 1065

OUTCASTE,
sons born before father's expulsion are not ——, 149*y*, 549
but subsequently born share his expulsion, *ib.*, *ib.*
outcaste's daughters are not expelled, *ib.*, *ib.*

OUTCASTE—*continued.*
outcastes and their children are disqualified from inheriting, 149, 541, 544, 551
doctrine does not apply to families sprung from sons, 149*y*
See ADOPTION II., 816, 1817; III., 845; IV., 944; DISQUALIFICATION; EXCLUSION; MAINTENANCE

OWNERSHIP,
origin of, 173
is a matter of secular cognizance, *ib.*
law of —— discussed by commentators at an early period, 234
in what —— consists, 187
possession necessary to the completion of ——, 104*g*
constituted by right of exclusive use, 303*l*
complete —— in the taker is the general principle of Hindu law, 656*n*
power of alienation not essential to ——, 303*l*, 305*r*
comparison of European laws, 303*l*
under Hindu law not lost by absence, 672
nor without owner's will, 174, 602
subject to public law, 187
restrictions still recognized in the North of India, 177*a*
arising from possession, 644
of the transferee cannot be greater that that of the transferor, 7
of village communities over common lands, 672*k*
tribal —— of lands the source of individual ——, 128*f*, 672*k*
tribal —— not found in Bombay Presidency, 399
unobstructed, 317*o*
obstructed, 318
collective in Malabar, 608*h*
See ADOPTION VII., 1013, 1014; GIFT; POSSESSION; PROPERTY; SALE

PAISACHA MARRIAGE, 484, 486
See MARRIAGE

PAKSHA CEREMONIES, 1012*o*
The Jains have no ——, 812*h*

PALAK KANYA,
quasi adopted or foster daughter, 828*y*, 907
may be discarded, 834*k*

PALAKA PUTRA, 827, 906, 1009, 1065
See FOSTER SON

PALLA, 283, 480
provision must be made for ——, 373
In Gujarat —— resumed on widow's remarriage, 395*h*

PANDITS (or SASTRIS),
opinions of ——, 2
testimony of ——, 13
See ADOPTION I., 785; IV., 941; VI., 963

PARADESI,
meaning of ——, 738*y*
See CASTE

PARASARA SMRITI, 43, 50

PARCENER. See COPARCENER; ILLEGITIMATE SON; PARTITION

PARENT,
to act with anxious care in giving a son, 833
parents entitled to maintenance, 253
order of ——s' succession, 421, 422
comparison of Salic law, 422*x*
See ADOPTION *passim*; FATHER; GIFT, 711*h*, 807*q*; GUARDIAN; INHERITANCE; MAINTENANCE; MOTHER; PARTITION

PARENTS' SAPINDAS,
succession of —— to Stridhana, 140, 484*ss*, 508

PARIBHASHIKA STRIDHANA,
according to the Mitakshara no distinction between —— and other kinds of Stridhana, 135, 283
succession to —— —— according to Vyav. May., 135

PARIT CASTE, 422

PARTIES TO SUITS,
all members of joint family must join as plaintiffs, 567*g*
one in possession before institution of suit is a necessary party, 635*k*
See FAMILY; FATHER; MANAGER; REPRESENTATION; SUIT

PARTITION,
defined, 559, 561
Vijnanesvara's definition defective, 561
is regarded by the Civil Law as a kind of exchange, 559
is a particular kind of intention, 193, 765
in —— there is a break of continuity of the person and familia, 62*y*
separate enjoyment for convenience does not constitute ——, 641, 711
how a source of property, 57, 63
division of the subject of ——, 561
will to effect ——, 611 631
favourably viewed by Hindu law, 624*h*
family is the basis of the law of ——, 560
governed by usage, 7
See CUSTOM; USAGE

PARTITION—*continued*.
according to caste laws, 612*ss*
son's right to claim —— derived from his co-ownership, 611, 658*w*
requires consent of all members (*Maroomakatayam*), 675*s*
Complete and Partial
son's right to —— denied by many castes, 612, 613
in Bengal son cannot obtain ——, 163
of self-acquired property when allowed, 610
of ancestral property held by father at will of son, 173, 609, 611, 726
confined to descendants of a common ancestor, 606
claimable by grandson, 611, 730
extends to the fourth in descent from the common ancestor if present, 622, 753*f*
not claimable by a grandson during the life of his father against the father's will?* 611, 645*b*
deferred till delivery of pregnant widow of deceased coparcener, 71, 609, 769
right to —— confined to demandant, 617
cannot take place between husband and wife, 85
between co-widows, 95
females cannot demand ——, 627
otherwise in Bengal, 629
mother cannot enforce ——, 710*q*
when a guardian may claim —— on behalf of the minor, 624, 708, 755
a co-sharer practising fraud does not lose his share, 630
See FRAUD
persons disqualified to inherit not entitled to ——, 629
may be enforced by purchaser of undivided share, 646, 651, 653
in such a case effect to be given to the particular transaction, 651
See COPARCENER
coparcener must claim —— of his whole share, 646
final —— re-opened for one excluded as outcast on his expiation, 56*c*
in —— the presumption is of all property held by coparceners being joint, 653
possible without property, 764
part reserved is divisible, 648
of lands redeemed may be enforced after a previous ——, 633
property omitted through inadvertence subject to ——, 648, 675, 758
comparison of Roman law, 648
of lands subject to public service, 256
of a vritti how made, 671*e*
woman's jewels excluded from ——, 204, 294*m*, 675*p*

---

* The rules presume an estate descended to the father or taken by him in partition, not a mere right which he may assert, as before partition. In the latter he cannot be superseded by his sons. See Mit. Ch. I. Sec. II. para. 6; Sec. V. para. 3 and *note*; and Yajn. II. 117, 120, 121. The Smriti rule as to the share claimable by a son after his father's death is extended to the case of a claim made by the son on his father after the father's separation but no further.

PARTITION—*continued.*
also reasonable gifts from father to son, 711*h*, 735
and to a wife or daughter, 205
is to be made of property as actually subsisting without allowance for previous inequalities of expenditure, 698, 769, 760
unless there has been dishonesty, 760
of liabilities on inheritance, 684, 698
valid incumbrances to be deducted, 686*h*
of debts and other liabilities, 717, 721
marriage expenses of unmarried members to be provided for, 713
regulated by the nature of the property as divisible or not, 704
in specie not essential, 633, 649
of divisible property how made, 704
of naturally indivisible property, 717, 718, 756
in —— of Bhagdhari and Narvadari no sub-division allowed, 684
may be made with reference to property itself impartible, 679, 680
in case of partible and impartible property of one family, 256, 679
compensation for impartible property taken by one sharer, 675
comparison of English law, 675*s*
may be postponed during a life-estate, 632, 765
or a mortgage, 633, 648
not constituted by mere arithmetical determination of share, 632, 641
not constituted by taking profits in shares, 641, 642
but is by a limitation of rights to particular parts without actual distribution, 649
not constituted by agreement to divide lands still to be recovered, 633
effectual though not by metes and bounds, 631*t*, 765
determination of shares on ——, 698
limited to coparceners in existence, 71, 72, 722
Equal and Unequal
in ancestral property father's and each son's shares are equal, 704
according to Bombay High Court and Privy Council —— as to all self-acquired property uncontrolled, 610*s*, 705, 706
in spontaneous —— of self-acquired property the head may reserve a double share, 704
he takes an equal share if —— is enforced, 704, 705
father to distribute equitably, 705
not bound to equality by custom, 706*v*
between brothers must be equal, 710, 734
collaterals *per stirpes*, 710
rights arising from sole possession of a portion by a coparcener, 711
compensation in such a case, *ib.*
contrary ruling, *ib.*
comparison of English law, 712*s*
in case of a house built by a member out of his separate funds, 711
See Possession
in —— between reunited coparceners the shares are equal, 715
mother in a —— takes an equal share, 710*g*, 627, 627*c*
with an only son a moiety, *ib.*
by a division of profits, 717

PARTITION—*continued*.
distribution of acquisitions by different parceners proportionate to contributions, 667*n*
unequal —— not now recognized, 705, 735, 746
except by consent, 767
of unequal gains must be equal, 669*z*
partial —— not provided for in the Hindu Law Books, 647
not claimable, 614, 645, 646, 717, 767*k*
effected only by consent, 614, 645, 683, 717
among sons cannot be effected against their will, 193, 617
Method of ——
in —— no account of past transactions is to be taken, 699*v*, 711
except from the time that —— is wrongly refused, 711*k*
deduction from share for prodigal expenses, 717
partial distribution brought to account in a fresh general ——, 711
against the branch previously benefited, 646
rights and duties arising on ——, 698
duly claimed gives a right to account from that time, 699*v*
in the case of enforced —— complete accounts must be taken from time of demand, 699
but not generally any further back, 702, 711*k*
account how taken, 703
in a suit for —— all the coparceners must be before the Court, 699
computation in case of one member's separation, 698, 699
if detrimental Court can refuse ——, 626
under English law the Court regards all equitable rights, 627*d*
decree for —— effects a severance, 615, 633
not a suit without a decree, 765
effect of decree suspended by appeal, 615, 765*d*
decree for —— of estate paying revenue to be executed by Collector, 723
Incidents of ——
repugnant conditions cannot be annexed to estates taken on ——, 724
the right to —— cannot be annulled by an agreement never to divide certain property? 608
trade partnership constituted by agreement in ——, 639*y*
signs of implied will to effect ——, 636, 771—778
may be proved like any other fact, 771
incompleteness of —— must be proved by those who assert it, 648, 649*b*
Consequences of—
once made is final, 638, 648, 759, 761, 762,
does not make members strangers, 226, 232
does not close all claims of father and son in case of pauperism, 723
does not deprive son of the right of inheritance, 359, 723
son born after —— sole heir to parent's share, 338
of newly discovered property, 758, 759
of a courtyard advisedly retained for common use refused, 755
so when division would prevent proper use, 757
consequences of partial ——, 711
partial —— separates the family as to the part divided, 645, 647*p*
but no further, 648

PARTITION—*continued.*
inchoate —— does not alter the rights of coparceners, 633
rights of tenants of united family after ——, 661*m*
evidence of— See BURDEN OF PROOF; EVIDENCE; PRESUMPTION, 636, 640
limitation now affects some cases of ——, 753
exclusive possession for 30 years bars an action for further ——, 643
mortgaged property redeemed by one member and held by him exclusively for 20 years is liable to ——, 641
See ADOPTION III., 901*i*; VII., 1046, 1047; VIII., 1075; CHARGES; COPARCENERS; DEBTS; DISQUALIFICATION; DISTRIBUTION; DIVISION; ELDER; ENDOWMENTS; EXPENDITURE, 760, 761; FAMILY; FATHER; FEMALE; FRAUD; FURNITURE, 671; GRANDSON; GRANT; IDOL; ILLEGITIMATE; INDIGENCE; MAINTENANCE; MOTHER; OWNERSHIP; PATRIMONY; PROPERTY; WIDOW

PARTNER,
partner's relations distinguished from those of a joint family, 560*c*
in business when inherits to a Banya, 125, 128

PARTNERSHIP,
joint family converted into ——, See PARTITION, 639*a*

PASHANDAS, 519
Jains are ——, 533
See CASTE

PASTURE GROUND. See GRANT; INAM

PATERNAL AUNT. See AUNT, PATERNAL

PATILKI VATAN. See VATAN

PATITA,
what actions make a man ——, 523
may inherit after penance, 56*c*

PAT MARRIAGE,
is legal by Act XV. of 1856, 391
of a widow allowed among Sudras, 399
children of —— —— generally legitimate, 368, 369, 391
See REMARRIAGE; PATNI

PAT WIFE,
said to have the same rights as a lagna wife, 391
during first husband's life-time without divorce is but a concubine, 392
See PAT MARRIAGE

PATNI,
meaning of ——, 82*x*
who is and who is not a ——, 87

PATNI—*continued.*
alone entitled to allotment, according to Smriti Chandrika, 82*x*
wife other than —— entitled to maintenance only, 82*x*, 87
alone has a right of inheritance according to the Sastra, 80, 87, 249, 398

PATNI BHAGA,
origin of ——, 373, 399, 745
prevalent in the Punjab and in Madras, 399
not now recognized elsewhere, 745

PATRIA POTESTAS,
under the Hindu law, 209, 275, 618
Roman. See ADOPTION VI., 1086*n*; FATHER; STRIDHANA
extreme formerly, 270, 275
gradually limited, *ib.*, *ib.*

PATRIMONY,
once alienable, 195
causes of this, 195*s*
recovered by father is separate property, 663
unless recovered with aid of ancestral estate, 665
mother's assent required to partition of —— in some castes, 612
father's assent required in many castes, *ib.*
according to the Smritis not divisible, 672*k*
See INHERITANCE; PARTITION; PROPERTY, 733

PATTADHIKARI,
=head of a Matha, 533

PAUNARBHAVA,
=son of a Paunarbhu, 604*h*

PAUPER. See ADOPTION V., 951; INDIGENCE; MAINTENANCE; PARTITION, 723

PENAL CODE, THE INDIAN. See ADULTERY

PENANCE,
questions on ——, 13
treated of in Yajnavalkya, 16
in case of adultery, 401, 556, 800
fornication, 401
an out-caste, 553
See DISQUALIFICATION, 56*c*

PENSION, 181
substituted for a saranjam must support junior members, 681
not attachable, 706*x*
See NIBANDHA; PROPERTY

PERMISSION. See ADOPTION *passim*; SANCTION

PERPETUITY,
rule against —— under English law rests on public policy, 198*e*
in favour of private persons disallowed, 185, 211*f*, 251
even under the form of a religious trust, 201*l*
in favour of an idol or charity, 185
See ENDOWMENT; TRUST
grants of land in —— not incompetent because raj impartible, 373
obstacle to —— in the presidency towns, 221
not in the mofussil, *ib.*

PERSONAL INHERITANCE,
(English Law), 706*x*

PERSONAL LAW,
governs duties, 7

PERSONAL PROPERTY,
(English Law), 706*x*
in stocks and shares, *ib.*

PER STIRPES. See PARTITION

PHALAVIBHAGA,
=division of produce, 717, 772
See PARTITION

PIGNORIS CAPIO, 697*l*

PILGRIMAGE,
not recognized as a cause for alienation, 306
expenses of a —— not awarded to a widow as against her brother-in-law, 697*g*

PIOUS ACTS,
are indivisible, 756

PITRIDVIT,
= Enemy of Father. See ENEMY OF FATHER, 547

PLACE OF ADOPTIOON, 988
See ADOPTION VI., 992

PLACE OF WORSHIP AND SACRIFICE,
indivisible, 716

POLITY, 20

POLLUTION,
arising from death; duration of ——, 848*w*
as effecting adoptive father and son. See ADOPTION III., 848; VII., 1022

POLYANDRY, 272
in Kamaun, 276*m*
still subsists in Cochin and Travancore, 272
and amongst many of the aborigines of India, 396
such as Tothiyars
the Nayars, 272, 396*x*
Seoraj, Lahoul, Spiti,
fraternal —— amongst the Thiyens, 397*z*
and Khasias, 276*m*
reduced to biandry, 272*w*
its effects on inheritance, *ib.*
transition to the ordinary system, 273
connected with niyoga, 276
in Sparta, 276*m*

POLYGAMY,
is referred to in the Vedas, 795*b*

POSSESSION,
its effect to under Hindu law, 640*d*
adverse and permissive —— discussed, 636*o*, 641, 643, 650*d*
partial —— extended to the whole when rightfully taken, 1065*g*
separate —— of part of joint estate, 589*g*, 711
by the mortgagee is acquired by a *bonâ fide* attornment of the mortgagor, 642*t*
not always given to a cultivator, 643
by Collector to protect revenue not adverse to real owner, 650*d*
in common by joint family, 625, 644
by co-sharer; its nature, 589
by one joint tenant is —— by all, 644
unless distinctly exclusive, *ib.*
exclusive —— constitutes separation, 589, 644
See BELOW
Necessary to bar co-parceners, 641, 642*t*, 643, 644*z*, 650*d*
mere non-enjoyment not equivalent to exclusion, 650*d*
change of —— when dispensed with, 180*v*, 1065
generally essential to change of ownership, 213, 216, 642*t*
comparison of Roman law, 642*t*
not necessary to validate gift to son, 635*k*, 738
change of —— replaced by registration, 635*k*
exception to change of —— being replaced, 635*k*
may be dispensed with when the deed is incontrovertible? 1065*g*
separate —— a sign of partition, 640, 641
once held essential to partition, 764
as to ownership of separate share, 104*g*
perfecting title may be acquired notwithstanding an irregularity in taking it, 642*t*

POSSESSION—*continued.*
giving by a single co-sharer to purchaser protected, 589
exclusive —— by a single co-sharer raises a presumption of its being his share in a past partition, 642
acquired *pendente lite* is subject to the decision, 635
before suit makes possessor a necessary party, *ib.*
is the strongest proof of ownership, 174
as a title prevails until a better is shown, 642*t*
title by —— arises concurrently with extinction of the right to sue, 644
long —— by a member with consent of other sharers gives him a right to retain the particular portion in partition, 711
by several in succession must be connected by lawful deprivation to give a prescriptive title to the last, 650*d*
acquired permissively or by tenancy does not become adverse by mere non-payment of rent for 12 years, 642*t*
by the mortgagee after payment is not necessarily adverse, *ib.*
suits for ——, *ib.*
refused to co-sharers excluded by one? 589*e*
See Coparcener; Gift; Limitation; Notice; Partition; Presumption; Property; Registration; Sale

POSSESSORY ACTIONS, 643
jurisdiction, *ib.*

POSTHUMOUS SON,
obtains a share after partition, 649
See Adoption VII., 1014; Son, 722

POVERTY QUALIFICATION. See Adoption V., 951; Daughter (*above*, Index)

PRABHU. See Adoption III., 850*l*; IV., 918; Caste, 488

PRAJAPATI
declares patrimony impartible. See Inheritance, 262
Property A; Patrimony

PRAJAPATYA MARRIAGE, 481, 484, 486
See Marriage

PRECEDENCE
of begotten son over adopted son, 1043, 1044
See Adoption VII., 1044; Eldership; Primogeniture

PRECEPTOR,
of a Brahmana, when inherits, 128, 451, 465, 469
inherits to a Naishthika Brahmachari, 134, 468

PRE-EMPTION
arises from former impartibility of patrimony, 672
right of —— may be exercised by a widow taking by inheritance, 298*l*

PREFERENCE
in adoption by a widow, rule of ——, 914

PREGNANCY
of widow postpones partition, 609
See ADOPTION III., 843, 902; PARTITION

PREPARED FOOD
indivisible, 756

PRESCRIPTION
under the Hindu law, 642*t*, 649*z*
comparison of Roman law, 649*z*
under the Bombay Regulation V. of 1827, 644
does not arise where successive possessions are unlawful, 650*d*
See LIMITATION; POSSESSION; OWNERSHIP

PRESENT
from a friend is separate property, 324
to a woman; succession to ——, 509
See STRIDHANA

PRESIDENCY TOWN,
residence in —— does not of itself subject a Hindu to English law, 3
testamentary law in —— ——. See WILL

PRESUMPTION
of union of a Hindu family, 653
of joint estate, 637, 653, 663, 666*m*
this is easily overcome, 670*b*
in favour of joint acquisitions in united family, 74, 654, 663, 666*m*
circumstances may rebut it, 74
in case of separate acquisitions asserted and denied, 670*b*
of separate acquisiition from conveyances in a single name and long enjoyment, 666*m*
of partition from separate possession, 641, 642
quiescent enjoyment of part, 631, 644
of allotment in partition against him who long holds a part of an estate exclusively, 689*e*
of death when arises, 626
in a benami transaction, 665
of acquiescence of co-sharers when lessee continues to hold under lease from a divided member, 711
of a debt contracted by the manager of a united family being joint, 687
in favour of widow's dealings approved by heirs, 1068
in favour of adotpion, 967*ss*
against the gift of only or eldest son except as dvyamushyayana, 1062*m*
See ADOPTION IV., VI.; BURDEN OF PROOF; EVIDENCE

PRIEST,
priest's fees and duties of ——, 377, 389
inherit from Yajamana, 658

PRIEST—*continued.*
widow may succeed to emoluments by custom, 389
she appointing an officiator, *ib.*
an intruder may be sued, *ib.*
See PROPERTY, SACRED

PRIMOGENITURE,
origin of ——, 819
under English law, 58
in ancient Hindu law, 65
was a right of headship rather than ownership, 677
connected with impartibility, 65*i*, 676*t*
instance of succession under rule of ——, 65*i*
junior son by birth entitled to precedence over elder son by adoption, 636*g*
provision for or succession by younger brother where —— prevails, 65*i*, 255
traces of —— still preserved, 676*t*
contests as to —— in India and Europe, *ib.*
See ADOPTION II., 853*e*; APPANAGE; BROTHER; CUSTOM; ELDERSHIP; PRECEDENCE; RAJ.

PRINCIPALITY
ruled usually by a single line of Chieftains, 675
various modes of succession to ——, 676

PRITIDATTA
is the affectionate gift of the husband, 135, 259, 486
See STRIDHANA

PRIVITY
connects successive possessions, 650*d*

PRIVY
is indivisible, 757

PROBATE
granted to adopted son, 1081
of a will in the Mofussil needless, 221, 618*x*
See ADOPTION VIII., 1081; WILLS, 220, 221

PROCEDURE,
Hindu, 233

PROCEEDINGS,
legal, 24
See ADOPTION VIII.; LIMITATION; SUIT

PROCREATION
by deputy was common in ancient times, 797*m*
on a Sudra a ground of expulsion, 401*i*

PRODIGAL. See EXPENDITURE, 786*n*; FATHER; INTERDICTION

PRODIGAL EXPENDITURE,
deduction for ——, 717
See COPARCENER; PARTITION

PRODIGALITY OF FATHER
a cause of rescission by son, 193*a*
See PRODIGAL; BURDEN OF PROOF

PROFITS. See RENTS AND PROFITS; PARTITION, 641

PROHIBITION. See ADOPTION III., 865, 866

PROHIBITIVE WILL
prevails over active in a combination, 568

PROFLIGACY. See ALIENATION; DEBTS; INTERDICTION; PARTITION; PRODIGAL

PROMISE,
promises are sacred, 189, 248, 281, 686*g*
promises now create only a moral not legal obligation, 193, 203
property promised morally inalienable, 203
gratuitous ——s generally void, 192
made by the father binding on the sons, 161, 686*g*
to wife if reasonable binds sons, 205
fulfilment of —— postponed to maintenance of family, 1089
See ADOPTION III., 850; FATHER; SON

PROPERTY,
A. ITS CHARACTERISTICS UNDER HINDU LAW.
nature of —— under Hindu law, 175
power of sale not a necessary incident of ——*
local sacrifices held a consecration for the benefit of the first occupants, 195
allodial rather than feudal, 175
takes its characteristics from the family law, 263
they are not qualities inherent in the land, &c., *ib.*
referred to religious connexion by the ancient law, 49
connected with family sacra, 551, 957
rights of —— under the Brahmanical system connected with spiritual union, 60*q*
possession of —— essential to an effective sacrifice, 59
partition attending dispersion of sacra, 672*k*
as viewed by Hindu law is in itself capable of alienation (Smr. Chand), 173*y*
sale of land once disallowed, 195, 672
religious gifts approved, 195, 196
irresumable, 128*f*, 175, 200

* *See* Bo. Gov. Sel. No. 114, p. 6, para. 12.

PROPERTY—*continued.*
these the source of the right of alienation, 191
comparison of history of the religious gifts under English law, 191*n*
under various other laws, 672*k*
See DEDICATION; ENDOWMENT; GIFT; GRANT; IDOL; SACRA
ownership regarded as indestructible without the owner's will, 672
See OWNERSHIP
conceived as not transferrable without consent, 602, 1023
how far volition passes —— depends on personal law, 7
partition originally a mere distribution for use, 672
may be freed from special custom by mutual consent, 681
intention to free —— from custom must be expressed, *ib.*
Limitations of ——, 169*ss*
by owner restricted, 179
must be in favour of an existing person, 182, 185, 981
cannot generally be made inalienable, 188
limitation of female ownership, 293*ss*, 425
limited rights of widows, 90, 91, 298, 983
of wives, 85, 309
See DAUGHTER; FEMALE; STRIDHANA; SUCCESSION
ownership and succession of tribes and village communities, 128*f*
succession of Brahmana community, 128
a stranger cannot be introduced as a co-sharer without assent of co-members, 672*k*
Mirasi rights, 177, 672*k*
Bhagdari and Narvadari estates *, 176
private property generally subordinated to the will of the sovereign, 179*n*, 185
religous gift usually inalienable, 195
limited to a corporation or family, 198, 199
limitations unrecognized by the law are refused effect by the Courts †, 181, 183
See DEDICATION; ENDOWMENT; CUSTOM; GRANT; INAM; JAGIR
B. SOURCES OF PROPERTY.
right to —— acquired by occupancy, 360
inheritance and partition how sources of ——, 57, 63, 561
See ENDOWMENT; GIFT; GRANT; INAM; INHERITANCE; LIMITATION; OCCUPATION; OWNERSHIP; PARTITION; POSSESSION; PRESCRIPTION; REVERSIONER
C. JURAL RELATIONS CONNECTED WITH PROPERTY GENERALLY.
I. *Resting on Volition of Owner*
a. Transfer and Creation of Rights by act inter vivos
generally alienable, 706
illegal restriction on a coparcener's dealing with his share disallowed, 661

---

* *See* Bom. Gov. Rec. No. 114. At p. 5 is an instance of the village changing the seat of cultivation triennially, which illustrates Tac. Germ. 26. *See* too 5th Rep. 723.

† *Kumar Tarakeswar Roy* v. *Kumar Soshi Shikhareswar*, L. R. 10 I. A. 51.

PROPERTY—*continued.*
personal —— = self-acquired, 1089
the right to give it away, 601*x*, 706, 1089
self-acquired and separate may be given or bequeathed, 129, 182, 447, 706
or otherwise disposed of by the owner, 192
interests unknown to the law cannot be created, *ib.*
See ABEYANCE; ALIENATION; COPARCENER; GIFT; MORTGAGE; PARTITION; PERPETUITY; PURCHASE; SALE; TRUST
β Disposal by Will
See BEQUEST; DEDICATION; DEVISE; ENDOWMENT; GIFT; TESTAMENTARY POWER; TRUST; WILL
II. *Descent and Disposal governed by Law*
a. Under the Law of Inheritance
is inherited for religious benefits, 551, 660*g*
taken as a "universitas," 160
ancestral —— descends in direct male line with its accretions, 654
descent of ancestral —— obstructed and unobstructed, 60
See BANDHU; DAUGHTER; DAYA; DESCENT; DEVOLUTION; FATHER; FEMALE; GOTRAJA SAPINDA; GRANDSON; INHERITANCE; MOTHER; PERPETUITY; SAPINDA; SON; STRIDHANA; SUCCESSION; WIDOW
β Under the Law of Partition
why land and dwelling house were considered indivisible, 672, 717
endeavours to preserve —— —— in the laws of the various countries, 673
self-acquired —— when mixed with ancestral —— becomes ancestral ——, 655
a grant of land in charity, if not for particular purpose, is divisible ——, 743
ancestral —— partible at will of father, 609
distribution of ancestral —— once allowed merely for use, 672*k*
consequences of this, *ib.*
See BROTHER; COPARCENER; DEBT; DISTRIBUTION; ELDERSHIP; FAMILY; FATHER; MOTHER; NEPHEW; OBLIGATION; PRESUMPTION; PRIMOGENITURE; SISTER; SON; STRIDHANA; WIDOW; WIFE
γ Under the Law of Adoption
See ADOPTION VII., VIII.; SON; WIDOW
III. *Liabilities annexed to Property or attending interests therein*
burdens on ——, 161, 238, 685
not hypothecated for father's debts, 73
yet is assets for payment of debts in the hands of the heir, 168, 192, 660
zamindari descended from father is liable to pay his debts, 76
even self-acquired, not alienable so as to deprive family of maintenance, 601, 1089
attachment of impartible —— for debts discussed, 161
of family estate, 602
provision for concubine a charge on ——, 164
See APPANAGE; CHARGE; CREDITOR; DAUGHTER; DEBT; DISQUALIFICATION; FAMILY; FATHER; FEMALE; MAINTENANCE;

PROPERTY—*continued.*

MANAGER; MORTGAGE; PURCHASER; REVERSIONER, 89*v*; SISTER; WIDOW; WIFE

D. CLASSES OF PROPERTY.

I. *According to Natural Character*

a. Immoveable Property

what is immoveable —— under Hindu law? question discussed, 706*x*
immoveable —— in legislation, 706*ss*
immoveable —— includes a hakk, *ib.*
and arrears? *ib.*
  may include property purchased with capital or profits of ancestral moveable ——, 654*h*
immoveable —— does not include an annuity from Government land revenue, 706
but one to a temple out of extra assessments held a charge on —— ——, *ib.*
  regarded as inalienable except with assent of family? 601
  disposable by owner, 705, 740
power of disposition supported by a Sastri, 741
and allowed by the High Court of Bombay, 705
naturally indivisible —— how disposed of, 754—757
immoveable —— not to be aliened so as to reduce family to indigence, 564, 1089
a compound is divisible —— under ordinary circumstances, 757
restrictions on widow's disposal of —— ——, 709
  See ALIENATION; STRIDHANA; WIDOW; BELOW *β*.

a. a. Moveable Property

  not identical with "personal property" under English law, 706
  disposable by owner, 739, 740
widow's power to dispose of —— ——, 709
  See PERSONAL PROPERTY; STRIDHANA; WIDOW

β. Incorporeal Property

Nibandha declared immoveable, 176*p*
  includes a religious fund, 716*m*
  See HAKK, 706*x*; NIBANDHA, 176*p*, 706; PENSION; SARANJAM

γ. Indivisible or Impartible Property; see below D. II.

indivisible —— described, 653
legally —— —— described, 675
kinds enumerated, 671, 715, 716, 756
legally indivisible, so to be disposed of in partition as to secure maximum of advantage to all coparceners, 716
  may be sold and proceeds distributed or equitably adjusted by agreement, 673, 717, 756
impartibility not a reason for exoneration from debts, 163

D. II. *According to purposes served*

a. Sacred Property

sacred ——, 128*f*, 185, 195, 199, 520
dedicated to an idol, 155
  confined to priestly family, 389
sacred —— inalienable under most religious systems. 1850

PROPERTY—*continued.*
comparison of Roman law, *ib.*
subject to special limitations as to inhertance, partition, and alienation, 743
temple allowances are hereditary and divisible, (subject to special customs) in some cases, 681
trust property partible subject to trust, *ib.*
a widow may enjoy —— —— appointing a substitute, 389
intruder subject to a suit *ib.*
See ALIENATION; ASCETIC; CUSTOM; DEDICATION; DIVISION; ENDOWMENT; GIFT; GOSAVI; GRANT; IDOL; KRISHNARPANA; MAHANT; PERPETUITY; SROTRIYAM; TEMPLE; TRUST; VRITTI

β. Charities and Public Dedications
DEDICATED—is a trust, 161
generally inalienable, *ib.*
See CHARITY; DHARMA; GRANT; TRUST; WILL

γ. Political Tenures
IMPARTIBLE—on account of political condition, 675
may be joint, 679
includes a pensoin commuted for a resumed saranjam, 603
may form part of family estate, 679
and be taken into account in partition, *ib.*
not necessarily inalienable, 680*v*, 681*f*,
seniority by birth gives superiority of title to ——, 74, 75
is inherited by the nearest male members in preference to daughters, 679
claim to a raj as being —— —— refuted by enjoyment opposed to impartibility, 681*f*
the Tarwad's —— —— in Malabar, 608*h*
See GRANT; JAGIR; RAJ; SARANJAM; ZAMINDAR

δ. Official Tenures
vatan is divisible ——, 767, 768
a vatan —— impartible, held not to have become partible by cessation of official functions, 765
See HEREDITARY OFFICE; JOSHI; VATAN

D. III. *According to Relations of the Persons interested*
a. As Members of a Family
a. In equal Relations

I 1. *Ancestral Joint Property*
ANCESTRAL—described, 654, 656, 661, 663, 665
joint —— regarded by Hindu law as an attribute of common origin, 560
implies concurrence of rights over the aggregate, *ib.*
depends on indivision of family, 561
comparison of Roman and French laws, 554*k*
a joint trade is joint ——, 324
acquired by use of patrimony is joint ——, 654, 663
purchased out of the income of ancestral —— is itself ancestral, 665
immoveable —— acquired by means of ancestral moveable —— ranks as ancestral immoveable ——, 654*h*, 665, 666

PROPERTY—*continued.*
acquired through instruction at the family expense is joint ——, 680
self-acquired does not rank as joint where acquirer received only sustenance and elementary education from family, 670
acquired while acquirer was drawing an income from family is joint ——, 668
JOINT —— causes absorption of interest on death without male issue, 560
the whole property of each member presumed to be joint ——, 653, 663, 666*m*, 670*b*
See FAMILY; PRESUMPTION

PROPERTY, ANCESTRAL,
gift to united brethren without discrimination is joint ——, 605*t*, 654
becomes ancestral as soon as it devolves undisposed of on descendants, 655
ancestral —— co-extensive with objects of unobstructed inheritance, 656
father and son have equal ownership in ancestral ——, 345, 371, 549, 657, 665, 726, 727
whether ancestral —— is alienable by father for purpose not illegal or immoral, 576, 577
joint —— inalienable by co-sharer under the Mitakshara, 1089
gift of immoveable ancestral —— allowed by Mitakshara to a separated parcener, 448
may be joint though impartible, 679
indivision excludes several ownership according to Daya Bhaga, 701
conditions under which partition may be claimed, 609
ancestral, partible at will of son united with father, head of a family, *ib.*
after partition retains its character between the parcener and his sons, 659, 661
comparison of English law, 661*m*
share taken on partition is ancestral —— to the branch taking it, 661
undivided —— not answerable for separate debts, 75
includes property mortgaged but not recovered, 633
recovered by one of several sons, 65, 727
immoveable —— mortgaged by the father and sold in execution subject to son's claim for partition 642*p*; comp., 576, 579, 596
effect of a single parcener's sale, 637*q*
father has no exclusive right in —— devolving on him by brother's death? 655
See COPARCENER; ELDERSHIP; PARTITION; POSSESSION; RESIDENCE, 648; SALE; SAVINGS, 153; WIDOW, 299
a. 1. 2. *Separate and Self-acquired Property*

PROPERTY, SEPARATE AND SELF-ACQUIRED,
defined, 324, 325, 664, 666, 669
is of two sorts, 664
as between father and son, *ib.*
as between coparceners, 666
independently acquired ranks as separate estate, 74, 667*o*
undivided members may have ——, 660*g*
separate —— includes: property inherited from females, brothers, collaterals, or great-great-grandfather, 655, 656, 666

PROPERTY, SEPARATE AND SELF-ACQUIRED—*continued.*
nature of property thus taken discussed, 656
inherited in any right other than lineal inheritance through males is self-acquired ——? 659, 665
separate —— includes: property sold, which a coparcener repurchases out of his own means, 662
savings and accumulations by junior members out of their allotments in a zamindari, 153, 683
gains of science without aid of patrimony, 666
a reward for extraordinary achievement, 667*o*
gains of valour without aid of patrimony, 666
gains of chance, *ib.*
nuptial gifts, 773
present from friends, *ib.*
grant of village, 664
bequests, 221, 222
property recovered from stranger holding adversely to family of acquirer, 662
ancestral property recovered by father, 661, 665
the recovery being through his own ability, 661, 666
mother's estate is not ——? 656*n*, 658
zamindari inherited through mother not ——, 658
received from father-in-law or maternal grandfather is —— (in Dera Gazi Khan), 656*n*, 666*m*
of half-caste received from his European father is self-acquired, 221
property renounced in favour of younger sons is their separate ——, 661*k*
source of fund employed determines if property is separate or otherwise, 670
property divided is treated as separate —— of the member as against separated members, 661
the acquirer has absolute power of disposal over separate ——, 447
presumption that —— is self-acquired from long enjoyment and separate dealings, 666*m*
unequal distribution of separate —— is admissible, though opposed to commentaries, 205*ss*, 601, 706, 739
separate —— may be given or willed to wife to the exclusion of sons? 734, 760
contrary opinion of the Hindu authorities, 735*ss*, 759, 978
especially as to immoveables, 601*x*, 737
See above D. I. *a.*
he may give her even ancestral separate —— to a moderate extent, 204
when son, grandson, or great-grandson can demand share in separate ——, 611, 725, 726, 732
acquired by different parceners how to be distributed, 667*o*, 673
presumptions which arise in such cases. See BURDEN OF PROOF; PRESUMPTION
See ADOPTION VII.; ALIENATION; COPARCENER; DISTRIBUTION; FATHER; MOTHER; TESTAMENTARY POWER, 95*ss*, 618
1. 3. *Recovered Property*
meaning of "recovered" —— 663, 727
nature of ——, 662
recovered by father when ranks as self-acquired, 661, 665

PROPERTY, SEPARATE AND SELF-ACQUIRED—*continued.*
and when as ancestral, 665
ancestral —— recovered without the aid of the patrimony becomes separate ——, 663, 667*o*
ancestral —— recovered by another coparcener with the aid of patrimony is ancestral ——, 661
subject to deduction of one-fourth for the acquirer, *ib.*
looked on jealously by custom though approved by the Sastras, 699
a. 2. *In Subordinate Relations*
gift ancestral immoveable —— restricted by Sastri in case of a married man, 447
and his testamentary power, 1021*s*
nuptial gifts are separate ——, 324, 666, 774
property acquired by a woman usually her husband's, 85
See ADOPTION VII.; CONCUBINE; DAUGHTER; FEMALE; ILLEGITIMATE SON; MARRIAGE; SISTER; WIDOW; WIFE
β. As members of Communities and Corporations
transferred by a mahant by breach of trust can be recovered, 188*h*
See BHAODARI, 407, 684; ENDOWMENT; MATHA
γ. As members of Castes and Classes
See BRAHMANAS; MAHARS
δ. Co-Ownership; Co-Possession; Co-Responsibility
See COPARCENER; FAMILY; MANAGER; OWNERSHIP; REPRESENTATION; POSSESSION; SUIT
Ancestral. See above D. III. and the references
Divisible. See PROPERTY A; C. II. *β*; D. I. *γ*; D. II. *a*; D. III. *a*. I. 2, and the references
Immoveable. See PROPERTY D. I. *a*. 1. 1, 1. 2; ALIENATION
Impartible or Indivisible. See PROPERTY D. I. *γ*; C. II. *β*; D. II. *γ*; D. III. *γ*, and the references
Inalienable. See PROPERTY A. D. II. *a*, and the references
Religious or Sacred. See PROPERTY D. I. *β*; II. *a*, and the references
Self-acquired or Separate. See PROPERTY D. III. *a*, 1. 2; ALIENATION; DEBT; INHERITANCE; PARTITION; PRESUMPTION

PROSTITUTION,
property acquired by —— belongs to the husband, 483

PUBERTY. See ADOPTION II., 832*z*; III., 891; AGE

PUBLIC POLICY, 188, 189

PUJARI,
= worshipper, 521

PUNARBHU, 367, 604, 799
son of a —— regarded as illegitimate, 369
legitimized by Act XV. of 1856, 368
See PAT.; REMARRIAGE, 368, 369

PUNJAB,
Punjab Laws Act IV. of 1872 and XII. of 1878, presumption in favour of Hindu and Mohammedan law applicable to Hindus and Mohammedans, 5

PUPIL,
when inherits, 127
when inherits to a Sannyasi, 133, 468
See DISCIPLE; GURU; STUDENT.

PURCHASE,
by a coparcener is presumed to be on the joint account, 654
of son disallowed, 806
of children by dancing women once common, 834*k*
by Gosavis of disciples, 834
See ADOPTION II.
of wife disapproved, 263, 358
See WIFE.

PURCHASER,
for value favoured, 192
of family property; his responsibilities, 579, 591
from father or manager bound to inquiry, 595
in good faith from a widow exonerated, 93
with notice of widow's claim, 75
without —— ——— ———, *ib.*
of an undivided interest, becomes a tenant in common with other co-sharers, 566, 587, 588, 652
not entitled to any particular portion of the estate? 566, 587, 646, 651
has to work out his right by partition, 566, 587, 651, 652, 653, 717
must join all the members as defendants, 652
on partition may be allowed the particular portion so far as justice allows, 651
cannot be put into possession, 616, 652
but in possession allowed a joint possession with other co-sharers, 589, 616, 652
will not be ousted, 589
not affected by subsequent partition to which he was not a party, 588
under decree against a coparcener must sue for partition, 592, 646, 746
contrary rule as to a father in Madras. *ib.*

PURI CASTE, 530
See GOSAVIS.

PUROHITA, 180

PUROHITS, 197, 235*h*

PUT,
escaped by a single adoption, 1013

PUTRA,
in the Smritis does not strictly include an adopted son, 807*x*
See Son.

PUTRESHTI. See Adoption VI., 957, 993, 995

PUTRIKA-PUTRA, 419, 803, 805
two senses of ——, 802*n*
not enumerated by Manu, 806*m*, 945*h*
but named separately, *ib.*
was ranked above Kshetraja, 691*a*
placed on the same footing as aurasa, 945*h*
sister's daughter or son cannot be —— ——, 933
the daughter herself might be called —— and perform obsequies, 945*h*
not recognized at the present day, 806
See Adoption II., 793; IV., 815; Appointment, 803.

PUTRIKA-SUTA, 79, 81

QUASI-ADOPTION. See Adoption, 960

QUASI-GOTRASHIP,
amongst the lower castes, 831*o*

QUIT-RENT, 644

RAJ,
may exist for purposes of property without special political status, 679
inheritance to such a —— resembles that to a principality, *ib.*
succession to ——, 66, 153, 678
compared with European system, 676t
illegitimate son excluded from ——, 140
regranted before adoption to widow, 1016
See Custom; Descent; Devolution; Eldership; Principality; Property II.

RAJAH. See Adoption VI., 991

RAJPUT CASTE, 365, 430

RAKSHASA MARRIAGE, 484, 486
See Marriage.

RAMANANDA, 537

RAMAVAT CASTE, 539

RANGARI CASTE, 335

RATIFICATION,
no —— of that which is not done on account of the principle, 350, 1034
requires knowledge, 1078
of a lease made by widow, 94*l*, 350
by conduct of son of payment of mortgage to his mother, 571
in cases of adoption, 971
See ACQUIESCENCE; ADOPTION VI., 898; VII., 1034; ESTOPPEL; RELATION, 1071*l*; WIDOW.

RATIONALIST,
ranks as an Atheist, 787

RAVALNATHA, 494*e*

RE-APPEARANCE. See ABSENCE; ABSTENTEE

REASON OF LAW,
when consulted, 624, 626, 639, 667, 702, 768
See INTERPRETATION

REASONABLE INQUIRY. See PURCHASER; MANAGER; MINOR; CREDITOR

RECORDS. See AUTHENTICATION, 895

REGISTRATION,
cases of —— referred to, 642*t*
case of gift discussed, 635*k*
effect of ——, 189, 190
as notice, 189
omission to register, *ib.*
replacing possession for transfer of ownership, 634
partition deed for Rs. 100 and more to be registered, 631*r*
but partition otherwise proveable, *ib.*
See ADOPTION VI., 1004; VIII., 1071

REGULATIONS. See separate List

RELATION—(TERM OF ENGLISH LAW),
cannot validate an act void for want of power, 861, 1070
the invalidity of an adoption is not cured by a supervening state of things in which it would have been valid, 905*f*

RELATIONS. See KINSMEN

RELATIONSHIP,
remote ——, 235
analogies of European law, *ib.*
of the adopted son dependent on the Samskaras, 762, 1057
See ADOPTION IV.

RELATIVES,
provision for —— at the time of partition, 685, 1056
blood —— of wife. See ADOPTION IV., 921
See INHERITANCE; KINSMEN; MAINTENANCE; PARTITION

RELIGION,
as determining personal law, 4

RELIGIOUS CEREMONIES. See CEREMONIES

RELIGIOUS COMMUNITY, 517, 520
See CUSTOM; PROPERTY

RELIGIOUS ENDOWMENT. See ENDOWMENT

RELIGIOUS SERVICES, 520

RELINQUISHMENT,
of a share, recognized, 752, 762
induced by fraud is not binding, 763
by son. See SON, 324, 722
by widow. See WIDOW, 89, 92
See ADOPTION VII., 838; 1033

REMAINDER,
only to a person in existence, 180
estate by way of ——, 1021
not to be governed by English law, 90, 90*f*

REMARRIAGE,
of widows in higher castes void by Hindu law, 391
of widows disallowed by Hindu law except under caste custom, 367*ss*, 394, 402, 421
valid amongst Sudras, 400
divests widow's estate, 554
in some castes on —— by widow, payment must be made to the family and sometimes to the caste, 395*h*
in some castes widow on —— has to give up all her first husband's property except pritidatta, 394
does not prevent inheritance from son by first husband, 430
does not deprive her of her right to give in adoption, 892
offspring of a woman by —— formerly considered illegitimate, 368
son by —— now legitimate, 391
legalized by Act XV. of 1856, 343, 368, 369, 391, 402, 421, 426
a woman remarried without divorce deemed a concubine, 556
such —— a penal offence, *ib.*
See ADOPTION III., 892; PAT. MARRIAGE; WIDOW

RENT AND PROFITS,
receipt of —— separately not conclusive of partition, 641, 717
division of —— is a recognized mode of partition, 641, 717, 754, 772
of a Vatandari village, 717

RENUNCIATION,
by an elder brother gives estate to a younger, 427, 661*k*
of adoption not allowed, 1017
of marriage on payment of a fine, 400
disallowed, 401
See ADOPTION VII.; RELINQUISHMENT

REPARTITION,
when —— may be claimed, 649, 763
not generally claimable, 759, 763
exceptions, 757
variation in value does not give a right to claim ——, 757
See PARTITION

REPRESENTATION (= DECLARATION),
inducing change of position must be made good, 189, 1079
(for inheritance) by descendants, 62
sons and grandsons take by ——, 69
female —— not generally recognized, 414
rule as to —— not affected by residence abroad, 70
extent of ——, 327, 604, 622
law of —— extends to remote relations, 71
failure of three intermediate links bars the right of ——, 70, 327
can be claimed up to seventh degree, 70
said not to extend to collaterals, 430, 431
grandsons take by —— when mother dies between death of grandfather and actual partition, 104
nature of this succession discussed, 656*n*
limits of —— by descendants, 606
not recognized in heirship to a deceased brother, 104
of family by father, 653
See FATHER
exception under circumstances in favour of infant sons, 653*y*
of family by father as defendant, 575*m*
of father by adopted son in partition, 835*a*
See ADOPTION VII.; FAMILY; MANAGER; POSSESSION
of joint family in suits, 573
See SUIT, 1037
representative character ascribed to father or coparcener sued, 570, 577*ss*, 585, 591
in other cases denied, 583*ss*
See SUIT

REPUDIATION. See WIFE, 556*w*

REPUGNANT PROVISIONS,
void, 621, 661, 664

RESERVE. See ADOPTION VI., 978, 979, 985; VII., 1020

RES SACRÆ, 185
See SACRA; PROPERTY, SACRED

RES JUDICATA,
binds the same parties, though a different portion of the property was the object of the former suit, 1082
binds when the decision bore on the same jural relation, 1083*x*
instance of —— maintained, though erroneous, 665*e*
See ADOPTION VIII., 1082

RESIDENCE,
as affecting the law to which subject, 3
abroad does not affect representation, 70
daughter entitled to ——, 64
of the widow should be in the family dwelling, 64, 75, 245, 247, 673, 751, 775
enforced by caste laws as a condition of maintenance, 249*p*
in husband's family a duty not now enforced, 248, 251
widow cannot be deprived of her right by a sale, 75, 245, 328, 673
comparison of custom of London, 675*n*
widow's occupation is notice of the right, 752*d*
purchaser with notice of widow's right to —— bound 245
separate —— when allowed, 249
See ADOPTION VI. 992; VII. 1026, 1038; MAINTENANCE; WIDOW

RESIDUE, UNDIVIDED,
succession to —— how regulated, 648

RESIGNATION. See RELINQUISHMENT; RENUNCIATION

RESPONSES
importance of —— of law officers, 3
See ADOPTION I., 785; V., 949

RESTRICTION. See TRANSFER, 664*b*

RESUMPTION,
of grants by native rulers, 378
of land by Government gives right to a parcener, deprived of it, to claim contribution from others, 764

RETROSPECTIVE EFFECT OF ADOPTION, 350, 878, 887*ss*, 1013*ss*, 1034

REUNION
with whom possible, 129, 133, 602
how effected, 129
effect of ——, *ib.*
original status restored, 132
according to the Viramitrodaya, 133
See FAMILY

REUNITED COPARCENER
succession to ——, 129
reunited coparceners when succeed, 130
sons take their father's estate, 129, 130
in preference to sons still separate, *ib.*
See INHERITANCE; REUNION, 129

REUNITED FAMILY. See FAMILY, REUNITED

REVERSIONER (= EXPECTANT HEIR),
has no vested interest during widow's life, 83, 87*l*
cannot generally obtain a declaration of his title during widow's life, 89, 371
but may in case of an attempted alienation.*
may protect the estate against improper alienation or waste, 90
cannot question alienation in which he concurred, 710*f*
what —— can sue the widow, 90
when bound by a decree against the widow, 89*v*
interest of —— is not liable to attachment and sale, 91, 190*z*, 299

REVOCATION. See ADOPTION VI. 960; GIFT

RIGHTS,
beyond the pale of religious connexion not recognized by ancient laws, 49*b*
creation of —— only in favour of a person in existence, 185
of widows restricted in Bengal, 953
of maintenance cannot be assigned by a widow, 191, 246, 250, 253, 288
proprietary —— acquired by occupancy, 361
restoration of conjugal —— when refused, 85*p*
See BIRTH; INHERITANCE; PROPERTY; WIFE

RITES AND CEREMONIES OF ADOPTION. See ADOPTION VI. *passim*

RIVAL WIFE. See WIFE

ROADS
common —— when indivisible, 671
may be used by all coparceners, 716

ROTATION
proceeds of hereditary office to be enjoyed by ——, 716, 743
an inam village, indivisible, may be enjoyed by ——, 754
property dedicated to family idol to be enjoyed by ——, 755
places of worship and sacrifices are indivisible and to be enjoyed by ——, 716, 743

ROTURIERS, 74*t*

---

* See *Iari Dutt Koer* v. *Musst. Hansbutti Koerain*, L R. 10 I. A. 150

SACERDOTAL PRIVILEGES, *520r*

SACRA, 56, 165*o*
privata, 165*o*, 185*o*
follow the inheritance, 816
connexion of —— with inheritance, 62*y*, 689*z*, 957
rights of property connected with ——, 957, 959, 973, 975, 988, 1011, 1052, 1058
devolve on the person who takes the estate, 839
perpetuation of the ——, 880, 883, 884
Sudras have no —— in the higher sense, 923
change of —— in adoption, 910, 1033
non-performance of —— does not deprive the heir of his estate, 816
See ADOPTION III., 879, 880, 883, 884; IV. 923; VII., 1011, 1046

SACRAMENTS
treated of, 20, 24
to be performed in adoptive father's family, 939
See ADOPTION; MARRIAGE, 942; PROPERTY, SACRED; SAMSKARAS

SACRED WRITINGS. See INTERPRETATION

SACRIFICE,
performance of —— taught, 31
motive for ——, 84, 791
expensive ——s may be performed by one member only with the assent of others, 564
See ASSENT
separate performance of —— a sign of partition, 637, 672*k*
sacrifices forbidden to the Sudras, 824
except vicarious, *ib.*
former prevalence of animal ——, 791*e*, 811*x*
Sarnta ——, 820
Roman domestic ——s, 638*s*
See ADOPTION IV., 939; VII. *passim*

SADRISAM
= likeness, suitableness, 937
See ADOPTION II. 830

SAGOTRA. See ADOPTION IV., 943; VI., 999

SAGOTRA SAPINDA. See SAPINDAS

SAHODHA SON, 805

SAKHA
a version of the Veda, 31

SAKULYA. See SAPINDA, GOTRAJA
defined, 464

SALE
of patrimony once disallowed, 195
arose through gifts, *ib.*
formerly had to take the shape of gift, 191, 196
delivery and acceptance necessary for a ——, 191
of land still unrecognized in some districts, 673
consent of townsmen or co-mirasdars formerly required, *ib.*
of family lands not a process of Hindu Law for enforcing payment of debts, 602
made for common liability causes a deduction from common property, 618
of a son in extreme need. See ADOPTION, 950, 951
and gift of a child forbidden by Apastamba, 792*n*
of children recognized amongst the Romans, 805*k*
of expectant interest of doubtful validity, 190*z*
in execution of a father's interest does not pass son's, 592*e*
of a single co-parcener's interest extends to it only, 652
effect given to —— by partition, 615, 653
purchaser at a Court —— can only seek for partition, 652*w*
acquires only the judgment debtor's right to claim a severance of his share,* 615
See ADOPTION VII., 1036; ALIENATION; COPARCENER; FATHER; PURCHASER; WIDOW

SALE IN EXECUTION,
rights of enjoyment of otherwise indivisible property (*e.g.*, well or tank) are transferrable in execution, 757

SALIC LAW,
compared with Hindu law, 82*w*, 422*x*

SALVATION
may be attained by asceticism, 814*a*
See ADOPTION II., 789, 791, 811, 812, 825, 957, 975; ASCETIC

SALVEE CASTE, 689*y*

SAMANAGOTRA,
the same as gotraja, 120
means belonging to the same family, *ib.*

SAMANODAKAS,
who are ——, 122, 123
meaning of ——, 123
gotraja, when succeed, *ib.*, 455
cease with the fourteenth degree, *ib.*, *ib.*
not mentioned in the Mitakshara as heirs to a woman's property, 503

* *Baboo Hurdey Narain Sahu* v. *Baboo Rooder Perkash Mitter*, L. R. U. I. A. 26.

SAMBANDHA, 48

SAMSARA
= moral and ceremonial duties, 600*t*

SAMSKARA *
= the initiatory rites (Manu. II., 26*ss*, 39, 67, 169, 170), 519
neglected by Gosavis, *ib.*
Munja or Upanayana (Manu. II., 169)
See INITIATION
performance of —— as affecting status, 838*s*
adoption. See ADOPTION II., 838*s*, 1012; VII., 1022, 1027; CEREMONIES; INITIATION; MARRIAGE

SAMSKARAKAUSTUBHA,
of Anantadeva, 24, 781
See separate List of Hindu Authorities

SAMSRISHTI,
succession to a ——, 129

SAMVARTA SMRITI, 43

SANCTION
of grantor deemed necessary to adoption of an heir to the holding of grantee, 836*n*
See ADOPTION III., 853, 854, 856, 859, 868, 880, 882

SANKARA,
was the father of Nilakantha, 21
author of Dvaitanirnaya, *ib.*

SANKARACHARYA, 518

SANNYASI, 56, 61
who may become ——s, 518*h*
Sudras and women cannot become ——s, 519
duties of a ——, *ib.*
succession to a ——, 133, 467
custom governs succession to ——s, 520
See ADOPTION III., 850; ASCETIC, 517*ss*

SANTHALS. See under TRIBES, 270

SAPINDA—S
described, 112
who are ——s, 113, 114

---

* An account of the Samskaras now practised will be found in R. S. V. N. Mandlik's Vyav. May. Introd. pp. xxx. ss.

SAPINDA—S—*continued.*
interpretation of —— according to Balambhatta, 119
relationship based on descent from common ancestor, 112
not on presentation of funeral oblations, 113
in the case of females on marriage with descendants of a common ancestor, *ib.*
when —— ceases, 113, 509*q*
bhinnagotra —— same as bandhu, 123
who are bhinnagotra ——s, 126
paternal aunt pronounced not a gotraja —— but a bandhu? 122*p*
contra, 122
relationship through females restricted to four degrees, 127
Sapindas of the husband when inherit, 141, 487
of the widow when inherit, 141
gotraja —— 435*ss*
who are ——s, 484
Kamalakara's rule of determining nearness of ——s, 485
sagotra ——s of the husband when succeed to the widow, 487
bhinnagotra ——s when succeed to the widow, 503
of the widow, inherit to her, 505
sagotra ——s of widow, succession of, 508
See ADOPTION VI., 991
bhinnagotra ——, 512
duty of —— as to adoption, 783, 796*k*, 871*g*
son of —— preferred for adoption, 800, 924
See ADOPTION III., 872, 894*ss*; VI., 987; VII., 1051; KINSMEN

SAPINDA'S SUCCESSION, 450, 451
See GOTRAJA SAPINDA

SABRATIBANDHA DAYA SUCCESSION. See SUCCESSION, OBSTRUCTED

SARANJAM,
is usually impartible, 174, 681, 683*z*
holder of a —— can make a grant for his own life, 664*b*
is attended with an obligation to maintain the younger members, 681
pension substituted for —— has the same legal character, *ib.*
succession to a ——, is according to primogeniture, 683*z*
grant to a lady out of —— resumable after death of grantor, 697

SARANJAMDAR,
consent of Government thought necessary to choice by —— in adoption, 952

SAROGEES. See ADOPTION III., 890; IV., 919

SASTRIS, 3
importance of their opinions, 785
reason of some inconsistencies in their answers, 401, 785*g*

SATATAPA (VRIDDHA) SMRITI, 46

SAUDAYIKA,
woman's control over —— absolute, 86, 258
limited by the Smriti Chandrika, 285

SAVINGS,
out of part of zamindari allotted to a junior member are not joint property, 153
made by a widow. See WIDOW, 299
of a widow out of the estate inherited from her husband are accretions to it unless distinctly appropriated otherwise, 299, 300, 301
out of allotments to juniors not joint property, 682
See ACCUMULATIONS; STRIDHANA

SAXON LAW,
as to pious gifts compared with Hindu law, 191*n*

SCHOOLS,
ancient, origin of ——, 31
Brahminical, origin of intellectual life in India, 48
of Hindu law, 12—54

SCIENCE. See GAINS, 667; PARTITION

SEBAITS. See MAHANT; PROPERTY D. II.; SUIT

SECOND ADOPTION. See ADOPTION III., 843

SECTARIANS,
fabrications of ——, 48

SECURITIES,
created by father binds sons unless of a profligate character, 73

SEISIN,
once essential to gift of land under English law, 214*w*
See POSSESSION

SELF-ACQUIRED
= in any way acquired except by succession, descent and participation of right, 658

SELF-ACQUIRED PROPERTY,
as between father and son, 664
between coparceners generally, 666
See PROPERTY, SEPARATE AND SELF-ACQUIRED

SELF-GIVEN. See ADOPTION II. and III.

SENIORITY,
in origin postponed to nearness in blood, 66
by birth gives superiority of right, 74, 75

SENIORITY—*continued.*
where property is impartible, 78
See ELDERSHIP, 676; PRIMOGENITURE

SEPARATE PROPERTY, 73*ss*, 664*ss*
See PROPERTY, SEPARATE AND SELF-ACQUIRED

SEPARATED HOUSEHOLDER,
becomes the origin of a new line of succession, 73
free to dispose of ancestral estate in the absence of sons, *ib.*
heirs to a ——, 74
See FATHER; INHERITANCE; PARTITION; PROPERTY; SEPARATION; SON

SEPARATION,
defined, 608
how effected, *ib.*
signs of ——, 411, 636, 637, 644
cannot be prevented by creditors, 609
times of ——, *ib.*
may be made at any time on terms agreed to, 611
at the will of a son, 609
of the father from his father and brothers does not involve —— of the father and his son, 338
sons born after —— preferred to sons separated as heirs to their parents' share, 64, 338
does not deprive a son of inheritance, 340
See ADOPTION VII., 1032; COMMENSALITY; EVIDENCE; PARTITION; SACRIFICE; SON, 709

SERVICE-LAND
aliened or divided freed from special rule of descent, 683

SERVICES, RELIGIOUS
secure future beatitude, 957

SETTLEMENT
of land made with holder binds owner, 665
See WIDOW, 1078

SET OFF
of barred debts against claimants on a fund, 572*l*

SEX. See FEMALE

SEXUAL ASSOCIATIONS
in the lower castes, 357, 394*ss*
in ancient times, 794, 796

SHARE ALLOTTED TO FEMALES,
nature of the property, 712, 715
See ADOPTION VII.; DAUGHTER; FATHER; MOTHER; PARTITION; SISTER; STRIDHANA; WIDOW

SHISHYA, 525

SIMPI (TAILOR) CASTE. See CASTE, 483, 1003

SIPUJ, 534

SIRPAVA. See ALLOWANCES

SISSEE ABORS. See TRIBES, 276

SISTER
entitled to maintenance, 227, 241, 412, 690
sister's provision in undivided family extends to a quarter share, 333
See BELOW
sister's maintenance and marriage a charge on brother's estate, 714a
indigent widowed ——s entitled to provision in some castes, 691e, 692n
to provision from brother's widows, 692
is a gotraja, 121
not so according to Smriti Chandrika, 442
in Gujarat is first of the gotraja sapindas, 107, 109
in Madras regarded as a bandhu, but postponed to sister's son, 463w
sister's succession, 435, 463w
perhaps a trace of female gentileship, 399n
position of full ——, 435
competent to inherit in Western India, 118d
exclusion of —— by custom, 435
her right admitted by Balambhatta, 121n
is analogous to that of brothers, *ib.*
sister's take equally, 436
succeeds before remote kinsmen, 430, 436
preferred to a paternal first cousin, 436
in Bombay and Gujarat precedes half-brother, 104, 430, 436, 437, 439
placed next to the grandmother by Nilakantha, 108, 109
postponed to gotraja sapindas by Vijnanesvara, 107, 108
ex. gr. to the widow of the paternal uncle, 121, 122
sister's succession to a sister, 471
half —— preferred to step-mother, 440
See HALF-SISTER, 436
in some passages allowed an equal share with brothers, 627d
takes absolutely by inheritance, 282, 313
property inherited by —— is Stridhana (in Bombay), 436
is entitled on partition to a share equal to one-fourth of a brother's, 412, 714
sister's share in a partition is her absolute property, 714
is only a marriage portion? (Smriti Chandrika), 288

SISTER—*continued.*
contra the Viramitrodaya, *ib.*
sister's Sulka inherited by her full brothers, 266*ss*, 311
See ADOPTION IV., 921; VII., 963, 969

SISTER'S DAUGHTER
sister's daughter's right of inheritance admitted by Balambhatta, 121*m*
succeeds to a woman, 513
postponed to sister's son, 463
pronounced not an heir, 446

SISTER'S DAUGHTER'S SON
his succession admitted in Bengal, 466
but questionable, *ib.*

SISTER'S GRANDSON, 467

SISTER'S SON
is a bandhu, 462, 463
has no right so long as a sister survives, 463
sister's sons take before sister's daughters, *ib.*
postponed to sister-in-law, 121
cousin's son, 331
fifth descendant from grandfather, 464
as successor preferred to paternal aunt's son, *ib.*
maternal ——, *ib.*
succeeds to his maternal aunt, 512
heir to his uncle amongst aboriginal tribes, 801*k*
See ADOPTION IV., 918, 919, 921, 924, 944; BANDHU; SAPINDA; SUDRA, 924; VAISYAS, 924

SISTER-IN-LAW
preferred to sister's son and to a male cousin, 121
son of wife's sister may be adopted. See ADOPTION IV., 942

SMRITIS, 12, 16, 25—50
natural at a particular period of development, 50
enumerated, 27
classification of ——, 30, 38, 46
are versions not forgeries, 45
come nearer than the Vedas to modern practice, 784
interpretation of ——, 48, 781*i*
governed by the Mimamsa, 505
See INTERPRETATION
are not codes but manuals, 48, 50
are above reasoning, 787
rules contained in the ——, 233, 234, 235
could not be repealed, 795*g*
rest on a religious not a utilitarian basis, 49*b*
deemed superior to usage, 787*a*
not entirely consistent, 814*a*

SMRITIS—*continued.*
when they conflict, Equity decides, 13
form one body, 16, 781*c*
are supplementary to each other, 16, 49
have frequently been altered, 29
contain much that is given in the Dharmasutras, 40
which —— are redactions of Dharmasastras, 45
hardly applicable to marriage relations of the lower castes, 401
or to adoption amongst these classes
See ADOPTION II.; IV.; V., 941, 948, 953; VII.

SOCAGE,
law of ——, 74*t*, 734*o*

SODA CHITI. See DIVORCE

SODAKA,
same as Samanodaka, 123

SLAVE
under the old law incapable of property, 262, 275, 324

SLAVERY
abolished by Act V. of 1843, 483
kinds of ——, 45
See ADOPTION II.; VII.

SMRITI CHANDRIKA. See SEPARATE LIST OF HINDU AUTHORITIES

SON,
importance of a ——, 789, 790*t*, 810, 811
guardianship of a —— during minority, 964*s*
See AGE; GUARDIAN; MINOR
continuator of family sacra, 657
procreation of a son an imperative duty, 812*h*, 812
substituted —— indispensable failing one begotten, 780
a single adoption discharges the sacred debt, 1012
takes the place of a father disqualified or retired, 610*v*
born in wedlock is legitimate though begotten before it, 324
includes son's son's son, 64
entitled in extreme need to maintenance, 258, 1090
even in preference to fulfilment of promise, 1090
status of —— necessarily unconditional, 959
not transferrible like a chattel, 833, 951, 952*q*
can be disinherited only for adequate reasons, 549, 551, 739, 790
but then could be replaced, 790*t*
begotten son not to be replaced according to some passages, 793*v*
identified with father for all lawful obligations, 162
son's liability to pay father's debts. See DEBTS, 75, 161, 164, 165, 550, 568, 596, 685*f*, 686, 1088
limited by caste laws, 686*h*,

SON—*continued.*
separated —— not liable unless he inherits property, 165
sons liable to pay with interest, grandsons without, 1089
is represented by his father in a suit, 574
is bound by a compromise made *bonâ fide* by his father, *ib.*
becomes head of family on father's incapacity or retirement, 610*v*
sons and father are joint owners in ancestral estate, 73, 371, 549, 657, 665
and in property acquired by father, 665, 666
co ownership arises only on actual birth, 731
or adoption. See ADOPTION VII.
cannot contest prior alienations by father, 731, 740
son's ownership, according to Daya Bhaga, arises only on the death of their father, 559*a*
not deprived of a real right by a transfer, 7
See TRANSFER
may prevent improper alienation of ancestral property by the father, 198*a*, 594, 737
See INTERDICTION
cannot generally charge property during father's life, 241
share of the —— how far liable in execution against the father, 576*ss*
sons take by representation, 61
but not brother's sons (see below), 103
takes impartible estate as "purchaser," 162
sons succeed to an Avibhakta Grihastha, 61, 323
sons and grandsons take solely the self-acquisitions of the father and grandfather, 324
sons succeed to a separated person, 73, 338
separated —— is preferred to father's widow, 340, 341, 722
sons may claim partition of ancestral property? 173, 609, 611, 617, 726, 727, 733
many exceptions to this by caste law, 611*ss*
cannot contest a partition made before his birth, 1078
sons cannot obtain partition in Bengal, 163
sons cannot demand partition with grandfather against father's will, 645*b*, 726
cannot enforce partition of father's self-acquired property, 741
allowed to sue to establish his right in a share inherited from his uncle by his father, 633
predeceased (childless); his interests merge in his father's, 169, 324, 670*t*, 882
may relinquish his share and become separate, 324, 722
does not thus lose his right of succession, 340, 722, 723
sons not reunited postponed to reunited, 129, 130
separated ——s postponed to ——s united or born after separation, 64, 324, 338, 347, 709, 722, 731
importance of eldest ——, 819
elder —— by younger wife preferred to a younger by an elder wife (generally), 324
See ELDERSHIP

SON—*continued.*
succeeds to his mother, 479
when ——s inherit to their mother, 140
sons take unobstructed inheritance according to Vyav. May., 103, 285, 658
See MOTHER
sons succeed to mother's self-acquired property (Bengal), 308*m*
sons are not co-sharers with mother (Smriti Chandrika), 100
sons are coparceners by birth, 61, 212*h*
sons take equally, 74, 314, 344
Sudra's ——s legitimate and illegitimate inherit *inter se* as brothers, 264
sons cannot be separated *inter se* against their will, 193, 617
sons of brothers of the full blood inherit, 105
half-blood inherit, *ib.*
when ——s of brothers of the —— —— inherit with brothers, *ib.*
sons of half-brothers are sapindas according to the Vyav. May., 106
sons of deceased brothers represent their fathers in partition and succession to ancestors, 327, 753
sons take the place of adoptive father, 76
See ADOPTION VII.
illegitimate ——s, not affected by their mother's connexion with other men than their father, 366
sons in the religious sense not possible to a Sudra, 365
illegitimate ——s of a Sudra inherit, 69, 76, 77, 355, 357, 421
get half-a-share if legitimate descendants are living, 360, 362
illegitimate —— of a Sudra preferred to a widow and daughter, 358
sons born in sin entitled to maintenance only, 78, 368, 401
sons of a concubine are *inter se* brothers of the whole blood, 78
and inherit *inter se* as brothers, 364
illegitimate ——s of a European could not form a true joint family, 4
illegitimate ——s of higher castes can claim maintenance only, 77, 164, 355, 358
Subsidiary Sons
twelve kinds of subsidiary ——s, 805
relative places assigned to the different kinds of ——s, 803, 804
division of sons into kinsmen-heirs, and kinsmen-not heirs, 803
subsidiary ——s of each class exclude those lower in the scale, 365
sons of uncertain origin excluded from succession, 807*x*
adopted sons succeed on failure of legitimate issue of the body, 67, 76, 347
See ADOPTION *passim*; DEBT; FATHER; GIFT; ILLEGITIMATE; OUT-CASTE; PRIMOGENITURE

SON'S DAUGHTER
postponed to daughter-in-law? 495

SON, POSTHUMOUS
inherits, 129, 769
partition re-opened by birth of —— ——, 649, 769

SON'S SON
son's son's succession to grandmother failing sons, 479

SON'S SON'S SON'S SON
inherits as a gotraja, 607

SON'S WIDOW
postponed to brother, 427

SON-IN-LAW
in some tribes taken into the family of a sonless man, 398*h*
affiliation of ——, 1065
admitted in some Narvadari villages as successor to a proprietor *
See GHAR-JAWAHI; ILLATAM, 398*h*

SONAR. See under CASTE, 473

SONIS. See under CASTE, 689*y*

SOURCES. See HINDU LAW, 9, 946

SPARTAN LAW
comparison of —— —— with Hindu law, 276*m*

SPIRITUAL RELATIONS, 126
See ASCETIC

SRADDHA †, 59
described, 1012*o*
importance of ——, 62
separate performance of —— is a sign of partition, 637
wife's share in ——s, 87
Jains have no ——s, 811
forbidden to Sudras, 825*n*, 832*y*
Sraddhas may be performed by all castes by custom, 825*n*
subordinate character of a —— celebrated for mother and her ancestors, 946*w*, 1027
in case of nephew adopted, 1023
by adopted son in default of original heirs, 1024
repetition of ——s a supposed ground fro repeated adoptions, 1027*q*
See ADOPTION II.; DHARMA-PUTRA; PROPERTY, 59; SACRA

SRAUTA SACRIFICE, 820*b*
SRAVAKS,
(Jains), 533, 534

SROTRIYAM GRANT
is separate property, 667*o*
descendible to grantee's sons only, *ib.*

---

* Bo. Gov. Rec. No. 114, p. 134.

† For the Sraddhas in actual use *see* R. S. V. N. Mandlik's Vyav. May. Introd. pp. xxxvi. ss.

SROTRIYAS
= learned Brahmanas, 128

SRUTIS
are fountain heads of law, 50
contents of ——, *ib.*
are above reasoning, 787

STATE
the source or sanction of private property, 179, 185
succession of —— to property, 94, 129
See ESCHEAT; KING; PROPERTY A.; D. II. γ.

STATUS
law of personal —— dependent on religion, 4
of son cannot be made subject to contingencies, 959
See ADOPTION VII., 1010, 1019

STATUTES. See SEPARATE LIST

STATUTE OF LIMITATION
bars suit for partition after long separate holding, 641
when —— —— operates by prescription, 644, 648
effect of —— —— in a suit for partition, 753
See LIMITATION; PRESCRIPTION

STATUTE LAW
supersedes Hindu law in contracts, 7

STEP-BROTHER. See HALF-BROTHER'S SON, 511

STEP-BROTHER'S SON. See HALF-BROTHER'S SON, 511
See BROTHER, 510

STEP-DAUGHTER. See DAUGHTER, 502
step-daughter's succession, 485
step-daughter's son heir to a widow, 491

STEP-GRANDMOTHER, 712

STEP-MOTHER
not included in the term "mother," 102
step-mother's right to maintenance or an allotment, 443*y*, 605*v*
and to residence, 341, 709*b*, 751
maintenance of —— a duty of step son as well as of her own son, 228, 629, 1039
step-mother's allotment, 712*w*
her right to inherit, 442
excluded by Strange, *ib.*
admitted by Balambhatta, *ib.*

STEP-MOTHER—*continued.*
stands next to paternal grandmother according to Mitakshara, 443
postponed to half-sister, 441
daughter, 409
grandmother, 442
regarded as successor to step-son and his widow, 490
adoptive. See ADOPTION VII., 1039
her step-son may inherit her stridhana, 443, 1040
step-mothers though sonless are entitled to equal shares on partition, 443, 746
this questioned by Viramitrodaya, *ib.*
doctrine of the Vyavahara Mayukha, 442

STEP-SISTER. See SISTER; HALF-SISTER
step-sister's son is excluded by sister's son, 463

STEP-SON
not entitled to succeed to his step-father, 480
succeeds to his step-mother, 442, 488, 1040
as heir to step-mother postponed to husband, 489

STIPULATION
by adoptive parents for annuity for giving their son, illegal, 961

STRANGERS
to agreements or awards cannot use admissions in them, 189*n*
cannot be intruded into sacred offices, 185*o*

STRIDHANA,
Different Conceptions of ——, 257*ss*
different senses of ——, 257, 258*ss*
Vijnanesvara's definition, 258, 301, 315
Nilakantha's definition, 258, 259
growth of woman's right to ——, 263*ss*
enumeration of ——, 258
enumeration of Manu not exhaustive, 137
the Sarasvati Vilasa on ——, 317
Apararka on ——, 712*w*
Nilakantha's classification into Paribhashika and other kinds, 134, 135, 258, 485
according to Mitakshara, 135, 138
no distinction between Paribhashika and other kinds, 135
has no technical meaning, 136
includes every kind of acquisition by a woman, 308, 313
recognition of every kind of acquisition by women by the Court in Madras. 314*w*
in Bengal, 315
but restricted by decisions so as to exclude property inherited from a male, as well as from a female, 314*ss*, 319, 320

STRIDHANA—*continued.*
the female now takes but a life estate? the law in Bombay and Mithila, 289, 319, 320
See DAUGHTER; FEMALE; SISTER, 422, 424, 436
distinction drawn between females born and those married in the family, 302*f*, 312, 313, 320
correctness of this discussed, 320, 321
in Bengal property inherited by a daughter from her father is not ——, Mithila, 288, 288*f*
nor is the share taken by a mother in a partition as representative of a deceased son, 288
See MOTHER
immoveable property bought by a widow out of savings from her maintenance is her ——, 299, 300. 475
if she indicates her intention of so holding it, 299, 299*r*, 300
so is property bought from a fund bequeathed by her husband, 300
mode of acquiring ——, 278
according to Mitakshara, 258, 301, 315
gifts from parents, 278, 481
husband, 279, 293, 296, 313, 324
ornaments given for ordinary wear are ——, 295
immoveable property given by the husband is ——, 296, 297, 309*t*
subject to restrictions on disposal, 710*f*, 984
a husband separate in estate can give or devise to his wife with absolute ownership, 984
gifts from sons, brother, and others, 281, 282
by inheritance, 137, 138, 139, 261, 263, 281, 311, 317, 709, 712
property inherited by a widow from her husband is ——? 313, 436
includes inheritance from second husband, 480
according to the Privy Council property inherited by a woman from a male or a female, except in Bombay and Mithila, is not —— and is not transmissible as her own, 138, 318, 320
proof that according to the Mit. inherited property is —— from the case of brother's succession, 263*x*, 308, *cf*318
from the treatment of the subject by the Vyav. May., 135, 138, 263*x*
the principal commentators adopt this doctrine, 316
Mit. followed by Viv. Chint. and Saras. Vil., 263, 316, 317
doctrine recognized as that of the Mit. by the Viram., Daya Bhaga, and Smr. Chan., 138, 263*z*
wife's share in a partition is ——, 290*v*, 294, 709, 713, 750. *cf* 709*d*
and a widow's share, 290*v*, 294
a mother's share is ——, 287*w*, 311, 712*w*, 714*z*, 714
so is a sister's share, 283*t*, 312, 318, 709
and a daughter's, 283*t*, 284
marriage gifts are wife's ——, 271
Adhivedanika, 259, 277
Adhyagnika, 277
Adhyavahana, *ib.*
Anvadheyika, 135, 277, 486
Pritidatta, *ib.*, *ib.*, *ib.*

STRIDHANA—*continued.*
Saudayika, 258
Sulka, 277
Yautaka, 485
nature of the woman's estate (see above)
gifts to a wife from strangers belong to husband? 281, 282, 285. *cf* 286*p*
mother does not take absolutely, 312, 313, 1036
but daughter and sister do, 261, 288, 289, 312, 313, 316, 320, 333
exception in Madras, 288
Bengal, 314, 316
Allahabad, 318, 319
so a maternal great-niece, 312*m*
mother's property in Yajn. = Stridhana in Mit., 309*n*
wife's power to alienate controlled by husband, 86
her power of disposal over gifts, bequests, and heritage, 288, 709*d*, 710*f*
her power over —— (Saudayikam) unfettered except as to immoveables, 86, 284, 285
according to the chief native authorities, 283—285
over —— generally except immoveables taken from her husband, 285, 286, 289
widow's estate not a trust nor an estate for life, 297, 398
she represents the inheritance, 398
widow's share in partition at her absolute disposal? 288, 289, 290*v*, 295
authorities discussed, 713*x*, 714
daughter has full power over —— devolved from her mother (Bombay), 288
and over her allotment in a partition, 284, 295
or a gift from father, 295
testamentary power as to —— commensurate with the right of disposal during life, 294
husband may dispose of wife's —— in distress, 283
may take —— in cases of wife's flagrant misconduct (Viram.), 283*v*
Succession to ——
the subject discussed, 137, 311*ss*
in Bombay, 318*ss*
property inherited by a sister from her brother is —— and goes to her daughters, 436
descends to daughters unprovided for, 477
heirs to the different classes of ——, 135, 295, 309, 486
Anvadheya, 135
Paribhashika, *ib.*
Pritidatta, *ib.*
Sulka, 139
Yautaka, 309
succession to —— according to Sri-Krishna and Vijnanesvara, 307, 308 484
according to Bengal law, 309, 481
Jagannatha, 309
immoveable property given by husband descends as ——, 309*t*
if an absolute estate has been given, 293, 297*c*, 983

STRIDHANA—*continued.*
so as to all inheritance save from husband, 313. *Cf* 314
contrary decisions, 138, 319, 421, 422
rule of succession to a male applied, 135, 138, 496
husband's sister preferred to his cousin, 503
husband's sister's son wrongly preferred to his cousin, 498, 501
widow's sapindas inherit after husband's, 505
See ADOPTION VII., 1034, 1038; DAUGHTER; EJECTMENT, 287*x*; FEMALE; INHERITANCE; MOTHER; SAPINDA; SISTER; STEP-MOTHER; SUCCESSION; WIDOW; WIFE; WOMAN

STUDENT. See FELLOW-STUDENT, 128; PUPIL, 468
to become a householder after instruction in the Veda (Manu. III. 2—4), 790*y*
See GRIHASTHA

STUDY
of Vedas and of Manu. prohibited to Sudras (Manu. II. 16), 824

SUBODHINI,
a commentary by Visvesvarabhatta, 18

SUBSIDIARY SON. See ADOPTION; KSHETRAJA; PUTRIKA PUTRA; SON

SUBSTITUTION
under Roman law, 303*l*

SUCCESSION
depends on status, 4, 5
See CUSTOM; HINDU LAW; LEX LOCI, 4
mode of determining —— in litigation, 5
regulation of —— according to the performance of funeral oblations peculiar to Bengal, 59
division of ——, 60, 61
to an Avibhakta Grihastha, 61
joint and undivided —— is the rule, 64
according to the Viramitrodaya, 126
tribal ——, 128*f*, 672
special rules of ——, 150, 177
to a raj or principality, 152, 675
miras, 177
regulated according to propinquity, 110*e*
differently according to various authorities, *ib.*
as affected by forms of marriage, 504
collateral —— of adopted son, 350, 1035, 1040, 1046
on the death of a widow goes to her husband's heirs next to those specified, 83
origin of —— of persons spiritually related, 60
not suspended for one not begotten or adopted, 63, 542, 545, 1050
of co-sharers impaired by adoption in a family, 949

SUCCESSION—*continued.*
to impartible property governed by seniority, 65, 75
limited to a series of single heirs is not equivalent to primogeniture *, 65i
See ELDERSHIP; PRIMOGENITURE; VATAN
illegitimate son excluded from ——, 153
except of a Sudra, 69
See ILLEGITIMATE SON
line of —— prescribed by law cannot be altered, 179r
unrecognized—disallowed,† 178
to an endowment determined by custom, 199
to bhagdari lands in Gujarat, 407
females in Maratha country not excluded from —— to inam property, *ib.*
See FEMALE; GRANT; INAM
through females only in some tribes, 274f
of parents, 421
on the death of mother who has inherited from son goes to his next heir, *ib.*
to undivided residue, 648
to priestly offices and emoluments, 389, 407
See ADOPTION VII., 1027, 1031, 1038, 1039, 1040, 1046, 1050, 1051, 1052, 1056, 1061, 1064; BROTHER; COPARCENER; CUSTOM; ENDOWMENT; FAMILY; FEMALE; INHERITANCE; MATHA; PRIEST; PRINCIPALITY, 675, 676; PROPERTY; RAJ; VATAN
UNOBSTRUCTED, 60, 63, 129, 269
extends to three descendants in the male line, 61, 64
according to Mit. and Madanaparijata —— extends to grandsons only, 61, 63
rules of —— apply to reunited family, 129
See FAMILY; INHERITANCE

SUCCESSION ACT (INDIAN) X. OF 1865, 1083
See SEPARATE LIST
governs Native Christians, 4
made applicable to wills of Hindus, 221
allows a remoter disposition than the Hindu law, *ib.*
See WILLS

SUDRAS, 61, 69, 76, 77, 79, 80, 81, 82, 97, 129, 265, 323, 356, 367, 392, 408, 413, 417, 426, 471, 479, 494, 511, 519, 521, 529, 535, 537, 545, 553, 603, 708, 712, 769
See ADOPTION II., 800, 801, 823, 824, 831; III., 849, 857, 873, 874
are Gribasthas, 61r
excluded from duties and rights of the higher castes (Manu. I. 91; II. 103), 823, 824, 831, 998
have not the higher sacra, 923
cannot become Sannyasis, 521
may become Gosavis, 519

---

* *Achal Ram* v. *Udai Partab Addiya Dat Singh*, L. R. 11 I. A. 51.

† *Kumar Tarakeswar Roy* v. *Kumar Shoshi Shikhareswar*, L. R. 10 I. A. 51.

SUDRAS—*continued.*
Vairagis, 537
forbidden to study the Vedas and to perform sacrifices, 61*r*, 832*y*
ex. gr. the datta homa, 824
recite mantras, *ib.*
their Sraddhas allowed, but defective, 790, 823, 825*n*, 832*y*
union among —— not of a sacred character, 916
incapable of having a son in the religious sense, 365
can adopt sister's son, 924
daughter's son, *ib.*
their rules of adoption partly admitted into the Brahminical system, 922
begetting a son on a —— woman entails loss of caste but not mere intercourse, 401*i*
See ADOPTION IV., 943, 944; V., 954; VII., 1044, 1045, and *passim*; BROTHER; CASTE; CEREMONIES; CUSTOM; DAUGHTER; FAMILY; ILLEGITIMATE SON

SUIT,
mere —— against one coparcener does not affect others, 588
unless the coparcener is a representative, 574
See JOINDER, 568; PARTIES; REPRESENTATION
representation of minor in a ——, 625
See ADMINISTRATION; MINOR, 703; NEXT FRIEND
and sale for a co-sharer's debt pass his right to share, 580, 585
in a —— against a family all are to be made defendants, 591
exceptions, *ib.*
by or against the father alone. See FATHER
as affecting sons, 577*ss*, 581, 583, 585
should name sons or specify representative character, 582
a compromise by father suing held binding on sons, 571*d*
sale under decree against father as affecting sons, 578*ss*, 584
a nephew not bound, 583*r*
against a manager affects only his share, 591
against sons for father's debt, 587
adopted son representative for ——, 1037
by son against father, 633
for property as divided does not bar one for it as undivided, 565, 723
for partition, 698*ss*
to enforce partition deed not allowed to be changed into one for maintenance, 712*w*
for partition by coparcener conveys no right to his widow, 765
perhaps not even a decree? *ib.*
to a —— for partition by the purchaser of the father's right the mother is a proper party *
for family idol, 716*m*
by Sebaits, 160
adoption pending ——, 1033
See ADOPTION VIII.; ATTACHMENT; CHARGE; COPARCENER; DEBT; DECREE; FAMILY; FATHER; GUARDIAN; LIABILITY; MANAGER; OBLIGATION; SALE

---

* *Hurdy Narain Sahu* v. *Rooder Perkash Misser*, L. R. 11 I. A. 26.

SUITS, POSSESSORY, 643
See POSSESSION

SULKA, 259, 277
definition of ——, 266
kinds of ——, *ib.*
not the same as Morgengabe, 267
goes to uterine brothers, 266—269, 311, 486*m*

SUPERSTITIOUS USES,
English law of —— not enforced, 211

SURETYSHIP *inter se* BY COPARCENERS
is a sign of partition but not conclusive, 636, 773

SURVIVOR. See ADOPTION, 887

SURVIVORSHIP,
rule of —— recognized, 71
alternative to that resting on recognized oblations, 72
no —— amongst daughters in Western India, 98
in united family, 428, 429
excludes an executor, 220
regulates succession in a reunited family, 132
See ADOPTION VII., 1032; BROTHER; COPARCENER; DAYA; FAMILY; INHERITANCE; PROPERTY; SUCCESSION

SUTAK, 1022

SUTAR, 249*p*

SUTRAS, 31—50
are strings of rules, 32
Apastambha Sutra, 32, 33
Hiranyakesi Sutra, 32
characterized by their shortness, 41

SVAIRINI
= disloyal wife, 604, 797
is one who deserts her husband and cohabits with another man, 368
son of —— occupied a place above adopted son, *ib.*

SVAMYA AND SVATANTRATA, 206

SVARJIT
= property acquired by one's self, 657

SVAYAMVARA, 271

SVYAMDATTA SON,
meaning of ——, 805, 956
not now recognized, 807
See ADOPTION V., 949

SWATHIS,
a Himalayan tribe, 733*g*

SWEDEN,
right of free occupancy in ancient ——, 672*k*

TAILOR, 362, 483

TANKS,
when indivisible, 671
may be used by all coparceners by turn or agreement, 716, 757

TAPODHANA CASTE, 410

TARWAD, *ib.*

TAULKIYA-AODICHYA CASTE, *ib.*

TEMPLE ALLOWANCES,
hereditary and divisible, 681
subject to special rules, *ib.*
See ADOPTION III., 945; ENDOWMENT; NIBANDHA

TEMPLE PROPERTY, 520, 521
See PERPETUITY; PROPERTY D. II. *a.*

TEMPLE SERVANT,
interest of —— —— alienable, 716*m*

TENANT. See LESSEE; LANDLORD
discharged by payment to one of several co-sharers, 570*s*
joint —— has not a devisable interest under English law, 618*x*
covenant by one joint —— to sell severs the joint tenancy in equity, 651*h*
See COPARCENER
rights of ——s after a partition, 661*m*

TENURE
rare under Hindu law, 174
of land supporting an office, 683
See GRANT; JAGIR; SARANJAM; VATAN

TESTAMENT. See WILL

TESTAMENTARY POWER, 209, 1021*s*
depends on the state of the family and the nature of the property, 173
regulated by Hindu law, 618

TESTAMENTARY POWER—*continued.*
not regulated by analogy to English law, 181
but to the Hindu law of gifts, 181 279
over self-acquired property absolute, 192, 214, 296, 618*x*, 705, 734, 982
limitations to this? 982, 983
collateral heirs no bar to the exercise of the ——, 193
not to defeat other's rights, 214, 215
or claims to subsistence, 215, 982
or to make illegal dispositions, 215
as to Stridhana is commensurate with the right of disposal during life, 294*g*
See ADOPTION III., 866; VI., 982; ALIENATION; COPARCENER; FAMILY; GIFT; MAINTENANCE; SON; SURVIVORSHIP

TEUTONIC LAWS,
comparison of —— —— with Hindu law, 191*n*, 262*w*, 303*l*

TEXTS. See INTERPRETATION, 8
to be received cautiously, 784, 785
interpretation of —— influenced by philosophical systems, 8
sometimes manipulated to suit later notions, *ib.*
how construed, 197*d*, 257*k*

THEODOSIAN CODE,
referred to, 399*l*

THIYENS. See TRIBES, 272, 397

TIME. See ADOPTION, 861, 871, 872

TIRTH-UPADYA,
Tirth-upadya's right partible by custom, 716*m*

TITHE. See POSSESSION, 644

TODA GIRAS, 180
not exempt from attachment, 703*x*

TONSURE,
period of ——, 831
as affecting fitness for adoption. See ADOPTION II., 830; III., 891; IV., 939, 941; VI., 1001*r*; VII., 939

TOOLS AND IMPLEMENTS,
when indivisible and when not, 671, 674
to be kept by those having them, 717

TOTHIYARS. See TRIBES, 396

TRADING *inter se* BY COPARCENERS,
a sign of partition. See EVIDENCE; PARTITION

TRADITIONS
as regards the Smritis, 26, 27
untrustworthy, 28
Brahminical, about the Dharmasutras, 36
an element of customary law, 787

TRANSACTION
of father how far binding on son, 571*d*
as to admissions of an adoptive mother, 1042
See COPARCENER; FATHER; MANAGER; OBLIGATION; REPRESENTATION; SUIT

TRANSFER
depends on individual will, 57
restrictions on —— inconsistent with estate disallowed, 193, 664*b*
of Saranjam not allowed, 664
different ceremonies for —— of immoveable and moveable property, 1065
irregular —— by father may be prevented by son, 738
or set aside, 740*e*
See ALIENATION; GIFT; GRANT; INTERDICT; POSSESSION; PROPERTY; SALE

TRAVANCORE. See FEMALE GENTILESHIP, 398; POLYANDRY, 272

TREASURE TROVE,
law of —— ——, 758

TRIBES,
Bhils, 269*i*
Bhooteah, 276*m*
Cacharis, 269*i*
Duflas, 276*m*
Garoo, 274*f*, 398
Gonds, 269*i*
Jats, 269*i*, 400*z*
Kangra tribes, 358
Kathis, 269*i*
Khasias, 276*m*, 398
Kholls, 269*i*, 270*m*
Khonds, 357
Koches, 269*i*, 398
Maravers, 406*z*
Meeris, 276*m*
Motati Kapus (Madras), 1065*c*
Nairs or Nayars, 272*w*, 396*x*, 398, 401*e*, 402*q*
Oraons, 269*i*
Pahans, *ib.*
Santhals, *ib.*
Sissee Abors, 276*m*
Talabda Kolis, 1056

TRIBES—*continued.*
Thiyens, 272, 397*z*
Tothiyars, 396*x*
Vazirs, 397*e*

TRIORDHA DIKSHA
= consecration, 533

TRUST,
not unknown to Hindu law, 200
legislation affecting ——s amongst Hindus, 416*h*
instances of ——s, 200, 201
native usage determines whether a —— has been created, 202
may be annexed to gift, 416
to husband for wife, 200
for daughter, 201
not allowed to create a perpetuity for a family or an estate, 200*l*
dissoluble only by assent of all interested, *ib.*
trusts uncertain and illegal ineffectual, 200, 201, 202
trusts how dealt with, 201, 202
charitable ——s enforced, 211*f*
enforcement of ——s, 201, 416
religious and charitable ——s common, 200
treated with special favour by Hindu law, 221
in favour of an idol, 160
heritable —— may be resigned by father to son, 519
not to be altered in constitution by majority, *ib.*
property transferred by a Mahant by a breach of —— can be recovered, 188*h*
beneficiaries may sue for the enforcement of the duties of ——, 377
subject to the consent of Advocate General or his substitute, *ib.*
See ENDOWMENT; GIFT, 416; GRANT; PROPERTY D. II.

TRUSTEE
of a religious endowment cannot alienate or encumber it except under special circumstances, 521*w*
See ENDOWMENT
widow is not a —— for son to be adopted, 1069
but continuing a suit after adoption may be deemed a trustee, *ib.*
the possessor of land who has settled for assessment is —— for owner, 664*b*

UNCERTAINTY
vitiates a trust, 200

UNCHASTITY
makes a woman only temporarily impure, 798*r*
disqualifies mother from inheriting to son, 554
does not prevent inheriting from maternal grandmother, *ib.*
disqualifies daughter from inheriting, 149*z*
but not among Lingayats, 554

UNCHASTITY—*continued.*
disables a widow for inheriting from her husband or son, 553, 554
but subsequent —— does not divest a widow's estate, 83, 554
See WIDOW
prevents one widow getting her share from the other, 554
of widow opens daughter's right to inherit, *ib.*
causes forfeiture of the right to maintenance, 555
maintenance allowed resumable on —— *ib.*

UNCLE
as manager; presumption in favour of his transactions, 592
may be commissioned by sister to give nephew in adoption, 954
when —— succeeds to nephew, 334, 444, 445
paternal —— succeeds to niece, 511
maternal —— postponed to the widow of the paternal uncle, 121, 122
inherits as bandhu, 125, 126, 460
inherits as a bhinnagotra sapinda, 459
preferred to maternal aunt's son, 461
See ADOPTION II., 809; IV., 914; NEPHEW

UNCLE'S (PATERNAL) DAUGHTER'S SON
an heir according to Bengal law, 460*n*

UNCLE'S (PATERNAL) GRANDSON, 451

UNCLE'S SON, 444*ss*, 511
See ADOPTION IV., 921

UNCLE'S (MATERNAL) SON
is a bandhu, 462
succeeds to a woman, 512

UNCLE'S SON'S WIFE, 454

UNCLE'S (PATERNAL) WIDOW
her succession, 453, 454
different law of N. W. Provinces, 454

UNCLE'S WIFE. See WIDOW OF PATERNAL UNCLE

UNDIVIDED FAMILY. See FAMILY

UNION, SPIRITUAL, 957

UNITY OF ESTATE
presumed in a united family, 670
See FAMILY, JOINT; PRESUMPTION

UNIVERSITAS, 162, 165, 209

UNMARRIED FEMALE. See DAUGHTER; FEMALE; SISTER

UNMARRIED MAN
may adopt. See ADOPTION II., 814a, 822, 823; III., 842x

UNMARRIED SON. See ADOPTION III., 880

UNOBSTRUCTED OWNERSHIP
its character, 96, 317o
See DAYA
of a son in his mother's estate asserted and denied, 205n, 711aa

UNOBSTRUCTED SUCCESSION. See INHERITANCE; SUCCESSION

UPADHI, 186

UPAKURVANA. See BRAHMACHARI

UPANAYANA, 941, 943. See ADOPTION III., 809h; IV.
meaning of —— rite, 939s, 997
no —— ceremony in many castes, 940

UPANISHADS, 49

USAGE
importance of ——, 2
tends to conform to received Scripture standards, 9, 401, 402, 785
governs inheritance, partition, and adoption, 7
is to be followed failing statute law, 7, 785
caste —— approved as to the members of families.*
gentu —— to govern succession and contracts of Gentus.†
See ADOPTION IV., 945; VI. 977, 985; CUSTOM, 197

USANAS. See INHERITANCE, 262
Dharmasastra, 34

VADILKI. See ELDERSHIP, 676

VAGHREE CASTE, 241p

VAIRAGIS. See GOSAVIS, 539
who are ——, 536
position and rights of —— with respect to temples, *ib.*
sometimes hold temple property like Mahants, *ib.*
may retain their property, 537
may marry, 539

VAISNAVAS
have forged some Smritis, 47

* St. 21 Geo. III. Ch. 70, Sec. 18.
† St. 21 Geo. III. Ch. 70, Sec. 17.

VAISVADEVA
= food oblations placed in fire, 637, 764, 773
separate performance of —— may be a sign of partition, 687
but is not conclusive, 637, 773

VAISYAS
said to have disappeared, 825*i*
a class of Grihasthas, 61
may become Sannyasis, 518
can adopt sister's son, 924
See ADOPTION III., 849

VALOUR
gains of —— as separate property compared with *peculium castrense*, 667*o*

VAMSA-PARAMPARA
= lineal succession not collateral, 345

VANAPRASTHA, 518*h*, 527, 531

VANDI CASTE, 374

VANI CASTE, 389, 476, 490

VASISTHA DHARMASUTRA, 32, 41
has been recast, 33
See ADOPTION V., 946, 947, 949; VI., 994

VATAN
nature of ——, 175, 684, 768*o*
law relating to ——, 768, 768*o*
compared with a fief, 768*o*
succession to ——, 765, 683*z*
devolution of —— is governed by special law, 180
females can succeed to a ——, 326*i*
not presumably impartible, *ib.*
Desgat —— is partible, 377
of a Kulkarni, 336, 413, 456, 477
Desaigiri, 424
Yardi, 336
Zamindar's —— is divisible, 671*e*
Patilki, 365
Joshi, 456
once aliened or divided is freed from special rule of descent, 683*z**
subject to statute, 180
profits of a vatandari village may be divided, 717
impartible —— does not become partible by disuse of services, 681

VATANDAR JOSHI. See JOSHI, 377

* Subject to Bombay Act III. of 1874 and other statutes.

VATANDARS' ACT
(Bom. Act III. of 1874) see separate List of Acts

VATANDAR VILLAGE. See DISTRIBUTION; VATAN

VATSA, 953

VAZIFA. See ALLOWANCES

VAZIRS. See TRIBES, 397*e*

VEDAS
the fountain of intellectual life in India, 48
the remote fountain of law, 50
superior to custom, 785
the four ——, 50
each of the —— consists of Mantras and Brahmanas, *ib.*
antiquity of ——, 839*b*
of little importance as a direct source of modern law, 50
character of their different parts, *ib.*
not to be recited by the Sudras, 1003
nor by a boy uninitiated, 1088

VEHICLES
when indivisible and when not, 671, 674
to be kept by those having them, 717, 756

VERSION OF NARADA
discussed, 44, 45

VESTED INTEREST. See ADOPTION III, 878*ss*, 886

VESTED REMAINDER. See REMAINDER, 90, 91

VIBHAKTA GRIHASTHA, 56, 61, 73—128, 338—467

VICE
as a ground of disinheritance, 149, 689*y*

VIDYADHYAYANA, 31

VIJNANESVARA, 17, 951
age of ——, 18

VINIYOGA
a disposal of widow by husband's family, 406, 691*d*

VIRAMITRODAYA
is a commentary by Mitramisra, 21

VIRA SAIVA, 533

VISHNU SMRITI, 33, 36

VISVESVARA (BHATTA), 17
is the author of the Subodhini, 18

VOLITION
how far —— passes property, 7

VRITTI
meaning of ——, 671*e*, 681*f*, 759*w*
is a family estate subject to inheritance and partition, 389
is heritable, 658*x*
Yajamana ——, 327, 388
is partible, 377, 671*e*, 681*f*, 766, 767
Bhatt's —— is divisible, 671*e*
inalienable outside the family, 389
widow may alien — for necessary sustenance, 407
mortgaged —— sold in execution of a decree, 680
intruder into a —— is liable for damages, 389
each invasion of a —— is a fresh cause of action, 328*o*
whether the representative of a priestly family can sue his Yajamana, 389
widow may alien —— for necessary sustenance, 407

VYAHRITIS
= mystic formulas of sacrifice, 994

VYASA, 953

VYAVAHARA MAYUKHA
ranks above the Mitakshara in Gujarat, 13, 109
is the sixth Mayukha of Bhagavanta Bhaskara, 20
composed by Nilakantha, *ib.*
dedicated to king Bhagavantadeva, *ib.*
must in some places be explained by the Dvaitanirnaya, 21

WATAN. See VATAN, 180

WAYS, COMMON
when indivisible, 671
may be used by all coparceners, 716, 756

WELFARE SPIRITUAL, 953. See ADOPTION, I., 789, 790; V.

WELLS
when indivisible, 671
may be used by all coparceners, 716, 756
use of —— as appendant to share of property, 756, 757

WHOLE BLOOD
limit of the preference of the —— over the half-blood, 116

WIDOW—*continued.*
duty to maintain —— avoided in some castes by giving licence to remarry, 395*h*
husband's debts have preference over her right, 250
the Sastris make the right depend on residence in the family, 248, 250 693, 713
so the Vyav. Mayukha and Viramitrodaya, 247, 249
so do the caste laws, 249*p*
but separate maintenance may be claimed, 251, 252
only on refusal or failure by the family? 250
decision of the Judicial Committee that it may, 249
High Court, Bombay, 693
the right to an allotment in strictness limited to the patni, 250
cases on the subject discussed, 248*ss*
distinction of Bengal law as to the right of —— to maintenance, 249
right of a widowed daughter-in-law. See DAUGHTER-IN-LAW; MAINTENANCE
Right to Residence
of coparcener entitled to residence in the family house, 64, 73, 75, 245, 673, 751, 775, 776
not deprived of her right by a sale, 75, 245, 328, 673
nature of the right, 244*h*
ought to reside with son, 247
entitled to residence as against adopted son, 1038
residence as a condition may be dispensed with occasionally, 247, 248, 251
as in case of ill-treatment, 247, 251
not compellable to reside, 251
widow's leaving her husband's family revolting to Brahmanical morality, 396
Position under the Law of Inheritance
heritable rights of a —— derived from a moral unity with her husband, 84
and her participation in husband's sacrifices, 397
regarded as taking by survivorship? 1020
amongst the lower classes her right depends on custom, 403
postponed to mother by some caste customs in Gujarat, 372, 383
and amongst Khojas, 152
takes husband's estate by inheritance, 88
not as a trustee, 88, 298
fully represents the inheritance, 297, 371
widow's estate discussed, 297, 304
compared with that under Teutonic laws, 303*k*
under decisions anomalous, 425
accumulations remain her absolute property though invested in land, 298, 299
See ACCUMULATIONS; STRIDHANA
not a tenant for life, 297
in what sense —— has a life estate, 298
may exercise right of pre-emption, 298*l*
must protect the estate as well as represent it, 89*v*, 306
must make good her transactions out of her property, 307

WIDOW—*continued.*
ornaments of —— not partible, 675*p*
See ORNAMENTS
succeeding to her husband's share of a Mahal is entitled to a partition of her share, 381*q*
Inheritance in Joint Family
cannot claim joint property against surviving members, 64
has no estate in joint family property, 64, 328, 329, 334, 335, 384, 430, 766
of a joint cousin succeeds in preference to distant separated relations, 455
of the last survivor of coparceners inherits, 328, 379*ss*, 415
as last survivor of a branch takes estate as separate property, 428
of a collateral does not take absolutely? 455
Inheritance in Divided Family
takes husband's property in a divided family, 260, 384
of separated coparcener takes his share, 606*x*
succeeds to her son's property on the same terms as to her husband's, 138
preferred to daughter-in-law, 476
takes in preference to a remote heir, 119*h*
of a predeceased son inherits after the paternal grandmother according to Balambhatta, 119
she is postoned to a brother, 427
of the paternal uncle takes as a gotraja sapinda, 121, 453
of last of a collateral line takes her husband's place, 119*h*, 455*v*
postponed in N. W. Provinces to aunt's sons? 454
of sapinda postponed to sapinda of same propinquity as her husband, 445
of descendants and collaterals inherit immediately after their husbands (in the absence of a male of the same branch?), 122
of brother's son preferred to another brother's great-grandson, 122*s*
of a Sudra postponed to illegitimate son, 80
and to daughter and daughter's son, *ib.*
succeeds to a fellow-widow, 490
two or more ——s, nature of their succession, 603
two or more ——s may divide, though authorized to adopt, 1068
inherit equally, 83
may divided the estate according to Vyav. May., Viram., and Mit., 83, 95
this doctrine recognized by Courts in Bombay. 95
bound to pay husband's debts, 94
can be sued only by the nearest reversioner, 90
may be sued by remoter reversioners for sufficient cause, *ib.*
may relinquish her right in favour of second "reversioners" with the consent of the first? 89, 92
reversioners cannot obtain a declaration of right during life-time of the ——, 89
competition between —— and holder of a certificate of administration, 371
Power of Disposal and Relinquishment
what estate —— takes by inheritance, 91
as to immoveables, *ib.*
moveables, *ib.*
her estate in a gift or bequest from her husband similar, 304

WIDOW—*continued.*
unless expressly enlarged, 297*c*, 709, 983, 984
restrictions are inseparable from widow's estate, 94, 714*b*
widow's powers not enlarged by absence of "reversioners," 94
growth of restrictions traced, 291
only two texts bear on her power over inheritance, 290
may give away property inherited from husband (Sastri), 291*y*
except for improper purposes, *ib.*
or immoveables, 291*y*, 294, 296, 301
widow's power of disposal absolute by custom in absence of male kindred, 714*b*
See CUSTOM
cannot bequeath inheritance? 294, 455
widow's right over money given for maintenance absolute, 295
may dispose of her ——'s estate, 93
may dispose of immoveables bought with her moveables, 307
See ACCUMULATIONS
may alien a vritti for necessary sustenance, 407
cannot dispose of immoveables without great necessity, 374
cannot dispose of immoveables by mere gift, 93, 297*c*
may sell or incumber husband's estate for some purposes, 91, 92, 94*l*, 306, 375
as to pay husband's debts, 94, 375
but not beyond her life-time without a special justification, 93, 291*ss*, 301, 375, 709
mere recital in the deed of sale of the object not sufficient proof of it, 94
concurrence necessary of relations interested, *ib.*
as manager cannot alienate without necessity, 349, 570
See ADOPTION VII., VIII.
cannot transfer family jewels as her separate property, 295
her complete ownership in moveables, 296, 298, 709
subject to husband's debts, 298
purchaser in good faith from —— protected, 93
duty of the creditor of ——, 94*d*
fraud on expectant heirs defeated, 306
See GIFT; STRIDHANA; WIFE; WILL
Loss and Destruction of her Right
adultery bars the succession of a ——, 83, 553
right to maintenance forfeited by her unchastity, 555
even an allowance assigned to —— for maintenance is resumable in case of her unchastity, *ib.*
See FORFEITURE; UNCHASTITY
Succession to Widow
of the nearest male sapinda of a predeceased husband is an heiress of a deceased ——, 96, 122*s*
after ——'s death estate not liable for her debts, 94
See DAUGHTER; FEMALE; SAPINDA; SON; STRIDHANA; SUCCESSION
Partition
cannot claim a division in Bombay, 342, 627, 766
but may in Bengal, 629

WIDOW—*continued.*
is entitled to a share on partition among her sons, 338
widow's share on partition not to be defeated, 616*g*
right over share in partition absolute, 292, 295, 305*r*
See FEMALE; MOTHER; PARTITION; STRIDHANA
Under the Law of Adoption
position of —— until adoption, 349, 372
widow's right and duties as to adoption. See ADOPTION *passim*
must adopt a boy designated by her husband, 813*t*
in Bombay adopts without express power, but cannot be compelled, 372, 814
the elder of two widows has a preferential right of adoption, 873
gift made by —— before adoption set aside, 349
but alienation for value upheld, 350
settlement on —— with concurrence of adopted son upheld, 1078
provision for —— in cases of adoption, 973*ss*
woman's right to maintenance secured in awarding property to adopted son, 1038
of adopted son predeceased entitled to maintenance, 1033
of son cannot be divested of her estate by adoption by a mother, 92, 887
cannot continue suit for adult adopted son against his will, 1081
Remarriage
remarrying is deprived of inheritance from her first husband, 93, 406, 553
but forfeits only the right actually inherited, not her right of inheritance to her son then living, 102
remarried —— can now inherit to her second husband, 82, 391, 402
entitled to maintenance, 342
contracting, remains liable after remarriage, 85*r*, 392

WIDOW OF COUSIN
preferred to widow of cousin's son, 454

WIDOW OF GRANDSON
is excluded by daughter's son, 419
but preferred to son's daughter, 119*h*

WIDOW OF NEPHEW
preferred to brother's great-grandson, 122*s*

WIDOW OF PATERNAL UNCLE, 452

WIDOW OF UNCLE, 454
excluded by sister, 436

WIDOWER, 842

WIFE
capture of ——. See CAPTURE; MARRIAGE
purchase of —— disapproved, 358
See BRIDE-PRICE, 263
purchase of —— still prevails amongst the lower castes, 399

WIFE—*continued.*
amongst them she is regarded as property, 397, 403*v*
purchase or hiring of another man's —— formerly allowed, 798*o*
completely passes into her husband's family by marriage, 85
shares the benefit of husband's sacred fire, 87
first married takes precedence over others, 82*x*
of different caste once allowed (Manu. II. 238; III. 12)
now disapproved except by special custom, 77*n*, 403*t*
importance of the ——, 84
of the patni, 87
position of pat and lagna ——, 391*ss*
may be discarded amongst the lower castes, 358, 399—401
repudiation rare in practice, 401
allowed only in case of an outcaste, 358, 556*w*
marriage of a second —— no ground for desertion, 401
become a widow may perform Kriya and Sraddhas in default of a son, 789*q*
exequal ceremonies of —— performed by her husband's family, 87
her duty to live with husband not enforced where dangerous, 85*p*
in some castes may desert her husband with sanction of caste, 400
this disallowed by the Bombay High Court, 401
deserting husband without sufficient cause not entitled to separate maintenance, 402, 555, 556
person harbouring run-away —— liable to suit by husband, 401
is subject to her husband's control even as to her Stridhana, 86, 307
simple disobedience does not disable the —— from inheriting, 405
general incapacity of —— as to contracts, 246, 247
exception of contracts jointly with husband, 85*p*, 391
wife's authority as to household expenses, 86*s*
annulled by adultery, *ib.*
property becomes her husband's, 246
as *ex. gr.* earnings by service, 278
contract with husband void, 246*w*
separate property. See STRIDHANA, 85*p*
rights of the —— in her husband's property, 87, 88, 372
wife's right and husband's not mutual, 86
is a subordinate co-owner with husband, 372
wife's interest in husband's property distinguished from son's, 1030
entitled to a provision, 193, 254, 255, 372
though put away, 840*f*
from whom entitled to support, 227
of a disqualified person entitled to maintenance on partition, 690
claim of —— to support not extinguished by allotment to her of a share, 723
cannot be deprived of maintenance by husband's alienation, 372
wife's right to maintenance not subject to disposal or release, 254
but may be defined, *ib.*
See MAINTENANCE
under gift from husband takes moveables absolutely, immoveables for life, 293, 294, 295, 297*c*
but a heritable right if expressly given, 297*c*, 710*f*, 984

WIFE—*continued.*
gift in case of two wives, 297, 297*a*
inherits to her separated husband, 385
See WIDOW
what —— can inherit, 81, 87, 250, 398
wives of ancestors to the seventh degree succeed to their descendants, 118
for unauthorized acts liable in Stridhana, 86
and when needlessly living apart, 85*r*
but not in person, 86
may eject husband from her separated property, 287*x*
See ADHIVEDANIKA
lands purchased out of separate funds saleable by ——, 307
and devisable, *ib.*
wife's succession to co-wife, 545
See ADOPTION *passim*; BRIDE; FEMALE; GIFT; INHERITANCE; MAINTENANCE; PARTITION; SAPINDA; WILL; WOMAN

WIFE'S BROTHER. See ADOPTION IV., 921

WIFE'S SISTER'S SON. See ADOPTION IV., 919

WILL—
History and Development
origin of the law of ——s, 181
recognition of ——s, 618*x*
definition of —— (in Mofussil) independent of Act X. of 1865, 220
absence of ——s under Hindu law, 209*ss*
wills disapproved by native judicial officers, 618*x*
and by the castes when the testator has issue, 621*a*
allowance of ——s a development of principles of the Hindu law, 181, 182
unlimited —— opposed to Brahmanic family system, 618*x*
comparison between the Hindu and English laws of ——s, 182, 620
first intention of Roman ——s, 210
comparison of the Roman, Athenian and English laws, 210
extent of power limited by the Hindu law of gifts, 618
See BELOW
as to property at testator's disposal operates in analogy to gift, 179, 181, 182
bequest by husband to wife treated as a gift, 297*c*, 710*f*, 984
See BEQUEST; WIFE
speaks at the death of testator, 180
woman's testamentary power equal to that of alienation, 294*g*, 710*f*
See FEMALE; STRIDHANA
by a widow in Bengal, 184
daughter's testamentary power, 618
Indian statutes as to ——s discussed, 219
effects of Act XXI. of 1870 and V. of 1881 on ——s, 219, 220, 618, 618*x*
executors excluded by survivorship, 215, 220
Forms
form of a —— according to Hindu law, 217, 218, 618*x*
nuncupative ——, 618, 740

WILL—*continued.*
attestation of —— under Hindu law intended to be assent to the transaction, 218
Extent of Operation
power of bequest limited by power of alienation, 220
does not go so far, 1029*f*
subject to rights of maintenance, 215, 220
wills valid which provide for maintenance of family, 595
uncertain —— void, 618
application of Indian Succession Act to ——s, 618, 620
control by —— of property bequeathed limited, 179, 181, 223
with a condition against alienation operates, but the condition is void, 188
wills can only confer estates and interests recognized by law, 179, 183, 188, 220
of ancestral property disallowed, 618
cannot be made of an undivided share, 217*p*
of self-acquired property now recognized, 181
fails in favour of persons not in existence at testator's death, 182
or of persons not ascertainable at testator's death, 620, 1081
or if the testator's intention cannot be ascertained, 224
effect to be given to a —— if reasonably possible, 183, 223
effect of a —— on the mutual relations of persons taking under it, 193, 194, 221
bequest for specific charity maintained, 224
cy près doctrine admitted, 224k, 224
private perpetuity disallowed, 188, 224, 618
even under colour of religious endowment, 618
a charitable perpetuity may be created by —— in the Mofussil, 221
but not it seems in Presidency towns? *ib.*
bequest may be made to a boy designated for adoption, 814
to two simultaneously adopted held void, 1072
adoption by —— not allowed, 995
disinheritance of a son by —— not feasible under the Mit. law, 984*n*, 1032*a*
even of posthumous son, 1040
principle applied to adopted son, 978, 1040
disinheriting a widow disallowed by the Sastris, 1021*s*
partly disinheritng daughter approved by Sastri, 410
so as to one devising part should there be no son, 595, 978
See COPARCENER; FAMILY; FATHER; ILLEGAL; PERPETUITY
Construction
interpretation of Hindu ——s, 183, 184, 222, 223
governed by Hindu law, 222, 618
Tagore case, 219
English words not to be construed by vernacular equivalents, 223*d*
Proof
custom governs mode of proof of ——, 218
Evidence of
proof of instrument by single witness by assent, *ib.*
See EVIDENCE

WILL—*continued.*
validity of —— whether adjudiacable on application for certificate of administration, 1080, 1081
probate needless in Mofussil, 221, 619
powers of the different courts, 619
opposition to grant of probate to adopted son not competent to creditors of next heir, 1081
See ADOPTION III., 861; VI., 978, 995; VII., 1020; FEMALE; INTERPRETATION; MAINTENANCE

WILL TO EFFECT SEPARATION
when expressed, 630
when implied, 636

WITNESSES
testimony of —— proves partition, 776
See ASSENT; ATTESTATION; EVIDENCE

WOMAN
never independent, 289*ss*
should perform sacrifices vicariously, 824
gradual elevation to the position of, 396*ss*
in Panjab does not transmit right of succession to village lands, 406
excluded from inheritance to land under Salic and Burgundian laws, 82*w*
property acquired by a married —— usualy her husband's, 85
by partition, gains full ownership according to Colebrooke, 295
and according to Mit. by inheritance, 315
contracts made by a —— jointly with her husband bind her Stridhana, 85*r*, 391
contracting as a widow remains liable after remarriage, 85*r*
her ownership of Stridhana subject to qualifications, 86
adoption of —— under Roman law, 833*h*
See FEMALE; ORNAMENTS; STRIDHANA; WIDOW; WIFE, &c.

WOMAN'S PROPERTY. See FEMALE; STRIDHANA; WIDOW; WIFE, &c.

WORKS
Hindu law ——, 9—13, 51—54, 781*ss*, 949
their relative position, 13—54

WORSHIP
place of —— not divisible, 743
division of place of —— by turns of occupation, *ib.*
division of right to ——, 716, 716*m*
worshipper at a temple, his position, 521

WUTTUN. See VATAN

YAJAMANA. See PRIEST, 658

YAJAMANA VRITTI, 331, 388

YAJNAVALKYA
Institutes of ——, 15, 16, 38, 43
difficulty of understanding ——, 40
See INHERITANCE, 262
translations of —— Bk. II. v. 47, 50, 175. 1087, 1089

YAMA, 35

YARDI VATAN. See VATAN

YASKA,
author of the Nirukta, 35, 36

YATI
heirs to a ——, 133, 533
See SANNYASI. 56, 133

YAUTAKA, 486
See STRIDHANA

YELLAMA, 494D

YOGI. See CASTE, 727

ZAMINDARI
once aliened or divided is freed from special rule of descent, 683z
income of —— chargeable with debts, 161
held not attachable after Zamindar's death, *ib.*
inheritance to —— resembles that to a principality, 679
governed by family custom, *ib.*
statement of succession to —— extensively construed, 682
inherited through mother not self-acquired property, 658
See CUSTOM; INAM; PRINCIPALITY; RAJ